Praise for Robert M. Gates's

Duty

"A refreshingly honest memoir and a moving one."
—*The Wall Street Journal*

"Probably one of the best Washington memoirs ever. . . . Historians and policy wonks will bask in the revelations Gates provides on major decisions from late 2006 to 2011, the span of his time at the Pentagon. . . . Gates is doing far more than just scoring points in this revealing volume."   —*The New York Times Book Review*

"Touching, heartfelt . . . fascinating. . . . Gates takes the reader inside the war-room deliberations of Presidents George W. Bush and Barack Obama and delivers unsentimental assessments of each man's temperament, intellect and management style. . . . No civilian in Washington was closer to the wars in Iraq and Afghanistan than Gates."   —*The Washington Post*

"A breathtakingly comprehensive and ultimately unsparing examination of the modern ways of making politics, policy, and war. . . . Students of the nation's two early twenty-first-century wars will find the comprehensive account of Pentagon and White House deliberations riveting. General readers will be drawn to [Gates's] meditations on power and on life at the center of great political decisions."   —*The Boston Globe*

"If you read only one book by a Washington insider this year, make it this one. It should be savored by anyone who wishes to know more about the realities of decision-making in today's federal government."   —*Library Journal*

"Gates has offered . . . an informed and . . . earnest perspective, one that Americans ought to hear, reflect on and debate."
                                                                  —*The Atlantic*

"Engaging and candid. . . . Young people who want to understand and live up to the highest ideals of American statesmanship would do well to read this book carefully; Gates has much to teach about the practical idealism that represents the best kind of American leadership."   —*Foreign Affairs*

"*Duty* . . . is an invaluable contribution to our understanding of what makes Washington tick."   —*Financial Times*

"A compelling memoir and a serious history. . . . A fascinating, briskly honest account [of a] journey through the cutthroat corridors of Washington and world politics, with shrewd, sometimes eye-popping observations along the way about the nature of war and the limits of power. . . . Gates was a truly historic secretary of defense . . . precisely because he did get so much done." —*Slate*

Robert M. Gates

Duty

Robert M. Gates served as secretary of defense from 2006 to 2011. He also served as an officer in the United States Air Force and worked for the Central Intelligence Agency before being appointed director of the agency by President George H. W. Bush. He was a member of the National Security Council staff in four administrations and served eight presidents of both political parties. Additionally, Gates has a continuing distinguished record in the private sector and in academia, including currently serving as chancellor of the College of William and Mary. He holds a Ph.D. in Russian and Soviet history from Georgetown University.

ALSO BY ROBERT M. GATES

From the Shadows:
The Ultimate Insider's Story of Five Presidents
and How They Won the Cold War

Duty

Duty

MEMOIRS OF A

SECRETARY AT WAR

Robert M. Gates

VINTAGE BOOKS
A Division of Penguin Random House LLC
New York

FIRST VINTAGE BOOKS EDITION, MAY 2015

Copyright © 2014 by Robert M. Gates

All rights reserved. Published in the United States by Vintage Books, a division of Penguin Random House LLC, New York, and distributed in Canada by Random House of Canada, a division of Penguin Random House Ltd., Toronto. Originally published in hardcover in the United States by Alfred A. Knopf, a division of Penguin Random House LLC, New York, in 2014.

Vintage and colophon are registered trademarks of Penguin Random House LLC.

The Library of Congress has cataloged the Knopf edition as follows:
Gates, Robert Michael.
Duty : memoirs of a Secretary at war / by Robert M. Gates.
pages cm
Includes index
1. Gates, Robert Michael, 1943–
2. United States. Department of Defense—Officials and employees—Biography.
3. Cabinet officers—United States—Biography.
4. Iraq War, 2003–2011—Personal narratives.
5. Afghan War, 2001—Personal narratives, American.
6. War on Terrorism, 2001–2009—Personal narratives, American.
7. United States—Military policy—Decision making.
8. Civil-military relations—United States—History—21st century.
9. United States—Politics and government—2001–2009.
10. United States—Politics and government—2009–   I. Title.
II. Title: Memoirs of a Secretary at war.
E897.4P48B76 2012   355.6092—dc23   [B]   2013026348

Vintage Books Trade Paperback ISBN: 978-0-307-94963-9
eBook ISBN: 978-0-307-95948-5

Book design by Cassandra J. Pappas

www.vintagebooks.com

Printed in the United States of America
10   9   8   7   6   5   4   3   2   1

This book is dedicated to the men and women
of the United States Armed Forces.

Contents

Author's Note

This is a book about my more than four and a half years at war. It is, of course, principally about the wars in Iraq and Afghanistan, where initial victories in both countries were squandered by mistakes, shortsightedness, and conflict in the field as well as in Washington, leading to long, brutal campaigns to avert strategic defeat. It is about the war against al Qaeda and Osama bin Laden, those responsible for our national tragedy on September 11, 2001. But this book is also about my political war with Congress every day I was in office and the dramatic contrast between my public respect, bipartisanship, and calm, and my private frustration, disgust, and anger. There were also political wars with the White House, often with the White House staff, occasionally with the presidents themselves—more with President Obama than with President Bush. And finally, there was my bureaucratic war with the Department of Defense and the military services, aimed at transforming a department organized to plan for war into one that could wage war, changing the military forces we had into the military forces we needed to succeed.

George W. Bush and Barack Obama were, respectively, the seventh and eighth presidents I worked for. I knew neither man when I began working for them, and they did not know me. To my astonishment (and consternation), I became the only secretary of defense in history to be asked to remain in the position by a newly elected president, let alone one of a different party. I came to the job in mid-December 2006 with the sole purpose of doing what I could to salvage the mission in Iraq from disaster. I had no idea how to do it, nor any idea of the sweeping changes I would need to make at the Pentagon to get it done. And I had no idea how dramatically and how far my mission over time would expand beyond Iraq.

As I look back, there is a parallel theme to my four and a half years at war: love. By that I mean the love—there is no other word for it—I came to feel for the troops, and the overwhelming sense of personal responsibility I developed for them. So much so that it would shape some of my most significant decisions and positions. Toward the end of my time in office, I could barely speak to them or about them without being overcome with emotion. Early in my fifth year, I came to believe my determination to protect them—in the wars we were in and from new wars—was clouding my judgment and diminishing my usefulness to the president, and thus it played a part in my decision to retire.

I make no pretense that this book is a complete, much less definitive, history of the period from 2006 to 2011. It is simply my personal story about being secretary of defense during those turbulent, difficult years.

Duty

CHAPTER 1

Summoned to Duty

I had become president of Texas A&M University in August 2002, and by October 2006 I was well into my fifth year. I was very happy there, and many—but not all—Aggies believed I was making significant improvements in nearly all aspects of the university (except football). I had originally committed to staying five years but agreed to extend that to seven years—summer 2009. Then my wife, Becky, and I would finally return to our home in the Pacific Northwest.

The week of October 15, 2006, the week that would change my life, started out routinely with several meetings. Then I took to the road, ending up in Des Moines, Iowa, where I was to give a speech on Friday, the twentieth.

Just past one p.m. that day I received an e-mail from my secretary, Sandy Crawford, saying that President Bush's national security adviser, Steve Hadley, wanted to speak to me on the phone within an hour or two. Hadley's assistant was "quite insistent" that the message be passed to me. I told Sandy to inform the assistant I would return Steve's call on Saturday morning. I had no idea why Steve was calling, but I had spent nearly nine years at the White House on the National Security Council (NSC) staff under four presidents, and I knew that the West Wing often demanded instant responses that were rarely necessary.

Hadley and I had first met on the NSC staff in the summer of 1974 and had remained friends, though we were in contact infrequently. In January 2005, Steve—who had succeeded Condoleezza Rice as George W.

Bush's national security adviser for the second Bush term—had asked me to consider becoming the first director of national intelligence (DNI), a job created by legislation the previous year, legislation—and a job—that I had vigorously opposed as unworkable. The president and his senior advisers wanted me to make it work. I met with Hadley and White House chief of staff Andy Card in Washington on Monday of inauguration week. We had very detailed conversations about authorities and presidential empowerment of the DNI, and by the weekend they and I both thought I would agree to take the job.

I was to call Card at Camp David with my final answer the following Monday. Over the weekend I wrestled with the decision. On Saturday night, lying awake in bed, I told Becky she could make this decision really easy for me; I knew how much she loved being at Texas A&M, and all she had to say was that she didn't want to return to Washington, D.C. Instead, she said, "We have to do what you have to do." I said, "Thanks a lot."

Late Sunday night I walked around the campus smoking a cigar. As I walked past familiar landmarks and buildings, I decided I could not leave Texas A&M; there was still too much I wanted to accomplish there. And I really, really did not want to go back into government. I called Andy the next morning and told him to tell the president I would not take the job. He seemed stunned. He must have felt that I had led them on, which I regretted, but it really had been a last-minute decision. There was one consolation. I told Becky, "We are safe now—the Bush administration will never ask me to do another thing." I was wrong.

At nine a.m. on Saturday—now nearly two years later—I returned Steve's call as promised. He wasted no time in posing a simple, direct question: "If the president asked you to become secretary of defense, would you accept?" Stunned, I gave him an equally simple, direct answer without hesitation: "We have kids dying in two wars. If the president thinks I can help, I have no choice but to say yes. It's my duty." The troops out there were doing their duty—how could I not do mine?

That said, I sat at my desk frozen. *My God, what have I done?* I kept thinking to myself. I knew that after nearly forty years of marriage, Becky would support my decision and all that it meant for our two children as well, but I was still terrified to tell her.

Josh Bolten, a former director of the Office of Management and Budget, who had replaced Card as White House chief of staff earlier that year, called a few days later to reassure himself of my intentions. He asked if I had any ethical issues that could be a problem, like hiring illegal immigrants as nannies or housekeepers. I decided to have some fun at his expense and told him we had a noncitizen housekeeper. Before he began to hyperventilate, I told him she had a green card and was well along the path to citizenship. I don't think he appreciated my sense of humor.

Bolten then said a private interview had to be arranged for me with the president. I told him I thought I could slip into Washington for dinner on Sunday, November 12, without attracting attention. The president wanted to move faster. Josh e-mailed me on October 31 to see if I could drive to the Bush ranch near Crawford, Texas, for an early morning meeting on Sunday, November 5.

The arrangements set up by deputy White House chief of staff Joe Hagin were very precise. He e-mailed me that I should meet him at eight-thirty a.m. in McGregor, Texas, about twenty minutes from the ranch. I would find him in the parking lot at the Brookshire Brothers grocery store, sitting in a white Dodge Durango parked to the right of the entrance. Dress would be "ranch casual"—sport shirt and khakis or jeans. I look back with amusement that my job interviews with both President Bush and President-elect Obama involved more cloak-and-dagger clandestinity than most of my decades-long career in the CIA.

I did not tell anyone other than Becky what was going on except for the president's father, former president George H. W. Bush (the forty-first president, Bush 41), with whom I wanted to consult. He was the reason I had come to Texas A&M in the first place, in 1999, to be the interim dean of the George H. W. Bush School of Government and Public Service. What was supposed to be a nine-month stint of a few days a month became two years and led directly to my becoming president of Texas A&M. Bush was sorry I would be leaving the university, but he knew the country had to come first. I also think he was happy that his son had reached out to me.

I left my house just before five a.m. to head for my interview with the president. Call me old-fashioned, but I thought a blazer and slacks more appropriate for a meeting with the president than a sport shirt and jeans. Starbucks wasn't open that early, so I was pretty bleary-eyed for the first part of the two-and-a-half-hour drive. I was thinking the entire way about questions to ask and answers to give, the magnitude of the challenge, how life for both my wife and me would change, and how to approach the job of secretary of defense. I do not recall feeling any self-doubt on the drive to the ranch that morning, perhaps a reflection of just how little I understood the direness of the situation. I knew, however, that I had one thing going for me: most people had low expectations about what could be done to turn around the war in Iraq and change the climate in Washington.

During the drive I also thought about how strange it would be to join this administration. I had never had a conversation with the president. I had played no role in the 2000 campaign and was never asked to do so. I had virtually no contact with anyone in the administration during Bush's first term and was dismayed when my closest friend and mentor, Brent Scowcroft, wound up in a public dispute with the administration over his opposition to going to war in Iraq. While I had known Rice, Hadley, Dick Cheney, and others for years, I was joining a group of people who had been through 9/11 together, who had been fighting two wars, and who had six years of being on the same team. I would be the outsider.

I made my clandestine rendezvous in McGregor with no problem. As we approached the ranch, I could see the difference in security as a result of 9/11. I had visited other presidential residences, and they were always heavily guarded, but nothing like this. I was dropped off at the president's office, a spacious but simply decorated one-story building some distance from the main house. It has a large office and sitting room for the president, and a kitchen and a couple of offices with computers for staff. I arrived before the president (always good protocol), got a cup of coffee (finally), and looked around the place until the president arrived a few minutes later, promptly at nine. (He was always exceptionally punctual.) He had excused himself from a large group of friends and family celebrating his wife Laura's sixtieth birthday.

We exchanged pleasantries, and he got down to business. He talked first about the importance of success in Iraq, saying that the current strategy wasn't working and that a new one was needed. He told me he was thinking seriously about a significant surge in U.S. forces to restore security in Baghdad. He asked me about my experience on the Iraq Study Group (more later) and what I thought about such a surge. He said he thought we needed new military leadership in Iraq and was taking a close look at Lieutenant General David Petraeus. Iraq was obviously uppermost on his mind, but he also talked about his concerns in Afghanistan; a number of other national security challenges, including Iran; the climate in Washington; and his way of doing business, including an insistence on candor from his senior advisers. When he said specifically that his father did not know about our meeting, I felt a bit uncomfortable, but I did not disabuse him. It was clear he had not consulted his father about this possible appointment and that, contrary to later speculation, Bush 41 had no role in it.

He asked me if I had any questions or issues. I said there were five subjects on my mind. First, on Iraq, based on what I had learned on the Iraq Study Group, I told him I thought a surge was necessary but that its duration should be closely linked to particular actions by the Iraqi government—especially passage of key legislative proposals strengthening sectarian reconciliation and national unity. Second, I expressed my deep concern about Afghanistan and my feeling that it was being neglected, and that there was too much focus on trying to build a capable central government in a country that essentially had never had one, and too little focus on the provinces, districts, and tribes. Third, I felt that neither the Army nor the Marine Corps was big enough to do all that was being asked of them, and they needed to grow. Fourth, I suggested we had pulled a bait and switch on the National Guard and Reserves—most men and women had joined the Guard in particular expecting to go to monthly training sessions and summer training camp, and to be called up for natural disasters or a national crisis; instead, they had become an operational force, deploying for a year or more to join an active and dangerous fight and potentially deploying more than once. I told the president that I thought all these things had negative implications for their families and their employers that needed to be addressed. He did not disagree with any of my points about the Guard. Finally I told him that while I was no expert and not fully informed, what I had heard and read led me to believe the Pentagon was buying too many weapons more suited to the Cold War than to the twenty-first century.

After about an hour together, the president leaned forward and asked if I had any more questions. I said no. He then sort of smiled and said, "Cheney?" When I sort of smiled back, he went on to say, "He is a voice, an important voice, but only one voice." I told him I had had a good relationship with Cheney when he was secretary of defense and thought

I could make the relationship work. The president then said he knew how much I loved Texas A&M but that the country needed me more. He asked me if I would be willing to take on the secretary's job. I said yes.

He had been very candid with me about many things, including his vice president, and he encouraged comparable candor on my part. I left confident that if I became secretary, he would expect and want me to tell him exactly what I thought, and I knew I would have no trouble doing that.

I was in a daze on the drive back to the university. For two weeks, becoming secretary of defense had been a possibility, one I continued to half-hope would not become a reality. After the interview, while the president had not told me to pack my bags, I knew what lay in front of me.

About half past five that afternoon, I received an e-mail from Bush 41: "How did it go?" I responded, "I may be off-base, but I think it went exceptionally well. I was certainly satisfied on all the issues I raised (including the ones you and I talked about). . . . Unless I miss my guess, this thing is going to go forward." I went on, "Mr. President, I feel sad about possibly leaving A&M but I also feel pretty good about going back to help out at a critical time. You know, other than a handshake when he was governor of Texas, I really had never spent any time with your son. Today we spent over an hour together alone, and I liked what I saw. Maybe I can help him." I asked him to be circumspect about how much he knew, and he quickly replied, "I do NOT leak! Lips sealed says this very happy, very proud friend of yours."

Literally minutes later Bolten called to tell me the president had decided to move forward. A one p.m. press announcement was planned for Wednesday, November 8, followed by a televised three-thirty presidential appearance with Secretary Rumsfeld and me in the Oval Office.

Cheney, as he wrote in his memoir, had opposed the president's decision to replace Rumsfeld, who was an old friend, colleague, and mentor. I suspected as much at the time and was relieved when Bolten passed along to me that Secretary of State Rice had been enthusiastic about my nomination and that the vice president had said I was "a good man." As Bolten said, coming from Cheney, that was high praise.

I kept Becky informed of all this—I didn't dare do otherwise—and expressed only one misgiving to her as that Sunday ended. The Bush administration by then was held in pretty low esteem across the nation. I told her, "I have to do this, but I just hope I can get out of this administration with my reputation intact."

THE ANNOUNCEMENT

On Monday, the ponderous wheels of a major confirmation process began to move, still in secret. My first contact was with the White House counsel, Harriet Miers, to begin going through all the ethics questions associated with my membership on corporate boards of directors, my investments, and all the rest. The political side of confirmation began on Tuesday, when I was asked to provide lists of members of Congress I thought would be positive in their reactions, as well as former officials, journalists, and others who could be expected to comment favorably on my selection. I was asked to be at the White House at midmorning on the eighth.

I was flown to Washington in an unmarked Air Force Gulfstream jet that landed at Andrews Air Force Base, just outside Washington, where it taxied to a remote part of the airfield. I was picked up (again) by Joe Hagin.

A few minutes later I arrived at the White House and was shown to a small office in the West Wing basement, where I would begin making courtesy phone calls to congressional leaders, key members of Congress, and other notables in and out of Washington. I was introduced to David Broome, a young White House legislative assistant who would be my "handler" and shepherd me through the confirmation process. I had some experience on the Hill myself, of course, but David was a very smart, practical, and astute observer of Capitol Hill, as well as a U.S. Marine Corps reserve officer. I felt very comfortable with him.

I made a number of calls, and the reactions to my impending nomination were overwhelmingly positive. I learned that even the Republicans were very nervous about Iraq and eager for a change from the current approach—especially given that many of them attributed their party's loss of control of Congress in the election the day before mostly to the public's growing opposition to the war. Not knowing where I would come down on Iraq, they still welcomed me. The Democrats were even more enthusiastic, believing my appointment would somehow hasten the end of the war. If I had any doubt before the calls that nearly every-one in Washington believed I would have a one-item agenda as secretary, it was dispelled in those calls.

At about twelve-thirty p.m. Texas time, about a half hour into the president's press conference announcing the change at Defense, an e-mail I had prepared was sent to some 65,000 students, faculty, and staff at Texas A&M with a personal message. The hardest part for me to write went as follows: "I must tell you that while I chose Texas A&M over returning to government almost two years ago, much has happened both here and around the world since then. I love Texas A&M deeply, but I love our country more and, like the many Aggies in uniform, I am obli-gated to do my duty. And so I must go. I hope you have some idea of how painful that is for me and how much I will miss you and this unique American institution."

A couple of hours later, it was showtime. The president, Rumsfeld, and I met briefly in the president's private dining room before Rumsfeld led the way into the Oval Office, followed by the president, then me. It had been nearly fourteen years since I had been in the Oval Office.

The president opened his remarks with a statement about the need to stay on the offensive in both Iraq and Afghanistan to protect the Ameri-can people. He spoke of the role of the secretary of defense and then reviewed my career. He then made two comments that would frame my challenges as secretary: "He'll provide the department with a fresh per-spective and new ideas on how America can achieve our goals in Iraq" and "Bob understands how to lead large, complex institutions and trans-form them to meet new challenges." He went on to generously praise Rumsfeld's service and his achievements as secretary and to thank him for all he had done to make America safer. Rumsfeld stepped to the podium next and spoke about the security challenges facing the country but focused especially on thanking the president for his confidence and support, his colleagues in the Department of Defense, and above all our men and women in uniform for their service and sacrifice. I thought the statement showed a lot of class.

Then it was my turn. After thanking the president for his confidence and Don for his service, I said:

I entered public service forty years ago last August. President Bush will be the seventh President I have served. I had not anticipated returning to government service and have never enjoyed any position more than being president of Texas A&M University.

However, the United States is at war, in Iraq and Afghanistan. We're fighting against terrorism worldwide. And we face other challenges to peace and our security. I believe the outcome of these conflicts will shape our world for decades to come. Because our long-term strategic interests and our national and homeland security are at risk, because so many of America's sons and daughters in our armed forces are in harm's way, I did not hesitate when the president asked me to return to duty.

If confirmed by the Senate, I will serve with all my heart, and with gratitude to the president for giving me the opportunity to do so.

Press coverage and public statements in the ensuing days were very positive, but I had been around long enough to know that this was less a show of enthusiasm for me than a desire for change. There was a lot of hilarious commentary about a return to "41's" team, the president's father coming to the rescue, former secretary of state Jim Baker pulling all the strings behind the scenes, and how I was going to purge the Pentagon of Rumsfeld's appointees—"clean out the E-Ring" (the outer corridor of the Pentagon where most senior Defense civilians have their offices). It was all complete nonsense.

For the next three weeks, while I continued to go through the motions of a university president, I was caught up in preparations for confirmation. Even though I was a former CIA director who had had access to the "crown jewels" of American secrets, I had to fill out the infamously detailed Federal Form SF 86—"Questionnaire for National Security Positions"—just like anyone else applying for a job in government. Like any senior appointee, I had to fill out the financial disclosure statements, among others. I'd done all these before, but the climate in Washington had changed, and inaccurate answers—even innocent mistakes—had tripped up other nominees in recent years. So I was advised to engage a Washington law firm that specialized in completing these forms to ensure there would be no errors. Because I wanted no hiccups to delay my confirmation, I took the advice and, $40,000 later, turned in my paperwork. (I could only imagine the cost for nominees who had far more complex—and bigger—financial disclosures.) I also had sixty-five pages of questions from the Senate Armed Services Committee to answer. The good news on the latter was that the Pentagon has a large group of people who do the bulk of the work in preparing answers to these questions, although the nominee must review and sign them and be prepared to talk about those answers in a confirmation hearing.

When in Washington to prepare for confirmation hearings, I worked out of an ornate suite of offices in the Eisenhower Executive Office Building, a gigantic granite Victorian gingerbread building next to the White House, where I had had a rather smaller office thirty-two years before. There I received materials to read on major issues, on the military departments (Army, Navy—including its Marine Corps component—and Air Force), and on the organization of Defense, including a diagram I found incomprehensibly complex, foreshadowing bureaucratic problems I would soon face. My overall strategy for the hearings was not to know too much, especially with regard to the budget or specific procurement programs about which different senators on the committee had diametrically opposed interests. I knew the hearings would not be about my knowledge of the Department of Defense but, above all, about my thinking on Iraq and Afghanistan as well as my attitude and demeanor. My coaches couldn't help me with that.

During these three weeks I first met Robert Rangel, the "special assistant" to Rumsfeld—in reality, his chief of staff. Before going to the Pentagon in 2005, Rangel had been on the staff of the House Armed Services Committee, including a several-year stint as staff director. I quickly concluded that Robert knew more, and had better instincts, about both Congress and the Department of Defense than anyone I had ever met. He would be invaluable to me, if I could persuade him to stay on.

The most dramatic event in the days before my hearing, one that more than any briefing clarified in my gut and my heart what I was about to take on, took place one evening when I was having dinner alone at my hotel. A middle-aged woman came up to my table and asked if I was Mr. Gates, the new secretary of defense. I said yes. She congratulated me on my nomination and then said to me with tears in her eyes, "I have two sons in Iraq. For God's sake, please bring them home alive. We'll be praying for you." I was overwhelmed. I nodded, maybe mumbled something like, I'll try. I couldn't finish my dinner, and I couldn't sleep that night. Our wars had just become very real to me, along with the responsibility I was taking on for all those in the fight. For the first time, I was frightened that I might not be able to meet that mother's and the country's expectations.

In the days prior to my confirmation hearing on December 5, I went through the ritual of visiting key senators, including, above all, those on the Senate Armed Services Committee. I was taken aback by the bitterness of the Republican senators over the president's decision to announce the change at Defense only after the midterm election. They were all convinced that had the president announced a few weeks before the election that Rumsfeld was leaving, they would have kept their majority. The Republicans also groused about how the Bush White House dealt only—they said—with the leadership and ignored everyone else. Several were critical of senior military officers. While some of the Republicans, among them John McCain, expressed strong support for the war in Iraq and thought we should ramp up our effort, it was revealing that at least half the Republican senators were very concerned about our continuing involvement in Iraq and clearly saw the war as a large and growing political liability for their party.

The Democratic senators I met with expressed their opinions starkly: opposition to the war in Iraq and the need to end it; the need to focus on Afghanistan; their view that the Pentagon's relationship with Congress was terrible and that civilian-military relations inside Defense were just as bad; their disdain for and dislike of George W. Bush (the forty-third president, hereafter occasionally referred to as Bush 43) and his White House staff; and their determination to use their new majorities in both houses of Congress to change course in the war and at home. They professed to be enormously pleased with my nomination and offered their support, I think mainly because they thought that I, as a member of the Iraq Study Group, would embrace their desire to begin withdrawing from Iraq.

The courtesy calls foreshadowed what the years to come would be like. Senators who would viciously attack the president in public over Iraq were privately thoughtful about the consequences of failure. Most made sure to acquaint me with the important defense industries in their states and pitch for my support to those shipyards, depots, bases, and related sources of jobs. I was dismayed that in the middle of fighting two wars, such parochial issues were so high on their priority list.

Taken as a whole, the courtesy calls to senators on both sides of the aisle were very discouraging. I had anticipated the partisan divide but not that it would be so personal with regard to the president and others in the administration. I had not expected members of both parties to be so critical of both civilian and military leaders in the Pentagon, in terms of not only their job performance but also their dealings with the White House and with Congress. The courtesy calls made quite clear to me that my agenda would have to be broader than just Iraq. Washington itself had become a war zone, and it would be my battlespace for the next four and a half years.

The Confirmation

During the car ride from my hotel to the Capitol for my confirmation to be secretary of defense, I thought in wonder about my path to such a moment. I grew up in a middle-class family of modest means in Wichita, Kansas. My older brother and I were the first in the history of our family to graduate from college. My father was a salesman for a wholesale automotive parts company. He was a rock-ribbed Republican who idolized Dwight D. Eisenhower; Franklin D. Roosevelt was "that damn dictator," and I was about ten before I learned that Harry Truman's first name wasn't "goddamn." My mother's side of the family were mostly Democrats, so from an early age bipartisanship seemed sensible to me. Dad and I talked (argued) often about politics and the world.

Our family of four was close, and my childhood and youth were spent in a loving, affectionate, and happy home. My father was a man of unshakable integrity, with a big heart and, when it came to people (versus politics), an open mind. He taught me early in life to take people one at a time, based on their individual qualities and never as a member of a group. That led, he said, to hatred and bias; that was what the Nazis had done. He had no patience for lying, hypocrisy, people who put on airs, or unethical behavior. In church, he occasionally would point out to me important men who fell short of his standards of character. My mother, as was common in those days, was a homemaker. She loved my brother and me deeply, and was our anchor in every way. My parents told me repeatedly when I was a boy that there were no limits to what I might achieve if I worked hard, but they also routinely cautioned me never to think I was superior to anyone else.

My life growing up in 1950s Kansas was idyllic, revolving around family, school, church, and Boy Scouts. My brother and I were Eagle Scouts. There were certain rules my parents insisted I follow, but within those bounds, I had extraordinary freedom to wander, explore, and test my wings. My brother and I were adventuresome and a bit careless; we were both familiar sights in hospital emergency rooms. I was a smart aleck, and when I sassed my mother, a backhand slap across the face was likely to follow quickly if my father was within earshot. My mother was expert at cutting a willow switch to use across the backs of my bare legs when I misbehaved. The worst punishments were for lying. On those relatively infrequent occasions when I was disciplined, I'm confident I deserved it, though I felt deeply persecuted at the time. But their expectations and discipline taught me about consequences and taking responsibility for my actions.

My parents shaped my character and therefore my life. I realized on the way to the Senate that day that the human qualities they had imbued within me in those early years had brought me to this moment, and looking ahead, I knew they would be tested as never before.

I had been through three previous confirmation hearings. The first, in 1986, for deputy director of central intelligence, was a walk in the park and culminated in a unanimous vote. The second, in early 1987, for director of central intelligence, occurred in the middle of the Iran-Contra scandal; when it became clear that the Senate would not confirm me with so many unanswered questions about my role, I withdrew. The third, in 1991, again to be DCI, had been protracted and rough but ended with my confirmation, with a third of the senators voting against me. Experience told me that unless I really screwed up in my testimony, I would be confirmed as secretary of defense by a very wide margin. An editorial cartoon at the time captured the mood of the Senate (and the press) perfectly: it showed me standing with upraised right arm taking an oath—"I am not now nor have I ever been Donald Rumsfeld." It was a useful and humbling reminder that my confirmation was not about who I was but rather who I was not. It was also a statement about how poisonous the atmosphere had become in Washington.

Senator John Warner of Virginia was chairman of the Armed Services Committee and thus chaired the hearing; the ranking minority member was Carl Levin of Michigan. The two would switch places in a few weeks as a result of the midterm elections. Warner was an old friend who had introduced me—he was my "home-state senator"—in all three of my preceding confirmation hearings. I did not know Levin very well, and he had voted against me in 1991. Warner would deliver opening remarks, followed by Levin, and then I would be "introduced" to the committee by two old friends: former Senate majority leader Bob Dole of Kansas and former senator and chairman of the Senate Intelligence Committee David Boren, by then longtime president of the University of Oklahoma. Then I would make an opening statement.

Warner focused, right out of the gate, on Iraq. He reminded everyone that after his recent visit to Iraq, his eighth, he had said publicly that "in two or three months, if this thing [the war] hasn't come to fruition and if this level of violence is not under control and if the government under Prime Minister Maliki is not able to function, then it's the responsibility of our government internally to determine: Is there a change of course that we should take?" He quoted General Peter Pace, chairman of the Joint Chiefs of Staff, as having said the day before, when asked if we were winning in Iraq, "We're not winning, but we're not losing." Warner commended the various reviews of Iraq strategy under way inside the administration and, in that context, advised me on how to do my job: "I urge you not to restrict your advice, your personal opinions regarding the current and future evaluations in these strategy discussions. . . . You simply have to be fearless—I repeat: fearless—in discharging your statutory obligations as, quote, 'the principal assistant to the president in all matters relating to the Department of Defense.'" Warner was publicly signaling his weakening support for the president on Iraq.

Levin's opening statement was very critical of the administration on Iraq and clearly set forth the views that he would bring to the table as chairman of the committee and with which I would be forced to contend beginning in January:

> If confirmed as secretary of defense, Robert Gates will face the monumental challenge of picking up the pieces from broken policies and mistaken priorities in the past few years. First and foremost, this means addressing the ongoing crisis in Iraq. The situation in Iraq has been getting steadily worse, not better. Before the invasion of Iraq, we failed to plan to provide an adequate force for the occupation of the country, or to plan for the aftermath of major combat operations. After we toppled Saddam Hussein in 2003, we thoughtlessly disbanded the Iraqi army and also disqualified tens of thousands of low-level Baath Party members from future government employment. These actions contributed to the

chaos and violence that followed, and to alienating substantial portions of the Iraqi population. We have failed, so far, to secure the country and defeat the insurgency. And we have failed to disarm the militias and create a viable Iraqi military or police force. And we have failed to rebuild the economic infrastructure of the country and provide employment for the majority of Iraqis. The next secretary of defense will have to deal with the consequences of those failures.

Levin went on to tell me that Iraq was not the only challenge I would face. He spoke of a resurgent Taliban in Afghanistan; an unpredictable nuclear power in North Korea; Iran aggressively pursuing nuclear weapons; the Army and Marine Corps in need of tens of billions of dollars to repair and replace equipment; the declining readiness of our non-deployed ground forces; the continuing pursuit of weapons programs we couldn't afford; the challenges in recruitment and retention of our forces; the problems of our military families after repeated deployments; and a department "whose image has been tarnished by the mistreatment of detainees in Abu Ghraib and Guantánamo and elsewhere."

Finally, the man I would have to work with as committee chairman said that the Department of Defense's effectiveness had been reduced by a civilian senior leadership that "has too often not welcomed differing views, whether from our uniformed military leaders, the intelligence community, the State Department, American allies, or members of Congress of both political parties. The next secretary will have to work hard to heal these wounds and address the many problems facing the department and the country."

I remember sitting at the witness table listening to this litany of woe and thinking, *What the hell am I doing here? I have walked right into the middle of a category-five shitstorm.* It was the first of many, many times I would sit at the witness table thinking something very different from what I was saying.

After very kind words from both Dole and Boren, it was my turn. I tried to open on a light note but one that reflected I hadn't lost my perspective. Senator Warner had long felt strongly that a nominee's family should accompany him or her to the confirmation hearing. Becky had accompanied me only to my very first hearing; I never thought of congressional hearings as family fare. I explained to Senator Warner that Becky had a choice: she could either attend my confirmation hearing or accompany the Texas A&M women's basketball team to Seattle to play the University of Washington. I said she was in Seattle, and I thought that was a good call. Then I got serious:

> I am under no illusion why I am sitting before you today: the war in Iraq. Addressing challenges we face in Iraq must and will be my highest priority, if confirmed. . . . I am open to a wide range of ideas and proposals. If confirmed, I plan, urgently, to consult with our military leaders and our combat commanders in the field, as well as with others in the executive branch and in Congress. . . . I will give most serious consideration to the views of those who lead our men and women in uniform.

Then I delivered a warning.

> While I am open to alternative ideas about our future strategy and tactics in Iraq, I feel quite strongly about one point: developments in Iraq over the next year or two will, I believe, shape the entire Middle East and greatly influence global geopolitics for many years to come. Our course over the next year or two will determine whether the American and Iraqi people and the next president of the United States will face a slowly but steadily improving situation in Iraq and in the region or will face the very real risk and possible reality of a regional conflagration. We need to work together to develop a strategy that does not leave Iraq in chaos and that protects our long-term interests in, and hopes for, the region.

Those three sentences captured my views on Iraq and what needed to be done, views that would guide my strategy and tactics in Washington and in Iraq for the next two years. As I would say repeatedly, whether you agreed with the launching of the war or not, "We are where we are."

I concluded my opening remarks with statements from the heart. "I did not seek this position or a return to government. I'm here because I love my country and because the president of the United States believes I can help in a difficult time. I hope you will reach a similar conclusion." And finally, "Perhaps the most humbling part of the position for which this committee is considering me is knowing that my decisions will have life-and-death consequences. Our country is at war, and if confirmed, I will be charged with leading the men and women who are fighting it. . . .

I offer this committee my solemn commitment to keep the welfare of our forces uppermost in my mind." When I made that pledge, I could not imagine all that would be required to fulfill it.

In the news coverage of the give-and-take that followed, two exchanges were highlighted. The first was early in the hearing, when Senator Levin asked me whether I believed we were currently winning in Iraq and I simply answered, "No, sir." The answer was widely celebrated as both realistic and candid and in contrast to earlier administration testimony. If one answer clinched my confirmation, that was it. There was something of an uproar that morning at the White House and in the Defense Department at the answer, and after a break for lunch, I decided to add to my earlier answer what Pete Pace had said the day before, that while we weren't winning, we weren't losing either. Above all, I did not want the troops in Iraq to think I was suggesting they were being beaten militarily.

The other exchange was with Senator Edward Kennedy, who talked about the sacrifices of our troops and asked whether, in the policy debates to come, I'd be a "stand-up person" for our national security and for the troops. I replied,

Senator Kennedy, twelve graduates of Texas A&M have been killed in Iraq. I would run in the morning with some of those kids, I'd have lunch with them, they'd share with me their aspirations and hopes. And I'd hand them their degrees. I'd attend their commissioning, and then I would get word of their death. So this all comes down to being very personal for all of us. The statistics, 2,889 killed in combat in Iraq as of yesterday morning: that's a big number, but every single one of them represents an individual tragedy not only for the soldier who has been killed, but for their entire family and their friends.

I then went on to say,

Senator, I am not giving up the presidency of Texas A&M, the job that I've probably enjoyed more than any I have ever had, making considerable financial sacrifice, and frankly, going through this process, to come back to Washington to be a bump on a log and not say exactly what I think, and to speak candidly and, frankly, boldly to people at both ends of Pennsylvania Avenue about what I believe and what I think needs to be done. . . . I can assure you that I don't owe anybody anything. And I'm coming back here to do the best I can for the men and women in uniform and for the country.

The remainder of the hearing covered broadly strategic matters as well as the parochial concerns of individual senators. There were perplexing questions, like the one from Senator Robert Byrd of West Virginia, who asked if I supported going to war with Syria. (I said no.) And there were some light moments, such as when Senator Ben Nelson of Nebraska asked what I thought about steadily increasing the bounty on Osama bin Laden by a million dollars a week. I responded, "Sort of terrorist Powerball?"

The open hearing concluded about 3:45 p.m. and was followed by an uneventful and largely congratulatory secret hearing at four. That evening the Armed Services Committee voted unanimously to recommend my nomination to the full Senate for confirmation. The next afternoon, December 6, the Senate voted to confirm me 95 to 2, with three senators not voting. The votes against me were Senators Jim Bunning of Kentucky and Rick Santorum of Pennsylvania, both Republicans. They didn't think I was nearly aggressive enough in how we should deal with Iran, including potential military action. However, I thought we had our hands full with the wars we were already in without looking for new ones. Avoiding new wars would be at the top of my agenda under both Presidents Bush and Obama. I would always be prepared to use whatever military force necessary to defend American vital interests, but I would also set that threshold very high.

I was not sworn in and did not take up my responsibilities as the new secretary of defense for twelve days after confirmation, probably an unprecedented delay. I felt very strongly about presiding at Texas A&M's December commencement ceremonies. I also needed a little time to wrap things up at A&M and get moved to Washington, D.C. On reflection, particularly in a time of war, I probably should not have waited. But there was virtually no criticism, and I used the time to good effect.

I was given an office suite in the Pentagon to use until I was sworn in. I filled out paperwork so I could get paid, had my official photo taken, received my badges and ID card, and went through all the procedures experienced by every new employee of the Department of Defense—including one I had not expected. One morning I went to use the bathroom adjacent to my office. I had just shut and locked the door and unzipped my pants when there was a frantic pounding on the door and someone shouted, "Stop! Stop!" Alarmed, I zipped up and opened the door. A sergeant standing there handed me a cup, saying a urine sample was required for a drug test. Even the secretary of defense was not exempt from that.

Both before and immediately after confirmation, I spent a lot of time thinking about how to approach running the Pentagon, the largest and most complex organization on the planet, with some three million civilian and uniformed employees. Unlike many who assume senior executive positions in Washington, I actually had experience leading two huge public bureaucracies—the CIA and the intelligence community, with about 100,000 employees, and the nation's seventh-largest university, with about 65,000 faculty, staff, and students. But the Pentagon was a whole other thing. Beyond the sheer monstrousness of the bureaucracy, I would have to deal with the troubled relationship between the civilian leadership of the department and many in the military leadership, and the fact that we were engaged in two major wars, neither of which was going well.

There were a large number of people eager to help me—some days too many. It seemed everyone in the Pentagon wanted to see me or send me briefing papers. I was seriously at risk of drowning in all this, so I was deeply grateful to Deputy Secretary Gordon England, chairman of the Joint Chiefs Pete Pace, and Robert Rangel for protecting me and for channeling people and briefings that I did need to see into a sensible structure. The number of those outside the Pentagon reaching out to offer me advice without wanting anything for themselves reflected the fact that many Washington insiders believed the department was in real trouble and that I had to be successful for the country's sake. I asked to have dinner with John Hamre, who had been deputy secretary of defense during President Clinton's second term and had subsequently led the Center for Strategic and International Studies. John's counsel was really useful. Among other things, he observed that decision making in the Pentagon is "like the old Roman arena—gladiators come before the emperor to battle and you decide who is the winner. Someone needs to make sure the process within the arena is fair, transparent, and objective."

John made two other comments that would profoundly influence my approach to the job. He emphasized the importance of having advocates both for today's requirements and for those of tomorrow. I would quickly discover that those concerned with potential tools for future wars far outnumbered, and had far greater influence than, the advocates for today's requirements. I would become the foremost advocate for getting the troops already at war what they needed. John also made clear the importance of having independent advocates for supply (recruiting, training, and equipping the troops) and for demand (the needs of commanders in the field). Commanders in the field might be limiting their requests for troops, he felt, out of the belief that the number of troops they wanted were not available. As a result, I would insist that field commanders tell me how many troops and how much equipment they felt were required and let me deal with how to get them.

I also turned to Colin Powell, an old friend. I had known Colin for nearly twenty-five years and had worked closely with him during the Reagan and George H. W. Bush administrations. As a career Army officer and former chairman of the Joint Chiefs of Staff, Colin not only knew the Pentagon well but retained many good contacts (and sources) in uniform. I e-mailed one specific request to him: "One place you could help right away is to assure any senior officers you talk to that I don't think I have all or even many of the answers to tough problems. I am a good listener, and I prize candor above all. I also will respect their experience and their views."

Of course, I received a lot of advice that I didn't think was sound, and a lot of back-channel commentary pro and con on many senior civilian and military officials. I heard from many people who were interested in filling positions they thought would be vacated by my anticipated purge of Rumsfeld's civilian team, and I was advised by several people to appoint my own transition team to oversee all the personnel and policy changes I would undoubtedly make.

Instead, I used the interregnum period to make a critical decision about leading the department that would turn out to be one of the best decisions I would make: I decided to walk into the Pentagon alone, without bringing a single assistant or even a secretary. I had often seen the immensely negative impact on organizations and morale when a new boss showed up with his own retinue. It always had the earmarks of a hostile takeover and created resentment. And of course the new folks didn't have a clue how their new place of employment worked. So there would be no purge. In a time of war, I didn't have time to find new people, and we couldn't afford the luxury of on-the-job training for novices. We also didn't have time for the necessary confirmation of new political appointees. I kept *everybody*, including notably Robert Rangel as de facto chief of staff, and Delonnie Henry, the secretary's confidential assistant, scheduler, and all-around utility infielder. If someone didn't work out or the chemistry was bad, I would make changes later. Continuity in wartime, it seemed to me, was the name of the game, and I wanted tacitly to express my confidence that the team was made up of capable and dedicated professionals. I would not be disappointed.

I did need to fill one senior vacancy, the undersecretary of defense for intelligence. The incumbent, Steve Cambone, had already resigned. Even before confirmation, I had asked another old friend and colleague, retired Air Force Lieutenant General Jim Clapper, to take on the job. Jim had been the director of the Defense Intelligence Agency when I was director of the CIA. He had subsequently retired from the military and later become director of the National Geospatial Intelligence Agency (NGIA), a clumsily named organization responsible for all U.S. photographic satellites and photointerpretation. Because Clapper had favored a strong director of national intelligence, with real control over the entire intelligence community, including Defense agencies, he had run afoul of Rumsfeld and, for all practical purposes, been forced out of the NGIA job. He had been out of government for only months when I asked him to come back. There had been a lot of criticism in the press and in Congress of the Pentagon intelligence operation, and I was confident that bringing in a man of Jim's experience and integrity would help correct that situation quickly. I also trusted him completely. He reluctantly agreed to take the job but imposed one condition: I had to call his wife, Sue, and tell her how important it was for him to do this. That was a first for me, but I did it, and Sue was very gracious about my disrupting their lives once again for national service.

As I said, leaving Texas A&M was very difficult for both Becky and me. At the end of my last day in my office, more than ten thousand students, faculty, and staff gathered to say good-bye. The president of the student body spoke, I spoke, and we all sang the Aggie "War Hymn." There were three commencement ceremonies, at the end of which my duties at Texas A&M were officially done.

We flew to Washington, D.C., on Sunday, December 17, to take up my new duties.

My swearing-in ceremony was at one-fifteen p.m. the next day. Both the president and the vice president were there, as was my entire family. I had asked Supreme Court Justice Sandra Day O'Connor to administer the oath, partly because she had done so fifteen years earlier, when I was sworn in as director of central intelligence. She was unable to do so this time because of travel plans, and so I asked Vice President Cheney to administer the oath. I saw it as a small gesture toward him of friendship and respect. Becky held the Bible my parents had given me on my sixteenth birthday.

Fifty-eight days after I first spoke with Steve Hadley, I was the secretary of defense charged with fighting two wars and the leader of the finest military in the history of the world. In my remarks, I said that I would travel soon to Iraq to meet with our commanders to seek their advice—"unvarnished and straight from the shoulder"—on how to proceed in the weeks and months ahead. I also noted that progress in Afghanistan was at risk and that we intended to keep our commitment there. Returning to the theme I had expressed at my confirmation hearing, I said,

> How we face these and other challenges in the region over the next two years will determine whether Iraq, Afghanistan, and other nations at a crossroads will pursue paths of gradual progress toward sustainable governments, which are allies in the global war on terrorism, or whether the forces of extremism and chaos will become ascendant. All of us want to find a way to bring America's sons and daughters home again. But as the president has made clear, we simply cannot afford to fail in the Middle East. Failure in Iraq at this juncture would be a calamity that would haunt our nation, impair our credibility, and endanger America for decades to come.

A mirthful note was added many hours later. In my remarks at the swearing-in, I had said that my ninety-three-year-old mother was present for the ceremony. Comedian Conan O'Brien picked up on that on his show that night. He joked that my mother had come up to me after the ceremony, offered her congratulations, and then told me, "Now, go kick the Kaiser's ass."

CHAPTER 2

Iraq, Iraq, and Iraq

My highest priority as secretary was to turn the situation around in Iraq. Political commentators before and after my confirmation were virtually unanimous in saying that my tenure as secretary would be judged almost entirely by what happened there, a rather daunting challenge given the rising tide of violence and the deterioration of the security situation, dysfunctional Iraqi politics, and the obvious failure of American military strategy there by mid-December 2006.

The United States was engaged in two major wars every single day I was secretary of defense for four and a half years. I participated in the development of our strategies both within the Pentagon and in the White House, and then had primary responsibility for implementing them: for selecting, promoting—and when necessary, firing—field commanders and other military leaders; for getting the commanders and troops the equipment they needed to be successful; for taking care of our troops and their families; and for sustaining sufficient political support in Congress to provide time for success. I had to navigate the minefields of politics, policy, and operational warfare, both in the field and in Washington. The military battlefields were in Iraq and Afghanistan; the political battlefields were in Washington, Baghdad, and Kabul. I was, next to the president, primarily responsible for all of them.

I did not come to the Iraqi battlefield as a stranger.

The Gulf War

I was one of a small group of senior officials in Bush 41's administration who were deeply involved in planning the Gulf War in 1991. At its conclusion, I believed that we had made a strategic mistake in not forcing Saddam personally to surrender to our generals (rather than sending an underling), in not making him take personal responsibility and suffer personal humiliation, and maybe even in not arresting him at the surrender site. On February 15, 1991, Bush, as he wrote in his memoir, had ad-libbed at a press conference that one way for the bloodshed in Iraq to end was "to have the Iraqi people and military put aside Saddam." The entire Bush team was convinced that the magnitude of their defeat would prompt the Iraqi military leaders to overthrow Saddam.

To our dismay, almost immediately after our military offensive ended, both the Shia in the south and the Kurds in the north spontaneously rose up against Saddam. They had interpreted the president's words—aimed at the Iraqi military—as encouragement of a popular uprising. We should have been more precise in saying what we were after, even though I don't think it would have forestalled the uprisings. We were criticized widely for allowing the regime to continue to use their helicopters to put down the uprisings (the Iraqis said they were needed because we had destroyed most of their highway bridges), although it was Iraqi army ground forces and armor that brutally ended the rebellions. Meanwhile Saddam used the time provided by those uprisings and their suppression to murder hundreds of his generals who might have done the same to him. Neither the Kurds nor the Shia—especially the latter—would forgive us for not coming to their assistance after they thought we had encouraged them to take up arms.

Another lingering criticism was that Bush 41 had not sent our military on to Baghdad to force regime change. Our view was that such action was not sanctioned by the UN Security Council resolutions on the basis of which we had constructed a broad coalition, including Arab forces. Thus the coalition would have shattered had we gone on to Baghdad. While that might not have mattered in the short term, by breaking our word then, we would have had an awful time trying to assemble another such coalition to deal with an international problem. Further, I made the point many times that Saddam was not just going to sit on his veranda and let U.S. forces drive up and arrest him. He would have gone to ground, and we would have had to occupy a significant part of Iraq in order to find him and/or defeat a determined and ruthless resistance movement that he almost certainly would have put together, with home field advantage.

So the war ended in February 1991 with Saddam still in power, Iraq under severe international sanctions limiting imports and controlling the export of Iraqi oil, and the Shia and Kurds even more brutally repressed. In the ensuing years, Saddam did everything possible to evade the sanctions, diverting proceeds from the "oil-for-food" program (under which the Iraqi regime was allowed to sell just enough oil to buy food and medicine) into his own pocket and overseeing a vast operation smuggling oil across the border into Iran for sale. He used a lot of that money to build dozens more gigantic, tasteless palaces that we would later occupy.

None of us doubted in the early 1990s that, just as soon as he could, Saddam would resume the programs he had had under way before the war to develop biological, chemical, and nuclear weapons. The intensive inspections program instituted after the war uncovered evidence that the Iraqis had, in fact, been considerably further along in developing nuclear weapons than U.S. intelligence had estimated before the war. We were so confident he had deployed chemical weapons that our first troops to cross the border wore chemical protection suits (which were unbearably hot and uncomfortable even in February). As long as the inspections effort continued and the sanctions were strictly enforced, his opportunities to resume the programs for weapons of mass destruction would be very limited.

But as the years went by, Saddam became much more aggressive in limiting the reach of the inspectors, and the inspections for all practical purposes ended in 1998. Adherence to the sanctions also gradually weakened as a number of governments—France, Russia, Germany, and China, among others—angled for oil contracts and other business opportunities with the Iraqis. By 2003, most governments and intelligence services had concluded that Saddam had been successful in resuming his weapons programs. That view was reinforced by his boasting and his behavior, intended to persuade his own people—and his neighbors—of that success. The result was unanimous adoption in the fall of 2002 of UN Security Council Resolution 1441, which demanded a full accounting of progress in Iraq's weapons programs and a rigorous international inspection effort. Serious consequences were threatened for noncompliance. Saddam nonetheless continued to play games with the inspectors and the international community. As Condi Rice would write years later, "The fact is, we invaded Iraq because we believed we had run out of other options. The sanctions were not working, the inspections were unsatisfactory, and we could not get Saddam to leave by other means." Particularly later, as the war dragged on, fewer and fewer people accepted that logic.

THE IRAQ STUDY GROUP

After I retired as director of central intelligence in January 1993, I had no access to classified information—and didn't want any. I was happy to leave Washington, D.C., in my rearview mirror, and one of many reasons to move to the Pacific Northwest was to avoid being asked to serve on any of the countless special commissions, blue ribbon panels, or study groups whose work almost invariably ends up collecting dust on some policy maker's shelf. But I did read a lot of newspapers, and based on what I read—and my knowledge of Saddam's behavior in the 1980s and early 1990s—it seemed highly likely to me that he had resumed working on weapons of mass destruction, that the sanctions were largely ineffective, and that the man was a very dangerous megalomaniac. So I supported Bush 43's decision to invade and bring Saddam down.

However, I was stunned by what I saw as amazing bungling after the initial military success, including failing to stop the looting of Baghdad, disbanding the Iraqi army, and implementing a draconian de-Baathification policy (Saddam ran the Baath Party) that seemed to ignore every lesson from the post-1945 de-Nazification of Germany. I was equally surprised that, after Vietnam, the U.S. Army seemed to have forgotten as quickly as possible how to wage counterinsurgency warfare.

I gave a speech on May 1, 2003, less than six weeks after the war began, that summed up my views:

The situation we face now [in Iraq] reminds me a little of the dog catching the car. Now that we have it, what do we do with it?

I believe the postwar challenge will be far greater than the war itself. Only in recent days has the American government begun to realize the extraordinary potential power of the Shia Muslim majority in Iraq, and the possibility that a democratic Iraq might well turn out to be a fundamentalist Shia Iraq. . . . The Kurds will, at minimum, demand autonomy in the north. And what happens to the [minority] Sunni Muslim population in the center, having oppressed both the Kurds and the Shia . . . for so long? Finally, the challenge of rebuilding Iraq, providing food and services, and rebuilding the economy after a dozen years of privation and decades of Baathist socialism will be no small task—though I believe a more easily achievable task than our political aspirations for the country.

For all these reasons, I believe the United States should agree to begin replacing our forces with a large multinational peacekeeping force—perhaps from NATO—as quickly as the security situation allows. . . . We will be making a big mistake if we keep a hundred thousand or so American soldiers in Iraq for more than a few months.

Even as the security situation continued to deteriorate, the Iraqis—with a lot of help from us and others—held what were broadly considered two reasonably fair elections in 2005, one on January 30 and another on December 16, both with a pretty good turnout, considering the circumstances. Forming a coalition government composed of several Shia parties, the Kurds, and politically acceptable Sunnis after the December election, however, was a major challenge. As those negotiations were dragging on, the bombing of a historic Shia mosque, the Askariya Shrine at the Golden Mosque of Samarra, on February 22, 2006, ignited horrific sectarian violence that escalated around the country. By October some three thousand Iraqi civilians were being killed every month. Attacks against U.S. troops increased from an average of 70 per day in January 2006 to an average of 180 per day in October.

As the security situation in Iraq deteriorated through 2006, the political situation in Washington did as well. The president's approval ratings further declined, public opinion polls on the war turned increasingly negative, and a Congress that had prided itself for decades on bipartisanship in national security matters became increasingly divided about the war along party lines—most Democrats opposed, most Republicans supportive (but increasingly uneasy).

The growing divide at home and the deteriorating situation in Iraq prompted Congressman Frank Wolf, a longtime Republican from northern Virginia, early in 2006 to propose creating a bipartisan group of well-known Republicans and Democrats from outside the government to see if a new strategy could be developed for the United States in Iraq that could win the support of the president and both parties in Congress. He proposed that it be funded—to the tune of a little over a million dollars—through the congressionally chartered Institute of Peace. The effort ultimately would also be supported by the Center for Strategic and International Studies, the Center for the Study of the Presidency and Congress, and the James A. Baker III Institute for Public Policy at Rice University. Former secretary of state Jim Baker and former Indiana congressman Lee Hamilton agreed to cochair what would be known as the Iraq Study Group.

Baker called me in February to ask me to be one of five Republicans in the group. While he and I had had a few disagreements during Bush 41's time in office (when I was deputy national security adviser), I had great respect for him and thought he had been a very effective secretary of state. I had written of Jim that I was always glad he was on our side as a negotiator. My first question to him was whether the president supported this initiative, because if he didn't, it would be a waste of time. Jim said that when he was approached about cochairing, his first call had been to Bush 43 to ask the very same question. He did not want to be involved in an effort that the president or others saw as undermining the administration. He assured me that 43 was on board. I later decided that the president wasn't so much supportive as acquiescent, perhaps hoping we could make useful suggestions or provide some political help at home.

Because the recommendations of the Iraq Study Group, released the day of my confirmation hearing, would play a major part in the debate over Iraq in 2007–8, it is important to know something about how the group did its work and how the thrust of the group's final recommendations surprised me.

The other Republicans involved were retired Supreme Court justice Sandra Day O'Connor, former attorney general Ed Meese, and former Wyoming senator Alan Simpson. The Democrats were led by Hamilton and included former Office of Management and Budget (OMB) director and White House chief of staff Leon Panetta, former Virginia senator Chuck Robb, Washington lawyer Vernon Jordan, and former secretary of defense William Perry. Hamilton had chaired both the House Select Committee on Intelligence and the House Foreign Affairs Committee, and I had known him for nearly twenty years. Lee is a man of extraordinary integrity and intellectual honesty, and I looked forward to working with him.

What you won't find in the report of the Iraq Study Group was how much fun we had. Simpson is simply hilarious, Panetta and Jordan both have a great sense of humor, Baker is a fount of wicked one-line asides, Hamilton has a very dry Indiana sense of humor, and everyone was easy to get along with. We understood the seriousness of our purpose but saw no reason why it should be boring.

The group launched its effort with a meeting on March 15. We met a total of eight times in Washington. Our efforts focused on the strategic environment in and around Iraq; security in Iraq and key challenges to enhancing it; political developments within Iraq following the elections and formation of the new government; and the economy and reconstruction. We put together a list of experts on each of the four main subject areas, received large three-ring notebooks of papers to read, and sat through innumerable briefings. We heard a broad range of views as we talked with all the key figures in the administration, including the president, former senior government officials, and a number of our most senior military leaders, as well as brigade-level officers, intelligence community leaders and experts, members of Congress, foreign officials, journalists, and commentators.

We asked a lot of questions. Justice O'Connor had no experience in foreign affairs or national security issues, but she was probably the best questioner. It was extraordinary to listen to her. From her years as a Supreme Court justice, she had an amazing ear for faulty logic, questionable evidence, inconsistency, and flawed analysis. In a kindly but firm way, she punctured a number of expert balloons.

For me, the most significant learning experience was the trip that seven of us made to Baghdad from August 30 through September 4. On the way to Kuwait, we stopped at the airport in Shannon, Ireland, to refuel. While there, Panetta and I made a dash for the airport liquor store, anticipating that such beverages would be hard to come by in Baghdad. (These two future secretaries of defense didn't realize that we would be in violation of the military's General Order no. 1 forbidding the consumption of alcohol in Iraq.) Hamilton used the one bed on the plane on the way out, and Baker would use it on the way back; the other slept on the floor. The other five of us slept in our seats or on the floor.

In Kuwait, where it was ghastly hot and windy, we transferred to a military cargo plane to fly to Baghdad, where it would be even hotter. The passengers on that flight were a study in contrasts. There were several dozen extremely fit young soldiers headed into the war zone with their helmets, body armor, and assault rifles. I could only imagine what they were thinking, especially given the steadily rising level of violence. And there were the seven of us, in our sixties and seventies, looking incredibly silly in our blazers and khakis, stylistically complemented by our own protective armor and helmets. Our appearance reminded me of the 1988 campaign photo of Michael Dukakis in a tank wearing a tanker's headgear. The soldiers must have wondered why in God's name these civilian bozos were going to Iraq. On arrival at the airfield in Baghdad, we transferred to helicopters to fly over Baghdad to the embassy complex. Each helicopter was manned on each side by a soldier with a .50 caliber machine gun. During the flight, we newcomers were startled when the helicopter began firing flares; we would learn that these defensive measures were intended to deflect heat-sensing weapons but would sometimes be triggered automatically by electrical transmission lines. Neither explanation was particularly comforting.

We stayed overnight at the embassy complex, the centerpiece of which was one of Saddam's huge palaces, complete with swimming pool and large pool house. We were quartered in the pool house. When the power (and air-conditioning) went out about two a.m., it was brutally hot. I decided to see if something could be done to get the power back on. I went outside in a T-shirt and shorts to find help. A young soldier, also in T-shirt and shorts—and carrying his assault rifle—was passing by, and I tried to explain the situation to him. He was, justifiably, monumentally indifferent to our minor discomfort and walked on without comment or a second glance.

We had meetings in Baghdad from August 31 to September 3. We were there to talk directly to our commanders on the ground, to our ambassador and embassy staff, to diplomats from other countries, and of course, to as wide a circle of Iraqi leaders as possible. We spent twelve hours each day in meetings. We didn't hear much about the grim situation in Iraq from the Americans and foreign diplomats that we hadn't heard before, although what they had to say was more pointed and graphic. General George Casey, the U.S. commander in Iraq, said the Iraqis had to tackle four difficult legislative issues: establishing a federal structure, de-Baathification, getting the militias under control, and apportioning the revenues from oil sales. He also said that a precipitous U.S. withdrawal would have "horrific" strategic consequences. Casey said it was important to try to impose targets and deadlines on the Iraqis and that we "should know by the end of the year whether the Iraqi leadership will make it or not." In the absence of the ambassador, the number-two man in our embassy, Dan Speckhard, told us it was important to bring about an improvement in the security environment that would be noticeable to Iraqis, especially in Baghdad.

We also spent some time talking with Lieutenant General Pete Chiarelli, commander of the Multinational Corps–Iraq, who was the direct commander of our troops in the fight. Chiarelli impressed us all with his thoughtful analysis about why we needed to protect the population and get the Iraqis services and jobs—to get young Iraqi men to pick up a shovel instead of a rifle. He spoke of the need for more U.S. civilian aid workers and development experts as well as military efforts, and he observed that something like restoring sewer service to an entire neighborhood could have a far more beneficial effect than a successful military engagement. Chiarelli, echoing Speckhard, spoke at length about the need to improve security in Baghdad as the prerequisite for success.

Below General Casey, no one in uniform suggested to us the need for more U.S. troops (we pursued the subject vigorously), probably because Casey and his boss, Central Command Commander General John Abizaid, were opposed, seeing additional troops as taking pressure off the Iraqis to assume more responsibility for their own security. Chiarelli did say that security in Baghdad could not improve without more U.S. forces being deployed there, and as I would later learn, other generals, including Ray Odierno, were pushing behind the scenes for more forces.

Believing we were not getting the full story, Bill Perry met privately with both Casey and Chiarelli but heard nothing new. I met privately with CIA's chief of station in Baghdad, whose views ran close to those we had heard from Chiarelli. I asked him how the relationship between the CIA and the military was going, and he said, "Oh, sir, it's so much better than when you were DCI." I was not offended because what he said was true and, in fact, a vast understatement. The close and growing collaboration, in fact, was bringing about a revolution in the real-time integration of intelligence and military operations.

Despite the holding back, we heard some pretty candid views in our conversations with U.S. military and embassy officials. The essence of their message was that the Battle of Baghdad had to be won, and a larger number of troops had to be sent to sustain improved security in those parts of the city where insurgents and extremists had been eliminated or suppressed and to restore infrastructure (though no new U.S. troops were needed in Iraq); measures to evaluate Iraqi progress in security, the economy, and reconciliation were needed by the end of the year; action had to be taken against Shia who engaged in violence if there was to be reconciliation; there had to be genuine outreach to the Sunnis; Syria needed to be neutralized; the Shia extremist alliance with Iran had to be broken; progress needed to be made in the Middle East peace process; and regional help with aid was needed. All agreed the United States must not fail in Iraq. The points, to a considerable extent, would shape many of the recommendations of the Study Group.

We also met with the Baghdad bureau chiefs of the major U.S. news organizations. Their evaluation of the Iraqi scene was stark and very pessimistic. We heard from them that the situation was deteriorating, not only because of conflict between Shia and Sunni but because of internal Shia divisions as well; that the U.S. military and the State Department were "in denial"; that there were not enough troops to provide security; that there had been a big exodus of the Iraqi middle class and intellectuals the previous summer; and that a "de facto" partitioning of the country was taking place.

Our meetings with the Iraqis made clear to us the magnitude of the political challenge. We met first with Prime Minister Noori Al-Maliki, head of the small Dawa Party and a compromise choice for the job precisely because he was seen as weak. He downplayed Iraq's continuing problems but said they were due to the activities of Baathists and Saddamists who remained in the country and in the government. He seemed out of touch with reality.

The Sunnis complained (with considerable justification) that the Ministry of the Interior was full of Shia extremists and death squads, with direct links to groups attacking both coalition forces and Sunnis. They pointed to Iran's involvement in Iraq and said that when tensions between Washington and Tehran increased over the nuclear issue, Tehran became more active in helping extremists on the ground in Iraq. The Shia leaders we met with, including religious leaders, told us that Saudi Arabia, Syria, and Iran were all interfering in Iraq. Neither the Shia nor the Sunnis were specific in their complaints; nor did they bother to mention the destructive impact of their own extremist groups. (After we met with Shia coalition leader Abd Al-Aziz Al-Hakim, I told Baker the vibes in the room made me feel that he would just as soon put us up against a wall as talk to us.)

Dr. Saleh al-Mutlaq, a Kurd from the Iraqi Front for National Dialogue, gave us the most thoughtful and realistic assessment. He said Iraq was a deeply traumatized society and that expectations about transition were "highly unrealistic." Iran wanted a weak Iraq and a quagmire for the United States, he said, with our 140,000 troops as "hostages." The Shia had to realize they could not control all the levers of power, and the Sunnis had to realize they would not return to power. He expressed concern that the Shia were trying to sideline the Sunnis. "It is politics at the heart of our problems; all other problems derive from that."

Our visit was critically important because you just have to see and hear some things in person to understand them fully. No number of briefings in Washington could take the place of sitting in the same room with the Iraqis, or some of our own people on the scene, for that matter. We had been treated respectfully and reasonably openly by all we met with, including President Jalal Talabani, who hosted a sumptuous dinner for us featuring a table full of very expensive scotch.

All in all, it was a depressing visit. I returned believing that one more major miscalculation had to be added to the bill of particulars against the decision to go to war: we had simply had no idea how broken Iraq was before the war—economically, socially, culturally, politically, in its infrastructure, the education system, you name it. Decades of rule by Saddam, who didn't give a damn about the Iraqi people; the eight-year-long war with Iran; the destruction we wreaked during the Gulf War; twelve years of harsh sanctions—all these meant we had virtually no foundation to build upon in trying to restart the economy, much less create a democratic Iraqi government responsive to the needs of its people. We were going to insist that our partner, the first democratically elected government in Iraq's four-thousand-year history, resolve in a year or so the enormous and fundamental political problems facing the country? That was a fantasy.

The Study Group held one more informational meeting in mid-September and then met on November 13 to begin formulating its recommendations. I had resigned from the group on November 8, when my nomination was announced. My place was taken by former secretary of state Larry Eagleburger.

While still in Baghdad, Bill Perry had drafted a three-and-a-half-page preliminary outline of the actions he thought the United States should take to improve the situation in Iraq. He began his memo with a dramatic statement: "The consequences of failure in Iraq would be catastrophic—much more consequential than failure in Vietnam." He addressed the various political and economic steps he believed should be taken but focused mostly on the security situation and the prospects for Operation Forward Together, a joint effort by the Iraqi army, the U.S. military, and the Iraqi police to restore security in Baghdad. Bill wrote,

> It will be important for the Iraqi government to provide a signifi-cant number of Iraqi army forces to support the police in keeping the cleansed [secured] areas from being reinfected. Most importantly, a larger contingent of American troops committed to this program would give us a higher probability of succeeding in this critical effort. . . . We recognize the difficulties entailed in such a commitment, but we also recognize how critically important this effort is to everything else we are doing in Iraq.

Bill made clear he was calling for a "short-term troop increase," per-haps using forces being held in reserve in Kuwait and Germany.

Soon after we returned from Baghdad, Chuck Robb (who would have to miss the mid-September meeting) weighed in with his own memo. Characterizing Perry's memo as an "excellent starting point," he said that

> I believe the Battle for Baghdad is the make or break element of what-ever impact we're going to have on Iraq and the entire region for at least a decade—and probably much longer. In my judgment, we cannot afford to fail and we cannot maintain the status quo. . . . My sense is that we need, right away, a significant short-term surge in U.S. forces on the ground, augmented where possible by coalition partners, and, with very few exceptions, they will have to come from outside the current theater of operations.

On October 15, just six days before Hadley's call to me about becom-ing secretary of defense, I sent an e-mail to Baker and Hamilton with my own proposed recommendations. I led off by saying that I thought Robb's line "We cannot afford to fail and we cannot maintain the status quo" should be the first sentence of our report. Then I wrote:

1. There should be a significant augmentation of U.S. troop levels (from outside Iraq) for a specific period of time to clear and hold [provide a sustained secure environment in] Baghdad and give the Iraqi army time to establish itself in these areas. Probably 25,000–40,000 troops would be needed for up to six months.
2. Prior to the deployment, clear benchmarks should be established for the Iraqi government to meet during the time of the augmentation, from national reconciliation to revenue sharing, etc. It should be made quite clear to the Iraqi government that the augmentation period is of specific length and that success in meeting the benchmarks will determine the timetable for withdrawal of the base force subsequent to the temporary augmentation.

My other recommendations—based on everything I had heard in Washington and Baghdad—were to convene a regional conference, including both the Syrians and the Iranians, to discuss the stabilization of, and aid to, Iraq, as well as a "high-visibility" return of the United States to the Israeli-Palestinian peace process. Both of these moves would be intended to create a more favorable political climate in the Middle East for us and perhaps improve the political environment in Baghdad. I also recommended the appointment of a "very senior" person by the president, resident in the White House, to coordinate all aid and reconstruction efforts in Iraq, reflecting my sense that there was too little coordination and integration of effort on the civilian side of the U.S. war effort. Finally, I proposed that we stop rotating officers at the battalion commander level and above in Iraq for the duration of the surge and that the State Department fill its open positions in Iraq, with involuntary assignments if necessary; both measures I thought were necessary to address the too-rapid turnover of American military officers with experience in Iraq and the insufficient number of civilians.

By mid-October, the only three members of the ISG to put their personal recommendations on paper—two Democrats and one Republican—had gone on record that a surge of U.S. forces from outside Iraq was needed to stabilize the situation in Baghdad, which in turn was critical to our success in Iraq. Yet when the group's recommendations were drafted in mid-November, there would be no mention whatsoever of a surge or augmentation of U.S. forces in Iraq in the executive summary of the report. Indeed, only on page seventy-three of the ninety-six-page report was it said that the group could support a short-term redeployment or surge of American combat forces to stabilize Baghdad, or to speed up the training and equipping mission.

I have never discussed this outcome with my former colleagues on the ISG but can only speculate that the Democrats' winning control of both houses of Congress in the midterm elections, and the desire for unanimity to make the report more politically potent, resulted in relegating a recommended surge of U.S. troops to the distant background. I was disappointed in this outcome.

THE SURGE

Despite the president's always-confident public posture, by spring 2006 I believe he already knew the strategy in Iraq was not working. Generals Casey and Abizaid had been focused throughout most of 2006 on transitioning security responsibility to the Iraqis, and earlier in the year Casey had said he hoped to reduce the U.S. presence from fifteen brigade combat teams to ten by the end of 2006. (Combat brigades average about 3,500 soldiers, plus a significant number of others in support, including logistics, communications, intelligence, and helicopters.) Declining security after the Samarra bombing had made such reductions untenable, but a big part of the continuing military resistance to more U.S. forces was the belief that their very presence, as targets, worsened the security situation, and that the more the United States did, the less the Iraqis would do. The commanders were set on transition.

Meanwhile, in Washington, by late summer, despite the rhetoric of success, there were at least three major reviews of Iraq strategy under way inside the administration. The principal one was being done by Steve Hadley and the NSC staff; the others were at the Department of State, by Secretary Rice's counselor Philip Zelikow, and at the Pentagon, under the auspices of the chairman of the Joint Chiefs of Staff, Pete Pace.

After confirmation, though not yet sworn in, I first spoke my mind during a private breakfast on December 12 with the president and Hadley in a small dining room adjacent to the Oval Office. I said the president needed to send a message to Maliki that we had reached a decisive moment, a watershed for both countries' leaders: "This is the time. What kind of country do you want? Do you want a country? Chaos is the alternative." I said we needed to force the issue in Baghdad: Could Maliki deliver and, if he couldn't, then who could? I said that our people in Baghdad were too bullish; they said there was "some reduction in sectarian violence," but it was like the tide, coming and going and coming back again. What's the follow-on economically and politically? I asked. I said that Syria and Iran needed to be made to understand that there is a price to pay for helping our enemies in Iraq. I suggested the Saudis had to get into the game, too: they said they were worried but they took no action. Finally, I asked what would happen if a surge failed. "What's Chapter 2?"

We had been discussing when Bush might make a speech if he decided to change the strategy and order a surge. He had decided to hold off until I was sworn in and could go to Iraq as secretary and return with my recommendations. I urged that he not let events drive the date of the speech. If he was not ready, then he should delay. "Better a tactical delay than a strategic mistake," I said.

On December 13, the president came to the Pentagon to meet with the Joint Chiefs of Staff in their conference room, long dubbed "the Tank." The vice president, Don Rumsfeld, and I were there. I said little at the meeting because Rumsfeld was still the secretary and spoke for the Department of Defense. But the meeting offered me a good chance to get a feel for the chemistry in the room among the principal players, and for how the president conducted meetings. The session also gave me a chance to observe the chiefs and their interactions with Bush and Cheney. Bush raised the idea of more troops going to Iraq. All of the chiefs unloaded on him, not only questioning the value of the additional forces but expressing concern about the impact on the military if asked to send thousands more troops. They worried about "breaking the force" through repeated deployments and about the impact on military families. They indicated that tour lengths in Iraq would need to be lengthened to sustain a larger force.

I was struck in the meeting by the service chiefs' seeming detachment from the wars we were in and their focus on future contingencies and stress on the force. Not one uttered a single sentence on the need for us to win in Iraq. It was my first glimpse of one of the biggest challenges I would face throughout my time as secretary—getting those whose offices were in the Pentagon to give priority to the overseas battlefields. Bush heard them out respectfully but at the end simply said, "The surest way to break the force is to lose in Iraq." I would have to deal with all the legitimate issues the chiefs raised that day, but I agreed totally with the president.

I couldn't help but reflect on an e-mail I had seen a year or so earlier at Texas A&M from an Aggie deployed in Iraq. He had written that, sure, he and his buddies wanted to come home—but not until the mission was completed and they could make certain that their friends' sacrifices would not be in vain. I thought that young officer would also have agreed with the president.

Hadley and I subsequently had a long telephone conversation on December 16 in preparation for my trip to Iraq. He said I would report to the president on the trip on December 23, and then the national security team would meet at the ranch in Crawford on December 28 to decide the way ahead. He went through the proposed agenda for the Crawford meeting. It was all about a surge, and the strategy for Baghdad. Did Casey have the resources to provide sustained protection for the Iraqis in Baghdad, and did he understand that the surge was "a bridge to buy time and space for the Iraqi government to stand up"? Could we surge both in Anbar province—where Sunni sheikhs were beginning to stand up to al Qaeda and the insurgency because of their wanton viciousness—and in Baghdad, or could we handle Anbar with special forces and Sunni tribes willing to work with us? How would we describe the broader transition strategy—security, training, or both? If we embedded our forces with Iraqi units, would it reduce the number of U.S. troops in the fight?

On December 19, the day after I was sworn in, I talked with David Petraeus. I wanted to pick the brain of the Army's most senior expert on counterinsurgency. I also wanted to get better acquainted with the leading candidate to replace George Casey. I asked him what I should look for in Iraq, what questions I should ask. Fundamentally, he said, the question was whether our priority was security for the Iraqi people or transition to Iraqi security forces. We probably couldn't do the latter until we had improved the former.

A few hours later I departed on my first trip to Iraq as secretary. I was accompanied by Pete Pace and by Eric Edelman, the undersecretary of defense for policy. Going to Iraq as secretary of defense was quite different than going as a member of a study group. For security purposes, I flew in a military cargo plane, but inside the vast hold was a sort of large silver Airstream trailer—a capsule nicknamed the "Silver Bullet"—for me and a handful of others. I had a small cabin to myself with a desk and a sofa that folded out into a bed. The bathroom was so small you could not use it with the door closed. There was a middle section with a desk and seat for a staff member, and a small refrigerator, and another section where two or three additional people could sit. It was tight quarters for a twelve-hour flight but significantly better than the seats out in the cargo bay, and a lot quieter as well. Still, because there were no windows in the plane, it was a lot like being FedExed halfway around the world.

Upon arrival in Baghdad, I was met by Generals Abizaid and Casey and helicoptered to Camp Victory, a huge complex that included the Al Faw palace, our military headquarters, and the Joint Visitors Bureau (JVB). The JVB guesthouse was another of Saddam's palaces and was ornately decorated in what I would call "early dictator," with huge furniture and a lot of gold leaf. My bedroom was roughly the size of a basketball court and featured a huge chandelier. The bathroom was long on ornamentation and short on plumbing. I would stay at the JVB many times, and after the National Guard took over its management, living conditions would improve. Still, the relative plushness made me uneasy because I knew what kind of conditions our troops were enduring. My staff and I had no cause to complain—ever.

I spent a lot of my two and a half days in Iraq with our commanders. It was during this trip that I would first meet several of the Army's warrior generals I would come to know, respect, and promote in the years to come, including Lieutenant Generals Ray Odierno, Stan McChrystal, and Marty Dempsey.

I had lengthy meetings and meals with all of the senior Iraqi government officials. These conversations were much more productive than what I had experienced when visiting as a member of the Study Group, which was not surprising, given how important I had become to their future.

I began a practice on this first trip that I would continue on all future visits to Iraq and Afghanistan, and also at every military facility and unit I would visit as secretary—I had a meal with troops, usually a dozen or so, either young officers (lieutenants and captains), junior enlisted, or middle-level noncommissioned officers. They were surprisingly candid with me—partly because I would not allow any of their commanders in the room—and I always learned a lot.

As I prepared to fly from Baghdad to Mosul, I gave my first press conference in Iraq, outdoors in front of the JVB. What I said probably had less of an impact on the reporters than the racket made by a firefight going on in the background.

On the flight back to Washington, I prepared to meet with the president the next morning at Camp David. I told him then that I had promised the Senate to listen on this trip to our senior commanders, and I had. Their central theme was still the transitioning of security responsibility to the Iraqis. I said I thought that we were at a "pivot point" in Iraq, that the emerging Iraqi plan being worked on by Casey looked like a turning point in terms of the Iraqis wanting to take leadership on security with strong U.S. support. From extensive discussions with the commanders, I said, it was clear to me that there was broad agreement from Abizaid on down on a "highly targeted, modest increase" of up to two brigades in support of operations in Baghdad, contingent on a commensurate increase in U.S. civilian and economic assistance. The incremental increase would be designed to prolong "holding" operations long enough for the Iraqis to get nine more brigades fully in place in Baghdad and start gaining control of the situation on the ground.

With regard to Anbar province, where the sheikhs had come on board, I reported that our commanders believed they had made significant progress. Abizaid had told me that Marine commander Major General Rick Zilmer was "kicking the crap out of al Qaeda" there. Both Odierno and Zilmer believed that two more Marine battalions in Anbar would allow them to build on their success. However, I said, Casey was not persuaded of the need for an increase in troops in Anbar, and the province seemingly was of no importance to Maliki. Casey's view was that enduring success required more Iraqi security forces and an Iraqi government presence. He said he would continue to work the issue with Odierno.

Maliki was a major problem, I told the president. In my private conversation with him, he had been "very queasy" about any surge. He had warned me that an influx of U.S. troops seemed counter to Iraqi expectations of reduced troop numbers and would make the coalition forces an even bigger target for terrorists. Both Casey and Odierno thought they could get Maliki to buy in, perhaps agreeing to one additional brigade by January 15 to support Baghdad security operations, with a second brigade moving to Kuwait by February 15 to reconstitute a U.S. reserve force. I suggested to the president that the key to addressing Maliki's reluctance would be to couple his strong desire to have the Iraqis take the lead with the necessity that they not fail. Our commanders were concerned that the Iraqis, while eager to lead, might not be able to successfully carry out the operation. Odierno, clearly more pessimistic than Casey about potential Iraqi performance, had warned me regarding Casey's plan, "There is no guarantee of success," and that it was crucial to follow up clearing operations with a prolonged and effective "hold" period, coupled with an immediate infusion of job-creating economic assistance.

I reiterated that Casey and Abizaid did not want more than these approximately 10,000 additional troops. Parroting their line, I said it would be difficult to resource a more aggressive approach due to stresses and strains on the force—and without imposing it on an Iraqi government clearly reluctant to see a large increase in the footprint of U.S. forces in Iraq; to do so would be to undermine much of what had been accomplished over the past two years.

I believe that a president's senior advisers always owe him as many options as possible and have an obligation to consider what might be done should a plan fail. So I told President Bush that "prudence obliges us to give you some thoughts on a Plan B, should the Baghdad effort fail to show much success." I had asked Pete Pace to work with Casey to develop such a plan, which might involve using the existing U.S. forces in Iraq for different purposes, including redirecting some of McChrystal's special operations toward targeting death squad leaders in Baghdad. A redeployment of U.S. forces already in Iraq, if it proved practical, would have a smaller U.S. footprint and would be more easily acceptable to the Maliki government.

I concluded, "Ultimately, Pete Pace, John Abizaid, George Casey, and I believe we probably have enough U.S. forces and Iraqi capability in place to avoid a catastrophe. The worst case is that we continue to make very little progress. If that was to be the result, then we would need to think about more drastic options to prevent our long-term failure in Iraq."

As I look back, I am sure the president was deeply disappointed by my report—though he never said so. I was basically echoing what Abizaid and Casey had been telling him for months, though they had grudgingly come around to accepting a modest increase in U.S. forces. The president clearly was headed toward a significant increase in U.S. troops. Though I had put on the table the idea of a bigger surge while in Baghdad in September and mentioned that to Bush in my job interview, when I spoke with the president that Saturday I did not mention my recommendation to Baker and Hamilton that we surge 25,000 to 40,000 troops. I had been in the job less than a week, and I was not yet prepared to challenge the commander in the field or other senior generals. That would soon change.

One thing I had to learn, and quickly, was the history that senior officers in the military services had among themselves—their relationships often went back decades or even to their West Point or Annapolis days—which affected their judgments of one another and of one another's proposals and ideas. I also needed to figure out quickly how to read between the lines in listening to military commanders and their subordinates, particularly to identify code words or "tells" that would let me know whether these men were putting on a show of agreement for me when, in fact, they strongly disagreed. I caught a whiff of disagreement between Casey and Odierno in Baghdad, but as I said, it later became clear that Ray strongly disagreed with his boss about the way forward, especially the surge. I would come to rely heavily for these insider insights on the chairman of the Joint Chiefs, first Pete Pace and then Admiral Mike Mullen, and also my senior military assistants.

My views on how we could change the situation in Iraq for the better were evolving quickly. I knew for sure that whatever people had thought about the decision to go to war in Iraq, at this point we could not fail. A defeat of the U.S. military and an Iraqi descent into a vicious civil war that likely would engage other countries in the region would be disastrous, destabilizing the region and dramatically boosting Iran's power and prestige. In the months of furious criticism of Bush's surge that would follow, I never heard the critics address the risk that their preferred approach of a precipitous withdrawal of our troops would, in fact, lead to these very consequences.

I recommended to the president that Lieutenant General David Petraeus replace George Casey, who had been in Iraq for thirty months and whose strategy Bush no longer supported. Everybody I asked, including Casey, thought Petraeus was the right man. Two weeks earlier

I had received a ringing endorsement of him from an unlikely source, my predecessor as president of Texas A&M, Ray Bowen. Ray had met him on a visit to Mosul in August 2003 and observed that Petraeus had learned how to gain the confidence of the Iraqi people and that he displayed "superior understanding" of Iraq, its people, and the issues surrounding the U.S. presence. The president clearly had also heard good things about Petraeus—as he had made clear during my job interview in early November—and so he immediately agreed.

We also discussed who should be the next chief of staff of the Army. General Pete Schoomaker had been brought out of retirement to assume the job and was more than ready to re-retire. The president said he did not want Casey, after all his service to the country, to leave with a cloud over his head because of the situation in Iraq. We agreed to ask George to become the chief of staff.

Some senators in the confirmation process to come, above all, John McCain, would not be as generous with Casey as the president had been. Indeed, during my first trip to Iraq as secretary, I received word that McCain wanted urgently to speak with me. The telephonic connection was finally made during a dinner Casey was hosting for me. I took the call in his bedroom in Baghdad and, in a surreal moment, listened to McCain tell me just how strongly he opposed making Casey chief of staff of the Army.

The meeting of the national security team with the president at the ranch near Crawford on December 28 brought nearly all of the issues to a head. The United States would commit up to five additional brigade combat teams, or approximately 21,500 troops, half of them by mid-February and the rest at a rate of about 3,500 each succeeding month. While Abizaid and Casey were still talking about sending two brigades with the others to come later as needed, both Petraeus and Odierno wanted all five committed and sent. I agreed with the new commanders' recommendation (reversing my earlier support of Casey's approach), persuaded by the argument that if you sent two brigades, then added others later, it would look like the strategy was failing and therefore reinforcements had to be sent. Better to go all in at the outset. I never kidded myself that I was a military expert at the operational level. On this occasion, as later, when I heard the field commanders' recommendations and was persuaded by the reasoning behind them, I was prepared to go all out to provide what they needed.

My lack of understanding of the actual number of troops required for a surge of five brigades led me to underestimate the overall size of the surge in my discussions with the president. The 21,500 represented just the combat brigades but not the so-called enablers—the personnel for helicopters, medevac, logistics, intelligence, and the rest—that would add nearly 8,500 more troops, for a total surge of about 30,000. (Never again would I forget about the enablers.) When first told about the larger numbers, I said, "This is going to make us look like idiots. How could military professionals not have anticipated this?" I sent an impatient memo to Deputy Secretary England and Pete Pace afterward asking if we were now confident in our estimate of the required support capability: "Explaining the most recent additional OIF [Operation Iraqi Freedom] forces and associated funding will be challenging enough. We simply cannot afford another surprise in the weeks ahead. . . . I do not want to be hit with another request three weeks from now." I was taking a crash course in asserting myself with senior officers.

We agreed in Crawford that the Iraqis would take the lead in quelling sectarian violence, but we would insist on the government's allowing the Iraqi army to carry out operations in a nonsectarian way—for example, the politicians (meaning Maliki) would not try to secure the release of politically "protected individuals." We would support the Iraqi forces even while continuing aggressive operations against al Qaeda in Iraq, the Shia kill squads from Jaish al Mahdi, and the Sunni insurgency. The point was made that most of our casualties were coming not from the sectarian violence but rather from improvised explosive devices (IEDs) planted by these groups. We also discussed an increase in the size of the Army and Marine Corps, but no decisions were made by the time we left Crawford.

On January 2, 2007, I reached Petraeus in his car on a Los Angeles freeway. He pulled into a parking lot to take the call, and I asked him if he would take the job as commander in Iraq. He didn't hesitate in saying yes. Like me, I don't think he had any idea how hard the road ahead would be, both in Iraq and in Washington.

On January 3, I met with the president to discuss two key personnel issues. I wanted him to know that Casey would likely face a lot of criticism in the confirmation process, though I thought it would work out if we stood strongly behind him. I also raised the question of who should succeed Abizaid, who was retiring. I said there was a need for a fresh perspective at Central Command and offered three names—General Jack Keane, retired vice chief of staff of the Army (and a key proponent of the surge); Marine General Jim Jones, who had just retired as commander of European Command and supreme allied commander Europe; and Admiral William "Fox" Fallon, commander of Pacific Command. I told him that Pace and others had told me that Fallon was perhaps the best strategic thinker in the military. I observed that in dealing with many of Centcom's challenges—Iran, the Horn of Africa, and others—the Navy had a big role to play. I also pointed out that the commander of Centcom would be Petraeus's boss, and I thought we would need a strong and seasoned four-star officer to make that work. Centcom would be Fallon's third position as a four-star. Fallon would also be the first admiral ever to command there, which I liked because I thought no command should "belong" to one or another service. The president accepted my recommendation, which included pairing Fallon with Army Lieutenant General Marty Dempsey, just coming back from Iraq, as the deputy commander. He also wanted to accelerate the announcement of the changes in leadership both in Baghdad and at Central Command to January 5 so he could send the message that the entire team dealing with Iraq was being changed (including a new ambassador).

At that meeting, I also told the president that I was working on a proposal to increase the size of the Marine Corps by 27,000 for a total of 202,000, and the Army by 65,000 for a total of 547,000. The increase would be spread over several years, with a first-year cost of $17 to $20 billion and a five-year cost of $90 to $100 billion. I also reported that I was looking at our policies with regard to mobilization of the National Guard and Reserves, particularly to ensure that their deployments were limited in duration—probably to a year—and to make sure they had the promised time at home between deployments. He immediately told me to proceed.

The president held a last National Security Council meeting on the new strategy in Iraq on January 8. My briefing materials framed just how dire the situation had become: "The situation in Baghdad has not improved, despite tactical adjustments. The police are ineffective or worse. Force levels in Baghdad are inadequate to stabilize the city. Iraqi support for the Coalition has declined substantially, partly due to the failure of security over the past year. We are on the strategic defensive and the enemy [Sunni insurgents and Shia militias] has the initiative." We had to face four key realities: (1) the primary challenge was extremists from all communities; the center was eroding and sectarianism was spiking (a change from when the Sunni-based insurgency was the primary challenge); (2) political and economic progress in Iraq was unlikely absent a basic level of security; (3) Iraqi leaders were advancing their sectarian agendas as hedging strategies, in pursuit of narrow interests and in recognition of past history; and (4) the tolerance of the American people for the effort in Iraq was waning (a gross understatement, if there ever was one). I think the meeting was, in some ways, a final gut check, for everyone at the table, of the necessity of undertaking the surge and changing our primary military mission from transition to protecting the Iraqi people. The president needed to know the team would hang together in what was certain to be a very rough period ahead.

The president announced his decisions on the surge in a nationwide television address on January 10. He would send five brigades to Baghdad and two battalions of Marines to Anbar. Condi Rice would surge civilian resources, as the chiefs had been asking. Maliki had provided assurances that our forces could operate freely and would say so publicly. My recommended increases in the size of the Army and Marine Corps would be adopted.

And then all hell broke loose.

In a span of forty-five years, serving eight presidents, I can recall only three instances in which, in my opinion, a president risked reputation, public esteem, credibility, political ruin, and the judgment of history on a single decision he believed was the right thing for our country: Gerald Ford's pardon of Nixon, George H. W. Bush's assent to the 1992 budget deal, and George W. Bush's decision to surge in Iraq. In the first two cases, I think one can credibly suggest the decisions were good for the country but cost those two presidents reelection; in the latter case, the decision averted a potentially disastrous military defeat for the United States.

In making the decision to surge, Bush listened closely to his military commander in the field, *his* boss at Central Command, and the entire Joint Chiefs of Staff, giving them ample opportunities to express their views. Then he rejected their advice. He changed his secretary of defense and the field commanders and threw all his weight behind the new team and his new strategy. Like some of his most esteemed predecessors, at least in this instance, he trusted his own judgment more than that of his most senior professional military advisers.

Bush has been criticized by some, particularly in his own party, for his delay in acting to change course in Iraq until the end of the year. My view is that, given the strong opposition of most senior military leaders and commanders and others in the government to the surge right up to his decision in December, changing strategies earlier in 2006 would have been even more difficult and given the president pause. I am in no position to judge whether not acting earlier was influenced by the forthcoming midterm elections. But I do know that once Bush made his decision, I never saw him look back or have second thoughts.

THE WASHINGTON BATTLESPACE

In beginning a partnership with Dave Petraeus that would last nearly four and a half years in two wars, I would often tell him that Iraq was his battlespace and Washington was mine. We each knew who our enemy was. My enemy was time. There was a Washington "clock" and a Baghdad "clock," and the two moved at very different speeds. Our forces needed time to make the surge and our broader plan work, and the Iraqis needed time for political reconciliation, but much of Congress, most of the media, and a growing majority of Americans had lost patience with the war in Iraq. The weeks and months to come were dominated in Washington by opponents of the war trying to impose deadlines on the Iraqis and timelines on us for withdrawal of our troops. My role was to figure out how to buy time, how to slow down the Washington clock, and how to speed up the Baghdad clock. I would repeatedly tell Petraeus that I believed he had the right strategy and, therefore, "I'll get you as many troops as I can for as long as I can."

All through December, the debate over a possible surge had raged in Washington, mainly in the media, since Congress was in recess. Naturally, the opposition of the Joint Chiefs and Casey to a troop increase leaked, as did debates within the administration and, especially, within the Department of Defense. A central theme of the press coverage of my initial visit to Iraq as secretary focused on the concerns expressed to me by commanders and even junior officers about a surge—about the size of the U.S. military footprint, about reducing pressure on the Iraqis to assume responsibility for security—concerns I openly acknowledged. It became increasingly apparent that within the Bush administration, the civilians favored the surge and most of the military did not. It was now being asked whether I could somehow bridge this divide. The criticism in December was just a warm-up for what was to come.

We knew we were in a precarious position with Congress. Everything depended on the Republican minority in the Senate holding firm in using that body's rules to prevent legislative action by a now Democratic-controlled Congress to impose deadlines and timelines that would tie the president's hands. Republican defections could be fatal to the new strategy.

To buy time, I developed a strategy in January for dealing with Congress that, at times, caused both the White House and Dave Petraeus heartburn. It was a three-pronged approach. The first was to publicly hold out hope that if the overall strategy worked—and we would know within months—we could begin to draw down troops toward the end of 2007. This caused a number of the strongest advocates of the surge, both within and outside the administration, to question whether my heart was really in the surge or if I understood that it needed time to work. They were looking at the Iraq battlefield, not the Washington battlefield. I believed the only way to buy time for the surge, ironically, was to hold out hope of beginning to end it.

The second part of my plan was to call for a review and report in September by Petraeus on our progress in Iraq and the effect of the surge. I calculated that I could counter calls from Congress for an immediate change in course with the very reasonable and I believed proper argument that we should be allowed to get all the surge troops into Iraq and then a few weeks later address whether they were making a difference. This would buy us at least until September. If the surge wasn't working by then, the administration would need to reassess the strategy in any case. The September report would take on a life of its own and become a real watershed. (This tactic of using high-level reviews to buy time was one I would use often as secretary.)

The third element focused on the media and on Congress itself. I would continue to treat critics of the surge and our strategy in Iraq with respect and to acknowledge many of their concerns—especially about the Iraqis—as legitimate. So when members of Congress would demand that the Iraqis do more either militarily or in terms of key legislative actions to demonstrate that reconciliation was proceeding, I would say in testimony or to the press that I agreed. After all, that is exactly what I had called for in my e-mail to Baker and Hamilton in mid-October. Further, I would legitimize their criticism by saying that their pressure was useful to us in communicating the limited patience of the American people to the Iraqi government—although I steadfastly opposed as "a bad mistake" any legislated specific deadlines. I always tried to turn down the temperature of the debate.

I divide the debate over Iraq during the last two years of the Bush administration into two phases. The first, from January 2007 until September 2007, continued to be about the war itself and, above all, the surge, and whether it made any sense. It was a bitter and nasty period. For the second phase, from September 2007 until the end of 2008, I changed my modus operandi, making the subject of the debate the pace of troop withdrawals so as to extend the surge as long as possible but also to try to defuse the Iraq debate as a major issue in the presidential election. Most of the Democratic presidential candidates at least tacitly acknowledged the need for a long-term—if dramatically reduced—U.S. presence in Iraq. My hope was that a new administration would proceed deliberately—not under pressure to take dramatic or precipitous action in terms of withdrawals—and thereby protect long-term U.S. interests both in Iraq and in the region.

The strategy largely worked, for a number of reasons, all dependent on the actions and steadfastness of others. The first was the spread of the "Awakening" movement led by Sheikh Sattar and his Sunnis in Anbar, together with the success of Petraeus and our troops in quickly beginning to change the conditions on the ground in Iraq for the better and in ways that within a few months became impossible to deny. We began to see signs that the surge was working as early as July. The second was the president's firmness and his veto power. A third was that the Republican minority in the Senate, for the most part, stayed with us and prevented the passage of legislation mandating timelines and deadlines for withdrawal of our forces. A fourth was that in matters of national security, Congress absolutely hates to challenge the president directly in a way that would saddle them with clear and full responsibility if things went to hell. Finally, negotiations with the Iraqis during 2008 on a Strategic Framework Agreement placing an end date on our troop presence was critical in defusing the issue of withdrawal in the 2008 presidential election—and buying still more time.

But that was all still very much in the future when, on January 11 and 12, 2007, Condi testified before the Senate Foreign Relations Committee on the surge, and Pete Pace and I testified before the two Armed Services Committees. Although we all were grilled intensively, I think Condi had the more difficult session—mainly, I think, because she had been in the administration at the time the decision was made to invade Iraq and so was the target of members' frustration about the entire course of the war. I suspect another reason she had a harder time was that at least four members of the Foreign Relations Committee were planning on running for president and saw the hearing as a platform. Senator Chris Dodd of Connecticut accused the administration of using our soldiers as "cannon fodder," Senator Joe Biden of Delaware said the new strategy was "a tragic mistake" and "more likely to make things worse," and Senator Barack Obama of Illinois said, "The fundamental question that the American people—and, I think, every senator on this panel, Republican and Democrat—are having to face now is, at what point do we say 'Enough'?" The Republicans weren't particularly supportive either. Indeed, Senator Chuck Hagel of Nebraska said that the surge would be "the most dangerous foreign policy blunder in this country since Vietnam."

Pace and I had a somewhat different experience, partly because the Republicans on the Armed Services Committees were generally more supportive of the president's war policies, especially John McCain. There was still a lot of criticism from the Democrats and tough questions from Republicans. I may also have gotten off a little easier because it was my first hearing after confirmation, and I was not my predecessor. I also won broad support when I announced my proposal to expand the size of the Army and Marine Corps during the hearings. And I think I caught them (as well as the White House, Petraeus, and others) off guard when I indicated that I hoped we could begin drawing down troop levels by year's end.

As is often the case, the members asked very few questions that we had not asked ourselves. There was broad skepticism about Maliki and the other Iraqi leaders delivering on their promises this time, unlike so often before; we wondered about this as well. This skepticism was only magnified by the fairly tepid support for the plan by Maliki and other Iraqi leaders in their public statements. Asked how long the surge would last, I went out on a limb in responding, "Months, not years." Both Pace and I took questions on our military leaders' apparent opposition to the plan.

All who testified had not expected a friendly environment, but I think Rice, Pace, and I—and the White House—were taken aback by the vehemence of the reaction and the criticism. It would not soon improve. There would be innumerable efforts to pass binding and nonbinding resolutions opposing the surge, to tie the size of the U.S. troop presence to the Iraqis' passage of legislation, and to use funding bills to limit what the president could do or to force his hand. All would fail, but not before causing those of us in the administration a lot of anxiety and huge budgetary disruptions in the Pentagon as Congress dribbled out war funding to us a few months at a time throughout the year.

One area that would truly test my patience was the senators' focus on benchmarks, and their demands that the Iraqi Council of Representatives enact, by specific deadlines, legislation in key areas such as de-Baathification, the sharing of oil revenues, and provincial elections. This was an approach I also had recommended to Baker and Hamilton, but I had not fully understood then just how tough these actions would be for the Iraqis, precisely because they would fundamentally set the country's political and economic course for the future. Remember, they had no experience with compromise in thousands of years of history. Indeed, politics in Iraq from time immemorial had been a kill-or-be-killed activity. I would listen with growing outrage as hypocritical and obtuse American senators made all these demands of Iraqi legislators and yet themselves could not even pass budgets or appropriations bills, not to mention deal with tough challenges like the budget deficit, Social Security, and entitlement reform. So many times I wanted to come right out of my chair at the witness table and scream, *You guys have been in business for over two hundred years and can't pass routine legislation. How can you be so impatient with a bunch of parliamentarians who've been at it a year after four thousand years of dictatorship?* The discipline required to keep my mouth shut left me exhausted at the end of every hearing.

Almost immediately after the president's January 10 announcement of the surge, both Republican and Democratic members of Congress began looking for ways to reverse it or at least express their disapproval.

In the Senate, Republican John Warner put forward a bipartisan resolution opposing the surge but supporting the forces going after al Qaeda in Anbar province. The Democratic leadership supported Warner's nonbinding resolution, believing that if they could get that passed, they could then move toward stronger steps, such as attaching conditions to war spending. But Warner could not rally the necessary sixty votes to prevent a filibuster, so the resolution quietly died. Too many senators just couldn't bring themselves to support a bill that seemed to undercut the troops.

On the House side, Democrat Jack Murtha, chairman of the Appropriations Defense Subcommittee and a wily old congressional operator, was more subtle. He proposed that units meet strict combat readiness criteria before deployment, a maneuver that Pace and I argued, in a hearing on February 6, 2007, would tie our hands and effectively cut the number of U.S. forces in Iraq by a third. Murtha's plan was to offer an amendment to our wartime supplemental appropriation request of $93 billion, then on the Hill and in need of passage by April to avoid disruptions. We would wrestle with Murtha's proposal and variants of it all through the spring as the Democrats turned to the spending bill as a vehicle to manifest their opposition to the surge.

Toward the end of January, the nominations of Casey to be Army chief of staff and Petraeus to be commander in Iraq were both before the Senate. As predicted, there was opposition to Casey, mostly among the Republicans. McCain was the most strongly opposed, as previewed, saying he thought Casey was the wrong man for the job. Warner was ambivalent. Senator Susan Collins of Maine was not supportive, saying Casey was too removed from the Army and that she had not seen anything positive in his record as commander in Iraq. Senator Saxby Chambliss of Georgia flipped from being supportive to opposing. Even some of those prepared to vote for Casey didn't think he was the best candidate. While I had no chance of getting McCain to change his mind, he did tell me he would not try to organize opposition to Casey. I also talked to Warner and others. This was, of course, discouraging to George after all his service, and on January 20 I suggested to the president that he convey to Casey his ongoing support, and he quickly did so. I was especially concerned about Casey's morale given that Petraeus was moving so fast toward confirmation in the Senate. I told Casey about the negative reactions but explained: "You're in charge in Iraq, and they hate what's going on there." I reassured him that the president was "strong as horse-radish" behind him, and so were Pace and I. I said I hoped he would be confirmed by February 9 or 10. Majority leader Harry Reid said he would get Casey confirmed, and he was, on February 8. Still, fourteen senators voted against him. There was not a single vote against Petraeus.

The president then, I think, made a mistake. Privately to Republicans and then publicly, he hammered the Democrats, asking how they could unanimously support Petraeus but oppose both the general's plan and the resources needed to implement it. It was a logical argument but created huge resentment among Democrats. It would make them far more cautious in confirming senior officers in the months ahead for fear the same argument would be turned on them.

Congressional maneuvering to use the war funding bill to force a change in strategy intensified in late February and March. On March 15, Murtha's subcommittee set a timetable for the withdrawal of U.S. forces from Iraq by the end of August 2008 and, as Murtha had foreshadowed, imposed requirements for unit readiness and deployment duration. On the same day, the Senate voted 50–48 against a binding resolution spon-sored by Harry Reid that would have required a redeployment from Iraq to begin within 120 days of enactment of the bill, set a goal of completing the withdrawal of most troops by the end of March 2008, and limited the mission of the remaining troops to training, counterterrorism opera-tions, and protecting U.S. assets. I pushed back hard for the first time both in private meetings with members of Congress and in the press on March 22, outlining the consequences, for the war effort and our troops, of legislative maneuvering that was bound to draw a presidential veto and thus delay funding for weeks. My warnings notwithstanding, the next day, March 23, the House voted 218–208 for the war funding but set a deadline for U.S. withdrawal from Iraq of August 31, 2008. On the twenty-sixth, the Senate passed the war funding bill with a deadline of completing troop withdrawals by March 31, 2008. On April 25 and 26 the House and Senate, respectively, approved the conference report calling for troop withdrawal to begin by October 1, 2007, and be completed 180 days later. The president vetoed the bill on May 1. We finally received the war funding on May 25 without any restrictive language, but con-gressional efforts to change the strategy would continue, as would our budgetary contortions caused by funding delays. I told members of Congress I was trying to steer the largest supertanker in the world through uncharted waters, and they were expecting me to maneuver it like a skiff.

I tried not to let the shenanigans on the Hill distract me from moving forward with my plans for Iraq, chiefly extending the surge as long as possible into 2008. On March 9, I told my staff that if we were not in a better place in Iraq by October, the strategy would have to change. On March 20, in a videoconference with Petraeus, I said that when I visited Baghdad in mid-April, I wanted to discuss with him how he would define success with respect to the surge. In that regard, he said he thought the surge should last at least until January 2008, a year from its start.

I told Pace on March 26 that I wanted to meet privately with the president before going to Iraq in April to make sure "I know where his head is on October." I told Pete I believed we needed a long-term presence in Iraq, and to achieve that, Iraq had to "be moved off center stage by mid-fall" politically in the United States. That meant, in turn, that the security situation had to improve to the point where Petraeus could honestly say we were making progress and that he could begin to pull out a brigade at a time starting in October, which would have the effect of extending the surge until February. Pace correctly said that it should not just be Dave who defined success; Petraeus should tell us his view, but the president and I needed to make the final call.

As you enter the Oval Office, to the right of the president's desk—a gift from Queen Victoria to President Rutherford B. Hayes in 1880, built from the timbers of the British ship *Resolute*—is a disguised doorway that leads to the president's private lair, the most exclusive "inner sanctum" in Washington. There is a bathroom (which Bush 41 named for a staff member he didn't like) on the right side of the passageway, a very small office to the left, and straight ahead a modest-size dining room with a small galley, where White House stewards prepare coffee, tea, and other drinks. At one end of the dining room is a door leading to the hallway between the Oval Office and the vice president's office, and on the other end, French doors leading to a small patio, where the president can sit outside in private. I had been in this dining room on many occasions while working for Bush 41; it's where we sat to watch the launching of the air war against Iraq in January 1991 on television. I never saw either President Bush in the Oval Office or even in these adjacent rooms without a coat and tie. On the several occasions, I had breakfast with Bush 43 in that dining room, I always wanted to order a "real" breakfast—bacon, eggs, toast. But Bush ate a healthy breakfast of cereal and fruit, and so I reined in my proclivity for greasy fare and made do with an English muffin.

I met privately with the president in that dining room on March 30 and told him I thought we had to turn the corner in Iraq by fall one way or another. I said we needed to get the issue of Iraq off the front burner politically by the presidential primaries in February 2008 so that the Democratic candidates did not lock themselves into public positions that might preclude their later support for sustaining a sizeable military presence in Iraq for "years to come," which I believed necessary to keep things stable there. I had been talking to Petraeus and the Joint Chiefs, I told him, and we all thought we probably could begin a drawdown of troops in October but pace it so Petraeus could keep most of the surge through the spring of 2008. I again emphasized that whether the strategy could be shown to be working by October or not, a change would be needed by then to accomplish our long-term goal of a sustainable troop presence in Iraq.

The president said he agreed with me. He also said he didn't know how long he could hold the Republicans to sustain vetoes. The initiative for any drawdown would have to come from Petraeus, and the president asked, "How will he define success?"

The president then said, I thought somewhat defensively, that he was not cutting Cheney or Hadley out of this discussion, though he and I needed to talk privately on occasion. He said he would not raise the issue of drawdowns again, but I should feel free to see him or call him.

I left the breakfast believing we were in agreement on the need to start a withdrawal in October and the initiative had to come from Petraeus. My challenge was to get Dave to agree to that.

EXTENDING THE SURGE

Before I could pursue the strategy of extending the surge beyond October, I had to address a painful reality. In January, I had announced several initiatives to give members of the National Guard and Reserves more predictability in their deployments; they would henceforth deploy as units—many had deployed before as individuals to larger, cobbled-together units—and not be mobilized for longer than a year. These decisions had been very well received by Guard and Reserve leaders, the troops themselves, and Congress. At the same time, I understood there was a similar challenge in establishing clear, realistic long-term policy goals for the deployment of active duty forces, particularly for the Army. As early as December 27, 2006, I had asked Robert Rangel and my first senior military assistant, Air Force Lieutenant General Gene Renuart, for the pros and cons of calling up units with a shorter time at home than current policy. In terms of morale (and the forthcoming announcement of the surge), I asked whether we were better off approving such early call-ups only for engineering battalions (in demand especially as part of the counter-IED effort) as a "one-off," or changing the policy for the whole force in Iraq as long as we had the current level of forces there. Also, I wondered about the domestic and congressional political dimensions of such a change. I was told that unless current policies were altered, the level of deployed forces in Iraq and Afghanistan would require active duty units to redeploy before they had spent a full twelve months at home. This had been a major factor in my decision to recommend significant growth in the size of the Army and Marine Corps. This was even before the president ordered the surge. Something would have to give.

The Army had presented only two options: extend troop deployments from twelve to fifteen months or shorten soldiers' time at home to less than one year. This was the most difficult decision I would make in my entire time as secretary, difficult because I knew how hard even the one-year deployments were, not only because of the absence from family but because, for those in combat units in Iraq (and Afghanistan), the fighting and the stress of combat were constant. There was no respite from primitive living conditions, the heat, and not knowing what the next moment might bring in terms of danger, injury, and death. Missing one anniversary, one child's birthday, one holiday was hard enough. My junior military assistant, then-major Steve Smith, told me that a fellow midgrade officer had said that a fifteen-month tour was more than just twelve plus three. Steve also reminded me that fifteen-month tours brought to bear the "law of twos"—soldiers would now potentially miss two Christmases, two anniversaries, two birthdays. Still, Pete Chiarelli, who had become my senior military adviser in March, told me that the troops were expecting this decision—the fifteen-month tours—and with the directness I so valued, went on to say, "And they think you're an asshole for not making it."

I once received a letter from the teenage daughter of a soldier who had been deployed for fifteen months. She wrote,

> First of all, fifteen months is a long time. It is just long enough so when the family member comes home it's kind of awkward. Not kind of, really awkward. There are so many things they missed out on and so much more to do. Secondly, they are not really "home" for a year. Sure, they are in the states [sic], but not home. My father was off doing training for the entire summer. So I really hadn't been able to see him very much. That's not even the worse [sic], the worse [sic] is when he is supposed to be home and he's been called to do something at the last minute. . . . Thank you for your time and I hope that you will take all that I have said into account when future decisions are made about the deployments. Megan, AKA Army brat.

I don't know if Megan's father ever knew she wrote me, but if he did, I hope he was very proud of her. I certainly was. After all, not many teenagers can make the secretary of defense feel like a heel. But her letter, and others like it, were so important because they did not let me forget the real-life impact of my decisions and the price our military families were paying.

After consulting with the Joint Chiefs and then the president, on April 11 I announced the deployment extension. All combat tours for the Army in Iraq, Afghanistan, and the Horn of Africa would be extended to fifteen months. I had no idea when we could revert to twelve-month tours. Both Republicans and Democrats were critical of the decision because to them it reflected the failure and costs of the president's war in Iraq.

Experience would show that the fifteen-month deployments for both Iraq and Afghanistan would be even worse for the troops and their families than I expected. While I couldn't prove it statistically, I believe those long tours significantly aggravated post-traumatic stress and contributed to a growing number of suicides, a belief reinforced by comments made to me by both soldiers and their spouses. While I could guarantee them a full year at home between tours, it wasn't enough.

While the troops may have been expecting the decision, a number of soldiers and their families shared their frustration and their anger with reporters. I couldn't blame them. They were the ones about to suffer the consequences of the "law of twos."

GETTING TO SEPTEMBER

The difficulty of extending the surge to September 2007 (when Petraeus would submit his report on progress), much less to the spring of 2008, was underscored by the rhetoric coming from both Republicans and Democrats in Congress. The frequently used line "We support the troops" coupled with "We totally disagree with their mission" cut no ice with people in uniform. Our kids on the front lines were savvy; they would ask me why the politicians didn't understand that, in the eyes of the troops, support for them and support for their mission were tied together. But the comments that most angered me were those full of defeatism—sending the message to the troops that they couldn't win and, by implication, were putting their lives on the line for nothing. The worst of these comments came in mid-April from the Senate majority leader, Harry Reid, who said in a press conference, "This war is lost" and "The surge is not accomplishing anything." I was furious and shared privately with some of my staff a quote from Abraham Lincoln I had written down long before: "Congressmen who willfully take actions during wartime that damage morale and undermine the military are saboteurs and should be arrested, exiled, or hanged." Needless to say, I never hinted at any such feelings publicly, but I had them nonetheless.

The president met with his senior team on Iraq on April 16, with Fallon, Petraeus, and our new ambassador in Iraq, Ryan Crocker, participating by videoconference. Crocker was a great diplomat, always eager to take on the toughest assignments—Lebanon, Pakistan, Iraq, Afghanistan. He quickly earned the president's confidence, though Ryan's consistent realism would lead to Bush teasing him as "the glass-half-empty" man, and sarcastically calling him "Sunshine." Crocker had forged a remarkably strong partnership with Petraeus. The ambassador described the disruptive impact of the recent bombing of the parliament building on the Iraqi Council of Representatives, and the prospects for progress on a de-Baathification law setting forth terms for amnesty for some Baath Party members and on the law for distributing oil revenues, two of the key benchmarks, as I've said, for both the administration and Congress in terms of national reconciliation. The president told Crocker to make clear to the Iraqis that they needed "to show us something." Congressional delegations would come back from visits, he said, say there was no political progress and that the military therefore couldn't do its job, and urge that the troops be withdrawn. "The political elite needs to understand they need to get off their ass," the president said. "We don't need perfect laws, but we need laws. We need something to back off the critics."

Petraeus reported that despite continuing extremist attacks that attracted considerable publicity, our troops were making slow, steady progress and that the preceding week there had been the lowest number of sectarian murders since June 2006. He warned that we were headed into a tough week as U.S. forces moved into areas where we had not had a presence before. He described his plans for deploying the remaining troops and Marines coming to Iraq. At the end of his briefing, Petraeus said he appreciated the announcement on extending tours to fifteen months: "It gives us much greater flexibility. It was the right call and not a big surprise for most units."

Just before leaving for Iraq, I met with Pete Pace about how to approach Petraeus. I told him I didn't want Petraeus walking out of our meeting thinking, *I've been told to wrap this thing up by October* and *I have to recommend an off-ramp by October.* We agreed that we were going to need a long-term presence in Iraq and that we had to set the conditions for that.

I arrived in Baghdad at midafternoon on April 19. Pace, Fallon, and Petraeus all met me at the plane. We immediately jumped in helicopters and flew to Fallujah. The security situation was still too tenuous for me to go into the city, so I was briefed at our military headquarters on progress in Anbar province. It was very encouraging. On leaving, I shook hands and had pictures taken with a number of troops, including one group of officers holding a Texas A&M flag. I ran into Aggies in the war zones all the time, and it was always special for me, although encountering in combat zones those I had given their diplomas was always unsettling.

We returned to Petraeus's headquarters and got down to the business of war strategy—specifically, how to lower the level of violence and buy time for internal political reconciliation. We all agreed that accomplishing those goals required extending the surge beyond September. I had a two-hour private dinner with Pace, Fallon, Petraeus, and Chiarelli, followed by a two-hour session with the same group the next day. We addressed three questions: how to sustain politically at home a significantly higher number of troops for a year; how to maximize the possibility of keeping a substantial number of troops in Iraq for years to come; and how to establish a long-term security and strategic relationship with Iraq. The answers to all three questions had to take into account the twin realities of growing opposition in the U.S. Congress and the growing desire of the dominant Shia in Iraq—especially those within the government, including Maliki himself—to be rid of the "occupiers." The key would be Crocker's and Petraeus's evaluation of success in September.

I emphasized to Dave that his recommendations were to be his own, not dictated by me or anyone else, but with a view to prolonging the surge to a year or more and enabling a sustained U.S. presence. Petraeus said he likely would recommend drawing down one brigade in late October or early November, a second in early to mid-January, and then a brigade every six weeks or so after that. This would allow him to keep 80 percent of the surge through the end of 2007, and 60 percent through the end of February. This would signal to both Americans and Iraqis that a corner had been turned (one way or another) and, hopefully, enable rational decision making regarding a long-term presence. Pace and Fallon both endorsed this approach.

As usual, when I visited Iraq—this was my fourth visit in four months—I met with all the senior Iraqi government officials. It was getting to the point where I could write their talking points for them, from President Talabani's unrealistic optimism and usually empty promises to take action on problems to Sunni vice president Tariq Al-Hashimi's constant complaints of being ignored, insulted, and sidelined, as well as his concerns about Maliki's dictatorial approach. What was new on this trip, though, was that in a private meeting, Prime Minister Maliki aimed a litany of complaints at me personally that he offered "as a brother and partner." While expressing appreciation for President Bush's steadfast support, he said that my statements expressing disappointment in Iraqi government progress toward reconciliation, particularly the oil law and de-Baathification, would encourage the Baathists to come back. He said he understood that the United States was keen to help the Iraqi government, but the realities were very tough. He couldn't fill ministerial positions, among other problems. He went on to say that "benchmarks give the terrorists incentives and encourage the Syrians and Iranians." He concluded that the political situation was very fragile and that we needed to avoid certain public statements that only helped our "enemies."

When he concluded, I was seething. I told him that "the clock is ticking" and that our patience with their lack of political progress was running out. I angrily told him that every day that we bought them for reconciliation was being paid for with American blood and that we had to see some real progress soon. After the meeting, I stewed over the fact that I had been arguing the case for this guy for months in Congress, trying to avoid mandatory benchmarks and deadlines, trying to buy him and his colleagues some time to work out at least some of their political issues.

As usually happened, a visit to our troops revived my morale. I went to a joint U.S.-Iraqi military and police facility in Baghdad meant to provide neighborhood security. It was a centerpiece of Petraeus's strategy, getting U.S. forces out of large bases and into local areas with Iraqi partners. I had imagined a police station like those in most U.S. cities, in the middle of a densely occupied urban area. The one I visited was instead in the middle of a huge open area—in essence, a small fort with concrete outer walls protecting a large concrete building in the center. In the entryway were pictures of Iraqis who had been killed operating out of this facility. I was escorted to a medium-size conference room crowded with Iraqi army officers and police as well as U.S. soldiers and officers, nearly everyone in body armor and carrying weapons. And right there in the middle of a war zone, in the equivalent of Fort Apache, Baghdad, I got a PowerPoint briefing by Iraqi officers. *PowerPoint! My God, what are we doing to these people?* I thought. It took a lot of self-control to keep from bursting out laughing. But what these men—both Iraqis and Americans—were trying to do, and the courage it took, was no laughing matter. I came away immensely impressed, not least by the awful conditions in which our young soldiers were having to work day and night.

I reported the results of my meetings with Petraeus to the president at Camp David on April 27. In testimony before the Senate Appropriations Committee some two weeks later, in response to questions, I showed a little leg on the possibility that the September evaluation might open the way to reducing forces in Iraq. Because the full surge was not yet on the ground in Iraq, this led to a minor firestorm in the press. It was said that I was on a different page from the president and the rest of the administration, that I was ready "to throw in the towel" if we could not see the surge working by September. In fact, this was what the president, Condi, Steve Hadley, Pace, I, and the commanders had been working on for weeks. It was consistent with my approach of holding out the carrot of *possible* troop reductions to get us at least through September and, hopefully, into the spring of 2008 with much of the surge still in place. Most outside observers and "military experts"—even the vice president—seemed to have no idea of how thin a thread the entire operation hung by in Congress through the spring and summer. George W. Bush understood.

The president once again came to the Pentagon on May 10 to meet with the chiefs and me in the Tank, which is actually a rather plain, utilitarian conference room. When the chiefs meet, the chairman and vice chairman sit at the head of a large blond-wood table, the heads of the Army and Navy sit on the side to their left, and the commandant of the Marine Corps and chief of staff of the Air Force to their right. The flags of the services hang behind the chairman, video screens are at the other end of the room, and on the wall to the chairman's left hangs a picture of President Lincoln and his generals. To the chairman's right and up a step is a long narrow table for staff. When the president visited, he and the other civilians—including the secretary—would sit with Lincoln at their backs, with the chiefs at one end and on the other side of the table.

That day in the Tank, the president was very candid and reflective. He told the group assembled, "Many people have a horizon of an inch; my job is to have one that is a mile." He went on to say, "We're dealing with a group of Republicans that don't want to be engaged. They think democracy in the Middle East is a pipe dream. We are dealing with Democrats who do not want to use military force." He said that the psychology of the Middle East was "in a bad place," and we needed to assure everyone that we were going to stay. He was concerned that drawing down to ten brigade combat teams in Iraq—about 50,000 troops—might be excessive, and we should look at the implications before September. Bush observed that "many in Congress don't understand the military."

The same day I met with Senator Carl Levin, chairman of the Armed Services Committee, to see if he would have any problem supporting Pace for a second two-year term as chairman, historically a routine matter. While Pete's first term wouldn't be over until the end of September, senior military nominations are complicated at Defense and the White House, and in Congress, so we tried to get them on track months in advance. I wanted Pace to continue for a second term. We worked very well together, I trusted his judgment, and he was always candid with me. It was a good partnership. But my call on Levin turned out to be anything but routine. He told me he would make no commitment to support Pace and that renominating him was not a good idea. He said there was likely to be opposition; he would check around among the Democrats on the committee. I was stunned.

The next day I talked to John Warner, the ranking Republican on the committee. He was unenthusiastic and said the reconfirmation could be a problem; he would check around among the Republicans. The same day I talked to John McCain. He said someone new was needed, but he would not lead the opposition fight. Warner called back on the fifteenth to tell me that he had talked to Saxby Chambliss and Lindsay Graham, and all three of them thought putting Pace up again was a bad idea. Levin called the next day and told me Pete was highly regarded personally, but he was considered too closely tied to past decisions. Levin also told me that Democrats had been furious when the president used their confirmation of Petraeus against them. Indeed, Levin was explicit about this publicly: "A vote for or against Pace then becomes a metaphor for where do you stand on the way the war is handled."

I then talked with Mitch McConnell, the Republican leader of the Senate. He thought that Pace's nomination would lead to a further erosion of Republican support on subsequent votes to change course on Iraq. More and more Republicans were feeling "quiet anger" that Bush was letting Iraq "sink the entire government." His bottom line: if the Republican leadership of the Armed Services Committee was against Pace's renomination, we probably ought to listen to them.

A week later Lindsay Graham told me that Pace's confirmation hearing would be backward-looking; it would become a trial of Rumsfeld, Casey, Abizaid, and Pace—a rehash of every decision over the previous six years. The focus would be on mistakes made, and the process would probably weaken support for the surge. A new person could avoid all that.

I had kept Pete informed of everything I was doing and everything I was hearing. He was predictably stoic, but I could tell he was disappointed that people in the Senate who he had thought were friends and supporters were, in fact, not. (I reminded him of Harry Truman's line that if you want a friend in Washington, buy a dog.) That said, he wanted to fight. I had two concerns with going forward. The first was for Pete personally. From firsthand experience, I knew better than most just how nasty a confirmation hearing could get. And based on what I was hearing from both Republicans and Democrats on the committee, there was at least a fifty-fifty chance Pete would be defeated for a second term after a long and bloody destruction of his reputation. I felt strongly that Pete should end a distinguished career with flags flying, reputation intact, and the gratitude of the nation. Iraq had become so polarizing that the reconfirmation process would very likely take down this good man. My second concern was that a bitter confirmation fight in the middle of the surge could jeopardize our entire strategy, given how thin support was on the Hill. Senator McConnell's warning had struck home.

I shared this thinking with Pete and with the president, and the latter reluctantly agreed with me. And so, in one of the hardest decisions I would make, I recommended to Bush that he not renominate Pete. Pete and I agreed that the new candidate should be Admiral Mike Mullen, the chief of naval operations. In my announcement on June 8, I said, "I am no stranger to contentious confirmations, and I do not shrink from them. However, I have decided that at this moment in history, the nation, our men and women in uniform, and General Pace himself would not be well-served by a divisive ordeal in selecting the next chairman of the Joint Chiefs of Staff." Although I never said as much to President Bush or anyone else, in my heart I knew I had, for all practical purposes, sacrificed Pete Pace to save the surge. I was not proud of that.

There would be stories later that I had fired Pete and the vice chairman, Admiral Ed Giambastiani. *The Wall Street Journal* editorialized that I had ceded the secretary's job to Senator Levin. In truth, it was the lack of Republican support for Pace and their weakening support for the surge and the war that worried me most. I had asked Giambastiani to stay on as vice chairman for another year, on the assumption that Pace would be confirmed for a second term. When I had to turn to Mullen, Ed had to give up his job because by law the chairman and vice chairman cannot be from the same service. I hated to lose Ed from the team, so I asked him if he would be interested in becoming the commander of Strategic Command. He declined and proceeded to retire.

In my job interview, I had raised with the president the need for stronger coordination of the civilian and military efforts in the war, and for the empowerment of someone in Washington to identify bureaucratic obstacles to those efforts and force action. I saw this person as an overall coordinator on war-related issues, someone who could call a cabinet secretary in the name of the president if his or her department was not delivering what had been promised. I told the press on April 11, "This czar term is, I think, kind of silly. The person is better described as a coordinator and a facilitator . . . what Steve Hadley would do if Steve Hadley had the time—but he doesn't have the time to do it full-time."

Hadley had come to the same conclusion and agreed with me that a coordinator was needed. The president, Cheney, and Rice were initially quite skeptical, but Hadley was able to bring them around. He offered the job to several retired senior military officers. All of them turned him down, one saying publicly that the White House didn't know what it was doing on Iraq. Steve then asked Pace and me for an active duty senior military officer to fill the role. Pete and I twisted the arm of Lieutenant General Doug Lute of the Joint Staff to take the job. I felt we owed him big-time when he reluctantly said yes. Doug would prove an important asset in the Bush administration (though a real problem for Mullen and me in the Obama administration).

During late May and early June, Fox Fallon began to make waves. I had heard indirectly that he and his staff were second-guessing and demanding detailed analyses of many of the requests coming in from Petraeus. Fox believed the drawdown could go faster than Dave was proposing. Fallon made the mistake of taking a reporter, Michael Gordon of *The New York Times,* into a meeting with Maliki. I thought it was bizarre; it made Condi furious. On June 11, I received the "upraised eyebrow" treatment from the president when the subject came up, which I always read as *What in the hell is going on over there?* He wanted to know what action was being taken with Fallon. Subsequently, the president read that Fallon was talking about reconciliation in Iraq, a matter he told me was only Crocker's business. I asked Pace to have a cautionary conversation with Fallon. Bush—and Obama—were very open to candid, even critical comments in private from senior officers. Neither had much patience for admirals and generals speaking out in public, however, particularly on matters that were considerably broader than their responsibilities. This episode of public outspokenness by a senior officer provoking a White House response would be the first of many I would have to confront.

I visited Iraq again in mid-June to discuss strategy with Petraeus, to visit the troops, and to meet with the Iraqi leaders. I again urged action on key Iraqi legislation and pushed Maliki not to allow the Council of Representatives to take a monthlong holiday. I was as blunt with him as I would ever be. During that visit, I told Petraeus that we would lose the support of moderate Republicans in September and that he needed to begin to transition "to something" in October. He outlined an operational rationale for a drawdown: the population security objectives had been met; there had been success in Anbar; Iraqis wanted a drawdown; Iraqis were assuming more responsibility for security (thirteen of eighteen provinces); and the Iraqi security force was improved. He asked me about starting the drawdown with a nonsurge brigade, and I told him that that decision was his to make.

I believe Petraeus knew what I was trying to do in terms of buying more time for the surge, and that he agreed with it, but I may have pushed a little too hard during that visit. We in the administration knew the initiative in September would need to come from Dave. For some reason, he felt compelled to tell me with half a chuckle, "You know, I could make your life miserable." I have a pretty good poker face—all those hours testifying in front of Congress required it—so I don't think Dave knew how taken aback I was by what I interpreted as a threat. At the same time, I understood he had been given an enormous task, the pressures on him for success were huge, and like any great general, he wanted all the troops he felt he needed for as long as he needed them. Fortunately for all of us, Dave was also politically realistic enough to know he needed to show some flexibility in the fall or potentially lose everything to an impatient Congress. But he didn't have to like it. He had just told me as much.

At the end of June, Fallon came to my office to offer his view of what the next steps ahead should be for Iraq. As he sat at the little round table that had belonged to Jefferson Davis when he was secretary of war and went through his slides, it became clear he was in a very different place than Petraeus was, and, I thought, a very dangerous place for our strategy and success in Iraq, as well as a precarious place politically for himself. He said there had been no progress on reconciliation despite constant promises; the central government was inexperienced, corrupt, and complicit in interfering in security operations to the advantage of Shia factions; the cycle of violence continued unabated, with more than one hundred U.S. soldiers being killed every month; insurgents and terrorists were targeting U.S. political resolve; the Iraqi forces were growing slowly but faced shortcomings in training, logistics, and intelligence;

and finally, the U.S. ability to respond to crises elsewhere in the world was foreclosed because our ground forces were completely committed in Iraq. Therefore, he concluded, a fundamental change in Iraq policy was necessary, and "acting now" would avoid a contentious debate in September. He called for the United States to shift its mission to training and enabling, with a gradual removal of U.S. forces from the front line. Fallon recommended reducing our brigade combat teams from twenty to fifteen by April 2008, to ten by the beginning of December 2008, and to five by the beginning of March 2009.

I knew his recommendations would never fly with the president, and I disagreed with them as well, as I told him. But I could not disagree with Fox's assessment of the situation on the ground. And while there would be rumors about differences between Fox and Petraeus on the way forward, I give Fox a lot of credit for the fact that his proposals of June 29 never leaked. Had they, there would have been a political firestorm, both in the White House and on Capitol Hill.

The rest of the summer I was largely focused on trying to retain what congressional support we had and to keep Congress from tying our hands in Iraq. The president's veto of the war funding bill setting a deadline for troop withdrawals did not deter the Democratic leadership in both Houses from continuing to try to legislate a change in Iraq strategy. Once again their approach was to focus on our military's readiness and the amount of time troops spent at home. Another approach, which appealed to moderate Republicans such as Lamar Alexander, was to try to legislate the recommendations of the Iraq Study Group, such as ending the combat mission and shifting to supporting, equipping, and training the Iraqis within a year. (The president saw the ISG recommendations as a strategy for withdrawing from Iraq rather than a strategy for achieving success there.)

By early July, our ability to stave off congressional action had weakened even further, with Senate Republicans such as Pete Domenici breaking with the president. The situation became so dicey that I canceled a planned trip to Central and South America in July so I could stay in Washington to meet with members of Congress and work the phones. My strongest argument, especially with the Republicans, was the need to wait at least until Petraeus and Crocker could report in September. As I had hoped early in the year, that bought us time. It was hard to argue that after all we had been through in Iraq, we couldn't wait another six weeks to hear how the president's new strategy was going. I also started using the line that it seemed odd to me that critics of the war who had complained so vehemently that Bush had ignored the advice of some of his generals at the outset of the war were now themselves prepared to ignore—or not even wait for—the generals' advice on the endgame.

That summer I was also focused on orchestrating how the Department of Defense would formulate and communicate its recommendations to the president in September on the next steps in Iraq, drawdowns in particular. I felt very strongly that the president should hear face to face from all of his senior military commanders and advisers. I believed that no single general should have to bear the entire weight of such a consequential recommendation; I also did not want the president to be captive to that person's views. I hoped that the process I designed would have the added benefit of minimizing whatever differences there were among the senior military leadership, differences I knew Congress would learn about and exploit.

In the middle of all this, typical of Washington, I had to deal on a continuing basis with personality-based journalism and rumors. For example, a reporter with a reputation for having good sources in the military wrote that the president was setting up Petraeus to be the scapegoat if the surge strategy failed. It was totally untrue and made the president furious. Then I was told that "folks in the White House" were hearing that Fallon was undercutting Petraeus and that retired Army vice chief of staff (and strong surge supporter) Jack Keane was saying Fallon was "bad-mouthing" Petraeus to the chiefs.

On August 27, Petraeus and Fallon began briefing the chiefs and me on their views of the way ahead in Iraq. This was where the rubber met the road. Petraeus said that there had been progress in security, but national reconciliation had been slower than we had hoped for, that the government was inexperienced and struggling to provide basic services, and that the regional picture was very difficult. In July, there had been a record number of security incidents—more than 1,700 per week. But civilian casualties were down 17 percent from the previous December, all deaths were down 48 percent, and all murders were down 64 percent. Attacks in Anbar had dropped from more than 1,300 in October 2006 to just over 200 in August 2007.

Dave recommended that in December 2007, we begin to transition from surge operations and gradually transfer responsibility for population security to the Iraqi forces. Specifically, Petraeus said he expected to redeploy U.S. forces from Iraq beginning in September 2007, bringing out the Marine Expeditionary Unit by September 16 and a total of five brigade combat teams (BCTs) and two Marine battalions between December 2007 and July 2008, and withdrawing combat support and service units as soon as feasible. That would bring U.S. forces in Iraq down to the presurge fifteen BCTs. He called for the United States to exploit progress in security with aggressive action on the diplomatic, political, and economic fronts. He proposed providing, no later than mid-March 2008, another assessment of mission progress and his recommendation for further force reductions beyond July 2008.

Petraeus said that a decision on going from fifteen to twelve BCTs would need to be made no later than March 2008. He went on to say that further drawdowns past July 2008 "will happen" but at a pace determined by assessments of factors "similar to those considered in developing these recommendations."

So there it was. I met with the Joint Chiefs in the Tank on the twenty-ninth, and then Pace and I met the next day in the Oval Office with the president, vice president, White House chief of staff Josh Bolten, Steve Hadley, and Doug Lute. Pace presented Petraeus's plan, as well as the views of Fallon and the chiefs. He said there was consensus among the military commanders and advisers on Petraeus's recommendations, carefully noting that the chiefs and Fallon leaned toward more emphasis on speeding the transition to Iraqi security forces while Petraeus was still leaning more toward continued U.S. military emphasis on providing security for the Iraqi population.

I had organized the meeting to "prepare the ground" for the president's meetings with Petraeus, Fallon, and others the next day. I wanted him to know beforehand what he would hear so he wouldn't have to react on the spur of the moment; particularly on a subject as important as this, no president should ever have to do that, except in a dire emergency. I also wanted the president to be able to ask questions, including political ones, that might be less convenient (or inappropriate) to ask in the larger forum the next day. And as so often, he had a lot of questions. Was this recommendation driven by stress on the forces? Did this represent a change of mission? He was unhappy with the so-called "action-forcing" pressures on the Iraqis that suggested they could be "driven" to reconciliation, measures intended to bring pressure on the Iraqis to pass laws we (and Congress) believed necessary for reconciling the Shia, Kurds, and Sunnis. He thought the troop reductions must be explicitly "conditions-based." He embraced the idea that a shift in strategy had been made possible by the success of the surge and conditions on the ground—not because of pressure from Congress, not because of stress on the fighting force, not as an effort to pressure the Iraqi government. I said that the changed situation on the ground enabled the beginning of a transition and noted that the surge brigades would not be the first to come out. Those would come from areas where the security situation was better, and the surge around Baghdad would be prolonged for a number of months. The vice president asked whether these steps put us on a path where we could not succeed. Pace responded, "No. They put us on a path where we can." In the end, the president was comfortable with Petraeus's recommendations. I think Cheney was reconciled but skeptical; I do not believe he would have approved the general's recommendations had he been president.

On August 31, Condi and Fallon were to join the same group that had assembled the previous day in the White House. There was a hiccup before the meeting. Pace and I got calls from the White House about six-thirty a.m. raising hell over Fallon's slides, which had been provided in advance and which stated that our presence in Iraq was a big part of the security problem there and created additional antagonism toward us in the region. He was focused strongly on the transition to Iraqi security control. Pace called Fallon and told him some of his slides didn't square with views he had earlier expressed to us. Fallon removed a couple of slides, the tempest was quelled, and the meeting went forward at 8:35.

Bush spent nearly two hours in a Situation Room videoconference with Crocker and Petraeus in Baghdad. Petraeus again gave his overall assessment of the situation, including a number of encouraging political and economic developments not reflected in the Iraqis' failure to pass key legislation advancing internal reconciliation. He went through his recommendations. Again, the president objected to what he called the "action-forcing" aspects. He said he didn't believe the United States could force Iraqis to reconcile their long-standing internal hatreds. There was a lot of candid give-and-take. Crocker, Petraeus, and Fallon all directly disagreed with the president, saying that without U.S. pressure the Iraqis "just can't act"; there wasn't enough trust or confidence or experience. I said there was a difference between real reconciliation and making progress on issues. I thought our role was more like a mediator between a union and a company—we could help make them deal with issues and reach agreements; we didn't need them to love one another. On troop levels, and particularly drawdowns between December and July, the president wanted to make sure that we couched them in terms of what we "expect" to happen versus what "will" happen, and that our decisions would be based on conditions on the ground. He wanted to proceed cautiously. Ironically, he was willing to be more aggressive with drawdowns after July. Fallon's remarks were helpful, and he endorsed Petraeus's recommendations.

That same afternoon the president met with the Joint Chiefs of Staff. Pace reviewed the chiefs' assessment of nine different options on the way ahead in Iraq, from a further increase in troops to a faster drawdown. Pete told the president that the chiefs had independently come out where Petraeus and Fallon were.

The president asked the chiefs if they had been driven to those recommendations by strains on the force, about which there was considerable discussion. Pace said no, that the recommendations were "resource-informed" but not "resource-driven." Bush asked, "Why do people join the military if they don't want to fight and defend the country?" The vice president chimed in, "Are we close to a time when we have to make a choice between winning in Iraq and breaking the force?" And the president said, "Somebody has got to be risk averse in this process, and it better be you, because I'm sure not." At the end, the president said, "I will do what Petraeus has recommended."

The president made a brief statement to the press after the meeting. I had talked with Hadley and Ed Gillespie, the president's counselor and communications guru, and suggested that a less strident tone than usual and more of an outstretched hand to the critics would be useful for the upcoming congressional hearings. They agreed and drafted such a statement. But the president got wound up and made a very tough statement, engaging his critics. Afterward I turned to Hadley and Gillespie and asked, "So this is his happy face?"

The Iraq process came out pretty much as I had planned—and hoped for—early in the year and as the president and I had discussed privately months before. We would not finish drawing down to presurge troop levels until the summer of 2008. The president would continue to speak of "winning." I was satisfied that our chances of failure and humiliating retreat had been vastly reduced. After all the earlier mistakes and miscalculations, maybe we would get the endgame right after all.

Two days later, on September 2, the president and Condi flew secretly to Al Asad Air Base in western Iraq to meet with Petraeus and Crocker, senior Iraqi government officials, and a number of the Sunni sheikhs who had played such a critical role in organizing resistance to al Qaeda and the insurgency in Anbar province. Pace went on his own. I flew separately in a C-17 and took Fallon with me.

Two conversations at Al Asad remain vivid for me. The first was between Crocker and the president. The president made the comment that the Iraqis' struggle was akin to what we went through with civil rights. (I detected Condi's influence in that analogy.) He then said to Crocker, "Where's your head?" Ryan made clear he thought Iraq was very different and much worse than our civil rights struggle. He said it was important to understand what thirty-five years of Saddam had done to Iraq—he had "deconstructed" it. It was a country and a people who had been reduced to their fears, and they were sectarian. It was going to take time, and "the cycle of fear" had to be broken. The U.S. action in 2003 had not been regime change, Ryan said. "It was much more. . . . And there is no Nelson Mandela because Saddam killed them all." "This is winnable," he said, "but it will take U.S. commitment and a long time." Ryan said there had been successes, but "if we walk away there will be a humanitarian disaster on the scale of Rwanda, it will open the way to al Qaeda to return to ungoverned spaces, and it will open the way for Iran with consequences for all Arab states." Crocker was as stark and plainspoken to the president as possible.

The second conversation was with the sheikhs and the provincial governor. It was all about the locals wanting money from the capital for their pet projects, as if they were members of Congress.

The headline from the trip was the president's statement to the press that "General Petraeus and Ambassador Crocker tell me if the kind of success we are now seeing continues, it will be possible to maintain the same level of security with fewer American forces."

A sad footnote to the Al Asad meeting was that a few days later, Sheikh Sattar, who had led the Anbar "Awakening" that played such an important role in the success of the surge, was assassinated.

The final hurdle was for Crocker and Petraeus to run the gauntlet on Capitol Hill on September 10 and 11. They testified over two long days against a backdrop of noisy protesters—the so-called Code Pink Ladies, a group of antiwar women dressed in pink clothes, some of whom had to be ejected from the hearing rooms. Crocker and Petraeus were in command of the facts, and they were brutally honest about the challenges in Iraq. Their caution and candor gave skeptics and critics plenty to chew on—and they did. There were some memorable lines. Crocker, in response to a question from Senator McCain about whether the Iraqis would do what we asked of them, said: "My level of confidence is under control." Senator Clinton said to Petraeus: "The reports that you provide to us really require the willing suspension of disbelief." "Buy time? For what?" said Senator Hagel. The Democrats were predictably furious that there had been so little progress on the political front in Iraq. Many Republicans, who had hoped for more positive testimony or indications of a dramatic change in strategy, were critical as well. Some of those who had been quietly supportive of the president's war policies, like Senator Elizabeth Dole, called for "action-forcing" measures, while others called for a legislated change in mission.

The quiet competence and honesty of both Crocker and Petraeus had a big impact, especially as they were subjected to incredibly hostile questioning, especially in the Senate, as noted above. The Senate Republican leadership expressed renewed confidence after the hearings that they would be able to prevent Democratic legislation on the war from passing. Meanwhile a full-page ad by an antiwar group, MoveOn.org, accused Petraeus of distorting the facts to please the White House and was headlined, "General Petraeus or General Betray Us?" I found it despicable and said so. Such an attack on a man who had devoted his life to defending the country infuriated the Republicans and embarrassed the Democrats and, in my view, made it harder for the critics to press their case. At the end of the two days, it was pretty clear that while few members of Congress were happy, the Democrats did not have the votes to change the war strategy. In that respect, Pace's and my testimony on the twelfth and the president's speech on the thirteenth announcing the drawdowns—the "return on success"—were anticlimactic.

All year long I had deliberately played my cards very close. As one journalist had written in August, "Even in his private meetings with lawmakers, top aides and his own senior commanders . . . he has avoided showing his hand. . . . He is the . . . administration official whose views are the least understood." I believed that I would maintain maximum leverage in the process, especially with Congress, if the other players did not know exactly what approach I supported. The only person to know, outside my immediate staff and Pace, was the president. I acknowledged all this in a press conference on September 14: "As the debate here in Washington proceeded in recent months and, more importantly, as we considered future U.S. actions in Iraq, I have kept a fairly low public profile in the belief I could thereby be more effective inside the Pentagon, in working with my National Security Council colleagues, in advising the president and in dealing with the Congress."

I then shared my view on the multiple objectives that the next steps in Iraq had to address. Above all, we had to maximize the opportunity created by the surge to achieve our long-term goals and avoid even the appearance of American failure or defeat in Iraq. We would need to reassure our friends and allies in the region—and signal potential adversaries—that we would remain the most significant outside power there for the long term. We had to reinforce to the Iraqis that they had to assume ever-greater responsibility for their own governance and security. And at home, we had to work toward winning broad, bipartisan support for a sustainable U.S. policy in Iraq that would protect long-term American national interests there and in the region. We had one further objective: to preserve the gains made possible by our men and women in uniform and thus reassure them that their service and sacrifice truly mattered.

I concluded, "Some say the Petraeus strategy brings our forces out too slowly, that we must withdraw faster. I believe that, whatever one may think about how we got to this point in time in Iraq, getting the next part right—and understanding the consequences of getting it wrong—is critical for America. I believe our military leadership, including a brilliant field commander, is best able and qualified to help us get it right."

Knowing that the next face-off would come in March, I decided at that press conference to dangle another carrot. I said that I "hoped" that Petraeus would be able to say in March "that he thinks the pace of drawdowns can continue at the same rate in the second half of the year as in the first half of the year." I wanted to underscore that the trend line on troops would remain downward and, as I had hoped early in 2007, make the debate in 2008 about the pacing of drawdowns and a long-term security relationship with Iraq rather than about the war itself or our strategy. I believed strongly this approach would be in the long-term best interest of the United States, and I hoped that it would be reflected in the presidential campaign.

A last gasp of those who wanted to change the strategy came in mid-September, with renewed interest in proposed legislation by Senator Jim Webb that would require troops to spend as much time at home as on their most recent tours overseas before being redeployed. This was another way to force the president to accelerate the troop withdrawals. In practical terms, because the amendment focused on individual soldiers instead of units, actually making it work would have been nearly impossible. I said in my September 14 press conference that such an amendment might require extending tours of units already in Iraq, calling up additional National Guard and Reserve troops, and would further stress the force and reduce its combat effectiveness. Pace and I pointed out that the amendment would require us to examine the deployment record of each individual soldier to ensure that he or she had been home long enough—and that could force the breakup of units with some soldiers who met the time limit and others who did not. This amendment had attracted fifty-six votes in the Senate in July and only four more were needed for passage. I worked the phones hard, as determined on this issue as I had been on anything since becoming secretary. After I gave a speech in Williamsburg, Virginia, on the seventeenth, I offered Senator John Warner a helicopter lift back to Washington. I used our time together to explain to the former secretary of the Navy the impossibility of managing what Webb was proposing. He agreed not to support it, which was important given Warner's seniority on the Armed Services Committee and status as Webb's partner in the Senate from Virginia.

That same day I told some journalists that the critics of the war were moving the goalposts on the president: they had asked for a troop drawdown, and now that was happening; they had asked for a date for the drawdown to begin, and now they had one; they had wanted a timetable for continued drawdowns, and Petraeus had provided one; and they had wanted a change of mission, and the president had announced one. I said that I thought it was in the interest of the critics to let the president get the situation in Iraq in the best possible shape so the new president would not be handed a mess there. I didn't make much of an impact.

House Speaker Nancy Pelosi invited me to breakfast on the eighteenth. Five days before, she had issued a news release saying, "The president's strategy in Iraq has failed," and "The choice is between a Democratic plan for responsible redeployment and the president's plan for an endless war in Iraq." With those comments as backdrop, at the breakfast I urged her to pass the defense appropriations bill before October and to pass the War Supplemental in total, not to mete it out a few weeks or months at a time. I reminded her that the president had approved Petraeus's recommendation for a change of mission in December and told her that Petraeus and Crocker had recommended a sustainable path forward that deserved broad bipartisan support. She politely made clear she wasn't interested. I wasn't surprised. After all, one wouldn't want facts and reality—not to mention the national interest—to intrude upon partisan politics, would one?

I had just concluded a very hard eight-month fight with Congress, "improvising on the edge of catastrophe," to paraphrase the historian Joseph Ellis. But I had gotten what I wanted. On September 21, Congress failed to pass a single one of the amendments to change our strategy.

Pace and I were to testify together one last time on September 26 before the Senate Appropriations Committee. Before the hearing that afternoon, I had breakfast with the Democratic majority leader in the House, Steny Hoyer, and a number of Democratic members. I then had lunch with the Senate Democratic Policy Group, led by Majority Leader Harry Reid. Both sessions were friendly, serious, and thoughtful.

The contrast with the hearing that afternoon could not have been more dramatic: it was the wildest hearing I experienced in my entire professional life. The Pink Ladies and others were out in force, and the huge hearing room was rowdy and noisy. An ancient and frail Senator Robert Byrd was in the chair. The hearing, supposedly about the defense budget, was basically one more opportunity for the Democrats to vent on Iraq. Byrd took it to a whole new level. Like an evangelical tent preacher, he played to the crowd, engaged them, and enraged them, virtually encouraging the protesters to heckle Pete and me. Byrd would shout rhetorical questions at us, like "Are we really seeking progress toward a stable, secure Iraq?" The crowd would respond in unison, "No!" When he referred to the "nefarious, infernal war in Iraq," the protesters shouted back, "Thank you. Thank you." He strung out his words for dramatic effect—the war had cost a "trillllunnn" dollars, and so on.

The Democrats on the committee grew uncomfortable about the lack of decorum. A couple of them spoke out about the need for order in the room. Then Senator Tom Harkin asked Pete about his "hurtful" views on gays in the military. (Pete had given an interview the previous March expressing his personal view that homosexual conduct was immoral.) Pace repeated his views—it was, after all, his last hearing, and he had nothing to lose. That did it. The room went berserk. Byrd had completely lost control of the hearing and realized it. He pounded the gavel so hard, I thought he might collapse. He then said the hearing was adjourned, was quickly reminded by aides to "suspend" it, and then ordered the room cleared of all spectators. As the Capitol police went about their work, Republican Senator Judd Gregg walked out, saying to Harkin, "You should be ashamed." Harkin jumped up out of his chair and shouted back, "I don't need any lectures from you."

I thought the whole thing had been comical—*Saturday Night Live* meets Congress. I didn't dare turn around to look at the crowd, or I would have burst out laughing. Politically, it was so over the top, it had been the Senate version of MoveOn.org's newspaper ad. I told my staff the next day that it had been "a civil hearing . . . aside from the riot." The hearing seemed a fitting culmination to my 2007 battle with Congress over the Iraq War. Sadly, one of the political casualties of both of those wars was sitting next to me at the witness table for the last time.

CHAPTER 3

Mending Fences, Finding Allies

I could not make headway on implementing the Iraq strategy without extinguishing—or at least controlling—a number of political and bureaucratic brushfires: with the senior military, Congress, the media, and other agencies, including the State Department and the intelligence community. Figuring out how to do this required a lot of time and energy during my first months as secretary. As you can imagine, I was also determined to establish a special bond with our troops, especially those on the front lines. How could I communicate to them and give them confidence that the secretary of defense personally had their backs and would be their advocate and protector in the Pentagon and in Washington?

In Washington, nearly every day began with a conference call at 6:45 a.m. with Hadley and Rice. Then I would usually spend endless time in meetings. In the White House, there were meetings with just Steve and Condi; meetings with the two of them and Cheney; meetings with that cast plus the director of national intelligence, the director of CIA, and the chairman of the Joint Chiefs; "principals" meetings with a cast of thousands, all of them taking notes (I was usually pretty quiet in those meetings); and meetings with the president. All those dealt just with routine business. If there was a crisis, more meetings were added. It was frustrating how often we would cover the same ground on the same issue, huge quantities of time consumed in striving to establish a consensus view. Some of the sessions were a waste of time; moreover, they often failed to highlight for the president that under a veneer of agreement, there were significant differences of view. As I would often say, sometimes we chewed the cud so long that it lost any taste whatsoever. I drank a huge amount of coffee, and the only saving grace of late-afternoon meetings at the White House was homemade tortilla chips with cheese and salsa dips. Still, all too often I found myself bored and impatient.

My meeting "problem" was even worse at the Pentagon. My days there began with a "day brief" in my office to acquaint me with what had happened overnight and the bureaucratic challenges ahead that day; the day ended with a "wrap up" at the same Jefferson Davis round table, where we surveyed the bureaucratic battle damage of the day. That table was one of three antiques in the office. (I would joke with visitors, four, if you included me.) There was also an elaborately carved long table behind my desk that had belonged to Ulysses S. Grant. My huge partners desk had been General John J. Pershing's, spirited away from the Old Executive Office Building next to the White House to the Pentagon by the second secretary of defense, a political hack named Louis Johnson. The rest of the office was in "late government" style, that is, brown leather chairs and a sofa, exquisitely accented by stark fluorescent lighting. Two portraits were on the wall behind my desk: my personal heroes, General George C. Marshall and General Dwight D. Eisenhower.

Robert Rangel conducted both the morning and evening meetings, which included just the two of us and my senior military assistant. Rangel had the best poker face of anyone I've ever known, so when he started in, I had no idea whether he was going to give me good news (quite rare) or set my hair on fire with some disaster (routinely). The rest of the day was filled with secure videoconferences with commanders in Baghdad and Afghanistan; meetings with my foreign counterparts (sometimes two or three a day); meetings on the budget or various weapons programs; meetings on civilian and military personnel; meetings on service-specific issues; meetings on issues of special concern to me that I wanted to track closely (usually having to do with the troops in the field). I usually ate lunch alone so I didn't have to talk to anyone for at least forty-five minutes during the day. For a mental break, I would usually do the daily *New York Times* crossword puzzle while I ate my sandwich. In the mix were all the calls and meetings with members of Congress and congressional hearings. Pace and subsequently Mike Mullen sat in with me on many, if not most, of these meetings. PowerPoint slides were the bane of my existence in Pentagon meetings; it was as though no one could talk without them. As CIA director, I had been able to ban slides from briefings except for maps or charts; as secretary, I was an abject failure at even reducing the number of slides in a briefing. At the CIA, I was able on most days to protect an hour or so a day to work in solitude on my strategies for change and moving forward. No such luck at Defense. One tactic of bureaucracies is to so fill the boss's time with meetings that he or she has no time to meddle in their affairs or create problems for them. I am tempted to say that the Pentagon crew did this successfully, except that many of my meetings were those I had insisted upon in order to monitor progress on matters important to me or to put pressure on senior leaders to intensify their efforts in accomplishing my priorities.

In truth, nothing can prepare you for being secretary of defense, especially during wartime. The size of the place and its budget dwarf everything else in government. As I quickly learned from 535 members of Congress, its programs and spending reach deeply into every state and nearly every community. Vast industries and many local economies are dependent on decisions made in the Pentagon every day. The secretary of defense is second only to the president in the military chain of command (neither the vice president nor the chairman of the Joint Chiefs of Staff is in the chain at all), and any order to American forces worldwide goes from the president to the secretary directly to the combatant commanders (although as a practical matter and a courtesy, I routinely asked the chairman to convey such orders). More important than any of the meetings, the secretary makes life-and-death decisions every day—and not just for American military forces. Since 9/11, the president has delegated to the secretary the authority to shoot down any commercial airliner he, the secretary, deems to be a threat to the United States. The secretary can also order missiles fired to shoot down an incoming missile. He can move bombers and aircraft carriers and troops. And every week he makes the decisions on which units will deploy to the war front and around the world. It is an unimaginably powerful position.

At the same time, no secretary of defense who wants to remain in the job can ever forget that he works for the president and serves only at the pleasure of the president. To be successful, the secretary must build a strong relationship of mutual trust with him and also with the White House chief of staff and other senior executive staff members—and, most certainly, with the director of the Office of Management and Budget.

The secretary of defense is also part of a broader national security team—the vice president, secretary of state, national security adviser, director of national intelligence, and director of the CIA among them, and the part he chooses to play on that team can have a big impact on the nation's, and a president's, success. Further, money fuels the Defense machine, and because every dime must be approved by Congress, the secretary needs to have the savvy and political skill to win the support of members and to overcome their parochial interests for the greater good of the country.

In short, despite the tremendous power inherent in the job, the secretary of defense must deal with multiple competing interests both within and outside the Pentagon and work with many constituencies, without whose support he cannot be successful. He is constantly fighting on multiple fronts, and much of every day is spent developing strategies to win fights large and small—and deciding which fights to avoid or concede. The challenge was winning the fights that mattered while sustaining and even strengthening relationships, while reducing the number of enemies and maximizing the number of allies.

Making Peace at Home

Before becoming secretary, I had heard and read that Defense's relationships with Congress, the media, and other agencies of the government—and the national security team—were in trouble. I had also heard rumors of real problems between the civilian leadership and senior military officers. Then I arrived in Washington for confirmation and really got an earful about how bad things were—from members of Congress in both parties, from reporters I had known a long time, from friends in government, and from a number of old associates with close ties to many in the Pentagon, both civilian and military. To this day, I don't know how much of this gossip was simply animosity toward Rumsfeld, how much was institutional ax-grinding, and how much was just sucking up to the new guy by trashing his predecessor (an old habit and a highly refined skill in Washington). But I also knew that in Washington, perception is reality, and that I had to tackle the reality that the Department of Defense had alienated just about everyone in town and that I had a lot of fences to mend. It would be critical to success in Iraq.

I started closest to home, in the executive corridors of the Pentagon itself, the E-Ring, the outermost corridor in the building and home to the most senior military and civilian officials. An hour after I was sworn in on December 18, I held my first staff meeting with the senior civilian leadership and the Joint Chiefs of Staff. I wanted them to know right away how I intended to operate. This is part of what I said:

First, contrary to rumors in the press, I am not planning any personnel changes and I am not bringing anyone in with me. I have every confidence in you and in your professionalism. The last thing anyone needs, in the seventh year of an administration and in the midst of two wars, is a bunch of neophytes surrounding a neophyte secretary.

Second, decision making. I will involve you, and I will listen to you. I expect your candor, and I want to know when you are in disagreement with each other or with me. I want to know if you think I'm about to make a mistake—or have made one. I'd rather be warned about land mines than step on one. Above all, I respect what each of you does and your expertise. I will need your help over what I expect will be a tough two years.

Third, on tough issues, I'm not much interested in consensus. I want disagreements sharpened so I can make decisions on the real issues and not some extraneous turf or bureaucratic issue. I'm not afraid to make decisions, and obviously, neither is the president.

Fourth, on style, you will find me fairly informal and fairly irreverent. I prefer conversation to death by PowerPoint. I hope you will look for opportunities for me to interact with soldiers, sailors, marines, and airmen—and opportunities for me to do my part to communicate our pride in them and gratitude for their service.

Fifth, we will succeed or fail depending on whether we operate as a unified team or separate fiefdoms. I will work in an open, transparent manner. I will make no decision affecting your area of responsibility without you having ample opportunity to weigh in. But once decisions are made, we must speak with one voice to the Congress, the media, and the outside world.

Sixth, no policy can be sustained without bipartisan congressional support. This will be a challenge with the change of majority party. But I want this department to be seen as eager to work with Congress and responsive to their requests insofar as we can be. The media is our channel of communication to the American people and the world. We need to work with them in a nonhostile, nonantagonistic way (however painful it is and will be at times).

Seventh, my priorities are clear: Iraq, Afghanistan, the war on terrorism, and transformation. Much else is going on. I want to continue the division of labor with Deputy Secretary [Gordon] England that existed under Secretary Rumsfeld—with all the really hard stuff going to Gordon! He and I will be joined at the hip. I expect to have the same close relationship with the chairman and the chiefs.

I then told them that General Pace, undersecretary for policy Eric Edelman, and I would be leaving the next day, the nineteenth, for Iraq, would return on the twenty-second and report to the president on the twenty-third. One important reason I took Pace and Edelman with me was to signal to civilians and military alike in the Pentagon that the chairman was going to be a close partner in my leadership of the department, and that the military needed to recognize that my civilian senior staff would play a critical role as well.

I repeated these points and expanded upon them in a meeting with the entire Defense leadership, civilian and military—including the combatant commanders from around the world—on January 24. I told them I was grateful Gordon had decided to stay on as deputy and that he would be the department's chief operating officer. I made clear to the senior military officers that Eric would have a key role in representing their interests in interagency meetings and at the White House and they should regard him as an asset and work closely with him.

I emphasized that when dealing with Congress, I never wanted to surprise our oversight committees, and I wanted to pick our fights with the Hill very carefully, saving our ammunition for those that really mattered. I encouraged anyone in the department who had special relationships or friendships with members of Congress to cultivate them. I felt that would benefit all of us.

Meetings and conferences, I said, should be more interactive. A briefing should be the starting point for discussion and debate, not a one-way transmission belt. If they had to use PowerPoint, I begged them to use it sparingly, just to begin the discussion or illustrate a point. I asked my new colleagues to construct a briefing while asking themselves how it would move us forward, and what the follow-on action might be. (Again, changing the Pentagon's approach to briefings was a singular failure on my part. I was not just defeated—I was routed.)

I told them I had decided to make a change in the selection process for flag-rank officers—generals and admirals. Rumsfeld had centralized this in the secretary's office. I said I would continue to review all positions and promotions at the four-star level and some at the three-star level, but otherwise I was returning the process to the services and the Joint Staff. I said that I still wanted the same things Rumsfeld had been looking for—joint service experience, operational experience, bright younger officers, and those willing to reexamine old ways of doing business. And I would be checking the services' homework.

I decided to adopt the same strategy with the military leadership I had used with the faculty at Texas A&M and with the intelligence professionals when I was running the CIA: I would treat them with the respect deserved by professionals. I would approach decisions by seeking out their ideas and views, by giving them serious consideration, and by being open and transparent. Everyone would know the options under consideration, and everyone would have a chance to weigh in with his or her point of view (more than once if they thought it important), but I often would not reveal my own views until the end of a decision-making process. I never fooled myself into believing that I was the smartest person in the room. As I had told Colin Powell, I am a very good listener and only through the candor and honesty of both my civilian and military advisers could I work my way through complex issues and try to make the best possible decision. In everything I did as secretary, I sought the advice of others—though I did not always heed it—and depended upon others for effective implementation of my decisions.

Good arguments could get me to change my mind. Early on I had to decide on a new U.S. commander in Korea. The position had been filled for nearly sixty years by Army generals. I thought the time had come to rotate the position to another military service. Because our Air Force and Navy would play a big role in any conflict on the Korean peninsula, I decided to appoint an Air Force officer as the new commander. Army chief of staff George Casey balked and made a strong case that the timing for the change wasn't good, especially as we were negotiating with South Korea on a transfer of operational control of forces from the

United States to the Koreans. He was right, so I recommended that the president nominate another Army general.

As I signaled at my first staff meeting, I worked hard from the beginning to make the chairman of the Joint Chiefs of Staff my partner within the framework of the chain of command, consulting with him on virtually everything and making certain, through him, that the service chiefs and commanders all knew I wanted and expected candor and their best advice.

I have long believed that symbolic gestures have substantive and real benefits—"the stagecraft of statecraft," as I think George Will once put it. Rumsfeld rarely met with the chiefs in the Tank, instead meeting in his conference room. I resolved to meet regularly with them in their space. I ended up doing so on a nearly weekly basis. Even when I had no agenda, I wanted to know what was on their minds. Instead of summoning the regional and functional combatant commanders (European Command, Pacific Command, Strategic Command, Transportation Command, and all the others) to the Pentagon to give me introductory briefings on their organizations, I traveled to their headquarters as a gesture of respect. This had the additional benefit of familiarizing me with the different headquarters' operations and of giving me the chance to speak with a number of staff I wouldn't otherwise have met. I resolved that I would try to attend change-of-command ceremonies for the combatant commanders, symbolic recognition of their important role and of the institutional culture.

My approach in dealing with the military leadership had a far more positive impact than I had expected. I had much less of a problem with end runs to the Hill and leaks than many of my predecessors. Of course, over time, demonstrating that I was willing to fire people when necessary probably didn't hurt either.

As for Congress, the two most important people on the Hill for me were the chairman of the Senate Armed Services Committee, Carl Levin, and the ranking Republican on the committee until 2009, John Warner, as we've already seen. While the House Armed Services Committee and its chairman, Ike Skelton, and the two Appropriations Committees were also important, I had a lot more business with the Senate Armed Services Committee, if only because it handled all of my department's civilian and military leaders' confirmations. My confirmation hearings got me off on the right foot with Levin and Warner, and I tried to keep them informed of what I was doing and planning, particularly with personnel. Levin was a formidable adversary on Iraq, but my willingness publicly to acknowledge the legitimacy of some of his concerns—such as the failure of the Iraqis to reconcile politically—and even to concede that his criticisms were helpful in putting pressure on the Iraqis, kept our differences from becoming personal or an impediment to a good working relationship. Levin was strongly partisan, and I thought some of his investigations were attempts to scapegoat my predecessor and others. But he always dealt fairly and honestly with me, always keeping his word. If he said he would do something, he did it. Warner was always pleasant to deal with, even if he sometimes was in my view a little too willing to compromise on Iraq. The next ranking Republican was John McCain. Ironically, while McCain and I agreed on most issues—especially Iraq—he was, as we have seen, prickly to deal with. During one hearing he might be effusive in his praise, and in the next he would be chewing my ass over something. But I always tried to be respectful and as responsive as possible to all members of the committee, however difficult that sometimes would prove to be. I saved my venting for the privacy of my office.

I dealt with many other members of Congress as well. I disagreed with Speaker of the House Pelosi on virtually every issue, but we maintained a cordial relationship. I would also meet from time to time with House Majority Leader Hoyer and other Democrats he would gather. My approach to Congress seemed validated when, at a Hoyer-hosted breakfast, Tom Lantos, chairman of the House Foreign Affairs Committee, opened his remarks with a French phrase he directed at me and translated as "It is the tone that makes the music." "You bring things and people together with your tone," he said. "Thank God. Your principal contribution will be setting a new tone in respecting different views on the Hill and throughout the country."

With all the major issues we had to deal with, my personal contacts with Senate Majority Leader Reid were often in response to his calls about Air Force objections to construction of a windmill farm in Nevada because of the impact on their radars. He also once contacted me to urge that Defense invest in research on irritable bowel syndrome. With two ongoing wars and all our budget and other issues, I didn't know whether to laugh or cry.

I came to believe that virtually all members of Congress carried what I called a "wallet list," a list they carried with them at all times so that if, by chance, they might run into me or talk with me on the phone, they had a handy list of local projects and programs to push forward. And some became pretty predictable. If Senator McConnell of Kentucky was calling, it was probably to make sure a chemical weapons disposal plant in his state was fully funded. Anyone elected from Maine or Mississippi would be on the phone about shipyards. California, C-17 cargo planes; Kansas, Washington, or Alabama, the new Air Force tanker; Texas, when were the brigades coming back from Europe and would they go to Fort Bliss?

In the privacy of their offices, members of Congress could be calm, thoughtful, and sometimes insightful and intelligent in discussing issues. But when they went into an open hearing, and the little red light went on atop a television camera, it had the effect of a full moon on a werewolf. Many would posture and preach, with long lectures and harshly critical language; some become raving lunatics. It was difficult for me to sit there with a straight face. But I knew from reading a lot of history that such behavior dated back to the beginning of the republic. And as amusing or infuriating as members sometimes were, I never forgot the importance of their roles. And all but a handful would treat me quite well the entire time I was secretary.

I had not dealt much with the media while director of the CIA or as president of Texas A&M, so regular press conferences and routine exposure to reporters were new to me. In a departure from the usual practice at the Pentagon, I wanted a press spokesman who had been a practicing journalist and who would not also have the job of administering the huge Defense Department public affairs operation. Marlin Fitzwater, Bush 41's press secretary, had made the point to the president that he could not do his job if he was not included in many of the president's meetings or if the press lacked confidence that he really knew the president's mind on issues. I thought Marlin was right, and I adopted his approach for Defense. I hired Geoff Morrell, who had been with ABC television news and had covered the Bush 43 White House. He became a key member of my team.

I continued the practice of appearing at press conferences together with the chairman. Both of us sat behind a table, which I thought was more casual (and more comfortable). I departed from this practice a few times early on, when I had a major personnel announcement (especially a firing), in which case I would go out alone and use a podium. It became a standing joke with the Pentagon press corps that if the podium was on the stage, someone was going to get the ax. I thought about faking them out a few times but thought better of it.

A practice I developed in talking with student groups and others at Texas A&M was never to condescend to a questioner, or question the question. I would follow the same practice with reporters. The Pentagon is fortunate in having, on the whole, an experienced and capable group of reporters assigned to it, most of whom are interested in the substance of issues and not personalities. I never had a real problem with them. Sure, I'd get frustrated occasionally, but probably not as often as they did: while I was candid and straightforward most of the time, they could not get me to talk about something I didn't want to talk about.

I hated leaks. I rarely blamed reporters for printing leaks, though; my anger was reserved for those in government entrusted to keep secrets who did not. When I announced the extension of Army tours in the Centcom area from twelve to fifteen months, I had to rush the announcement because of a leak. I was furious because we had orchestrated the decision to give commanders forty-eight hours to explain the decision to their troops. I told the press that day, "I can't tell you how angry it makes many of us that one individual would create potentially so much hardship not only for our servicemen and women, but also for their families, by . . . letting them read about something like this in the newspapers."

My views on the role of Congress and the media were a little out of the ordinary for a senior official of the executive branch, and I pushed those views forward whenever possible, especially at the service academies. In my commencement address at the Naval Academy on May 25, 2007, I told the about-to-be new ensigns and lieutenants:

> Today I want to encourage you always to remember the importance of two pillars of our freedom under the Constitution—the Congress and the press. Both surely try our patience from time to time, but they are the surest guarantees of the liberty of the American people. The Congress is a coequal branch of government that under the Constitution raises armies and provides for navies. Members of both parties now serving in Congress have long been strong supporters of the Department of Defense, and of our men and women in uniform. As officers,

you will have a responsibility to communicate to those below you that the American military must be nonpolitical and recognize the obligation we owe the Congress to be honest and true in our reporting to them. Especially if it involves admitting mistakes or problems.

I went on to discuss the media:

The same is true with the press, in my view a critically important guarantor of our freedom. When it identifies a problem . . . the response of senior leaders should be to find out if the allegations are true . . . and if so, say so, and then act to remedy the problem. If untrue, then be able to document that fact. The press is not the enemy, and to treat it as such is self-defeating.

Many members of Congress and many in the media read these remarks. They were, I believe, the foundation of an unprecedented four-and-a-half-year "honeymoon" for me with both institutions.

The final relationships to fix were interagency, particularly with the State Department, the intelligence community, and the national security adviser. This was the easiest for me. I had first worked with Steve Hadley on the NSC staff in 1974, and Condi Rice and I had worked together on that staff during Bush 41's presidency, as mentioned earlier. I knew that for much of my career, the secretaries of state and defense had barely been on speaking terms. The country had not been well served by that. I had known the director of national intelligence, Mike McConnell, when he was the two-star head of intelligence for the Joint Staff. Nearly nine years on the NSC staff had also ingrained in me the importance for a president of having the team pull together. It had worked well in Bush 41's administration, and it needed to in Bush 43's. I readily conceded that the secretary of state should be the principal spokesperson for the United States, and I also knew that if she and I got along, it would radiate throughout our departments and the rest of the government. Symbolism was important. When Condi and I would meet together with leaders in the Middle East, Russia, or Asia, it sent a powerful signal, not just to our own bureaucracy but to other nations, that trying to play us off against each other wasn't likely to work.

There was another factor that made me comfortable assuming a less publicly assertive role. I wrote earlier about the unparalleled power and resources available to the secretary of defense. That ensures a certain realism in interagency relationships: the secretary never has to elbow his way to the table. The secretary can afford to be in the background. No one can ignore the eight-hundred-pound gorilla in the room.

The fractious relationship among Defense, the director of national intelligence, and the director of the CIA needed to be repaired as well. Undersecretary of Defense for Intelligence Jim Clapper; McConnell, the DNI; General Mike Hayden, the CIA director; and I now undertook to figure out how to remedy the deficiencies of the 2004 Intelligence Reform Act and bring the intelligence community closer together. It was an arduous process—more than it should have been—because of so much scar tissue and enmity in the various bureaucracies. This was one of those rare instances where a unique set of personal relationships stretching back decades allowed us significantly to mitigate otherwise intractable bureaucratic hostility. And it is still another reminder that when it comes to government, whether it works or not often depends on personal relationships.

If there was any doubt that things had changed among the agencies with my arrival, it was put to rest with a speech I made at Kansas State University in November 2007, where I called for significantly more resources for diplomacy and development—for the State Department and the Agency for International Development. No one could ever recall a secretary of defense calling for an increase in the State Department budget. With Rice, Hadley, and me working together, cooperation among the agencies and departments improved significantly. Indeed, as early as February 2007, Steve told me I was already making a huge contribution, that I had "opened up the process for the president" and had had a real impact on other departments and the interagency process. My unspoken reaction was that I had enough fights on my hands without looking for more.

THE BUSH TEAM

I joined the Bush administration at the end of its sixth year. Neither the president nor the vice president would ever again run for public office. That fact had a dramatic impact on the atmosphere and the nature of the White House. The sharp-elbowed political advisers and hard-core ideologues who are so powerful in a first term were pretty much gone.

All eyes were now on legacy, history, and unfinished business, above all, on Iraq.

In all the books and articles I have read on the Bush administration, I have seen few that give adequate weight to the personal impact of 9/11 on the president and his senior advisers. I'm not about to put Bush or anyone else "on the couch" in terms of analyzing their feelings or reactions, but my views are based on many private conversations with key figures after joining the administration, and on direct observation.

Beyond the traumatic effect of the attack itself, I think there was a huge sense among senior members of the administration of having let the country down, of having allowed a devastating attack on America take place on their watch. They also had no idea after 9/11 whether further attacks were imminent, though they expected the worst. Because the senior leadership was worried there might be warning signs in the vast collection apparatus of American intelligence, nearly all of the filters that sifted intelligence reporting based on reliability or confidence levels were removed, with the result that in the days and weeks after 9/11, the White House was flooded with countless reports of imminent attacks, among them the planned use of nuclear weapons by terrorists in New York and Washington. All that fed the fear and urgency. That, in turn, was fed by the paucity of information on, or understanding of, al Qaeda and other extremist groups in terms of numbers, capabilities, leadership, or anything else. Quickly filling those information gaps and protecting the country from another attack became the sole preoccupation of the president and his senior team. Any obstacle—legal, bureaucratic, financial, or international—to accomplishing those objectives had to be overcome.

Those who years later would criticize some of those actions, including the detention center at Guantánamo and interrogation techniques, could have benefited from greater perspective on both the fear and the urgency to protect the country—the same kind of fear for national survival that had led Lincoln to suspend habeas corpus and Franklin D. Roosevelt to intern Japanese Americans. The key question for me was why, several years after 9/11 and after so many of those information gaps had been filled and the country's defenses had dramatically improved, there was not a top-to-bottom review of policies and authorities with an eye to culling out those that were most at odds with our traditions, culture, and history, such as renditions and "enhanced interrogations."

I once asked Condi that question, and she acknowledged they probably should have done such a review, perhaps after the 2004 election, but it just never happened. Hadley later told me, though, that there had been a review after the election, some of the more controversial interrogation techniques had been dropped, and Congress had been briefed on the changes. Like most Americans, I was unaware.

Most of the members of the Bush team I joined have been demonized in one way or another in ways that I either disagree with or believe are too simplistic. As for President Bush, I found him at ease with himself and comfortable in the decisions he had made. He knew he was beyond changing contemporary views of his presidency, and that he had long since made his presidential bed and would have to sleep in it historically. He had no second thoughts about Iraq, including the decision to invade. He believed deeply in the importance of our "winning" in Iraq and often spoke publicly about the war. He saw Iraq as central to his legacy, but less so Afghanistan, and he resented any suggestion that the war in Iraq had deprived our effort in Afghanistan of adequate resources. Bush relied a lot on his own instincts. The days of funny little nicknames for people and quizzing people about their exercise routines and so on were mostly long over when I came on board. This was a mature leader who had walked a supremely difficult path for five years.

Bush was much more intellectually curious than his public image. He was an avid reader, always talking about his current fare and asking others what they were reading. Even in his last two years as president, he would regularly hold what he called "deep dives"—in-depth briefings and discussions—with intelligence analysts and others on a multitude of national security issues and challenges. It was a very rare analyst or briefer who got more than a few sentences into a briefing before Bush would begin peppering him or her with questions. They were tough questions, forcefully expressed, and I can see how some might have seen the experience as intimidating. Others found the give-and-take with the president exhilarating. At the same time, the president had strong convictions about certain issues, such as Iraq, and trying to persuade him otherwise was a fool's errand. He had a very low threshold for boredom and not much patience with structured (or long) briefings. He wanted people to get to the point. He was not one for broad, philosophical, or hypothetical discussions. After six years as president, he knew what he knew and rarely questioned his own thinking.

Bush was respectful and trusting of the military but, at least in my time, not reluctant to disagree with his senior leaders and commanders, especially as it became clear in mid-2006 that their strategy in Iraq wasn't working. He visited the Pentagon fairly regularly, willing to meet as often as needed with the chiefs to give them the opportunity to lay out their views and talk with him. He welcomed their candor, and while he would react to or rebut things they said, I never heard him do so in a rude or curt manner or in such a way as to discourage future candor. At the same time, he would get impatient with senior officers who were publicly outspoken on sensitive issues. Whether it was the DNI, Admiral Mike McConnell, in a *New Yorker* article calling some of our interrogation techniques torture, or Fox Fallon expounding on avoiding conflict with Iran, or Mike Mullen on several occasions going against the company line on both Iraq and Afghanistan, the president would turn to me and say, "What is it with these admirals?"

The president and I were not close personally, but I felt as though we had a strong professional relationship. He invited Becky and me to Camp David on several occasions, but we were unable to go either because of my foreign travel or Becky being in the Pacific Northwest. Declining the invitations became a source of embarrassment to me, especially when the invitations stopped coming. I was always concerned the president might think we were avoiding what would have been a real honor when, in fact, it was always just poor timing.

The one somewhat touchy area between us—never openly discussed— was my close relationship to the president's father. When Bush 41 was in Washington in late January 2007 and wanted to come over to the Pentagon to see me and meet some of the military leaders, I got a call from Josh Bolten that Bush 43 thought such a visit might become a news story and he did not want that. Josh urged me to call off the visit. I said I would defer to 43's wishes. So 41 and I had breakfast the next day at the White House instead. A few weeks later I was returning from a meeting at the White House when my secretary called to tell me that 41 was on his way to the Pentagon. I barely arrived in time to welcome him, and he went around shaking hands and talking with the folks in my immediate office. He was there only about fifteen to twenty minutes, but I think he wanted to make a point about his own independence.

My only real problem with the Bush White House involved its communications/public relations advisers. They were always trying to get me to go on the Sunday TV talk shows, write op-eds, and grant interviews. I considered their perspective—and that of Obama's advisers too—to be highly tactical, usually having to do with some hot-button issue of the moment and usually highly partisan. I believe that when it comes to the media, often less is more, in the sense that if one appears infrequently, then people pay more attention when you do appear. Bush's advisers occasionally would try to rope me into participating in White House attacks on critics of the president, and I would have none of that. When the president gave a speech to the Israeli Knesset in the summer of 2008 in which he came close to calling his critics appeasers, the White House press folks wanted me to endorse the speech. I directed my staff to tell them to go to hell. (The staff told them more politely.) In terms of picking fights, I intended to make those decisions for myself, not cede the role to some staffer at the White House.

President Bush was always supportive of my recommendations and decisions, including on those occasions when I told him I wanted to fire some of his senior-most appointees in the Defense Department. He gave me private time whenever I asked for it, and we were in lockstep on strategy with respect to Iraq, Iran, and other important issues where some in the administration, the press, and Congress sometimes thought I was freelancing. I kept him well informed about everything I was doing and what I intended to say publicly.

I enjoyed working for and with President Bush. He was a man of character, a man of convictions, and a man of action. As he himself has said, only time will tell how successful he was as president. But the fact that the United States was not successfully attacked by violent extremists for the last seven years of his presidency, and beyond, ought to count for something.

I met Dick Cheney in the mid-1980s when he was a member of the House Select Committee on Intelligence. I had been a junior National Security Council staffer during the Ford administration, when he was deputy White House chief of staff and then chief; I was far too much of an underling to have any contact with him. In my opinion, one cannot understand Cheney without having been in the White House during the Ford years. It was the nadir of the modern American presidency, the president reaping the whirlwind of both Vietnam and Watergate. The War Powers

Act, the denial of promised weapons to South Vietnam, cutting off help to the anti-Soviet, anti-Cuban resistance in Angola—Congress took one action after another to whittle down the power of the presidency. Cheney saw it all from the Oval Office. I believe his broad assertion of the powers of the presidency after 9/11 was attributable, in no small part, to his experience during the Ford years and a determination to recapture from Congress powers lost fifteen years before and more.

Because Dick is a calm, fairly quiet-spoken man, I think a lot of people never fully appreciated how conservative he always was. In 1990, in the run-up to the Gulf War, the question arose as to whether to seek both congressional and UN Security Council approval for going to war with Saddam Hussein. Cheney, then secretary of defense, argued that neither was necessary but went along with the president's contrary decisions. And when the Soviet Union was collapsing in late 1991, Dick wanted to see the dismantlement not only of the Soviet Union and the Russian empire but of Russia itself, so it could never again be a threat to the rest of the world.

He and I had always had a cordial relationship. When I was acting director of central intelligence in early 1987, I met with Cheney to ask his advice on how to deal with the White House and Congress; he was the only member of Congress I consulted. We got along well during 41's administration, sharing a concern—well placed, as it turned out—about the prospects for Gorbachev's survival and agreeing on the need to reach out to other reformers, including Boris Yeltsin. Much later, perhaps around 2004 or 2005, Becky and I had joined the Cheneys and one other couple as guests of former U.S. ambassador to the United Kingdom Anne Armstrong and her husband, Tobin, at their vast and historic ranch in south Texas for bird shooting. Neither Becky nor I am a bird hunter, but we went out with the party and watched the shooting from a safe distance. We socialized before, during, and after meals and had a great time. (We were later invited to participate in another such hunting weekend at the Armstrong ranch with the Cheneys a year or so later. I had a speech commitment in Los Angeles and so we had to decline. The Austin lawyer invited in our stead would be the victim of the hunting accident involving the vice president.)

By the time I joined the administration, Dick was increasingly concerned about unfinished business, with regard to Iran in particular, and eager to deal with it because the next president, in his view, might not be tough enough to do so. He was a strong supporter of the surge in Iraq and provided access to its most vocal advocates outside government, including retired general Jack Keane, especially when they thought others in the government (mainly me, Rice, Mullen, and Fallon) weren't sufficiently committed. Cheney never wavered in his support for "enhanced interrogation techniques" or for the ongoing importance and value of the prison at Guantánamo. On these and other issues, he was increasingly isolated inside the senior ranks of the administration, a reality he conceded with some humor and grace. He got to the point where he would often open his remarks with "I know I'm going to lose this argument" or "I know I'm alone in this."

Cheney's manner in the inner circles of the government belied the "Darth Vader" image that his public speeches and positions helped create. I never heard him sound off in anger; rather, he would present his point of view lucidly and calmly. He asked thoughtful questions of experts and intelligence professionals, and I considered him a less aggressive questioner than the president. Based on what I heard from folks at the Defense Department, I think the vice president let some of his staff be the "bad guys" in interagency affairs rather than taking on that role himself. Again, my observations come from the last two years of an eight-year run. How much his approach changed after Condi became secretary of state and Hadley the national security adviser (Hadley had worked for Dick at Defense during 41's administration), and then again after I replaced Rumsfeld (they had been extraordinarily close), I simply do not know. What was clear was that on the important issues, the vice president remained as committed as ever, and however calm his demeanor, he was not prepared to retreat on any of the controversial policies of the Bush administration. While we agreed on a number of important national security issues—above all, Iraq and Afghanistan—when I thought he was prepared to risk a new military engagement, I pushed back, just as I would in the Obama administration.

I knew Condi Rice and I would get along fine. (She, Hadley, and I are now consulting partners.) Under Bush 41, when I was deputy national security adviser, Condi had been the Soviet expert on the NSC. We both had doctorates in Russian and Soviet studies (she could still speak Russian, not me), and we agreed on just about everything relating to the collapsing Soviet Union from 1989 until 1991, when she returned to Stanford. Indeed, when 41 authorized me in the summer of 1989 to form a very secret, small group to begin contingency planning for the collapse of the Soviet Union, I asked Condi to lead the effort.

Condi is really good at just about anything she tries, a source of resentment for those like me who have no athletic, linguistic, or musical talent. But she and I quickly developed a strong working relationship that radiated throughout our respective bureaucracies, as I've said. We would get together for dinner every few months, always at her favorite restaurant in the Watergate building. On virtually all of the major issues during the Bush administration, she and I were pretty much on the same page. On North Korea, where I was far more pessimistic than she or her negotiators about any chance for denuclearization, I saw no harm in trying—unlike the vice president, who opposed any talks.

Rice was very tough-minded and very tough. She has a razor-sharp tongue, and she spares few who cross her. On one occasion, in a meeting with the vice president, Hadley, and me, Dick made some comment about the need to protect the Republican base in the Senate. Condi shot back, "What's that—six senators?" Another time, when the senior leadership of the government was meeting in the Roosevelt Room of the White House to discuss closing Guantánamo (Condi and I were about the only advocates for closure at the table), Attorney General Mike Mukasey said we should let the whole thing just play out in the courts. Without missing a beat, Condi said, "Mike, every time you go to court, you lose." She was also skeptical of guidelines for interrogation that still allowed humiliation through nakedness, as well as other techniques she found questionable.

Condi and I testified together on a number of occasions. The worst was a four-hearing marathon that we had to endure right after the president's decision on the surge. A number of members of the House Foreign Affairs Committee were rude, nasty, and stupid—in the process, making the Armed Services Committees look almost statesmanlike. I was so angry at the boorishness and antagonistic tone of members of the Foreign Affairs Committee that about half an hour before the end of the hearing, I just shut down. I made clear I was finished trying to answer their questions. But not Condi. She leaned forward in the saddle and took them on (she clearly had more experience with this crowd) with intensity and logic. Of course, logic doesn't count for much when the critics are baying at the moon.

Condi was very protective of State Department turf and prerogatives, and she bristled quickly at any hint that State wasn't pulling its weight in the wars in Iraq and Afghanistan. More than once, I got an earful about some general or admiral who had complained publicly about the lack of civilian support in the war effort. My sense from our military leaders in Iraq and Afghanistan was that the civilian experts made a real difference; there were just too few of them. Early in my tenure, I received a memorandum from the State Department asking for military officers to fill what were supposed to be civilian positions in Iraq. Given what our folks were already being asked to do there, I wasn't happy and said so publicly. Still, she and I never let those dust-ups impact our cooperation. It was my great good fortune to have two formidable women—Condi and Hillary Clinton—serve as secretary of state during my tenure as secretary of defense. On controversial issues in both the Bush and Obama administrations, I worked hard to make sure Condi and Hillary were on my side—and vice versa.

Steve Hadley and I first started working together on the NSC staff in 1974. He worked amazingly hard and, I thought, ran an interagency process that well served the president but that also was regarded as fair and even-handed by the rest of us. He was deeply loyal to Bush 43. As befits a good lawyer, he was meticulous in every respect. When I joined the government in late 2006, I thought Steve was exhausted, spent. But he kept on trucking, fueled by green tea. As secretary, I had a lot of respect for him, even if he did convene all those damn meetings.

The other key member of the national security team with whom I would work most closely was the chairman of the Joint Chiefs of Staff. As I've said, I worked with Pace for nine and a half months and with Mike Mullen for three years and nine months. They had very different backgrounds (beyond the former being a Marine, the latter a sailor) and very different personalities. Both are observant Roman Catholics, both are men of extraordinary integrity and honor, and both have good senses of humor. Their views on homosexuals serving in the armed forces were diametrically opposed—Pace adamantly against, Mullen becoming a historic advocate in favor. Both were superb advisers to me and to the presidents they served.

I was sold on Mullen to succeed Pace when Pete Chiarelli, my new senior military assistant, told me that he had paid a courtesy call on Mullen and had asked him what worried him the most about our forces, and he, the chief of naval operations, had replied, "The state of the Army." I got to know Mullen better than Pace because of the length of our time together, and we shared more foxholes together. Despite the occasional bump in the road, I could not imagine a stronger, better chairman or a better partner.

At the outset of his tenure, Mike took on several issues where I actually agreed with him but, consistent with my practice of avoiding fights I didn't need, thought he would spend political capital and ultimately lose. I think Mike felt the role of the chairman had been diminished over a period of years, and he was determined to strengthen it and make the chairman a much more publicly visible senior military leader. He soon took on a significant public calendar of speeches, television shows, and other appearances. Some of my staff and some at the White House became restive over this and recommended that I rein him in. While his public schedule occasionally made me uneasy, I trusted him, felt we had a strong partnership, and decided I would not make an issue of it. Mike strongly objected to Jack Keane's advisory role in Iraq, specifically with Petraeus, and called Keane in to tell him he couldn't go to Iraq anymore. Keane complained to the vice president, and the next thing I knew, Cheney was on the phone asking me why all the administration's critics could travel to Iraq but not one of its foremost defenders. I ended up leaving the matter in Petraeus's hands—if he could use him and found value in his visits, then Keane could go over. Mike objected to retired military officers taking an active role in politics and spoke out forcefully against it. He also wanted to eliminate the use of the term "Global War on Terror" by the military, early on in his tenure, perhaps to stake out his independence from the White House. Again, I didn't really disagree, but I knew it would raise hackles throughout the administration and was another hassle we didn't need. All that said, over nearly four years, there were only a few issues or decisions of consequence where we disagreed.

Mike had many strengths. He gave me great advice on military appointments and those personal relationships among senior officers that count for so much. He was a powerful advocate of accountability, especially after a screw-up, and thus an important ally when it became necessary to fire or replace senior officers. One of his greatest strengths was his ability to bring the service chiefs together as a unified front when we had to deal with tough issues like the budget, thereby mostly avoiding internecine fighting among the services. He also made sure they had the chance to present their views directly to me and, whenever necessary, to the president. He had the gift of fostering unity, and I believe it well served the military, both presidents, the country, and me.

Perhaps for the first time ever, the chairman and the secretary of defense were next-door neighbors. Confident that I was going to be in Washington for only two years, for an exorbitant amount of money I rented a house on the Navy compound next door to where Mullen lived as chief of naval operations. He remained there as chairman, even though there is a very large house at Fort Myer, in Virginia, just across the Potomac from D.C., reserved by law only for the chairman. As a result, on weekends, Mike and I fairly often would wander over to each other's porch to talk through some sensitive issue or crisis or our agenda. It must have been a strange sight for others working in the compound on a weekend to see the chairman of the Joint Chiefs of Staff in a T-shirt, shorts, and sandals sitting on the porch talking to the secretary of defense wearing jeans and a sport shirt and smoking a cigar.

One little problem was that, as chairman, Mike had several noncommissioned officers who worked at his house, cooking, cleaning, and so on. I, on the other hand, despite being secretary of defense and his boss, was a civilian and therefore not entitled to the household help that top generals and admirals receive. There was a lot of good-humored back-and-forth between us about the situation. I'd see Mike headed out on a weekend, and as I told my staff, "I was out there watering my damn flowers." One night there was a terrible rain and windstorm, and a big limb came down in my yard. It lay there for several days, and I finally told one of my security officers, "After dark, drag the thing over to Mullen's yard—it'll be gone in an hour." Sure enough, it was. At my farewell ceremony, Mike suggested that I had blown leaves over onto his yard. Not true, but only because I didn't have a leaf blower.

The other senior military officer with whom I would work most closely was Marine General James ("Hoss") Cartwright. During my first months on the job, I had been extremely impressed with Hoss, then the commander of Strategic Command (responsible for U.S. nuclear forces and, at that time, cyber warfare). When the president decided to nominate Mike as chairman, Hoss was my pick for vice chairman. He had extraordinary technical expertise and a rare ability to explain highly technical matters in a clear and straightforward manner to the layman. I settled on Hoss before consulting Mike, who had reservations. I told him I had made up my mind and asked him to make it work. For four years, both were highly professional and the relationship did work more or less, but the chemistry between them at the beginning was not good and would only get worse. Both Bush 43 and President Obama developed a high regard for Hoss. He represented the chiefs at the "deputies"-level meetings at the White House and had to spend an inordinate amount of time there each day alongside the civilian undersecretary of defense for policy, who was my representative. This group, which Brent Scowcroft and I had created in 1989 and I had chaired as deputy national security adviser under Bush 41, would hash out policy options in preparation for meetings of their bosses and play a key role in crisis management. Cartwright performed superbly in that forum, as well as in his other responsibilities as the second-ranking American military officer, including procurement, budget issues, and other critical administrative matters. He and Mike had very different styles, and getting the Joint Staff to be open and work hand in glove with its civilian counterparts in the department was an ongoing challenge (something I suspected was not a new phenomenon at Defense). When Mike was traveling, Hoss would accompany me to all meetings at the White House, including my private meetings with the president. He was very smart and had great common sense—and a sense of humor. I valued him and his contribution the entire time we worked together, although I would come to have some issues with him under President Obama.

Becoming "the Soldiers' Secretary"

As president of Texas A&M, I had devoted a lot of time and effort to looking after the interests of the students. They would often send me their complaints by e-mail, and whenever I thought they had a legitimate gripe, which was pretty often, I would be sure the university responded. I invited the student body president to be a regular participant in my executive staff meetings. I participated in countless student events. In many huge universities, the president is just a name to the students. I wanted them to think of me as their advocate in that huge bureaucracy. By all accounts, I was successful in establishing that kind of relationship and reputation. As mentioned earlier, ten thousand students turned out to say good-bye on my last day there.

I wanted the same kind of personal relationship with our troops. At Texas A&M, I would walk the campus all the time and see eighteen-to-twenty-five-year-olds in T-shirts, shorts, and backpacks. Now suddenly I was in Iraq and Afghanistan and seeing young men and women the very same age in full body armor, carrying assault rifles and living in wretched conditions. The contrast had a profound impact on me. Having been a university president made my transition to secretary of defense more difficult emotionally, and it would continue to affect me as long as I was in the job—especially as I reflected that one group of young people had set aside their dreams, made sacrifices, and were risking their lives to protect the dreams of another group the same age, and all the rest of us as well.

Establishing a personal relationship with two million troops required innovation. When I suggested establishing a designated e-mail account so they could communicate directly with me, as the students had at A&M, my chief of staff, Robert Rangel, looked at me as though I had lost my mind. Two million potential e-mails! That was the end of that.

There were no shortcuts to what I wanted to achieve. Young people are inherently skeptical, if not cynical, about the rhetoric of older people and those in authority, because too often their actions do not correspond. In the military, that is compounded many times over. The only way I could make any impact on the troops and dent their indifference to who might be secretary of defense would be through actions that demonstrated how much I cared about them.

Coincidentally, many decisions intended to help the troops were also necessary for success in our military campaigns. Our fundamentally flawed and persistent assumption from the outset, that the Iraq War would be a short one, caused many problems on the ground and for the troops. As the months stretched into years, those at senior levels nevertheless clung to their original assumption and seemed unwilling to invest substantial dollars to provide the troops everything they needed for protection and for success in their mission, and to bring them home safely—and if wounded, to provide them with the very best care. Who wanted to spend precious dollars on equipment for today's troops that, after Iraq, would just be surplus? So for years in Iraq, our troops traveled in light vehicles like Humvees (the modern equivalent of a jeep) that, even with armoring, were vulnerable to weapons such as improvised explosive devices (IEDs), rocket-propelled grenades (RPGs), and explosively formed projectiles (EFPs). These vehicles that could all too easily be blown up or become funeral pyres for our troops. While investments had been made in remotely piloted vehicles (drones), there were no crash programs to increase their numbers or the diversity of intelligence, surveillance, and reconnaissance capabilities for commanders. And here at home, while the quality of military medical care was absolutely the best in the world, outpatient and posthospitalization treatment of the wounded and their families was a scandal waiting to happen. Too few in the Pentagon responsible for training, equipping, and deployment decisions looked out sufficiently for the interests of the troops as individuals. This would become a principal preoccupation of mine for my entire tenure.

During my first months as secretary, I made these issues my own. As mentioned, I recommended an increase in the size of the Army and Marine Corps by 65,000 and 27,000 respectively. In September 2007, I would authorize a further, temporary increase in the Army of 22,000 soldiers. On January 19, I signed a directive that the National Guard thereafter would deploy as units (rather than individuals being shifted around to fill out units from other states) and that deployments would be limited to a year. Protecting that limit would be a challenge, and whenever the Joint Staff wanted to break it, I would send them back to the drawing board. I would repeat, over and over, "I gave my word to them they wouldn't have to go for more than a year. Why would they ever believe me again if I break my word on this?" With respect to deploying as units, I would argue, if I'm an ordnance disposal specialist, I want to deploy with the team I trained with, know, and trust, not a bunch of strangers I just met. On a few occasions, harsh reality forced me to violate my commitment to one-year tours, but only under extraordinary circumstances. As hard as the decision was to extend tours in Iraq and Afghanistan to fifteen months, my only consolation was that it at least guaranteed those troops a year at home and provided predictability. I wanted to end the practice of stop-loss, a practice in the Army of involuntarily extending a soldier's duty time. The overwhelming majority of those stop-lossed were NCOs, whose continued service was considered essential to unit cohesion. Stop-loss had been going on for some time, but the numbers increased fairly significantly as a result of the surge in Iraq, and during my tenure it peaked at about 14,000 soldiers. I considered the practice the equivalent of involuntary servitude and a breach of faith with those affected, and I was determined to end it. A few months before I retired, not one soldier was on stop-loss.

As I've said, every place I went, I learned a lot from the young troops I insisted upon spending time with. Having conversations with maintenance NCOs on board ships and at Air Force bases and hearing about shortages of manpower "to do the job right" played a big role in my decision to stop further reductions in both Air Force and Navy personnel. Visiting Creech Air Force Base in Nevada, where many of our drones operating overseas are controlled, I learned that the crews had more than an hour commute each way to their homes at Nellis Air Force Base and little in the way of amenities—places to eat and work out—at Creech. Those problems would be fixed. At Camp Pendleton, I observed Marines training in a fake Iraqi town before their deployments, and I learned that the commanders did all their training on how to use drones in simulators because there were no real drones available. We largely corrected that, though it took considerable time.

I tried to meet with families and spouses of soldiers whenever possible. Most of those meetings were emotionally draining. I visited Fort Campbell, Kentucky, a few weeks after becoming secretary. Soldiers from the 101st Airborne were preparing to deploy. I met with some of their spouses, whose tears showed that they had been down this road before and that they were feeling the stress of multiple deployments. Some were very young, still teenagers, but with one or two babies. Many of those women were scared and frustrated with problems that only added to their stress, like marginal medical care on post, long waits to see a doctor, or the need to drive sixty miles to get care from a pediatric specialist.

The compliments that always meant the most—until the day I left my job as secretary—were from the troops and their families.

The hardest part of being secretary for me was visiting the wounded in hospitals, which I did regularly, and it got harder each time. At the outset, I wasn't sure I could handle it. People would tell me not to worry, that "they will lift you up" with their courage, determination, and resilience. But I would think, particularly as time went along, *Yes, they do, but there is one difference between all of you—members of Congress, military officers, whomever—and me: I'm the one who sent them in harm's way.* It tore me apart to see fit young men who'd had limbs blown off, suffered devastating gunshot wounds, and experienced every sort of trauma to their bodies and their brains—wounds both visible and invisible. Some were in comas or unconscious. Many had their families there, often including a young wife and little children, a family whose life would never be the same. I approached one soldier's room and a doctor emerged to suggest that I not go in because the young man had an open, gaping leg wound and he refused to cover it while I visited him. I steeled myself and went in. He was neither bitter nor self-pitying. I visited a young soldier at Walter Reed who was the first quadruple amputee, losing both legs above the knee and both arms below the elbow. He said he just wanted to drive a car again. And his father told me, "We have been to the valley of despair and the mountain of hope." The father asked me to make sure his son received the most advanced prosthetics, and I promised he would. I met a soldier from Texas A&M who had been shot in the throat. He rasped out to me that he was able to choose the music played in the operating theater during his surgery, and he had them play the Aggie "War Hymn" over and over. I kidded him that he should have made sure his surgeon wasn't a rival University of Texas Longhorn.

In May, I made my first visit to Brooke Army Medical Center in San Antonio, where the military's finest burn treatment facility is located. I was to visit the Center for the Intrepid, a new rehabilitation facility for amputees paid for by private donations, and also the burn center. I told Pete Chiarelli that I didn't think I was strong enough to visit the burn unit. He was silent, and I asked him, "Do the kids at the burn unit know I'm coming?" He said yes. I closed my eyes and told him, "Well, then I have to do it."

I walked into the rehab center at the burn unit, and standing in front of me was Marine First Lieutenant Dan Moran, wearing a Texas A&M Corps of Cadets T-shirt and holding his graduation picture of me handing him his diploma. His beautiful wife and four-week-old baby were with him in the unit. He asked me to sign the graduation picture and then asked if I would present his Navy commendation medal with V for Valor to him at some point at Texas A&M. I said of course. (On October 27, Bush 41 and I presented Dan with his medal at halftime during an A&M home football game, with 85,000 in attendance cheering their lungs out for this young hero. If only all our wounded and veterans could get such recognition.)

The burn unit was nearly full. There was a young soldier who had been there for nearly two years with horrific burns; we did a fist bump because he had no fingers. After a long and heroic struggle, he would die a few months later. I visited a sergeant in an isolated room, badly burned, missing limbs, in a coma. There were others, ambulatory and sharp, who still faced dozens of surgeries in the months and years to come. There are no words to describe their courage. Because Brooke is not in Washington or on a coast, not very many VIPs from any walk of life visit there. The patients would talk about how rarely they got official visitors. After my visit, one Army sergeant told the press that it meant a lot when someone "comes here in person." He said, "I don't need more medals or money, just someone to say thanks."

I would never have forgiven myself had I fallen victim to my self-doubt and not gone to the burn unit. I would visit again on a number of occasions. There are no adequate words to describe the compassion, commitment, and skill of those at Brooke—and at all our military hospitals—caring for our sons and daughters.

Soon afterward I visited the U.S. military hospital at Landstuhl, Germany, where nearly all wounded from Iraq and Afghanistan were sent before returning stateside. I was told I was the only secretary of defense to visit that hospital since the start of the wars in Iraq and Afghanistan. There, for the first time, I presented Purple Hearts, six of them. One was to a young soldier who was unconscious, and I had my initial experience with a mother in my arms crying. The next time I saw him, months later, he was sitting in a chair having lunch at a Pentagon event for wounded warriors. With a certain insouciance, he said, "Bet you don't recognize me!"

I increasingly felt a personal responsibility for those kids in the hospitals, and it weighed more and more heavily on me. Yet in the hospitals there was still hope. Not so for those who were killed, or for their families.

Every morning, first thing, I would receive written notifications of servicemen and women killed and wounded in combat during the preceding twenty-four hours. There were no names, just a description of what had happened and the raw numbers. Immediately upon taking office, I starting signing condolence letters to parents, a spouse, or a child of someone killed in action. It wasn't long before just a signature didn't seem enough, and at night, I started hand-writing notes at the end of each letter. As the surge in Iraq progressed, I was soon signing well over a hundred letters a month. Sometime later even the notes didn't seem enough. I was determined not to let these men and women ever become statistics for me, and so I asked for a picture of each, and the hometown news accounts of the life and death of their local heroes. I could look at the picture and read accounts from family, friends, coaches, and teachers about how fun-loving they had been, how they loved to fish and hunt, how they excelled at athletics, about their willingness to help others. Or I learned how they had been aimless until joining the military, where they found purpose and direction for their lives. And so virtually every night for four and a half years, writing condolence letters and reading about these mostly young men and women, I wept.

That was in private. But after only a few months as secretary, my emotions over the sacrifices of these amazing men and women in uniform began occasionally to ambush me in public. The first time was in a speech at the Marine Corps Association dinner on July 18, 2007. I was cruising along just fine until near the end of the speech, when I began to talk about a Marine company commander, Capt. Douglas Zembiec, and his actions in the first battle of Fallujah (Iraq) in April 2004. He said his men had "fought like lions," and he was later himself dubbed the "Lion of Fallujah." I talked about him volunteering to go back to Iraq in early 2007, but "this time, he would not return—to his country or to his wife, Pamela, and his one-year-old daughter." I began to lose my composure at that point, though I was able to say that more than one thousand people—including many enlisted Marines—had attended his funeral at Arlington, where an officer told a reporter, "Your men have to follow your orders; they don't have to go to your funeral." I simply could not go on. Press accounts would say that I was clearly struggling and suffering. I was. But I finally pulled myself together and closed with these words: "Every evening I write notes to the families of young Americans like Doug Zembiec. For you, and for me, they are not names on a press release, or numbers updated on a web page. They are our country's sons and daughters."

This was the real face of war. I never spoke to anyone about the emotional toll on me of the visits to the front lines, the hospitals, and the cemeteries, of sending kids into danger and hardship—a burden that would only grow over four and a half years of war. I would do my duty, I would do everything I could for us to win in Iraq and Afghanistan. But I knew the real cost. And that knowledge changed me.

WALTER REED

On February 18 and 19, 2007, *The Washington Post* ran a two-part series by reporters Dana Priest and Anne Hull on the administrative nightmare and squalid living conditions endured by wounded warriors at Walter Reed Army Medical Center in Washington, D.C. The series documented a bureaucratic labyrinth faced by soldiers who were in recuperation, seeking further treatment, or deciding whether they could stay in the military despite their wounds. The reporters described, in detail, Building 18, where a number of recuperating soldiers were housed, as rife with mold, filth, leaks, soiled carpets, rodents, cockroaches, and overall shabbiness. There were clearly not enough caseworkers to help outpatients and not enough help for outpatients and families to navigate through the huge hospital complex or the massive and confusing paperwork. I was shocked by the conditions described in the articles. At my morning staff meeting on February 20, I said we had a big problem on our hands, a failure to take proper care of our wounded warriors and their families. That had to be addressed immediately.

Over the next two days, I learned enough to substantiate much of what had been in the *Post* and to devise how we would respond. On February 23, I met with the president at nine a.m. to confirm for him the seriousness of the conditions at Walter Reed and to tell him I intended to announce that day the formation of an outside group led by Togo West, secretary of the Army and secretary of veterans affairs under President Clinton, and Jack Marsh, secretary of the Army under President Reagan, to look at the situation in depth and recommend remedial actions. I would give them only forty-five days to report their findings. I told the president I intended to hold people accountable and that that could result in some high-level firings. He was entirely supportive. I then went directly from the White House to Walter Reed, where I personally walked through Building 18. In the few days since the articles came out, the place had been cleaned up some, but it was still depressing. I was then briefed on outpatient care and the resource challenges and bureaucratic obstacles that had led to the conditions reported by the newspaper.

I held a press conference at Walter Reed, during which I said I was dismayed to learn that some of our injured troops were not getting the best possible treatment at all stages of their recovery, especially in their outpatient care. "This is unacceptable, and it will not continue," I said. In a departure for a senior government official, I also said, "I am grateful to reporters for bringing this problem to our attention, but very disappointed we did not identify it ourselves." Speaking of our wounded warriors, I asserted, "They should not have to recuperate in substandard housing, nor should they be expected to tackle mountains of paperwork and bureaucratic processes during this difficult time for themselves and their families. They battled our foreign enemies; they should not have to battle American bureaucracy." I made clear that the problem was not about world-class medical care but about outpatient facilities and administration. I then named the members of the review group and said they were empowered to inspect circumstances not only at Walter Reed but at Bethesda National Naval Medical Center in Maryland and at any other centers they chose to examine. I expressed my "strong belief that an organization with the enormous responsibilities of the Department of Defense must live by [the] principle of accountability at all levels. Accordingly, after the facts are established, those responsible for allowing this unacceptable situation to develop will indeed be held accountable." I later noted that several of those officers and NCOs most directly involved had already been relieved by the Army, and that "others up the chain of command were being evaluated."

Senior Army officers responded in different ways. The vice chief of staff, General Dick Cody, said, "We were absolutely disappointed in the status of the rooms and found the delays and lack of attention to detail to the building's repairs inexcusable." From that day forward, Cody made the problems of our wounded warriors his highest priority, and with his leadership, the Army began to move in the right direction. Unfortunately, there were others who were defensive and seemed to downplay the problem. The Army's top medical officer, Lieutenant General Kevin Kiley, called the newspaper reports a "one-sided representation" and seemed to question the tone rather than the facts. His response set my teeth on edge, but not nearly as much as comments from Secretary of the Army Fran Harvey, who was quoted as saying, "We had some NCOs who weren't doing their job, period." To blame the widespread outpatient problems at Walter Reed on "some NCOs" was, in my view, unconscionable.

I wanted change at Walter Reed, and under pressure from me, the Army's first step, on March 1, was to relieve the hospital commander, Major General George Weightman. Weightman had been in the job only about six months but accepted the action with dignity. He publicly acknowledged the problems and apologized to the families. Secretary Harvey then made what was, in my opinion, a huge mistake. He appointed Kiley as temporary hospital commander. In our own examination of the situation during the preceding days and in congressional hearings that week, it became pretty clear that Kiley had been informed of the problems at Walter Reed and that some of them could be traced back to his command there. His appointment was greeted with dismay by many wounded warriors and their families. He had not acted to remedy the situation, and his public comments continued to seem to downplay it. Indeed, Harvey recounted to the press a call he had received from Kiley criticizing the *Post* series and saying, "I'm willing to defend myself. . . . I want to have an opportunity to defend myself, and it was wrong and it was yellow journalism at its worst, and I plan on doing it. Trust me." Kiley's appointment, on top of Harvey's placing blame on a few NCOs, confirmed to me that the secretary of the Army did not understand the magnitude of the problem and could not lead the effort to fix it. On March 2, after talking with the president, I called in Harvey and asked for his resignation, saying Kiley's appointment was the last straw. He was stunned and clearly felt he was being thrown under the bus to placate the media and Congress. I received his letter of resignation that afternoon. Fran Harvey was a good man who had rendered distinguished service to the country. I fired him because once informed of the circumstances at Walter Reed, he did not take the problem seriously enough. I said the same thing to reporters.

I held a press conference on March 3 to announce that I had directed the Army—Pete Geren would be acting secretary—to appoint a new commander at Walter Reed that same day, rescinding the Kiley appointment. I went on to say, "I am disappointed that some in the Army have not adequately appreciated the seriousness of the situation pertaining to outpatient care at Walter Reed. Some have shown too much defensiveness and have not shown enough focus on digging into and addressing the problems. Also, I am concerned that some do not properly understand the need to clearly communicate to the wounded and their families that we have no higher priority than their care, and that addressing their concerns about the quality of their outpatient experience is critically important." I reaffirmed my full confidence in the Walter Reed doctors, nurses, and staff, who I said were "among the best, and most caring, in the world."

At my suggestion, the president appointed a bipartisan commission to examine the full range of treatment of wounded warriors by the Departments of Defense and of Veterans Affairs. He appointed former

The journey begins: my wife, Becky, holds the Bible as I am sworn in as secretary of defense on December 18, 2006.

My first visit to Iraq as secretary on December 19, the day after I began my job. General Pete Pace, chairman of the Joint Chiefs of Staff, is to the right of the officer gesticulating.

Breakfast with President George W. Bush in the White House family dining room. He ate healthy cereal and fruit. I did not.

With Russian president Vladimir Putin at the Munich Security Conference in February 2007. This is his happy face. (I think I made him nervous.)

Just another dinner with fellow government workers, visitors, and spouses.

Pace and I share a rare light moment before a Senate Armed Services Committee hearing. (Note the antiwar protester in pink in the background.) I came to despise such sessions.

Meeting in Baghdad with Iraqi prime minister Nouri Al-Maliki, on the right; in the center is Sadi Othman, an interpreter and adviser to General David Petraeus. Chosen because he was weak, Maliki would become too strong and not particularly interested in reconciling the opposing factions in Iraq.

Comforting the mother of a grievously wounded soldier at the U.S. military hospital at Landstuhl, Germany. Her son would recover.

On a helicopter with Petraeus in Iraq. Our partnership in two wars would last four and a half years.

President Bush meets with the Joint Chiefs of Staff in their conference room (the Tank). From the end of the table, moving clockwise from me: Steve Hadley (National Security Adviser), General George Casey (Army), General Buzz Moseley (Air Force), General Jim "Hoss" Cartwright (vice chairman), General Pace (chairman), and Admiral Mike Mullen (Navy). Not visible is General Jim Conway (Marine Corps).

With President Bush at Al Asad Air Base in Iraq, for a meeting with the Iraqi Presidential Council. From left, Iraqi Vice President Adel Abdul Mahdi (Shia), Prime Minister Maliki (mostly hidden), President Jalal Talabani (Kurd), and Vice President Tariq Al-Hashimi (Sunni). There was no love lost among them.

Aboard a C-17 cargo plane converted into a hospital plane. Such was the skill of the doctors and nurses on board that I heard of only one patient who died en route home.

I present Marine First Lieutenant Dan Moran his Navy Commendation Medal with V for valor at a Texas A&M home football game as 85,000 fans cheer him. I had handed him his diploma in 2003 when I was president of the university— a job I loved—and next saw him in the burn unit at Brooke Army Medical Center in San Antonio.

With Marines during basic training. I visited all of the services' basic training facilities to see new recruits preparing to go to war.

Visiting the plant in Charleston, South Carolina, where skilled and dedicated workers complete the assembly and equipping of mine-resistant, ambush-protected vehicles (MRAPs). They knew they were saving lives.

Watching an MRAP being loaded for airlift to Iraq.

Enlisting new recruits in my hometown of Wichita, Kansas. They volunteered to serve knowing they would go to war.

At Kansas State University in late 2007, I called for more money for the long-underfunded State Department and U.S. development programs abroad. Coming from the secretary of defense, the speech made a big splash.

Becky and I arrive at Pacific Command in Hawaii, my arm in a sling. I had never broken a bone or had surgery before I was secretary of defense. I managed to do both within two years after taking the job.

With President Bush and Secretary of State Condoleezza Rice at the NATO summit in Bucharest, Romania, in 2008. It was the only time I saw him sit patiently through hours of boring speeches. He lasted longer than most of his colleagues.

Lieutenant General Pete Chiarelli was one of my closest confidants. A tireless advocate for the troops, he was always exceptionally candid with me.

The dedication and opening of the Pentagon 9/11 Memorial. To my left, the president, former secretary of defense Donald Rumsfeld, Admiral Mullen, and Jim Laychak (president of the Pentagon Memorial Fund).

I was the only secretary of defense to take an entire motorcade to a Burger King. Geoff Morrell, left, and Ryan McCarthy of my office enjoy my lack of discipline.

President Bush, Vice President Dick Cheney, and I are joined in the Oval Office by White House chief of staff Josh Bolten, at far left, and National Security Adviser Steve Hadley. It really wasn't four against one. Well, sometimes it was.

In Baghdad in September 2008, for the change of command from Petraeus to General Ray Odierno. I can't remember the reason for the levity, but there wasn't much of it in Iraq.

Holding an informal press conference at Bagram Air Base in Afghanistan in September 2008. Twenty years earlier, as the deputy director of the CIA, I had been providing weapons to the Afghan resistance to attack Soviet aircraft at that base.

A birthday present from Deputy Secretary of Defense Gordon England. I was uncertain about the symbolism: did he think I needed the costume for my many battles?

Just another tourist
in Kosovo.

Visiting my heroes who
had fallen in Iraq and
Afghanistan, in Section
60, Arlington National
Cemetery, late 2008.
There would be many
more.

In Kandahar,
Afghanistan, checking
out an M-29 Reaper
drone, which represented
a major innovation in
reconnaissance and
weaponry.

It wasn't all drudgery and conflict: attending a Little League baseball game at the White House with President Bush and Admiral Mullen.

President Bush and I say our farewells in the Oval Office a few days before the end of his presidency.

One editorial cartoonist properly captures the venality of certain members of Congress, and another depicts the reaction to my announcement that I wanted to kill or cap three dozen major weapons and equipment programs.

With General David McKiernan, commander of U.S. and coalition forces in Afghanistan. He was a fine officer, but I relieved him on this visit.

Speaking to a group of Marines in Helmand province, Afghanistan, with the ever-present backdrop of MRAPs, a life-saving vehicle I championed. I would take an individual picture with every soldier and Marine present on such visits.

Senate majority leader Bob Dole, a wounded warrior himself from World War II, and former secretary of health and human services Donna Shalala to cochair the commission. At George Casey's suggestion, I urged the president to include in the membership of the panel a young wounded warrior and the widow of one of our fallen.

At my senior staff meeting on March 5, I went back to the comments I had made on my first day, December 18, and again to the senior civilian and military leaders in mid-January. I repeated that when Congress or the press makes an accusation, we need to look into it and not be defensive. Further, I said I would not allow junior or midgrade officers and NCOs to be fall guys for systemic problems. "Your antennae need to be up for other issues, such as equipping the troops." I went on to speculate that the Department of Veterans Affairs likely had many problems if Walter Reed had the problems it did. I told the staff that the idea of a White House commission to look at the entire wounded warrior problem had been mine, and I expected full cooperation. I reiterated that acute care at Walter Reed was the best in the world, and that the problem was outpatient care. "The easiest thing in the world to fix is the facility; the biggest issues are bureaucracy and resources," I said. "However, we will ensure it is not a resource issue. We'll get the resources."

There was still one loose end, Lieutenant General Kiley. I told my assistant Rangel on March 6 that I wanted General Cody, Major General Eric Schoomaker (the new commander at Walter Reed), the chairman of the Joint Chiefs, and Acting Secretary Geren to talk about Kiley's future. I said that it needed to be an Army decision, but I did not feel he was helping the Army. Kiley retired soon thereafter.

I sent a message on March 9 to every American serviceman and woman all over the world informing them of my reaction to the situation at Walter Reed, describing the remedial actions being taken, and pledging to them that, "other than the wars themselves, I have no higher priority than taking care of our wounded warriors."

The outpatient problem at Walter Reed was just the most visible of our shortcomings and failures in taking care of our wounded and their families. Because no one had expected a long war or so many wounded, no one had planned for or allocated the necessary resources in terms of caseworkers, established facilities on posts and bases to care for the wounded, fixed the bureaucratic abyss between the Departments of Defense and Veterans Affairs, and so much more. At my first cabinet meeting, the secretary of veterans affairs had introduced himself, and I offered him any and all assistance, knowing that his department had to have been pushed to the wall with all the seriously wounded veterans coming into its system as a result of two wars. I was staggered when he said his department was in good shape and had no problems. I'd been around long enough to know that when the head of a cabinet department says his organization has no problems, he is either lying or delusional. I knew the secretary wasn't a liar. The scandal at Walter Reed was caused by a failure of leadership, but the awful outpatient conditions there were also a product of budget and personnel cuts, an unwillingness to invest money in a hospital complex that was slated for closure, and outsourcing to contractors. As I had foreshadowed to my staff, fixing the bureaucratic problems would prove a lot harder than getting adequate resources.

I received a lot of praise in the media and in Congress for acting so decisively. But as usual, the reaction that meant the most to me came from a soldier. I received an e-mail, a few weeks after these events, from someone who had sat next to an Army medic on an airplane flight. The medic was quoted as saying that he and his buddies had been "amazed and hopeful with Gates when he jumped into the Walter Reed Hospital mess. With the first appointment of a new administrator [Kiley], it looked like more of the same. Gates firing the guy in under twenty-four hours meant a lot to them." The medic "was so grateful for Gates's efforts to straighten out the hospital mess. Gates gave him hope."

I spent a lot of time and energy during my first months mending fences and making allies. I won praise for my calm, respectful approach to doing business and dealing with people—and for patching up relationships across Washington. But the Walter Reed scandal gave me an unanticipated opportunity to demonstrate early on that when it came to incompetence, negligence, or anything negatively affecting our men and women in uniform, I could and would be utterly ruthless. Such ruthlessness would be needed when, beginning in the spring of 2007, I resolved to make senior civilian and military leaders in the Pentagon lower their eyes from future potential wars and turn aside from day-to-day politics and bureaucratic routine to focus on the wars right in front of them, in Iraq and Afghanistan. Effectively waging war on our enemies on those battlefields would also require successfully waging war on the Pentagon itself.

CHAPTER 4

Waging War on the Pentagon

As of January 2007, I had a new commander headed to Iraq, a new strategy, and 30,000 additional troops. Their success would require a sense of total commitment in the Department of Defense that I was staggered to learn did not exist. It was one thing for the country and much of the executive branch of government not to feel involved in the war, but for the DoD—the "department of war"—that was unacceptable.

Even though the nation was waging two wars, neither of which we were winning, life at the Pentagon was largely business as usual when I arrived. I found little sense of urgency, concern, or passion about a very grim situation. No senior military officers, no senior civilians came to me breathing fire about the downward slide of our military and civilian efforts in the wars, the need for more or different equipment or for more troops, or the need for new strategies and tactics. It was clear why we had gotten into trouble in both Iraq and Afghanistan: after initial military successes in both countries, when the situation in both began to deteriorate, the president, his senior civilian advisers, and the senior military leaders had not recognized that most of the assumptions that underpinned early military planning had proven wrong, and no necessary adjustments had been made. The fundamental erroneous assumption was that both wars would be short and that responsibility for security could quickly be handed off to Iraqi and Afghan forces. From the summer of 2003 in Iraq and from 2005 in Afghanistan, after months, even years, of overly optimistic forecasts, as of mid-2006 no senior civilians or generals had been sacked, there were no significant changes in strategy, and no one with authority inside the administration was beating the drum that we were making little if any progress in either war and that, in fact, all the signs were pointing toward things getting worse. (I was later told that some NSC, CIA, and State Department staff were making this case but without effect.)

The historian Max Hastings wrote in his book *Inferno* that "it is characteristic of all conflicts that until enemies begin to shoot, ships to sink and loved ones—or at least comrades—begin to die, even professional warriors often lack urgency and ruthlessness." At the end of 2006, we had been at war in Afghanistan for over five years and in Iraq for nearly four years. The enemy had long been shooting, and many of our soldiers had died, yet our civilian and military leaders and commanders still lacked "urgency and ruthlessness." I considered it my responsibility to do something about that.

Symbolically, there was no one of high rank in Defense whose specific job it was to ensure that the commanders and troops in the field had what they needed. The chairman of the Joint Chiefs of Staff spoke for the armed services and was the senior military adviser to the president, but he had no command authority over the military services or civilian components, and no money. The senior civilians who were my top deputies in the Office of the Secretary of Defense, the undersecretaries, had a policy advisory role and direct authority only within their own areas of responsibility. The very size and structure of the department assured ponderousness, if not paralysis, because so many different organizations had to be involved in even the smallest decisions. The idea of speed and agility to support current combat operations was totally foreign to the building. It was quickly apparent that only I, as secretary, had the authority to change that. If that gargantuan, labyrinthine bureaucracy was to support the war fighter effectively and with speed, the initiative would have to come from the top. More often than not, that meant bypassing the bureaucracy and regular procedures and running the effort directly from my office. That personal effort to support the commanders and the troops would dominate my entire tenure as secretary.

The Department of Defense is structured to plan and prepare for war but not to fight one. The secretaries and senior military leaders of the

Army, Navy, and Air Force departments are charged with organizing, training, and equipping their respective forces. The last of these chores is all about acquiring the weapons systems, ships, trucks, planes, and other matériel that the services likely will need in the future, a far cry from a current combat commander's need for "make do" or "good enough" solutions in weeks or months. The military departments develop their budgets on a five-year basis, and most procurement programs take many years—if not decades—from decision to delivery. As a result, budgets and programs are locked in for years at a time, and all the bureaucratic wiles of each military department are dedicated to keeping those programs intact and funded. They are joined in those efforts by the companies that build the equipment, the Washington lobbyists that those companies hire, and the members of Congress in whose states or districts those factories are located. Any threats to those long-term programs are not welcome. Even if we are at war.

For the wars in Iraq and Afghanistan, the needs of the field commanders and their troops were forwarded as requests to the regional (Centcom) combatant commander, who reviewed them and, if he was in agreement, pushed them to the Pentagon. Each request then had to pass through a Joint Chiefs of Staff filter, a military department filter, a department comptroller (the money person) filter, multiple procurement bureaucracy filters, and often other filters, any of which could delay or stop fulfillment of the requested equipment. These current, urgent requests were weighed against the existing long-term plans, programs, and available budgets and all too often were found to be lower in priority than nearly everything else—which meant they disappeared into a Pentagon black hole.

There is an express lane for the most pressing war fighter needs, a process to address "joint urgent operational needs." These requests are evaluated at a very senior level, including the deputy secretary of defense and the vice chairman of the Joint Chiefs. Those that are approved are sent to the appropriate military service, which is asked to come up with the money. Another black hole. If the money is authorized, all too often it will be months or years after the "urgent" request is made. Worse, even during two wars, protecting future needs, bureaucratic lethargy, an unwillingness to challenge Congress on pet programs, a peacetime mind-set, and weak leadership in refereeing fights over who should pay for matériel that everyone agreed was needed all too often resulted in no action at all—even as we had kids dying on battlefields because those needs were not being met. All that was intolerable to me.

Although I had decades of experience in the national security arena, I never made any claim to expertise as a military strategist or defense reformer. I had, however, as I said earlier, successfully led and run huge organizations. I had been brought in to turn around a failing war effort. My fight to sustain minimal support in Congress so that the troops would have time to accomplish that turnaround was tough enough, but I soon realized I would also have to fight the Pentagon itself. I decided I had to be the principal advocate in Defense for the commanders and the troops. I would be both "urgent" and "ruthless."

To complicate matters, all the services regarded the counterinsurgency wars in Iraq and Afghanistan as unwelcome military aberrations, the kind of conflict we would never fight again—just the way they felt after Vietnam. The services all wanted to get back to training and equipping our forces for the kinds of conflict in the future they had always planned for: for the Army, conventional force-on-force conflicts against nation-states with large ground formations; for the Marine Corps, a light, mobile force operating from ships and focused on amphibious operations; for the Navy, conventional maritime operations on the high seas centered on aircraft carriers; for the Air Force, high-tech air-to-air combat and strategic bombing against major nation-states.

I agreed with the need to be prepared for those kinds of conflicts. But I was convinced that they were far less likely to occur than messy, smaller, unconventional military endeavors. I was also convinced, based on history and experience, that we were utterly unable to predict what kinds of future conflicts we would face. In fact, after Vietnam, when we used our military—in Grenada, Lebanon, Libya (twice), Panama, Haiti, the Balkans, and elsewhere—it was usually in relatively small-scale but messy combat. The one time we used large conventional formations with limited objectives—against Iraq to liberate Kuwait in 1991—the war ended in one hundred hours. The war in Afghanistan, from its beginning in 2001, was not a conventional conflict, and the second war against Iraq began with a fast-moving conventional offensive that soon deteriorated into a stability, reconstruction, and counterinsurgency campaign—the dreaded "nation-building" that the Bush administration took office swearing to avoid. In not one of those conflicts had we predicted even six months beforehand that we would be militarily engaged in those places. I felt strongly that we had to prepare our forces in the future, both in training and in equipment, to fight all along the spectrum of conflict, from counterterrorism to taking on well-armed nonstate groups (such as the terrorist group Hizballah) to fighting conventional nation-states. Developing this broad range of capabilities meant taking some time and resources away from preparations for the high-end future missions the military services preferred. I would take on that fight in mid-2008, but in 2007 and early 2008, my focus was on getting the troops in Iraq and Afghanistan the equipment and support they needed.

MINE-RESISTANT, AMBUSH-PROTECTED VEHICLES

On April 19, 2007, while on an official visit to Israel, I noticed in the Pentagon's daily press summary, "The Early Bird," an article by Tom Vanden Brook in USA Today that began, "In more than 300 attacks since last year, no Marines have died while riding in new fortified armored vehicles the Pentagon hopes to rush to Iraq in greater numbers this year, a top Marine commander in Anbar province said." The article described the vehicles' raised, V-shaped hulls that deflected the force of blasts from homemade bombs buried in roadways—improvised explosive devices (IEDs). It quoted Marine Brigadier General John Allen, deputy commander of coalition forces in Anbar, as saying there had been eleven hundred attacks on these vehicles in the preceding fifteen months, with an average of less than one injured Marine per attack. I flew on to Iraq that afternoon for twenty-four hours for the key meeting with David Petraeus about troop drawdowns in the fall, returned home for thirty-six hours, and then, on the twenty-second, began a trip to Russia, Poland, and Germany. But I continued to think about this new kind of vehicle and asked for a briefing on it once I was back in Washington.

IEDs had been a problem in Iraq from the early days of the war. As time went by, the bombs became bigger and the insurgents more clever in how they planted, hid, and detonated them. By the end of 2006, the number of IEDs deployed by our enemies in Iraq accounted for up to 80 percent of soldier casualties. To make matters worse, Iran was providing its surrogates in Iraq with "explosively formed projectiles," a fairly sophisticated warhead that, when fired, in essence became a molten metal slug capable of penetrating the armor of our heaviest vehicles, including the Abrams tank. To develop countermeasures against IEDs and get solutions, and training, to the field quickly, the Army created a task force that changed form several times, but ultimately, in February 2006, at Secretary Rumsfeld's direction, it became the inelegantly named but critically important Joint Improvised Explosive Device Defeat Organization. It received billions of dollars to develop surveillance and jamming systems to defeat the IED bomb-building networks and to detect and disable IEDs before they exploded. The organization was an early example of a secretary and deputy secretary of defense concluding they had to go outside the normal bureaucratic structure to get a critical combat task accomplished.

Despite these efforts, more and more of our troops were being burned, maimed, and killed by IEDs, many of them in Humvees. Humvees could be reinforced with armor on the sides, but there were few practical options left to further armor the underbelly of the vehicle. Soldiers were reduced to putting sandbags on the floors of the Humvees to try to protect themselves. It didn't help much. Too many Humvees became funeral pyres for our troops, and I would see some of the surviving victims at the burn unit at Brooke Army Medical Center in San Antonio. Over time more and more side armor was attached to the Humvees, as additional protection from attacks by rockets, grenades, and other weapons, but it still provided little or no protection from bombs that blew up under the vehicles.

I received my first briefing on the mine-resistant, ambush-protected (MRAP) vehicle I had read about in *USA Today* on April 27, 2007. The secretary of defense's conference room is not a big one by Washington (and Pentagon) standards, and it is quite plain, which suited me fine. I always tried to set an informal atmosphere so people would be more inclined to speak up; I don't think I ever wore a suit jacket to a meeting of Defense officials in that room. The table seats about twenty, with another twelve or so chairs lining the wall. There is a screen for the omnipresent PowerPoint slides, and combat photographs line the walls—including one of Doug Zembiec, "the Lion of Fallujah," whose story had caused me to choke up publicly at the Marine Corps Association annual dinner. There was also a coffee cart, essential to my alertness and my self-discipline—for some reason, a coffee cup in my hand made it easier for me not to fly off the handle in briefings that were often frustrating and maddening. There was always a behind-the-scenes battle involving myriad people pushing and shoving to be in meetings I held, and it fell to my two senior assistants to decide who could or could not attend. I guess people felt they needed to be there to demonstrate to others that they were "on the inside" on issues or to protect their sector's equities. Unfortunately, those in the room rarely gave me the background details—especially about bureaucratic infighting—on the matter at hand that would have helped me understand how the problem had ended up on my desk.

So it was with MRAPs. I learned the background story the same way I heard about the vehicle in the first place: from the newspaper. Two and a half months after my first briefing, I read in *USA Today* that the Pentagon had first tested MRAPs in 2000 and that the Marine Corps had requested its first twenty-seven of them in December 2003 for explosive disposal teams. At the end of 2004, the Army had solicited ideas for a better armored vehicle—to sell to the Iraqis, not for U.S. use. The first of those vehicles, nearly identical to MRAPs, were delivered to the Iraqis at the end of summer 2006. Meanwhile, in February 2005, Marine Brigadier General Dennis Hejlik in Anbar province signed a request for more than a thousand of the same kind of vehicles for his men. According to the newspaper, Hejlik's request was shelved; fifteen months later, a second request won Pentagon approval. The first vehicles arrived in Anbar in February 2007, two years after the original request.

Multiple explanations have been put forward for the delay in getting MRAPs into Iraq. The most significant is that no one at a senior level wanted to spend the money to buy them. The services did not want to spend procurement dollars on a vehicle that was not the planned long-term Army and Marine Corps replacement for the Humvee—the joint light tactical vehicle. Most people believed the MRAPs would just be surplus after the war, which most also thought would soon end. Some argued that the threat from IEDs was evolving, and that only in 2006 had our troops begun encountering the explosively formed projectiles (EFPs) that could cut through our heaviest armor. Others contended that only in 2006 had road-implanted bombs become the primary threat, which ignores the fact that in the summer of 2004 more than 1,000 IEDs exploded in Sadr City alone, and another 1,200 were dug up. Procurement of the heavy MRAP vehicles may also have been delayed because they were seen to be contrary to Secretary Rumsfeld's goal of lighter, more agile forces. There were doubts whether industry could produce MRAPs in numbers and on a schedule that would meet the need. Finally, most opposed acquiring MRAPs simply because they thought the vehicles were a waste of money; the enemy would just build bigger IEDs.

Whatever the reason, there were hardly any MRAPs in Iraq when I was briefed in April 2007. But I knew damn well that our troops were being burned and blown up in Humvees well before I became secretary and that had they been in MRAPs, many soldiers would have escaped injury or death.

My briefer at that April 27 meeting was the assistant commandant of the Marine Corps, General Bob Magnus. (The Marine Corps had taken the lead in developing MRAPs.) In November 2006, the Corps had solicited proposals for an armored vehicle that could protect against roadside bombs, and in January 2007 it had awarded nine companies contracts to develop prototypes. Magnus explained the importance of the vehicles and said that 3,700 were on order for the Marine Corps and 2,300 for the Army, but that there was no money available to pay for them. Only 1,300 were to be built by the contractor in 2007. Business as usual.

On May 2, I met with the secretaries of the Army and Navy, Deputy Secretary England, Pace, and others on the need to dramatically increase the funding, size, and speed of MRAP procurement. I didn't often get passionate in meetings, but in this one I laid down a marker I would use again and again concerning MRAPs: "Every delay of a single day costs one or more of our kids his limbs or his life." To my chagrin, not a single senior official, civilian or military, supported my proposal for a crash program to buy thousands of these vehicles. Despite the lack of support, the same day I issued a directive that made the MRAP program the highest-priority Department of Defense acquisition program and ordered that "any and all options to accelerate the production and fielding of this capability to the theater should be identified, assessed, and applied where feasible." This directive began an all-out push to produce MRAPs, an effort that would become the first major military procurement program to go from decision to full industrial production in less than a year since World War II.

Congress was fully supportive of the project. More than a month before my decision, Senator Joseph Biden on March 28 had offered an amendment, which passed 98–0 in the Senate, providing an additional $1.5 billion for MRAPs and pulling forward money from the FY2008 budget into 2007. At the end of April, Congress approved $3 billion to buy MRAPs during the following six months, and a House Armed Services subcommittee added another $4 billion for FY2008. Congress gave us every cent we requested. Indeed, given how large the MRAP procurement would eventually become, without congressional willingness to add money to the war funding bills for the vehicles, they would never have been built—at least not in the numbers we bought. Without this support from Congress, funding for the MRAPs would have had to come out of the military services' regular budgets, which would have caused a bureaucratic and political bloodbath. Congress's habitual lack of fiscal discipline in this instance was a blessing.

On Saturday, May 19, at Aberdeen Proving Ground in Maryland, I saw these huge new vehicles for myself. There were a number of different models from different manufacturers being tested. I watched in awe as a test model was blown up by a large IED and the passenger compartment remained intact. The soldiers inside would have survived. The experts at Aberdeen were identifying the weaknesses and strengths of the different models to inform the program managers, who would decide what to buy, and also to give feedback to the manufacturers about their vehicles. I had nothing to contribute except to reiterate my now-familiar exhortation: "Hurry up! Troops are dying."

At the end of May, I approved putting the MRAP program in a special, very small category of Defense procurement, effectively setting aside many bureaucratic hurdles typical of military programs. It gave the MRAP program legal priority over other military and civilian industrial production programs for key components such as specialty steel, tires, and axles. I also directed establishment of a department-wide MRAP task force and asked to be briefed every two weeks. I emphasized that getting MRAPs to Iraq as fast as possible was essential and that everyone needed to understand that speed and multiple models meant we would face problems with spare parts, maintenance, training, and more. I said we would deal with those problems as they arose and that we should be candid with the president and with Congress that those potential problems were risks we were prepared to take to get better protection to the troops faster. We also reminded everyone that the MRAP wasn't immune to successful attack and the enemy would adapt his techniques to the new vehicle. But it would provide better protection than anything else we had.

The magnitude of the challenge became clear at my first meeting with the task force on June 8. The initial approved requirement for MRAPs of all models at that point was 7,774 vehicles. In just a matter of a couple of weeks, though, the total proposed requirement had skyrocketed to 23,044 at a cost of a little over $25 billion—I think because the field commanders quickly recognized the value of the MRAP and realized that the vehicles were actually going to get built. But how to produce the huge quantities of critically needed materials for the vehicles, from specialty ballistic steel to tires? How to get the MRAPs to Iraq? Where to base them? How to maintain them? It fell to the task force led by the director of defense research and engineering (and soon to be undersecretary for acquisition, technology, and logistics), John Young, to find the answers to these questions, and find them they did.

On a trip to the Middle East in late summer 2007, I experienced a gut-wrenching validation of the need for MRAPs. While visiting Camp Arifjan in Kuwait, a gigantic logistics center supporting the war effort in Iraq, toward dusk, I was taken to the "boneyard"—an area covering many acres that contained the wrecked remains of thousands of American tanks, trucks, Humvees, and other vehicles. Nearly all had been destroyed by enemy attacks in Iraq. I separated myself a bit from the group and wandered through the endless sandy rows of equipment, each vehicle bearing witness to the suffering and losses of our troops. I imagined their screams and their shattered bodies. As I departed, I knew it was too late to help them, but by God, I would move heaven and earth to try to save the lives of their comrades.

Ultimately, we would buy some 27,000 MRAPs, including thousands of a new all-terrain version for Afghanistan, at a total cost of nearly $40 billion. The investment saved countless lives and limbs. Over time, casualty rates in MRAPs were roughly 75 percent lower than they were in Humvees, and less than half those in Abrams tanks, Bradley fighting vehicles, and Stryker armored vehicles. And there would continue to be improvements. For example, underbelly blasts had such upward force that too often soldiers in MRAPs would suffer badly broken legs and fractured pelvises, so the flooring and seats were redesigned.

On January 18, 2008, I visited the Space and Naval Warfare Systems Center in Charleston, South Carolina, where MRAPs received a final fitting out before being shipped to Iraq. I toured the factory and talked to the workers, many of them veterans themselves. These men and women were skilled salt-of-the-earth patriots who were passionate about what they were doing. Each of those I talked with knew that the vehicle he or she was working on would very likely save the lives of our soldiers. One of them, a bearded, heavyset fellow in jeans and a plaid shirt, invited me to sit in the driver's seat of the MRAP he was just finishing. He reached into the glove compartment and brought out a laminated card that would accompany the vehicle to Iraq. It had the signatures of the team that had worked on that vehicle. He said they knew lives depended on the quality of their work, and they wanted the soldiers riding in that vehicle to know that each member of that team took personal responsibility for that specific MRAP. He said such a card went with every MRAP.

Beginning in late 2007, every time I visited Iraq, units were proud to show me their MRAPs. Unit commanders especially loved them as they saw their soldiers walk away from attacks that previously would have been fatal. I learned from soldiers that the ride was very uncomfortable, that the vehicles were so heavy (the weight ranged from roughly fourteen tons to nearly thirty tons, depending on the model) that they were not very useful off-road, and that rollovers were a real risk. They were so tall that, when going through towns, the antennas could snag electric wires. Our ingenious troops simply improvised, using long pieces of plastic pipe to lift the electric wires as they went under. Others jerry-rigged ambulances out of MRAPs, and one brigade commander had a desk put in one to use as a mobile command post. But mostly they just delivered soldiers from one place to another with far greater safety than they previously had. Time and again, commanders would walk me over to a damaged MRAP, and there would be two or three soldiers standing by it who would tell me about surviving an attack on that vehicle. A journalist passed along to me the story of a colonel watching a live video feed showing one of his unit's vehicles overturned and in flames after an IED attack and praying out loud, "Please, just save one of my guys." And then he watched, astonished, as all three men inside emerged injured but alive. They had been in an MRAP.

Toward mid-2008 our attention turned to the need to get MRAPs into Afghanistan because of the growing IED threat there. As we began to ship growing numbers of the vehicles over time, it became clear that, having been designed for the relatively flat terrain and roads of Iraq, the heavy and hard-to-maneuver vehicles weren't suitable for off-road use or for rocky and mountainous Afghanistan. Again, the MRAP task force—and industry—responded quickly by designing a lighter, more maneuverable vehicle—the MRAP-ATV (all-terrain vehicle).

There are a lot of heroes in the MRAP story, from those in the Marine Corps who kept pressing for an MRAP-like vehicle for years, to program director Marine Brigadier General Mike Brogan and his team, John Young and all those who worked with him on the MRAP task force, my own staff—especially Chiarelli, who was passionate about getting the troops more protection and who daily reminded everyone that I was watching like a hawk—our industry partners, all those great folks in Charleston, and Congress, which on this rare occasion did the right thing and did it quickly. On May 21, 2008, I wrote letters to all the key contributors thanking them for a great achievement. I hand-wrote, "Your efforts—and those of your team—have saved lives and limbs. On behalf of all who return home alive and whole because of your efforts, you have my most profound gratitude."

As usual in a huge bureaucracy, the villains were the largely nameless and faceless people—and their leaders—who were wed to their old plans, programs, and thinking and refused to change their ways regardless of circumstances. The hidebound and unresponsive bureaucratic structure that the Defense Department uses to acquire equipment performs poorly in peacetime. As I saw, it did so horribly in wartime. And then, as I've already said, there was the department's inexplicable peacetime mind-set in wartime. My role had been to push all these obstacles to the sidelines so that senior leaders like John Young could act urgently to save lives.

To those who contended then, and still do, that MRAPs were unnecessary and a costly one-dimensional, one-time-use vehicle that detracted from more important long-term priorities, I offer only this response: talk to the countless troops who survived IED blasts because they were riding in an MRAP.

Intelligence, Surveillance, and Reconnaissance

Time and again I would have to tackle that damnable peacetime mind-set inside the Pentagon. By fall 2007 my impatience was boiling over. On September 28, I called a meeting of all the senior department officials—civilian and military—to read them the riot act. I told them that for our field commanders and troops engaged in the fight, "the difference between getting a decision tomorrow versus next week or delivery of a piece of technology next week versus next month is huge. This department has been at war for over six years. Yet we still use the processes that were barely adequate for peacetime operations and impose a heavy cost in wartime." I told them that whether the issue was MRAP fielding rates, increasing intelligence, surveillance, and reconnaissance (ISR) coverage, or fixing troop rotations, it was obvious to me that business as usual "rarely meets the needs of our troops in the field." I challenged them to look for opportunities to apply a sense of urgency and a willingness "to break china" if it involved getting something to the fight faster or in larger quantities: "The difference between getting something in the hands of our combat forces next month versus next year is dramatic. . . . We must all show up every day prepared to look at every decision and plan affecting our combat operations through the lens of how we can do it faster, more effectively, and with more impact."

A month later I told the secretaries of the three military departments: "I need you and your team to continue to poke and prod and challenge the conventional wisdom if that is what it takes to support our kids in the field."

On January 14, 2008, I sent Mike Mullen a very tough note that cited several examples "where a formal request addressed to me took numerous months (in one case over six) to wind its way through the Centcom/ Joint Staff staffing process before it was brought to me for action." I directed him to develop and implement a process by which I would be informed immediately of *any* request specifically addressed to me by our commanders in Iraq and Afghanistan.

The immediate problem that provoked those expressions of impatience was the difficulty we were having in meeting our field commanders' need for intelligence, surveillance, and reconnaissance (ISR) capabilities: a mix of unmanned drones, propeller-driven reconnaissance aircraft, analysts, linguists, and data fusion capabilities that collected and fed critical battlefield information—including intercepted phone calls of terrorist leaders and live video transmission of insurgents planting IEDs—to military commanders, who could then act on it.

In the case of the MRAPs, accelerating production and delivery was essentially a matter of empowerment and finding the money. In the case of ISR, I encountered a lack of enthusiasm and urgency in the Air Force, my old service.

The fusion of extraordinary technical intelligence capabilities with military operations in real time and in direct support of small units in both Iraq and Afghanistan produced a genuine revolution in warfare and combat. While aerial intelligence support for commanders on the ground dates back at least to the Civil War and the use of balloons, over the last quarter of a century this support has taken on an entirely new character. I saw an early example of this as deputy at the CIA in the spring of 1986, when we were able to feed real-time satellite information about Libyan air defense activity directly to the pilots who were conducting the attacks on Tripoli. That was horse-and-buggy technology compared to what has been done in Iraq and Afghanistan.

While I was CIA director, in 1992, I tried to get the Air Force to partner with us in developing technologically advanced drones, because of their ability to loiter over a target for many hours, thus providing continuous photographic and intercepted signals intelligence coverage. The Air Force wasn't interested because, as I was told, people join the Air Force to fly airplanes and drones had no pilot. By the time I returned to government in late 2006, the Predator drone had become a household word, especially among our enemies, though the Air Force mind-set had not changed. In Iraq, the Army had converted small two-engine propeller planes into intelligence-collection platforms that could provide live video coverage—"full-motion video"—of an area over a prolonged period. This capability, Task Force ODIN (Observe, Detect, Identify, and Neutralize), became a critical asset not only in spotting individuals planting IEDs but in allowing analysts to track people and vehicles and thus to identify the networks producing and planting bombs. It was amazing to watch a video in real time of an insurgent planting an IED, or to view a video analysis tracing an insurgent pickup truck from the bomb-making site to the site of an attack. It was even more amazing—and gratifying—to watch the IED bomber and the pickup truck be quickly destroyed as a result of this unprecedented integration of sensors and shooters.

A number of other intelligence-collection platforms—various kinds of manned aircraft, aerostats (dirigibles), fixed cameras, and many other sensors—were developed. Initially, the full panoply of these platforms was used primarily by Special Forces in their operations, but over time, as other commanders saw what these ISR capabilities were, the demand for more of them for regular combat operations and for force protection grew exponentially.

There were impediments to meeting the demand. One was the limited production capacity of the single company that was making both the Predators and the ground stations necessary to process the collected information. Another was the need for more linguists to translate collected communications. A third was the limited number and availability of other kinds of collection capabilities. For example, one highly effective platform was the Navy's P-3 aircraft, designed principally for hunting enemy submarines. Unless we essentially deprived ourselves of that capability in Pacific Command and elsewhere, only a handful of these aircraft would be available for Iraq and Afghanistan. They were also getting very old, limiting the number of hours they could fly.

The small number of trained crews available to pilot the drones, particularly in the Air Force, was another significant problem. The Army flew its version of the Predator—called Warrior—using warrant officers and noncommissioned officers. The Air Force, however, insisted on having flight-qualified aircraft pilots—all officers—fly its drones. The Air Force made clear to its pilots that flying a drone from the ground with a joy stick was not as career-enhancing as flying an airplane in the wild blue yonder. Not surprisingly, young officers weren't exactly beating the door down to fly a drone. When I turned my attention to the ISR problem in mid-2007, the Air Force was providing eight Predator "caps"—each cap consisting of six crews (about eighty people) and three drones, providing twenty-four hours of coverage. The Air Force had no plans to increase those numbers; I was determined that would change.

There was an unseemly turf fight in the ISR world over whether the Air Force should control all military drone programs and operations. The Army resisted, and I was on its side; the Air Force was grasping for absolute control of a capability for which it had little enthusiasm in the first place. I absolutely loathed this kind of turf fight, especially in the middle of ongoing wars, and I was determined the Air Force would not get control.

In the ISR arena, each military service was pursuing its own programs, there was no coordination in acquisition, and no one person was in charge to ensure interoperability in combat conditions. The undersecretary of defense for intelligence, the CIA with its drones (mainly flown by the military), and the director of national intelligence all had their own agendas. It was a mess.

Whatever the complications, the surge of troops in Iraq and mounting difficulties in Afghanistan required a surge in ISR capabilities. Indeed, in nearly every one of my weekly videoconferences with Dave Petraeus, first in Iraq and later in Afghanistan, he would raise the need for more ISR. I asked Ryan McCarthy of my staff, a former Army Ranger and combat veteran of Afghanistan, to be my eyes and ears in this effort—and my cattle prod when necessary.

The first order of business during the summer of 2007 was to scour the world for additional capability. I was prepared to strip nearly every combatant command of much of its ISR to provide more to Petraeus. Every region of the globe is assigned a regional four-star headquarters. These commanders—sometimes compared to proconsuls during the Roman Empire—are loath to give up any military assets assigned to them. Nonetheless we rounded up every drone we could find that was not already deployed in Iraq and grabbed P-3 aircraft from around the world to send to Iraq and Afghanistan. An even more capable drone than the Predator was its larger cousin, the Reaper, and we worked to maximize its production and deployment to the theater as well. At the same time, we had to ramp up new production and accelerate training of new crews. I directed the Air Force to increase its Predator capacity from eight caps to eighteen, and I told its leaders that I wanted their plan by November 1.

Several developments late that fall confirmed for me that the Air Force leadership didn't accept the urgency of the need for ISR "downrange" or the need to think outside the box about how to get more. This was especially puzzling to me because the Air Force was making an invaluable contribution to the war effort by providing close air support to ground troops under fire, in medical evacuations, and in flying huge quantities of matériel into both Iraq and Afghanistan. In late October 2007, Air Force Chief of Staff Mike "Buzz" Moseley directed a study on how the Air Force could get to eighteen caps by October 2008—far too slowly, in my view. Then, at a time when we were trying to put every intelligence platform possible into the war, the Air Force proposed ending all funding for the venerable U-2 spy plane by the end of summer 2008. The U-2, the same kind of spy plane piloted by Francis Gary Powers and shot down by the Soviets in 1960, was still providing remarkable intelligence. I thought proposing to ground it at this juncture was just plain crazy. Further, nearly every time Moseley and Air Force Secretary Mike Wynne came to see me, it was about a new bomber or more F-22s. Both were important capabilities for the future, but neither would play any part in the wars we were already in.

I saw firsthand some of the challenges when I visited Creech Air Force Base in Nevada very early in 2008. Creech is the headquarters of the 432nd Reconnaissance Wing and the 15th and 17th Reconnaissance Squadrons, and it was the control center where pilots actually flew many of the drones based in Iraq and Afghanistan. The base is in the middle of nowhere and, when I first visited, quite spartan. In the operations building, there were multiple cubicles, each with an Air Force pilot at a work station. The whole enterprise resembled a very sophisticated video arcade—except these men and women were playing for keeps. On screens in front of them, the pilots in Nevada could see exactly and simultaneously what the Predator or Reaper was seeing in Iraq or Afghanistan. Each pilot had a joy stick and an instrumentation panel for remotely flying a vehicle thousands of miles away. It was one of the most astonishing—and lethal—displays of technological prowess I have ever seen.

I was taken to a new hangar to see both a Predator and a Reaper. They both look like giant bugs, with long spindly legs, a broad wingspan, and a camera pod that looks like a huge, distended eyeball. The Reaper is quite a bit larger than the Predator and, when armed, can carry a weapons load comparable to some of our fighters. Looking at those aircraft, I could not understand why I was having such a hard time persuading the Air Force leadership that these "remotely piloted vehicles" were an integral part of the Air Force's future and should become a significant and enduring part of its combat capability.

I spent some time with the drone pilots, who had a number of gripes. They had a two-hour round-trip commute every day from their homes at Nellis Air Force Base after a grueling day of flying multiple missions. There was no place where you'd want to eat at Creech. There was no physical fitness facility. There was no promising career path for the airmen who flew the drones without going back to flying airplanes—they weren't being promoted, and they were ineligible for the kind of air combat recognition and medals that airplane pilots could receive. Within months of my visit, the Air Force extended the hours of the child care center at Nellis, funded a medical and dental clinic at Creech, and began construction of a new food outlet and dining facility.

As the need for more ISR kept growing through the winter of 2007–8, it was clear my haranguing wasn't working. On April 4, 2008, I sent a memo to Admiral Mullen, a strong supporter and valuable ally in what I was trying to do with ISR, expressing my determination to press aggressively on all fronts necessary to get ISR support to Iraq and Afghanistan. I asked him for a briefing on initiatives under way and for his thoughts on any additional opportunities to increase ISR support over the ensuing thirty to ninety days. Ten days later I told Mullen that we needed a more comprehensive approach addressing how to maximize capabilities in the short term.

I soon established the ISR task force, led by the director of program evaluation Brad Berkson and Marine Lieutenant General Emo Gardner. I asked them for options for additional ISR capability in 30-, 60-, 90-, and 120-day phases. Each major Defense component with a stake in the outcome would have a senior representative on the task force, which would report to me directly once a month, beginning in two weeks.

Mullen, Undersecretary for Intelligence Clapper, Berkson, and I also agreed we needed to find more ISR resources in the United States and in other commands—for example, did we need as many pilots and drones in the training program instead of deployed in the field?—and that we had to look hard at whether the commands in Iraq and Afghanistan could more efficiently use the ISR resources they already had. For me, these bureaucratic fights always came back to my obsession to protect the troops currently in the fight and to do so urgently.

My first briefing by the task force soon thereafter underscored the problem and fed my frustration. Of nearly 4,500 U.S. drones worldwide, only a little more than half were in Iraq and Afghanistan. We needed to change that. We also needed to increase the number of translators for intercepted communications, unattended ground sensors to provide early warning of approaching insurgents, and people and hardware for quickly processing the information we collected and getting it to the commanders and troops who needed it. In August, I approved seventy-three new initiatives at a cost of $2.6 billion. On occasion, I would overreach. At one briefing when I was told we would soon have twenty-four "caps" (each with enough drones and crews to provide twenty-four-hour coverage), I asked whether the theater could manage ninety-two caps. I was told, "No, that would eclipse the sun."

During the summer, Berkson and McCarthy launched themselves into the field, visiting Creech as well as Iraq and Afghanistan. They were not welcomed. As they counted the number of Predators in hangars at Creech, one Air Force officer there complained to the Pentagon about my micromanagers telling him what he did and did not need. But Berkson and McCarthy found two to three caps' worth of capability in their visit to Creech and reported that the pilots there were "flying" only sixty hours a month. They could do more and subsequently did. Command staffs in Baghdad and Kabul were equally sore at having someone from Washington "grading their homework." But what was important was that they found more capability.

The congressional appropriations committees were uneasy with the ISR task force because the funding did not go through the traditional budgetary process. They almost always ultimately approved, but it took too long, and they continued to press for dissolution of the task force and a return to regular procedures. I changed the structure of the task force a couple of times—and renamed it in the Obama administration—which amounted to a bit of a shell game with the Hill for more than three years, to ensure I had a mechanism at my disposal in Washington that could effectively serve the commanders in the field.

We would focus on getting more ISR capabilities to Iraq and Afghanistan for the remainder of my time as secretary. By June 2008 the Air Force was able to tell me it was dramatically increasing the number of patrols by armed drones. The following month I approved reallocating $1.2 billion within Defense to buy fifty MC-12 planes—dubbed "Liberty" aircraft—equipped to provide full-motion video and collect other intelligence, primarily in Afghanistan. These relatively low-cost, low-tech, twin-propeller aircraft—the kind traditionally despised by the Air Force—were more than capable of getting the job done. Allocating ISR assets between Iraq and Afghanistan was an ongoing challenge for Central Command, but one simple reality helped guide decisions: Predators were man hunters, whereas the Liberty aircraft were a superb asset in the counter-IED world. We would develop and deploy many other kinds of cameras and platforms, both airborne and at fixed sites on the ground, to provide our troops with intelligence that supported combat operations but that also protected their bases and outposts, especially in Afghanistan. There were almost sixty drone caps when I left office.

The difficulty in getting the Pentagon to focus on the wars we were in and to support the commanders and the troops in the fight left a very bad taste in my mouth. People at lower levels had good ideas, but they had an impossible task in breaking through the bureaucracy, being heard, and being taken seriously. The military too often stifled younger officers, and sometimes more senior ones, who challenged current practices. In a speech I gave to Air Force personnel a few days after I established the ISR task force, I made it clear that I encouraged cultural change in the services, unorthodox thinking, and respectful dissent. I spoke of earlier Air Force reformers and the institutional hostility and bureaucratic resistance they had faced. I asked the midlevel officers in the audience to rethink how their service was organized, manned, and equipped. I repeated my concern that "our services are still not moving aggressively in wartime to provide resources needed now on the battlefield." In a line about ISR that I penciled in on my way to the speech, I said, "Because people were stuck in old ways of doing business, it's been like pulling teeth."

At West Point the same day, I delivered a lecture to the entire corps of cadets with a similar message about military leadership, knowing that my remarks there would be read throughout the Army. I told the cadets,

> In order to succeed in the asymmetric battlefields of the twenty-first century—the dominant combat environment in the decades to come, in my view—our Army will require leaders of uncommon agility, resourcefulness, and imagination; leaders willing and able to think and act creatively and decisively in a different kind of world, in a different kind of conflict than we have prepared for for the last six decades. . . . One thing will remain the same. We will still need men and women in uniform to call things as they see them and tell their subordinates and superiors alike what they need to hear, not what they want to hear. . . . If as an officer—listen to me very carefully—if as an officer you don't tell blunt truths or create an environment where candor is encouraged, then you've done yourself and the institution a disservice.

Mindful of an article published earlier by an Army lieutenant colonel that was highly critical of senior officers, I added: "I encourage you to take on the mantle of fearless, thoughtful, but loyal dissent when the situation calls for it."

Because of the ISR issue and other concerns I had with the Air Force (more later), my speech to them was generally seen as a broadside against its leadership. At a press conference soon afterward, I was asked if that was my intention. I said there had been a lot of praise for the Air Force in my speech and that I had criticized the military bureaucracy across the board, particularly with regard to getting more help to the war fighter now. Everyone recognized that both speeches represented my first public assertion that supporting the wars we were already in and those fighting those wars, as well as preparing for future conflicts, would require cultural change in all the services. It was only the opening salvo.

WOUNDED WARRIORS

I believe that exposure of the scandalous problems in the outpatient treatment of wounded troops at the Walter Reed Army Medical Center mortified the senior military leadership of the services and the whole Department of Defense. I was always convinced they had been unaware of the bureaucratic and administrative nightmare that too often confronted our outpatient wounded, as well as the organizational, financial, and quality-of-life difficulties that faced our wounded troops and their families. The scandal prompted numerous reviews and studies of the entire wounded warrior experience, while the department and the services simultaneously began remedial actions.

During my entire tenure as secretary, I never saw the military services—across the board—bring to a problem as much zeal, passion, and urgency once they realized that these men and women who had sacrificed so much were not being treated properly after they left the hospitals. Senior generals and admirals jumped on the problem. I don't think that was because I had fired senior people. I was always convinced that once the military leadership knew they had let down these heroes, they were determined to make things right for them. The established bureaucracies, military and civilian, in the Departments of Defense and Veterans Affairs, however, were a different story.

The Army was the service, along with the Marine Corps, that had suffered the overwhelming preponderance of casualties, physical and psychological, in the post-9/11 wars. I met with Army Chief of Staff Casey in early March and told him not to wait on the reviews or studies but to act right away to fix Walter Reed and look at the rest of the Army's treatment of wounded warriors. With respect to evaluating soldiers for disability, I told him, "When in doubt, err on the side of the soldier." Casey and Army Vice Chief of Staff Dick Cody leaped on the problem without further urging from me. On March 8, I was briefed on the Army's action plan. Under Cody's supervision, other personnel changes had already been made at Walter Reed, a Wounded Warrior Transition Brigade was created (to give wounded soldiers an institutional unit to look after them while in outpatient status), a "one-stop soldier and family assistance center" was established, and all outpatient soldiers were moved into proper quarters. The Army was establishing a wounded warrior and family hotline, organizing teams to examine circumstances at the Army's twelve key medical centers, and looking into how to improve the Army's physical disability evaluation system. General Casey took the lead in aggressively tackling the problem of traumatic brain injury and post-traumatic stress. In June, Casey briefed me on a program to train every soldier in the Army on the causes and symptoms of post-traumatic stress in an effort not only to help them cope but also to begin to remove the stigma of mental illness. As he told me, "We've got to get rid of the mentality that if there are no holes in you, then you're ready for duty." The other services were not far behind the Army's lead.

On March 9, I had sent a message to every man and woman in the U.S. armed forces on the Walter Reed situation. I described the actions taken so far, including establishment of the two outside review panels. I told them we would not wait on those reports before tackling the problems. I told them I had directed a comprehensive, department-wide review of military medical care programs, facilities, and procedures, and that I had told the senior civilian and military leadership that in dealing with this challenge, "Money will not be an issue." I went on: "After the war itself, we have no higher priority than caring properly for our wounded." It was a sentiment and an admonition I would repeat often over the next four years.

Shortly thereafter I created the Wounded Warrior Task Force, charged with reporting to me every two weeks actions that were being taken across the Defense Department to address the needs of wounded warriors and their families. The goals of the task force were ambitious: (1) to completely redesign the disability evaluation system; (2) to focus on traumatic brain injury and post-traumatic stress; (3) to correct the flaws in case management of wounded warriors and their support; (4) to expedite Defense–Veterans Affairs data sharing; (5) to ensure proper facilities for wounded warriors; and (6) to reexamine the entire process for transitioning wounded warriors to Veterans Affairs. These were also the primary issues addressed by the West-Marsh independent review I had appointed and by the presidential Dole-Shalala commission. I was in a hurry and was not concerned about the three efforts stumbling over one another; each had a somewhat different mandate.

I wanted to ensure that good ideas were being shared across the services and around the Defense Department. As with MRAPs and ISR, I intended to make clear from my personal engagement the priority I attached to this endeavor, and that I was going to make sure everyone was moving aggressively to fix any problems we found. Gordon England and I also reenergized a joint Department of Defense–Veterans Affairs oversight group—the Senior Operations Committee—cochaired by each department's deputy secretary in an effort to make significant improvements in the process of transitioning from active duty to retired or veteran status.

I believe that at the outset of the Afghan and Iraq wars, neither Defense nor VA ever conceived of, much less planned for, the huge number of wounded young men and women (overwhelmingly men) who would come pouring into the system in the years ahead. Many of our troops would not have survived their wounds in previous wars, but extraordinary medical advances and the skills of those treating the wounded meant that a large number with complex injuries—including traumatic brain injuries and multiple amputations—faced prolonged treatment, years of rehabilitation, or a lifetime of disability. The Defense and VA bureaucracies, accustomed to dealing with older vets from Vietnam and earlier wars or retirees with all the ordinary problems of aging, seemed incapable of adjusting to wartime circumstances, just like the rest of Defense and the rest of government. There were three areas where I fought the military and civilian bureaucracy on behalf of the wounded, and all three stemmed from my strong belief that those wounded in combat or training for combat should be dealt with as a group by themselves and be afforded what I referred to as "platinum" treatment in terms of priority for appointments, for housing, for administrative assistance, and for anything else. I wanted them to have administrative staff for whom they were the sole "customers." The Defense and VA health care bureaucracies just could not or would not differentiate the wounded in combat from all others needing care.

Wounded Warrior Transition Units were being created by all the services at posts and bases throughout the United States so the wounded would have a home unit to watch over them. The first fight was over who should be allowed into them. I was shocked to learn, only months into the program, that the Army units of this kind were nearly filled to capacity. My intent in approving these units had been that they be reserved for those wounded or injured in battle or training, but the Army had allowed in those with noncombat injuries and illnesses as well. So a transition unit berth that I had hoped would go to a soldier wounded in Iraq might instead go to a soldier who had broken his leg stateside in a motorcycle accident. I obviously wanted the latter to get first-class medical care, but that was not why we created these units. In talking to wounded warriors at various Army posts around the country, I was told that deploying units would often transfer soldiers with behavioral or drug problems to these units. Eventually I persuaded the new Army secretary, Pete Geren, to be more faithful to my original intent but agreed it could be done through attrition, so that no soldier was forced to leave a transition unit.

The second fight was over bureaucratic delays in making disability decisions. In the case of those severely and catastrophically wounded, there was no need to take months to determine if they were entitled to full disability benefits. Similarly, a decision to transition wounded troops unable to remain on active duty to the VA ought not take nearly as much time as it took. I called this approach "tiering." President Bush was supportive of giving wounded warriors the benefit of the doubt on disability evaluations, erring on the side of the soldier initially and then making adjustments later if needed. Because the number of wounded warriors in the system was such a small subset of all those needing medical care and evaluation, I believed even more strongly that the system should be tilted in their favor. "We need to look at this from the perspective of the soldier, not the perspective of the government," I told a group of West Point cadets in September. We were able to get a pilot program going in the Washington, D.C., area to expedite the disability evaluation process, but it was always limited by legislation and bureaucracy. I pushed for these changes for years, but the unified opposition of the military and civilian bureaucracies—and the lack of support for my efforts from their leaders—largely defeated me. Any new approach, anything different from what they had always done, anything that might require congressional approval, and any differentiation between troops wounded in combat and others who were ill or injured was anathema to most officials in Defense and VA.

The third fight was over the disability evaluation system itself. To be considered for a disability retirement, a wounded warrior had to be evaluated as at least 30 percent disabled. This seemed to me to involve a ridiculous level of precision. How can you quantify whether a person is 28 percent disabled or 32 percent? I knew there were rules and guidelines, and I knew some veterans tried hard to game the system to get more money. But when it came to wounded warriors, when it was a close call or there was doubt, I wanted to err on the side of the soldier, and generously. I argued that we could institute a five-year review process to reevaluate the level of disability and correct any egregious errors made initially. I had no luck.

I also pressed for more support of families of the fallen and severely wounded, in addition to advancing state-of-the-art medical care for the signature injuries of the current conflicts—post-traumatic stress, traumatic brain injury, lost limbs, and eye problems and sight restoration. I predicted that these injuries would "continue to be the signature military medical challenge facing the Department for years to come."

In mid-July, at a meeting with the senior civilian and military leadership, I was briefed on statistics that I thought proved my point about tiering. I was told that, as of that date, 1,754,000 troops had been engaged in Iraq and Afghanistan. Thirty-two thousand had been wounded in action, half of whom had returned to duty within seventy-two hours. Ten thousand troops had been medically evacuated from Iraq and Afghanistan, not all of them for combat-related injuries, and a total (as of July 15) of 2,333 had been catastrophically injured or wounded. In short, the number of troops wounded in combat at that point in the wars represented a small fraction of all those being treated.

I felt a great sense of urgency in addressing these issues, in no small part because I assumed I had only six months remaining as secretary. I knew that if I didn't make progress in these areas, and if my successor was not as committed as I to fixing these problems, very little would happen. I knew one of the chief obstacles to proper treatment of wounded troops and veterans was the bureaucratic territoriality of both the Defense and Veterans Affairs Departments. A wounded soldier had to go through two separate disability evaluations, and getting health records from one department to the other was always a challenge. The secretaries of veterans affairs whom I worked through most of the Bush and Obama administrations (respectively, James Peake and Eric Shinseki) were committed to working out these problems. Unfortunately, if there is one bureaucracy in Washington more intractable than Defense, it is VA. Only when the VA secretary and I personally directed an outcome was any progress made at all. Unless successor secretaries are equally committed to change, whatever progress we made will be lost. And again, as far as I was concerned, a big part of the problem was the system's unwillingness to differentiate in the process between someone wounded in combat and someone retiring with a hearing problem or hemorrhoids.

Wounded warriors and their families would often mention how difficult it was to get information on what benefits were available to them. When I raised this at the Pentagon, I was sent a two-page list of Web sites where wounded warriors could go to find all they wanted to know about support and benefits. But the effort required to access and read all that material—and the assumption that every wounded warrior family had a computer, especially when assigned to medical facilities away from home—seemed to me symptomatic of what was wrong with the system. In January 2008, I formally asked the personnel and readiness organization in the Pentagon to prepare a paper booklet for wounded warriors that could serve as a ready reference for benefits and care. I received a response a month later in the form of multiple brochures and handouts, a list of more Web sites and 1-800 call centers, all developed to address the needs of the wounded warrior community. I wrote back, "This is *precisely* the problem. We need *one*, easy to read, tabbed and indexed comprehensive guide. Like I originally asked for months ago." Two weeks later I received a memo laying out plans for the handbook and all that would need to be included in it, and I was informed that it would be available on October 1. I hit the ceiling. I wrote back on the memo, "Strikes me that if it takes six months to pull all this together, we have a bigger problem than even I thought." And we did.

Many of these matters came under the purview of the undersecretary of defense for personnel and readiness (P&R). For that office, it seemed the status quo was satisfactory. Virtually every issue I wanted to tackle with regard to health affairs (including the deficiencies in Tricare, the military health insurance program, which I heard about continuously from those in uniform at every rank), wounded warriors, and disability evaluations encountered active opposition, passive resistance, or just plain bureaucratic obduracy from P&R. It makes me angry even now. My failure to fix this inert, massive, but vitally important organization will, I fear, have long-range implications for troops and their families.

Beyond the Defense and Veterans Affairs bureaucracies, there were two other obstacles to reforming the disability system for wounded warriors. The first was Congress, which has over the years micromanaged anything dealing with veterans and responds with Pavlovian reliability to lobbying by the veterans service organizations (VSOs, including the Veterans of Foreign Wars and the American Legion). Nearly any change of consequence requires new law—a huge challenge. In October 2008, I directed development of a "stand-alone" legislative proposal that would give us the authority to create an express lane for catastrophically and severely wounded warriors.

In December, Mullen and I met again with the people in Defense working on the wounded warrior problem to discuss what initiatives we might suggest to the new presidential administration. I said that I had reached out to the new veterans affairs secretary, Eric Shinseki, who was eager to work with us on the disability evaluation issue. There were two choices: either Defense and VA worked this problem out together or we would go the legislative route. Mullen noted that we needed to improve support for families of the wounded, and I responded that we needed legislative relief to reduce their financial burden. Finally, I said we needed to make sure the National Guard and Reserves were provided for in any legislation. We knew that the legislative path would be tough because of the veterans organizations.

I greatly admire the VSOs for their work on behalf of veterans, for their patriotic and educational endeavors, and for their extraordinary efforts to help military families. That said, again and again they were a major problem whenever I tried to do something to help those still on active duty—for example, my attempt to bring about the changes in the disability evaluation system as described above. The organizations were focused on doing everything possible to advantage veterans, so much so that those still on active duty seemed to be of secondary importance, especially if any new benefits or procedures might affect veterans. The best example of this was their opposition to legislation implementing some of the excellent recommendations of the Dole-Shalala commission. That was unforgivable.

Another example: Senator Jim Webb authored a new GI Bill that was immensely generous in its educational benefits for veterans. I felt the benefits were so generous they might significantly affect retention of those on active duty. I wanted Congress to require five years of service to qualify for the benefits so we could get at least two enlistments out of troops before they left the service. When I called House Speaker Pelosi to press for this change, she told me, "On matters such as this, we always defer to the VSOs." (When I visited Fort Hood in the fall of 2007, a soldier's wife suggested to me that a service member ought to be able to share his or her GI Bill education benefits with a spouse or children. I thought it was a great idea and suggested it to President Bush, who included it in his 2008 State of the Union Address. There was little enthusiasm for it on Capitol Hill, but we were able, ultimately, to get it included in the final GI Bill—a benefit I saw as somewhat offsetting our inability to require five years of service to qualify for the education benefit.)

I found it very difficult to get accurate (and credible) information from inside Defense about whether we were making progress in helping wounded warriors and their families. The bureaucrats in the personnel and readiness office would regularly tell me how well we were doing and how pleased our troops and families were. Meanwhile I was hearing the opposite directly from the wounded. I insisted that we get more comprehensive and accurate feedback from the wounded, other troops, spouses, and parents. "I want an independent evaluation of soldiers and families and a list of programs where you need money," I said.

I would never succeed in cracking the obduracy and resistance to change of the department's personnel and health care bureaucracy, both military and civilian. It was one of my biggest failures as secretary.

The War About War

In the spring of 2008, the vital issue of the military services' preoccupation with planning, equipping, and training for future major wars with other nation-states, while assigning lesser priority to current conflicts and all other forms of conflict, such as irregular or asymmetric war, came to a head. It went to the heart of every other fight with the Pentagon I have described. In my four and a half years as secretary, this was one of the few issues where I had to take on the chairman and the entire Joint Chiefs of Staff.

Their approach, it seemed to me, ignored the reality that virtually every American use of military force since Vietnam—with the sole exceptions of the Gulf War and the first weeks of the Iraq War—had involved unconventional conflicts against smaller states or nonstate entities, such as al Qaeda or Hizballah. The military's approach seemed to be that if you train and equip to defeat big countries, you can defeat any lesser threat. I thought our lack of success in dealing with the Iraqi insurgency after 2003 disproved that notion. I didn't disagree with the importance of preparing for war against other nations. While that kind of conflict was the least likely, it would have the most significant consequences if we were not prepared. However, I thought we also needed explicitly to budget, train, and equip for a wide range of other possible adversaries. It was never my purpose to relegate state-to-state conflicts and the sophisticated weapons to fight them to second-level status compared to the wars we were currently fighting, but rather to ensure that we maintained our nontraditional capabilities. I wanted them to have a place in the budget and in the Defense culture that they had never had.

In short, I sought to balance our capabilities. I wanted to institutionalize the lessons learned and capabilities developed in Iraq and Afghanistan. I didn't want the Army, in particular, to forget how to do counterinsurgency—as it had done after Vietnam. I did not want us to forget how we had revolutionized special operations, counterterrorism, and counterinsurgency through an unprecedented fusion of intelligence and combat operations. I did not want us to forget that training and equipping the security forces of other nations, especially developing nations, might be an important means of avoiding deployment of our own forces. My fights with the Pentagon all through 2007 on MRAPs, ISR, wounded warriors, and more made me realize the extraordinary power of the conventional war DNA in the military services, and of the bureaucratic and political power of those in the military, industry, and Congress who wanted to retain the big procurement programs initiated during the Cold War, as well as the predominance of "big war" thinking.

As mandated by law in 1986, the president must produce a National Security Strategy, a document that describes the world as the president sees it and his goals and priorities in the conduct of foreign affairs and national security. The secretary of defense then prepares the National Defense Strategy, describing how Defense will support the president's objectives through its programs. The NDS provides a framework for campaign and contingency planning, force development, and intelligence. Given finite resources, the NDS also addresses how Defense would assess, mitigate, and respond to risk, risk defined in terms of "the potential for damage to national security combined with the probability of occurrence and a measurement of the consequences should the underlying risk remain unaddressed." Finally, drawing on the NDS, the chairman of the Joint Chiefs of Staff prepares his own document, the National Military Strategy, providing even more specific guidance to the military services and combatant commands in terms of achieving the president's goals.

Each of these three documents takes many months to write, in part to ensure that every relevant component of the government and the Defense Department can weigh in with its own views on the drafts. There is a high premium on achieving consensus, and countless hours are spent wrangling over the texts. The disputes are occasionally genuinely substantive, but more often they reflect efforts by each bureaucratic entity to ensure that its priorities and programs are protected. Ironically, and not atypically, the practical effect of the content of these documents is limited at the most senior levels of government. Personally, I don't recall ever reading the president's National Security Strategy when preparing to become secretary of defense. Nor did I read any of the previous National Defense Strategy documents when I became secretary. I never felt disadvantaged by not having read these scriptures.

The NDS became important to me in the spring of 2008 in part because my name would go on it, but also because I wanted it to reflect my strongly held views on the importance of greater balance between conventional and unconventional war in our planning and programs. The key passage in the draft concerned the assessment of risk:

> U.S. predominance in traditional warfare is not unchallenged, but is sustainable for the medium term given current trends. . . . We will continue to focus our investments on building capabilities to address these other [nontraditional] challenges. *This will require assuming some measure of additional, but acceptable, risk in the traditional sphere* [emphasis added]. We do not anticipate this leading to a loss of dominance or significant erosion in these capabilities.

This passage, and especially the italicized sentence, led to a rebellion; the chairman of the Joint Chiefs, the secretaries of the Navy and Air Force, and the chief of staff of the Army all refused to agree to that language. There was "no margin to accept additional risk in traditional capabilities to invest in other capability areas," they argued.

I met with the Joint Chiefs and combatant commanders in mid-May.

I asked how they differentiated between "risk" associated with current wars and "risk" associated with our ability to respond to future threats. "Why do you assume that state competitors will rely on traditional capabilities to challenge us?" I asked. I did not disagree with them on the need to prepare for large-scale, state-to-state conflict, but I was not talking about moving significant resources away from future conventional capabilities. I just wanted the defense budget and the services formally to acknowledge the need to provide for nontraditional capabilities and ensure that the resources necessary for the conflicts we were most likely to fight were also included in our budgeting, planning, training, and procurement. I was moving the needle very little. But even that was too much, given the threat it posed to the institutional military's modernization priorities.

Ultimately, I agreed to somewhat water down my language in the NDS, but I would continue to advocate publicly for more balance in our defense planning and procurement. This may seem abstract and like prosaic bureaucratic infighting, but these matters, which rarely engage the general public, have very real consequences for our men and women in uniform and for our national security, especially when budgets are tight and hard choices must be made.

At the end of September 2008, at the National Defense University in Washington, D.C., I summarized the issues and concerns that had been at the root of my war with the Pentagon for nearly two years.

The balance we are striving for is:

- Between doing everything we can to prevail in the conflicts we are in, and being prepared for other contingencies that might arise elsewhere, or in the future;
- Between institutionalizing capabilities such as counterinsurgency and stability operations, as well as helping partners build capacity, and maintaining our traditional edge—above all, the technological edge against the military forces of other nation-states.

I do not want to leave the impression that I fought my wars inside the Defense Department alone. With the exception of the NDS and one or two other issues, Mike Mullen was a steadfast ally. Most combatant commanders and all field commanders engaged in Iraq and Afghanistan obviously were supportive. On many issues, especially those involving wounded warriors, the senior military leadership was either right beside me or well in front of me, once the problems were identified. Senior civilians in the department like Edelman, Young, Clapper, and those who worked for them, provided critical support and leadership. My adversaries were those with a traditional mind-set, the usual opponents of any idea "not invented here," those fearful that what I was trying to do threatened their existing programs and procurements. Moreover, the size and complexity of the department itself made doing anything differently than had been done in the past a huge challenge. My wars inside the Pentagon in 2007–8 had been to address specific problems and shortcomings in supporting those fighting in Iraq and Afghanistan. The broader, bigger issues I had addressed only rhetorically. But when I found out I would remain as secretary under President Obama, I began to plan how I would actually begin to implement my ideas in the budget. As Gordon England put it, "We do what we fund." And I would, for the first time, take charge of that process.

THE BLAME GAME

In Washington, everyone wants a scalp when things don't go right. But, in truth, there isn't a simple answer as to who should bear responsibility for the failure to act earlier in the areas I have been discussing. When I sought to fix the problems I have described, I came to realize that in every case, multiple independent organizations were involved, and that no single one of them—one of the military services, the Joint Chiefs, the undersecretary for acquisition, the comptroller—had the authority to compel action by the others. The field commanders had been talking about withdrawing troops from Iraq throughout 2005 and 2006. If that was to be the case, why would the Army's civilian and military leaders take money away from future programs to buy a new kind of armored vehicle for use in a war that presumably was ending? The Air Force had never liked the idea of aircraft without pilots—why invest heavily in them at the expense of other programs? No one anticipated the huge influx of grievously wounded soldiers and Marines, nor the repeated tours of duty in Iraq and Afghanistan that would take a heavy toll on their bodies, their minds, and their families. Walter Reed hospital was scheduled to be shuttered as part of the base realignment and closure process. So why spend money for upkeep and facilities for outpatients or add administrative staff to work there?

There never was intentional neglect of the troops and their well-being. There was, however, a toxic mix of flawed assumptions about the wars themselves; a risk-averse bureaucracy; budgetary decisions made in isolation from the battlefield; Army, Navy and Air Force focus in Washington on the routine budget process and protecting dollars for future programs; a White House unaware of the needs of the troops and disinclined to pay much attention to the handful of members of Congress who pointed to these needs; and a Congress by and large so focused on the politics of the war in Iraq that it was asleep at the switch or simply too pusillanimous when it came to the needs of the troops. A "gotcha" climate in Washington created by investigative committees, multiple inspector general and auditing organizations, and a general thirst for scandal collectively reinforced bureaucratic timidity and leadership caution. All this translated into a ponderous and unresponsive system, the antithesis of the kind of speed, agility, and innovation required to support troops at war.

In my mind, what blame there is to be apportioned for failure to support the troops should be directed at those in senior positions of responsibility who did not scream out about these problems, and those who had authority but failed to act.

In the first category must be counted the field and combatant commanders; the service secretaries and chiefs of staff whose troops were at risk; the chairmen and vice chairmen of the Joint Chiefs; civilian political appointees at all levels in Defense; and the Armed Services Committees of both houses of Congress.

In the second category must be, principally, the secretaries and deputy secretaries of defense. Only they had the authority to ignore every organizational boundary and parochial budgetary consideration and force action. Only they, by taking ownership of problems, could remove risk from individuals and organizations. Only they could sweep aside with the stroke of a pen most bureaucratic obstacles and ponderous acquisition procedures and redirect budget resources. Secretary Rumsfeld did this successfully when he created the Joint Improvised Explosive Device Defeat Organization, the counter-IED organization. He did not act on other issues that I found critically important. I failed in some key respects in my efforts to transform the care of wounded warriors, especially providing administrative and financial support over and above that given others in uniform, and in fixing an outdated, complicated, and opaque disability evaluation system. I'm sure I fell short in other areas as well.

Secretary Rumsfeld once famously told a soldier that you go to war with the army you have, which is absolutely true. But I would add that you damn well should move as fast as possible to get the army you need. That was the crux of my war with the Pentagon.

CHAPTER 5

Beyond Iraq:
A Complicated World

No president, not even in wartime, has the luxury of being able to focus on just one problem. Bush 43 was no exception. Indeed, during the last two years of his administration, while fighting two major wars, we faced serious challenges with Russia, Syria, Iran, Israel, Pakistan, China, North Korea, NATO, Eastern Europe, Georgia, and, of all things, piracy. These problems collectively would take as much, if not more, of the president's time, and that of his senior national security team, than the wars in Iraq and Afghanistan. And several of them would provoke serious disagreements among us.

The world had changed dramatically since 1993, when I retired as CIA director. At that time, the United States had routed Saddam Hussein's army—then the fourth largest in the world—in less than one hundred hours during the Gulf War. Eastern Europe had been liberated, Germany was reunified, the Soviet Union had recently collapsed, and China was quiescent, its leaders focused on economic growth and developing trade. As victor in the Cold War, the United States stood supreme, the only surviving superpower—a political, military, and economic colossus.

What we did not realize then was that the seeds of future trouble were already sprouting. There were early stirrings of future great power rivalry and friction. In Russia, resentment and bitterness were taking root as a result of the economic chaos and corruption that followed the dissolution of the Soviet Union, as well as the incorporation of much of the old Warsaw Pact into NATO by 2000. No Russian was more angered by this turn of events than Vladimir Putin, who would later say that the end of the Soviet Union was the worst geopolitical event of the twentieth century. China, seeing the USSR's collapse, as well as America's military prowess in the Gulf War, resolved to expand its own military power. Al Qaeda's first attack on the World Trade Center in New York was launched in February 1993, and other attacks would follow throughout the 1990s. Meanwhile other nations increasingly resented our singular dominance and our growing penchant for telling others how to behave, at home and abroad. The end of the Soviet threat also ended the compelling reason for many countries to automatically align with the United States or do our bidding for their own protection. Other nations looked for opportunities to inhibit our seeming complete freedom and determination to shape the world as we saw fit. In short, our moment alone in the sun, and the arrogance with which we conducted ourselves in the 1990s and beyond as the sole surviving superpower, caused widespread resentment. And so when the World Trade Center came down on September 11, 2001, many governments and peoples—some publicly, many more privately— welcomed the calamity that had befallen the United States. In their eyes, an arrogant, all-powerful giant had been deservedly humbled.

I believe the widespread resentment of the United States, publicly suspended briefly in the immediate aftermath of the attacks on 9/11, was rekindled and exacerbated by President Bush's "You are either with us or you are against us" strategy as we launched the war on terror. The invasion of Iraq and subsequent revelations about renditions, prison abuses at Abu Ghraib, the detention facility at Guantánamo, and "enhanced interrogations" all fueled further anti-American feeling. This animosity, I think, began to recede by 2006–7, particularly in Europe, where leaders hostile to the United States and our Iraq policy had left office. Chancellor Gerhard Schroeder in Germany was replaced by the more conservative Angela Merkel in September 2005, and President Jacques Chirac in France was replaced by the openly pro-American Nicolas Sarkozy in May 2007. So by the time I reentered government in December 2006, the overall relationship with most European countries—and others—was on the upswing, though bruises remained from the acrimony engendered in the run-up to the war in Iraq. Still, our relationships with many countries were worse than when I had left government with the first President Bush in January 1993.

The passage of fourteen years had led to another significant change in the international environment. As I told Bush 43 and Condi Rice on more than one occasion, when I had been in government before, problems or crises more often than not would arise, be dealt with, and go away. The Yom Kippur War in October 1973, a serious crisis that risked confrontation with the Soviet Union, was over in a few days. Even the Iranian hostage crisis, as painful and protracted as it was, ended in 444 days. Now hardly any issue or problem could be resolved and put aside; instead problems accumulated. And while the national security apparatus to deal with such problems is gigantic, ultimately they all had to be addressed by just eight people: the president, the vice president, the secretary of state, the secretary of defense, the chairman of the Joint Chiefs of Staff, the director of national intelligence, the director of CIA, and the national security adviser.

Much of the time we spent together was in the White House Situation Room, which in no way resembles the high-tech, flashy "situation rooms" portrayed in movies and on television. Indeed, many of the military's four-star commanders—as well as the CIA—have significantly more technologically advanced conference rooms and operations centers with more gee-whiz gizmos. When I left in 1993, the Situation Room was a simple windowless conference room. It had several screens for television or displaying maps, but mostly people just used an easel for charts because the screens were too user-unfriendly. The table normally seated ten, four on either side and one at each end—one of whom was the president, with the presidential seal on the wall behind him.

The Situation Room complex had been upgraded during the Bush 43 years, sort of. It had been relocated and now had two windows, which I thought pointless because both were always covered for security reasons. The biggest improvement was the videoconferencing capabilities: the president or others could now hold face-to-face meetings with colleagues or counterparts half a world away. The president used the videoconferencing regularly for conversations with our commanders and ambassadors in Iraq and Afghanistan. The screens for maps were slightly better than before. The new conference table could seat up to fourteen, with perhaps another twenty seats around the walls for staff and others. It was close quarters, and the backbenchers were physically at risk if a principal at the table unexpectedly pushed his or her chair back too quickly. The growing number of these straphangers attending all but the most sensitive meetings (and all taking notes) was an unwelcome change from when I had last served in government, especially in terms of preventing leaks. This became more problematic during the Obama administration, especially in our deliberations about the Afghan War.

Seating was always by protocol rank, in both the Bush and Obama administrations. The president sat alone at the head of the table, with the vice president on his right and the secretary of state on his left. During the Bush administration, I sat next to Secretary Rice; during the Obama years, I was on the other side of the table and sat next to Vice President Biden—awkward placement given how often we disagreed.

The table had hidden electronic connections down the center for laptops and other devices. I never saw anyone use them. We mostly worried about spilling our coffee into the electronics and frying everything—and maybe everybody—at the table. I came to dread the long hours sitting in there—endless meetings, repetitive debates, the stress of spending so much time trying to find the least bad solution to a problem. (There were almost never "good" options available.) A few months into the Obama administration, I proposed adding a bar for the early evening sessions. A lot of heads nodded agreement, but wisely, nothing ever came of it. By then, some enterprising soul put curtains up over the covered windows. Obama came in and accusingly asked, "Who did that?" The curtains were gone the next day. The Situation Room remains a spartan place, perhaps fitting given the life-and-death, war-and-peace decisions that are taken there.

I also spent a great deal of time on airplanes. The plane I used for nearly all of my international travel is a several-decades-old Boeing 747, designated the E-4B and modified as the National Airborne Operations Center—a flying war room. There are no windows, as the entire plane is shielded against all manner of electronic interference. The airplane can be refueled in midair so, barring a maintenance problem, I would always fly nonstop wherever I was going—eighteen hours to Singapore from Washington, fourteen to Baghdad, seventeen to Kabul. I had a spacious office/bedroom (bunk beds) at the front of the plane, quite utilitarian, and, of course, secure telephone connections to anywhere in the world.

The only disconcerting aspect to my quarters was that the pipes from the midair refueling port went through the ceiling, and I could hear the gushing of the thousands of pounds of jet fuel we were taking on—and hope there was no leak. There is a nice conference room, where my senior staff traveled; a large but usually crowded press cabin; and then row after row of electronic stations, where other staff would be located. In addition to flight crews, the plane carried a full complement of technical specialists to keep the old bird flying and a security contingent to guard it when on the ground. Being on the plane was like being in the office in most respects—I was always reachable by telephone, and through the magic of modern electronics, my office in-box at the Pentagon managed to find its way to the plane. My most junior military assistant on board usually brought another load of paperwork to me just as I was settling down to read a book or take a nap. The generals and admirals wanted no part of my impatience with the endless stream of work.

I had been flying in the plane for over a year before I discovered that I could actually choose the meals we ate. For the next several years, everyone on board had to share my singularly unhealthy eating preferences: primarily bacon cheeseburgers, Reuben sandwiches, and barbecue. In fact, the crew dubbed the plane "The Big Brisket." In four and a half years, I traveled to 109 countries, spent the equivalent of thirty-five work weeks on the plane (250 travel days), and personally ate sixteen pounds of brisket. The Air Force keeps track of important things like that.

I was proud to fly in that airplane. When the huge blue and white plane, with the words *United States of America* emblazoned on the side and a big American flag on the tail, landed anywhere, I felt it made a statement about American presence and power. A high point for me came in Munich when we spotted President Putin's pilots in the cockpit of his plane taking pictures of ours.

RUSSIA

One of my first trips in that plane was in early February 2007, to Seville, Spain, for a NATO defense ministers meeting and then on to the Munich Security Conference. While in Seville, I met with Sergei Ivanov, who had been Russian defense minister for nearly six years and would soon become first deputy prime minister. Ivanov was in Seville for a meeting of the NATO-Russia Council. He is a cosmopolitan person, very smooth, fluent in English, and more candid than most Russian officials. In our meeting, he told me that Russia wanted to withdraw from the Intermediate Nuclear Forces Treaty signed during the Reagan administration, which prohibited the United States and the Soviet Union (later Russia) from deploying medium-range ballistic missiles (with a range of 300 to 3,400 miles). Ivanov said it was ironic that now the United States and Russia were the only two countries in the world that could not deploy these types of missiles. He said Russia would not deploy them in the west but wanted to place them in the south and the east—to counter Iran, Pakistan, and China. I responded that if Russia wanted to abrogate the treaty, "You are on your own. The United States will not support discarding the INF treaty." We agreed to disagree on missile defense in Europe—though he consented to send Russian experts to Washington to continue discussions on the subject—and on Russian arms sales to China, Iran, and Venezuela. We also agreed to keep open the channels of communication between us. He then invited me to visit Russia.

Every year senior government officials, political figures, academicians, and security experts from the United States, Europe, and elsewhere gather at the Munich Security Conference to network, exchange ideas, listen to speeches, and generally be seen hobnobbing with other influential people. The "three amigos" of the U.S. Senate—John McCain, Lindsey Graham, and Joe Lieberman—were always there. I found the gathering incredibly tedious and, after my second time, demurred on going again.

In 2007, though, I was still new to the job and felt obligated to go. In the spacious meeting room of the old hotel, senior government officials sat at long, narrow tables laterally arranged in rows with a center aisle. Behind the rows of tables were perhaps twenty or twenty-five rows of chairs for other participants, who had a good view of the dais—and the backs of all of us at the tables. I sat on the aisle in the front row. Just across the aisle from me were, in order, Russian president Putin, German chancellor Angela Merkel, and Ukrainian president Viktor Yushchenko. Yushchenko, who very much wanted to distance Ukraine from Russia and even join NATO, had been quite ill and his face was badly pitted—the result, he strongly believed, of the Russian intelligence services attempt to fatally poison him. When Merkel went to the podium to open the conference, she left only an empty chair separating Yushchenko and

Putin. From my vantage point only a few feet away, I could see Yush-chenko glaring at Putin with undisguised hatred. I am confident the sentiment was reciprocated.

Putin spoke next and, to everyone's surprise, launched a diatribe against the United States. He claimed the United States had used its uncontested military power to create and exploit a "unipolar" world and that, because of U.S. dominance, the world had become more destabilized and was seeing "more wars and regional conflicts." He said that the "almost uncontained hyper-use of force" by the United States and its disdain for the basic principles of international law had stimulated an arms race as insecure countries turned to weapons for security, including weapons of mass destruction. Putin asked why the United States was creating frontline bases with up to 5,000 troops on Russia's borders; why NATO was expanding aggressively toward a nonthreatening Russia; and why a missile defense system was being deployed in Poland close to the Russian border. He concluded by saying that Russia, "with a thousand years of history," hardly needed advice on how to act on the international scene. In response to a question, he backed off a little bit by describing President Bush as a decent man and someone he could do business with. Still, the overall impact of Putin's remarks, particularly on the European participants, was like an ice-cold shower. He was clearly trying to drive a wedge between the Europeans and the United States with his anti-American remarks, but all the questions he was asked were hostile in tone and content. He had misread his audience. As Putin was returning to his seat, he came up to me, smiled, shook hands, and repeated Ivanov's invitation for me to visit Russia.

I felt the harshness of his remarks had handed me an opportunity. So even as he was speaking, I began to rewrite the opening of my prepared remarks, to be delivered the next day. My speech would mark my first public appearance abroad as secretary of defense, and there was considerable anticipation among the participants as to how I, known as a Cold War hard-liner, would respond to Putin. Some U.S. officials there, including several from the State Department, felt strongly that I should be tough.

Consulting with my deputy assistant secretary for Europe, Dan Fata, whose judgment I trusted, I decided not to respond in kind to Putin but instead to use humor as a weapon.

Speaking of issues going back many years, as an old Cold Warrior, one of yesterday's speeches *almost* filled me with nostalgia for a less complex time. *Almost*. Many of you have backgrounds in diplomacy or politics. I have, like your second speaker yesterday [Putin], a starkly different background—a career in the spy business. And, I guess, old spies have a habit of blunt speaking.

However, I have been to re-education camp, spending four and a half years as a university president and dealing with faculty. And as more than a few university presidents have learned in recent years, when it comes to faculty, it is either "be nice" or "be gone."

The real world we inhabit is a different and much more complex world than that of twenty or thirty years ago. We all face many common problems and challenges that must be addressed in partnership with other countries, including Russia. For this reason, I have this week accepted the invitation of both President Putin and Minister of Defense Ivanov to visit Russia.

One Cold War was quite enough.

By the nods and smiles throughout the hall, I knew I had taken the right tack. The rest of my speech focused on NATO and a number of problems around the world, including the need for alliance members to invest more in defense and to do more in Afghanistan. I also held out an olive branch to our oldest allies. Secretary Rumsfeld had once referred to the differences between "old Europe" (our original NATO partners) and "new Europe" (those former states of the Warsaw Pact that had joined the alliance), with the clear implication of American preference for the latter. I decided to clear the air on that distinction but also make a point about the alliance that I would make often for the rest of my time as secretary:

Over the years, people have tried to put the nations of Europe and of the Alliance into different categories: The "free world" versus "those behind the Iron Curtain"; "North" versus "South"; "East" versus "West"; and I am told that some have even spoken in terms of "old" Europe versus "new."

All of these characterizations belong to the past. The distinction I would draw is a very practical one—a "realist's" view perhaps: it is between Alliance members who do all they can to fulfill collective commitments, and those who do not. NATO is not a "paper membership" or a "social club" or a "talk shop." It is a *military* alliance—one with very serious real world obligations.

The reaction in Europe and at home to my speech was uniformly positive. I received a note from Sir Charles Powell, who had been Prime Minister Margaret Thatcher's national security adviser, that captured the general view. I had "struck absolutely the right note of wicked humor in swatting Putin and put him in his place," he wrote.

When I reported to the president my take on the Munich conference, I shared with him my belief that from 1993 onward, the West, and particularly the United States, had badly underestimated the magnitude of Russian humiliation in losing the Cold War and then in the dissolution of the Soviet Union, which amounted to the end of the centuries-old Russian Empire. The arrogance, after the collapse, of American government officials, academicians, businessmen, and politicians in telling the Russians how to conduct their domestic and international affairs (not to mention the internal psychological impact of their precipitous fall from superpower status) had led to deep and long-term resentment and bitterness.

What I didn't tell the president was that I believed the relationship with Russia had been badly mismanaged after Bush 41 left office in 1993. Getting Gorbachev to acquiesce to a unified Germany as a member of NATO had been a huge accomplishment. But moving so quickly after the collapse of the Soviet Union to incorporate so many of its formerly subjugated states into NATO was a mistake. Including the Baltic states, Poland, Czechoslovakia, and Hungary quickly was the right thing to do, but I believe the process should then have slowed. U.S. agreements with the Romanian and Bulgarian governments to rotate troops through bases in those countries was a needless provocation (especially since we virtually never deployed the 5,000 troops to either country). The Russians had long historical ties to Serbia, which we largely ignored. Trying to bring Georgia and Ukraine into NATO was truly overreaching. The roots of the Russian Empire trace back to Kiev in the ninth century, so that was an especially monumental provocation. Were the Europeans, much less the Americans, willing to send their sons and daughters to defend Ukraine or Georgia? Hardly. So NATO expansion was a political act, not a carefully considered military commitment, thus undermining the purpose of the alliance and recklessly ignoring what the Russians considered their own vital national interests. Similarly, Putin's hatred of the Treaty on Conventional Armed Forces in Europe (limiting the number and location of Russian and NATO nonnuclear military forces in Europe) was understandable. It had been negotiated when Russia was weak, and the provisions limited Russia's freedom to move troops from place to place in its own territory. As I later told Putin directly, I would not stand for restrictions on my ability to redeploy troops from Texas to California.

Throughout my career, as I said, I had been characterized as a hard-liner on the Soviet Union. Guilty as charged. Many of the problems between post-Soviet Russia and the United States grew out of Russian leaders' efforts to seek domestic political advantage by portraying the United States, NATO, and the West more broadly as a continuing threat to Russia; bullying their neighbors, particularly those that had once been part of the Soviet Union; using oil and gas supplies as a means of politically pressuring and extorting money from the nations on their periphery and in Europe; crudely abusing human and political rights at home; and continuing to support a number of thuggish regimes around the world. But during the Cold War, to avoid military conflict between us, we had to take Soviet interests into account, maneuvering carefully wherever those interests were affected. When Russia was weak in the 1990s and beyond, we did not take Russian interests seriously. We did a poor job of seeing the world from their point of view, and of managing the relationship for the long term. All that said, I was now President Bush's secretary of defense, and I dutifully supported the effort to bring Georgia and Ukraine into NATO (with few pangs of conscience because by 2007 it was clear the French and Germans would not allow it). On missile defense, however, I did look for ways to accommodate Russian interests and persuade them to become partners. Still, I was always clear that we would move ahead, with or without them.

The relationship between the United States and Russia during my time as secretary under George W. Bush would be dominated by the president's decision to emplace missile defenses against Iran in eastern Europe, U.S. efforts to expand NATO to include Georgia and Ukraine, and Russia's invasion of Georgia. Our commitment to missile defenses in Europe would also dominate U.S.-Russian relations during Obama's first term.

Russian opposition to the United States developing missile defense capabilities has deep roots. During the first strategic arms limitation talks under President Nixon, the Soviets ultimately sought to prohibit only the development and deployment of missile defenses, which they believed the United States could build and they couldn't—thus giving us a significant advantage in the strategic nuclear relationship. The result was the Anti-Ballistic Missile Treaty signed in 1972, along with an agreement limiting offensive strategic weapons essentially to the programs both countries already had planned. President Reagan's Strategic Defense Initiative (SDI), announced in 1983 and calling for a nationwide missile defense using very sophisticated technology, both angered and, I believe, terrified the Soviets. As I joked at the time, there appeared to be only two people on the planet who actually thought SDI would work—Reagan and Mikhail Gorbachev. The Soviets were under enormous economic pressure by that time and knew they could not compete with such a system.

President Bush's 2002 abrogation of the 1972 ABM treaty (thereby allowing the United States to develop any kind of missile defenses it wanted), and our subsequent development of ground-based interceptors and radars based in Alaska and California, our efforts to bring Georgia and Ukraine into NATO, and our support for the independence of Kosovo (which the Russians strongly opposed), taken together with Russian opposition to the United States in Iraq and elsewhere, all had brought the bilateral relationship to the low point of Putin's February 2007 tirade in Munich. The personal relationship between Bush and Putin, however, remained civil.

I made a difficult situation with Russia worse by signing off—the day after I was sworn in as secretary in December 2006—on a recommendation to the president that the United States locate ten long-range missile defense interceptors in Poland and an associated radar installation in the Czech Republic. Construction would, we hoped, begin in the second half of 2008. The system would provide significant protection from Iranian missiles for the United States and many of our European allies, although I acknowledged that the negotiations could be difficult: Poland would want significantly greater military assistance, and the makeup of the Czech government was uncertain. The Russians saw the proposed deployments as putting their nuclear deterrent at risk and as a further step in the "encirclement" of their country. The president approved my recommendation a few weeks later.

I took up the invitation to visit Russia and landed at Moscow's Sheremetyevo Airport on a Monday morning in April. My first meeting was with the new Russian minister of defense, Anatoly Serdyukov, who had been in the furniture business, had run the Russian tax service, and was personally and politically well connected. The meeting was at the Russian Ministry of Defense, a massive building with no distinguishing features, characteristic of Soviet architecture. The conference room was also nondescript. Serdyukov knew little about defense matters and had been brought in to reform the Russian military—a daunting, even dangerous, proposition. In our meetings, he was tightly scripted and chaperoned by the chief of the Russian general staff, General Yuri Baluyevskiy. Our meeting, like the others I would have in Moscow, focused almost entirely on missile defense.

Reading from a script, Serdyukov immediately said that our proposed system would diminish Russia's nuclear deterrent and have a negative effect on world peace. We had said the system was a counter to Iran and North Korea, but he contended that neither country had missiles capable of reaching Europe or the United States; nor was that likely in the foreseeable future. Russia, he said, was very concerned that our system could intercept Russia's ballistic missiles. I responded that the concerns of both sides needed to be taken into account, that the opportunities for cooperation between us were unprecedented, and that we both needed to think ten or twenty years into the future. My undersecretary for policy, Eric Edelman, reassured the Russians that the radar in the Czech Republic would be too close to get a fix on missiles launched from Russia; the system had no capability again Russian ICBMs; and debris from the missiles would burn up in the atmosphere. The Russian military experts seemed increasingly intrigued and interested. We repeated a long list of potential areas for cooperation previously mentioned to the Russians, including working together on research and development, sharing data gathered by the system's radar, jointly testing the system's components, and possibly using a Soviet-era radar in Azerbaijan. I invited the Russians to visit our missile defense sites in Alaska and California and suggested that, with the permission of the Polish and Czech governments, the Russians would be allowed to routinely inspect missile defense installations in those countries. What I put on the table went well beyond anything presented previously to the Russians. The Russians' real worry was clearly not about the current system we were describing but about the possibility that at some point in the future we might introduce additional capabilities that would threaten their deterrent. While Serdyukov and Baluyevskiy were unyielding, they agreed to further discussions among technical experts from both sides.

I then moved on to the Kremlin to meet with Putin. I had last entered the Kremlin in 1992 as CIA director, and driving through the gate then, in the U.S. ambassador's limousine with American flags flying on the front of the car, had felt like a victory lap. By 2007 the world had moved on, and so had I. Putin and I encountered each other at a table in his ornate, very large office with plentiful gold leaf and spectacular chandeliers— all courtesy of the tsars and preservation efforts by the Communists. As I reported to President Bush, the meeting with Putin was cordial, far different in tone from Munich. He blessed the idea of the experts meeting on missile defense and invited me to return to Russia. He recited a litany of woes besetting Russia, which he blamed on the West. His talking points were predictable: We have a similar view of threats and challenges; many in the United States don't think Russia is a partner; why are you putting bases near our borders?; North Korea and Iran will not have missiles that are threatening anytime soon; why is the United States supporting "separatists" in Georgia?; tensions are not surprising given that we have "looked at each other through the barrel of a shotgun"; we want to be partners, even strategic allies. The issue that really stuck in his craw was the conventional forces in Europe treaty, which he called the "colonial" treaty, "imposed on Russia." I tried to put a positive spin on the potential to work together.

With fifteen minutes to go in the meeting, an aide came in and whispered something in Putin's ear. He abruptly, but not impolitely, concluded the meeting, and I was ushered out of his office. Former Russian president Boris Yeltsin had died.

Later that afternoon I met again with Sergei Ivanov, in his new deputy prime minister's office in the Russian White House. We covered much of the same ground, although Ivanov added some candor about Iran. "You know, the Iranians don't need a missile to get a nuclear weapon into Russia," he said, clearly prepared to ratchet up the sanctions pressure on Iran if Tehran didn't suspend uranium enrichment.

While the press reported that I had received a "cool" reception in

Moscow, I told President Bush that my meetings had been warm, businesslike, and surprisingly constructive. I can see now that our two countries were just kicking the can down the road on missile defense, playing for time. The Russians recognized that they were being presented with a fait accompli, and that our offers of cooperation were more like take it or leave it. They hoped they could build enough opposition in Europe to stop the project. We wanted Russian participation, but we would not let their opposition slow our plans, though I would spend four more years working on this problem.

On my way home, I stopped in both Warsaw and Berlin to brief those governments on my meetings in Moscow. President Lech Kaczynski in Warsaw made clear he wanted to move fast on missile defense, concluding negotiations well before Poland's 2009 election. His defense minister, Aleksander Szczyglo, was standoffish, saying that the U.S. proposal (to emplace ten long-range interceptor missiles in Poland) would be "carefully considered" and that we shouldn't "prejudge the negotiations." In a refrain I would hear repeatedly for years, he said that for any plan to be accepted, it must increase Poland's security.

After the trip, I reported to the president that both Poland and the Czech Republic had domestic political problems associated with the proposed system, with two of the governing coalition parties in Poland opposed to missile defense and the Czech government faced with a hung parliament and elections in the offing. Polls showed that more than half of the Czechs were against deployment of the missile defense radar on their soil. In Poland, one poll had 57 percent opposed. Secretary Rice, in Moscow in mid-May, and the president soon afterward at his ranch in Crawford and during visits to Poland and the Czech Republic, both underscored U.S. resolve to go forward. Putin by then had offered data sharing from the Russian radar in Azerbaijan as an alternative. At a NATO defense ministers meeting in Brussels in June, in the presence of Russian defense minister Serdyukov, I stated explicitly that we would go forward with the missile defense project despite Putin's offer.

On October 12, 2007, Condi and I met in Moscow with our counterparts—a "two plus two" meeting—as well as with Putin. We came bearing proposals even more attractive to the Russians than those I had put forward the previous April, including the possibility that the interceptors might not be made operational until there was a demonstrated Iranian nuclear-armed ballistic missile capability.

Putin invited us to his dacha outside Moscow. En route, we passed through some very swanky new estates and shopping centers, with stores like those in a high-end shopping center in a wealthy American suburb or in a fashionable part of London, Paris, or Rome. Life was clearly good for at least some Russians, especially those who lived in Putin's neighborhood. His dacha was large and perfectly nice, but it seemed very utilitarian to me, more like a corporate guesthouse. He kept us waiting for about twenty minutes, which the U.S. press played up as a slight to us both. When he came in, he apologized, explaining that he had been on the telephone with Israeli prime minister Ehud Olmert, talking about the Iranian nuclear threat.

We met in a plain, medium-size conference room, dominated by a large oval table. Each of us was provided with mineral water, coffee, and a little plate of pastries. Condi and I were accompanied by our very able ambassador, Bill Burns, and an interpreter. Putin was joined by the foreign minister, Sergei Lavrov; the defense minister, Serdyukov; the chief of the general staff, General Baluyevskiy; and an interpreter. We had no sooner sat down than the room was flooded with press, shoving and pushing. Putin's press audience in place, he harangued us for nearly ten minutes, mainly about missile defense. He was sarcastic: "We may decide someday to put missile defense systems on the moon, but before we get to that, we may lose a chance for agreement because of you implementing your own plans." He warned us against "forcing forward your previous agreements with Eastern European countries." Condi and I weren't too happy about being used as stage props but kept our game faces and, in the brief moment we were allowed to respond before the Russians shooed out the press, tried to put a positive spin on the opportunities to work together. After the press left, the secretary of state and I looked at each other and just rolled our eyes. Putin's dacha, Putin's show.

When we got down to business, Putin continued to insist that our plans were aimed at Russia because Iran was not a near-term threat to either the United States or Europe. He shared with us a map featuring circles that showed the ranges of different Iranian missiles and the few countries they could reach. He said the circles, which appeared to be hand-drawn with a grammar school compass and colored pencils, represented the best estimates of Russian intelligence. I flippantly told him he needed a new intelligence service. He was not amused. As prearranged with Condi, I then laid out our new offerings, meant to persuade the

Russians that the Polish and Czech sites were no threat to them, and to get them to work with us. We offered a new proposal for joint cooperation in developing a missile defense architecture that would defend the United States, Europe, and Russia; accepted Putin's offer for radar information sharing, with a view to creating an integrated command and control of U.S. and Russian missile defenses; proposed transparency measures, including personnel exchanges that would allow the Russians to monitor our system and for us to participate in their system; and, as I said, suggested the possibility of tying our missile defense deployments in Europe to development of the Iranian missile threat, including joint monitoring of Iranian developments and a commitment to make our system operational only when warranted by the evolving threat. Putin seemed genuinely interested in these ideas and acknowledged that we had made some interesting proposals. Indeed, all the Russian officials except for General Baluyevskiy seemed convinced that the United States was sincerely interested in cooperating with Russia, and we agreed that experts would meet to flesh out our ideas.

During the meeting with Putin, I wrote a note to Condi that Baluyevskiy reminded me of "the good old days," and she wrote back, "He was once considered a forward-leaning moderate. Shows how much has changed." After several hours of meetings with our counterparts later that same day, I wrote Condi another note: "I don't have the patience for diplomacy. I'd forgotten how much I really don't like these guys." A little later Condi, Ambassador Burns and his wife, and I were hosted for dinner by Sergei Ivanov and his wife. After dinner I told Condi, "Well, I do like some of them."

The next morning I gave a speech at the General Staff Academy, another monument of Stalinist architecture, to several hundred Russian officers. From the moment I walked into the room, I knew this would be a tough event. The general in charge was an old bull out of Red Army central casting, and the pale, frowning faces in the audience radiated skepticism and resentment. I talked about reform efforts under way in both our militaries and the opportunities for cooperation in the future. These officers were not buying what I was selling: they were deeply suspicious of the United States, our military, and me, and they probably hated the reform efforts in their own military. During the question-and-answer period, a colonel asked me why the United States wanted to take over Siberia. After years of handling off-the-wall questions from members of Congress, I thought I was pretty quick on my feet, but that question really threw me. So I simply said that there was no truth to that idea. Bill Burns told me later that Madeleine Albright had given a speech a few weeks before in which she posed the question of how Russia could develop Siberia as it became depopulated and Russia's overall population continued to shrink. That the colonel and others had reached the conclusion they did based on her question was, to me, a measure of Russian paranoia.

Like Sisyphus trying to roll that rock uphill, we kept at it with the Russians on missile defense in 2008. The Russians felt that the written version of what Condi and I had offered at Putin's dacha "diluted" what we had said. The only change made in the written version was to note that the presence of Russian officers at our sites in Poland and the Czech Republic would, of course, require the consent of those governments. Nonetheless I told Ivanov at the Munich Security Conference in February that we had been thinking about how to achieve progress on missile defense and strategic arms control before President Bush left office. If an outline of agreements on these issues could be achieved, I said, Condi and I would be willing to move up the next "two plus two" meeting and come to Moscow again. The two presidents subsequently talked, and on March 12 Bush sent Putin a letter laying out opportunities for agreement and progress in the bilateral relationship before his term ended. Our ace in the hole was that Putin desperately wanted Bush to visit Sochi, future site of the Olympics, after the NATO summit in Bucharest in early April. Bush made no commitments, waiting to see how Putin would behave in Bucharest.

Condi and I converged on Moscow on March 17 and later that day met with President-elect Dimitri Medvedev and then separately with Putin. The atmosphere during this visit was even better than the previous October. The Russians were interested in moving forward with continuity as the Bush administration came to an end and Medvedev assumed the Russian presidency. Still, I told my staff beforehand that I thought the odds for progress on a Strategic Framework Agreement on this trip were a hundred to one against, and that the obstacles in the path of progress with Russia on NATO membership for Georgia and Ukraine as well as for Kosovo independence were too great to be overcome.

I was struck by how diminutive Medvedev was, about my height— five foot eight—but probably thirty pounds lighter. He was on top of his brief, knowledgeable and impressive, but I had no doubt Putin was calling the shots.

We met with Putin in the Kremlin, in a beautiful oval room with high, lime-green and white walls—and more gold leaf. Our session was scheduled for an hour but lasted two. He said he had carefully analyzed the president's letter, and there were many issues to discuss. During the meeting, Condi handed Putin a draft Strategic Framework Declaration addressing some twenty proposals for cooperation or agreement in four areas: promoting security (including strategic arms limits and missile defense); preventing the spread of weapons of mass destruction; combating global terrorism; and strengthening economic cooperation. We managed to clarify some of the proposals relating to missile defense that had become muddled since the October meeting, including Russian presence at the sites in Poland and the Czech Republic, and discussed the next steps for negotiating additional limits on strategic nuclear forces. With regard to the latter subject, I said we were prepared to consider a legally binding treaty but that it should be short and adaptable to changing circumstances. I noted that I had been involved in the first strategic arms treaty in 1972 and that the last thing we needed was an agreement the size of a telephone book. To which Putin responded, "You are really old." I laughed and nodded in agreement.

The next day we met with our counterparts, Foreign Minister Lavrov and Defense Minister Serdyukov. Lavrov did almost all the talking for the Russians, and all I can say is that it was a good thing Condi had to deal with him. My patience and my limited diplomatic skills would both have failed me. We rehashed missile defense issues, and our proposals for greater partnership, again and again. Lavrov cut to the chase when he observed, "We take it as reality that you will build the third site [in Poland and the Czech Republic; the first site was in California, the second in Alaska], but want to make sure it will not be turned and targeted against Russia." A few minutes later he candidly described what was eating at the Russians: "I would not call it a positive development that we cannot stop your third site even as we see it as destabilizing. Our position is pragmatic, not positive."

At a joint press conference after the meeting, both sides tried to put lipstick on the pig, calling the talks "fruitful" and positive. In truth, the only two areas in which real headway was made was the Framework Declaration, which the Russians desperately wanted signed by Bush and

Putin at Sochi after the NATO summit, and the follow-on Strategic Arms Agreement. Inviting Georgia and Ukraine to join NATO, Lavrov said simply, "would destroy bilateral relations between our two countries." Independence for Kosovo, he said, "would be a violation of international law." While the president would go to Sochi and the Framework Declaration would be signed, it was clear by now that the Bush administration would accomplish nothing further with Russia.

I was convinced the Russians would never embrace any kind of missile defense in Europe because they could see it only as a potential threat to themselves. What I hadn't counted on was the political opposition to the missile defense system in Poland and the Czech Republic. As early as January 2008, the new Polish center-right government led by Prime Minister Donald Tusk made clear they would not consider hosting the interceptors unless the United States agreed to an accompanying defense package of shorter-range missile defenses for Poland and made a greater commitment to come to Poland's aid than provided under the NATO charter. In June 2008, Polish defense minister Bogdan Klich told me that to bring the negotiations to closure, it would be "important for President Bush to make a political declaration and commitment of assistance to Poland similar to those the United States provided to Jordan and Pakistan." For their part, the Czechs were making demands about bidding on our contracts associated with site construction and also letting us know that U.S. companies and citizens working on the project would be subject to Czech taxes. Our presumptive partners for missile defense in Europe were stiff-arming us.

GEORGIA

As the Soviet Union was collapsing and Georgia (an ancient country in the Caucasus that had been annexed by Russia early in the nineteenth century) declared its independence, two pro-Russian Georgian provinces, South Ossetia and Abkhazia, declared *their* independence. Bloody conflict followed until 1994, when Russia was finally able to negotiate a cease-fire sustained by Russian peacekeeping troops in both provinces. A fragile peace lasted until January 2004, when an aggressive and impetuous Georgian nationalist, Mikheil Saakashvili, was elected president. In the summer of 2004, Saakashvili sent Interior Ministry troops into South Ossetia, on the pretext of putting down "banditry," to reestablish Georgian control. The Georgians were forced into a humiliating withdrawal, but their violation of the status quo infuriated the Russians. When Saakashvili sent troops into a third independence-minded province in the summer of 2006, it signaled that he was prepared to fight to regain the two pro-Russian separatist provinces. Russian hatred of Saakashvili was stoked further when, in 2007, he went to the border of Abkhazia and promised loyalists there they would be "home" within a year.

The Russians used Kosovo's declaration of independence (it had been a part of Yugoslavia and had long historical ties to Serbia) in February 2008, which the United States and Europeans supported and a pro-Serb Russia opposed, as a pretext to turn up the temperature on Georgia. The West's logic in supporting Kosovo's independence, said the Russians, ought to apply as well to Abkhazia and South Ossetia. Putin in April said Russia might possibly recognize the independence of the two provinces. On April 21, Saakashvili telephoned Putin to demand that Russia reverse course on recognition and cited statements by Western governments opposing it. Putin had used highly colloquial Russian in telling Saakashvili where he could put the Western statements. Soon thereafter Georgia mobilized its troops, and in response, Russia sent 400 paratroopers and a howitzer battery to staging areas near the cease-fire line. Acts of violence in both provinces increased during the summer. On August 7, Georgia launched a massive artillery barrage and incursion to retake the South Ossetian capital of Tskhinvali.

The next day Russian forces poured into South Ossetia, routed the Georgians, and drove deep into Georgian territory, a punitive attack aimed at the destruction of the Georgian military infrastructure. They attacked military facilities—especially those that had been certified by NATO—and destroyed coastal patrol boats, military equipment, communications, and a number of villages. The deputy chief of the Russian general staff said at the time that the Russian mission was to weaken Georgia's military, but plainly the Russians were also sending a warning to other governments in Central Asia (and Ukraine) about the risks of trying to integrate with NATO.

The Russians had baited a trap, and the impetuous Saakashvili walked right into it. The Russians, Putin in particular, wanted to reassert Russia's traditional sphere of influence, including in the Caucasus. I was asked by a reporter if I trusted Vladimir Putin "anymore"? I responded,

"'Anymore' is an interesting word. I have never believed that one should make national security policy on the basis of trust. I think you make national security policy based on interests and on realities." After meeting with Putin in 2001, President Bush had said he looked into Putin's eyes and "got a sense of his soul." I said to some of my colleagues privately that I'd looked into Putin's eyes and, just as I expected, had seen a stone-cold killer.

As the invasion unfolded, President Bush, Condi, Steve Hadley, Admiral Mullen, and I were all on the phone with our counterparts in both Russia and Georgia—urging the Russians to stop and withdraw to the cease-fire lines while urging the Georgians not to do anything else stupid or provocative. When I talked with Serdyukov on August 8, I told him we were alarmed by the escalation of hostilities and urged him "in the strongest terms to halt the advance of your forces and stop the missile and air attacks inside Georgia." I asked him point-blank if they intended to take all of Georgia. He said no. I was equally blunt with my Georgian counterpart. I told him, "Georgia must not get into a conflict with Russia you cannot win" and that Georgian forces needed to cease hostilities and withdraw to defensible positions. Above all, direct contact between Georgian and Russian forces had to be avoided. I assured him we were pressing the Russians not to introduce more forces into Georgia and to respect Georgia's territorial integrity. These calls continued over the next several days.

The Georgians requested the immediate return home from Iraq of 1,800 Georgian troops who had been sent there to help us. We had much earlier agreed that if Georgia wanted to bring these troops home, we would not object. At the same time, we were very concerned that the Russians might interfere with our airlift of these Georgian troops and subsequent humanitarian aid to Georgia. The last thing we wanted was a military confrontation with the Russians, or to have them target one of our transports. Accordingly, Admiral Mullen was in close touch with his Russian military counterpart, now General Nikolai Makarov, and our embassy people in Georgia were in contact with Russians on the ground to provide them with precise information on when each of our planes would enter Georgian airspace, and to state our expectation that they would be left alone. We gave assurances that we were not providing the Georgians with additional military capability to take on the Russians.

The airlift of Georgian troops began on August 10 and was completed the next day, and on August 13 I directed that the humanitarian assistance begin. There was no interference from the Russians.

French president Nicolas Sarkozy negotiated a cease-fire that was supposed to take effect on August 12, and Medvedev said on that date that the Russians were complying. It was not true. On August 17, Russia pledged to begin withdrawing troops the next day. At that point, Russian troops were forty miles west of Tbilisi, the Georgian capital, and occupied large areas of the country. The Russians did not withdraw until mid-October. Meanwhile, in September Russia recognized both Abkhazian and South Ossetian independence. They were joined only by Nicaragua and the Palestinian terrorist group Hamas. Rice would later chide Lavrov about this "triumph" of Russian diplomacy.

While there was broad agreement in our government and elsewhere that Saakashvili's aggressiveness and impetuosity had given the Russians an opportunity to punish Georgia, the violence and extent of Russian military (and cyber) operations were eye-openers for many. I said at a press conference on August 14 that "Russia's behavior over the past week has called into question the entire premise of [our strategic] dialogue and has profound implications for our security relationship going forward—both bilaterally and with NATO." I went on to say, "I think all the nations of Europe are looking at Russia through a different set of lenses." However, reflecting the challenges we faced with both Russia and Georgia, I observed dryly, "Both parties have been undisciplined with the truth in their dealings with us."

President Bush and all his senior advisers knew that if we took strong unilateral political and economic action against Russia, we ran the risk of the United States, rather than the Russians, becoming isolated over the invasion. A statement by the European Union criticizing the invasion by was predictably tepid. So as much as most of us wanted strong action against Russia, we suppressed our feelings and agreed to march in lockstep with our NATO allies. (It reminded me of my initial crisis in government when, during my first week on the job at CIA in August 1968, the Soviets invaded Czechoslovakia. As horrified as the Europeans said they were by the brutal invasion, for them, everything was back to business as usual with the Soviets within three or four months.)

The Bush administration was out of time, energy, and patience to try to get the relationship with Russia back on track. With less than five months left, nobody really cared. There was one ancillary, modest gain after the Russian invasion: six days later, the Poles signed a deal with us to allow ten missile defense interceptors to be based in their country.

Syria

Syria had been a problem for the United States for the last two decades of the Cold War. The regime, controlled by the Assad family, had fought several wars with Israel, invaded Jordan, allied with Iran, and supported a number of terrorist and militia groups causing trouble in the Middle East. In the spring of 2007, the Israelis presented us with compelling evidence that North Korea had secretly built a nuclear reactor in Syria. The administration was divided about how to respond, our options constrained by the fact that the Israelis had informed us of this stunning development and therefore were in a position to significantly influence—if not dictate—what could be publicly divulged and when. The case for the existence of the reactor and the North Korean role in building it depended heavily on Israeli intelligence. Our debates during the ensuing months as to whether to take military action, and about how closely to work with the Israelis, were important regarding Syria, but they also prefigured in many respects the arguments regarding the Iranian nuclear program in 2008 and later.

Contacts between North Korean nuclear organizations and high-level Syrians were believed to have begun as early as 1997. In 2005, we found a large building under construction in eastern Syria, but its purpose became clear only with photographs of the inside of the building provided by the Israelis in 2007. The design was very similar to that of a North Korean reactor at Yongbyon, and our analysts concluded that the reactor would be capable of producing plutonium for nuclear weapons.

Syria for years had been a high-priority intelligence target for the United States, as was anything having to do with possible development of weapons of mass destruction, nuclear weapons in particular. Early detection of a large nuclear reactor under construction in a place like Syria is supposedly the kind of intelligence collection that the United States does superbly well. Yet by the time the Israelis informed us about the site, the reactor construction was already well advanced. This was a significant failure on the part of the U.S. intelligence agencies, and I asked the president, "How can we have any confidence at all in the estimates of the scope of the North Korean, Iranian, or other possible programs" given this failure? Surprisingly, neither the president nor Congress made much of it. Given the stakes, they should have.

As the Bush national security team discussed what to do about the reactor, I asked Lieutenant General Martin Dempsey, acting commander at Central Command, to provide us with a number of military options and different target lists associated with each. I sent Dempsey's report to National Security Adviser Steve Hadley on May 15 for the president to see. The report also focused on how we might disrupt Syrian support for Hizballah in Lebanon and, specifically, how we might prevent Hizballah from toppling the weak Lebanese government in retaliation for a military strike on Syria. Successfully restraining Hizballah would require using American ground forces, and that the president would not do. I told Hadley there were a number of other considerations to be taken into account as well, including the impact in the broader Middle East of a military strike on Syria—after all, we were already in two wars in or near the region. We also had to consider whether the kings of Saudi Arabia and Jordan would publicly support a strike. And what about the risk to the 7,000 Americans in Syria?

In the coming weeks, Cheney, Rice, Hadley, and I frequently discussed our options in Syria. Cheney thought we should attack the site, the sooner the better. He believed not only that we had to prevent Syria from acquiring nuclear weapons, but also that a military strike would send a powerful warning to the Iranians to abandon their nuclear ambitions. We could also, he said, hit Hizballah weapons storage sites in Syria at the same time to weaken them—always a key priority of the Israelis. By attacking, we might even be able to rattle Assad sufficiently so as to end his close relationship with Iran, thus further isolating the Iranians. Cheney often raised the question of what our actions, or inaction, would have on our relationship with the Israelis and their own decisions about what to do. As always, Dick laid out his views logically and analytically. He, Rice, Hadley, and I—often joined by Mike Mullen, Director of National Intelligence Mike McConnell, and CIA director Mike Hayden—would sit around the conference table in Hadley's White House office and, while eating lunch or munching on chips and salsa, go over the choices facing the president. Cheney knew that, among the four of us, he alone thought a strike should be the first and only option. But perhaps he could persuade the president.

Our first long meeting as a group with the president was on the evening of June 17. Cheney, Rice, Hadley, and I were joined by Mullen, White House chief of staff Josh Bolten, and several NSC staff members. My views then, and for the next four years, were shaped by several overriding considerations: we already had two ongoing wars in Muslim countries, our military was overstretched, we were already considered by most countries as too quick to use military force, and the last thing America needed was to attack another Arab country. I also thought we had both time and options other than an immediate military strike. Using notes, I spoke bluntly:

- Without specific proof of a state taking hostile action against Americans (Libya—1986; Panama—1989; Afghanistan—2001), I am aware of no precedent for an American surprise attack against a sovereign state. We don't do "Pearl Harbors." Remember, President Reagan condemned the Israeli attack on Iraq's Osirak reactor in 1981.
- U.S. credibility on weapons of mass destruction is deeply suspect at home and abroad as a result of the Iraq legacy.
- Israeli credibility is equally suspect, if not more so, in the Middle East, Europe, and maybe significant elements of the U.S. public. An act of war based principally on information provided by a third party is risky in the extreme. U.S. and Israeli interests are not always the same.
- Any Israeli action will be seen as provocative, aimed at restoring their credibility and deterrent after their indecisive war with Hizballah [in 2006] and at shoring up a weak Israeli government. Israeli action could start a new war with Syria.
- Any overt U.S. preemptive attack will cause a firestorm in the Middle East, Europe, and the U.S. Efforts to prove our case against Syria and North Korea, based on current available intelligence, will be unsuccessful or regarded with deep skepticism. U.S. military action will be seen as another rash act by a trigger-happy administration and could jeopardize our efforts in Iraq, in Afghanistan, and even with respect to missile defense in Europe. It would be seen as an effort to offset or distract from failures in Iraq.

I told the group that I agreed the reactor should not be allowed to become active, but that we shouldn't use it as a pretext to try to solve all our problems with Syria and placate Israel by hitting other targets, as

Cheney had suggested. We should focus just on the reactor. I said that my preferred approach was to begin with diplomacy and reserve a military strike as the last resort. We should expose what the Syrians and North Koreans had done and focus on their violations of UN Security Council resolutions, the nonproliferation treaty, and more. At the United Nations, we should demand an immediate freeze on activity at the site and prompt inspection by representatives of the five permanent members of the Security Council (United States, United Kingdom, France, Russia, and China). We should be specific in saying that the United States would not allow the reactor to become operational but were turning to the Security Council and the International Atomic Energy Commission to negotiate its destruction or permanent immobilization. I said this approach would require Syrian president Bashar Hafez al-Assad either to accede or to prove that the facility was not what we said it was. If he did the latter, we would have used diplomacy to defuse a crisis; if, as we believed, he could not, then we could hold other governments' feet to the fire—to put up or shut up on nonproliferation. As I would later tell the president, the option to delay operational status of the reactor by destroying the pump house (without a water supply, the reactor could not become operational) or by destroying the reactor itself would remain available to us throughout the diplomatic process. I concluded my remarks by saying, "I suspect no one in the world doubts this administration's willingness to use force—but better to use it as a last resort than as a first step." The next day, after a videoconference with Petraeus and our ambassador to Iraq, Ryan Crocker, the president pulled me aside and thanked me for my comments the evening before. He knew that Hadley, Rice, and I had discussed the "Tojo option"—referring to the Japanese prime minister who ordered the surprise attack on Pearl Harbor—earlier that morning and simply said, "I'm not going to do that."

In the latter part of June, the debate intensified as the Israelis pressed us to act or to help them do so. The president was very pro-Israel—as was Cheney—and greatly admired Prime Minister Ehud Olmert, and I was genuinely worried that Bush might just decide to let the Israelis take care of the reactor, forgoing any benefit of a sequenced approach and still leaving the United States with all the consequences of an attack. The administration's senior leaders again staked out our positions in a meeting with the president on June 20. Cheney said we should hit the reactor immediately. Rice and I argued for a sequenced approach, beginning with diplomacy, but if that failed, we should take military action. General Pace supported that approach, saying it "gives you two chances to win." Hadley observed that if we gave Assad too much time, he would organize the Arab world against us. I warned the president that Olmert was trying to force his hand.

In early July, I communicated my views privately to the president. I told him that I had recently read various statements on the use of force by former defense secretaries Cap Weinberger and Don Rumsfeld, as well as by Colin Powell and Tony Blair, and that the only thing they all agreed on was that the use of force should be a last resort after all other measures have failed. I warned that a preemptive U.S. strike to destroy the reactor would lead to a "huge negative reaction" at home and abroad, risking a fatal weakening of remaining support for our efforts in Iraq, and that our coalition support there could evaporate. At the same time, if we let the Israelis take care of the problem, we would be regarded as complicit or a coconspirator and that this option also ran the risk of igniting a wider war in the Middle East and an unpredictable reaction in Iraq. I urged Bush to "tell Prime Minister Olmert that we will not allow the reactor to become operational but Israel must allow us to handle this in our own way. If they do not, they are on their own. We will not help them." Further, I told the president he should tell Olmert very directly that if Israel went forward on its own militarily, he would be putting Israel's entire relationship with the United States at risk.

The president talked to Olmert on July 13, and while he declined to put the matter to him in the way I had urged, he did push the prime minister hard "to let us take care of this." Olmert responded that the reactor represented an existential threat to Israel that it could not trust diplomacy to fix, even if the effort was led by the United States. In the course of the conversation, the president pledged not to expose knowledge of the reactor publicly without an Israeli okay.

All the president's national security team met the next morning, and the focus was on the Israelis. I was furious. I said that Olmert was asking for our help on the reactor but giving us only one option: to destroy it. If we didn't do exactly what he wanted, Israel would act and we could do nothing about it. The United States was being held hostage to Israeli decision making. If there was a secret attack, all the focus would be on what the Israelis did, not what Syria and North Korea had done. I warned that if a wider war occurred after the attack, the United States would be blamed for not restraining the Israelis. "Our proposal [the first step being diplomatic/political] will emerge, making it look like the U.S. government subordinated its strategic interest to that of a weak Israeli government that already had screwed up one conflict in the region [against Hizballah in 2006] and that we were unwilling to confront or cross the Israelis."

I am, and always have been, strongly pro-Israel. As a moral and historic imperative, I believe in a secure, viable Jewish state with the right to defend itself. But our interests are not always identical, as I said earlier, and I'm not prepared to risk vital American strategic interests to accommodate the views of hard-line Israeli politicians. The president said that he was impressed with Olmert's "steadfastness" and that he was unwilling to preempt the prime minister through a diplomatic initiative or even to put much pressure on him. Rice called me late that afternoon to express her deep unease over the situation. I said I might talk to the president again, and she said, "Use my name and count me in."

Hadley, Rice, Vice Chairman of the Joint Chiefs General Cartwright, McConnell, Hayden, Bolten, and I met on Monday, the sixteenth. Bolten asked if the president was in the "right place" on the reactor issue and Israel. I was emphatic in saying no. I said he was putting U.S. strategic interests in Iraq, in the Middle East, and with our other allies in the hands of the Israelis and that he must insist to Olmert that he let the U.S. handle the Syrian problem. Olmert should be told that vital American interests were at stake, as I had argued earlier, and if necessary, the problem would be dealt with, one way or another, before Bush left office. I repeated what I had said about Olmert boxing us in. Notwithstanding, it was clear that the vice president, Elliott Abrams of the NSC staff, my own colleague Eric Edelman, Condi's counselor Eliot Cohen, and others were all for letting Israel do whatever it wanted. I'm inclined to think that the president himself was sympathetic to that view, perhaps mainly because he was sympathetic to Olmert's view of the reactor as an existential threat to Israel, though I never heard him say so. By not confronting Olmert, Bush effectively came down on Cheney's side. By not giving the Israelis a red light, he gave them a green one.

On September 6, the Israelis attacked the reactor and destroyed it. They insisted on keeping the existence of the reactor secret, believing—correctly, as it turned out—that the lack of public exposure of the reactor and embarrassment over its destruction might persuade Assad not to retaliate militarily. But Condi and I were frustrated that Syria and North Korea had undertaken a bold and risky venture in violation of multiple Security Council resolutions and international treaties to create a covert nuclear capability in Syria, probably including other sites and labs, and had paid no political price for it. Nor could we use their gambit to our advantage in detaching Syria from Iran or in seeking harsher sanctions on Iran.

Within a week, the Syrians began a massive effort to destroy the ruined reactor building and to remove all incriminating nuclear-related equipment and structures. They worked at night or under the cover of tarpaulins to mask what they were doing. As the Israelis insisted, we kept silent as we watched the Syrians work. Finally, in April 2008, when the Israelis decided the risk of Syrian military retaliation had greatly diminished, we went public with the photographs and intelligence information on the Syrian reactor. By then, any real opportunity to leverage what the Syrians and North Koreans had done for broader political and non-proliferation purposes had largely been lost. The absence of any Syrian reaction to the Israeli attack—after the absence of Iraqi reaction to the bombing of their Osirak reactor by Israel in 1981—reinforced the views of those in Israel who were confident that any attack on Iranian nuclear sites would provoke, at most, only a very limited response.

On our side, a very sensitive and difficult security challenge had been debated openly with no pulled punches. The president heard directly from his senior advisers on a number of occasions and had made a tough decision based on what he heard and on his own instincts. And there had been no leaks. Although I was unhappy with the path we had taken, I told Hadley the episode had been a model of national security decision making. In the end, a big problem was solved and none of my fears were realized. It is hard to criticize success. But we had condoned reaching for a gun before diplomacy could be brought to bear, and we had condoned another preventive act of war. This made me all the more nervous about an even bigger looming national security problem.

IRAN

The Islamic Republic of Iran has bedeviled every American president since the overthrow of the shah in February 1979. Events in Iran contributed to Jimmy Carter losing his reelection bid in 1980 and nearly got Ronald Reagan impeached in 1987. Every president since Carter has tried in one way or another to reach out to the leadership in Tehran to improve relations, and every one of them has failed to elicit any meaningful response.

I was a participant in the first of those efforts. In October 1979, Carter's national security adviser, Zbigniew Brzezinski, represented the United States in Algiers at the twenty-fifth anniversary of the Algerian revolution. I accompanied him as his special assistant. He received word that the Iranian delegation—the prime minister, defense minister, and foreign minister—wanted to meet with him. Brzezinski received approval from Washington and met in a hotel suite with the Iranians. I was the notetaker. He offered recognition of the revolutionary regime, offered to work with them, and even offered to sell them weapons we had contracted to sell to the shah; we had a common enemy to the north of Iran, the Soviet Union. The Iranians brushed all that aside and demanded that the United States return the shah, who was then receiving medical treatment here, to Tehran. Both sides went back and forth with the same talking points until Brzezinski stood up and told the Iranians that to return the shah to them would be "incompatible with our national honor." That ended the meeting. Three days later our embassy in Tehran was overrun and more than fifty Americans taken hostage. Within a few weeks, the three Iranian officials with whom we had met had been purged from their jobs.

On April 24, 1980, the United States attempted a daring military operation to rescue those hostages. As executive assistant to the head of CIA, Admiral Stansfield Turner, I was aware of the planning and was with him in the White House the night of the mission. The operation ended in a fiery disaster in the desert sands of eastern Iran, with eight Americans killed when a helicopter collided with a C-130 transport plane on the ground. It was a humiliating failure. The only good to come out of it was that this tragedy soon led to the creation of the Joint Special Operations Command and the superb military capabilities—both in people and in equipment—that would kill Osama bin Laden thirty-one years later.

Nineteen-eighty also saw the beginning of an eight-year war between Iraq and Iran, which began in September with an attack by the Iraqis. The U.S. approach during the Reagan administration was ruthlessly realistic—we did not want either side to win an outright victory; at one time or another we provided modest covert support to both sides. This effort went off the rails with the clandestine sale of antitank missiles to the Iranians, with the profits secretly being funneled to help the anti-Communist Contra movement in Nicaragua. This was the essence of the Iran-Contra scandal, which broke publicly in November 1986, nearly wrecked the Reagan administration, and derailed my nomination to be director of central intelligence early in 1987. I had learned to be very cautious in dealing with Iran.

During the last two years of the Reagan administration, the United States would actually confront the Iranians militarily in the Persian Gulf, when we provided naval protection to Kuwaiti oil tankers. Several of our ships struck Iranian mines, we responded with retaliatory strikes, and in one tragic incident, a U.S. Navy ship accidentally shot down an Iranian passenger airplane.

From the early 1980s, the fact that Iran has been the principal foreign supporter of the terrorist organization Hizballah, providing money, intelligence, weapons, training, and operational guidance to its fighters— including the suicide bombers who destroyed the U.S. embassy and Marine barracks in Beirut during the early 1980s—has further poisoned the air between our two countries. Until al Qaeda attacked the United States on September 11, 2001, Hizballah had killed more Americans than had any terrorist group in history.

In 2004, Brzezinski and I were asked to cochair a task force on U.S. policy toward Iran under the auspices of the Council on Foreign Relations. One reason I had moved to the Pacific Northwest after retiring as CIA director was to avoid getting roped into projects like this. But because of my respect for, and friendship with, Brzezinski and council president Richard Haass, I agreed.

The task force issued its report in July 2004, acknowledging the failure of repeated efforts over the preceding twenty-five years to engage with Tehran but expressing the view that the U.S. military intervention in both Afghanistan and Iraq, on Iran's eastern and western borders, respectively, had changed the "geopolitical landscape" and might offer new incentives for a mutually beneficial dialogue. The report recommended selective diplomatic engagement as a means to address issues such as Iran's nuclear program. The report also proposed withdrawing U.S. objections to an Iranian civil nuclear program in exchange for stringent safeguards; suggested using economic relationships as positive leverage in dealing with Iran; and recommended U.S. advocacy of democracy in Iran "without relying on the rhetoric of regime change." The recommendations acknowledged the likelihood of Iranian obstinacy preventing progress.

With "reform" president Hojjatoleslam Mohammed Katami in office—someone who in 1998 had called for a "dialogue with the American people"—and "reformers" winning a landslide victory in the Iranian general election in 2000, the recommendations of the report did not seem particularly radical, despite Iran's continued support for anti-Israeli militants. However, given events over the ensuing two years, including the election of a hard-line president in Iran and Iranian support for Shia extremists killing our troops in Iraq, by the time I came back to government in late 2006, I no longer supported most of the recommendations in the report. It so quickly slid into oblivion that after I was nominated to be secretary, someone asked Steve Hadley if the administration had been aware of the positions I had taken in the report vis-à-vis Iran. I was told Steve was quite taken aback and asked, "What report?"

On December 23, 2006, five days after I became secretary of defense, the UN Security Council voted to impose limited sanctions on Iran, thus internationalizing some of the economic sanctions the United States had imposed on Tehran during the Clinton administration and first years of the Bush administration. In his January 10, 2007, speech announcing the strategy change and the surge in Iraq, Bush also said that henceforth U.S. troops would target Iranian agents inside Iraq who were helping the insurgency; more significantly, he also announced that he was sending a second aircraft carrier to the Persian Gulf and deploying Patriot missile defense batteries to the region as well. During a White House meeting on January 21, Rice passed me a note saying, "The Iranians are getting *very* nervous. Now is the time to keep the heat up."

The trouble was that the Iranians were not the only ones getting nervous. A number of members of Congress and commentators worried publicly whether the Bush administration was getting ready to launch another war, a worry that only grew every time we announced some new nefarious act by the Iranians. I tried to strike the right balance in a press conference on February 2, saying that the second carrier was intended to increase pressure on the Iranians in response to their training and providing weapons to Shia extremists fighting the United States in Iraq (we believed the Iranians either killed or trained the killers—murderers,

actually—of five American soldiers in Karbala on January 20), as well as
to serve as a response to their continued nuclear activities. I underscored
that "we are not planning for a war with Iran." On February 15, I said,
"For the umpteenth time, we are not looking for an excuse to go to war
with Iran." Cheney's affirmation a few days later that "all options are still
on the table"—the administration's position—hardly helped dampen
the speculation.

Ayatollah Khamanei, Iran's "supreme" leader, had weighed in publicly on February 8, warning that Iran would retaliate against our interests if attacked by the United States. At the same time, the commander of
the Iranian Revolutionary Guards navy announced the test-firing of an
antiship missile "capable of sinking a large warship." Trying to downplay
its significance, I told the press at a NATO defense ministers meeting in
Seville that we had watched the test, and "other than that, I think it's just
another day in the Persian Gulf."

About the same time, the administration went public with evidence
that the Iranians were supplying sophisticated IED bomb-making materials to Iraqis trying to kill our troops. We couldn't prove that the most
senior Iranian leaders knew about this, but I found it inconceivable that
they did not; I was eager for us to be even more aggressive in picking up
their agents—or killing them—in Iraq. Tensions with Iran rose further
in March 2008, when the Iranian Revolutionary Guards navy seized fifteen British sailors and marines accused of intruding into Iranian territorial waters. (I immediately directed that no U.S. sailors or Marines were
to patrol or board other boats in the Gulf without cover from helicopter
gunships or without a U.S. warship within firing range. I wasn't about to
risk any of our sailors or Marines falling into Iranian hands.) Four days
later the United States began a naval exercise in the Gulf, including two
aircraft carriers and a dozen other warships—it was the first time two
carriers had held a joint exercise in the Gulf since 2003.

These actions set off another round of speculation that President
Bush was laying the groundwork for attacking Iran. *The Economist* spec-
ulated that Bush "might not be prepared to leave office with the Iranian
question unresolved." In an editorial, the magazine explained why Bush
might act:

One is Iran's apparent determination to build nuclear weapons, and a
fear that it is nearing the point where its nuclear programme will be

impossible to stop. The second is the advent of Mahmoud Ahmadine-jad, a populist president who denies the Holocaust and calls openly for Israel's destruction: his apocalyptic speeches have convinced many people in Israel and America that the world is facing a new Hitler with genocidal intent. The third is a recent tendency inside the Bush admin-istration to blame Iran for many of America's troubles not just in Iraq but throughout the Middle East. . . . Given his [Bush's] excessive will-ingness to blame Iran for blocking America's noble aims in the Middle East, he may come to see a pre-emptive strike on its nuclear programme as a fitting way to redeem his presidency.

Frankly, I shared some of *The Economist*'s concerns. One thread running through my entire time as secretary was my determination to avoid any new wars while we were still engaged in Iraq and Afghani-stan. Remember the old saw "When you find yourself in a hole, the first thing to do is stop digging"? Between Iraq and Afghanistan, I thought the United States was in a pretty deep hole. Were we faced with a seri-ous military threat to American vital interests, I would be the first to insist upon an overwhelming military response. In the absence of such a threat, I saw no need to go looking for another war. I kept a 1942 quote from Winston Churchill in my desk drawer to remind me every day of certain realities: "Never, never believe any war will be smooth and easy, or that anyone who embarks on the strange voyage can measure the tides and hurricane he will encounter. The statesman who yields to war fever must realize that, once the signal is given, he is no longer the master of policy but the slave of unforeseeable and uncontrollable events."

I therefore opposed military action as the first or preferred option to deal with the Syrian nuclear reactor, to deal with Iran's nuclear pro-gram, and later, to intervene in Libya. I was convinced Americans were tired of war, and I knew firsthand how overstretched and stressed our troops were. There were those inside the Bush administration, led by Cheney, who talked openly about trying to resolve problems—like ours with Iran—with military force before the end of the administration. I'd been told that some at State believed that if the Israelis struck Iran mili-tarily, always a possibility, there likely would be a regional conflict, so we should "do it" ourselves. Bush fortunately opposed such actions. But I wasn't entirely sure where he stood at the time, and so I consistently opposed anything that might draw us into a new conflict.

During my time in the Bush administration, I worried about the influence of the Israelis and the Saudis in the White House, particularly Prime Minister Olmert and King Abdullah, and their shared desire to have problems like Iran "taken care of" while Bush was still president. Cheney had a very close relationship with both men, so they had a direct pipeline into the White House. As I said, the president also had very high regard for Olmert as well as a good personal relationship with the king. Between April and August 2007, I would have extremely frank discussions with both those foreign leaders.

On April 18, 2007, I arrived in Israel. I met with both the defense minister and the foreign minister in Tel Aviv and the next day drove to Jerusalem to meet with Olmert. The drive has always fascinated me, in no small part because as you wind through the hills, you can see the wreckage of military vehicles that have been preserved since the 1948 war—a reminder of the security threat Israel has faced for its entire modern existence. The drive is also a reminder of how small Israel is. Olmert and I met privately (with one associate each) in his rather spartan office for most of our time together. It was our first encounter, and he was very gracious. With respect to Iran, we agreed on the importance of continuing to share intelligence on the nuclear program and reviewed the impact of sanctions and other measures to delay the program. Olmert left no doubt that Israel saw a nuclear-armed Iran as an existential threat—as was Syria's reactor—and would not allow the program to succeed. He agreed that there was still time for sanctions and other pressures on Iran to work, but he insisted that all options had to remain on the table. I agreed with that, but there was no discussion of military planning or options.

We talked at length about Israel's security, and I pledged that the United States would ensure that Israel maintained its qualitative military edge (QME) over any potential regional adversaries by providing them with some of our most sophisticated military equipment, including tactical aircraft, weapons, and missile defenses. We agreed to set up a mechanism to address Israel's QME concerns. I asked Olmert not to oppose the sale of military equipment, including weapons, to Saudi Arabia. In arguments that I would use for the next four-plus years, I urged him to think more strategically about the region; that Saudi Arabia was focused on the threat from Iran, not on acquiring capabilities to threaten Israel. When I left Jerusalem, I well knew that there were different clocks ticking on the Iranian nuclear program. The challenge was how to slow down both the Iranian nuclear and the Israeli military clocks, while speeding up the sanctions/pressure clock.

My opportunity for candor with King Abdullah came three months later. In a rare, if not unprecedented, joint trip of the secretary of state and secretary of defense, Condi and I met up in Sharm el-Sheikh, Egypt, on July 31 to meet with President Hosni Mubarak and other Egyptian officials, and then meet with our counterparts from the Gulf Cooperation Council (a political and economic union consisting of Saudi Arabia, Bahrain, Kuwait, Oman, Qatar and the UAE), as well as representatives from Egypt and Jordan. Our joint participation was intended to send several messages—above all, the importance of all the governments involved to work together to support the Iraqi government and to oppose Iranian activities in the region. We knew a number of the attending governments were deeply worried about the United States withdrawing from Iraq too soon, and we could provide reassurance on that score. We also wanted our joint appearance to hammer home the message that the U.S. Departments of State and Defense were working with the same agenda. The stage was set for the trip with the announcement in Washington the day before the meeting that the Bush administration would propose ten-year military assistance packages of $20 billion for Saudi Arabia, $13 billion for Egypt, and $30 billion for Israel. One unintended consequence of the highly unusual joint travel of the secretaries of state and defense was that nearly everyone in the region thought we were coming to tell them we were going to attack Iran. All the governments but one—which will become clear momentarily—were relieved when we made clear that that wasn't the case.

After the meetings in Sharm el-Sheikh, Condi and I flew together on my plane to Jeddah, Saudi Arabia, to meet with the king. Our meeting with the king at his palace was preceded by a sumptuous banquet. The room where we ate was the equivalent size of five or six basketball courts, with an Olympic-size pool in the middle. The buffet must have had fifty or more dishes. But the most striking aspect of the room was a floor-to-ceiling aquarium, about 50 to 75 feet across and 30 feet high, that formed the wall behind where we dined. Among the many kinds of fish in the tank were a number of big sharks. When I asked one of the Saudis how they prevented the sharks from eating the other fish, he replied that it was important to feed the sharks on a careful schedule.

The king's usual practice was to begin a meeting with a large delegation on both sides in attendance, and then for the guest(s) to ask to meet privately. Condi and I did so and had a long meeting with the king, with only an interpreter present. It was one of the most memorable meetings during my tenure as secretary. It was also the only encounter with a foreign leader in which I lost my cool. Abdullah, a heavyset man in his eighties with a history of health problems, was very sharp and did not mince words as he smoked one cigarette after another. He wanted a full-scale military attack on Iranian military targets, not just the nuclear sites. He warned that if we did not attack, the Saudis "must go our own way to protect our interests." As far as I was concerned, he was asking the United States to send its sons and daughters into a war with Iran in order to protect the Saudi position in the Gulf and the region, as if we were mercenaries. He was asking us to shed American blood, but at no time did he suggest that any Saudi blood might be spilled. He went on and on about how the United States was seen as weak by governments in the region. The longer he talked, the angrier I got, and I responded quite undiplomatically. I told him that absent an Iranian military attack on U.S. forces or our allies, if the president launched another preventive war in the Middle East, he would likely be impeached; that we had our hands full in Iraq; and that the president would use military force only to protect vital American interests. I also told him that what he considered America's greatest weakness—showing restraint—was actually great strength because we could crush any adversary. I told him that neither he nor anyone else should ever underestimate the strength and power of the United States: those who had—Imperial Germany, Nazi Germany, Imperial Japan, and the Soviet Union—were all now in the ashcan of history. I was pretty wound up. And then we were done.

Nearly four years later, in my last meeting as secretary with the king, he referred—smiling—to that discussion in Jeddah as the night I "turned the table over." He told me that he had been seeking clarity from the United States on what we were likely to do about Iran and had been unable to get it—until that night. He said my candor demonstrated to him that he could trust what I said.

Our efforts through the summer and fall to gain approval of more international sanctions—and pressure—on Iran and to persuade China and Russia, among others, to curtail their dealings with Iran were dealt a self-inflicted, grievous blow on December 3, 2007. U.S. intelligence agencies on that date issued a national intelligence estimate, *Iran: Nuclear Intentions and Capabilities.* The first sentence of the key judgments said it all: "We judge with high confidence that in fall, 2003, Tehran halted its nuclear weapons program." It went on to say that Iran was keeping open the option to develop nuclear weapons and that, while it had not restarted the nuclear weapons program as of mid-2007, "we do not know whether it currently intends to develop nuclear weapons." Because I believed the estimate would be leaked and quoted out of context, I recommended, and the president approved, that we issue an unclassified version of the key judgments. In my entire career in intelligence, I believe no single estimate ever did more harm to U.S. security interests and diplomatic efforts. Because in virtually all other countries of the world intelligence services work for the government in power and are expected to toe the official line, the independence of our intelligence community in preparing assessments is hardly understood at all. Accordingly, most governments wondered what in hell the Bush administration was up to in releasing an intelligence report that was directly at odds with the positions it had been taking diplomatically. My French counterpart, Defense Minister Hervé Morin, characterized the situation best when he told me that the intelligence estimate was "like a hair in the soup."

Then on January 6, 2008, a group of five small armed Iranian speedboats approached three U.S. warships in the Gulf at a high rate of speed. The rules of engagement for our Navy ships in the Gulf were clear: they were not to take actions that might be seen as provocative by the Iranians, but they were to do whatever was necessary to protect their ships. If the Iranians were to approach within a range considered threatening, the Navy was free to fire. The captain of one of our ships was within seconds of giving the order to fire when the boats turned away. After some back-and-forth with the White House, we released a video of the entire incident two days afterward. That same day I was on the phone with the president talking about a number of issues when he asked me what I would recommend if an Iranian fast boat, loaded with explosives, sank a U.S. warship. I gave him an initial response—still highly classified because it remains an active option—and we agreed we'd discuss it further.

Just when I would begin to wonder what else could go wrong, something always did. A week or so later I met with the president to review senior military personnel issues and appointments through the end of the administration. It was clear that something was bugging Bush, and that was when he asked me, "What is it with these admirals?" As mentioned earlier, I knew he was unhappy with Admiral Mike McConnell, the director of national intelligence, for an interview he had given *The New Yorker* in which he characterized waterboarding as torture—always a sensitive subject with Bush. Then the president expressed concern as to whether the chairman of the Joint Chiefs, Admiral Mullen, and the Central Command commander, Admiral Fallon, would continue to support what he was trying to accomplish in Iraq after a new president was elected. If not, should he replace them while he still could? Bush was clearly miffed at some of the things Fallon had been saying about how the United States must not go to war with Iran and at what Mullen had been saying about Iraq preventing us from providing adequate resources to the war in Afghanistan. The next day the president took me by surprise when he told me he had asked Petraeus if he would like to take Central Command. Dave had said no, that he wanted to go to Europe and also didn't want to push someone out prematurely. Soon afterward I got a call from Hadley, again about the "Navy guys." I asked Steve if someone on the NSC staff was "gunning" for Fallon. He replied, "The president and vice president are very concerned." I asked if it was because of his purported remarks on Iran. Steve said, "Yes, mainly."

A few weeks later Fallon called late in the afternoon to warn me that *Esquire* was going to publish an article about him in the next few days that likely would cause some heartburn. The press characterization of the article—usually more important in Washington than any article itself— was essentially that only Fox Fallon was keeping Bush from attacking Iran. It indeed caused heartburn and then some—mainly because it was untrue. It was clear, though, that the president had lost confidence in Fallon, the cumulative effect of a number of press statements that together seemed to portray a commander seriously at odds with his commander in chief on both Iraq and Iran.

Three days later, on March 6, Mullen and I met with the president, who asked, "Do we have a MacArthur problem? Is he challenging the commander in chief?" To me, he said, "I know what you'd do if he challenged you." I told Bush that he did not have a "MacArthur problem," that Fallon wanted to come in and apologize to him. The president responded, "No, I don't want to humiliate the guy, but he kind of boxed me in." When Mullen said that Fallon should volunteer to resign, Bush said, "But no signals, no coaching. If he acts, it needs to be without any pushing or hinting, solely on his own. He's given a lot of distinguished service to the country." He concluded, "Let's let it ride and continue to think about it." The president and I had another exchange on Fallon the next day. He said he had decided not to do anything and to wait and see if Fallon did "the right thing." I replied, "At some point I may need to act. I can't have a combatant commander who does not have the trust and confidence of the president." Bush said, "I didn't say I'd lost trust and confidence in him," and I said, "Right. I would say he's lost mine." We agreed not to take any action for the time being.

In truth, Fallon's actions as a commander had been wholly consistent with administration policy, but his interactions with the press left a different, and unacceptable, impression. I received a very gracious, handwritten letter of apology from Fox on March 7 that also made clear that he hoped to retain his command. However, Admiral Fallon, probably with a nudge from Mullen, on March 11 sent the chairman and me an e-mail requesting approval to step aside as Centcom commander. "The current embarrassing situation, public perception of differences between my views and administration policy, and the distraction this causes from the mission, make this the right thing to do," he wrote. Fallon had been in the job five days less than a year. Later in the day at a press conference, I praised his forty-plus years of service to the nation and concluded, perhaps stretching the truth a bit, that "Admiral Fallon reached this difficult decision entirely on his own. I believe it was the right thing to do even though I do not believe there are, in fact, significant differences between his views and administration policy." Fallon, with great class, had done the right thing.

Once again partisan leaders in Congress lived down to my expectations, using Fallon's resignation to attack the administration. Harry Reid called the resignation "yet another example that independence and the frank, open airing of experts' views are not welcomed in this administration." Nancy Pelosi said Fallon's resignation was "a loss for the country, and if it was engineered by the administration over policy differences, that loss is compounded."

Presidents and Congress expect senior military leaders to provide their personal and professional military opinions candidly and honestly. There is no requirement for them to do so through the news media.

Admiral William Fallon would not be the last senior officer on my watch to lose his job through a self-inflicted wound with the press.

We needed a new Centcom commander, and Mullen and I quickly agreed it should be David Petraeus. The problem with making unanticipated changes in senior military leadership is that there is always a daisy-chain effect, affecting other positions; for instance, who should replace Petraeus in Iraq? I was obsessed with not losing any momentum there, and that meant the new commander had to be someone with current experience and knowledge not only of the campaign plan but also of the Iraqi players. Ray Odierno, just back from his assignment as corps commander in Iraq in charge of day-to-day operations and already nominated to become vice chief of staff of the Army, seemed the best choice. After discussing the situation with the president, I announced on April 23 that I would recommend nominating Petraeus to take Centcom and Ray to return to Baghdad. It was a huge sacrifice on Odierno's part—and his family's—to have to return to Iraq only six months after leaving, but he did not hesitate. Because we wanted Petraeus in Iraq for as long as possible, we delayed the change of command until early fall. Lieutenant General Marty Dempsey was doing an excellent job as acting commander at Centcom, and we had confidence he could carry that burden of command alone in the interval.

For the next two months, command changes notwithstanding, Iran was front and center on my agenda. On April 8, 2008, I met with the chairman, Dempsey, and the undersecretary for policy, Eric Edelman, on our next steps. I observed that while most revolutions tend to lose their radical edge over time and degenerate into old-fashioned dictatorships, with the election of Ahmadinejad as president and with the radical students associated with seizing our embassy in 1979 assuming leadership roles, Iran was regaining its revolutionary edge. Dempsey said that Centcom had a "containment" strategy for Iran that integrated all previous military planning. He wanted to present it for review by the Joint Staff. I said it would be very hard "for this administration" to adopt a containment strategy that would require the United States to live with a nuclear-armed Iran. A couple of weeks later Mike Mullen advised me that Centcom and the Joint Staff were planning for potential military courses of action, among several options, as the Iranian government exercised "increasingly lethal and malign influence in Iraq." Meanwhile the president directed the CIA and Defense to accelerate efforts to develop an array of options between traditional diplomacy and conventional military power to set back the Iranian nuclear program.

Debate within the administration heated up considerably in May, prompted by several Israeli military requests that, if satisfied, would greatly enhance their ability to strike the Iranian nuclear sites. In a meeting with the Joint Chiefs and me in the Tank on May 10, in the middle of a conversation on Afghanistan, the president suddenly asked if anybody was thinking about military action against Iran. He quickly added that the goal was of course to prevent Iran from getting a nuclear weapon and that he "just wanted you to be thinking about it—not a call to arms."

Two days later the national security team met with the president in his private dining room adjacent to the Oval Office. The participants included Cheney, Rice, Mullen, Bolten, Hadley, Hadley's deputy Jim Jeffrey, and me. We addressed two questions: How do we answer the Israelis and what should *we* do about the Iranian nuclear program? In many respects, it was a reprise of the debate over the Syrian nuclear reactor the year before. Hadley asked me to lead off. When making my case to the president on a significant issue like this one, I always wrote out in advance the points I wanted to make, because I did not want to omit something important. Given Bush 43's green light to Olmert on the Syrian reactor, I was very apprehensive as the meeting began.

I recommended saying no to all the Israelis' requests. Giving them any of the items on their new list would signal U.S. support for them to attack Iran unilaterally: "At that point, we lose our ability to control our own fate in the entire region." I said we would be handing over the initiative regarding U.S. vital national interests to a foreign power, a government that, when we asked them not to attack Syria, did so anyway. We should offer to collaborate more closely with Israel, I continued, doing more on missile defense and other capabilities, "but Olmert should be told in the strongest possible terms not to act unilaterally." The United States was not reconciled to Iran having nuclear weapons, but we needed a long-term solution, not just a one-to-three-year delay. I went on to say that a strike by the United States or Israel would end divisions in the Iranian government, strengthen the most radical elements, unify the country behind the government in their hatred of us, and demonstrate to all Iranians the need to develop nuclear weapons. I warned that Iran was not Syria—it would retaliate, putting at risk Iraq, Lebanon, oil supplies from the Gulf (which would lead to skyrocketing oil prices), and the end of the peace process, as well as increasing the likelihood of a Hizballah war against Israel. Addressing what I knew to be Cheney's desire to deal with the Iranian nuclear program before Bush left office, I observed that our current efforts to isolate Iran, significantly increase their economic problems, and delay their nuclear program might not be successful in bringing about a change of policy in Tehran during the Bush presidency, but they would leave his successor a robust array of tools with which to apply pressure. Finally, I pointed out that the president's own conditions for preemptive war had not been met, our own intelligence estimate would be used against us, and we would be the ones isolated, not Iran.

Cheney spoke next, and I knew what was coming. Matter-of-factly, he said he disagreed with everything I had said. The United States should give Israel everything it wanted. We could not allow Iran to get nuclear weapons. If we weren't going to act, he said, then we should enable the Israelis. Twenty years on, he argued, if there was a nuclear-armed Iran, people would say the Bush administration could have stopped it. I interjected that twenty years on, people might also say that we not only didn't stop them from getting nuclear weapons but made it inevitable. I was pretty sure Condi did not favor accommodating Israel's requests, but the way she expressed her concerns about not leaving our ally in the lurch or feeling isolated led Mullen and me after the meeting to worry that she might be changing her mind. Mullen talked about the difficulty of carrying out a successful attack. Hadley remained silent. At the end, the president was noncommittal, clearly frustrated by the lack of good options for dealing with Iran. He had a lot of company in the room on that score.

That afternoon I flew to Colorado Springs to celebrate the fiftieth anniversary of the North American Aerospace Defense Command. Aboard the plane, I became increasingly worried that the president might be persuaded by Cheney and Olmert to act or to enable the Israelis to act, especially if Condi's position was softening. I decided to communicate once again with Bush privately. I said,

> We must not make our vital interests in the entire Middle East, the Persian Gulf, and Southwest Asia hostage to another nation's decisions— no matter how close an ally. Above all, we ought not risk what we have gained in Iraq or the lives of our soldiers there on an Israeli military

gamble in Iran. Olmert has his own agenda, and he will pursue it irrespective of our interests. . . . We will be bystanders to actions that affect us directly and dramatically. . . . Most evidence suggests we have some time. . . . The military option probably remains available for several years. . . . A military attack by either Israel or the United States will, I believe—having watched these guys since 1979—guarantee that the Iranians will develop nuclear weapons, and seek revenge. . . . A surprise attack on Iran risks a further conflict in the Gulf and all its potential consequences, with no consultation with the Congress or foreknowledge on the part of the American people. That strikes me as very dangerous, and not just for sustaining our efforts in the Gulf.

In the end, the president deflected the Israeli requests but simultaneously directed a dramatic intensification of our bilateral intelligence sharing and cooperation on ways to slow down the Iranian program. In the years ahead, I would enthusiastically oversee a dramatic expansion of our military cooperation with Israel, direct an intensification of our military planning efforts vis-à-vis Iran, and significantly increase U.S. military capabilities in the Gulf. Whatever our differences internally or with Israel on what to do about the Iranian nuclear program, there was no disagreement that it posed a huge threat to the stability of the entire region.

It probably was not coincidental that a few weeks later, in mid-June, the Israelis held a military exercise that they knew would be monitored by many nations. In what appeared to be a rehearsal for a strike on Iran, one hundred Israeli F-15 and F-16 fighters flew from Israel over the eastern Mediterranean to Greece and returned. The exercise included the deployment of Israeli rescue helicopters and the use of refueling tankers. Flight tactics and other elements of a potential strike were rehearsed. The distance the fighters flew was 862 nautical miles. The distance from the Israeli airfield to the Iranian uranium enrichment facility at Natanz was 860 nautical miles. Israel wanted to signal that it was prepared for a strike and could carry it out.

I think my most effective argument, and one that even the vice president came grudgingly to acknowledge, was that an Israeli attack that overflew Iraq would put everything we had achieved there with the surge at risk—and indeed, the Iraqi government might well tell us to leave the country immediately. I discussed this with the president in a meeting on

June 18, and he emphatically said he would not put our gains in Iraq at risk. I responded that the Israelis had to be told this.

Given the connections the Israelis had in the Bush White House, they quickly knew of my role in the policy debate. They intensified the dialogue between Defense Minister Ehud Barak and me to see if I could be persuaded to change my view. I had known Ehud since I was CIA director and he was chief of the Israeli Defense Forces fifteen years earlier. I liked and respected him and always welcomed our meetings—well, almost always. Our first get-together after the Iran policy debate was on July 28. Then, and subsequently, we worked out some significant enhancements for Israeli security, including sending to Israel a U.S. X-band missile defense radar system and contributing to the development of several Israeli missile defense programs, perhaps most importantly one named Iron Dome to defend against short-range missiles. Barak and I would sustain our dialogue, and our friendship and cooperation, for the rest of my time as secretary.

Iran would get at least one more senior military officer in trouble with President Bush. In early July, Admiral Mullen apparently told reporters that, in essence, the U.S. military was too stressed to take on Iran. This mightily displeased the president, as Hadley told me. I called Mullen and advised him to "cool it" on Iran. I did not tell him that the president had said it "looked like Mullen was auditioning for a job with the next commander in chief while he still works for this one!" I just couldn't understand the lack of political awareness by senior officers of the impact at the White House of their remarks to the press.

FREQUENT FLYER

I traveled to scores of countries over a two-year period working for Bush 43. I made more than a dozen trips for various NATO meetings, at which I almost always hammered away on three themes: the need for greater European investment in defense, the need for the Europeans to do more in Afghanistan, and the need for NATO to reform its structures and way of doing business. For a decade or so, member states had committed to spend at least 2 percent of their gross domestic product on defense (reduced from the earlier guideline of 3 percent). By 2007–8, just five of twenty-eight members met that guideline, including Greece and Croatia; all others spent less. Given the economic downturn during this period, telling the Europeans to increase their defense spending was about as useful as shouting down a well.

I found the NATO meetings excruciatingly boring. On every topic, representatives of each of twenty-eight countries could speak their piece, reading from a prepared script. My secret to staying awake was revealed publicly at one meeting by the French defense minister, who was in a rant about how boring the meetings were—he confessed to doodling to pass the time and then outed me for doing crossword puzzles.

At the NATO summit in Bucharest, Romania, in April 2008, President Bush lasted longer at the meeting table than most of his counterparts—at least five hours—but as the afternoon wore on, he was eager to get a little downtime before a long formal dinner and "native" entertainment. Condi and I, sitting behind him, also wanted to leave. But who would stay and represent the United States until the bitter end? I offered the president and Condi a deal: I would stay at the table by myself until the meeting was over in exchange for not having to attend the formal dinner. They agreed immediately. Over time I made some good friends among my ministerial colleagues, and I would continue to value the alliance greatly. But I didn't have the patience for those long meetings.

I made three trips to Asia during my first fourteen months as secretary. The first, in early June 2007, was to Singapore for the "Shangri-La" Asia Security Summit, named for the hotel where it was held every year. My maiden speech in Asia focused on urging the Chinese to explain the purpose behind their major military buildup, but I also tried to turn down the temperature in the relationship with China by calling for a bilateral dialogue on a range of issues. During this trip, I again visited the troops in Afghanistan. In Bishkek, Kyrgyzstan, where Manas airfield had become a vital link in our aerial resupply of soldiers in, and troop movements to, Afghanistan, the amazingly corrupt government of Kurmanbek Bakiyev saw our continued need for the airfield as a rich source of revenue or, as I called it, extortion. The Kyrgyz were once again making noises about closing Manas to us, and we had to have it open, so I had to see Bakiyev and let him pick our pockets again. He, his officials, and his generals looked and acted just like the old Soviets, whose vassals they had been. Bakiyev reeled off a list of areas where we were ignoring Kyrgyz sovereignty and Kyrgyz people, and how we were "cheating" them of revenues. In the crassest kind of insult in that part of the world, the big crook didn't even offer me a cup of tea. He was, without question, the most unpleasant foreign leader I had to deal with in my years as secretary, and I celebrated when he was overthrown in April 2010.

My trip ended at the American cemetery in Normandy on June 6, the sixty-third anniversary of D-Day, where French defense minister Morin and I presided over the commemoration ceremonies. It was rainy, windy, and cold, just like that historic day in 1944. After the ceremony, I walked alone among the countless rows of white crosses, deeply moved by the sacrifice they represented but also reflecting on the new gravestones being erected at home above the remains of young men and women I was sending in harm's way, making their own sacrifice for our country just as the GIs had done at Normandy. It was a hard day.

I went to China, South Korea, and Japan in early November 2007 on my second trip to Asia. President Bush and Chinese president Hu Jintao had agreed that the military-to-military relationship between our two countries needed to be strengthened, and so I made my first pilgrimage to Beijing in more than fifteen years. My first visit had been as a CIA officer at the end of 1980, when bicycles still reigned supreme on the capital's streets. Now traffic was horrible, and the pollution made the air nearly unbreathable. The Chinese were preparing to host the Olympic Games the next year, and it was plain they had a lot of work to do to avoid all the visitors having to wear gas masks. In all of my meetings, the same three topics were discussed: international and regional security issues, with me spending a lot of time on Iran; state-to-state relations between our two countries; and specific issues in the military relationship. Bush and Hu had agreed in April 2006 to pursue bilateral discussions of nuclear strategy, but it was pretty plain that the People's Liberation Army hadn't received the memo. Still, I pushed for beginning a "strategic dialogue" to help us understand each other's military intentions and programs better.

My third trip to Asia, at the end of February 2008, was an around-the-world jaunt including stops in Australia, Indonesia, India, and Turkey. This trip was made difficult by the lamentable fact that a week before we departed, I slipped on the ice outside my house in Washington, D.C., and broke my shoulder in three places. I had been lucky in that the bones had remained where they needed to be, so I didn't need surgery or a cast, just immobilization in a sling. The arm caused some awkward moments during the trip. At a very nice dinner given in my honor by Australian prime minister Kevin Rudd, I was doing fine at table conversation until Rudd began a long soliloquy on the history of Australia. I had made it just past World War I when the combined effect of a painkiller, jet lag, and a glass of wine caused me to fall asleep. This led to not-so-subtle attempts by my American colleagues at the table to rouse me. Rudd was very gracious about the whole thing; my team less so, as they took raucous delight in making fun of my undiplomatic snooze. I was shocked when I got out of bed the next morning to see that my entire upper body was totally black and blue and yellow. The U.S. Air Force doctor traveling with me called in a couple of Australian physicians, and everyone was puzzled that the bruising had appeared a week after my fall, but in typical Aussie fashion and with good cheer, they said it would take care of itself. The rest of the trip was uneventful, if long.

Most of my many other trips abroad during the Bush years, apart from the frequent visits to Iraq and Afghanistan, fell into the category of what former secretary of state George Shultz called "gardening"—shoring up or nurturing relationships with friends, allies, and others. The highlight for me always was meeting and talking with our men and women in uniform around the world. Each encounter seemed to provide a much-needed transfusion of energy and idealism from them to me, which I would need when I returned to Washington.

CHAPTER 6

Good War, Bad War

B y fall 2007, the unpopular war in Iraq—the "bad war," the "war of choice"—was going much better. However, the war in Afghanistan—the "good war," the "war of necessity"—while continuing to enjoy strong bipartisan support in Washington, was getting worse on the ground. The politics in Washington surrounding the two wars both frustrated and angered President Bush. In a meeting with the Joint Chiefs and me in the Tank on May 10, 2007, he said, "Many in Congress don't understand the military. Afghanistan is good. Iraq is bad. Bullshit."

The war to oust the Taliban from power in Afghanistan and to destroy al Qaeda began auspiciously less than a month after the September 11, 2001, attacks on the United States. Within a matter of weeks, the Taliban had been defeated, and their leaders, along with al Qaeda's, had fled to the border areas inside Pakistan. On December 5, 2001, Hamid Karzai was selected by an informal group of Afghan tribal and political leaders to serve six months as chairman of an "interim administration." In June 2002, he was chosen by a grand assembly *(loya jirga)* as interim president for two years, then was elected to a full five-year term the following October. From the beginning, Karzai had strong support from the United States and the international community, which set about trying to help him and his government establish their authority and an effective national government beyond Kabul. When I became secretary, the

United States had about 21,000 troops in Afghanistan, while NATO and coalition partners together had about 18,000 troops.

When interviewing with Bush in early November 2006, I had told him that based on what I read, I thought the war in Afghanistan was being neglected. I also said there was too much emphasis on building a strong central government in a country that had virtually never had one, and too little emphasis on improving governance, security, and services at the provincial and district levels, including making better use of local Afghan tribal leaders and councils. On my first trip to Afghanistan in January 2007, I quickly came to believe that, as in Iraq, from early on we had underestimated the resilience and determination of our adversaries and had failed to adjust our strategy and our resources as the situation on the ground changed for the worse. While we were preoccupied with Iraq, between 2002 and 2005 the Taliban reconstituted in western Pakistan and in southern and eastern Afghanistan. Headquartered and operating in Pakistani cities including Peshawar and Quetta, virtually unhindered by the Pakistani government, the Taliban recovered from their disastrous defeat and again became a serious fighting force. They received invaluable, if unintended, assistance from the sparseness of Afghan government presence outside Kabul—Karzai was referred to as the mayor of Kabul—and the corruption and incompetence of too many Afghan government officials at all levels in the provinces.

The first significant American encounter with a revitalized Taliban came in eastern Afghanistan on June 28, 2005, when four Navy SEALs were ambushed in a well-organized attack, and a helicopter with SEAL and Army Special Forces reinforcements sent to assist them was shot down. Three of the SEALs on the ground were killed, as well as sixteen U.S. servicemen on the helicopter. One of the three SEALs on the ground, Navy Lieutenant Michael Murphy, posthumously received the Congressional Medal of Honor for his heroism. American casualties that day were the worst yet in a single engagement in the Afghan War and a wake-up call that the Taliban had returned. The following spring, 2006, the Taliban increased the level of their attacks in both the south and east of Afghanistan. They were further enabled by a deal Pakistani president Pervez Musharraf cut at about the same time with tribes on the border, in which he pledged to keep Pakistani troops out of their tribal lands as long as the tribes prevented al Qaeda and the Taliban from operating in those lands. The feckless deal effectively gave the Taliban safe haven in those areas. The Taliban "spring offensive" was characterized by assassinations, the murder of teachers and burning of schools, the shooting of workers building roads, and other acts of targeted violence. The Taliban were joined in their depredations by other extremist groups, most notably those led by Gulbuddin Hekmatyar (to whom we had provided weapons when he was fighting the Soviets) and Jalaluddin Haqqani.

By the end of 2006, U.S. commanders in Afghanistan were telling the press that the number of Taliban attacks had surged by 200 percent in December from a year earlier and that since Musharraf's deal with the tribes had gone into effect in early September, the number of attacks in the border area had gone up by 300 percent. Military briefers reported that suicide attacks had grown from 27 in 2005 to 139 in 2006; the number of roadside bombings in the same period had risen from 783 to 1,677; and the number of direct attacks using small arms, grenades, and other weapons had gone from 1,558 to 4,542. Two thousand six had been the bloodiest year since 2001. When I became secretary, the war in Afghanistan, as in Iraq, was clearly headed in the wrong direction.

Recognizing the deterioration, just prior to my becoming secretary, President Bush had ordered an increase in the number of U.S. troops from 21,000 to 31,000 over a two-year period—what he called a "silent surge." He also doubled funding for reconstruction, increased the number of military-civilian teams (provincial reconstruction teams) carrying out projects to improve the daily life of Afghans, authorized an increase in the size of the Afghan army, and ordered more U.S. civilian experts to Afghanistan to help the ministries in Kabul become more effective (and less corrupt). Bush also encouraged our allies to do more in all these areas, and to drop the "national caveats" that limited the combat effectiveness of their troops.

It was against this backdrop that I made my first visit to Afghanistan in mid-January 2007, less than a month after being sworn in. As on my first trip to Iraq, General Pace joined me. It was nearly midnight when we landed and rode in a heavily armored motorcade to the main U.S. base in Kabul, Camp Eggers. There was snow and ice everywhere, and the temperature was about twenty degrees. My accommodations at Bader House consisted of a small second-floor bedroom with dim lighting and a bed, couch, easy chair, desk, and drapes that all looked like they had been salvaged from an old college dorm. The staff shared one room with four bunk beds. We all knew we were "living large" compared to our troops, and no one complained.

The first morning, I met with our ambassador, Ronald Neumann; then the senior American commander, Lieutenant General Karl Eikenberry; then other U.S. commanders; and finally with the commander of the International Security Assistance Force (the NATO-dominated coalition), British general David Richards. I heard a consistent message from everyone: the Taliban insurgency was growing, their safe havens in Pakistan were a big problem, the spring of 2007 would be more violent than the previous year, and more troops were needed. I was told that NATO nations had not provided some 3,500 military trainers they had promised, and Eikenberry—who was due to rotate out less than a week after my visit—asked that the deployment of a battalion of the 10th Mountain Division (about 1,200 troops) be extended through the spring offensive.

I told Eikenberry that if he thought more troops were needed, I was prepared to recommend that course of action to the president. At the same time, Pace made clear that additional troops for Afghanistan would increase the strain on the U.S. military at least in the short run. While I said I wanted to keep the initiative and not allow the Taliban to regroup, Pace had put his finger on a huge problem. With the surge in Iraq and 160,000 troops there, the Army and Marine Corps didn't have combat capability to spare. My intent upon becoming secretary had been to give our commanders in Iraq and Afghanistan everything they needed to be successful; I realized on this initial visit to Afghanistan I couldn't deliver in both places at once.

That afternoon we helicoptered east across the snow-covered mountains to Forward Operating Base Tillman, at an elevation of some 6,000 feet in eastern Afghanistan, only a few miles from the Pakistani border and near a major Taliban infiltration route. When we landed, I couldn't help but reflect that a little over twenty years before, as deputy director of the CIA, I had been on the Pakistani side of the border looking into Afghanistan and doing business with some of the very people we were fighting now. It was a stark reminder to me of our limited ability to look into the future or to foresee the unintended consequences of our actions. That was what made me very cautious about committing military forces in new places.

I was met by Captain Scott Horrigan, the commander at FOB Tillman, who gave me a tour. His troops were partnered with about 100 Afghan soldiers in this fortified outpost in the mountains, named for Corporal Patrick Daniel Tillman, a professional football player who had enlisted in the Army and was killed in Afghanistan in a friendly-fire tragedy in 2004. The walking tour across snow, rocks, and mud brought home to me just how much we were asking of our young officers and troops in these isolated posts. Captain Horrigan was overseeing road building, negotiating with local tribal councils, training Afghan soldiers—and fighting the Taliban. His base was attacked by rocket and mortar fire at least once a week. The range of his responsibilities and the matter-of-fact way he described them and conducted himself took my breath away. I thought to myself that the responsibilities this young captain had and the authority and independence he enjoyed would make any return to garrison life—not to mention the civilian world—very hard. More than any headquarters briefing, the quiet competence, skill, and courage that he, his first sergeant, and their men displayed gave me confidence that we could prevail if we had the right strategy and proper resources.

In a dramatic shift of setting and circumstance, I met that evening for the first time with President Karzai in the presidential palace in Kabul. Karzai owed his position—and his life—to American support, yet he was very much a Pashtun leader and an Afghan nationalist. Accordingly, distrust and dislike of the British, who had famously failed to pacify Afghanistan in the nineteenth century, was in his DNA. I would meet with him many times over the next four and a half years, often alone, in every subsequent visit. He and I were able to speak very frankly to each other. His wife had given birth to a son a few days before my initial visit, and in future meetings I would always ask about the boy, of whom he was very proud. While dealing with Karzai could be incredibly frustrating and maddening, especially for those who had to do it nearly every day, I quickly understood the importance of actually listening to him—something too many of my American colleagues, including all our ambassadors during my time as secretary, did too rarely—because he was very open about his concerns. Long before issues such as civilian casualties, the actions of private security contractors, night raids, and the use of dogs on patrols became nasty public disputes between Karzai and the international coalition, he would raise these matters in private. We were far too slow in picking up on these signals and taking action. Karzai knew he needed the coalition but he also was sensitive to actions that would anger the Afghan public, undermine their tolerance for the presence of foreign troops in their country, and reflect badly on him in the eyes of his countrymen. "I know I have many flaws," Karzai once told me, "but I do know my people."

Wholly dependent upon the largesse and protection of foreign governments and troops, he was exceptionally sensitive about any foreign action or commentary that did not show respect for Afghan sovereignty, Afghan citizens, or himself. He was especially allergic to foreign criticism of him or his family, particularly on the issue of corruption. He tracked the foreign press zealously (or his staff did) and once showed me an article critical of him in *The Irish Times*. I thought to myself, *Who in the hell reads* The Irish Times *outside Ireland?* But all too often, in both the Bush and Obama administrations, American officials failed to calibrate their criticisms of Karzai in terms of what was said, how often, at what level, and whether publicly or privately. The result was to make a challenging relationship more difficult than it needed to be.

I returned from the January 2007 trip determined to provide more American troops, to try to persuade our NATO allies to provide more troops, and to see if we could get better cooperation from the Pakistanis on the border. I wasn't optimistic about my chances for success.

Getting more American troops was a challenge. With the surge in Iraq, our ground forces were stretched very thin. The expression I most often heard from senior officers when discussing this was "We are out of Schlitz"—meaning there was nothing more available. Thinking it very important to blunt the Taliban offensive in the spring of 2007, within days of my return to Washington I recommended, and the president approved, extending the deployment of the 10th Mountain Division battalion for another 120 days, as Eikenberry had requested. I also asked the president to approve accelerating the deployment of units of the 82nd Airborne Division. All together this provided roughly another 3,200 U.S. combat troops, bringing our number to about 25,000, the highest level yet in the war. I could send no more troops for the rest of 2007, given our commitments in Iraq. The commanders still had an outstanding request to NATO for 3,500 additional trainers for the Afghan army and police.

President Bush was sensitive to the charge that the war in Iraq— and the surge—were holding us back or distracting us in Afghanistan. This was an ongoing source of his irritation with Mike Mullen, whose public commentary suggested just that. In late September, the president expressed his displeasure to me over a statement Mullen had made in an interview to the effect that Iraq was "a distraction." And he also disliked Mullen's later repeated characterization to Congress that "in Iraq, we do what we must. In Afghanistan, we do what we can." Mike was describing reality, however politically uncomfortable, but it was public statements like these that I think led the president to question whether Mullen would continue to support the effort in Iraq under a new commander in chief.

We needed to persuade our NATO allies to do more. As I said earlier, I attended my first NATO defense ministers meeting in Seville in early February 2007, where I asked the Europeans to deliver the combat troops, trainers, and helicopters they had promised. I pressed them to lift restrictions on the kinds of missions their forces could undertake. I told them it was important for the spring offensive in Afghanistan to be an "alliance offensive." Several ministers, including my German colleague, Franz Josef Jung, countered that a more "balanced, comprehensive" approach was needed in Afghanistan and that the alliance should be focusing more on economic and reconstruction efforts than on boosting force levels. This was a refrain I would hear constantly in the future. The approach favored by the Europeans, however, looked a lot like nation-building, the work of decades in Afghanistan and not the kind of mission accomplished in the middle of a war. The Europeans—especially those deployed in the more peaceful west and north of Afghanistan—wanted to focus on a very broad long-term mission, just as there was growing sentiment in the Bush and then the Obama administration that we had to narrow our objectives to those that could be realistically achieved in the time that an increasingly impatient and war-weary American people would give us. No one ever focused explicitly on this divergence of views between the United States and our NATO allies either in our meetings or publicly, but it was an important underlying source of friction and frustration.

When the Europeans agreed to take on Afghanistan as a NATO mission in 2006, they had thought they were signing up to something akin to armed peacekeeping, as NATO had undertaken in Bosnia, not a full-fledged counterinsurgency. Their publics did not want to be in a war and had very low tolerance for casualties, and most governments faced significant political opposition at home to their military commitment. While I would pester and nag the Europeans for years to do more, I actually was surprised they were so steadfast in supporting the mission, given their domestic politics, especially in the several countries where coalition governments held on to power by a thread. The hardest fighting, and greatest sacrifices, fell to those countries deployed in the south and east (the United States, Britain, Canada, Denmark, the Netherlands, Australia, Estonia, and Romania), but the French, Germans, Italians, and Spanish contributed thousands of troops elsewhere in Afghanistan. Getting many of those troops to venture outside their fortified base camps, however, was a continuing challenge. Over time national caveats would diminish, the numbers of allied troops would gradually increase, and no one would bail out.

I wanted to get the Pakistanis to do more to end safe havens and to stop Taliban infiltration from their side of the border. As important to the United States as Pakistan is, both in Afghanistan and in the region, I would travel there only twice because I quickly realized my civilian counterpart had zero clout in defense matters (dominated by the chief of the army staff). My first and only significant visit was on February 12, 2007, about three weeks after my initial trip to Afghanistan. The purpose was to meet with President Musharraf, who was then also still chief of the army staff, to see if he would step up Pakistan's military efforts along the Afghan border, especially in anticipation of the Taliban's spring offensive. I talked about the need for the United States, NATO, Afghanistan, and Pakistan to do more. His response was one that we would hear ad nauseam. The international media and some foreign leaders portray all problems in Afghanistan as coming from Pakistan, he said, but we needed to take on the Taliban where they come from and operate, which was in Afghanistan. He went on to say that only the Pakistani intelligence services seemed to catch high-ranking Taliban and al Qaeda and that "Pakistan is the victim of the export of the Afghan Taliban." After he reviewed his plans for border control, the refugee camps, and military action in Waziristan (in northwestern Pakistan, on the Afghan border), we retired to a small room for a private meeting. I gave him a list of specific actions we wanted Pakistan to take, actions we could take together, and actions the United States was prepared to take alone. In private, Musharraf acknowledged Pakistani failures and problems on the border, but he asked me what a lone Pakistani border sentry could do if he saw thirty to forty Taliban moving toward the Afghan border. I responded, You should permit the sentry to warn us, and we will ambush the Taliban. He said, "I like ambushes, we ought to be setting them daily." *If only*, I thought.

I went through our very specific list of requests: capture three named Taliban and extremist leaders; give the United States expanded authority to take action against specific Taliban and al Qaeda leaders and targets in Pakistan; dismantle insurgent and terrorist camps; shut down the Taliban headquarters in Quetta and Peshawar; disrupt certain major infiltration routes across the border; enhance intelligence cooperation and streamline Pakistani decision making on targeting; allow expanded ISR flights over Pakistan; establish joint border security monitoring centers manned by Pakistanis, Afghans, and coalition forces; and improve cooperation for military planning and operations in Pakistan. Musharraf kept a straight face and pretended to take all this seriously. While the Pakistanis would eventually deploy some 140,000 troops on their border with Afghanistan and endure heavy losses in fighting there, and while there was some modest progress on joint operations centers and border security stations, we'd still be asking for virtually all these same actions years later.

The real power in Pakistan is the military, and in November 2007 Musharraf handed over leadership of the army to General Ashfaq Parvez Kayani. At that point, I turned the Pakistani account over to Mike Mullen, who would travel to Pakistan regularly to talk with Kayani.

It became clear to me that our efforts in Afghanistan during 2007 were being significantly hampered not only by muddled and overly ambitious objectives but also by confusion in the military command structure, confusion in economic and civilian assistance efforts, and confusion over how the war was actually going.

The military command problem was the age-old one of too many high-ranking generals with a hand on the tiller. U.S. Army General Dan McNeill had replaced British general Richards on February 1, 2007, as commander of ISAF (International Security Assistance Force) in Kabul. McNeill was the first U.S. four-star commander dedicated to Afghanistan. There he had command of all coalition forces, which included about two-thirds of U.S. forces in country. Because his was a NATO command, McNeill reported to U.S. Army General John Craddock in his NATO role as supreme allied commander Europe. McNeill commanded only about half of some 8,000 to 10,000 additional U.S. and other coalition soldiers assigned to Afghanistan, who, under the rubric of Operation

Enduring Freedom (OEF), reported to a separate U.S. three-star general, who in turn reported to the four-star commander of Central Command in Tampa. A significant percentage of the Special Forces operating in Afghanistan reported to yet another commander, also in Tampa.

This jerry-rigged arrangement violated every principle of the unity of command. And to make things worse, Craddock and McNeill did not get along with each other. Craddock guarded his NATO turf zealously; whenever I wanted the ISAF commander to brief the defense ministers at our meetings, Craddock was recalcitrant unless I insisted. I can think of only one occasion in my years as secretary when I directly overruled a senior military officer. It was right after General Stan McChrystal was appointed to command ISAF: on his way to Kabul, I wanted him to join me at a meeting of NATO defense ministers, whose troops he would be commanding, and say a few words. I passed word to Craddock to make it happen. We sat next to each other at a formal luncheon, and he passed me a note formally objecting to McChrystal appearing before the ministers, saying he didn't think it set a good precedent. I scribbled back to him on his note, "Noted. Now make it happen."

I heard about this command and control problem in the Pentagon from Undersecretary Eric Edelman, Assistant Secretary Mary Beth Long, and from Doug Lute at the NSC, on my visits to NATO and in Afghanistan. I asked Pete Pace to recommend how to fix it, and he came back to me exasperated with the complexity and the politics. The apparent trouble was that OEF had the mission not only of training and equipping the Afghans but also of carrying out covert ("black") special operations. The Europeans, especially the Germans, characterized our interest in putting everything under one American commander as having sucked them into Afghanistan as an alliance project and then wanting to take it over again. They also saw it as an effort to make NATO complicit in black special ops, which their publics wouldn't stand for. Pace concluded that, as Craddock put it, the command and control "is ugly, but it works on the ground." Actually, it didn't. This problem would not fully be resolved until the summer of 2010, nearly nine years after the war started.

International civilian assistance and reconstruction efforts were also confused. Scores of countries, international organizations, and nongovernmental organizations were engaged in trying to help the Afghans develop an effective government, improve the infrastructure, strengthen the economy, and carry out humanitarian projects. It was—and is—

a massive endeavor, made significantly more difficult because no one knew what anyone else was doing. Each country and organization worked strictly within its own sector on its own projects. There was little sharing of information on what was working or not, little collaboration, and virtually no structure. To make things worse, the outsiders too often did not inform the Afghan government about what they were doing, much less ask the Afghans what projects *they* would like. Strictly speaking, this was not my area of responsibility as defense secretary, though historically the U.S. military, with its resources and organization, has taken on many traditionally civilian tasks in war zones. But the war was certainly my responsibility, and if we couldn't get the civilian side right, our chances of achieving the president's objectives were reduced, if not impossible.

A senior civilian coordinator was needed, someone with a broad international mandate to oversee all the economic development, governance, humanitarian, and other projects under way in Afghanistan and then to work with President Karzai and his government to bring some greater structure, coherence, and collaboration to those efforts—with significant Afghan involvement. We discussed this first at the NATO defense ministers meeting in Seville in February 2007, then for months afterward. I believed the coordinator had to be a European and, if possible, have a mandate from the United Nations, NATO, and the European Union, thus encompassing virtually all the international organizations and countries with projects ongoing in Afghanistan. The effort was sidetracked for months by a strong British push for Paddy Ashdown, a longtime member of Parliament who had served as high representative for Bosnia and Herzegovina from 2002 to 2006. The United States and other allies were all prepared to go along, mainly because the British felt so strongly about his appointment. The problem was that Karzai was familiar with Ashdown's role in the former Yugoslavia. Karzai told me during my visit to Kabul in December 2007 that his cabinet had unanimously rejected Ashdown as the senior civilian coordinator because Afghanistan was "not interested in a viceroy for development." He said he was wary of Ashdown because of reports of his high-handedness in the Balkans. Karzai said he wanted the scope of the coordinator's role and authority clearly defined and his writ limited to making international support more coherent and to lobbying for greater assistance.

In March 2008, Norwegian diplomat Kai Eide was named as senior civilian coordinator, operating under the mandate of the United Nations. Eide, who would develop a good relationship with Karzai and could speak frankly with him about delicate matters, often to good effect, would offer his appraisal of the current situation in Afghanistan at every NATO defense ministers meeting. Kai was frank about the challenges but usually fairly upbeat about how things were going. I got to know him pretty well and strongly supported his role so he was very forthright with me. Given the UN bureaucracy, it took months for him to get additional staff, let alone fulfill his mandate. Despite Kai's best efforts, the structured coordination of international assistance I had hoped for never developed, just like everything else in Afghanistan involving multiple governments.

No less confusing was determining whether we were making progress in Afghanistan. I was enormously frustrated by the divergent views of intelligence analysts in Washington, who were pretty consistently pessimistic, and the civilians and military on the ground in Afghanistan, who were both much more positive. In my years at CIA and the NSC, I had seen this movie a number of times—in Vietnam, in Afghanistan in the 1980s, and during the Gulf War, to mention only a few examples. It's hard to say whether the field or the Washington analysts were more accurate, but I gave a slight edge to the experts in Washington (probably reflecting my bias in having been a Washington-based analyst). However, my experience made me wary because, contrary to conventional wisdom, intelligence analysts far prefer showing that the decision makers don't know what they're doing rather than supporting them—especially when they can testify to that effect before Congress.

After months of reading and hearing the conflicting analysis, my impatience boiled over during a September 25, 2007, videoconference with McNeill in Kabul, Craddock in Brussels, and the chairman and others in Washington. I vented about the gap between D.C. intelligence evaluations versus "the take of the guys in the field." I said I didn't know how to get the most accurate assessment of the situation on the ground. I confessed, "I'm confused and I'm sure others are as well." I asked Jim Clapper, the undersecretary of defense for intelligence, to adjudicate the differences in analysis between those in Afghanistan and those in Washington. He reported a couple of days later that the disconnect was worse than we thought; there were differences in assessment between General McNeill's headquarters, Central Command, NATO, and both CIA and

Defense Intelligence Agency analysts in Washington. Not a good situation in the middle of a war.

In mid-October, Clapper reported that there was a "robust" dialogue under way among all of the different analytical communities with respect to the "real situation" in Afghanistan. He said that analysts from CIA and other agencies had gone to Afghanistan and, working with the experts there, had come up with forty-five to fifty questions to try to sharpen where they disagreed and what they could agree upon. I thought the intelligence folks were missing the point. Too much of the reporting was tactical—day-to-day combat reports—and anecdotal; everyone saw the same data, but interpretation of it varied widely. What was the broader picture?

In mid-June 2008, I again let loose my frustration in a videoconference with the generals in Kabul and Brussels and the senior Pentagon leadership in Washington: "You guys [in Kabul] sound pretty good, but then I get intelligence reports that indicate it is going to hell. I don't have a feel for how the fight is going! I don't think the president has a clear idea either of exactly where we are in Afghanistan." The differences in perspective and views were genuine, but still . . .

The lack of clarity fed my worry that things were not going well. Our insufficient levels of combat troops and trainers, inadequate numbers of civilian experts, confusing military command and control, the lack of multinational coordination on the civilian side, and deficient civil-military coordination were matched and then some on the Afghan side—corruption at every level, the mercurial Karzai, the scarcity of competent ministers and civil servants, problems between the capital and the provinces. Eric Edelman told me about these Afghan weaknesses as early as mid-March 2007. Eric also said that the Ministry of the Interior was probably involved in the drug trade and that Karzai spent far too much time in his palace and not enough time showing the flag around the country. Edelman, a career diplomat, ended his litany with a line perhaps designed to keep me from getting too depressed: "I'm not discouraged, but there are issues."

Two weeks later Rice, Hadley, and I met in Washington with NATO secretary general Jaap de Hoop Scheffer. His message was familiar: "I feel we can 'contain,' but cannot 'prevail'" against, the Taliban. He questioned the sustainability of the NATO commitment and told us the alliance needed better coordination, better integration of our forces, better training of the Afghan army, and more consistency in the public statements of NATO and contributing governments about the war. He added that someone with real clout was needed who could speak to Karzai on behalf of all the countries working in Afghanistan, someone who "can tell him what the truth is." We agreed with everything he had to say, and Hadley asked whether we really needed three senior representatives in Kabul—one each from NATO, the EU, and the UN, as at present. I asked if NATO should own the entire role, and Rice chimed in, "You can do it de jure or de facto, but make the NATO guy the strongest."

During my second visit to Afghanistan, in early June 2007, I continued to worry that we were strategically more or less in the same place as we had been in Iraq in 2006—at best, at a stalemate. In my comments to the press, I said, "I think actually things are slowly, cautiously headed in the right direction. I am concerned to keep it moving that way." In fact, I was *very* concerned. In a meeting on July 26 with the senior civilian and military leadership in the Pentagon, I said we were losing European forces because they didn't have the stomach for the fight; we were doing well in conventional military terms against the Taliban, but the level of violence was rising; a new U.S. president would have to decide whether to put more forces into Afghanistan without much NATO support; the Pakistanis weren't pushing al Qaeda or the Taliban from their side of the border so that we could take care of them in Afghanistan, nor would they let us go after them unilaterally in Pakistan. The one comparatively bright spot was the Afghan army, which for all its problems was significantly more competent and respected than any other Afghan government institution.

The problems I faced with command personalities, as well as figuring out what was going on in Afghanistan, were demonstrated in a videoconference on September 13. The deputy U.S. commander of the 82nd Airborne Division, Brigadier General Joe Votel, assured me we still held the initiative in eastern Afghanistan, but he went on to describe the situation there as deteriorating, with the Taliban and their allies increasing the number of suicide bombings, kidnapping of women and beheadings, and moving their support bases closer to Kabul. He said there were increased numbers of the enemy across the border in Pakistan; that attacks in the east were 75 percent higher than the previous year; and that collusion was growing among the disparate insurgent groups. General McNeill questioned Votel's "dire assessment" and asserted, "We're not going down the tubes here and the Taliban does not have the upper hand. We're killing a lot of them, getting to sufficient numbers of their leaders and having great effect. I think we're in pretty good shape when it comes to the Taliban." I thought to myself, *Well, that's just great. Even the military commanders on the ground don't agree on how we are doing.* Admiral Fallon then added, "I'm with Dan [McNeill] on the prospects in Afghanistan—it's not as gloomy as some would have you believe."

I arrived in Kabul on December 4 and helicoptered to Khowst province in eastern Afghanistan. The 82nd Airborne had, in fact, done a superb job there of fighting an effective counterinsurgency, and despite the increase in violence, it was clear, as Votel had said, that we still had the initiative. While in Khowst, I flew to a small village to meet with a group of provincial officials and tribal elders. We landed in a field outside the village, and there didn't seem to be a living green thing in sight. Everything was brown. As so often in visiting such remote places in Afghanistan, I asked myself, *Why are people fighting over this godforsaken place?* The officials and elders were already assembled in an open-sided but roofed structure and did me the favor of providing chairs to sit on. There were some stunning beards in the room, many of them white and streaked with red henna. It could have been a scene out of the eighteenth century—until one of the elders told me he had read my recent Kansas State University lecture on soft power on the Internet. It was a useful reminder that traditional customs and dress do not equate with technological backwardness—a lesson to remember in dealing with the Taliban as well. I came away from Khowst impressed with the effective partnering of military efforts with civilian experts from State, AID, and the Department of Agriculture. It was a genuinely comprehensive counterinsurgency, combining military operations with robust reconstruction efforts, with Afghans fully integrated. Khowst at that time was a model of a sort: open-minded and skilled U.S. military leaders, adequate numbers of U.S. civilian experts, Afghan involvement, and a competent Afghan governor.

My briefings in Kabul from the various regional commanders were uniformly upbeat. They said the situation overall was "no worse" than before, "just different." The commander in the south said that his forces there "had a better year than the media gives them credit for and than the European capitals think." The west was described as in pretty good shape, and the north has "no insurgency—organized crime and warlords are the biggest threat to security." In the east, "the counterinsurgency strategy continues to show progress." Each commander expressed frustration that the growing violence—due to more aggressive coalition efforts to root out the Taliban—was viewed in Washington as evidence of failure. Every commander wanted more troops, and McNeill said he was about four battalions short, plus trainers, of what he needed.

I then met privately with Karzai. I said he'd probably had enough people beating up on him and that I was there to listen. He talked about how the Russians, the Iranians, and the Pakistanis were all meddling in Afghanistan (undoubtedly all true) and that they and the Afghan Northern Alliance were all working against him. In what was, even for him, a particularly conspiratorial frame of mind, he talked about how "inclusiveness" (meaning working with the Northern Alliance) had put the country at risk and that these guys—"Putin's allies"—were now killing parliamentarians and even children. "This is not done by the Taliban or al Qaeda but by our own bad people," and his government needed to "consult with the United States on how to handle this." Because most of the Taliban operations were in southern Afghanistan, he said, the brunt of the war was being borne by the Pashtuns, and they felt we were targeting them. He said that to address this, we needed to work more closely with the tribes. It was classic Karzai—overdrawn and paranoid but not necessarily wrong.

I told the president on my return that there had been significant progress in Afghanistan, but the progress was too slow. The regional commanders were relatively upbeat, I said, but their briefings were discouraging in that they all were asking me to fill military capabilities or equipment needs NATO had not filled. I said we had to be prepared to continue to invest robustly in training and equipping the Afghan security forces, especially the army, and that more trainers and mentors were needed—areas where NATO was falling woefully short. I summarized: NATO didn't know how to do counterinsurgency, the allied mentoring and liaison teams didn't know what they were doing, the small Taliban presence in the north was being used by the warlords as a reason to rebuild their militias, in the west it would be better not to have the Italians there, and the south was a mess. My bottom line to Bush: Where we were in charge and Karzai had appointed competent, honest leaders, we were doing okay. Everything else was a holding action. We had to transition from European-favored comprehensive nation-building, toward a more focused counterinsurgency, no matter how much it upset the Europeans. If we had learned one lesson from the surge in Iraq, it was that we had to give the people a sense of security before anything else could work.

As we looked toward 2008, I was eager to have the NATO summit in April 2008 bless a longer-term strategy in Afghanistan, out of necessity. For more than a year, the defense ministers of the countries fighting in Regional Command–South (RC-South: the United States, Britain, Canada, Australia, Denmark, the Netherlands, Estonia, and Romania) had been meeting by ourselves to coordinate our countries' efforts better. We met again on December 13–14, 2007, in Edinburgh. This meeting included foreign ministers for the first time. Condi was represented by her undersecretary for policy, Nick Burns, who I had gotten to know when he worked on the NSC staff with Condi under Bush 41.

I proposed to ministers that the alliance prepare a three-to-five-year strategic plan comprehensively integrating both military operations and civilian development programs. I said such a plan would lift allies' eyes above heading for the exits at the end of 2008 and focus on the reality that success in Afghanistan was going to take some time. The prologue to such a plan should make clear why we were in Afghanistan and what we had achieved, framing the cause in a way not done before in Europe and providing essential political cover, and political ammunition, for governments. I proposed establishing milestones and goals so we would know if we were making progress. I volunteered the United States to prepare an initial draft and submit it to RC-South partners, then to alliance headquarters, and finally to the NATO summit meeting in Bucharest in April for approval. I also suggested that the British prepare a similar three-to-five-year plan just for the south, to include Helmand, Uruzgan, and Kandahar provinces, which we should review at a meeting in Canada in late January. There was broad support for both initiatives, with a number of useful suggestions from Nick Burns and other ministers. The initiative would never have succeeded without a lot of help from my civilian and military colleagues at the Pentagon and State. We were on course for a positive and useful statement on Afghanistan at the summit.

While home for Christmas 2007, I reflected on the fact that, despite all our problems, we had gotten a free ride from Congress on Afghanistan. The Democrats in Congress had spent the year trumpeting failure in Iraq and trying to change President Bush's strategy there; central to their approach was to contrast it with the war in Afghanistan, which they steadfastly supported—partly to demonstrate they weren't weak on national security. In not one of my congressional hearings all year did I hear criticism, much less concern, about the U.S. role or actions in Afghanistan. I consistently heard support for the war from both Democrats and Republicans and calls for our allies to provide more troops and remove restrictions on their use. The irony was that by the end of 2007, the war in Iraq was going much better and the situation in Afghanistan was getting worse. Many in Congress failed to acknowledge either of those realities. Consistent with the approach of the Democrats, they were saying more and more about the need to accelerate the troop drawdowns in Iraq so we could send more to Afghanistan.

In mid-January 2008, I announced we would be sending 3,200 Marines on a "onetime deployment" to Afghanistan in April, bringing our total number of troops to about 31,000. At the same time, I sent a letter to my ministerial colleagues in countries that we thought could do more in Afghanistan. I told them that the Marines were a bridging force to get us to the fall, and that the allies' failure to step up to the plate placed the entire alliance at risk.

I created a problem in the effort to get a summit statement of strong support for the Afghan mission by putting my foot in my mouth in an interview with Peter Spiegel of the *Los Angeles Times,* published on January 16. Spiegel asked about the counterinsurgency effort. I told him exactly what I thought: "I'm worried we're deploying [military advisers] that are not properly trained and I'm worried we have some military forces that don't know how to do counterinsurgency operations. . . . Most of the European forces, NATO forces, are not trained in counterinsurgency; they were trained for the Fulda Gap," the area of Germany where a Soviet invasion of Western Europe was thought most likely to take place.

A favorite saying of mine is "Never miss a good chance to shut up," but I blew that chance in this interview, and needless to say, all hell broke loose in the alliance. Edelman told me that the allies were very upset, that individual countries thought my criticisms had been aimed at them specifically. Eric called his counterparts in Britain, Canada, and the Netherlands, as well as the secretary general, all of whom were concerned about the impact of what I had said. The next day, at a press conference, I said my comments had been about an overall problem, that I was not drawing invidious comparisons between our troops and others, and that I hoped the allies would take advantage of counterinsurgency training opportunities. The United States had forgotten how to do counterinsurgency operations after Vietnam, I added, and had relearned at huge cost in Iraq and Afghanistan. The squall passed.

A trip to Europe in early February gave me a chance to mend fences. But I would not abandon speaking out publicly about challenges facing the alliance, heartfelt concerns grounded in my belief in its importance. The day before my departure Mike Mullen and I testified before the Senate Armed Services Committee, where I warned that the Atlantic alliance risked becoming a two-tiered organization, divided between some allies who were willing to fight and die to protect people's security, and others who were not, and that that put the organization at risk. Nearly simultaneously, Condi Rice made a surprise visit to Afghanistan, where she exhorted the allies to do more.

At the NATO defense ministers meeting in Vilnius, Lithuania, on February 7–8, recognizing that my stridency was becoming counterproductive, I softened my tone and my rhetoric but not my message. At the end of the meeting, several countries indicated they were considering increasing their troop commitments, including the French. On February 9, I returned to the Munich Security Conference and directed my remarks to the European people, not their governments. It was exceedingly unusual for an American defense secretary to address himself to foreign publics, but the president, Rice, Hadley, and I thought it would be useful to make the case for why success in Afghanistan mattered to the Europeans, especially since their own governments seemed loath to do so. I reminded the audience of the number of successful and attempted attacks by Islamic extremists in Europe and said the task facing the United States and its allies "is to fracture and destroy this movement . . . to permanently reduce its ability to strike globally and catastrophically, while deflating its ideology. . . . The best opportunity to do this is in Afghanistan."

I felt the outcome on Afghanistan was good at the April NATO summit. The allies unanimously endorsed a Strategic Vision Statement that committed the alliance to remain in Afghanistan for an extended period and to improve governance through greater training of Afghan officials, especially the police. Despite growing concern in Washington about nation-building, the United States acquiesced in the statement's expression of support for the "comprehensive approach," including both combat and economic reconstruction. President Bush pledged that the United States would send substantial additional troops to Afghanistan in 2009 but, at my suggestion, kept the number vague. We hoped the commitment would lead other nations to add to their forces. In fact, a number of allies did promise additional forces; France committed to send at least another 700 troops. As a result of the summit and the statement, the risk of significant allied defections at the end of 2008 was much reduced. Amazing to me as an old cold warrior, the Russians even agreed in Bucharest to allow nonlethal alliance military equipment going to Afghanistan to cross Russia. All that said, new troop commitments were modest or vague or both. And the "comprehensive approach" committed us to broad, ambitious goals that I and other U.S. officials were increasingly coming to see as unachievable in wartime.

The level of U.S. troops in Afghanistan remained a major concern for me for the rest of 2008. During my first year on the job, the number of troops had grown from 21,000 to 31,000. General McNeill had been asking for months for more soldiers, but by the time we arrived at the April summit, his request had grown to 7,500 to 10,000 more troops. The United States was the only possible source. Despite broad support in Congress for the war in Afghanistan, some questioned how President Bush could commit the United States to send more troops in 2009, when a new U.S. president would be in office. "I think that no matter who is elected president, he would want to be successful in Afghanistan," I said at one point. "So I think this was a very safe thing for him to say." As I told colleagues, as we drew down in Iraq, the United States could consider sending an additional three to five brigades (15,000 to 30,000 troops) to Afghanistan in 2009, but for the rest of my tenure (which I expected to end in January 2009), "I can't do jack-shit."

For the rest of 2008, we had to play "small ball," finding a few more helicopters in one place, a battalion we needed in another, ordnance disposal experts and ISR capabilities in yet another. The president told me he didn't want a "surge" in Afghanistan, and I told him we couldn't carry one out if we wanted to. In late July, as we worked the options for meeting commanders' needs in Afghanistan through November, there were a number of leaks of Joint Staff recommendations. I called Mike Mullen to express my unhappiness about that. I also had to tell Mullen that, once again, he had infuriated the president: on a television news show he said, in effect, that Bush had told him to focus on Iraq and *then* on Afghanistan. The president also kept saying to me that we needed to get allies who would not contribute troops—Japan, for one—to do more to fund the training and equipping of the Afghan forces. The results were minimal.

General Dan McNeill's assignment as commander of ISAF was to end in early June 2008. In anticipation of that change, Army chief of staff General Casey and Mike Mullen recommended that Army General David McKiernan be McNeill's successor. In 2003, McKiernan had commanded all coalition and U.S. ground forces in the invasion of Iraq. He had been appointed in 2005 as the commander of U.S. Army forces in Europe and had done a good job there. He was a fine soldier. With Casey's and Mullen's support for McKiernan (Vice Chairman of the Joint Chiefs General Cartwright was opposed), I saw no reason to challenge his appointment. With benefit of hindsight, I should have questioned whether McKiernan's conventional forces background was the right fit for Afghanistan. This was a mistake on my part.

McKiernan had been on the ground in Afghanistan less than three months when I met with him in Kabul. He told me that if he could take care of the safe havens in Pakistan, "we could secure Afghanistan in six months." I asked him if he thought we were winning. "Some places have governance, others have prosperity, and some have security," he said. "But few have all three. We are winning slower in some places than others." He told me he needed three additional brigade combat teams in addition to the 10th Mountain Division brigade due to arrive in January 2009—with support elements, a total of probably 15,000 to 20,000 more troops. (He would soon add a requirement for a combat aviation brigade, a significant addition of helicopters.) McKiernan said he could help beat back the "sky-is-falling narrative." He was making a not-so-subtle dig at Mullen's statement to the House Armed Services Committee on September 10 that he couldn't say we were winning in Afghanistan—again infuriating the White House and, apparently, the field commander.

By midsummer 2008, even before McKiernan's request for a significant increase in troops, I began to have misgivings about whether the foreign military presence in Afghanistan was growing to the point where most Afghans would begin to see us as "occupiers" rather than allies. Up to that point, all indications—polling and the like—suggested that most Afghans still saw us as allies. But more than anyone else at senior levels in Bush 43's administration, I had been involved with Afghanistan and

Pakistan during the 1980s and had watched the Soviets fail despite having nearly 120,000 troops there: their large presence (and brutal tactics) turned Afghans against them.

Historically, Afghanistan has not been kind to foreign armies. I began to worry aloud about where the tipping point in terms of the number of foreign troops might be and to act on that worry. On July 29, I asked for an analysis of the political and security implications of further troop increases. Ten days later I asked for a review of Afghan airfields, roads, and other infrastructure to determine whether they could support the additional forces being considered, over 20,000 more troops.

By the end of summer, I was deeply worried about our "footprint" and the Afghans' view of us. Although we were extremely careful to avoid civilian casualties—uniquely, I think, in the history of warfare—they did take place. Of course, the Taliban would hide among the population, use civilians as shields, and kill anyone who opposed them and many others who were just trying to avoid getting involved on either side. That said, we were clumsy and slow in responding to incidents where we caused civilian casualties, every one of which was a tragedy. Our procedure when incidents were reported was to investigate, to determine the facts, and then, if we were in fact responsible, to offer "consolation payments" to the families of victims. (Initial reports almost always exaggerated the number of people killed or hurt, as our investigations would show.)

I visited Afghanistan again in mid-September, primarily to publicly offer my "sincere condolences and personal regrets for the recent loss of innocent life as a result of coalition air strikes." The press conference at which I spoke those words was televised all across Afghanistan, and I was told by our commanders that the message had a beneficial effect—though, I suspected, a temporary one. I told McKiernan to change our approach: if we thought there was a chance we were responsible for civilian casualties, I wanted us to offer the condolence payments up front and then investigate to determine the facts. Some of our officers disagreed with my approach, but I believed that even if we overpaid, it would be a pittance compared to the bad publicity we were getting. I agreed with the Afghan defense minister to establish a Joint Investigative Group to meet continuously on this issue. I also invited the Afghan (as well as U.S.) media to a briefing I received on the procedures our pilots went through to avoid civilian casualties. Despite our best efforts and repeated directives from McKiernan, McChrystal, and Petraeus to our forces to avoid civilian casualties, the problem would continue to bedevil us.

In my private meeting with President Karzai, I filled him in on the measures we were taking to minimize civilian casualties. I told him that his penchant for going public with information—often inaccurate—was putting his allies in the worst possible light and doing real harm. I urged him to hold off speaking out about civilian casualty incidents until he learned the facts. I also reminded him that the Taliban were intentionally killing large numbers of Afghan civilians, not to mention deliberately placing them in harm's way, and that he should speak out about that. I was not optimistic I had made any impact.

There were other aspects of our operations that created problems with civilians, and thus with Karzai. Night raids to capture or kill Taliban leaders (and avoid civilian casualties), while militarily very effective, greatly antagonized ordinary Afghans. So did the use of dogs on patrols and especially in searching houses, as I mentioned earlier, which was culturally offensive to the Afghans and about which Karzai complained to me routinely. Our troops were not always as respectful of Afghans as they should have been, including our vehicles barreling down the roads scattering pedestrians and animals. I heard, anecdotally, about an Afghan elder who showed up at the gate of the main coalition base in Kandahar to complain about some insult to his family by troops. He was ignored for three days, returned home—and his three sons then joined the Taliban. While I did not have to deal with incidents as inflammatory as troops urinating on dead Taliban or posing with body parts or burning Korans, there were enough incidents to increase my misgivings about a dramatic increase in foreign forces in the country. No matter how skilled and professional the U.S. military was, I knew that some abusive and insulting behavior by troops was inevitable. Given Afghanistan's history, if the people came to see us as invaders or occupiers, or even as disrespectful, I believed the war would be lost.

All my overseas trips took a physical toll. Younger by a few years than my predecessor and my successor, I was nonetheless in my late sixties, and it usually took a week or so for me to recover from jet lag—and then I was off again. But the trips to Iraq and Afghanistan took a heavy emotional toll as well. I insisted on meeting and eating with troops on every trip, as I've said, and all too often I could see in their faces the cost of their deployments. There weren't many smiles. The troops all carried weapons, and I would later learn, to my chagrin, that they had to remove the ammunition before meeting with me. I suppose I understood the security precaution—there had to be more than a few who were resentful that I had sent them to such dangerous and godforsaken places—but I still didn't like the message of mistrust.

The troop visits got harder over time because, as I looked into each face, I increasingly would wonder to myself which of these kids I would next see in the hospital at Landstuhl or Walter Reed or Bethesda—or listed for burial at Arlington cemetery. For those on the front line who ate with me, I realized it might well be the occasion for the first hot meal or shower in days if not weeks. Each forward unit I visited seemed to have its own makeshift memorial in a small tent or lean-to dedicated to those who had been killed—pictures of them, mementos of each, challenge coins. I always went in alone. Although the morale of the troops and their NCOs and officers invariably seemed high, on each visit I was enveloped by a sense of misery and danger and loss. I would fly home with my heart aching for the troops and their distant families. With each visit, I grew increasingly impatient and angry as I compared their self-lessness and sacrifice with the self-promotion and selfishness of power-hungry politicians and others—in Baghdad, Kabul, and Washington. One young soldier in Afghanistan asked what kept me awake at night. I said, "You do." With each trip to the war zones and with each passing day at home, maintaining my outward calm and discipline, and suppressing my anger and contempt for the many petty power players, became a greater challenge. Images of the troops weighed on me constantly.

I didn't socialize in Washington. Every day I had a fight of one kind or another—usually several—and every evening I could not wait to get home, get my office homework out of the way, write condolence letters to the families of the fallen, pour a stiff drink, wolf down a frozen dinner or carry-out (when Becky was in the Northwest), read something totally unrelated to my work life, and turn out the light.

I got up at five every morning to run two miles around the Mall in Washington, past the World War II, Korean, and Vietnam memorials, and in front of the Lincoln Memorial. And every morning before dawn, I would ritually look up at that stunning white statue of Lincoln, say good morning, and sadly ask him, *How did you do it?*

I first publicly discussed my concerns about Afghanistan at a Senate Armed Services Committee hearing on September 22, 2008, five days after a visit to the country. I was accompanied by General Cartwright. I—and everyone else—thought it would be my last hearing as secretary of defense, and so most senators preceded their questioning with very kind words about my time in office. The eulogies complete, we got down to business. Levin asked me why we weren't responding promptly to the commander's request for more troops in Afghanistan. I replied that the requirements had been changing, and I mentioned McKiernan's request just the previous week when I'd been in Afghanistan. But, I continued, "We need to think about how heavy a military footprint the United States ought to have in Afghanistan, and are we better off channeling resources to build Afghan capacity?" I added that without extending tours and deployment schedules again, we didn't have the forces available, though we might be able to meet the force needs in the spring or summer of 2009.

Levin then asked a politically loaded question: Could we meet the Afghan needs more quickly by reducing forces in Iraq faster? General Cartwright said we would need additional support structure in Afghanistan, and we would need to restructure deployment and training cycles for Afghanistan because currently both were strongly weighted toward the heavy brigade combat teams in Iraq, and the forces needed in Afghanistan would be different. Senator Jeff Sessions of Alabama asked if we needed to be more humble "than we have been" in Afghanistan about how much we could change that country. The question went to the heart of many of my concerns. I told him, "We need to listen better to what the Afghan leadership is saying. If the Afghan people view foreigners as occupiers, it will never work—we need to make sure our interests are aligned with those of the Afghan people."

By fall 2008 the president also concluded that the war in Afghanistan was not going well and directed an NSC-led review of the war, directed by Doug Lute. On September 24, I met with Cartwright (Mullen was out of town); Edelman; the assistant secretary for special operations and low-intensity conflict, Mike Vickers (a former CIA officer I had worked with on Afghanistan in the 1980s, made famous by the book and movie *Charlie Wilson's War*), and others to go over the Defense Department contribution to the review. Central Command had advised us that they would not be able to flow the forces requested by McKiernan until June through October 2009. Lighter forces than the brigades coming up next in the rotation for deployment were required (fewer tanks and armor, among other things); facilities needed to be constructed—barracks, air fields, and parking areas for aircraft and helicopters; the infrastructure to support thousands of additional troops.

The intelligence community was nearing completion of a national intelligence estimate—the most authoritative level of analysis—that would portray the situation in Afghanistan as very bleak. Even before publication of the estimate, the view was becoming commonplace in Washington that Afghanistan had a "feckless, incompetent, corrupt government"; the coalition was treading water; Taliban assaults on towns, even when beaten back, were undermining a sense of security and confidence in the coalition and the government; and the insurgents were getting closer to Kabul. As concerned as I was about the course of the Afghan campaign, I complained at that September meeting about the bandwagon effect of pessimism, observing that in terms of perceptions, "this situation has gone from twilight to dark in six to eight weeks."

To change both the direction of events on the ground in Afghanistan and perceptions at home, we reviewed a number of options: a dramatic acceleration of the growth of the Afghan army; the pursuit of tribal engagement while avoiding the creation of warlords and militias and undermining the central government and army; leveraging competent local governors; providing development aid on the Pakistani side of the border; building commerce and other connections between Pashtuns on both sides of the border; concentrating our forces in those areas strategically most important—the south and east; and planning for a larger and longer-term U.S. troop commitment.

Just as in 2006, when the president decided things weren't working in Iraq, we ended up with reviews by at least three different organizations inside the administration on what to do in Afghanistan—one at State requested by Condi, several in Defense (the Joint Staff for the military, Eric Edelman's civilian policy unit in my office, Central Command, and probably others I didn't even know about), and the NSC review led by Doug Lute. The key effort was at the NSC, and the recommendations looked a lot like what I had discussed with my Defense colleagues in late September: President Bush described the outcome in his memoir as "a more robust counterinsurgency effort, including more troops and civilian resources in Afghanistan and closer cooperation with Pakistan to go after the extremists." Lute would lead a similar review a year later under Obama and come to very different conclusions.

Given that the administration literally had only weeks more in office, we debated whether to make the review public. Based on past experience, I thought anything publicly identified with the outgoing Bush administration would immediately be junked by a new administration. Everyone agreed that it was better to pass it along quietly. And so, with some 33,000 U.S. troops in-country, several thousand more en route, almost 31,000 coalition troops there, and the commander's pending request for another 20,000 troops or so, a troubled war in Afghanistan would be handed off to a new president. In December, Bush was prepared to approve the additional 20,000 troops, and Steve Hadley asked Obama's national security adviser–designate Jim Jones whether the new administration preferred that Bush make the troop decision (and take the heat) or hold off. The new team opted for the second course.

I made what was originally planned to be a farewell visit to the troops in Afghanistan on December 11, 2008. In comments to the press on the trip, I warned the incoming administration to be careful in carrying out a significant buildup in a country where the experience of foreign militaries "has not been a happy one. . . . I think there is a concern on the part of the Afghans that we sort of tell them what we're going to do, instead of taking proposals to them, and getting their input, and then working out with them what we're going to do. . . . This is their country, their fight, and their future." We too often lost sight of that and would suffer the consequences.

BUSH'S ENDGAME IN IRAQ

Although several different Democratic legislative efforts to change Bush's strategy in Iraq failed in September 2007, their criticism of the war did not flag; nor did their efforts to find new ways to get us out of there faster. There was now constant pressure to accelerate the troop drawdowns, and accusations that, despite the obviously improving security situation, the war was still a failure because the Iraqis weren't enacting laws necessary to advance political reconciliation. As our own economic crisis began, there were growing demands in Congress that the Iraqis pay more of the cost of the war. In September, Congress gave us only enough money to run the war for two months. In October, Senators Levin and Reid began an effort to have the Senate Appropriations Committee include language in our next funding bill calling for the withdrawal of most U.S. combat troops from Iraq within nine months of enactment of the legislation—and to give us only six months of funding. Such legislative maneuvering would continue for much of the following year, but I felt increasingly confident no legislation inhibiting our strategy would pass Congress while Bush was president.

During the fall months after the president's surge withdrawal announcement in September, even as the security situation continued to improve, we faced a number of Iraq-related problems both in Baghdad and in Washington. One was a blow-up over private security contractors (PSCs). As the contractor presence developed in Iraq after the original invasion, there was no plan, no structure, no oversight, and no coordination. The contractors' role grew willy-nilly as each U.S. department or agency contracted with them independently, their number eventually climbing to some 150,000. Out of some 7,300 security contractors Defense hired, nearly 6,000 did some kind of stationary guard duty.

The State Department, however, hired a large number to provide convoy security for diplomats, other government officials, special visitors, and some other civilians, and it was those hires who caused most of our headaches. As David Petraeus put it in one of our videoconferences, "They act like the Toad in *Wind in the Willows*—'out of my way!' " The behavior of some of those men was just awful, from killing Iraqi civilians in road incidents to roughly treating civilians. Obviously, their behavior undermined our efforts to win the trust and confidence of the Iraqis. I told Petraeus I felt strongly that everyone carrying a gun on our behalf in Iraq ought to be under his control, or at minimum, he should know what they were doing.

After some particularly egregious incidents in the summer and fall of 2007, there were growing demands from the Iraqis and from Congress (it took a lot to put those two on the same page) to bring these contractors under the supervision and coordination of State and Defense. This included a debate over whether to bring them under the jurisdiction of the military judicial system or the Justice Department. Turf issues between State and Defense, complicated by aggressive congressional involvement, made solving the matter much harder than it should have been. Secretary Rice and I on too many occasions had to untie bureau-cratic knots. There were months of negotiations on this issue, and we finally reached an agreement involving much closer State and Defense oversight of the contractors, coordination of their activities, and their placement under the jurisdiction of the military commander. The situation improved.

We also had to address the problem of Kurdish terrorists in northern Iraq crossing the border and killing Turkish officials, troops, and police. The Turks demanded that the Iraqi government stop this infiltration, even though Baghdad was helpless without the active cooperation of the leaders of Iraqi Kurdistan. The Turks launched a number of ground and air attacks across the border, and the situation was very close to getting out of hand. Petraeus worked hard to get the Turks to at least give us advance warning so we could ensure that Turkish and U.S. forces did not inadvertently clash, but Turkish notifications were haphazard and often after the fact. Some of the Turkish air strikes were very close to the Iranian border. On more than one occasion, the Iranians scrambled fighters to react, and one of our worries was that they might not be able to differentiate between Turkish and U.S. aircraft.

These incursions lasted for some months and included a major cross-border ground operation at the end of February 2008 that began just before I arrived for a visit in Ankara. The Turkish government was being assailed domestically for not being more aggressive. Nonetheless, my message was to stop the current operation, with its attendant risks, and get Turkish troops back across the border. When American report-ers with me asked if I thought the Turks had gotten my message, I said yes, "because they heard it four times." Our inability to help the Turks deal with the Kurdish terrorists, among other bilateral issues, led to a real downturn in the relationship that began to improve only when we provided some new ISR capabilities to help them monitor the border and target those terrorists with much more precision; when we persuaded the leadership in Kurdistan to cooperate better with the Turks; and when President Bush worked out a plan for broader cooperation with Turkish prime minister Recep Tayyip Erdogan.

One issue that caused a dispute within the administration in the fall of 2007 was what to do with five Iranian Quds Force officers we had captured in Iraq the preceding March. The Quds Force is a special unit of the Iranian Revolutionary Guards responsible for "extraterritorial operations." It reports directly to Ayatollah Khamenei. The leader of the group we captured, Qais Khazali, was a particularly bad guy who had been responsible for smuggling the lethal "explosively formed projectiles" and other arms into Iraq, training extremist Shia militias, forming death squads, fomenting sectarian violence, and carrying out kidnappings and assassinations. He also planned the attack in Karbala, Iraq, on January 20, 2007, in which five U.S. soldiers were murdered in cold blood. The Iranians obviously wanted these five Quds Force officers back very badly. They put great pressure on the Iraqi government, and within the Bush administration, some supported returning them. Among that group, much to my surprise, was Admiral Fallon, who told me he thought we ought to let the "Iranian hostages" go if we could get something for their release. I told him we had been approached by the Swiss to negotiate a deal, but that "I am not for it."

I told Petraeus in one of our regular videoconferences that the issue of release was being hotly debated in Washington. The Iranians apparently had made some sort of commitment to stem the tide of "illicit arms" flowing across the border, and Hadley and Lute were planning to take the question of releasing the Quds Force officers to the president. I told Petraeus there was a divide in the administration: Rice and Hadley wanted to "wring them dry" of information and then release them; Cheney and I wanted to keep them indefinitely. The issue would continue to come up from time to time, and while three of the five were released during the Bush administration, Qais Khazali was not released until January 2010, when he was exchanged for Peter Moore, a British computer consultant in Iraq kidnapped by the Quds Force. After what Khazali did to our soldiers at Karbala, I would never have let him go.

One of my more awkward moments as secretary arose during the fall of 2007, when the president promised Speaker Pelosi a copy of Petraeus's and Crocker's Joint Campaign Plan for Iraq—and I had to figure out a way to renege on his commitment. The issue grew out of a request Senator Clinton had made the previous May for our plans for drawing down in Iraq. Eric Edelman denied that request, which prompted the Democrats in Congress to rally around a request for our military plans in Iraq, a request that flew in the face of long-standing Defense Department denial to Congress of military and operational plans. This was another attempt to force the administration to commit to specific drawdown plans, regardless of conditions on the ground, which I thought irresponsible. Legislation had been introduced in the House in mid-July and in the Senate in early October requiring Defense to report regularly on the status of planning for redeployment of our forces from Iraq. A day after the Senate legislation was filed, I received a letter from the chairman of the House Armed Services Committee, Ike Skelton, urging me to begin the planning; he wanted to know what our "footprint" in Iraq would look like when the transition was complete, among other things, and insisted on detailed briefings.

I told Hadley we could not fulfill the president's commitment to provide the Joint Campaign Plan to Congress because of the precedent it would set. Over a period of weeks of tortuous negotiations with the Hill, we finally arrived at a compromise, through which I would send senior officers to brief congressional leaders on the key questions we would be addressing as we planned for the drawdowns.

In September, on Petraeus's recommendation, the president announced that, conditions on the ground permitting, all of the surge would be withdrawn from Iraq by midsummer 2008, a reduction of five combat brigades bringing us back to the presurge fifteen brigades. As a shield against pressure for faster and steeper drawdowns beyond that, I strongly endorsed Petraeus's proposal that the next review be in March, at which point he would present his recommendations for additional drawdowns during the second half of 2008. I even dangled a carrot in a press conference the day after the president's September speech. I said that I hoped Petraeus "will be able to say that he thinks the pace of drawdowns can continue at the same rate in the second half of the year as in the first half of the year"—in effect, suggesting a further drawdown to ten combat brigades, or about 100,000 U.S. troops, by the end of 2008. My strategy was to make the continuing reduction in our combat forces in Iraq unmistakable, in an attempt to keep Iraq from being a central issue in the presidential election. It would also provide the new president with political cover for a longer troop presence and a sustainable U.S. role in Iraq's future for the long term. I wanted to focus the Iraq debate on the pacing of drawdowns, a debate I thought the generals would win every time because it would be about battlefield conditions and the situation on the ground.

I felt strongly about a long-term U.S. troop commitment in Iraq for several reasons. Our presence could continue to play an important role in keeping sectarian conflict from boiling over again; we often mediated confrontations, especially between Arabs and Kurds. Our troops were also a deterrent to Iranian meddling. In this regard, a continuing U.S. military deployment in Iraq would also be reassuring to our friends in the region. There was a continuing need for U.S. participation in the counterterrorism mission and in training the Iraqis. And I did not want to put at risk all we had achieved at such great cost in lives by leaving a fledgling Iraqi government at the mercy of its neighbors and its internal divisions. More time was needed.

After the diversions of the fall, I met privately with Petraeus in Baghdad in December 2007, to discuss the March review and further drawdowns. On troop levels, I said, we shared the same objective but had different perspectives on time: he wanted the maximum possible number of troops in 2008 and early 2009. "I don't know if I can get to ten brigade combat teams [100,000 troops] by the end of 2008," he said. I was taking a longer view. I believed that a gradual but continuing reduction in force levels throughout 2008 was critical to getting political support at home for the longer-term presence: "If we end 2008 with thirteen to fifteen combat brigades in Iraq, I fear the next president will order everyone or nearly everyone out on a very short timeline, which will be highly destabilizing and possibly catastrophic." I told him I had noticed he "back-end loaded" the drawdowns in the first half of 2008 (he grinned sheepishly), that is, he had scheduled most withdrawals toward the end of the six-month period rather than spacing them out evenly. I asked if he couldn't do the same in the second half, even if he recommended in March that the drawdowns continue. I told him I intended the same decision-making process as the preceding September: he would make recommendations, as would Central Command, the Joint Chiefs, the chairman, and I. It would be great to be able to say again that all the senior military leaders agreed on the recommendations; if they didn't, the president would have to decide on the pacing.

I told Petraeus during our meeting that the president wanted him to remain in place until January 20, 2009. Petraeus said he would prefer to leave in the summer of 2008 and become commander of European Command (and supreme allied commander Europe). I said that I would try to arrange with the president to get him confirmed by the Senate for the Europe job in the summer if he would remain in Iraq until November.

When I talked with the president about my meeting with Petraeus, he mused that maybe we should keep the troop level at fifteen combat brigades but announce further reductions after the election "to force the new administration to follow our timetable." Observing that this would be an "unwelcome gift" if a Democrat was elected, Bush said, "You wouldn't believe what Clinton left for us." It was a refrain I would hear about Bush throughout my time in the Obama administration.

The president met with Petraeus in Kuwait on January 13, 2008, asking that his recommendations in March be strictly "conditions-based." Petraeus reported to me that the president shared his concerns about the strain on the force but again made his argument that the biggest blow to the military would be to lose in Iraq. The president, Petraeus said, told him that he would be fine if the U.S. force stayed at fifteen combat brigades "for some time"—a point the president later made to the press.

On January 29, I met alone with the president over breakfast to discuss drawdowns in Iraq. I told him I was focused on "setting the table" in both Iraq and Washington and trying to think forward at least a year. The critical question was how to preserve and expand our gains in Iraq while maximizing support at home for a sustainable long-term presence there. The challenge was that steps to do one could jeopardize the other, so how to find the right balance? I said our gains in Iraq were real but fragile. I was coming to believe that continuing the drawdowns in the second half of the year at the same pace as the first—the hope I had expressed the previous September—"may be too aggressive." At the same time, standing pat for the rest of the year at fifteen combat brigades would also be risky, signaling that the situation in Iraq had stopped improving. It would send the wrong message to both Iraqis and Americans and could have a potentially significant impact on the campaign debate in the United States and decisions after January 20, 2009. It would relieve both the military and political pressure on the Iraqis. Simultaneously, by making it look like we were staying as "occupiers," negotiation of the Strategic Framework and Status of Forces Agreements would be harder (the former would lay the foundation for future U.S.-Iraqi economic, political, and security cooperation; the latter would provide the legal basis for a U.S. military presence in Iraq over the longer term). Finally, no additional drawdowns would make it more likely that troop levels would fall off a cliff on January 20 if a Democrat was elected. I don't think the president had thought through these risks.

Pending Petraeus's recommendations, I said, the president might announce in April that we could take out "several" more combat brigades by January 2009. I urged him to consider one out in September–October and two more in late November–early December. This would allow us to keep fourteen combat brigades in Iraq until nearly the end of 2008, and a new president would be on a path to twelve brigades in Iraq on Inauguration Day. This would signal that things were getting better in Iraq and could forestall a precipitous withdrawal under a Democratic president.

The president said he would think about what I had said. Then he shocked me as the breakfast ended by saying that he wished he'd made the change in secretary of defense "a couple of years earlier." It was the only thing I ever heard him say even indirectly critical of Rumsfeld.

Before traveling to Iraq to continue the dialogue with Petraeus on troop drawdowns, I endured another hearing with the Senate Armed Services Committee. It continued my yearlong experience on the Hill of not a single Democrat having anything positive to say about the war in Iraq, even though Levin had publicly acknowledged the success of our military operations. Now Levin echoed the Pelosi-Reid theme that the surge had failed because it had not brought reconciliation among the Iraqi factions, a view disappointingly echoed by Senator Warner, the ranking Republican on the committee.

There was more discussion of possible legislation requiring increased time at home for the troops, a back-door political strategy to cut the number of troops that had been tried by Democrats but blocked by Senate Republicans the previous fall. Senators wanted to make sure the agreements we were negotiating with the Iraqis did not commit us to their defense, and Senator Edward Kennedy pushed for any agreements to be approved by Congress. After the hearing, Speaker Pelosi exploited Mullen's comment that the U.S. military was accepting significant risk by having so many troops deployed in Iraq and Afghanistan, saying that his testimony "confirms our warning that the war in Iraq has seriously undermined our nation's military strength and readiness" and that we needed "a new direction." There was no mention of Afghanistan. She was shameless and relentlessly partisan on the Iraq War. In fact, it was impossible to have a sensible discussion with Democrats in Congress on anything to do with Iraq in the presence of television cameras. I had never liked testifying; I was now beginning to really hate it. Every time someone in a hearing criticized the lack of reconciliation among Iraqi factions, I wanted to suggest the committee members get a mirror and take a long, hard look at themselves and maybe try a little reconciliation nearer to home. The posturing and partisanship were requiring me to exert more and more effort to be respectful, nonpartisan, and deliberative. January 20, 2009, seemed a long way off.

On February 11, I spent nearly two hours with Petraeus in Baghdad. I agreed that getting down to ten brigades before the end of the year was unwise militarily and also that a "pause" for "evaluation and consolidation" after the last surge brigade came out in July made sense. We agreed that the president should announce the pause in April and then, conditions permitting, resume the drawdown in the fall, giving Petraeus fourteen brigades through the end of the year. I said I would support keeping the "glide path" of withdrawals as modest as possible but that we had to keep drawing down. I told Dave I believed most Americans thought the war was a huge mistake and that a continued reduction in troops was key. I repeated my mantra about maintaining minimal public and congressional support for our long-term goals in Iraq. I thought Petraeus and I were on the same page.

On the plane ride home, I told the press aboard that I thought "the notion of a brief period of consolidation and evaluation probably does make sense." I was thinking of about forty-five days. My comments seemed to make nearly everyone mad. The White House was thinking of the pause in terms of months rather than weeks. Hillary Clinton said she was "disheartened" by what I said and called on the president "to end the war he started." Obama said he strongly disagreed with plans for a pause in the "long overdue removal of our combat brigades from Iraq." The chiefs weren't all that pleased either with my agreement to a pause. *The Washington Post*, on the other hand, editorialized that "at last, a Bush administration defense secretary listens to his commanders." And *USA Today* observed that "the success of the surge quiets the issue of Iraq in the election."

The day after I returned from Iraq, I passed along to the president what I thought would be Petraeus's recommendation, one I agreed with: an announcement by the president in early April of a pause for consolidation and evaluation, and resumption of a conditions-based drawdown in the fall. The plan was to announce on September 1 that another combat brigade was coming out and then at some point between October and early December announce that another one or two would come out.

That same evening I slipped on the ice and broke my shoulder, as

I mentioned earlier. I had been scheduled for a congressional hearing the next morning, which I could not attend. I had complained so much about hearings that some colleagues jokingly said I had purposely fallen just to avoid another "close encounter" with Congress. I received a very nice note from Ted Kennedy wishing me a quick recovery because "we need you my friend."

A little more than a week after senators trashed the Iraqis for inaction on key legislation (the pot calling the kettle black), the Iraqi Council of Representatives passed three significant pieces of legislation: a budget, a de-Baathification/amnesty law, and a provincial powers law. After months of deadlock, a grand bargain had been reached that had something for all the major factions. This was a vital step forward for the Iraqis and for our efforts to sustain support in the United States. Also in February, Lieutenant General Lloyd Austin replaced Ray Odierno as the corps commander in Iraq. Petraeus had been the primary architect of the new strategy in Iraq, but Ray had been instrumental in making it work on the ground and deserved great credit for its success. During one week that month fewer than five hundred violent incidents took place in Iraq for the first time since January 2006. In March, the command recorded the fourth-lowest number of incidents in a week since 2004. We still had very bad days—on March 10, five soldiers were killed by a deeply buried IED and a suicide bomber killed three more—but Petraeus was convinced that the insurgents were trying to crank up the violence in anticipation of his and Ambassador Crocker's congressional testimony in April.

As we approached the April decision point, Petraeus, the chairman, and I were talking every week, often more frequently. Dave gave us a preview of his recommendations in a videoconference on March 20. He said the postsurge mission would remain "security while transitioning." He spoke of a forty-five-day period of consolidation and evaluation beginning in mid-July, when we were down to fifteen combat brigades; moving two more brigades out by the end of the year; and removing a third just after the Inauguration.

I told Dave I thought the withdrawal of the first additional brigade as early in the process as conditions permitted would be helpful, as would a statement that we were going back to twelve-month deployments. "Trend lines and impressions are what count," I said. We should also make clear that "evaluation" is a continuous process; that is, we would not be withdrawing brigades if the situation in Iraq went to hell.

Just a few weeks before Petraeus's and Crocker's next appearance before Congress, Iraqi prime minister Maliki, frustrated and angered by Iranian-backed Shia extremist actions in Basra, ordered units of the Iraqi army into the city to reestablish control. The U.S. commanders were horrified that Maliki had taken such a risk without proper preparation. They scrambled to provide the logistics, planning, and military advice to support Maliki's effort; without such help, he almost certainly would have failed. But he didn't and therefore won significant recognition all across Iraq for acting like a "national" leader by suppressing his Shia brethren. The president told the chiefs, "We ought to say hurray to Maliki for going down to Basra and taking on the extremists." He characterized it as a "milestone event." "Maliki used to be a paralyzed neophyte—now he is taking charge." Bush was right.

In the same meeting where Bush expressed his opinion, he had a wide-ranging dialogue with the chiefs about Afghanistan and, independently, the health of our forces. Mullen observed that success in Iraq would allow a reallocation of forces to address competing demands, above all Afghanistan. "So is Iraq causing Afghanistan to fail?" Bush asked, not expecting—and not getting—an answer. The president asked about post-traumatic stress, and General Casey talked about the efforts under way to "de-stigmatize" it "from commanders on down." Bush ended by saying, "The worst thing for morale is if you have a president who is apologetic for the action and not confident that it was the right thing to do."

The congressional response to testimony by Petraeus and Crocker on April 8 and 9 was vastly different in both tone and substance from the preceding September. Petraeus spoke to the fragility of the security gains in Iraq and said that after the last surge brigade returned home during the summer, he had asked for a forty-five-day evaluation period, followed by an indefinite "assessment" period before making a recommendation on further troop drawdowns. On April 10, the president spoke to a veterans group, along with the Department of Defense civilian and military leadership and others, in the cross hall (the intersection between the north foyer and the hallway connecting the East Room and the State Dining Room) at the White House. He confirmed his approval to withdraw the last of five surge brigades from Iraq by July, and his strong support of Petraeus's request to halt further reductions until after a period of evaluation and assessment. The president said, "I've told him

[Petraeus] he'll have all the time he needs." He said the war was not "endless" and announced that all units deploying after August 1 would have twelve-month tours, not fifteen.

Mullen and I testified before the Senate Armed Services Committee a few hours after the president's statement. Petraeus naturally had wanted to err on the side of caution in terms of further drawdowns and the president wanted to support him. I described the halt in troop withdrawals as a "brief pause." "I do not anticipate this period of review to be an extended one, and I would emphasize that the hope, depending on conditions on the ground, is to reduce our presence further this fall." I said Petraeus would provide recommendations in that regard in September. The senators jumped on the difference between Petraeus's more open-ended period of evaluation and assessment and my characterization, and I responded, "One of the benefits of being the secretary of defense, I suppose, is that I'm allowed more to hope than the field commander is." My comments were portrayed as being at odds with—or contradictory to—both the president's and Petraeus's statements, and the truth is, they were, at least in tone. I was convinced we needed to keep the drawdown carrot dangling to lower the political temperature.

But my motives in staking out a more forward-leaning position were broader than that. As I've said, I was convinced a long-term U.S. military presence in Iraq was in our national interest. I believed that continued drawdowns in 2008 were critical to make that outcome politically possible after our elections. That meant keeping pressure on the president and Petraeus to continue the drawdowns while simultaneously resisting Democratic efforts to change the strategy even as I pressed them to support a long-term approach. I knew I was walking a political tightrope.

I ended my prepared statement at the hearing with a very personal one:

> I have eight months remaining in this position. We continue to find ourselves divided over the path forward in Iraq. . . . It was my hope sixteen months ago that I could help find a bipartisan path forward in our Iraq policy that would sustain a gradually much lower—but still adequate and necessary—level of commitment beyond this administration in Iraq [and] that would ensure [Iraq] is an ally against extremists and [able to] govern and defend itself. Now I fear that understandable frustration over slow progress and dismay over sacrifices already made

may result in decisions that are gratifying in the short term but very costly to us in the long term. We were attacked at home in 2001 from Afghanistan and are at war in Afghanistan today in no small measure because of mistakes we made—mistakes I, among others, made—in the endgame of the anti-Soviet war there. If we get the endgame wrong in Iraq, I predict the consequences will be far worse.

My comments notwithstanding, keeping the temperature down did not mean Iraq had disappeared as a campaign issue. After the president had spoken and Petraeus, Crocker, Mullen, and I had testified, Obama said, "There is no end in sight under the Bush policy. It is time to bring this war in Iraq to a close." And Hillary Clinton asserted, "It's time for the president to answer the question being asked of him: In the wake of the failed surge, what is the endgame in Iraq?"

A critical element of the "endgame" was the negotiation of a Strategic Framework Agreement (SFA) and Status of Forces Agreement (SOFA) with the Iraqi government. A successful SOFA—the legal basis for a continuing U.S. troop presence—negotiation was required during 2008 because at the end of the year the UN Security Council resolution authorizing our military presence in Iraq would expire. The Iraqis weren't interested in extending, or "rolling over," the resolution. Our negotiating team was led by Rice, Crocker, Brett McGurk of the NSC staff, and David Satterfield from State. Defense was represented on the team, and there was close coordination with both the department and Petraeus and his staff, but the military was more than happy to let State and the civilians do the heavy lifting in the negotiations. And it was heavy lifting. The obstacles to success were daunting, in substantial part because of the Iraqi political environment and strong opposition to any continuing U.S. presence in several quarters—above all, from the Iranian-supported Shia. Everyone soon realized the plan to sign the agreements on July 31 was completely unrealistic.

The forces agreement was clearly the more problematic, and I suggested that the more it looked like similar SOFA agreements we had with other countries, the more acceptable it would be to the Iraqis. I proposed we tell the Iraqis to talk to the South Koreans and Japanese about their experience with the SOFAs we had with them. That was a monumentally bad idea. Representatives of those countries shared with the Iraqis their frustrations about U.S. troops breaking local laws. Immunities for contractors would be difficult given the Iraqis' very unhappy experience with them. In a videoconference on February 5 with Mullen, Petraeus, Fallon, Edelman, and others, I set out the Defense Department priorities for the negotiations. Most important would be operational freedom of action (including legal protection for our troops) and keeping detainees (violent extremists we believed the Iraqis might release). "We could compromise on" contractors. The next day Edelman quoted Crocker as saying, with respect to protections for contractors, "This is radioactive and will blow up the SOFA."

By early summer, all avenues to our military remaining in Iraq seemed radioactive. I heard repeatedly that the SOFA "wasn't going to happen this year," the Iraqis hated the Coalition Provisional Authority decrees from 2003, and they hated the UN Security Council resolution. Without one of the three, we had no legal basis for our military remaining in Iraq after December 2008. Despite all the problems, by July 2008 both sides concurred we were close to agreement. The agreement would require us to withdraw our combat forces from Iraqi cities by mid-2009, with the timing of total withdrawal to be negotiated between Maliki and the president. Edelman told me, "This is as good as it is going to get," and Odierno said it was "enough to do the job."

In September, jurisdiction over Americans in uniform who broke Iraqi laws became an issue, as we tried to find the balance between assuring our troops that they would never end up at the mercy of Iraqi courts and assuring Iraqis that if someone committed a horrible crime, he could be tried in Iraq. In my last videoconference with Petraeus as commander in Iraq on September 9, I told him that Defense Department lawyers "are gagging" over the contemplated compromise and worried that it could impact other SOFA agreements elsewhere. Here, too, we found a compromise we could live with.

Petraeus told me an Iranian brigadier general had been arrested in Iraq for bribing legislators with $250,000 each to vote against the SOFA. Later in the fall, we learned that the head of the Iranian Quds Force, Major General Qassem Suleimani, had told President Talabani that Iraq should not sign any agreement with Bush.

The same day I talked to Petraeus, September 9, the president announced that another 8,000 troops would come home by February 2009 thanks to the continuing decline in violence. The next day Mike Mullen and I testified before Congress. I said that we had now entered the endgame in Iraq and it was important to get that right. I urged our political leaders to be cautious and flexible and take into account the advice of our senior commanders and military leaders. I said "to keep in mind that we should expect to be involved in Iraq for years to come, although in changing and increasingly limited ways."

On September 16, 2008, Ray Odierno took Petraeus's place as commander of the multinational force in Iraq. Immediately before the change of command ceremony, I promoted Ray to full general, a ceremony carried out in the headquarters videoconference room at Al-Faw palace in Baghdad so his wife and family could watch at the Pentagon in the middle of the night. I Velcroed Odierno's four-star patch onto the front of his fatigues and then, out of the corner of my eye, saw him discreetly remove the patch and re-Velcro it right side up.

While in Iraq for the change of command, I met with Maliki. He expressed his worry that if we were unable to reach agreement on the SOFA and the U.S. forces left, "the situation here would be very complicated. We need American forces here, at least for a while. If they leave, we lose all of our successes and accomplishments." He said that it was in Iraq's interest to have U.S. forces in Iraq and "to have a long-term relationship." In fact, all the key Iraqi leaders wanted the agreements; it was just that no one wanted to be the first to say so publicly.

On November 3, the day before the U.S. presidential election, I attended a meeting at the White House to try to wrap up the agreements. The Iraqis had made 120 suggested changes, of which there were three or four important issues. We made some adjustments and a few days later sent the agreement to the Iraqis one last time. The negotiating process was over as far as the United States was concerned. Both the Strategic Framework Agreement and the Status of Forces Agreement were signed on November 17, 2008, by Ambassador Crocker and Iraqi foreign minister Hoshyar Zebari in Baghdad. The SOFA required U.S. combat forces to withdraw from all Iraqi cities and villages by June 30, 2009, and for the removal of all U.S. forces by December 31, 2011. In Baghdad, on December 14, 2008, President Bush and Prime Minister Maliki signed the agreements.

As I watched the signing ceremony on television, I felt a great sense of relief. Considering the dire circumstances we faced in Iraq at the end of 2006, we had come a long way. The security situation in Iraq had improved dramatically, and while Iraqi politics were messy, and would remain that way, the factions were debating their differences, not shooting at one another. The path toward ending U.S. military involvement in Iraq was set, but thanks to the agreements, we would have three more years to help stabilize the country and work with its military. The end of the U.S. military combat role in Iraq would not be a calamitous failure or defeat but rather a handover to a democratically elected government with a U.S.-trained military. In December 2008 and thereafter, I believed we should and would have a residual military presence in Iraq after the end of 2011 to partner with the Iraqis in counterterrorism and in training their forces, even though that would require a follow-on agreement with the Iraqis.

Given how difficult the negotiations on the SOFA had been in 2008, and the near failure then of the Iraqi legislature to approve it, I should have been more realistic about the challenges we would face in getting Iraqi approval for a post-2011 U.S. military presence. For many Iraqis, we would always be seen as invaders and occupiers, not as liberators. Like us or not, though, we had given them a much different—and brighter— future, though at a very high cost for Iraqis and for Americans.

Inwardly, I was also proud of what had been accomplished on the battlefield that was Washington, D.C., since January 2007. Petraeus had told me the surge needed to last until January 2008; the last surge troops left Iraq in July 2008. Every effort by Congress to reverse or limit the surge, or to accelerate the rate of withdrawal, or to impose conditions on the Iraqis (and the president) had failed.

As the saying goes, success has many fathers, and that is certainly true of the turnaround in Iraq in 2007–8. Among them were the president, for his courageous shift in strategy and the surge; our military commanders and troops, whose skill, steadfastness, and sacrifice made success possible; U.S. civilian officials, including above all Ambassador Ryan Crocker; the Republican minority in the Senate, who, under great pressure, resisted all attempts to thwart what we were trying to do; and the sheikhs of Anbar and the many other Iraqis who at great risk and sacrifice worked to bring a better future to their country.

A new president would not confront significant problems in Iraq, at least for several years. But he would face a deteriorating war in Afghanistan. As Mike Mullen had testified on September 10, we were not winning in Afghanistan, "but I am convinced we can." Barack Obama assumed the presidency committed publicly to do just that.

CHAPTER 7

One Damn Thing After Another

Amid two major wars and myriad other national security challenges, I also had to deal with countless institutional issues at the Defense Department. Some were deadly serious and required dramatic actions; some were nuisances; some were mildly amusing. Many had significant political ramifications.

THE AIR FORCE

During the Bush administration, the Air Force, the branch of the military in which I had served briefly as a junior officer, was one of my biggest headaches. I thought the service did a superb job in Iraq and Afghanistan providing close air support, medevac, and transport as well as ordnance (IED) disposal and performing other important and often dangerous tasks on the ground. Earlier, I described my frustration in trying to get the Air Force leadership to provide more drones for intelligence, surveillance, and reconnaissance use in the wars. But there were other problems as well.

The most significant related to the Air Force's responsibility for our nuclear-armed bombers and intercontinental ballistic missiles. On August 30, 2007, a B-52 bomber took off from Minot Air Force Base in North Dakota at 8:40 a.m. carrying six air-launched cruise missiles, each armed with a nuclear weapon capable of explosive power more than ten times that of the atomic bomb dropped on Hiroshima. The plane landed at Barksdale Air Force Base in Louisiana at 11:23 a.m. It was parked there without any of the stringent security measures required for such weapons. At ten that evening, a member of the munitions crew at Barksdale discovered that the warheads were not mock training rounds but actual nuclear weapons that had been loaded in error. Only then was the incident reported to the National Military Command Center (NMCC) as a "Bent Spear" event—"an incident involving nuclear weapons, warheads, components or vehicles transporting nuclear material of significant interest." Air Force chief of staff General Mike Moseley reported the incident to me on August 31. I was incredulous at such a monumental screw-up. I immediately called Hadley and the president to inform them. With a justified edge to his voice, Bush told me to get to the bottom of this mistake and to keep him informed. The initial incident report from the NMCC stated, "No press interest anticipated." Wrong.

The Air Force immediately conducted an inventory to ensure that all its other nuclear weapons were accounted for, then launched an investigation. On October 19, Secretary of the Air Force Michael Wynne announced its findings, among them: "There has been an erosion of adherence to weapons-handling standards at Minot Air Force Base and at Barksdale Air Force Base." The Air Force relieved three colonels and four senior noncommissioned officers of their commands or positions. As with the outpatient treatment scandal at Walter Reed, I wondered why the disciplinary measures had been limited solely to midlevel officers and whether ultimate responsibility for that "erosion" belonged higher up the chain of command. Accordingly, I asked former Air Force chief of staff General Larry Welch (retired), a member of the Defense Science Board (an advisory board appointed by the president), to lead a board panel to study the incident as part of a broader examination of procedures and policies for handling nuclear weapons. He briefed his conclusions to the Senate Armed Services Committee on February 12, 2008: "The military units responsible for handling the bombs are not properly inspected and, as a result, may not be ready to perform their missions. . . . If you look at all the areas and all the ways that we have to store and handle these weapons in order to perform the mission, it just requires, we believe, more resources and more attention than they're getting." Structural changes combining nuclear and nonnuclear organizations had produced "markedly reduced levels of leadership whose daily focus is the nuclear enterprise and a general devaluation of the nuclear mission and those who perform the mission." At no time was the public in danger from the weapons—even had the plane crashed—but Welch's conclusions pointed to serious problems in the Air Force's management of its nuclear responsibilities.

I allowed the Air Force to determine what disciplinary measures and organizational changes were needed as a result of this incident. I should have reacted more forcefully when I received Welch's report.

On March 21, five weeks after Welch's testimony, I was informed that two days earlier a Taiwanese military officer had told his U.S. security assistance contact that four ICBM warheads had been discovered in a shipment the Taiwanese had received sometime before. U.S. military representatives immediately inspected the shipment and found four Minuteman ICBM nose cones ("forward assemblies") with associated electronics, and took custody of the container. (There were no nuclear weapons in the shipment.) The container was mislabeled, carrying the stock number for batteries. In August 2006, the Taiwanese had placed an order for U.S. military helicopter batteries, and when the shipment was received, it was placed in storage without being opened. When it was opened nearly two years later, the Taiwanese recognized the missile nose cones and contacted U.S. authorities.

Coming on the heels of the Bent Spear incident, it was clear that all hell was going to break loose. My staff and the multiple organizations in the Pentagon involved worked through the weekend trying to determine what had happened. I called the leadership of the Armed Services and Appropriations Committees on the twenty-fourth to inform them, and the Chinese ambassador was put in the picture by Defense at five p.m. the same day. We were very sensitive to the possibility that our mistake would be misconstrued or misinterpreted by the Chinese, and I wanted to do everything possible to underscore that it was a mistake, not a covert scheme to arm Taiwan with nuclear weapons. Throughout, I wanted complete transparency.

I had not pursued General Welch's concerns aggressively enough initially, and I would not make that mistake a second time. Because all our bombers carrying nuclear weapons and all our ICBMs are the responsibility of the Air Force, I wanted an independent non–Air Force officer to lead the inquiry. And so, I asked Admiral Kirkland Donald, the head of the Navy's nuclear programs, to "conduct an investigation into the facts and circumstances surrounding the accountability for, and shipment of, sensitive missile components provided to the Government of Taiwan on or around August 2006." I gave the admiral a sweeping mandate for the investigation and asked him for recommendations not only in terms of improvements in policies and procedures but also in terms of holding "accountable anyone at any level . . . who failed to perform his or her duties and responsibilities properly." I asked for his report as soon as possible but in no more than sixty days. That same day I directed the secretaries of the Air Force and Navy and the director of the Defense Logistics Agency (the support organization that had handled the shipment to Taiwan) to inventory all nuclear and nuclear-related materials held by their respective departments.

Admiral Donald gave me his preliminary report on April 15, reporting that nothing nefarious had taken place and that there was no evidence the Taiwanese had accessed or tampered with the nose cones. I asked him whether the standards of accountability had become lax over time. I recalled for him, and he heard me out patiently, that however briefly, I had been in the Strategic Air Command in the 1960s—General Curtis LeMay's SAC—when discipline and accountability standards were very high. At any SAC bomber or missile base at any time in those days, a planeload of inspectors from SAC headquarters in Omaha might arrive without prior notice and take the unit apart piece by piece. Failure to pass one of these Operational Readiness Inspections almost always led to the unit commander being fired. It seemed to me, I told Donald, that those standards were no longer maintained in the Air Force nuclear mission. Accompanied by General Cartwright, I briefed the president on Donald's preliminary conclusions the next day.

Donald's final conclusions confirmed that the safety, security, and reliability of our nuclear arsenal were solid. But as I said in a news conference shortly thereafter, his report made clear that there had been an "overall decline in Air Force nuclear weapons stewardship, a problem . . . not effectively addressed for over a decade. Both the Minot-Barksdale nuclear weapons transfer incident and the Taiwan misshipment . . . have a common origin: the gradual erosion of nuclear standards and a lack of effective oversight by the Air Force leadership."

The Defense Department and the Air Force and Navy must ensure the absolute safety and secure stewardship of the nation's nuclear arsenal. There is no room for error. For the American people, allies, potential adversaries—the whole efficacy of deterrence depends upon the perfect performance of that stewardship. The Donald report and its sobering conclusions required immediate and dramatic action to make clear that the deficiencies he identified would not be tolerated and that correcting them would become the top priority of the Air Force leadership and that of the Department of Defense. Donald already had identified nine generals (seven Air Force, two Army) and eight colonels who he thought should be held accountable.

For a problem of this magnitude, I decided I had to go higher, dismissing both Secretary Wynne and General Moseley. I consulted with Admiral Mullen, Gordon England, and General Cartwright. Mullen sent me an e-mail on June 2 in which he observed that "the decline in the nuclear mission in the Air Force is representative and symptomatic of a greater decline, for which I can tie responsibility directly to the two most senior leaders. . . . I believe our Air Force leadership has to be held accountable." Cartwright, who had special expertise on this issue because of his past leadership of Strategic Command, agreed. So did the president.

I have always believed that firing someone or asking for a resignation should be carried out face-to-face by the one making the decision. (The only two presidents I had worked for who were willing to do this were Ford and Carter.) I had to violate this principle for the first—and only—time in the case of Wynne and Moseley because of a leak. They were both at an Air Force conference at Wright-Patterson Air Force Base in Ohio, and I asked Gordon England, who was traveling west that day, to stop and talk to Wynne. I asked Mike Mullen to talk to Moseley. I took no pleasure from the dismissals. I enjoyed working with both men, but I didn't believe they really understood the magnitude of the problem or how dangerous it could be.

The simultaneous firing of both the service secretary and the service chief predictably stunned the Air Force, the rest of the department, and Washington. But there were no dire repercussions. There would later be allegations that I fired the two of them because of their foot-dragging on ISR, or more commonly, because we disagreed on whether to build more F-22 combat aircraft, or on other modernization issues. But it was the Donald report alone that sealed their fate.

At a press conference, I announced that I had asked former secretary of defense and energy and former CIA director Jim Schlesinger to lead a senior-level task force to recommend improvements to ensure that "the highest levels of accountability and control are maintained in the stewardship and operation of nuclear weapons and related materials and systems across the entire Department of Defense." The Schlesinger panel identified further problems, including neglect in the Office of the Secretary of Defense. I believe the Air Force gave nuclear issues too low a priority. It had been at war in the skies over Iraq for seventeen years and over Afghanistan for seven. After the end of the Cold War, I believe the nuclear mission became a second-class citizen in the Air Force, a backwater starved of proper resources and the best people. The later focus on the wars in Iraq and Afghanistan compounded the problem. It would be vital for the new secretary and chief of staff to correct that.

After I announced recommended replacements for those jobs, I left Washington to visit three Air Force bases, where I wanted to explain my decisions to airmen and give them a chance to ask questions or just vent. I have always felt it important, after making a tough, or especially, a controversial decision, to be willing to meet face-to-face with those most affected. At Langley Air Force Base in Virginia, headquarters of Air Combat Command, the airmen, fighter pilots, and those who support them were respectful but cool. Their questions were thoughtful: What is the balance between current and future threats? How much drone capability do you intend to buy? A fighter wing commander asked about procuring more F-22s and whether the focus was too much on "the here and now versus future threats." Why wasn't it more widely known how much the Air Force was doing in the current wars? What other priorities should the new Air Force leadership have to make sure they were "playing as well with others as you would like"? Above all, the session with hundreds of airmen gave me a chance to explain the firings firsthand. Woody Allen has said that 90 percent of life is just showing up. I felt that just showing up at Langley demonstrated my respect for those who probably most vigorously disagreed with my decision on Wynne and Moseley.

The reception at Peterson Air Force Base in Colorado Springs and at headquarters of Air Force Space Command was better, but the warmest reception was at Scott Air Force Base in Illinois, headquarters of Air Mobility Command and Transportation Command, the latter led by General Norton Schwartz, who I had announced would be nominated to be the new Air Force chief of staff. These were the airmen who flew troops and equipment all over the world, and Schwartz was one of them. When I mentioned his name, there was a huge burst of applause. At all three bases, though, most of the questions were about current and future priorities. As was not the case in Washington, their eyes were on the mission, not on personalities.

The firing of Moseley and Wynne led to one of the most awkward moments of my life. I received an invitation from Wynne to attend his farewell ceremony at the Air Force Memorial on June 20. I sought assurances that Mike genuinely wanted me to attend; he wasn't just following protocol. Even though I knew it would be an uncomfortable situation, I agreed to attend and speak. When I arrived, Moseley and Wynne and their wives greeted me. My experience has always been that spouses take actions like mine much harder than do their husbands, and that certainly proved to be the case here. Everyone was respectful, but if looks could kill, I'd have been a goner. Wynne, Moseley, and I marched out to three big leather chairs in front of bleachers filled with Wynne's family and friends. There was a lot of quiet murmuring about what the hell I was doing there, and I could feel the daggers pointed in my direction. As the ceremony went on, I kept waiting for a child to come up to me and give me a good kick in the shin and ask if I was the jerk who had fired his grandpa. I swore I would never put myself in that position again.

To my surprise, Schwartz's nomination proved difficult with Congress. Congressman Mike Rogers of Michigan called Schwartz to say he believed the general had misled him in 2003–4 as then-director of the Joint Staff when Rogers complained about unprotected arms caches in Iraq. He said he intended to so inform the White House and his congressional colleagues. A few weeks later Senator Levin told me we needed to meet early the following week to discuss the Schwartz nomination. I immediately agreed.

The meeting took place in my office on July 28 and included Senators Levin and Warner, Mike Mullen, and me. Senators coming to the Pentagon to discuss a nomination was highly unusual, if not unprecedented, at least in my experience, and the stuff of high Washington drama. They said there were concerns about Schwartz's forthrightness. Specifically, at a hearing on February 25, 2003, General Eric Shinseki, Army chief of staff, had famously testified that hundreds of thousands of troops would be needed after the invasion of Iraq. Schwartz, then a three-star general assigned to the Joint Staff, testified the next day that the number of troops would depend upon the circumstances—for example, whether the post-Saddam Iraqi army was helpful. He did not reveal that Rumsfeld had specifically given instructions that no one testifying should speculate on troop numbers.

Levin told me he thought Schwartz's answer had been evasive. He went on to say that Senator Bill Nelson of Florida was concerned about Schwartz's candor on several occasions between February and October 2003. He added that Senator Saxby Chambliss thought Schwartz wasn't strong enough for the job, a view shared by others. He said Schwartz needed to come up and testify again the next day and that Mullen and I needed to meet in executive session with the committee later the same day. No such meeting had taken place within the memory of anyone involved. On the twenty-ninth, prior to that session, Levin and Warner met with Shinseki to discuss the numbers debate in 2003, which the general said had been "all over the place." He also quietly told both senators that Schwartz would make a good chief of staff of the Air Force. Warner called to tell me about the meeting.

The executive session began at about five-thirty p.m. in a large conference room with the same configuration as the usual hearing room, the senators at a large U-shaped table, Mike and I at a small table some distance away. There were fifteen or sixteen senators, limited staff, and no press. Levin began by reading a long excerpt of Schwartz's testimony in 2003 and raising the issue of candor. Warner described the meeting with Shinseki, leaving out the retired general's endorsement of Schwartz. Levin then asked us to comment.

I was inwardly steaming. I did not believe for a second that Schwartz had tried to mislead anyone in 2003 and felt that the senators, especially Levin, at that time had placed him in an impossible position, in essence demanding that a staff officer offer an opinion on a matter over which he had no decision-making authority and had specifically been instructed not to speculate—all to score political points against Rumsfeld and the president. For Schwartz's sake, I curbed my anger and matter-of-factly came to his defense. I gave the senators my personal assurance that no one would be more forthcoming and candid with them than Schwartz. I told them I had led several very large institutions and had hired and fired a lot of people, had confidence in my judgment of people, and was confident Schwartz was the best man for the job. I added that not to confirm him would be a disaster for the Air Force, that the bench was thin and there was no obvious alternative. On the question of evasiveness in 2003, I said they needed to consider the context of the time, the fact that the troop numbers were changing constantly and that there had been no final decision by either the secretary or the president. Admiral Mullen was also strong in his defense of Schwartz's integrity, reinforcing my comments. After the two-hour session ended, Levin told me that Schwartz's nomination would have failed without the meeting.

Schwartz, Mike Donley as secretary, and General Duncan McNabb as the new commander of Transportation Command were confirmed on August 1. A few days later I received a note from Senator Warner praising Mullen's and my efforts on behalf of Schwartz. The whole affair left a very bad taste in my mouth nonetheless. Schwartz, a good man, had unnecessarily been put through a wringer. Politically motivated senators should have been put in the dock, not Schwartz.

There were two other episodes involving the Air Force that took a lot of my time during 2008. The most difficult was the effort to select the contractor to build a new tanker aircraft for the Air Force. The two competitors were Boeing and a partnership of Northrop Grumman and Europe's EADS/Airbus, and each had a support team in Congress from the states where the planes would be built. The Boeing team was comprised of members of the congressional delegations from Washington, Kansas, and, to a lesser extent, Missouri; the Airbus team was principally from Alabama. The contract was to build 179 tanker aircraft valued at $35 billion. It was the service's highest acquisition priority. Originally the contract had been awarded to Boeing in an unusual leasing arrangement, but irregularities mooted the decision. The Boeing CEO and CFO resigned and at least one senior civilian Air Force official went to jail for handling the contract bid while simultaneously seeking employment with Boeing. The egregious problems were exposed by a corruption investigation pushed by Senator McCain, who went on the warpath against the Air Force. On December 1, 2006, even before my confirmation hearing, McCain asked me to explain to him how I would ensure that the tanker competition would be conducted "fully, fairly, and transparently." When the contract was finally awarded to the Northrop/Airbus team in February 2008, it was protested by Boeing. The General Accounting Office issued a report in mid-June identifying 111 minor and major problems with the contracting process—half a dozen or so of real significance. Six days later I received a handwritten note from Jack Murtha, chairman of the House Defense Appropriations Subcommittee, with a straightforward statement: "You need to get rid of the AF acquisition team."

On July 9, I announced a limited rebid of the tanker contract that would be overseen not by the Air Force but by the undersecretary of defense for acquisition, logistics, and technology, John Young. Two months later, on September 10, I told Congress that I was terminating the tanker rebid because it had "become clear that the solicitation and award cannot be accomplished by January. Thus, I believe that rather than hand the next administration an incomplete and possibly contested process, we should cleanly defer this procurement to the next team."

I didn't think it appropriate or wise to try to award a contract of this size and sensitivity in the final days of an outgoing administration, especially because the contract had become the most politically explosive and emotional procurement I had ever seen. Each company bought full-page ads to try to persuade the department and Congress that it should be awarded the contract—ads I suspected we would end up paying for as part of the overhead charges in the competition. Members of Congress were outrageous in their claims and pressures, with Boeing supporters pushing "buy American" legislation—even though most of the Airbus planes eventually would have been built in Alabama by American workers—and pointing to Airbus's unfair advantage because of subsidies from European governments. Airbus accused Boeing of unfair practices in the failure of the first two contract awards. At one hearing, one of my staff was walking behind Senator Patty Murray of Washington and noticed that no one had bothered to remove the Boeing letterhead from her talking points. Both companies, and supporters of both in Congress, were all, in my view, reprehensible in the tactics and distortions they employed to drive the Defense Department to a decision in their favor. There was so much heat and so little light in the debate that I thought a cooling-off period would be beneficial. And so I punted the contract decision to my successor. To my great dismay, I would end up receiving my own punt.

A very different kind of Air Force–related issue came up in the spring of 2008, a time when I was preoccupied with drawdowns in Iraq, conflict with the chiefs over the National Military Strategy and "next-war-itis," growing concern over Afghanistan, and the Air Force's reluctance to expand its ISR efforts aggressively.

When it comes to the treatment of the remains of American servicemen and women killed in combat, no two places are more sensitive or more sacred than the mortuary at Dover Air Force Base and Arlington National Cemetery. Perfection in performance is expected at both, and both have been involved in recent years in inexcusable errors and lapses in judgment. The first of these lapses to come to my attention was at Dover. The remains of uniformed Americans who die overseas are flown to Dover AFB in Delaware, where the Air Force conducts autopsies for all the services and prepares the remains for onward transportation for burial. It is a solemn responsibility.

The morning of May 9 my senior military assistant, Pete Chiarelli, received an e-mail from an Army lieutenant colonel who, at the request of a fallen soldier's wife, had met his transfer case (casket) when it arrived at Dover. He wrote Chiarelli that the transfer from the plane had not been particularly dignified and that he had then followed the transfer vehicle carrying the remains of the soldier to an off-base crematorium that was marked as a pet crematorium. While he said there were separate facilities for pet and human remains, there was no indication of that on the exterior of the building. Chiarelli soon learned that the mortuary staff at Dover had contracted with a company that ran a local pet crematorium to cremate the remains of some seventy-five servicemen. There had never been any mixing of human and pet remains.

We had to act fast to fix this problem to prevent a huge public outcry. Beyond the facilities issue, when a number of the remains had been delivered to the crematorium, no U.S. military personnel stood vigil and ensured their dignified handling, which was contrary to policy. Cremations were stopped at this facility immediately, and new contracts signed with civilian mortuaries in the area. In each case, a uniformed military escort would stand vigil during the cremation. And the Air Force decided to build its own crematorium at the base. We informed the press of what had happened the evening of the same day we learned about it, along with the remedial measures, and our transparency was favorably reported. Unfortunately, this would not be the last problem at Dover.

OTHER CHALLENGES

In the winter of 2007–8, I was dealing with hot spots all around the world: Iraq, Iran, Afghanistan, Pakistan, North Korea, Russia, China, Venezuela, and the Israeli-Palestinian conflict. My days were filled with problems of mind-boggling variety. For example, sandwiched between my visit to Russia and meetings with the Israeli and Afghan defense ministers, on October 15, 2007, a Patriot missile at the U.S. base in Qatar was accidently fired during a training exercise and landed several miles away, in the backyard of the Qatari chief of defense, a general who had been incredibly kind to U.S. soldiers, opening his estate for recreational purposes. Fortunately, no one was hurt. *How the hell does a Patriot missile just go off?* I asked my staff rather rudely. I said all questions should be directed to Central Command.

Mike Mullen brought me a more serious challenge on January 10, 2008, when he informed me that a U.S. satellite was falling. While there was a 10 percent or less chance of it landing in a populated area, it carried a toxic propellant, hydrazine, that was a threat to humans. Over the next several weeks, Strategic Command, under the leadership of General Kevin Chilton, developed options for shooting down the satellite because of the hydrazine. Chilton briefed President Bush on the plans. If we used one SM-3 missile launched from an Aegis destroyer, the odds of success were estimated at 79 percent; using two missiles, the odds were 91 percent. The president approved shooting down the satellite (the operation was dubbed Burnt Frost) and delegated the decision and timing to me. The optimal window for the launch was February 20, when I was aboard the E-4B on my way to Asia. I had a final conversation with Generals Cartwright and Chilton from the plane about 1:40 p.m. my time, and after discussing weather issues and deciding to say nothing publicly until after the shot, I gave the go-ahead. The missile was launched about two and a half hours later and destroyed the tumbling satellite. General Cartwright gave the press the details; there was no debris larger than a football, and the likelihood that the propellant tank was destroyed was "very good." It was an impressive display of the capability of the SM-3 missile, a key component of our missile defense system. When I landed in Canberra, my Australian counterpart said, "Nice shot, Bob."

I devoted a lot of time during the Bush administration to trying to figure out how to close the detention center at Guantánamo Bay. My first major decision relating to the facility was shortly after I became secretary. In 2006, the Pentagon had asked for congressional approval to spend $102 million on a court complex at Gitmo for trying the detainees. The complex was to include two courtrooms, conference and meeting facilities, and housing for twelve hundred people. I directed that the proposal be killed and that plans be prepared for a temporary facility at about a tenth of the cost.

By 2007 the detention center had become almost luxurious, with exercise equipment including elliptical trainers, television rooms, reading rooms with literature and magazines in Arabic and other languages, and extraordinarily professional and well-trained prison guards. But due to highly publicized photographs of the initial rough conditions and reports of abusive interrogations of several high-value detainees during its first year in operation, Guantánamo still carried enormous negative baggage politically around the world. President Bush and Condi Rice had both said publicly that they would like to see it closed. I did as well.

The challenge all along was that some of the prisoners at Guantánamo were declared enemies of the United States who made it quite clear that, if released, they would like nothing better than to kill more Americans. They therefore could not be released. If Guantánamo were closed, where would they be sent? Secretary Rice and I, in conversations with both the president and Attorney General Alberto Gonzales in January 2007, urged that the prison be closed and suggested that perhaps the prisoners could be moved to military facilities in the United States, where they would remain in military custody and subject to military judicial proceedings. Cheney and Gonzales disliked that idea, with government lawyers arguing that bringing the prisoners to the United States could give them significant additional rights under the Constitution. Rice's and my initiative went nowhere. I did not share with my Bush administration colleagues the letter of praise for these efforts that I received from the executive director of the American Civil Liberties Union. As Bush 41 would say, Wouldn't be prudent.

At a hearing on May 20, 2008, Senator Dianne Feinstein asked me for a progress report on Guantánamo. "The brutally frank answer is that we're stuck and we're stuck in several ways," I said. Some detainees were ready to be sent home, but their governments didn't want them or could not guarantee their safekeeping. (A recent suicide bomber in Mosul had been a released detainee.) In Congress, there was a "not in my backyard" mentality with regard to moving the worst of the worst to military or civilian prisons in the United States.

The last effort inside the Bush administration to close Guantánamo was during the summer of 2008, after a Supreme Court decision knocked down the administration's position with respect to detainee rights, including denying them habeas corpus. There were two meetings in the latter half of June in the Roosevelt Room at the White House, the president's day-to-day conference room. It has several paintings of both Franklin and Theodore Roosevelt and the latter's Nobel Peace Prize medal, as well as the flags of the military services with historic battle streamers dating back to the Revolution. Chief of Staff Josh Bolten chaired the meetings, attended by Rice, Attorney General Mike Mukasey (who had replaced Gonzales the preceding November), me, the FBI director, a number of White House staff, including some from the vice president's office, and more lawyers than I could count. We went around and around on the implications of the Supreme Court decision, the legal complications of bringing detainees to the United States, the administration's losing streak in the courts, and the politics of the issue. Rice and I were the only two in the meetings who argued for an aggressive effort to get legislation that would permit us to close the prison. Some on the White House staff, such as the communications director, Ed Gillespie, were concerned how the Republican base would react and asked how we could protect the American people if we closed Gitmo. I responded that they should forget the politics and let the president seize a historic initiative.

Condi and I lost the argument, and the problem of closing the prison at Guantánamo would fall to the next president. He would find the challenge just as daunting. On October 20, 2008, I directed the Pentagon to begin contingency planning to close Gitmo if the new president was to order it on taking office in January. I said the planning should include legislative remedies to the risks posed by closing the facility, examination of the Navy brig in Charleston, South Carolina, as an alternative, and identifying the two or three safeguards we would need in legislation as we figured out what to do with the detainees.

Piracy and the effort to ban cluster munitions (weapons that eject multiple explosive bomblets designed to kill troops or destroy vehicles) consumed considerable time during the last months of the Bush administration. The munitions were widely used by the Soviets in Afghanistan, by U.S. forces along the Korean demilitarized zone, and by the Israelis against Hizballah in 2006. The United States had become increasingly isolated internationally on the cluster munitions issue, refusing to sign on to an international ban. At the end of June, the White House saw this as a burgeoning public relations problem and wanted me to speak out in defense of the munitions and why they were important. In a meeting, I said, "So you want me to be the poster boy for cluster munitions?" Cheney, with a bit of a smile, said, "Yes, just like I was with torture and Hadley was with land mines!" Steve told me he wanted to be able to tell the president that I had personally looked into this and believed that the munitions were vitally important.

I consulted with senior leaders at the Pentagon. Mike Mullen said cluster munitions were very important, very effective weapons. Eric Edelman said there was broad interagency agreement that the munitions had utility and that 90 percent of casualties from unexploded munitions are from conventional bombs. Banning cluster bombs therefore would increase the risk of innocent casualties because we would need to use more conventional bombs. The Marine commandant, General James T. Conway, observed that North Korea, Russia, Iran, and India all had cluster munitions and none would sign an agreement banning them. Our solution was to develop cluster munitions that would automatically deactivate after a certain time. We committed to replacing 99 percent of our cluster munitions over a ten-year period.

As for piracy, it had been a growing problem for years in the Strait of Malacca, between Indonesia, Malaysia, and Singapore, through which a huge percentage of global seaborne commerce passes. We had worked with those three governments, and over time they greatly reduced the level of piracy. But pirates operating out of Somalia became increasingly emboldened as they encountered little opposition either from the ships they seized and held for ransom or from local or international forces. Also, they lived and recruited in areas of Somalia where there was no governance, and no foreign country—especially the United States—would send military forces to clean out the nests. As we spent more and more time in the Situation Room trying to figure out how to resolve the problem, Condi at one point exclaimed, "Pirates? Pirates? For God's sake, the last American secretary of state to deal with pirates was Thomas Jefferson!" Over time the international community, led by NATO, assembled a substantial naval force in the region, including both Chinese and Russian navy ships, and shipowners began using more aggressive techniques to keep the pirates from boarding—removing ladders, using hoses, arming the crews, placing security teams aboard. These measures reduced the threat but did not end it. For poor Somalis, the risks of getting caught or killed paled compared to the money they could make.

The last two examples of unexpected challenges that consumed vast quantities of time and energy concern two individuals in uniform, one of whom had a bright future but baggage, the other a heroic Marine sergeant.

Lieutenant General Stan McChrystal was the commander of the Joint Special Operations Command from 2003 to 2008. In this capacity, he led U.S. Special Forces in both Iraq and Afghanistan in the conduct of clandestine operations to capture or kill members of al Qaeda and insurgent leaders. His operations were remarkably successful, including the capture of Saddam Hussein and the killing of Abu Musab al-Zarqawi, the leader of al Qaeda in Iraq, and played a major role in the success of the surge in Iraq and the counterinsurgency in Afghanistan. I had come to know and admire McChrystal during my first year as secretary, and I believed he was perhaps the finest warrior and leader of men in combat I had ever met. I was determined to promote him to a higher level of responsibility. But I thought Stan would have some difficulty getting confirmed for higher rank and position. He had been "the tip of the spear" for nearly five years in two theaters of war. Given how controversial Iraq had become, and the experience of both Pete Pace and George Casey, I saw trouble on that front. McChrystal had also been one of the subjects of an investigation into the death by friendly fire of Corporal Pat Tillman because he signed off on a Silver Star medal for valor for Tillman with a citation that made no mention of friendly fire as the cause of his death. The Pentagon investigation of the case recommended that eight officers be disciplined, one of them McChrystal. The Army did not agree and took no action against him.

On top of all this, Senator Levin had been conducting an in-depth investigation of the treatment of detainees (which I thought had Rumsfeld as its target) and expressed concern about abuse of detainees in Afghanistan by troops under McChrystal's command. Levin let me know there had been forty-five allegations of misconduct in his command and that he, Levin, intended to bring McChrystal in for a hearing. I had looked into McChrystal's actions in the Tillman case and the allegations of detainee abuse and, after extensive discussions with Mullen and others, determined to move forward with his advancement.

McChrystal had been rumored to be a candidate for several four-star positions, including commander of Special Operations Command, replacing Petraeus in Iraq, and commander of Central Command. However, I believed that I first needed to get McChrystal confirmed by the Senate for an unobtrusive, noncontroversial staff job, a confirmation that, in effect, would give him a clean slate. Then, my thinking went, when I pushed him for a higher-visibility job and a fourth star, it would be hard for the Senate to oppose him without suggesting they had done an inadequate job of vetting him previously. And so I enthusiastically supported Mullen's recommendation that Stan be nominated as director of the Joint Staff, an important position but one that operated under the Washington radar. It is a position from which most incumbents go on to a fourth star.

In February 2008, we moved on this plan. Senator McCain initially opposed McChrystal because of the Tillman case and Levin was opposed because of the detainee issue. The Senate Armed Services Committee intended to fight McChrystal's nomination. I told the president, "McChrystal is one of the heroic figures of these wars, and if we won't stand and fight for him, then who?" And so we fought. A nasty confirmation fight can get even a brave man down, and so I called Stan in early June to let him know that, based on personal experience, this was all about politics and that every senior officer who had fought in Iraq and Afghanistan was likely to face the same kind of challenge—a disgraceful reality. I told him that the president and I were prepared to fight for him. In a very rare Armed Services Committee hearing for a nominee to a three-star position, McChrystal did well in responding to the senators' questions. In August, he became the director of the Joint Staff. The path was clear for more senior command and a fourth star, which would follow in less than a year.

Of the estimated forty million men and women who have served in the armed forces since the Civil War, fewer than 3,500 have received the Medal of Honor, the highest honor the United States can bestow, some 60 percent posthumously. Too few have been awarded in the wars in Iraq and Afghanistan, in which there have been so many heroic, selfless deeds. President Bush was, I think, always disappointed that he was unable to present the Medal of Honor to a single living recipient. I once asked Chiarelli why so few had been recommended. He said because medals had been passed out so freely in Vietnam, succeeding officers were determined to raise the bar. They had raised it too high, he thought.

It was a big deal when a recommendation for the Medal of Honor came to my office. Everyone on the staff would read the file and be in awe.

Whether the recommended recipient was living or dead, the documentation was massive, with multiple eyewitness accounts, maps, photos, and the results of multiple investigations and reviews. The standard for a recipient is extraordinarily high: "There must be no margin of doubt or possibility of error in awarding this honor." There are many layers of approval. By the time a recommendation came to my desk, almost without exception, any questions had been resolved and any doubts put aside.

One such exception landed on my desk in mid-2008, with the recommendation that U.S. Marine Corps Sergeant Rafael Peralta receive the Medal of Honor for his heroism and self-sacrifice in the second battle of Fallujah on November 15, 2004. Peralta had volunteered for a house-clearing mission and, when entering the fourth house, had opened a door and was hit several times with AK-47 fire. As two other Marines entered behind him, an insurgent threw a grenade that surely would have killed them except that, according to eyewitnesses, Peralta pulled the grenade under his body, absorbing the blast. He was killed; the other Marines survived. The medal recommendation had been endorsed by the proper chain of approval, including the secretary of the Navy and the chairman of the Joint Chiefs of Staff. However, the documentation also included dissenting views from the medical forensic community and the undersecretary for personnel and readiness. As a result, I personally interviewed several senior officers in Peralta's chain of command, and in light of the unanimous support of the entire unformed leadership involved, I approved the recommendation. I was satisfied that Sergeant Peralta met all the criteria and deserved the Medal of Honor.

After I signed the recommendation to the president, I was informed that a complaint had been made to the department's inspector general that Peralta could not have consciously taken the action credited with saving the two other Marines' lives and therefore did not meet the criteria for the award. The inspector general intended to carry out an investigation unless I took some action to deal with the complaint. After consulting with a number of senior leaders, including Mike Mullen, I decided that the only way to clear the air quietly was to ask a special panel to look into the allegation. Chaired by a retired former Multinational Corps–Iraq commanding general, the panel included a retired Medal of Honor recipient, a neurosurgeon, and two forensic pathologists. The panel was given access to all available information, including detailed medical reports; interviewed numerous subject matter experts; conducted a recreation of the event; and inspected the available evidence. The panel concluded unanimously that, with his wounds, Peralta could not have consciously pulled the grenade under him. I had no choice but to withdraw my approval. Perhaps someday, should additional evidence and analysis come to light, the criteria for the award will be deemed to have been met, and Sergeant Peralta will receive the Medal of Honor. Regardless, there is no doubt he was a hero.

Every day, for four and a half years, issues like these came to me for decision, adjudication, or resolution. Nearly all, one way or another, affected the lives and careers of men and women who had rendered significant service to our country. Some decisions brought pain, others pleasure—for those affected and for me. In the evenings, when my wife would sometimes ask me how my day had gone, I'd just have to reply, "One damn thing after another."

CHAPTER 8

Transition

I did not enjoy being secretary of defense. As soldiers would put it, I had too many rocks in my rucksack: foreign wars, war with Congress, war with my own department, one crisis after another. Above all, I had to send young men and women in harm's way. Visiting them on the front lines and seeing the miserable conditions in which they lived, seeing them in hospitals, writing condolence letters to their families, and going to their funerals took a great toll on me. In Doris Kearns Goodwin's book *Team of Rivals*, she wrote of President Lincoln's secretary of war, Edwin Stanton, who, after making a decision that would lead to a soldier's death, was found "leaning over a desk, his face buried in his hands and his heavy frame shaking with sobs. 'God help me to do my duty. God help me to do my duty!' he was repeating in a low wail of anguish." I wrote out that passage and kept it in my desk.

I wrote earlier that my time as secretary had two themes, war and love—the latter referring to my feelings about the troops. Sometime in 2008 I began telling troops in the war zones and elsewhere that I felt a sense of responsibility for them as if they were my own sons and daughters. I did not exaggerate. Nothing moved me more than a simple "thanks" from a soldier, and nothing made me madder than when I learned that one of them was being badly treated by his or her service or the Pentagon bureaucracy. My senior military assistants spent a huge amount of time helping individual young men and women in uniform who encountered indifference or neglect when faced with a problem; usually I would learn of such things in a letter sent to me, or see something in the media, or hear something in a meeting with troops. Whether it was getting new washing machines for a remote forward operating base in Afghanistan or helping a young Marine with post-traumatic stress cope with the bureaucracy, no problem was too trivial. I wanted those troops to know I would do anything to help them—and I hoped that word would spread. I also wanted to set an example: if I could make time to try to help a single soldier, then by God so could everyone else in authority. I knew my overwhelming love and sense of responsibility for the troops, along with my deep conviction that we had to succeed in these wars, would lead me to stay on as secretary if asked by a new president.

After my initial months in the job, Gordon England gave me a small countdown clock, ticking off the days, hours, and seconds until noon on January 20, 2009, when I could set aside my duties and return home for good—as the label on the clock said, "Back to the real Washington," a reference to my home in Washington State. Journalists and members of Congress were always surprised when I could tell them exactly how many days I had left as secretary; I carried that clock in my briefcase and consulted it often.

With the election in 2008, we were facing the first presidential transition in wartime since 1968. I was determined to minimize any chance of a dropped baton and began planning for the changeover as early as October 1, 2007, when I asked Eric Edelman to tell the Defense Policy Board, chaired by former deputy secretary of defense John Hamre, that I wanted them to devote their summer 2008 meeting solely to transition issues. Sometimes there was a temptation by an outgoing administration to try to solve all problems before Inauguration Day, but this would be my seventh presidential transition, and I had yet to see a new administration that did not inherit problems.

Early in 2008, there was press speculation that I might be asked to stay on as secretary at least for a while to ensure the smooth handoff of the wars, no matter who was elected president. At the end of March, when I attended an eightieth birthday party for Zbigniew Brzezinski, he said he had told the Obama campaign that if Obama won, he should keep me on. I stared at Zbig and said, "I thought you were my friend." Press inquiries about whether I would stay if asked increased as the spring went along, and I usually would just pull out my countdown clock and show the questioner how long I had left. I devoted a fair amount of effort to quelling such speculation, often saying, "I learned a long time ago never to say never, but the circumstances under which I would do that are inconceivable to me." During those months, I was clear both privately and publicly that I did not want to remain as secretary, did not intend to try to stay, and wanted only to go home at the end of the Bush administration.

My strategy was to be so adamant about not wanting to stay on that no one would ask. Because I knew that, if asked, I would give the same answer I had given President Bush in November 2006: With kids doing their duty fighting and dying in two wars, how could I not also do mine? I maintained a disciplined, consistent, and negative response to questions on this throughout the presidential campaign, with one private lapse. In an e-mail exchange in early April with my old friend and former deputy secretary of state for Bush 43, Rich Armitage, I let my guard down: "The best part of the job [secretary of defense] is the same as at Texas A&M: the kids. They blow me away. They make me cry. They are so awesome. Only they could get me to stay." I then caught myself, and added, "Okay, that's really highly classified. Because if Becky saw it, she would kill me."

Even as I was trying to build a wall that would prevent me from being asked to stay, I was aware of the gossip and rumors circulating about me—and Mike Mullen. My press spokesman, Geoff Morrell, learned in late May 2008 from his contacts that the Obama campaign had "taken aboard" Mullen's argument that the wars in Iraq and Afghanistan simply wouldn't allow for a months-long interregnum. Morrell was told that Obama wanted a bipartisan cabinet and that my staying in place would show foreigners that U.S. resolve would be undiminished; it would also reassure the domestic audience that Obama could be trusted on national security. There was some criticism on my own staff, once again, about Mullen's "aggressive" legislative and public affairs "campaign." I believed that his being seen as holding an independent view of things would be helpful with a change of administrations because he and Petraeus would then be better able to stand up to a new president if he wanted to do something drastic in Iraq. As I told one of my senior aides, "Admiral Mullen is fundamentally in the right place on Iraq and Afghanistan." President Bush clearly wasn't as confident as I was about Mike's views on Iraq, because repeatedly over the ensuing months I would hear from various folks at the White House their concern that the chairman was already "positioning" himself for the next president.

In mid-June, there were several press articles about my efforts to organize a smooth transition, and speculation intensified about my being asked to remain in place for a while. Mullen and I often discussed how to handle the handover. I established a transition Senior Steering Group, chaired by my chief of staff, Robert Rangel. I did so to ensure that the vast preparations routinely undertaken by the Defense Department had coherence and coordination—and would be under my control. Mullen's involvement was important because he would still be in his position in a new administration and would be central to continuity and a smooth transition. Senior Pentagon civilians had to be prepared to remain in place beyond Inauguration Day so a new secretary wasn't sitting in his office virtually alone; that had been the case with Secretary Rumsfeld in 2001 as he waited for everyone else to be confirmed. Meanwhile one of Obama's senior campaign advisers, Richard Danzig, was quoted in an article as saying, "My personal position is Gates is a very good secretary of defense and would be an even better one in an Obama administration." In the same article, a McCain adviser said that McCain likely would ask me to stay on for several months to ensure a smooth wartime transition.

On June 18, there was a near disaster. Joe Klein, writing a piece for *Time* magazine, was told by Obama that "he wanted to talk to Gates about serving in his administration." Klein told my press spokesman, Geoff Morrell, that, and Morrell told me. I was really upset. I told Geoff that publication of such a quote would render me useless and impotent for the remaining six months of the Bush administration. I told him to tell Klein as much, and that if he ran the quote, I would issue an unequivocal statement saying there were no circumstances under which I would stay on beyond the end of Bush's term. Klein agreed not to run the quote because, he told Morrell, he didn't want to hurt that prospect. In the end, the *Time* story had Klein asking Obama if he would want to retain me as secretary and Obama responding, "I'm not going to let you pin me down . . . but I'd certainly be interested in the sort of people who served in the first Bush administration [Bush 41]."

About the same time I heard from John Hamre that it was too late for me "to avoid being on the short list for SecDef for either Obama or McCain." I e-mailed him back on Sunday, June 22:

> What folks don't understand is that they [McCain and Obama] are not on my short list. Or any list of mine. People have no idea how much I detest this job—and the toll taken by the letters I write [to the loved ones of soldiers killed in action] every day. Being secretary of defense when we are engaged in multiple wars is different than at other times.... Virtually all of the kids in Iraq and Afghanistan today are there by my order. Not to overdramatize, I will do my duty, but I can't wait to lay down this burden.

In the midst of all this press speculation and to-ing and fro-ing, a most bizarre episode occurred on the last day of June, when I took a telephone call from Senate Majority Leader Harry Reid. He told me that he was the one who had talked Obama into running for president (a lot of people were claiming that) but there was no candidate for vice president. Reid said he was thinking about me, and that was the reason for the call. It took a lot of willpower for me to keep from bursting out laughing. He asked me if I had a public position on abortion; I laughed, saying no. He asked if I was a longtime Republican. I said, actually no; I hadn't been registered with either party for many years. He asked how long I had been an academic. He wanted us to keep all this very private between us. "Possibly nothing will come of it," he said. I couldn't figure out if he was serious, if it was just idle flattery, or if he was delusional. It was so weird, I never told anybody, in part because I didn't think they'd believe me.

Washington, D.C., is always an ugly, jittery place in the months before, and weeks after, a presidential election. People outside government who want inside are jockeying for jobs in a new administration, and people on the inside are maneuvering to stay there—or beginning to look for new jobs outside. Sharp elbows and sharp tongues are everywhere. Gossip and rumors flow around town as freely as liquor at a lobbyist's reception. Even senior career officials and civil servants are tense, knowing they will soon be working for new faces with new agendas and will be forced to prove themselves anew to people who will be suspicious of them because they served with the preceding administration.

On July 15–16, I chaired the last Defense Senior Leadership Conference of the Bush administration, a gathering of the service chiefs, the combatant commanders, and the department's senior civilian leaders. We spent a lot of time on the prospective transition. I said that terrorists had tested the previous two administrations early—the first attack on the World Trade Center in 1993 came a month after Clinton took the oath of office, the 9/11 attacks less than eight months after Bush became president—so it was important that Defense be watchful well into 2009. I warned that a full civilian leadership team wouldn't be in place for some time after the inauguration and said I would try to persuade Bush 43 to allow us to brief both candidates after the conventions. The chairman and others spoke about trying to establish contact with the campaigns. I reminded them that in preceding transitions, the incumbent presidents' practice had been to funnel all contact with the campaigns through either the national security adviser or the White House chief of staff, and that the only organization allowed to brief the candidates before the election had been CIA. This presidential campaign would be more complicated for us, though, because both candidates would be sitting U.S. senators with security clearances and Senate staff authorized to ask for briefings. McCain sat on the Armed Services Committee, both Obama and Clinton on the Foreign Relations Committee. I said we had to be very careful about responding to their offices' requests lest we cross the line between their legitimate needs as senators and their desires as candidates. Rangel's Senior Steering Group for the transition would be the sole point of contact.

An example of such complications came less than two weeks later. Obama was going to Iraq, and on his return trip, we were informed by one of his staff, a retired Air Force major general named Scott Gration, that the candidate wanted to visit the U.S. military hospital at Landstuhl, Germany. All American wounded—and many of our coalition partners'—in both Iraq and Afghanistan were flown to Landstuhl to receive further treatment and stabilization before being flown back home. Gration said two campaign staff members would accompany Obama to the hospital. He was told that under Defense Department directives, the senator was welcome to visit the hospital with personal Senate or committee staff, but no campaign staff would be allowed to accompany him. There was a dustup with Gration, who I thought at the time was just trying to insert himself into the senator's visit and was not actually speaking for him. In any event, Obama ultimately decided not to visit the hospital because he didn't want there to be any perception that he was using troops—especially wounded ones—for political purposes.

About the same time, McCain's running mate, Sarah Palin, attended a National Guard event in Alaska. The press asked Morrell why she was allowed to do so. He pointed out that as governor of Alaska, she was the commander in chief of that state's National Guard.

Every day was a political minefield. The situation was not helped by rumors about my staying. These rumors were fed by occasions like Obama's meeting with the House Democratic Caucus during the last week in July, where Representative Adam Schiff asked him if he was considering having me stay on for at least a few months. According to the magazine Roll Call, there were "quite a few moans and groans" from Democrats present, presumably appalled by the idea of keeping on a Bush appointee. In early September, the same publication suggested that McCain might keep me.

In September, Mike Mullen came close to inadvertently setting off a political bombshell that, in my opinion, would have seriously damaged him, the military, and the Defense Department. I wrote earlier that one of the few major disagreements I had with Mike and the chiefs was their nonconcurrence in my National Defense Strategy, specifically my view that we could take some additional risk in terms of future conventional capabilities against other modern militaries in order to win the wars we were already fighting. The usual practice, once the NDS is published, is for the chairman of the Joint Chiefs to issue his own document, the National Military Strategy, intended to describe how the uniformed services would translate both the president's National Security Strategy and the NDS into military planning and resource needs. I read a draft of the NMS closely and could see that Mike was plainly distancing himself and the chiefs from several fundamental elements of Bush's National Security Strategy. A key component of that strategy for years had been "winning the long war," a phrase encompassing the war on terrorism and the wars in Iraq and Afghanistan. Mike made no reference to it. The draft, however, did imply that our forces were unable to respond to multiple military contingencies, just the opposite of what he and I had been telling Congress. Mike also omitted any reference to promoting democracy, walking away from Bush's "freedom agenda." He told me he wanted to issue the NMS in early or mid-October.

To me, his timing was terrible. On October 5, I handwrote him a long letter stating my reasons:

I believe it would be a serious mistake to issue this kind of document in the last weeks of a presidential election campaign. The NMS is already some seven months past due, and with such timing, I think you run a high risk of being accused of trying to influence the outcome of the election. Issuing a major pronouncement on the perils the nation faces and the military power required to deal with them in the closing weeks of the campaign could be seen as an effort by the military to shift the debate back to national security issues [versus the economy] and thus help Senator McCain.

I have seen all too often how paranoid campaigns get as election day approaches, and any surprise, any unexpected development, makes them crazy—and they think the worst case. . . . The irony, of course, is that you have made a huge effort to take and keep the military out of politics. Putting the NMS out now, especially with the distancing from several aspects of the NSS and NDS, likely will land you squarely in the middle of the campaign.

More broadly, I worry that issuance now—as opposed to a week or so *after* the election—would raise questions in people's minds about military motives, e.g., why now in the closing days of the campaign? Further, some would wonder, why is the senior military leadership asserting its independence from the civilian leadership—both the secretary and the president—just before an election? And what does that say about the civilian-military relationship going forward? The impact on both candidates could be quite negative. While leaks are always possible (and unclassified slides highlighting where you want to distance yourself from the current administration are tempting leak morsels indeed), that is not the same as formal issuance and roll-out.

In sum, Mike, I am convinced that issuance of the NMS so soon before the election would look politically motivated and would be a serious mistake. Accordingly, I am very strongly opposed to issuance prior to the election. The risk of creating a perceptions problem for our military among political leaders in both parties and the public—as well as problems for you regardless of the outcome of the election—is too great.

On the substance of the NMS, I objected strongly to omission of any reference to promoting democracy. I thought Bush's freedom agenda as publicly presented by the administration was too simplistic in that real, enduring freedom and democracy must be based on democratic institutions, the rule of law, and civil society—all of which are the work of decades. As with Jimmy Carter's human rights campaign, the only countries we could meaningfully pressure to reform were our friends and allies; the worst offenders, including Iran, Syria, and China, ignored our rhetoric. But I reminded Mike that promoting democracy around the world had been a fundamental tenet of American foreign policy since the beginning of the republic. "What has differed," I wrote, "has been how to accomplish or pursue that goal, and a new administration probably will approach it differently [from] the current one. But it will not abandon the goal." I concluded that omitting the goal from the NMS entirely—and in a way obviously intended to be noticed—"seems to me to go too far."

Mike made some modest changes in the military strategy document and agreed to hold it until after the election.

On October 14, President Bush made his last visit to the Pentagon to meet with the chiefs and me in the Tank. It was a reflective session, with each of the chiefs talking about how his service had changed during the Bush presidency. Mullen led off by saying the period had represented the biggest change in the U.S. military since World War II. We now had the most combat-hardened, experienced, and expeditionary force in our history, and if we could keep the young leaders, we would be ready for the future. He said that our forces were more balanced, more innovative, more agile, and better integrated and organized than ever before. I chimed in that the biggest danger to the military in the next administration would be pressure from Congress to reduce the number of soldiers in order to buy equipment. George Casey talked about the transformation of the Army from a force trained to fight Cold War–type set-piece battles to smaller "modular brigades" able to operate more flexibly; he also talked about changes in equipment. When Casey said the Army had gone from eight unmanned aerial vehicles (UAVs) in 2003 to 1,700 in Iraq in 2008, the president exclaimed, "Really? You've got to be kidding me."

Admiral Gary Roughead told Bush that in 2001 the Navy could put only one-quarter of our carriers to sea at once, but now we could put half of them out. He summarized the Navy's contributions in Iraq and

Afghanistan, as well as success in developing shipborne ballistic missile defenses. Cheney asked about the Chinese missile threat to our carriers, and Roughead told him, "We're making progress." General Conway said the Marine Corps welcomed the increase in force levels that I had recommended and that the president had approved, and he said the Corps would achieve the new ceiling in three years rather than the earlier estimate of five. He said the Marines had no equipment issues. He reported on success with the Osprey aircraft (a program Cheney had tried to kill because of cost overruns and development problems in the early 1990s when he was secretary), and the vice president, with a chuckle, wished the Marine Corps the best with it. Finally, General Schwartz reported that the Air Force would grow from 300 UAV pilots to 1,100, underscoring that the service finally had embraced the future role of drones. He closed by asking the president and vice president to visit a bomber or missile base, before leaving office, to give a speech on the importance of nuclear deterrence. Finally, Admiral Eric Olson talked about Special Operations Command (responsible for training and equipping unconventional forces such as the SEALs and Delta for all the military services), which at 55,000 he said was 30 percent larger than in 2001. He said special operators woke up that morning in sixty-one countries doing their jobs. The president and Olson both observed that these elite units had suffered a high casualty rate. (Olson's predecessor had told me eighteen months earlier that Delta Force had suffered 50 percent casualties—wounded and killed.)

Before Bush concluded the meeting, he said he didn't think the current strategy of being able to fight two major regional conflicts at once was useful any longer because we "likely won't have to do that." He went on: "If that is the standard for readiness, we will never be ready." He also said that we needed to focus on "nation-building" where "we have torn the nation apart and have a responsibility, but I'd be damned concerned about it in other places. Resist the next group that wants to do this—that is the State Department's responsibility, even though you [the military] may do it better."

No one in the Tank that day knew that the odds of my continuing to lead those same senior officers under a new president were increasing. The Obama camp had reached out to me privately. On July 24, Democratic Senator Jack Reed of Rhode Island told me he was leaving shortly for Iraq with Obama, would be spending a lot of time with him, and wanted to know whether, if Obama was interested in my staying at Defense, I would consider that. I told Jack, one of the handful of members of Congress whom I truly respected, that "if he believes the nation requires me to stay, I would be willing to have that conversation." A second call came on October 3, when Reed asked if I would be willing to meet with Obama. I told him that I didn't think it would be appropriate for me to meet before the election but would be willing to meet afterward. In the meantime, I told Reed, I would prepare some questions to focus a potential postelection conversation.

After the call with Reed, I asked Steve Hadley to tell President Bush I had had a feeler from Obama about staying on. Steve called back to say the president was very pleased and hoped that, if I was asked, I would stay because it would greatly benefit the country. I called Reed on October 15 to arrange delivery of my questions, and a few days later, Robert Rangel handed them to him in a sealed envelope.

On October 29, Reed told me the questions had elicited a very positive reaction and even more interest, on the part of Obama, in having a conversation with me. He said that Obama had asked whether I wanted the answers in writing, whether I wanted him to brief Reed, who would then brief me, or whether the questions were to serve as the basis for a conversation. I said the last. Reed responded that Obama "will want to talk right after the election." The more I thought about these contacts, the more I realized how extraordinary they were, truly unprecedented. Perhaps the most unusual aspect was a prospective appointee sending the prospective president-elect a list of questions to answer. Potential vice-presidential candidates, prospective cabinet members, and other possible appointees were always the ones who had to answer the president-elect's questions or the questions his minions prepared.

My questions might have seemed somewhat presumptuous, if not impertinent. But Obama and I were both embarking on uncharted waters in the middle of two wars. There was no precedent, since the creation of the Defense Department in 1947, for a sitting secretary to stay on in a newly elected administration, even when the same party held on to the White House. As we contemplated such a historic move, I wrote Obama, "I think it would be more complicated than it might seem. The questions . . . are intended to help both of us think it through." If this relationship was to work and benefit the country, we needed to understand each other clearly at the very beginning. I needed to know I could ask hard questions and get straight answers and that he would welcome straight talk and candor. And frankly, because I did not want to stay in the position, I felt free to press him both on my role and on the tough issues we would face. What did I have to lose?

A few days after the election, I was given the telephone number for Mark Lippert, one of Obama's closest aides, so we could set up a meeting with the president-elect. I contacted Lippert and asked him to work with Rangel on the arrangements. Like my interview with Bush, this meeting was to be highly clandestine. We agreed to meet at the fire station near the General Aviation terminal at Reagan National Airport on November 10.

That day Obama was headed back to Chicago. His plane was on the tarmac at the airport. My staff was told I was "behind closed doors" in a private meeting while I stepped into the private elevator from my office to the underground parking area, climbed alone into the backseat of an armored Suburban, and headed for the airport. The meeting was set for three-thirty p.m., and I arrived a little early. All the fire trucks had been moved out of the station so both our motorcades could enter. After we did, the doors closed. The empty, spotlessly clean firehouse seemed cavernous. I was escorted to a small conference room that had been meticulously prepared by one of Obama's aides for the meeting. There was an American flag in one corner. On the table were bottled water, almonds, two bananas, two apples, and a bottle of green dragon tea. I sat at the conference table thinking about my path to this meeting. I had a pretty good idea how it was going to end, partly because I knew that if he asked me to stay, I would agree. I had e-mailed my family the day after the election and foreshadowed what was to come: "Regardless of one's political leanings, yesterday was a great day for America—at home and around the world. The land where dreams come true. Where an African-American can become president. And where a kid from Kansas, whose grandfather as a child went west in a covered wagon . . . became the secretary of defense of the most powerful nation in history. Big decision coming at some point in the next few days. Pray it's the right one. But there is a debt to the Founders that must be paid."

Obama arrived about twenty-five minutes late. I heard a commotion outside, and then he was in the room. It was our first meeting. We shook hands, he took off his suit jacket, and I took off mine as well. He got straight to business, pulling from his suit pocket his copy of the questions I had sent. The first question was pretty simple: "Why do you want me to stay?" He said it was, first, because of the excellence of my performance as secretary, and, second, because he needed to focus over the next six months or so on the economy and needed continuity and stability in defense matters. My second question was: "How long do you want me to stay?" I had added parenthetically that I thought about a year would be optimal to get the full Obama team at Defense—and elsewhere in the national security arena—confirmed and fully knowledgeable in their jobs. Saying "about a year" would not make me a lame duck but would not lock in either of us. Obama replied, Let's leave it completely open publicly, with the private understanding of about a year. My third question: "We do not know each other. Are you prepared to trust me from day one and include me in your innermost councils on national security matters?" He answered, "I wouldn't ask you to stay if I didn't trust you. You'll be in on all the major issues and decisions—and the minor ones, too, if you want."

My fourth question was who the rest of the national security team would be. (I'd long believed that on the national security front, presidents should look at the key positions as a package—will it be a good team? I'd seen too many administrations where the senior leaders—especially secretaries of state and defense—disliked each other or couldn't work together.) He was, I thought, very open with me. He said he couldn't appoint Chuck Hagel (a former Republican senator from Nebraska) to a senior position if I stayed, so he was thinking about Jim Jones (a retired Marine general and former supreme allied commander Europe) for national security adviser or secretary of state. He mentioned Hillary Clinton for State, noting that she respected me but that her husband's many different commitments were a potential complication. I told him I thought Jones would be better at the NSC as opposed to State because placing a retired general there would convey the image of the militarization of foreign policy. (I was wrong in making that point. Two generals who became secretary of state—George Marshall and Colin Powell, the former a hero of mine, the latter a good friend of many years—had never been seen as "militarizing" foreign policy; quite the contrary.) I said the director of national intelligence should be somebody he trusted implicitly, someone with no policy agenda.

The fifth question was about how to avoid my isolation (as a holdover) in the administration and in the Department of Defense. Above all, what would be my role in the selection of appointees in Defense? In the questions I sent to Obama, I had written that I didn't see how I could enforce accountability unless appointees knew I had a role in their selection and that I could fire them. I added that I knew the civilian leadership needed to be an Obama team and that I would be open to his and his advisers' recommendations, but that I would need the freedom to reject a candidate. Also, because we were at war and needed to keep the department running smoothly, I asked if I would be able to keep a number of incumbents in place until the Obama nominees were confirmed. He said that might be possible.

The sixth question concerned the deputy secretary of defense and his role. I recommended John Hamre, chairman of the Defense Policy Board, who had served as deputy secretary in the Clinton administration. I told the president-elect I didn't think Hamre would take the deputy's job again without a good chance to succeed me as secretary. "My highest priority for any alternative candidate would be management experience, preferably in a large enterprise," I said. Obama said he would take a run at Hamre about being deputy secretary and mentioned Richard Danzig (secretary of the Navy under Clinton) but said, whatever the case, he would consult closely with me. He said he'd like to get Jack Reed, but Rhode Island had a Republican governor who would appoint his replacement in the Senate. He went on, "How did Rhode Island end up with a Republican governor? I took that state with sixty-five percent of the vote."

My seventh question was whether I could keep two or three current appointees, at least for the duration of my tenure. I mentioned Pete Geren, secretary of the Army; Jim Clapper, undersecretary for intelligence; and John Young, undersecretary for acquisition, technology, and logistics. Obama said that at first glance all seemed strong, and he would consider it. I also said I would want to keep my current immediate office staff and press spokesman.

The eighth question was: "Do you foresee any major change in the level of the defense budget for the first year of your administration?" He replied that he had campaigned on a strong budget for defense, but that was before the economic crisis: "I can't make tough decisions on domestic agencies—antagonizing my supporters—and leave Defense untouched." I reminded him of the deep cuts in Defense after each conflict going back a century and that recovery from those cuts was only at great cost in both blood and treasure. I also mentioned what I had told Bush 43, that there would be moves in Congress to cut troop levels in order to protect jobs at home associated with the procurement of equipment and weapons—a huge mistake, in my opinion. Obama assured me there would be no deep cuts, but Defense had to demonstrate discipline and make tough decisions.

The last substantive question I had asked posited that the two of us were probably "in the same place" on Afghanistan, but I needed to know "if there is some flexibility in how we achieve your goals in Iraq in order to best preserve the gains of the past eighteen months and so Iraq does not go south in 2009–10." Obama said he was prepared to be flexible. I asked him if he agreed it was important to go after violent extremists "on their ten yard line and not ours." Obama answered, "Yes. I'm no peacenik."

We had been talking for fifty minutes. Finally, I said to him, "If you want me to stay for about a year, I will do so." He smiled, stuck out his hand, and replied, "I do."

At the end of the written questions, I had offered him some reassurance: "I have asked you some far-reaching questions. In turn, I want you to know that should I stay, you would never need worry about my working a separate or different agenda. As I have with other presidents, I would give you my best and most candid advice. Should you decide on a different path, I would either support you or leave. I would not be disloyal." I repeated that promise at the end of the meeting, and I kept it for the next two and a half years.

The following three weeks were awkward, to say the least. I told President Bush almost immediately that I had been asked to stay. I was worried he might think ill of me for being willing to work for someone whose entire campaign had focused on attacking him and everything he had done in both domestic and foreign affairs. To the contrary, Bush was very pleased. I suspect he figured that the chances of preserving what had been gained at such high cost in Iraq were improved if I remained secretary of defense. I had told only three people about the meeting (other than Becky)—Rangel, Lieutenant General David "Rod" Rodriguez (who had succeeded Chiarelli as my senior military assistant in July), and my confidential assistant, Delonnie Henry. I was convinced that no one else knew but didn't take into account the analytical skills of my other two military assistants who, watching the president-elect's motorcade on television arrive at the airport and then veer away from his plane to a building, checked the peephole in my office door, saw that the office was empty after a so-called private meeting had run far beyond the allotted time, and concluded I had sneaked out to meet with Obama. Happily, they kept it to themselves. After the meeting with Obama, I told Rangel, press spokesman Geoff Morrell, and Henry that I wanted them to stay on with me, if they were willing. Rangel is a rock-ribbed Republican who had been staff director of the House Armed Services Committee when the Republicans were in the majority, but he and other key members of the core front-office staff, including Ryan McCarthy and Christian Marrone, all agreed to stay with me. They would be loyal to the new president and good team players within the administration, but that's not to say there wasn't periodic private muttering "inside the family" about some of the new White House staff, politics, domestic policies, and the incessant attacks on Bush—whom they had all loyally supported and served well. When I told Mike Mullen I would be staying, he seemed both pleased and relieved.

On November 12, when the Obama transition team leaders showed up at the Pentagon to get down to business, awkwardness set in. I was traveling overseas. No matter how well organized, well intentioned, and cordial a transition team is, its arrival in a cabinet department after an election always has the aura of a hostile takeover. *We're in, you're out. We'll now fix everything you screwed up over the past four or eight years.* Often smug arrogance is plainly visible behind the smiles. Fortunately, the leaders of the Obama Defense transition team were Michèle Flournoy and John P. White, both of whom had served in the Defense Department during the Clinton administration and were at once knowledgeable and straight-shooters. What they did not know was that Obama had already asked me to stay, and so this transition would be like none other in the history of Defense. Rangel told them the Pentagon would support their efforts. He said our department wanted to focus on their needs and had dedicated staff and office space to support them, along with materials to help the new team in their first months in office. Rangel also told them that a number of appointees were prepared to remain in place while key Obama nominees went through the confirmation process, although that was completely up to the incoming administration. He suggested that they appoint a senior person to join our front office who could quickly get up to speed on issues and crises we were dealing with, observe the decision-making process, and thus be able to understand better the situations around the world that Obama would inherit on January 20.

Upon my return, I met with Flournoy and White on November 20. Afterward Flournoy sent Rangel a list of questions regarding current operations and possible contingencies. They wanted an overview of current military operations globally; how we had been balancing risk between Iraq and Afghanistan and other challenges around the world; our strategy and operations for combating terrorism; future contingencies that Obama should know about before January 20; the cyber threat; options for dealing with Iran; options for dealing with Russia; and planned changes in U.S. global military posture. She asked that we proceed with staff discussions at the "secret" level, which would allow for informed discussion of most issues but nothing too sensitive. The challenge for me and my staff, at this point, was that we had no idea who from the transition team would end up in senior Defense positions; I had no intention of briefing sensitive military contingencies or operations to individuals who were in the building in November and December but might not be after January 20. Also, high-level security clearances would have to be obtained. Bush and Steve Hadley had been very specific about not opening the door to the transition team on current counterterrorism, intelligence, and Iran- and Pakistan-related operations.

I agreed to Flournoy's request with several caveats: I did not want the transition team briefed on the reviews of Afghan policy and strategy still under way; we would ask the Joint Chiefs for a list of operations that could be discussed at the secret level; and we would identify key operational plans—without getting into the specifics—that should receive priority attention by the incoming team. I told Rangel to let Flournoy know that any discussion of Iran options "would be incomplete" at the secret level.

My most important communication during the transition, though, was a long e-mail I sent on November 23 to John Podesta, overall head of the Obama transition effort, on the practical transition challenges associated with my staying on. First I told him that once I was publicly named, the transition team should report to both him and me, so I would know what issues, options, and recommendations they were framing and have an opportunity to shape what they were doing—or add my own thoughts for the president-elect. I said I understood that this would be Obama's Defense Department and that, apart from my personal front-office staff, speechwriters, press spokesman, and the rest, the only senior appointee I wanted to try to persuade to stay on was Jim Clapper. I said my sole criterion for potential appointees was competence to do the job. I wanted to interview those being considered and then make recommendations to the president-elect for his decision. As I had told Obama in our firehouse meeting, "If I am to lead the department and hold people accountable, the senior-most officials need to know I recommended them . . . for their jobs." I recommended, as I mentioned earlier, that I be authorized to ask incumbent appointees to remain in place until their successors were confirmed (which could take months). This was a rare if not unprecedented step. Virtually always, political appointees of the outgoing president are expected to leave by January 20.

I received a response from Podesta within a few hours. He saw no problem with the joint reporting arrangement for the transition team and, on personnel, thought the process I had proposed was fine. He promised a decision on Clapper within a few days. He said they might want to deal with incumbents on a case-by-case basis and would probably prefer to name some people as "acting" officials. The one place he pushed back a bit was on the press spokesman. He said he would need to get back to me because, when it came to dealing with the press, "the Obama team tend to be control freaks." I e-mailed him back that Morrell was nonpolitical and "I feel very strongly about keeping him." "I think I've been very flexible in terms of personnel," I wrote, "but I trust this guy to do and say what I want, and I want him to stay." Podesta quickly came back, "I'll smooth the way." I wanted Morrell to stay not only because of his competence in his job and his remarkable network of journalist friends and others around Washington, who were willing to tell him confidential tidbits they were hearing from their colleagues and government officials, but because he was one of the handful of people I could count on to criticize me to my face, to tell me when I had given a poor answer to a question, to question my patience (or impatience) with others in the Pentagon, and to question a decision. He was also one of the very few around whom I could let down my hair and be myself, vent without worry of a leak, and just relax. He could make me laugh as well. Frankly, I could not imagine continuing in my job without Rangel, Henry, and him.

At the firehouse meeting, Obama had told me that he intended to name his economic team first but hoped to name the national security team before Thanksgiving. As it turned out, the announcement was set for Monday morning, December 1, in Chicago. Becky and I spent Thanksgiving at home in the Northwest and flew to Chicago on Sunday. The next morning we drove to the Chicago Hilton and met the new team for the first time: Hillary Clinton, secretary of state–designate; General Jim Jones, national security adviser–designate; Janet Napolitano, secretary of homeland security–designate; Eric Holder, attorney general-designate; and Susan Rice, ambassador to the United Nations–designate. Jones was the only one I knew.

The president led off, and then each of us was given a minute to speak. I was the only one to clock in under a minute and my message reflected my innermost feelings:

> I am deeply honored that the president-elect has asked me to continue as secretary of defense.
>
> Mindful that we are engaged in two wars and face other serious challenges at home and around the world, and with a profound sense of personal responsibility to and for our men and women in uniform and their families, I must do my duty—as they do theirs. How could I do otherwise?
>
> Serving in this position for nearly two years—and especially the opportunity to lead our brave and dedicated soldiers, sailors, airmen, marines, and defense civilians—has been the most gratifying experience of my life. I am honored to continue to serve them and our country, and I will be honored to serve president-elect Obama.

I left Chicago immediately after the press conference and flew to Minot Air Force Base in North Dakota, home to Minuteman ICBMs and B-52 bombers, to deliver a previously planned message to airmen on the importance of their work. Minot had been part of the problem that led to my firing the secretary and chief of staff of the Air Force. I wanted to give the airmen there a pep talk. The visit was a tonic for me. Seeing our men and women in uniform immediately after the press conference was a vivid reminder for me of why I had agreed to stay on.

I gave my own press conference the next day to make clear I had no intention of being a "caretaker secretary." Lita Baldor of the Associated Press asked me a question I had never been asked publicly: Are you a registered Republican? I realized immediately that if I said I was an independent, I'd make two presidents angry—the one who first appointed me assuming I was a Republican, and the new one who wanted a Republican on his national security team and believed it would be me. I said I was not registered as a Republican but had always considered myself to be one. She also asked if I was resetting my countdown clock, and I said I'd thrown the damn thing away because it was obviously useless. I said the president-elect and I had left open the question of how long I would serve. Another reporter wanted to know how effective I could be working with a new civilian team who were all strangers to me. I reminded him that I had come to the Pentagon in December 2006 to work with a bunch of strangers, and that had seemed to work out okay. I said I was impressed by the president-elect reaching out to talk to Mike Mullen and also by Michelle Obama's desire to work with military families.

Much of the rest of that week, I huddled with my core staff working on what Gates 2.0 at Defense should look like, and what my priorities should be for the next eighteen months or so (I was thinking in those terms by then). I said I didn't want to make Jimmy Carter's mistake of having too many priorities: MRAPs could be taken off my plate now, but not ISR and certainly not the effort to better serve wounded warriors, which I thought was still a mess.

I had deep concerns about the acquisition of equipment, which I believed was a "tar pit." We had a shipbuilding strategy that seemed to change whenever the Navy secretary or chief of naval operations changed. A joint service acquisition process had to be created to avoid competing budget priorities or duplication. We needed to balance the development of advanced technologies with the ability to buy larger numbers of ships, planes, and other equipment. We had to get on top of the acquisition process, I warned, because if we didn't, "the Congress will fuck it up." We didn't need more studies on how to acquire more effectively—we had rooms full of those, and they hadn't done any good. What we needed, I said, was to focus on decision making, execution, and negotiating skills. I said we needed to show the new administration a path forward on closing Guantánamo, because in my view they were underestimating "the legal and political complexity of bringing detainees to specific states." This would require legislation; also, "pure law enforcement is not the way to go."

On the transition itself, I needed help on relationships with a totally different set of players in the national security arena. What was their thinking on issues such as Gitmo, acquisition, the budget? My staff and I laughed—sort of—about how I would deal with all the big issues I had punted to myself. I wanted the transition team to work for me as well as the president-elect, and I wanted to make sure my fingerprints were all over their final report to him, rather than have a paragraph tacked on at the end. I appointed Ryan McCarthy from my office to join the transition team to make sure that happened.

On Friday night, December 5, over martinis, steak, and red wine, a proven formula for deep thinking, my core team and I agreed that I would minimize my overseas travel for the first ninety days of the administration so I could get to know and establish strong relationships with the new national security team and focus on the 2010 budget.

I said that former deputy defense secretary John Hamre had heard from Paul Volcker that Obama would keep defense spending at a pretty high level for the first two years and then the ax would come down (a very prescient forecast, as it turned out). I intended to spend more time on the budget process and to be more involved on program decisions. I wanted the final say on big issues like the F-22 fighter and C-17 cargo plane production. And I wanted the service secretaries to wear two hats—to serve in their traditional role as advocate for their service, but also to remember that they worked for me and for the president and had to support what was best for the department as a whole and for the country. I said I thought our goals in Afghanistan were "too ambitious for us to achieve." I suggested we focus on creating an Afghan government that could prevent al Qaeda and others from once again attacking us from a safe haven in Afghanistan and leave more ambitious governance and development goals for the long term. We needed to concentrate on the south and east in Afghanistan, areas where the Taliban were strongest. I think all of us assembled agreed I had to continue to press forward on wounded warrior care and, more broadly, on medical care for all wounded, military families, and veterans. Finally, we discussed the need to accelerate planning for the closure of Guantánamo.

The next day the schizophrenic nature of my life during those weeks was highlighted when I attended the Army-Navy football game in Philadelphia. The preceding Monday I had shared a stage with president-elect Obama. On Saturday, I was walking around a football field side by side with George W. Bush as he waved to tens of thousands of cheering fans, troops, and families. During this period, a journalist asked me if it was difficult working for two commanders in chief. I responded that there is only one commander in chief at a time, but being at the beck and call of current and prospective presidents did involve some awkwardness in terms of getting to meetings each scheduled.

The following week Mike Mullen and I went to school on Barack Obama. I wanted to know how he approached decision making, how he dealt with advisers, and how he looked at the world. We spent time with several people who at least claimed to have some insights into the new president. We called the sessions "Obama 101," and our professors were Scott Gration (the retired Air Force general who had been an Obama campaign assistant), Richard Danzig (secretary of the Navy under Clinton), Robert Soule (also in the department under Clinton), and Flournoy. They said that Obama "pushes the envelope" in terms of the broader context in foreign policy: How does all this fit together? What does this achieve? What does this cost me? He was oriented toward diverse views, they told us. All of them urged us to read his book *Dreams of My Father*. They said he was a good listener and placed great emphasis on accountability. He was, they said, skeptical on missile defense and "way ahead of you" on Gitmo. Danzig referred to Obama's power to win over foreign constituencies and asked whether he should speak to the Islamic world.

Assuming they were to be advisers to him, I urged them not to go to the lowest common denominator in discussions with the president but to force debate. If all his advisers agreed, it would be harder for him to disagree. Use the NSC interagency process, I suggested, to strip away turf issues in order to get to the real issues and have a productive discussion. When Gration said the president wanted to revoke "Don't Ask, Don't Tell," Mullen said he had heard to the contrary. I said we would have to address it, but the president would be better off to deal with it when our forces were not under so much stress. On Guantánamo, I said straightforwardly that closure wasn't as simple as they thought. At the end of the meeting, I told the group assembled that with regard to the president-elect, "we will be totally engaged to make him successful."

I received a copy of the transition team report on December 11. There was a two-and-a-half-page executive summary for the president-elect and a seventy-one-page report for the secretary of defense. We had twenty-four hours to comment on the draft, and I decided not to offer any comments. Among other things, there were a number of pejorative statements in the report about the Bush administration—for example,

"Restore wise, responsible, and accountable presidential leadership on national security"—that I did not want to appear to endorse. Flournoy and White acknowledged that the report would have little value for me—except as a statement of Obama administration priorities—but would serve as a guide for incoming senior personnel. I thought to myself: *Well, actually, I will serve as the guide for incoming personnel.* I did find the issue summaries useful for insight into the Obama team's views on defense matters.

An additional paper I received contrasted my public positions on specific issues with those of the president-elect. We were close on Iraq after the signing of the Status of Forces Agreement, and in sync on Afghanistan, more funding for the State Department, counterterrorism efforts, increasing the size of the Army and Marine Corps, use of the National Guard and Reserves, aiding wounded warriors, procurement, and even, to a large extent, the defense budget. We were characterized as being in disagreement on the need for a new nuclear warhead (indeed, I had given a speech in October 2008 at the Carnegie Institute of Peace on the need for nuclear weapons and modernizing our current weapons; one of my staff who lingered afterward overheard some of the Carnegie folks saying that I had just ensured I would not be asked to stay on by Obama), and clearly he was more skeptical of missile defense than I was.

The first meeting of the new national security team was at the transition team headquarters in Chicago on December 15. The meeting space was like any other high-rise office building—lots of cubicles and a modest conference room. When I walked in and saw coffee and doughnuts, I thought I would get along just fine with these folks. The traffic coming in from Midway Airport was awful, and Hillary Clinton was late. She had dispensed with a police escort complete with lights and sirens, clearly having an elected official's sensitivity to ticking off everyone on the road. I did not have that sensitivity and was one of the first to arrive. In addition to those who had been present at the naming ceremony—Obama, Biden, Clinton, Holder, Napolitano, Jones, Rice, and me—we were joined by Mike Mullen, director of national intelligence Mike McConnell, Rahm Emanuel (White House chief of staff to be), Podesta, Tony Blinken (Joe Biden's national security adviser), Greg Craig (White House counsel to be), Mona Sutphen (deputy chief of staff to be), Tom Donilon (Jones's deputy to be), Jim Steinberg (deputy at State to be), and Mark Lippert and Denis McDonough (both to be at the NSC).

I thought carefully about how to approach this and subsequent meetings. I had observed enough presidential transitions to know that, for a holdover at any level, the worst thing to do in the early days is to talk too much and especially to voice skepticism about new ideas or initiatives. *(That won't work—that's been tried before and failed.)* An experienced "know-it-all" is truly a skunk at the garden party. So I spoke infrequently, usually only on questions of fact, and when asked. We sat at tables arranged in a hollow square, and Mullen and I sat together opposite the president-elect. All the men were in coats and ties.

Obama began by describing how he wanted the discussion to flow and his style of seeking information and opinion. Biden urged everyone to be willing to challenge assumptions. The transition team had prepared papers sent to us in advance on most of the issues to be discussed, providing a brief summary of each, campaign promises that had been made, and key issues. I thought the papers were of good quality, matter-of-fact, and devoid of campaign rhetoric. In retrospect, the one on Afghanistan was particularly interesting, observing that two lessons learned were the need for more military and civilian resources and the central role played there by Pakistan. The paper identified troop levels as a key early decision for the new president. In light of later developments, the last sentence of the transition's Afghan paper was remarkable: "From the beginning of the new administration, the president and his top advisers will need to signal firmly that the United States is in this war to win and have the patience and determination to do so."

Turning to the agenda, Jones gave a tutorial on the National Security Council and the interagency process, followed by an hour of discussion on Iraq. We then had an hour on Afghanistan, Pakistan, and India. Pakistan was described as the "biggest, most dangerous situation." During lunch, we spent an hour on the Middle East. We concluded with a discussion of early action items, including foreign travel, initial meetings with foreign leaders, national security themes for the inaugural address, new executive orders and Guantánamo (the most extended discussion), special envoys and negotiators, and early budget issues. Obama wanted to move promptly to close Gitmo and sign executive orders on interrogations, rendition, and the like, to signal a sharp departure from the Bush administration. Greg Craig, soon to be White House counsel, described the need to be both thoughtful and careful with the executive orders, noting that more than a third of those signed in the early days of the Clinton administration had had to be reissued because of mistakes. There was considerable discussion on whether to set a deadline for Guantánamo's closure. I argued in favor of a one-year deadline because, as I had learned at Defense, a firm deadline was necessary to move the bureaucracy.

All in all, I thought it was a good first meeting. There had been minimal preening by new people trying to impress the president-elect (or one another), and the discussion was, for the most part, realistic and pragmatic. I would have to ignore the many jibes aimed at Bush and his team, which hardly diminished over time, and comments about the miserable shape U.S. national security and international relationships were in. I knew that in four or eight years, another new team would be saying the same things about these folks. I also knew from experience that, when all was said and done, there would be far more continuity than the new team realized in its first, heady days.

The second meeting of the national security team took place on the afternoon of January 9, 2009, in Washington. Among other things, we turned to the Middle East, Iran, and Russia. The format was the same as in Chicago, with McConnell and Mullen providing ten-minute briefings followed by discussion. Particularly on Iran and Russia, there was a lot of discussion of the shortcomings of the Bush administration's policies and the need for a new approach to both countries.

Biden asked to meet with me privately after the meeting. We met in a small conference room, and he asked me for my thoughts on how he should define his role in the national security arena. I said there were two very different models—George H. W. Bush and Dick Cheney. Bush's staff had attended all interagency national security meetings, including the Principals Committee, thereby keeping him well informed, but almost always he shared his views only with the president. Cheney, by contrast, not only had his staff attend all lower-level interagency meetings, he routinely attended Principals Committee meetings and meetings of principals with the national security adviser. He was open about his views and argued them forcefully. His staff did likewise at other meetings. I told Biden I would recommend the Bush model because it more befitted the dignity of the vice president as the second-highest elected official in the country; and more practically in Washington, if no one knew what he was advising the president, no one could ever know whether he was winning or losing arguments. If he were to participate in all meetings below those chaired by the president, then he was just another player whose scorecard was public knowledge. He listened closely, thanked me, and then did precisely the opposite of what I recommended, following the Cheney model to a T.

On December 19, Hillary Clinton joined me for lunch in my office at the Pentagon. I thought it important that we get better acquainted, and she readily agreed. We ate at the small round table that had belonged to Jefferson Davis. I told her about the sordid history of relationships between secretaries of state and defense and the negative impact that had had on the government and on presidents. I told her that Condi Rice and I had developed a strong partnership, and it radiated not only down through our two departments but across the entire national security arena. I said I wouldn't try to compete, as had a number of my predecessors, as principal spokesman on U.S. foreign policy, and that as in the Bush administration, I would continue to press for more resources for the State Department. I hoped we could have the same kind of partnership I had had with Condi. Hillary had been around long enough, both in the White House and in the Senate, to understand exactly what I was talking about, and she readily agreed on the importance of us working together. Indeed, we would develop a very strong partnership, in part because it turned out we agreed on almost every important issue.

In mid-December and early January, I received guidance on who among the Bush appointees needed to go on January 20, who would be asked to stay until successors were confirmed, and who would be asked to stay on as Obama appointees. The transition team wanted Gordon England out on the twentieth. The president-elect and I both tried hard to persuade John Hamre to take the deputy secretary job, including, on my part, trying to lay a serious guilt trip on him for not saying yes, but he had commitments that he said he simply could not break. Bill Lynn, an executive with Raytheon and senior Defense official in the Clinton administration, was selected to take England's place. Edelman had already indicated he would be leaving, and Flournoy was chosen to be his successor as undersecretary for policy. Bob Hale was picked as the comptroller (the money manager), and Jeh Johnson as general counsel. I quickly developed very high respect for Flournoy, Hale, and Johnson, and we would work together very closely. Johnson, a successful New York attorney, proved to be the finest lawyer I ever worked with in government—a straightforward, plain-speaking man of great integrity, with common sense to burn and a good sense of humor. Flournoy would prove to be every bit as clear-thinking and strong as Edelman, a high bar in my view. Lynn and I would have a cordial relationship, but there was something missing in the chemistry between us. Bill's earlier experience in Defense, I thought, had made him very leery of bold initiatives, and I never had the feeling he supported, or believed in, much of my agenda for changing the way the department did business.

Except for those positions, I was given the go-ahead to ask most Bush appointees to remain in place until their successors were confirmed. I could not remember anything like that happening before. It was proof, in my view, that the new administration didn't want discontinuities that could prove dangerous when we were engaged in two wars. Three Bush appointees were asked to remain indefinitely: Clapper as undersecretary for intelligence, Mike Donley as Air Force secretary, and Mike Vickers as assistant secretary for special operations and low-intensity conflict.

On January 19, Bush's last full day in office, the core national security teams for both presidents gathered in the Situation Room so that the old team could brief the new one on the most sensitive programs of the American government in dealing with terrorism, North Korea, Iran, and other actual or potential adversaries. After some banter about which side of the table I should sit on, the remainder of the meeting was quite somber. I believe that, in broad terms, there weren't many surprises for the Obama team, although some of the details were eye-opening. I had not heard of such a conversation between administrations in past transitions—although presidents-elect received such briefings—and it was, I thought, a mark of Bush's determination to have a smooth transition and of the receptivity of the new president to such a meeting. Such cordiality was uncommon.

In the run-up to the inaugural, I became a real thorn in the side of those planning the great event. The Secret Service had overall responsibility for security, coordinating the efforts of the Washington, D.C., metropolitan police, the U.S. Park Service police, and the National Guard. As the inauguration neared, and speculation grew that upward of four million people could end up on the Mall, it seemed to me that the number of police and national guardsmen being assembled—as I recall, about 15,000 in total—would be woefully short if anything went wrong. Any number of events apart from a terrorist attack could spark a panic, and with only two or three bridges across the Potomac River, there could be a disaster. If there was trouble, the bridges would be jammed with people trying to escape, making it impossible for military reinforcements to get into the city. I kept pushing to have a significantly larger number of the National Guard called up and on standby at local military facilities. Those responsible kept telling me they could have large reinforcements called up within hours at more distant locations; I kept telling them that if something went wrong, they needed people fifteen to thirty minutes away. The organizers did agree in the end to increase the number of Guardsmen nearby. Fortunately, of course, nothing bad happened.

Simultaneously serving two administrations became even more weird in the two weeks before the inaugural. On January 6, the armed forces held a farewell ceremony and tribute for President Bush at Fort Myer, an Army post just across the Potomac from Washington. Appropriate to the occasion, my remarks paid tribute to Bush's accomplishments in the defense and military arenas—a record my new boss considered an unending litany of disaster. Then on the tenth, the entire Bush clan— and thousands of others of us—gathered in Newport News, Virginia, for the commissioning of the aircraft carrier *George H. W. Bush*. It was a wonderful day and a bittersweet occasion in that it would be one of the last public ceremonies at which Bush 43 would be present as president.

All the events associated with both the outgoing and incoming administrations were complicated for me by the fact that I had seriously injured my left arm. My first day home in the Northwest during Christmas break, there had been a snowstorm. I missed working outdoors and so bundled up and set about attaching a snowplow blade to my lawn tractor to clear our rather long and steep driveway. The blade was heavy, and as I lifted part of it, I heard a pop. I was sixty-five, and any physical exertion was accompanied by pops, but there are routine pops and there are not-so-routine pops. I knew this was the latter. But after a couple of minutes, the pain went away and I continued on with my chore. My arm was mobile and didn't hurt, and though I couldn't lift much, I decided I wasn't about to ruin my vacation with a bad-news diagnosis. So I postponed seeing a doctor until I returned to Washington, D.C. There I learned that I had popped the bicep tendon right off my forearm bone and that surgery was required. I checked my calendar and said I could probably work it in during February. The doctor said, How about tomorrow? We compromised on the Friday after the inaugural.

As I said previously, Barack Obama would be the eighth president I worked for, and I had never attended an inauguration. I intended to keep my record intact. For all events where the entire government will be present, one cabinet officer is selected to be absent to ensure continuity of government in the event of a catastrophe. I was able to persuade both the Bush and Obama staff chiefs that I was the only logical person to play that role during the inaugural. After all, I provided perfect continuity—a Bush appointee who would still be focused on the job on the morning of January 20 and the only Obama appointee already confirmed and in place.

I reported for work under a new president the following Monday. Wearing a sling.

CHAPTER 9

New Team, New Agenda, Old Secretary

I had been the secretary of defense for just over two years on January 21, 2009, but on that day I again became the outsider. I had crossed paths with a few of the older Obama appointees over the years, but I didn't really know well anybody in the new administration, and I certainly had no one I could call a friend—with the possible exception of the new CIA director, Leon Panetta. In the new administration, there was a web of long-standing relationships—from Democratic Party politics and from President Clinton's administration—about which I was clueless. The contest between Hillary Clinton and Obama for the Democratic presidential nomination further muddied the picture for me because there had been appointees from the Clinton administration who had supported Obama and thus earned the enmity of the Clinton crowd, and to say the least, there were lingering resentments in the Obama camp toward Hillary and those who had supported her. The "team of rivals" approach worked a lot better at the top than it did farther down the totem pole.

In addition to being the outsider, I was also a geezer in this new administration. While I had been just three years older than Bush, Obama was nearly twenty years younger than me. Many influential appointees below the top level in the new administration, especially in the White House, had been undergraduates—or even in high school—when I had been

CIA director. No wonder my nickname in the White House soon was Yoda, the ancient Jedi teacher in *Star Wars*. Those appointees, drawn mostly from the ranks of former congressional staffers, were all smart, endlessly hardworking, and passionately loyal to the president. What they lacked was firsthand knowledge of real-world governing.

Because of the difference in our ages and careers, we had very different frames of reference. My formative experiences had been the Vietnam War, the potentially apocalyptic rivalry with the Soviet Union, and the global Cold War. Theirs had been America's unrivaled supremacy in the 1990s, the attacks on September 11, 2001, and the wars in Afghanistan and Iraq. Bipartisanship in national security was central to my experience but not to theirs.

A number of the new appointees, both senior and junior, seemed to lack an awareness of the world they had just entered. Symbolic of that, I noticed at our first meeting in the Situation Room that fully half the participants had their cell phones turned on during the meeting, potentially broadcasting everything that was said to foreign intelligence electronic eavesdroppers. I mentioned it to Jim Jones, the new national security adviser, after the meeting, and the problem did not recur. But as Mullen and I returned to the Pentagon that day, I spoke my favorite line from the *Lethal Weapon* movies: "I'm getting too old for this shit."

As for the senior members of the team, I had met Vice President Biden a few times on the Hill but don't recall ever testifying in front of him or having any dealings with him. Biden is a year older than I am and went to Washington about six years after I did, when he was elected to the Senate in 1972. Joe is simply impossible not to like. He's down to earth, funny, profane, and humorously self-aware of his motormouth. Not too many meetings had occurred in the Situation Room before the president started impatiently cutting Biden off. Joe is a man of integrity, incapable of hiding what he really thinks, and one of those rare people you know you could turn to for help in a personal crisis. Still, I think he has been wrong on nearly every major foreign policy and national security issue over the past four decades. After one meeting at the White House, Mullen and I were riding back to the Pentagon together, and Mike turned to me and said, "You know you agreed with the vice president today?" I said I realized that and was therefore rethinking my position. Joe and I would disagree on many issues over two and a half years, especially Afghanistan, but the personal relationship always remained cordial. While Biden had been in Congress a lot longer than Vice President Cheney, both were very experienced politicians, and I found it odd that they both so often misread what Congress would or would not do. More about that later.

After our December lunch together, I was confident that Hillary and I would be able to work closely together. Indeed, before too long, commentators were observing that in an administration where all power and decision making were gravitating to the White House, Clinton and I represented the only independent "power center," not least because, for very different reasons, we were both seen as "un-fireable." A personnel decision by the president, however, soon complicated life for both of us.

The president wanted Jim Steinberg, who had been deputy national security adviser under President Clinton, to become deputy secretary of state. Having been a deputy twice myself, I suspect Jim did not want to return to government as a deputy anything. (My deputy secretary at Defense under Bush, Gordon England, had before that been secretary of the Navy. He once told me that "being secretary of anything is better than being deputy secretary of everything.") In order to persuade Steinberg to accept the offer, Obama agreed to his request that he be made a member of the Principals Committee and have a seat in National Security Council meetings as well as one on the Deputies Committee. As far as I know, no deputy had ever been given an independent chair at the principals' table.

Steinberg's presence on the Principals Committee gave State two voices at the table—two voices that often disagreed. Steinberg would often stake out a position in the Deputies Committee that was at odds with what Hillary believed, then express that position in meetings of the principals and even with the president. Let's just say that having two State Department positions on an issue was an unnecessary complication in the decision-making process. And I suspect the arrangement caused Hillary more than a little frustration, especially since—as I understand the situation—Steinberg, despite having been in her husband's administration, had not been her choice to be her deputy. Hillary had been promised she would have freedom to choose her own subordinates at State, but that promise was not fully kept, and that would be an ongoing source of tension between her and the White House staff, especially the politicos.

(Those on the National Security Staff [NSS] who bridled at Defense having two seats at the table forgot that the National Security Act of

1947 establishing the NSC specifically named the secretary of defense as a member and the chairman of the Joint Chiefs of Staff as an adviser. There was no mention of the deputy secretary of state.)

My experience working with Hillary illustrated, once again, that you are never too old to learn a lesson in life. Before she joined the Obama administration, I had not known her personally, and what views I had were shaped almost entirely by what I had read in the newspapers and seen on television. I quickly learned I had been badly misinformed. I found her smart, idealistic but pragmatic, tough-minded, indefatigable, funny, a very valuable colleague, and a superb representative of the United States all over the world. I promised myself I would try never again to form a strong opinion about someone I did not know.

I did know Jim Jones, the new national security adviser, but only through a few phone calls and having met perhaps twice. After I had turned down the job of director of national intelligence in January 2005, I was asked to call Jones—a four-star former commandant of the Marine Corps, he was then commander of European Command and supreme allied commander Europe—to try to talk *him* into taking the position. (That struck me as a bit odd.) I reached him on his cell phone in a restaurant in Naples. He was polite but not interested in the job. After he retired in the fall of 2006 and I became secretary a few months later, he conducted a review of the Afghan security forces and wrote a report on them at the behest of Congress and then, part-time, worked with the Bush administration to strengthen the Palestinian security forces on the West Bank and improve their cooperation with the Israelis. I had not been impressed with his Afghan report, and his demands for active-duty Marines to support him in the Palestinian project were insatiable.

Still, I was relieved by Jones's appointment as national security adviser because no one else in the White House at a senior level had been in the military or knew much about the military. Nor, apart from Jones's deputy at the NSC, Tom Donilon, did the senior people at the White House have any executive branch experience in national security affairs, except perhaps as midlevel staff in the Clinton administration. It took only a matter of weeks to see that Jim was isolated in the White House. Unlike so many others there, he had not been part of the campaign and was not an old friend of the president's. The NSC chief of staff, Mark Lippert, on the other hand, had worked for Senator Obama and was his sole foreign policy aide at the start of the presidential campaign. Denis

McDonough, the new NSC head of strategic communications, had also worked for Obama on the Hill and then became his chief foreign policy adviser during the presidential campaign. Both McDonough and Lippert had an independent relationship and rapport with the new president that Jones could not hope to have. Obama also gave them ready access, making Jones's position all the more difficult.

Early on, after one of my weekly meetings with Obama, Jones complained to me that the briefing memo the president was using for my meeting had been prepared by Lippert without Jones's knowledge. On the NSC staff under Henry Kissinger, Brent Scowcroft, and Zbigniew Brzezinski, such a breach of protocol and process would have been a firing offense. I can only imagine how Jones, after a lifetime in the Marine Corps—the most hierarchical organization there is—felt about repeated violations of the chain of command. Meanwhile Donilon had a close relationship with the vice president, and he and Chief of Staff Rahm Emanuel had been friends for a long time. Jones also had to deal with a number of others on the White House senior staff—Emanuel, presidential counselors Valerie Jarrett and David Axelrod, press secretary Robert Gibbs, and others—who weighed in independently with Obama on foreign policy issues. Perhaps a dozen people, including Jones's own subordinates, had more access to the president than he did and were invited to offer opinions on national security matters, often in his absence. Indeed, one White House official was quoted in the *Financial Times* as saying, "If you were to ask me who the real national security adviser is, I would say there were three or four, of whom Rahm is one, and of which General Jones is probably the least important."

Things boiled over during the president's first foreign trip, for the meeting of the G-20 in London on April 2 and the NATO summit in Strasbourg and Kehl (border cities in France and Germany) on April 3–4. Jim told Hillary and me several days later that at both summit meetings, others in the White House—he did not name names—were advising the president on foreign policy issues that they knew nothing about. With disdain, he described how one naïve White House staffer at a NATO summit reception persuaded the president to collar the Turkish and Armenian foreign ministers together to try to get them to work out their problems—in plain view of everyone. Since the two countries have one of the world's most bitter, intractable, and long-standing adversarial relationships, the effort was predictably unsuccessful and embarrassing. Jones vented that he had told Tom Donilon to return to Washington after the G-20 meeting, but other senior White House staff told Donilon to travel with the president for the entire trip, which Jones discovered only when he saw Donilon in the hallway of their hotel at the NATO summit. Jim said it was hard to get decisions on scheduling presidential travel and that Donilon and Lippert and others in the White House were constantly doing "end runs" around him.

The next morning Mike Mullen called to tell me he had talked with Jones, who was ready to quit. When I told Hillary about it, she was very worried Jim might indeed resign.

When I saw Jones alone late that afternoon, he said, "Yes, it can't go on like this." He lamented that he had no personal bond with the president, maybe because of their age difference. He described his difficulties in the White House and confided that he had seen the president alone only once since inauguration day. He complained again about Lippert and Donilon, telling me he had told Lippert he wanted something done, and Lippert, who was a lieutenant in the Naval Reserve, had pretty much ignored his retired four-star-general boss. "Rank insubordination," Jones called it. Jones said the president had told him he would be the last voice he heard on national security issues, but it wasn't true: "There are too many cooks, and I can't go on." I told Jim he was the glue holding the national security team together, the only person in the White House in the national security arena, other than the president and vice president, with gravitas and an international reputation. It would be a "catastrophic blow" for him to leave. I told him I was prepared to talk to the president if necessary: "We can't afford to lose you." Jim called me the next day to say he had arranged some time alone with the president and believed that things would get sorted out. He seemed upbeat, thanked me for our talk, and said it had helped a lot.

After this crisis, the national security process in the White House did get more orderly and somewhat more disciplined. Jim would survive at the White House for nearly two years, though he was never a good fit there.

Rounding out the major players on the national security team were CIA director Leon Panetta and the director of national intelligence (DNI), Dennis Blair. Panetta and I had gotten to know each other as members of the Iraq Study Group. There were some raised eyebrows at Leon's appointment, given his lack of experience in national security and unfamiliarity—except as OMB director—with the intelligence business. Based on what I had learned about him on the ISG, I had no problem with his appointment. I knew that most CIA directors had no previous experience in the business—in fact, up to that point only three career officers in its history had become director of central intelligence (Richard Helms, William Colby, and me). What counted was that Leon was smart and tough, had run large government organizations before, and above all, knew Congress—a perennial deficiency at CIA. And he plainly had the confidence of the new president and a long-standing friendship with the secretary of state. Occasionally Leon would doff his CIA hat and offer the president some hardheaded political advice on contentious national security issues; I thought he had more insight into the political realities in Washington than anyone at the table, including Obama and Biden. He was very careful about making clear when he was speaking not as CIA director but personally. His respect for the CIA professionals, his quick wit and easy laugh, and his wisdom and common sense made him a welcome addition.

I first met Blair in the mid-1970s, when he was a young Navy officer on assignment as a White House fellow and I was on the NSC staff. A Rhodes scholar, he was described to me then as one of the smartest officers in uniform. We would have little further contact until the Obama administration. Denny was a retired four-star admiral, his last position being commander of Pacific Command, responsible for military operations covering about half the earth's surface—about as close as you can get to being an imperial proconsul in the modern American military. Mike Mullen and I got along fine with Denny, but his relationships with others on the team and in the intelligence community were scratchy from the beginning. He actually believed that he was the boss of the U.S. intelligence community, with authority over most, if not all, its constituent elements, including CIA. In reality, despite the understandings and accommodations that Undersecretary of Defense for Intelligence Jim Clapper, former CIA director Mike Hayden, and former DNI Mike McConnell and I had reached in 2008, the DNI still did not have the statutory basis or political clout to assert complete authority over others in the intelligence community. If the freewheeling White House national security staff was a headache for Jim Jones, the national intelligence apparatus was a nightmare for someone who had been a four-star admiral and combatant commander. As I would often comment, the job of DNI is less akin to a chief executive officer than to the powerful chairman of a congressional committee—there are some inherent authorities, but mostly you have to persuade people to go along with you. Denny wasn't much into persuasion.

Unfortunately, his first big clash was with Panetta, who was both politically and bureaucratically savvy and determined to earn loyalty at CIA. Blair provided just the opportunity to do so. An earlier DNI proposal to designate the senior intelligence officer in capitals abroad—the CIA "chief of station"—also as the DNI representative had predictably languished at CIA for a year. The CIA had always filled this job. Implicit in the proposal was the notion that chiefs of station would be appointed by the DNI and might or might not be CIA officers. In the spring of 2009, Blair unilaterally issued a worldwide directive simply implementing the proposal. (As a former director of central intelligence, I thought Denny was crazy to make such a frontal assault on the agency and its new director.) Panetta immediately issued his own worldwide cable countermanding the DNI's directive, at which point Blair sent a letter to Panetta ordering him to retract his cable. A relationship that had begun as fragile had become poisonous. Leon prevailed, making it clear to all that the CIA director had more clout in the White House than the DNI did.

Blair did not have good chemistry with the president and other members of the national security team. He had a tendency to offer his views in meetings forcefully and with a certain finality, including on policy matters on which he shouldn't have taken a position in the first place, and that displeased the president. According to Jones and others, Obama also did not like the way Denny conducted himself in the morning intelligence briefings, often interjecting his own opinions. I could read the body language in the Situation Room when he spoke, and it was pretty clear that his only friends in the room were Mullen and me, and maybe Hillary.

I would spend a lot of time with two other Obama appointees, both in the White House. I had never met Rahm Emanuel, the new chief of staff, who was hell-on-wheels and became well known for terrorizing everyone, even cabinet officers. Armed with an inexhaustible supply of "f-bombs," he was a whirling dervish with attention deficit disorder. Jones told me once that Rahm would have an idea at ten in the morning and expect it to be implemented by four in the afternoon—regardless of complexity. I enjoyed Rahm. He made me laugh. He was a political animal to his core and often a source of considerable insight into politics and Congress. He was also far from the first bombast I had worked with in the White House. I would have some very serious differences with Emanuel over "Don't Ask, Don't Tell" (the law concerning gays in the military), the budget, and Afghanistan, but we got along personally. After I dropped several "f-bombs" of my own on him during a heated argument, he said admiringly that he didn't know I could talk like that and seemed to treat me with new respect. Actually, he—and everyone else in the Obama White House—always treated me with great courtesy and even deference.

The one other White House player I want to mention is John Brennan, whom Obama appointed assistant to the president and deputy national security adviser for homeland security and counterterrorism. Brennan was a career CIA officer and one of the few who had served in senior positions in both the analytical and the operational sides of the agency. I don't recall ever having met him at CIA, although during his early years as an analyst, he must have worked for me. Obama had wanted to nominate him to be CIA director, but his role at CIA during the Bush years resulted in significant pushback from the Hill, and so he ended up with a White House appointment that did not require Senate confirmation. In White House meetings I attended, Brennan would offer an opinion only when asked directly by Jones or by the president. Brennan came to have great influence in the Obama White House and, as best I could tell, was quite effective in his job, playing a central role in the grievous damage done to al Qaeda. (He would become CIA director in Obama's second term.)

A new phenomenon for me was the appointment of "special envoys" to work on important regional problems—Ambassador Richard Holbrooke for Afghanistan and Pakistan, former senator George Mitchell on Middle East peace, and retired Air Force Major General Scott Gration for Sudan. The Clinton administration had used special envoys or "representatives" to deal with difficult and time-consuming foreign policy issues such as the Balkans, where Holbrooke had rendered successful service in a brokered deal (the Dayton Accords) that brought about peace, if an uneasy one. Personally, I think the idea of high-profile personalities working on sensitive issues outside normal channels is a mistake because it leads to bureaucratic conflict in Washington and confusion abroad as to who speaks for the president.

Holbrooke's success in the Balkans in the 1990s had been a one-off due to the unique combination of the nature of that conflict, the leaders involved, and Richard's skills and personality, both aptly suited to the Balkans. His "in your face" approach seemed unlikely to work with countries like Pakistan and Afghanistan, where the leaders, culture, and political conditions were not susceptible to the Holbrooke style. Hardly had he been appointed before conflict arose with the National Security Staff (as the National Security Council staff was restructured and renamed in order to give it a broader range of responsibilities, including homeland security), Holbrooke enjoying Hillary's steadfast support. The president's curtness in addressing Richard made clear he was not Obama's cup of tea, further limiting his influence and effectiveness. Holbrooke soon alienated both the Pakistani and Afghan leaders and would become a peripheral participant in the war discussions, despite his valuable insights and strong team.

Mitchell came to his new appointment with success as a mediator in Northern Ireland under his belt, not an inconsiderable achievement. His chances for achieving success in the Middle East were slim. As we saw in the Camp David Accords in 1978, which led to the Israeli-Egyptian peace treaty signed in early 1979, only when both the Israelis and their Arab interlocutors are strong politically at home *and* willing to compromise is progress toward peace possible. In early 2009, those conditions did not exist. There was a weak Palestinian government on the West Bank composed of reasonably pragmatic politicians, and Hamas extremists in Gaza who were determined to destroy Israel. In Israel, the administration had to deal with Prime Minister Benjamin Netanyahu, leading a right-wing coalition government, who was unwilling to take meaningful steps toward a two-state solution. The Obama team was divided between the old Middle East hands, including Dennis Ross, who thought we should proceed step-by-step in the process with great caution, and those like Jim Jones and me, who preferred a bolder approach in which the United States would sketch out what a comprehensive agreement might look like so both sides could evaluate what they might have to give up and what they might gain. The balance tilted to the old hands, and George would shuttle endlessly back and forth to the region, with nothing to show for it. Scott Gration encountered an intractable situation in Sudan, and a split in our own government on how to deal with the regime there, but he did help secure a peaceful referendum that led to the creation of South Sudan.

That was the new core team. Then there was the president himself. Interviewers would persistently ask me to compare working for Bush and Obama, and how I could work for two men who were so different. I would remind people that Obama was the eighth president I had worked for, each very different from the others. Career officials, at least those lacking a partisan agenda, learn to adapt to different presidential styles and personalities. I did not have a problem making the transition from Bush to Obama.

My relationship with Obama would become quite strong, but it was always a business relationship. That had been true as well with Bush, although, as I mentioned earlier, he did invite Becky and me to Camp David on several occasions, none of which panned out. Obama would occasionally say we ought to get together for a martini, but it never happened. Until my last night in Washington as secretary, when he and Michelle hosted a small going-away dinner for us in the family quarters of the White House, we did not socialize. Just as I was not into mountain biking and so missed my sports bonding opportunity with Bush, I was a foot too short, too athletically inept, and too old to be considered for the Obama presidential basketball team, nor did I play golf. So, our two and a half years together were spent almost exclusively in the Oval Office and the White House Situation Room.

Although Obama to my mind is a liberal Democrat and I consider myself a moderately conservative Republican, for the first two years, on national security matters, we largely saw eye to eye. As with most presidential transitions, there was considerable continuity in this area between the last years of the Bush administration and the first years of Obama's presidency, as loath as partisans on both sides were (and are) to admit it. The path forward in Iraq had been mostly settled by the 2008 Strategic Framework Agreement with the Iraqis, and Obama essentially followed the path Bush had agreed to in December 2008, ending the war "responsibly," as he put it. Obama had campaigned on the need for more resources in Afghanistan, and he clearly was prepared to go after al Qaeda aggressively. For the first year we worked together, he was supportive of robust funding for Defense. We had a strong foundation for a productive partnership. On some lower priority issues, as I will examine later, while

I might disagree, I was willing to acquiesce or be supportive—as I had been in the Bush administration. Nobody in Washington wins on every issue, and as long as I was comfortable on the big stuff, I would be a team player on other matters. I don't recall Obama and I ever discussing his domestic policies, and that was probably just as well.

I found the president quite pragmatic on national security and open to compromise on most issues—or, to put it more crassly, to cutting a deal. So on some major contentious issues, as I will describe, I would hold my cards close and then try to pick the right moment to weigh in with an alternative to proposals on the table that would provide him with a solution we both could support. Usually, as I had done with Bush, I would preview my thinking with the president in private; most of the time I had confidence that he would ultimately agree to my proposal. I would later read that some on the National Security Staff were annoyed with my hanging back from stating my views in meetings, but I knew that my recommendations would carry more weight at the table if I was selective about when I expressed them, though there were occasions when I remained silent because I was undecided on an issue and simply wanted to listen to help me make up my mind. I usually went into meetings having spoken to Clinton, Jones, and others, so I had a pretty good idea what they were going to say. A meeting in the Situation Room was never just another gathering for me: outcomes were important, and I always had a strategy going in. More often than I liked, there were two or three such meetings a day, and all that strategizing required a lot of energy.

One quality I missed in Obama was passion, especially when it came to the two wars. In my presence, Bush—very unlike his father—was pretty unsentimental. But he was passionate about the war in Iraq; on occasion, at a Medal of Honor ceremony or the like, I would see his eyes well up with tears. I worked for Obama longer than Bush, and I never saw his eyes well up. Obama could, and did, express anger (I rarely heard him swear; it was very effective when he did), but the only military matter, apart from leaks, about which I ever sensed deep passion on his part was "Don't Ask, Don't Tell." For him, changing that law seemed to be the inevitable next step in the civil rights movement. He presumably was also passionate about health care reform, but I wasn't present for those discussions.

Where this lack of passion mattered most for me was Afghanistan. When soldiers put their lives on the line, they need to know that the commander in chief who sent them in harm's way believes in their mission. They need him to talk often to them and to the country, not just to express gratitude for their service and sacrifice but also to explain and affirm why that sacrifice is necessary, why their fight is noble, why their cause is just, and why they must prevail. President Obama never did that. He rarely spoke about the war in Afghanistan except when he was making an announcement about troop increases or troop drawdowns or announcing a change in strategy. White House references to "exit paths," "drawdowns," and "responsibly ending the wars" vastly outnumbered references to "success" or even "accomplishing the mission." Given his campaign rhetoric about Afghanistan, I think I myself, our commanders, and our troops had expected more commitment to the cause and more passion for it from him.

Having said that, I believe the president cared deeply about the troops and their families. He and Mrs. Obama, from the moment he was elected, were committed to helping our men and women in uniform. Michelle in particular, along with Jill Biden, the vice president's wife, devoted enormous time and effort to helping returning soldiers find jobs and to helping their families. The president visited military hospitals, encouraged the wounded, empathized with their families, and consoled those who had lost a child or a spouse in combat. And he would ensure that significant additional resources flowed to the Veterans Affairs Department and that it was protected from budget cuts. I never doubted Obama's support for the troops, only his support for their mission.

Obama was the most deliberative president I worked for. His approach to problem solving reminded me of Lincoln's comment on his approach to decision making: "I am never easy when I am handling a thought, till I have bounded it north, and bounded it south, and bounded it east, and bounded it west." As Obama would tell me on more than one occasion, "I can't defend it unless I understand it." I rarely saw him rush to a decision when circumstances allowed him time to gather information, analyze, and reflect. He would sometimes be criticized for his "dilatory" decision making, but I found it refreshing and reassuring, especially since so many pundits and critics seem to think a problem discovered in the morning should be solved by evening. As a participant in that decision-making process, I always felt more confident about the outcome after thorough deliberation. When the occasion demanded it, though, Obama could make a big decision—a life-and-death decision—very fast.

He once told me that one reason he ran for president was because he was so bored in the Senate. I never saw anyone who had not previously been an executive—and especially someone who had been a legislator—take so quickly and easily to making decisions and so relish exercising authority. And like Bush, once Obama made a tough decision, I never knew him to have a second thought or look back.

I always thought Obama was "presidential." He treated the office of the presidency with respect. I rarely saw him in the Oval Office without a coat and tie, and he always conducted himself with dignity. He was a man of personal integrity, and in his personal behavior—at least to the extent I could observe it—he was an excellent role model. We had a relaxed relationship, and frequently, in private, I would tease him, occasionally asking him, when he was beset by big problems, "Tell me again why you wanted this job?" His broad smile is well known, and I saw it often; what is less well known is how fast it can disappear, giving way to a glacial look. It dawned on me one day that the only other person I had worked with who changed expressions so dramatically and quickly had been Margaret Thatcher. It was no fun to be on the receiving end of such a change from either of them. (Like everyone else, I saw more glacial looks than smiles from Thatcher.) I often wished both Bush and Obama would be less partisan, but clearly the political world had changed since I retired the first time in 1993. I thought Obama was first-rate in both intellect and temperament. You didn't have to agree with all of his policies to acknowledge that.

Less than two weeks after the inaugural, at the end of his weekly meeting with Mullen and me, the president asked me to remain behind for a private conversation. He asked me whether everything was going okay. I told him I thought the team was off to a good start, the chemistry was good, and the principals were working well together. (The problems I described earlier had not yet surfaced.) As Obama had done before on several occasions with all the principals, he encouraged me always to speak up and to be sure to give him bad news or to express disagreement (as if I needed encouragement). He concluded with what I thought was a very insightful observation twelve days into his presidency: "What I know concerns me. What I don't know concerns me even more. What people aren't telling me worries me the most." It takes many officials in Washington years to figure that out; some never do.

A few months after the inaugural, the president convened a weekend "retreat" at the White House for the cabinet and senior White House staff to talk about how to accomplish his objectives. I was asked to participate in a panel addressing "Working More Effectively to Achieve the Administration's Priorities." I could already see a president and White House staff, as so many before them, seeking total control and trying to centralize all power—and credit for all achievements—in the White House. I decided to address this bluntly and to have a little fun. I told the cabinet secretaries and senior White House staff there were two realities to keep in mind. First, no one in the White House other than the president could execute any policy or action; only the cabinet departments or agencies could do that. How well the White House staff understood this would determine whether things got done at all, and with or without enthusiasm and speed. If the president's staff didn't respect the role of the cabinet secretaries and make them partners in policy making, implementation would suffer. Second, outside of the Office of Management and Budget, no one in the White House had to testify before Congress on policy or budgets. The cabinet secretaries and agency heads had to "own" the president's policies when it came to dealing with Congress, and the White House staff ignored this at its peril. Would a secretary's testimony be enthusiastic or tepid? "You can get very insulated against reality in this building."

I then talked about how the White House treated the cabinet day to day. I said cabinet secretaries frequently got calls from someone saying that "the White House wants" this or that, and that personally I often suspected the calls came from a fresh-faced junior staffer with a new White House pass who probably had his secretary call the dry cleaners saying "the White House is calling"; I referred to such people as "sniffing at the hems of power." I told the assembled cabinet and White House staff that when my office told me the White House was calling and wanted something, I ignored it. A building didn't make telephone calls. I said that, as a cabinet officer, I expected to be contacted only by a very senior White House person.

Finally, I had two warnings for my cabinet colleagues. First, there are too many staff assistants who think the way upward in their careers is to set their boss's hair on fire with lurid stories about the depredations or encroachments by other cabinet departments or the White House staff. The only way to defuse this kind of internecine feuding, I said, is for top officials to get to know and trust one another. Cabinet secretaries and senior White House staff working on the same issues need to have regular personal contact to build relationships, and if that is the case, staffs will soon realize that it is not career-enhancing to try to get their bosses into bureaucratic battles. My second warning was that at that very moment, one or more people in each of my colleagues' departments or agencies were doing something that was illegal or improper or engaging in behavior that they, as the boss, would hate. The key, I said, was to have mechanisms in place to find such people before they did too much harm. This warning, a couple of cabinet secretaries told me later, was the one that really made them sit up and take notice.

As I looked out on all the new appointees at the White House in mid-2009, I was struck by how diverse they—like their predecessors—were in their motives for joining the government. Some were acolytes who idolized the new president, had worked unbelievably hard for his election, and were totally devoted to him on a personal level. They were prepared to sacrifice years of their lives to try to make him successful. Others were "cause" people, individuals who had worked for him and were willing to serve under him now because of one or another specific issue—or the entire agenda—and saw him and their service as a way to advance policies they believed in. Still others had been successful in their careers and saw an opportunity to give back to the country by working for a man they supported, or simply wanted to do something different for a while. Still another group were just political "junkies"—they loved the political life, and working in the executive branch after eight years on the Hill or "in the wilderness" (outside government) was like a fresh tank of oxygen. And then there were a small number whose arms had to be twisted personally by the president to get them to abandon the comforts of private life in exchange for grueling hours and the opportunity to be all too often flayed personally and politically on the Hill and in the media.

I had been lucky financially when I reentered government in late 2006. Under the ethics rules, I had to sell all the stocks I owned in early 2007, at the very top of the market. However, those joining the Obama administration in early 2009 who owned stocks, and there were quite a few, had to sell at the bottom of the market. A number of those people took huge losses in their personal finances, and I admired them for their patriotism and willingness to serve at great sacrifice. I would disagree with more than a few of these appointees in the years ahead, but I never doubted their love of country (although, as in every administration, there was also ample love of self).

My most awkward moment in my early days working for President Obama occurred about three weeks after the inaugural. I called Bush 43 to tell him that we had had a significant success in a covert program he cared about a lot. There was so much anti-Bush feeling in the administration, I figured no one else would let him know. During our brief conversation, he asked how things were going, and I said just fine. Bush concluded by saying, "It is important that [Obama] be successful." I said, "Amen." To my chagrin and deep embarrassment, the next day Obama told me he was going to call Bush and tell him about the covert success. My heart in my mouth, I told him that was a great idea. As soon as I hung up the phone with Obama, I called 43 to tell him 44 was going to call and that I hoped Bush wouldn't mention that I had called. I knew I should have given 44 the chance to call. I never talked to Bush again about government business.

My New Agenda at Defense

By 2009, I had come to believe that the paradigms of both conventional and unconventional war weren't adequate anymore, as the most likely future conflicts would fall somewhere in between, with a wide range of scale and lethality. Militias and insurgents could get access to sophisticated weapons. Rapidly modernizing militaries, including China's, would employ "asymmetric" methods to thwart American's traditional advantages in the air and at sea. Rogue nations like Iran or North Korea would likely use a combination of tactics. Accordingly, I believed that our post–Cold War strategy of being prepared to fight two major regional conflicts at the same time, which determined much of our military's force structure, was outdated. We needed to sustain and modernize our strategic and conventional capabilities, but we needed also to train and equip for other contingencies.

Working for Obama, I was determined to use the additional time I had been given to shape forces, budgets, and programs along these lines. As the full extent of the country's economic crisis became apparent, I knew the defense budget was too fat a target for Congress and the president to ignore. I decided to try to preempt a crude, counterproductive, and potentially dangerous grab for defense dollars by showing that we could clean up our own budgetary and programmatic stable. My hope was that if the Pentagon could boldly demonstrate a willingness to reduce bureaucratic overhead and waste while enhancing military capabilities, we might suffer only a glancing blow from the coming budgetary train wreck. I was, shall we say, overly optimistic.

My priorities were clear: to continue taking care of the troops and their families; to achieve greater balance between preparing for future large-scale conflicts and supporting the fights we were already in and most likely to face in coming years, using the budget process to effect that rebalancing; to tackle the military acquisition process and weed out long-overdue, over-budget programs and those that were no longer needed; and to do all I could to enhance our prospects for success in Afghanistan. The first three priorities meant continuing my war on the Pentagon itself, the second and third meant more war with Congress, and the fourth would involve war with the White House. It was clear that every day of my entire tenure as secretary would involve multifront conflict. I wouldn't have had it any other way. Like both Obama and Bush, I bore easily.

With regard to taking care of the troops, during the fall of 2008 I had heard of a considerable disparity in the time required for medical evacuation from the battlefields in Iraq and Afghanistan—the standard in Iraq was one hour, in Afghanistan it was two hours. As I addressed the matter, I learned that non-U.S. NATO medevac helicopters didn't fly in "low illumination"—dusk or dark—or in bad weather or into "unsecured" landing zones. Of course, these were most of the times, places, and situations in which medevac would be needed most. Just as troubling, I learned that when U.S. Air Force helicopters in Afghanistan were needed for medevac, the request had to be approved by a senior commander, which caused added delay when every minute counted.

On November 12, I sent the chairman of the Joint Chiefs a memo asking for "a concerted effort" to get the medevac standard in Afghanistan down to one hour, carrying out "this task with a sense of urgency and priority." Much to my surprise, Mike Mullen, the Joint Staff, and both civilian and military medical bureaucrats pushed back hard that this capability was not needed. Given that the survivability rate of the wounded exceeded 95 percent and that Iraq and Afghanistan shared similar medevac death rates of 4 to 5 percent, they saw no need to take

President Barack Obama was always friendly and gracious toward me, even when we disagreed.

Briefing President Obama in the Oval Office with JCS vice chairman Cartwright, perhaps Obama's favorite general.

A U.S. ground-based interceptor missile in its silo at Fort Greely, Alaska. The GBIs there are the heart of our missile defense against limited threats from North Korea and Iran.

A press briefing aboard an E4B en route to Singapore. The plane, a converted Boeing 747, was dubbed by the crew "The Big Brisket" in recognition of my fondness for barbecue, which was often served on these flights.

CBS correspondent Bob Schieffer, Secretary of State Hillary Clinton, and I share a laugh while taping a joint interview at the Pentagon. She was a terrific colleague and a highly valued one—not least for her sense of humor.

With two presidents in a dressing room at Texas A&M University. Obama supported George H. W. Bush's Points of Light Foundation. They were the sixth and eighth presidents I worked for.

Afghanistan president Hamid Karzai and I always had a warm relationship, even when he was bitterly criticizing the United States. Many of his outbursts were provoked by our failure to heed concerns he voiced in private—and by internal politics in Afghanistan.

Talking with troops in Kabul. They never failed to inspire and reenergize me.

With General Stan McChrystal at his headquarters in Kabul. He was a supremely gifted combat commander, outflanked by politics and the media.

Walking the streets of Now Zad, a village in southern Afghanistan reclaimed from the Taliban by U.S. Marines at a very high cost. I wondered to myself if the cost was too high.

A tepee with memorials to a unit's lost comrades at Forward Operating Base Frontenac in Afghanistan.

Arrival and "dignified transfer" of a fallen soldier at Dover Air Force Base, Delaware. I had directed in April 2009 that such photos could be taken with the family's permission.

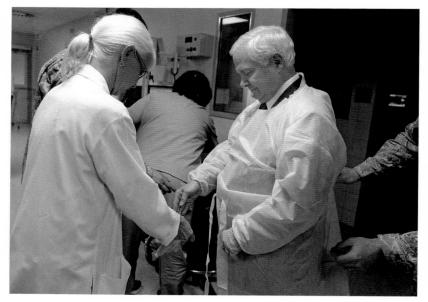

Gowning up to visit seriously wounded troops at Landstuhl Hospital in Germany, the first stop for wounded on the way home. Thanks to the doctors, nurses, and staff there, nearly everyone who went on from Landstuhl would survive.

Secretary Clinton and I at Panmunjom at the Korean demilitarized zone (DMZ). I was tempted to make a very undiplomatic gesture to the North Korean soldier observing us through the window. I refrained, barely.

With two great Marine warriors, General Jim Mattis, on my left, and General John Allen.

Congratulating would-be SEALs on their survival of "Hell Week." Only about a third of those who enter training for these elite units become SEALs.

Presenting medals and combat insignia in Afghanistan. The soldiers were so damn young and, as I said, my heroes.

Lunch with junior enlisted troops at Combat Outpost Senjaray, near Kandahar. I always learned a lot in these sessions, which were frequent.

Meeting privately at Forward Operating Base Connolly, eastern Afghanistan, with a platoon that had lost six soldiers in an attack by an Afghan soldier.

One unit in Afghanistan, to which I presented five Purple Hearts and multiple other medals.

I am pinning on the Purple Heart medal in Afghanistan, honoring those wounded in battle. It is the medal no one wants to earn but that I was deeply honored to present.

Out for a stroll in eastern Afghanistan with commander of the storied 101st Airborne Division, Major General J. F. Campbell, on my right. I had great respect for him as a soldier and a leader.

Landing at a forward operating base in eastern Afghanistan. Not much grows there except bad guys.

Watching flight operations on board the aircraft carrier *Abraham Lincoln*.

A cozy, casual meeting with China's new leader-to-be, Vice President Xi Jinping. We are on the far right; the others are U.S. ambassador to China Jon Huntsman, fourth from the right, and my staff.

The new world: the former director of the CIA and U.S. secretary of defense gives a press conference atop the Great Wall of China. I am being coached by my press spokesman, Geoff Morrell.

Locked and loaded with vodka, properly armed for a congressional hearing. Kevin Brown, with me, was my security officer and provisioner.

Mike Mullen and I, in a routine meeting with the president in the Oval Office. I never ate a single apple.

Jim "Hoss" Cartwright explains something complicated using a laptop. The light of understanding is not apparent on the faces of his audience—me, Vice President Joe Biden, and President Obama.

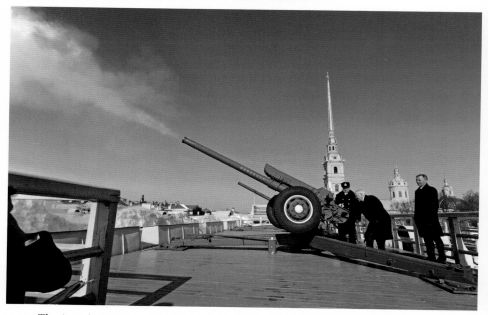

The American secretary of defense fires the noon cannon at Peter and Paul Fortress, St. Petersburg, Russia. The cannon blast has been a tradition since the time of Peter the Great. Stalin must have been spinning in his grave.

At the hospital at Camp Leatherneck in southern Afghanistan, where significant increases in medevac capabilities helped the doctors save lives.

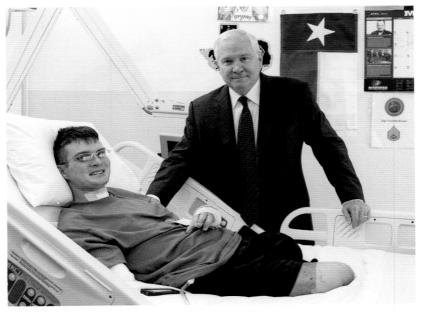

With Marine Staff Sergeant Timothy Brown at Walter Reed Army Medical Center. Over time, these visits got harder for me, knowing I had sent all the wounded in harm's way.

General Lloyd Austin, here with me in Baghdad on my last visit there, in 2011, was the last American commander in Iraq.

Mullen and I share the platform one last time at Arlington National Cemetery on Memorial Day 2011. He was a terrific partner.

Resplendent in my traditional Afghan war helmet, a gift from my intrepid staff during my last visit to Kabul.

A last helicopter flight in Afghanistan with Deputy Commander Lieutenant General "Rod" Rodriguez and Lieutenant General John Kelly. Rod was one of my earlier senior military assistants, and John was my last. All five officers who had that job under me were the cream of the crop.

Wherever I went in Iraq and Afghanistan, I found Texas A&M Aggies on the front lines, and they found me. Some I had presented with their diplomas, witnessed their commissioning, and then, as secretary, sent them to war.

On the anniversary of D-Day in June 2011, I spoke to troops in Afghanistan for the last time. They had no idea how hard that was for me.

President Obama presents me with the Medal of Freedom on my last day in office, June 30, 2011. My four and a half years at war were finally over.

measures to speed up medevac in Afghanistan. The Joint Staff surgeon, a one-star admiral, argued that with improvements in battlefield medicine, the two-hour standard was sufficient, and the chairman supported him. The Air Force was also opposed to a sixty-minute standard; the Navy was ambivalent. Only the Army and my own staff supported the change I was pushing. The bureaucrats had crunched the numbers, and that was that.

Their response really pissed me off. I told the senior military officers and civilians in one meeting that I didn't care what their statistics showed, that if I were a soldier who had just been shot or blown up, I'd want to see that medevac helicopter as fast as possible. I told them that if a soldier had been deployed to Iraq, he expected the wounded to be picked up within an hour. Why would he accept something less in Afghanistan? I said this medevac problem was about the troops' expectations and their morale, and by God, we were going to fix it.

The interim solution was to immediately add ten helicopters and three forward surgical hospitals in the southern and eastern parts of Afghanistan, where our troops were most heavily engaged in combat. By late spring, another fifteen helicopters and three more hospitals had been added. In January 2009, 76 percent of medevac missions in Afghanistan took longer than an hour; by July, that was down to 18 percent.

In May 2009, I visited the surgical hospital and helicopter medevac unit at Forward Operating Base Bastion in Helmand province in southern Afghanistan. One of the surgeons there told me that prior to the additional medevac assets, they often could not save the life of a soldier or Marine who had lost both legs; now they did so routinely. Those doctors are very special people, and the medevac crews are unsung heroes who fly into places and in conditions that would take your breath away to rescue their comrades-in-arms. We had just needed another little war inside the Pentagon to give them the tools to do their jobs most effectively.

About the same time the medevac issue emerged, the need for an MRAP-like vehicle designed for the unique conditions of Afghanistan became clear. With a casualty rate less than half that of the M1A1 tank and about one-fourth that of the Humvee, the MRAPs had proven their value on the flat terrain and relatively decent roads in Iraq. But these same vehicles were too heavy, hard to maneuver in a rugged landscape—they had virtually no off-road capability—and too wide for the narrow and usually primitive roads of Afghanistan. So again, under constant pressure from my office (and me), the MRAP task force—and industry—quickly designed a lighter, more maneuverable vehicle, the MRAP-ATV (all-terrain vehicle). We signed the initial production contract at the end of June 2009. The first MRAP-ATVs were delivered to the troops in Afghanistan in early November. The speed with which all this took place—less than a year—as with the original MRAPs, simply could not have been achieved through the regular bureaucratic process. And once again Congress had come through with the money.

A controversial issue affecting troops and their families arose early in the Obama administration. Since the Gulf War in 1991, the press had been prohibited from being present and photographing the flag-draped caskets of service members killed abroad when they arrived at the military mortuary facility at Dover Air Force Base in Delaware. The military services felt very strongly that these "dignified transfers" should be private, and they even discouraged families from traveling to Dover to witness the rite. Some of the media, on the other hand, argued that this policy was a politically inspired effort to prevent the American people from seeing the "real cost" of our wars abroad. Others contended that these returning heroes should be publicly recognized and honored. I disagreed with the no-media policy, but when I looked into changing it in early 2008, the resistance inside the Pentagon from both military and civilians was so strong, I dropped the idea.

Then on February 9, 2009, at a press conference, the new president said he wanted the matter to be reviewed. The next day, based solely on reading what he had said, I again directed a review of media access to the transfer of fallen service members at Dover and told a press conference of my own that I had done so. I said I thought a change made sense if the needs of the families could be met and privacy concerns satisfied. I imposed a two-week deadline for the review.

The review evoked a wide range of responses. Several groups representing military families and families of the fallen were opposed to any change in policy, I think fearing a media circus. The Marine Corps adamantly opposed any change. The Air Force and the undersecretary of defense for personnel and readiness—the civilian component of the department responsible for such matters—thought no action should be taken until data on family and service members' views was gathered. The Army and the Navy supported a change but with complete deference to the wishes of the families: if a family wanted no press coverage, that was final; if they were agreeable to media coverage, then it would be allowed at a respectful distance. Those opposed to a change were, I believed, sincere in their concern that asking the families about media coverage only added another tough decision at an incredibly difficult moment in their lives. The formal recommendation that came to me on February 19, reflecting a "universal consensus," was to delay any decision until service members, family members, support groups, and other interested parties had been heard from. I gave them a week to do so.

Political scientists, historians, and reporters are often completely unaware of events or experiences unseen by the public eye that influence important decisions. I often reminded colleagues that presidents and other senior officials listen to a wide array of voices other than those in official government channels. In the case of my decision on Dover, an HBO movie, *Taking Chance,* released that February, had an important impact. The story follows a Marine lieutenant colonel (played by Kevin Bacon) as he escorts the remains of Marine Lance Corporal Chance Phelps from Dover to his hometown in Wyoming, ordinary Americans making gestures of respect all along the way. After seeing the film, I was resolved that we should publicly honor as many of our fallen warriors as possible, beginning at Dover.

On February 24, Mullen and I briefed the president on the results of the review and outreach, and with his strong support, two days later I announced at a press conference that, having heard from the services and organizations representing military families, I had directed that "the decision regarding media coverage of the transfer process at Dover should be made by those most directly affected—on an individual basis by the families of the fallen. We ought not presume to make that decision in their place." For families wanting media coverage, it would be allowed at a respectful distance. For other families, the transfer would be private. The person designated by the fallen service member as the primary next of kin would speak for the family, although our long-term plan was to offer service members the opportunity to choose for themselves whether they would want media present for their return should they be killed. The transfer of Air Force Staff Sergeant Phillip Myers of Hopewell, Virginia, on April 6 was the first to be photographed by the media under the new policy. I attended Myers's funeral at Arlington on April 27.

It seemed to me that some families would want to greet their fallen child or spouse when he or she first returned to American soil at Dover. Defense Department policy was to discourage families from doing so, although some families made their way to Dover anyway, paying for their own plane reservations and hotel accommodations. I decided we should make the arrangements and assume the cost for the families who wanted to go. The Air Force outdid itself in implementing this decision. In January 2010, a new Center for the Families of the Fallen, a six-thousand-square-foot space with a comforting, serene environment, opened at Dover. That spring construction began on a small hotel as well as a meditation center and adjoining garden for the families. By 2010, some 75 percent of the families of returning fallen service members were going to Dover to be present when their hero returned to America, and about 55 percent allowed media coverage.

I made my first visit to Dover on March 16, in the middle of the decision process. As was often the case, the chartered Boeing 747 carrying the remains arrived at night. As we were waiting for the transfer to take place, I asked my staff how the four service members had been killed. I was emotional that night, and when I was told that the soldiers had been in a Humvee that was hit by an IED, I turned on my staff and through clenched teeth angrily demanded, "Find out why they didn't have their goddamned MRAPs yet."

Uniformed in fatigues and white gloves, the Air Force honor guard that would carry out the transfer marched by us, and we fell into line and cadence with them to move planeside. The night was cold, with wind and rain. The plane was bathed in floodlights, and the side cargo door was open high above the ground, allowing us to glimpse the first two plain aluminum flag-draped transfer cases. I had told my staff to arrange for me to be alone with the four, so I climbed the front steps of the plane and was escorted to the rear cargo area and the four fallen. They were Army Sergeant Christopher Abeyta, Specialist Robert Weiner, Private First Class Norman Cain, all from the 178th Infantry Regiment, and Air Force Staff Sergeant Timothy Bowles from Elmendorf Air Force Base, Alaska. Alone with them, I was overwhelmed. I knelt beside each for a moment, placing my hand on the flag covering each case. Tears flooded my eyes. I did not want to leave them, but I finally sensed the chaplain move close behind me, and so I rose, returned to the tarmac, and saluted as, one by one, with extraordinary precision, respect, and care—even tenderness—the honor guard transferred each case to a waiting vehicle. There was complete silence on the plane back to Washington.

A month later I was visiting wounded at Walter Reed. I walked into one room where a young soldier was sitting on his bed holding a copy of that day's *Washington Post* with a story about my March visit to Dover, including my intemperate question about why those four service members had not been in an MRAP. He read aloud from the story what I had demanded of my staff, and then he began to cry as he told me, "Your MRAP saved my life." I managed to keep my composure—barely. I didn't fully appreciate at the time the emotional toll my duties were taking on me.

Another issue I had tried to resolve early in my tenure was stop-loss, the practice of keeping soldiers on active duty after their scheduled service was completed. I knew that the practice was allowed by the contracts soldiers signed, but I considered it a breach of faith. Stop-loss was obviously unpopular among the troops, but it was also unpopular in Congress. Jack Murtha, chairman of the Defense Subcommittee of the House Appropriations Committee, pushed through legislation providing special compensation of $500 a month for the time any soldier was stop-lossed, retroactive to September 11, 2001. Ultimately we estimated there were some 174,000 eligible claimants, and Congress appropriated over $500 million for the retroactive pay.

A significant number of those stop-lossed were sergeants. Senior Army officers argued that their mustering out would deprive units of their experienced enlisted leadership. More than 14,000 soldiers were stop-lossed at one point. The surge in Iraq made ending the practice impossible in 2007 and 2008, but it remained on my to-do list. I returned to the issue early in the Obama administration. Thanks to the drawdowns in Iraq, Army chief of staff General George Casey and Pete Chiarelli came up with a plan to end stop-loss, which I announced on March 18, 2009, two days after my visit to Dover. Units of the Army Reserve would begin mobilizing and deploying without using stop-loss in August, the National Guard in September, and active duty units in January 2010. The goal was to reduce the number of those in stop-loss by 40 percent by March 2010, 50 percent by June, and to end the practice altogether by March 2011. The Army met these goals, and I was very proud of that.

There were a number of other matters affecting men and women in uniform and their families that remained high on my priority list. We still had to do better in getting needed equipment to the field faster; more intelligence, surveillance, and reconnaissance (ISR) was always on the list. We needed to keep improving the special units on active duty posts and bases—warrior transition units—created to provide a home for wounded troops while they recovered before returning to active duty or leaving the service. Ever more focus needed to be placed on post-traumatic stress and the shocking rise in suicides. We needed to expand and sustain programs for child care, family counseling, and others helping families. And we needed a much greater effort to eliminate sexual assault, a criminal act that destroyed trust, morale, unit cohesion—and lives.

Occasionally, amid so many issues and problems affecting our troops that wore me down, there would be an incident or moment that made me laugh or raised my spirits. Two such occurred in the first few months of the Obama administration. One morning in May, on the front page of *The New York Times,* there was a photograph of a soldier firing his rifle at Taliban attackers from the ramparts of Firebase Restrepo in Afghanistan. An Associated Press photographer had captured Specialist Zachary Boyd defending his firebase dressed in helmet, body armor, flip-flops, and pink boxer shorts with little red hearts in which were printed "I love New York." I burst out laughing. "Any soldier who goes into battle against the Taliban in pink boxers and flip-flops has a special kind of courage," I said publicly. "What an incredible innovation in psychological warfare!" I loved that picture so much that an enlargement hung on the wall outside my office for the next two years.

For inspiration, I would turn again and again to Lieutenant Jason "Jay" Redman, a Navy SEAL who had been shot seven times and had undergone nearly two dozen surgeries. He had placed a hand-drawn sign on the door to his room at Bethesda Naval Hospital. It read:

ATTENTION. To all who enter here. If you are coming into this room with sorrow or to feel sorry for my wounds, go elsewhere. The wounds I received I got in a job I love, doing it for people I love, supporting the freedom of a country I deeply love. I am incredibly tough and will make a full recovery. What is full? That is the absolute utmost physically my body has the ability to recover. Then I will push that about 20% further through sheer mental tenacity. This room you are about to enter is a room of fun, optimism, and intense rapid regrowth. If you are not prepared for that, go elsewhere. From: The Management.

I met with Jay and his family in early February 2009, when he returned to Washington to donate his sign to the hospital. I drew great strength from young Jay Redman and from so many like him I encountered. Their example kept me going.

I mentioned earlier our need to prepare for future potential large-scale conflicts against other modern military powers while preparing for and fighting the conflicts we were already in or most likely to face in the years ahead—combating insurgents, terrorists, smaller rogue states, or groups taking advantage of chaos in failed states and humanitarian disasters. This had been at the heart of my disagreement with the Joint Chiefs over the National Defense Strategy.

I resumed the dialogue on these issues with the senior military and civilian leadership of the department in early January 2009, before Obama was inaugurated. It was the last gathering of the Bush Defense team, and the night before we began, the president and Mrs. Bush invited the chiefs and combatant commanders and their wives, along with several wounded warriors, to the White House for a wonderful, if poignant, farewell dinner. The next morning we got down to business. The assigned reading was my speech at the National Defense University—which had subsequently been adapted and published in the journal *Foreign Affairs*—where I had laid out my views. I led off our meeting by saying that I was "determined . . . to 'operationalize' the strategic themes I have been talking about for the past two years." I warned that the strategic environment facing us had altered dramatically with a change in administrations, domestic and global financial crises, waning public support for increased defense spending, a strategic shift from Iraq to Afghanistan, seven years of constant combat operations and the resulting stress on the force, and resolve by Congress and the new administration to "fix" defense acquisition.

Circumstances had presented us with an immensely difficult bureaucratic challenge. In 2009, we had to carry out four complex, difficult periodic assessments required by Congress (the Quadrennial Defense

Review, the Nuclear Posture Review, the Space Review, and the Ballistic Missile Review), all intended to shape Defense planning and budgets. We also had to execute the FY2009 budget, get approval of the FY2009 war supplemental, build the FY2010 budget and supplemental within a few weeks, and by fall develop the FY2011 budget. For a bureaucracy as ponderous as ours and the long lead times to complete each of these endeavors, this was a staggering agenda. I told the senior military and civilian leadership of the department we did not have the time to do all these things sequentially, and so even as the congressionally mandated reviews were being drafted, we needed to use them to help shape the budgets. I made clear this presented us with an opportunity to use these parallel processes to accelerate the strategic and programmatic changes that needed to be made. I asked for their opinions and ideas on how to proceed. I posed some tough questions:

- Did I get it wrong at NDU? "You should know me well enough by now to know that I welcome real debate on these fundamental issues."
- What were the implications of our inability to anticipate where we would use military force next?
- How would we achieve the rebalancing I called for to deal with hybrid conflicts covering a spectrum of capabilities from the primitive to high tech—and, at the same time, be prepared to respond to future threats from "near peers" (e.g., China)? How much did these capabilities overlap?
- How should we assess real risk, and how would that drive investment?
- How should we look across the services in assessing risk? For example, could we mitigate risk caused by reducing one or another program in one service by doing more in a complementary capability in another service?

My first opportunity to translate some of these ideas into action actually had occurred in the fall of 2008 while preparing the FY2010 budget. Members of Congress from both parties had complained repeatedly about the wars being funded through "supplemental" appropriations, outside the regular "base" budget of the Defense Department. It took me a while to realize this was political bullshit. Most members of Congress loved supplementals because they could irresponsibly hang all manner of parochial, often stupid, and militarily unnecessary expenditures onto those bills—earmarks for their districts and states—with no regard for fiscal discipline. Even worse, members would often eliminate items we had requested in the supplementals to fight the wars and substitute their pet projects. The Pentagon was not innocent in this regard either, as a good deal of defense spending that would normally be in the base budget—from Army reorganization to an additional F-35 fighter—got shoveled into the war funding request, which would make weaning the military off supplemental funding all the more painful in the future.

In any event, given bipartisan criticism of the supplementals, I decided we should begin to move certain war-related costs that we knew should continue beyond the wars themselves—including, for example, the expansion of the Special Forces and programs to help military families—into the regular defense budget. Anticipating that we would be deploying the equivalent of several brigades to various hot spots around the world for years to come, for everything from small-scale conflicts to training and assistance missions, as an experiment we added $25 billion to the regular budget to pay for such operations, thereby reducing the need for future supplemental appropriations. In their last meeting with President Bush, the Joint Chiefs pressed their budget concerns, and the president encouraged them to make his last defense budget very forward-leaning in terms of modernization, reequipping our forces after the two wars, and funding "unplanned contingencies." His encouragement only abetted the traditional practice of a departing administration leaving behind a budget that would immediately be ripped apart by the new team. Only this time, of course, I was "the new team."

By the time we were finished putting together an FY2010 budget that incorporated what the Joint Chiefs had discussed with Bush and a good deal of spending previously covered by supplementals, it had exploded to $581 billion, $57 billion more than the earlier projected budget for FY2010. I knew immediately that that dog wouldn't hunt. What I had not taken into account was that an effort that I had seen as experimental and illustrative for the White House and Congress had been immediately embraced as firm financial guidance by the Joint Chiefs and others. Every element of the Pentagon had built its budget down to the last dime on the basis of a $581 billion request. And when we had to develop a real-world budget tens of billions of dollars lower, there was all manner of screaming and yowling out of the Pentagon about a huge "cut." Needless to say, as all this was playing out, more than a few Obama folks—with some justification—thought the Bush administration had sandbagged them, seeking to make Obama look weak on defense, as he inevitably would have to pare back the budget. Trying to begin moving away from supplementals had blown up in my face. I also realized I should have stopped the additions encouraged by Bush. These were both my errors. After all my years around Congress and my own building, I had, to my chagrin and embarrassment, been naïve about both.

This fiasco behind me, I set about to rebuild the 2010 budget. In a meeting with the president on February 2, I acknowledged the need to curtail the growth in defense spending, but in a refrain I returned to again and again, I said the cuts should be "strategy-driven, not accountant-driven," that we should do what was best for the country and not worry about the politics. The president agreed. The numbers we settled on in early February ($533.8 billion for the 2010 base budget and $130 billion for the war supplemental) were lower than I wanted but higher than what the Office of Management and Budget wanted.

I had a long private conversation with the president on February 11, during which I told him I "hoped and expected" to send him a new budget that cut many programs and reshaped spending to provide greater balance between current and future needs. This would involve making very difficult decisions, I said, and would be very controversial on the Hill. If we waited to speak out publicly until after the administration formally submitted its full budget to Congress in April, every major decision would have leaked, giving industry, lobbyists, and members time to galvanize support for sustaining every major individual program.

I recommended a highly unusual, if not unprecedented, political strategy. I told him, "I propose to review the major elements of the package with you and Peter [Orszag, director of OMB] *before* I even send it to OMB. Then I will go public and brief the recommended actions in their entirety—a holistic, coherent reform package. It will be harder to cherry-pick parochial interests if the package is seen as a comprehensive whole that serves the nation. We can capture the political high ground." Another advantage, I told him, was that he and OMB could gauge the reaction and, if necessary, turn down one or more of my recommendations. The president was very supportive but wanted Orszag on board. I used Obama's support to ensure that that was the case.

Rebuilding the 2010 budget gave me the opportunity not only to make "rebalancing" meaningful but also to weed out over-budget, overdue, or unjustifiable programs and to turn my attention to the herculean task of reforming the defense acquisition process. The history of cutting defense programs, especially big ones, is not pretty. When Dick Cheney was secretary in the early 1990s, two programs he tried to cut were the A-12 Navy and Marine Corps ground attack aircraft (nicknamed "the Flying Dorito" for its triangular shape) and the Marine Corps' tilt-rotor Osprey, a combination helicopter and airplane. The A-12 matter was still in litigation twenty years later, and Congress overruled Cheney to keep the Osprey flying. When other secretaries had tried to kill programs, the services would work behind the scenes with sympathetic members of Congress to keep the programs going and preserve the jobs they provided. When the services wanted to kill a program, Congress would usually just override them and fund the procurement over their objections. For most members of Congress, the defense budget is a huge cash cow providing jobs in their districts and states. Thus, even in those rare instances when the Pentagon tried to show some acquisition discipline, Congress made it tough, if not impossible, to succeed. To beat the system, I needed the radically different political strategy that I had described to the president.

I threw myself into the budget process. During February and March 2009, I chaired some forty meetings as we considered which programs should have more money and which were candidates to be eliminated or stop production. It was an intense period, partly because of the amount of work that had to be done, and partly because everyone knew that hundreds of billions of dollars in programs were at stake. Most of my meetings were with what we called the "small group"—deputy secretary Bill Lynn (after he was confirmed on February 11); the chairman and vice chairman of the Joint Chiefs, Mike Mullen and Hoss Cartwright; the director of program evaluation, Brad Berkson, and his deputy, Lieutenant General Emo Gardner; the acting comptroller, Mike McCord and (once confirmed) the comptroller, Bob Hale; the undersecretary for acquisition, technology, and logistics, John Young (a Bush holdover); the undersecretary for policy, Michèle Flournoy; and Robert Rangel and Ryan McCarthy of my staff. Gardner was the real workhorse on much of the effort. Every few days we would hold expanded meetings (the "large group") that included the service secretaries and chiefs and other senior civilians. And twice we brought in the entire senior Defense leadership, including the combatant commanders. One key point I would keep repeating, especially for the military, was that this was not driven by a reduction in the overall budget—money saved in some areas would be reinvested in programs of higher value.

All these meetings were a critical part of my strategy. One of the principal reasons previous secretaries—from Robert McNamara on—had failed to get Congress to go along with their recommended program changes was their exclusion of the military services from the decision-making process and the consequent opposition of the chiefs to their initiatives. I wanted the services intimately involved in the process, and I was prepared to give each service chief and secretary all the time he wanted to explain his views. Knowing that the services would often include programs in their budgets they didn't want but were sure Congress would insist on, I told the chiefs that this time around they should include only programs they really wanted "and leave the politics to me." I met at least four times with Army chief of staff George Casey and several times each with the other chiefs. Everyone had a chance to weigh in, not just on his own program but those of others as well. I wanted this to be a team effort, because when we were finished, I expected the chiefs, in particular, to support whatever decisions I made.

As I had told the president, previous efforts to cut programs had been leaked to Congress and the press early in the process, usually from the military service whose program was at risk. So at sensitive points in the debates, I prohibited circulation of briefing books and instead created limited access reading rooms where senior Defense officials had to go to prepare for the meetings. The huge staffs previously involved in the process were cut out. At the suggestion of Mike Mullen, I made everyone sign a nondisclosure statement. I signed the document and ultimately so did everyone else, after some grumbling. In other organizations, those agreements might not have meant much. But Mike and I knew what an oath and honor meant to military men and women—there was not a single leak during the entire process. I told no one except a small core group any of my final decisions until the day I announced them publicly. All of this drove the media and Congress nuts. Members of Congress would later complain about the use of "gag orders" and the lack of "transparency," and I shot back that previous "transparency" had been the result of a flood of leaks, not official briefings.

As grandiose as it sounds, the magnitude of what I intended to do was unprecedented. Other secretaries had tried to cut or cap a handful of defense programs. We were looking at more than sixty possibilities.

Ultimately I settled on nearly three dozen major programs that, if executed, would have cost about $330 billion over their lifetimes. Given my strategy to announce together all the changes I had in mind ahead of the regular budget process, we were lucky that by the time I was ready to go public, Congress was in recess. (In the hope of securing the neutrality, if not the support, of the leadership of the Armed Services and Appropriations Committees, we briefed them a few days before the announcement on the broad strategic context as well as the specifics. All those leaders supported most of my recommendations.) I believed the response of most media and pundits would be positive, so when Congress reconvened, those members attacking my decisions would be on the defensive. I thought announcing the changes all at once would "divide and conquer" members on the Hill. Previously, when only a few programs were proposed for elimination, affected members could build opposition coalitions by promising those who had no dog in the fight their vote on another issue in exchange. Going after dozens of programs made forming those coalitions much harder.

As for the larger defense industry companies, most of which have multiple contracts with the department, while many would lose in some areas, they would gain in areas where we would be increasing investments. This by and large minimized contractors' opposition to my decisions.

It was important to make sure the president not only was supportive in principle but would stand behind me with a veto threat if necessary. On March 30, I told the president, Rahm Emanuel, Jim Jones, and OMB director Peter Orszag about each of the major recommendations. The president approved them all. Rahm, thinking of the political challenge ahead, asked me for a list of states and districts that would be most affected by the cuts and how many jobs were affected by each decision. The advantage for the president in all this was that it fit nicely into his theme of Defense reform. And, if it went badly, he could disown one or more of my proposals.

I went public on April 6. I talked about reshaping priorities for Defense on their merits, not to balance the books. I announced we would spend $11 billion to protect and fund the growth of the Army and Marine Corps and halt manpower reductions in the Air Force and Navy; add $400 million for medical research and development; institutionalize and increase funding in the base budget by $2.1 billion for programs to take care of the wounded and those suffering from traumatic brain injury and post-traumatic stress; and increase funding by $200 million for improvements in child care, spousal support, housing, and education. All together, funding for taking care of our troops and their families was increased by $3 billion.

I said we would increase base budget funding for intelligence, surveillance, and reconnaissance by $2 billion to deploy fifty Predator-class drone orbits, increase the number of turboprop Liberty aircraft to go after IED networks, and fund a number of ISR enhancements and developmental platforms "optimized for today's battlefield"; $500 million more for acquiring and sustaining more helicopters and crews, "a capability in urgent demand in Afghanistan"; $500 million more for training and funding foreign militaries' counterterrorism and stability operations; add more money for expanding our special operations capabilities, both in terms of people and specialized equipment; and add money for more littoral combat ships, a key capability for presence, stability, and counterinsurgency operations in coastal regions.

For conventional and strategic forces, I said we would accelerate the purchase of F-35 fifth-generation stealth fighters and buy more F/A-18 fighters to keep the Navy's carrier wings fully equipped until the F-35s came on line; add $700 million to field more of our most capable theater missile defense systems; add $200 million to fund conversion of six additional Aegis ships to enhance ballistic missile defense capabilities; fund additional DDG-51 "Arleigh Burke" destroyers, a ship first built in the Reagan years but with additional modernization still best in class; add money to triple the number of students in our cyber warfare schools; proceed with the next generation Air Force tanker; and begin a replacement program for our ballistic missile submarines. I said we would also examine the need for a new Air Force bomber.

I realized that for the press and others, this was mostly ho-hum stuff. The real headlines were about the major programs to be cut or capped. The most significant was probably my decision to cap the F-22 stealth fighter at 187 aircraft. Ironically, I got tagged as the one who "killed" the F-22, but the program had had a long slide since the original proposal in 1986 for 750 aircraft. Over nearly twenty-five years, the F-22 program suffered almost as many cuts from as many hands as Julius Caesar had. Virtually every defense secretary except me wielded a knife. The manufacturers of the plane were very clever—the plane had suppliers in forty-four states, which made it important for eighty-eight senators. That made capping the number a battle royal.

Apart from cost, I had other problems with the F-22. It was an exquisite aircraft designed primarily to take on other fifth-generation aircraft (presumably Chinese) in air-to-air combat and penetrate and suppress sophisticated air defenses. But we had been at war for ten years, and the plane had not flown a single combat mission. I would ask the F-22's defenders, even in the event of a conflict with China, where we were going to base a short-range aircraft like the F-22. Did its defenders think the Chinese wouldn't destroy bases in Japan and elsewhere launching U.S. warplanes against them? All that said, one couldn't quarrel when pilots said it was the best fighter in the world. After a hard fight, and with a presidential veto threatened, the Senate voted 58–40 in July to accede to our proposal to end production at 187 aircraft. The House of Representatives ultimately went along.

My cancellation of the new VH-71 presidential helicopter drew considerable attention. This program was a poster child for acquisition going off the rails. Over the years, the White House had added more and more important requirements—like added survivability, range, and passenger load—but also trivial ones such as more than six feet of interior clearance so the president wouldn't have to stoop when he got on board, and a galley with a microwave oven. The Navy acquisition bureaucracy had also made expensive engineering changes that moved the helicopter further away from a commercial design intended to keep costs down. The development program for the helicopter had fallen six years behind schedule, and the cost had doubled to $13 billion. The five helicopters in the initial buy would have had half the range the White House wanted and just over half the range of the existing helicopters. I told President Obama he was about to buy a helicopter that in several respects was not as good as what he already had, that each would cost between $500 million and $1 billion—but that he could microwave a meal on it in the middle of a nuclear attack. As I expected, he thought the whole thing was a pretty bad idea. The concern on the Hill—especially from Jack Murtha and Bill Young—with the cancellation was that we had already spent $3.5 billion of the taxpayers' money, and it would just be wasted. They were right. The blame belonged squarely on the White House, the Defense Department, the Navy (managing the contract), and the contractor.

I also canceled a couple of big parts of the missile defense program that simply couldn't pass the giggle test. I guess they had survived until then because for some members of Congress, there was no such thing as a dollar wasted on missile defense. The first was the "kinetic energy interceptor," intended to shoot down enemy missiles (for example, from China and Russia) right after launch. It had been canceled a year earlier by the Ballistic Missile Development Office but restored by Congress. Its five-year development program had stretched to fourteen, there had been no flight tests, and there had been little work on the third stage and none on the kill vehicle itself. The weapon had to be deployed in very close proximity to enemy launch sites, a real problem with respect to large countries such as Russia, China, or even Iran. And the missile was so large and heavy, it would have to be deployed either on a future ship specifically designed for it or as a ground-based launcher. The program's cost had already increased from $4.6 billion to $8.9 billion. I put a stake through its heart.

The so-called airborne laser, also designed to shoot down ballistic missiles right after launch, met the same fate. This chemical laser was to be deployed aboard a Boeing 747, but the laser had a range of only about fifty miles, and so the 747 would have to orbit close to enemy launch sites (usually deep inside their territory), a huge, lumbering sitting duck for air defense systems. To maintain constant coverage, a fleet of some ten to twenty of the aircraft would have been needed at a cost of $1.5 billion each, along with an estimated annual operating cost per airplane of about $100 million.

I also killed the Army's Future Combat System, a highly sophisticated combination of vehicles, electronics, and communications with a projected cost in the range of $100 billion to $200 billion. The program, like so many in Defense, was designed for a clash of conventional armies. It was highly ambitious technologically, and there were serious doubts it would ever come to fruition at an acceptable cost. My major concern, though, was that the vehicle design did not take into account all we had learned in Iraq and Afghanistan about IEDs and other threats. I killed the vehicle part of the program, seeking a new approach, and the Army was able to use a number of the other technologies that had been developed.

General Cartwright patiently sat beside me through the entire presentation in the Pentagon press room, added his own remarks in support, and then helped me in answering questions. His technical understanding of the issues and problems affecting many of the programs was invaluable at that moment, as it had been in the decision-making process itself.

In the days following my press conference, I traveled to the war colleges of all four services—Quantico, Virginia, for the Marines; Maxwell AFB, Alabama, for the Air Force; Carlisle Barracks in Pennsylvania for the Army; and Newport, Rhode Island, for the Navy—to talk about what I was trying to do and to discuss decisions specific to each service. The middle-grade officers I addressed were the future of each of the services, and I hoped by engaging them directly I might be able to plant some ideas and perspectives that would have long-term impact. We'll see.

We fought Congress all summer and fall of 2009 over the 2010 budget and over all the program changes that I had recommended and the president had embraced. To stay on the offensive, Geoff Morrell, my press spokesman, suggested I give a major speech before the Economic Club of Chicago in mid-July, which Rahm Emanuel arranged with the help of William Daley, a member of the club's board (and Rahm's subsequent successor as Obama's chief of staff). Given that it was midsummer, I was amazed at the size of the crowd they assembled, its enthusiastic response to what we were trying to do, and the widespread press coverage we received. The event symbolized the full support of the White House.

When I had reviewed with the president at the end of March the specifics of what I was going to propose, both Biden and Emanuel said we'd be lucky to get half or 60 percent of what we wanted. When the dust settled, of the thirty-three major program changes I had recommended to the president, Congress ultimately acquiesced in 2009 to all but two. A year later we were successful in getting our way on those. It was unprecedented.

From some quarters, I received harsh criticism. One retired general said that I had "ripped the heart out of the future of the Army." Others said I had gutted missile defense. According to one retired Air Force general, "He has decimated the Air Force for the future." Former secretary of the Air Force Mike Wynne, not a member of my fan club, wrote, "I am sure . . . the Iranians are cringing in their boots about the threat from our stability forces. Our national interests are being reduced to becoming the armed custodians of two nations, Afghanistan and Iraq." At the same time, a significant number of members of Congress of both parties were supportive, as were most of the media, who were amazed that a secretary of defense was able to kill even one military program, much less thirty or so.

These battles would continue for as long as I was secretary and beyond. Meanwhile the new president and his team were focusing on other, more politically potent issues such as health care and foreign policy, and that would include addressing my fourth priority, getting Afghanistan on track.

The President's Agenda

As I said earlier, for the first several months under Obama, it took a lot of discipline to sit quietly at the table as everyone from the president on down took shots at Bush and his team. Sitting there, I would often think to myself, *Am I invisible?* During those excoriations, there was never any acknowledgment that I had been an integral part of that earlier team.

It was especially grating when the others would talk about how terrible our relations were with so many countries around the world, how our reputation as a country had been so damaged, how our standing had never been so low, and how much repair work lay ahead. While I would concede that the war in Iraq, in particular, had hurt many of our relationships, the world they described was not the world I had encountered when traveling as Bush's secretary of defense. Instead, I had found most countries in 2007–8 eager to strengthen their relationship with us. I thought our partnerships in Europe, Africa, and China were in pretty good shape, and the fairly sour state of affairs with Russia had more to do with their bad behavior—including the invasion of Georgia—than with missteps by the United States. Asian leaders, however, had told me they felt neglected by the Bush administration, and we obviously still had big problems in the Middle East.

Discussions in the Situation Room allowed no room for discriminating analysis: everything was awful, and Obama and his team had arrived just in time to save the day. Riding back to the Pentagon after White House meetings, Mike Mullen and I would discuss how everyone seemed completely oblivious to the possibility that both of us might take offense to some of the things being said. Just as likely, they didn't care. It was the dues we paid for staying on, but we didn't have to like it.

No president has the luxury of focusing on just a few issues, but it is hard to think of a president who entered office facing more challenges of historic magnitude than Obama. The nation's economic meltdown and the possibility of another great depression while we were engulfed in two wars certainly were at the top of the list. But there were myriad other pressing problems as well, among them the Iranian nuclear program and the related growing possibility of a new Middle East war; a nuclear-armed North Korea; a European economic crisis; increasingly nationalistic policies in both Russia and China; and Pakistan in possession of dozens of nuclear weapons and growing more dysfunctional by the day. Then there were Obama's own initiatives, such as reshaping the federal budget and far-reaching health care reform. During his first four months, he had to deal additionally with the launch of a long-range North Korean missile over Japan on April 5, which fortunately failed; the killing of three Somali pirates and the rescue of an American ship captain by Navy SEALs on April 12; a North Korean nuclear test (which apparently fizzled) on May 25; and working with the Canadians to rescue two of their UN envoys who had been kidnapped in Mali by al Qaeda. These and other such unforeseeable events made every day interesting, but they also made demands on the president's time and, accordingly, the time of his senior national security team.

Given the president's campaign pledges, Iraq had to be high on the agenda for prompt action. As a candidate, Obama had promised to withdraw all U.S. combat forces within sixteen months and, as provided in the Strategic Framework Agreement, to have all U.S. troops out of Iraq by December 2011. General Ray Odierno, the commander in Iraq, had started looking at different options for drawing down his forces well before the inauguration. As usual, there was a leak—almost certainly from the Pentagon—and *The New York Times* ran an article on January 15 discussing Ray's efforts. The story implied that there already was a difference of view between Obama and the military. This was not helpful. Geoff Morrell talked with Obama's adviser David Axelrod and press secretary–designate Robert Gibbs, who were very concerned about Obama appearing to be at odds with the military "right out of the gate," as had happened with President Clinton. They agreed that Morrell would tell the press that Mullen's and my discussions with Obama "had been broad in nature and they will not begin the process of presenting specific options on the way ahead in Iraq and Afghanistan until after the inaugural." In the months to come, there would be real, not imagined, problems between the White House and the military.

In a videoconference, Odierno told me he thought a recent preinaugural trip to Iraq by Biden and Senator Lindsay Graham had gone well, and he hoped if there was continued progress in both the security and political arenas, it might persuade the president to be flexible about his sixteen-month timeline. He said Biden told him that Obama would not be communicating directly with Prime Minister Maliki nearly as much as Bush had. I told Odierno I hoped to set up two sessions with Obama on the subject of drawdowns, one a videoconference with him and Petraeus, and the second a meeting at the Pentagon with the chairman, the chiefs, and me. I cautioned Odierno—and others—that Obama likely would not make a decision "on the spot," as Bush had done so often, but would probably want to consult with other advisers first.

Iraq was the subject of the first Obama National Security Council meeting on January 21, 2009. The president said he wanted to draw down troops in a way that "preserves the positive security trends and protects U.S. personnel." He asked for at least three options, one of which had to be his earlier sixteen-month timetable. In a press conference the next day, a reporter asked me what they should take from the fact that a White House statement after the NSC didn't mention sixteen months. I replied, "I wouldn't take anything from it."

In early February, ambassador to Iraq Ryan Crocker and Odierno submitted three options: (1) a twenty-three-month drawdown period, reducing U.S. forces to a residual training and advisory presence by December 2010, an option they recommended as offering the lowest level of risk and highest probability of achieving our objectives; (2) a nineteen-month drawdown, reaching the residual force level by August 2010, that would meet most but not all requirements for development of the Iraqi security forces; and (3) a sixteen-month-drawdown, which would be completed in May 2010, an option they said presented "extremely high risk" to overall mission accomplishment. Crocker and Odierno recommended a residual force of 50,000 to 55,000 troops, restructured into six advisory and assistance brigades, with the primary mission of training and advising Iraqi forces, deterring external threats, conducting counterterrorism operations, and protecting themselves and U.S. civilians. As provided in the Strategic Framework Agreement with the Iraqis, all

American forces would be out of their country by the end of December 2011.

I had discussed the options in detail with Odierno in January and knew what he could live with. I also knew Obama wouldn't accept a twenty-three-month drawdown. So in a private meeting with the president on January 26, I strongly recommended the nineteen-month-drawdown option. That moved his timetable back by 90 days and Odierno's up by 120 days. I told him this option would demonstrate that he was not blindly committed to a campaign promise, that it would show he had listened to his commanders and adjusted his approach, and that it would provide a definite date to move to an "advise and assist" mission. This also would provide maximum U.S. military strength through the March 2010 Iraqi elections. "You will be a prisoner neither to your campaign nor to your commanders," I concluded. He replied tersely: "I'm okay with that. It's also good politically." Obama and I had informally agreed on the Iraq drawdown timetable six days after the inaugural.

Unaware of the conversation between the president and me, the Deputies and Principals Committees met on several occasions during the first three weeks of February to discuss the options. On February 26, the president met with two dozen Democratic and Republican congressional leaders in the State Dining Room at the White House for "consultations" on the drawdown decision. As with virtually every president I worked for, such an occasion was less a consultation with Congress than a preview of what he was going to do and then hearing them out. All the president's senior advisers were there, including Mike Mullen and me. Everyone sat at one huge table.

Politically, it was not a great evening for the president. The Republicans were almost unanimously supportive, including John McCain. The Democratic leadership was shocked not so much by the timetable but by the fact that some 50,000 troops would remain in Iraq until nearly the end of 2011. I was sitting across from House Speaker Nancy Pelosi and thought she alternately looked like she had swallowed an entire lemon or was simply going to explode. She drummed her fingers on the table and had a white-knuckled grip on her pencil. She said she just could not understand why so many troops had to remain. Among the Democrats there, only Senator Dick Durbin, a close Illinois ally of Obama's, supported the president's plan.

The president flew to the Marine base at Camp LeJeune, North Carolina, the next day to announce his decisions and place them in a larger regional context. Mike Mullen, Jim Jones, and I accompanied him. His references to the sacrifice and bravery of the troops drew warm applause, but he got his biggest round of cheers when he told the Marines he was going to raise military pay. That day, February 27, General Odierno sent a message to all his troops: "After extensive consultation with the Iraqis, [the] U.S. military chain of command, and civilian leaders, the president announced his plan for the responsible drawdown of U.S. forces in Iraq. . . . The president has provided clear guidance regarding the change of mission for our forces, and his plan provides significant flexibility to military commanders on the ground to implement this guidance."

At the outset of the surge in Iraq in 2007, as we've seen, I had told Petraeus I would get him as many troops as I could for as long as I could. In Odierno's case, I was trying to ensure that he would *keep* as many troops as he could for as long as he could. While he was not entirely comfortable with the deal I struck, he would be able to hold on to significant troop levels until after the March 2010 Iraqi elections. He would manage it brilliantly.

The president moved quickly on the several foreign policy initiatives he had talked about during the campaign. Reaching out to Europe, he sent Biden, Jones, Holbrooke, and Deputy Secretary of State Steinberg to the Munich Security Conference in early February. Their tone, particularly on Biden's part, was that the Neanderthals were no longer in charge in Washington and the "good guys" were back. In exchange for more consultation and strengthening partnerships and international organizations, Biden said, the Obama administration was hoping for less criticism and more constructive ideas; for help in enforcing the rules of international organizations; for greater willingness to consider the use of force when absolutely necessary; and for concrete contributions, even if not military. He and the other senior Americans met to good effect with a number of European leaders at the conference. I was happy I didn't have to go. I had been to that conference twice under President Bush and that was enough. (On my second trip to Munich, I told my staff to pull me out of the dreaded formal dinner before dessert on the pretext of a call from the White House. Then I told them to get me just as the main course was served. Finally, just before going into the dinner, I said to come for me after the salad. As I left, heads turned, wondering what crisis compelled me to leave such a wonderful occasion so early. Pete

Chiarelli made me stop by my hotel room to "take the call" before we made a beeline for the hotel pub for beer and sausages.)

Given the perception of American neglect in Asia, I was both impressed and pleased that Hillary Clinton's first overseas trip as secretary of state was to Asia, beginning in Indonesia. I thought it sent an important message.

The more controversial among Obama's early initiatives were his efforts to reach out to countries where our relationships ranged from poor to outright hostility, principal among them Russia and Iran. In these cases, the president and Clinton played the primary role, although we spent a great deal of time discussing each matter in the Situation Room. I had a lot of bad memories relating to Iran from my earlier life in government. I had been on the advance trip to Tehran in late 1977 for a state visit by President Carter, a city I thought then—just over a year before the Islamic revolution—was the most tense I had ever experienced; I was present as notetaker in the fall of 1979 in Algiers, when Carter's national security adviser, Zbigniew Brzezinski, made the first (failed) U.S. attempt to engage the Iranian leadership (our embassy in Tehran was seized days later); I was in the White House with CIA director Stansfield Turner the evening of our failed attempt to rescue our embassy hostages in the spring of 1980; I witnessed the Iran-Contra disaster in 1986–87; and I was present in the Situation Room during the U.S.-Iranian naval incidents in the Persian Gulf in 1987–88 and the downing of a civilian Iranian airliner by a U.S. warship in 1988. I reminded the president and principals that every president since Carter had tried to engage with the Iranians, that every outstretched American hand had been slapped away, and that two presidents, Carter and Reagan, had paid a significant political price for it.

There were a couple of exchanges of letters between Obama and Iranian supreme leader Khamenei in the spring of 2009, and Obama videotaped a message to the Iranian people on March 20 on the occasion of the Iranian New Year. The return letters from Tehran were diatribes. There was a lot of criticism, especially from conservatives, about the outreach to Iran. I had no objection because I thought that when it failed—as I believed it would—we would be in a much stronger position to get approval of significantly stricter economic sanctions on Iran at the UN Security Council. That turned out to be the case. I was convinced that those sanctions held the only possible path to stopping the Iranian nuclear program, short of war. I underestimated the reaction to the initiative from the Israelis and our Arab friends, both of whom nurtured the dread that the United States would at some point cut a "grand bargain" with the Iranians that would leave both Israelis and Arabs to fend for themselves against Tehran.

Most support inside the administration for engagement ended with the Iranian regime's rigging of the outcome of the June 9 elections and the brutally harsh repression of protesters that ensued, although the administration would not fully abandon the idea until fall. The president was strongly criticized then and later for failing to speak out more clearly on behalf of the "Green Revolution." At the time, I was persuaded by the State Department's experts and by CIA analysts who briefed us in the Situation Room that too powerful an American voice on behalf of the protesters might provide ammunition for the regime to label the protest movement a tool of the United States and CIA and thus be used against them. In retrospect, I think we could and should have done more, at least rhetorically.

Another Iranian problem we faced had its roots in Bush's final days in office. On January 7, 2009, I was heading out of my office to celebrate with my infinitely patient wife our forty-second wedding anniversary when I heard Geoff Morrell talking to my chief of staff, Robert Rangel, right outside my door. Geoff had received a call from *New York Times* reporter David Sanger that afternoon alerting him that Sanger was writing an article that would say Israel had asked the United States early in 2008 for bunker-busting bombs and for permission for overflight of Iraq in order to strike the Iranian nuclear enrichment site at Natanz. Sanger claimed that the United States had refused both requests, believing that the Israelis would be able to delay the Iranian program only a short while but would put 150,000 U.S. troops in Iraq at risk. He also referred to a covert program intended to delay the Iranian nuclear program. Sanger wanted Morrell to ask me what I made of all this. I was furious. I called Bush's national security adviser, Steve Hadley, to report what Morrell had just told me. I suggested Hadley call executive editor Bill Keller of the *Times* to try to stop publication of the article. Hadley thought that would never work, and then, at Rangel's suggestion, I proposed bringing Jim Jones up to speed and then recommended that Hadley and Jones together call Keller. I don't think that ever happened. Sanger's article was published on January 11. A month later Obama was still so angry about the leaks to Sanger that he told me he wanted a criminal investigation. As long as I had been in Washington, I could not for the life of me understand why someone would leak information about programs that were an alternative to war. But the leaks would continue. I didn't know whether they were coming from the administration, from the Israelis, or from both. What I did know was that they were terribly damaging to the prospects for a nonmilitary outcome with Iran, and that that was unforgivable.

As an old "Russia hand," I had no objection to Obama's reaching out to Moscow as long as no unilateral concessions were involved. I was greatly reassured in an early meeting when Hillary said that she had no interest "ever" in doing something for nothing. She sent Russian foreign minister Sergei Lavrov a handwritten note on January 29 outlining a number of areas where the two sides could work together constructively, including a follow-on strategic arms agreement, global economic challenges, Middle East peace, Iran, North Korea, and Afghanistan. This was followed by a letter in early February from Obama to Russian president Medvedev setting forth a similar agenda, adding that both of them were young presidents with a different mind-set from those who came of age during the Cold War. (I wonder who he could have been talking about.) As reported publicly several weeks later, Obama wrote Medvedev that if we could satisfactorily resolve the Iranian nuclear problem, the need for missile defenses in Europe would be removed. This caused consternation in some conservative circles in the United States but in fact was very close to what Condi Rice and I had told Putin during the Bush administration. Although the administration would pursue a wide range of possibilities for cooperation in the months ahead, the focus of our dealings with Russia, as for so long before, narrowed principally to arms control and missile defense. There was progress on the former, failure and rancor on the latter.

Although by 2009 it was politically incorrect to describe Iran and North Korea as "rogue nations" or an "axis of evil," they still acted as if they were, even in small things. In March 2009, two American women journalists who had crossed on foot into North Korea from China were arrested for spying. A few months later, in July, three other American hikers—two men and one woman—crossed into Iran from Iraq and were arrested. Frankly, I had no patience with any of them; no sentient person goes tootling anywhere near either the North Korean or Iranian border. But we had to try to get them out nonetheless.

The North Korean government said it would release the two women only if a former U.S. president came to get them. Hillary, Jim Jones, several others, and I gathered in Jones's office in early August to discuss what to do. Hillary had asked President Carter to go, but he made clear that if he went, he would discuss broader aspects of the U.S.–North Korean relationship—as ever, an unguided missile—in addition to negotiating the terms of their release. When Clinton told Carter he could not go without a prior guarantee of the women's release by the North, the former president responded, "You can't dictate terms—they're a sovereign state!" I was against either Carter or former president Clinton going. I had no objection to lower-profile emissaries who had been suggested, such as former defense secretary Bill Perry, former secretary of state Madeleine Albright, or New Mexico governor Bill Richardson, but I was very much against giving the North a chance to humiliate a former U.S. president or allowing Pyongyang to dictate terms to one. I don't remember who it was who said the two women had a lot of media connections and the families could go public, charging that the administration had turned down a chance to get the women back. I was frustrated that the others seemed more sensitive to the domestic U.S. ramifications of not doing as North Korea wanted than to the foreign policy implications. Ultimately, President Clinton made the trip and secured the release of the two women. The Iranians released the woman hiker after about a year, but it was nearly three years before the two men were released. All of this took up an enormous amount of time and effort.

The president wanted very much to reach out to the Muslim world and looked for an opportunity to do so. There was general agreement he should give a major speech in the Middle East but considerable debate about the best location to do so. On June 4, 2009, eighteen months before the Arab Spring, he stepped to the rostrum of a huge auditorium at Cairo University and delivered one of his best speeches. He spoke forthrightly about tensions between Muslims and the United States around the world, about shared principles, the dangers to all of violent extremists, the Israeli-Palestinian-Arab conflict, the Iranian nuclear program, and the American commitment to governments that reflect the will of the people—democracy. I thought he threaded the needle well in terms of advocating for human and political rights while not losing sight of the importance in the region of the American relationship with Mubarak's Egypt. His talk was welcomed in most Muslim countries and raised our standing among the Arabs. His words were not well received in Israel, and he was criticized by the more hawkish neoconservatives in the United States, who accused the president of apologizing for his country. For me, the real downside of the speech was not that it was an acknowledgment of mistakes—free and confident nations do that—but that it raised expectations very high on the part of many Arabs that, for example, the United States would force Israel to stop building settlements and accept an independent Palestinian state. It wasn't long before perceptions of us reverted to the by-then normal distrust and suspicion.

In the early months of the Obama administration, there was another Defense-related agenda item high on the president's priority list—getting rid of the "Don't Ask, Don't Tell" (DADT) law. Early in President Clinton's administration, he had pushed hard to allow gays and lesbians to serve openly in the American armed forces but ran into opposition in Congress and a brick wall of resistance from the senior military leadership. The result was a compromise that left everyone unhappy: in essence, gays could continue to serve as long as they remained in the closet and kept their sexual orientation a secret, that is, as long as they did not engage in homosexual "conduct." Between 1993 and 2009, some 13,000 service men and women were discharged from the military for homosexuality, either self-admitted or as a result of being reported by someone. Obama was determined to allow gays to serve openly but was willing to wait a bit. He did not want to repeat the 1993 Clinton experience of having a confrontation with the Joint Chiefs early in his term. That suited me just fine. I think all of us at Defense, civilian and military, knew that a change in the law was inevitable at some point, but with our military engaged in two wars and already under great stress, the prevailing view was that waiting was the right thing to do.

I was conflicted. As director of central intelligence in 1992, I had lifted all the restrictions and practices that effectively had previously barred gays from serving in CIA. If a person was open about his or her sexual orientation and therefore not vulnerable to blackmail, they were welcome to serve as long as they met the same CIA standards as other employees. CIA officers, however, do not live and work together 24/7. They do not share foxholes for days at a time or live in the extremely close quarters of a warship. The military is therefore different from CIA— a perspective strengthened by my conversations with troops, particularly young soldiers, in Iraq and Afghanistan. At a lunch with ten or so junior enlisted soldiers, one asked about the prospects for DADT. In the conversation that followed, one of them told me very matter-of-factly that if gays were allowed to serve, "There will be violence." Another asked if "combat arms units"—those on the front lines—could be exempted. I heard such comments elsewhere as well. At the same time, I was mindful that there were gay men and women in uniform who were serving with courage and honor yet were required to live a lie, constantly in fear of being outed and having their careers ended. Still, when asked about changing the law in a television interview on March 29, 2009, I replied, "I think the president and I feel like we've got a lot on our plates right now, and let's push that one down the road a bit."

In the spring of 2009, though, we faced a growing risk that the courts would take control of the issue and make a decision requiring a change overnight. I felt that that was the worst possible outcome, and that risk increasingly shaped my view of the need to move forward. The president faced his first decision on a court case in early April. Major Margaret Witt had been a highly respected nurse in the Air Force Reserve for seventeen years. She never disclosed her sexual orientation to anyone in the military, but in 2004, the estranged husband of a woman Witt had begun dating reported the major to the Air Force. When informed in 2006 that the Air Force was beginning the process that would culminate in her discharge, she sued. Her suit was dismissed in district court, and she was discharged from the Air Force in July 2007. On her appeal, the Ninth Circuit Court in May 2008 reinstated certain aspects of the case and remanded it back to the district court. The Air Force in December urged appealing the Ninth Circuit Court's decision to the Supreme Court. In early April 2009, Obama chaired a meeting in the Roosevelt Room of the West Wing to discuss what to do. He clearly hated the idea of upholding a law he considered abhorrent. Some in the meeting said DADT was the law of the land and that was that. The president said if he had to take that approach, he was going to say publicly that he was going to change the law.

On the advice of the Defense Department's general counsel, the well-respected New York lawyer Jeh Johnson, I agreed we should not appeal to the Supreme Court, and that was subsequently the decision. Johnson's primary reason, and therefore mine (because I trusted and respected him like no other lawyer I had ever worked with), was that he thought the government's case as it stood was weak and that we might very well lose the appeal, resulting in my nightmare scenario of a Supreme Court–mandated overnight change in the DADT law for the military. I told the senior defense leadership that the decision not to appeal did not represent a change in policy but was a very technical and narrow legal decision about how to dispose of a specific case.

This discussion formed the backdrop of Mullen's and my first in-depth discussion of DADT with Obama on April 13. We understood his commitment to changing the law, but the question was how to fulfill that promise in a way that "mitigates the negative consequences." I was quite candid with him. He needed to remember, I said, that a high percentage of our service men and women come from the South, Midwest, and Mountain West, more often than not from small towns and rural areas. They come from areas with conservative values, and they are, broadly speaking, more religious than many Americans. While they join the military for a variety of reasons, they often enlist because of the encouragement or at least support of their fathers, coaches, and preachers. The demographic and cultural realities of the U.S. military could not be wished away, and we had to acknowledge and address them if a change in the law was going to be successful.

I went on to tell him that no one in the Pentagon had any idea what the impact of eliminating DADT would be on the force with regard to unit cohesion, discipline, morale, recruitment, and retention. We didn't know how quickly a policy could be implemented without major disruption to the services. The military had never had an open conversation internally about gays serving. What dialogue there had been was, I suspected, mostly among groups of soldiers in the barracks or in small groups over a few beers. If the policy was to change, I cautioned him in the strongest possible terms, it should not be by presidential order; it could not be seen by the military as simply the fulfillment of a campaign promise by a liberal president. DADT was the law. Any change had to come through a change in that law by the elected representatives of the American people. That, and only that, would have legitimacy. I said he could count on the fact that when the law and the policy changed, the military would implement it quickly and smoothly. He took all that in, I thought, with surprising equanimity.

"Let's do it but do it right," I concluded. I told the president I would appoint a task force to study the impact of changing the policy and how best to implement such a change. A few weeks later Rahm urged me to begin preparations throughout the force for repeal right away, to ease pressure from the "advocacy groups." I refused, telling him I would not throw the military into turmoil in the middle of two wars to prepare for a controversial change that might or might not happen. When the president went to Congress and got the law repealed, then I would act.

That said, Mullen and I were thinking about how to structure a dialogue within the military to have an open discussion for the first time ever about gays serving openly, what the challenges would be, and how they could be mitigated. I asked Jeh Johnson to examine ways in which I could change the regulations to make it harder to discharge gays and to place the responsibility for such a decision higher in the chain of command. At the end of June, in response to a question, I told the Pentagon press corps that Mullen and I were actively discussing a change in the DADT law with the president and the senior military leadership. Among other things, we were looking at how to prepare for a change without disrupting the force, and for areas where there might be some flexibility in how we applied the law; for example, if someone was "outed" by a third party, would we be forced to take action? Those two issues would be debated internally through the remainder of 2009.

CHAPTER 10

Afghanistan: A House Divided

On a crisp, sunny day in October 1986, I stood on a ridgeline in northwestern Pakistan near the Afghan border. I was the deputy director of CIA, and I was visiting a mujahideen training camp, escorted by officials of Pakistan's Inter-Services Intelligence directorate (ISI). There were thirty to forty fighters, all wearing brand-new parkas, and they were learning to shoot rocket-propelled grenades, using as their target whitewashed rocks on the mountainside in the outline of a Soviet T-72 tank. I assumed everyone there knew CIA was providing the funds for their war, and they were putting on a great show for the man who wrote the checks. The new parkas, the handpicked marksmen, the chilled Pepsis at lunch, and the professions of gratitude for the munitions and other supplies—it was a well-staged snow job. It would not be my last.

Behind Oz's curtain on the Pakistani frontier that day were harsh realities. I was there principally because the ISI was stalling on providing our new Stinger antiaircraft missiles and other supplies to the Tajiks of the Panjshir Valley and other non-Pashtuns fighting the Soviets in Afghanistan. It was the Pakistanis who decided which mujahideen groups—which warlords—got our weapons. CIA could cajole and exert pressure, but President Muhammad Zia ul-Haq and the ISI were the "deciders." While we were working closely with Zia to defeat the Soviets, he was at the same time enacting laws that would promote the Islamization of Pakistan and the strengthening of Islamic fundamentalism.

A lot of American weapons, accordingly, went to Afghan Islamic fundamentalists. Our lack of understanding of Afghanistan, its culture, its tribal and ethnic politics, its power brokers, and their relationships, was profound. After becoming secretary of defense twenty years later, I came to realize that in Afghanistan, as in Iraq, having decided to replace the regime, when it came to "with what?," the American government had no idea what would follow. We had learned virtually nothing about the place in the twenty years since helping defeat the Soviets there.

These experiences—these ghosts—led to my strong conviction, as I stated earlier, that the idea of creating a strong, democratic (as we would define it), more or less honest and effective central government in Afghanistan, to change the culture, to build the economy and transform agriculture, was a fantasy. Our goal, I thought, should be limited to hammering the Taliban and other extremists so as to degrade their military capabilities, and to building up the Afghan army and local security forces to the point where they could keep the extremists under control and deny al Qaeda a future safe haven in Afghanistan. We needed to be thinking in terms of three to five years to accomplish those narrow goals, but we also needed to figure out how to sustain a modest civilian and military presence for many years—as necessary in Afghanistan, I believed, as in Iraq. We couldn't just walk away again. As I thought about how to achieve those objectives, the memory of 120,000 Soviet troops and more than 15,000 dead Soviet soldiers stuck in my mind. If we had too many foreign troops in country, if there were too many civilian casualties and too little respect for Afghans and what *they* wanted and what *they* thought, the Afghans would come to see us, too, as occupiers, not partners. And we would lose, just as the Soviets had. My thinking along these lines was reflected consistently between December 2006 and late 2009 in my public statements, in my congressional testimony, and in my skepticism about adding significantly more troops there.

Prior to Obama's inauguration, Joe Biden visited Afghanistan and Iraq, as I said. Talking to U.S. diplomats, commanders, and soldiers in Kabul, Biden found confusion at all levels about our strategy and objectives. His previous encounter with Afghan president Karzai, at a dinner in February 2008, had gone badly and ended with the then-chairman of the Senate Foreign Relations Committee throwing down his napkin and walking out on the Afghan president. At dinner with Karzai in January 2009, there was another tempestuous conversation, during which Biden went after the Afghan president on both governance and corruption. One of Biden's messages to Karzai (and Maliki) was that Obama would not engage with them nearly as often as had Bush. There was concern among Obama's team that Bush's frequent videoconferences with both leaders had led to an unhealthy dependence on direct communications with the U.S. president that undercut the ability of Americans in country to do their jobs. I thought there was some validity to the concern, but I was torn. Bush had been a useful mentor for both, and when he raised issues, both leaders knew there was no higher-level appeal. Biden also met with International Security Assistance Force (ISAF) commander General David McKiernan, who made his case for 30,000 more troops, particularly to improve security before the Afghans' August election. Biden was deeply disturbed about what he had found in Afghanistan. (Things went much better on his visit to Iraq.)

Obama had pledged during the campaign to send more troops to Afghanistan to remedy the inadequate resourcing of the war during the Bush administration, which had begun shifting its focus and priorities to Iraq within months of the fall of the Taliban. I think that all the senior national security officials of the incoming administration shared the view that we were neither winning nor losing in Afghanistan and that we needed to take a hard look at what we were doing there. I had told President Bush in my job interview in November 2006 that I thought our goals in Afghanistan were too expansive, and my concerns had only increased over the ensuing two years. In my January 26 meeting with Obama, I told him that we should have "no grandiose aspirations" in Afghanistan; we just wanted to prevent the country from again becoming a source of threats to us or our allies, as it had been under the Taliban. In a hearing before the Senate Armed Services Committee the next day, I was even more explicit: "If we set out to create [in Afghanistan] a central Asian Valhalla, we will lose. We need to keep our objectives realistic and limited, or we will set ourselves up for failure."

The new administration's first NSC meeting on Afghanistan was on January 23. There was much discussion on the lack of a coherent strategy. Petraeus and Mullen both pushed strongly for quick approval of McKiernan's requested 30,000 troops. I was supportive of some more troops but ambivalent about the number, partly because of the rationale the military was advancing. The additional troops were supposed to blunt the Taliban's summer offensive and provide security for the

August elections, but many of them could not get there in time to do either. I was also still concerned about the size of our military "footprint." Biden quite logically objected to sending more troops even before we had figured out our strategy.

The president decided to reach outside the government to ask Bruce Riedel, a Middle East expert who had advised his campaign, to lead a sixty-day review of the situation in Afghanistan and recommend changes in strategy. Holbrooke and Defense Undersecretary Flournoy would cochair the effort, with Doug Lute and his staff at the NSC in support. Riedel had been a longtime analyst at CIA and had worked for me. He was one of the best, most realistic Middle East analysts.

The immediate problem facing the president was timing: if we were to get thousands of troops, whatever the exact number, trained, equipped, and into Afghanistan in time to deal with the Taliban's summer offensive and the elections, we needed a decision before Riedel's report would be finished, to the chagrin of the vice president and others in the White House. On his return flight from the Munich Security Conference in early February, Biden had told the press that he wasn't going to let the military "bully" the White House into making decisions about more troops for Afghanistan because of "artificial timelines." The president had wanted to announce his decisions on the troop drawdowns in Iraq before announcing more troops for Afghanistan, but that wasn't going to happen either. As the Deputies Committee, chaired by Tom Donilon, parsed the request for 30,000 troops and focused on when they could get to Afghanistan and what they would do, it became clear that the Joint Staff had not worked through how many could get there by summer. The request was eventually pared to about 17,000 additional troops.

This pressure for an early decision on a troop increase in Afghanistan had the unfortunate effect of creating suspicion in the White House that Obama was getting the "bum's rush" from senior military officers, especially Mullen and Petraeus, to make a big decision prematurely. I believed then—and now—that this distrust was stoked by Biden, with Donilon, Emanuel, and some of Obama's other advisers joining the chorus, including, ironically, Jim Jones and Doug Lute. The distrust may also have been attributable in part to the lack of experience with military affairs—particularly, in this case, training and logistical timelines—among the senior civilian White House officials from the vice president on down. I believe the military had no ulterior motives: failure to approve at least some troop movements quickly would, in itself, limit the president's options, rendering him unable to blunt the Taliban summer offensive or add security before the Afghan election. Nonetheless, the suspicion would only fester and grow over time.

Incidents unrelated to Afghanistan worsened it. In late February, for example, Admiral Tim Keating, commander of all U.S. forces in the Pacific, told a press conference about U.S. capabilities to shoot down North Korea's Tae Po Dong 2 missile and that a prospective launch would be "a stern test" of the new administration. The president was furious at what he called "freelancing" as well as the admiral's presumption in appearing to judge the president. In his view, Keating's remarks created serious problems for the administration: if the president ordered the missile shot down, Keating had telegraphed our punch and made non-attribution difficult to sustain; if the president decided not to act, people would wonder why. Mullen and I asked the president if he wanted Keating relieved. Obama said no, that everyone deserved a second chance, but he told me to recall Keating and reprimand him. Keating flew from Hawaii to Washington for a ten-minute meeting with me. I told him of the president's unhappiness but that we all wanted him to stay—and to learn from the experience. Tim asked me to convey his apologies to the president and tell him this kind of thing would never happen again. And it didn't (at least with Keating). This episode, along with the president's problems with the outspoken director of national intelligence, Denny Blair, and increasingly Mike Mullen, showed that presidential irritation with publicity-prone admirals was another source of continuity between the Bush and Obama administrations. All too early in the administration, suspicion and distrust of senior military officers by senior White House officials—including the president and vice president—became a big problem for me as I tried to manage the relationship between the commander in chief and his military leaders.

On February 13, the president chaired an NSC meeting to consider whether to wait until after the Riedel review to decide on more troops, to send 17,000 as soon as possible, to send some troops now and the rest later, or to send the full 30,000 McKiernan had requested. Riedel and all but two of the principals—Biden and Steinberg—supported sending 17,000 at once.

On February 16, in our regular weekly meeting, the president told Mullen and me that he would have preferred to announce the Iraqi drawdown first, as we knew, but that he had decided to authorize the 17,000 troops to help stabilize the situation in Afghanistan and prevent further deterioration. Obama then said to me, "I trust you and your judgment." The next day the White House announced the decision in a written press release. Although Obama later characterized the decision as the toughest he had made early in his term, he did not bother to announce it in person.

There would later be questions about why so many of the additional troops—Marines—were sent to Helmand province with its sparse population. Their deployment was intended primarily to prevent the security situation in the south from further worsening; that took precedence over providing election security. But an important reason the Marines deployed to Helmand was that while Marine Commandant Jim Conway was eager to get his Marines off their duffs in western Iraq and into the fight in Afghanistan, he also insisted that all the Marines deploy to a single "area of responsibility"—one battlespace—with Marine air cover and logistics. Only Helmand fit Conway's conditions. The Marines were determined to keep operational control of their forces away from the senior U.S. commander in Kabul and in the hands of a Marine lieutenant general at Central Command in Tampa. The Marines performed with courage, brilliance, and considerable success on the ground, but their higher leadership put their own parochial service concerns above the requirements of the overall Afghan mission. Despite several failed attempts through Pace and Mullen, I did not get this and other command problems in Afghanistan fully fixed until 2010. I should have seized control of the matter well before that. It was my biggest mistake in overseeing the wars in Iraq and Afghanistan.

The other major issue discussed at the February 13 NSC meeting was the timing of the Afghan elections. The Afghan constitution required that the presidential election be held by May 22, 2009, when Karzai's term would legally end, but the United States and our coalition partners were pressing hard to postpone the election to August 20. Holbrooke argued that a May election could undermine the opposition's ability to compete and the ISAF's ability to provide security. The president directed Holbrooke to tell Karzai that he, Obama, was aware of the constitutional problem of going beyond May and that we would work with him to help find a "bridge" to August elections. No one, including me, was indelicate enough to mention that the new administration, dedicated to building "the rule of law" in Afghanistan, had just decided to violate the Afghan constitution and to connive with Karzai on keeping him in power illegally for several months. In its most favorable light, the decision was intended to provide time for other presidential candidates to get organized so there would be a credible election in Afghanistan. For Holbrooke and others at the table, it provided the time necessary to identify a viable alternative to Karzai, who they thought had to go. If the Afghan constitution was an impediment to achieving this goal, the hell with it.

About the same time, Michèle Flournoy returned from her first visit to Afghanistan with some disquieting observations:

> I saw little to convince me that we have a comprehensive interagency plan or concept of operations. I still believe that many competing—and often conflicting—campaigns are ongoing in Afghanistan: counter-insurgency, counterterrorism, counternarcotics, and efforts at nation-building. Interagency planning, coordination and resourcing are, by far, the weakest link. . . . Commanders believe that the substantial planned increase of U.S. forces and capabilities, combined with growth in the ANSF [Afghan National Security Forces], will improve their ability to "clear" and "hold" some key areas. These forces alone will remain insufficient to "build" enough to reduce the insurgency and promote Afghan self-reliance.

She told me that the civilian-military assistance teams—the provincial reconstruction teams—intended to help bring services and better governance to areas the military had cleared of insurgents were "woefully underresourced." I was dismayed but not surprised by her assessment of deficiencies on the civilian side—after all, I'd been talking about this problem for two years.

I told my staff in early March that I was very disappointed in the Riedel review so far, which contained no new ideas. Among other things, his report called for significantly greater U.S. civilian advisory capacity without offering any concrete proposals as to where it could be found. Flournoy said that the draft report was all about *what* should be done but the *how* was missing. There were four options under discussion: (1) "whack-a-mole" counterterrorism—also referred to as "mowing the grass"—and walking away from any other goals; (2) counterterrorism plus some training of the Afghan security forces, cutting deals with warlords, and then getting out as soon as possible; (3) limited counterinsurgency (COIN); and (4) more ambitious COIN, going beyond McKiernan's request in terms of troop numbers.

During a single week in mid-March, there were three Principals Committee meetings and two sessions with the president on Afghanistan. That Friday we reviewed the final Riedel report, which recommended disrupting the terrorist networks in Afghanistan and especially Pakistan, promoting a more effective government in Afghanistan, developing the Afghan security forces, ending Pakistan's support for terrorist and insurgent groups, enhancing civilian control in Pakistan, and using U.S. diplomatic, military, and intelligence channels to reduce enmity and distrust between Pakistan and India. It was breathtaking in its ambition. Most significantly in terms of the conflicts to come between the White House and the military, the report stated, "A fully-resourced counterinsurgency campaign will enable us to regain the initiative and defend our vital interests." All the principals except Biden concurred in the recommendations of the report and also supported full deployment of the 17,000 troops already approved and another 4,000 trainers for the Afghan security forces. Except for the focus on the need to treat Afghanistan in a regional context and, above all, the critical importance of Pakistan to the outcome of the war, the Riedel report had much in common with the review Lute had overseen at the end of the Bush administration. They also had in common the weakness pointed out by Flournoy: far too much attention was paid to *what* should be done and far too little to *how* to get it done.

Biden argued throughout the process, and would continue to argue, that the war was politically unsustainable at home. I thought he was wrong and that if the president remained steadfast and played his cards carefully, he could sustain even an unpopular war. Bush had done that with a far more unpopular war in Iraq and with both houses of Congress in the hands of the Democrats. The key was showing that we were being successful militarily, at some point announcing a drawdown of forces, and being able to show that an end was in sight. Nearly two and a half years later, when I left, we still had 100,000 U.S. troops in Afghanistan. Contrary to Biden's gloomy forecast in early 2009, the president had been able to sustain the effort.

The president embraced most of the Riedel recommendations and announced the elements of his new "AfPak" strategy in a televised speech on March 27 with his senior advisers standing behind him. The goal, he said, would be "to disrupt, dismantle, and defeat al Qaeda in Pakistan and Afghanistan and to prevent their return to either country in the future." He said that the 17,000 soldiers he already had approved would "take the fight to the Taliban in the south and east, and give us a greater capacity to partner with Afghan security forces and to go after insurgents along the border." Although he added that they would also help provide security in advance of the Afghan elections, implicit in his remarks was the priority of taking the fight to the Taliban in their heartland. There would now be some 68,000 American troops in Afghanistan. Further, we would increase the training and size of the Afghan security forces.

He also called for a dramatic increase in the U.S. civilian effort— agricultural specialists, educators, engineers, and lawyers—to advance security, opportunity, and justice and to help the Afghan government serve its people and develop an economy not dominated by illicit drugs. This civilian component was central to any political strategy for denying the Taliban influence. He never used the words *counterinsurgency* or *counterterrorism* in the speech, but the strategy he announced was clearly a blend of both. Two days after the announcement, I told a television interviewer that I did not think there would be any need to ask the president to approve more troops until we saw how the troops soon to deploy were doing.

I fully supported the president's decisions although I was deeply skeptical about two fundamental elements of the strategy. Based on our experience in Iraq, I harbored deep doubt that the required number of civilian advisers from State, the Agency for International Development, the Department of Agriculture, and other agencies could be found and deployed. My doubts would prove justified. I also doubted we could persuade the Pakistanis to change their "calculus" and go after the Afghan Taliban and other extremists on their side of the border. When a Pakistani Taliban offensive that spring reached within sixty miles of Islamabad, the Pakistani army went after them in the border provinces of Swat and South Waziristan for their own protection. Their continuing toleration of the Afghan Taliban, including harboring their leaders in Quetta, was a hedging strategy based on their lack of trust in us, given our unwillingness to stay engaged in Afghanistan in the early 1990s. The

Obama administration worked hard to alleviate that mistrust, but history was working against us.

My definition of success was much narrower than Riedel's or the president's at that point: using military operations—a combination of selective counterinsurgency and counterterrorism—to degrade the Taliban's capabilities to the point where larger and better trained Afghan security forces could maintain control of the country and prevent the return of al Qaeda. I would take this position for as long as I was secretary. The president's broad new policy would help accomplish that goal. I had told Petraeus in Iraq that a key to success was recognizing the tipping point—when the Iraqis doing something barely adequately was better than us doing it excellently. I thought the same principle should apply in Afghanistan and, even in the Bush administration, I had called it "Afghan good enough."

In June 2008, on my recommendation to the president, General Dave McKiernan became the commander of ISAF in Afghanistan, a coalition force of American troops and troops from more than forty other countries. George Casey, Army chief of staff, and Mullen thought he was the right man for the job, and I had a very high opinion of him, in no small part because he had worked so well with our allies in Europe. Nonetheless, by mid-fall, I was openly expressing concern to my immediate staff about whether I had made a mistake. To this day, it is hard for me to put a finger on what exactly it was that concerned me, but my disquiet only grew through the winter. Perhaps more than anything it was two years' experience in watching generals like Petraeus, McChrystal, Chiarelli, Rod Rodriguez, and others innovate in blending both counterterrorism and counterinsurgency operations, and observing their flexibility in embracing new ideas, their willingness to experiment, and their ability to abandon an idea that didn't pan out and move on to try something else. McKiernan was a very fine soldier but seemed to lack the flexibility and understanding of the battlespace required for a situation as complex as Afghanistan. Based on his recent background and experience—commanding coalition ground forces during the opening phase of the Iraq War and then leading the U.S. Army in Europe—I wondered if I had put him into a situation that did not play to his strengths.

There were some specific issues. In trying to solve the command and control problem for coalition forces in Afghanistan, Mullen and I agreed that the best alternative was to replicate the structure we had in Iraq—a four-star commander of all forces, McKiernan, with a subordinate three-star commander to manage the war on a day-to-day basis. McKiernan, like McNeill before him, spent a significant amount of time with Karzai and other Afghan officials, coalition ambassadors, and visiting government officials, and on NATO-related issues—diplomatic and political duties. That role was critically important but made apparent the need for someone else who would be totally focused on the fight. McKiernan strongly resisted such a change. I was also concerned that we were not moving fast enough or decisively enough to deal with the problem of civilian casualties. As I said before, I don't believe any military force ever worked harder to avoid innocent victims, but it seemed like every incident was a strategic defeat, and we needed to take dramatic action. Soon after the president's March announcement, I told Mullen, "I've got kids out there dying, and if I don't have confidence I have the very best possible commander, I couldn't live with myself."

The issue came to a head in early April when Michèle Flournoy returned from Afghanistan and told me of her concern as to whether McKiernan was the best man for the job. The specific issues she raised paralleled my own list. Mullen and Petraeus both agreed a change was needed. Casey argued strenuously against firing Dave, calling it a "rotten" thing to do. He wrote a letter to the president expressing his views, a letter that he shared with me and I personally delivered.

I had talked on several occasions privately with the president about my misgivings and in mid-April told him I thought the time had come to make a change. Mullen, Petraeus, and I would unanimously recommend Lieutenant General Stanley McChrystal to succeed McKiernan. The president understood the potential for a political ruckus caused by firing the senior commander in the war, but he was willing to make the change.

Relieving McKiernan of command was one of the hardest decisions I ever made. He had made no egregious mistake and was deeply respected throughout the Army. Mullen had been talking with him about what was in the air for a few weeks and, in the latter part of April, flew to Afghanistan to try to persuade him to step down of his own accord. Dave made clear he wanted to remain in place until the end of his tour in the spring of 2010. I couldn't wait that long. I flew to Kabul on May 6 and went almost immediately into a private dinner with Dave, telling him why I wanted to make a change so quickly. He acceded with extraordinary dignity and class.

I would learn only later that this was the first time a wartime commander had been relieved since Truman fired Douglas MacArthur in 1951. During World War II, Generals George Marshall and Dwight Eisenhower routinely fired commanders, many of them perfectly capable officers, including several personal friends. General Matthew Ridgway did much the same in Korea before and after taking over from MacArthur. The act was common enough not to be a career-ender or blight on the reputation of the affected general or the Army itself. But by the time of the Vietnam War, it was practically unheard of in the Army. I hope that the McKiernan episode will contribute to reestablishing accountability for senior officers for wartime performance, including the precedent that personal misconduct or serious mistakes need not be required for relief.

On May 11, I announced that McKiernan was being relieved and that I would recommend McChrystal to take his place as senior commander. My senior military assistant, Rodriguez, would become the deputy commander in charge of the day-to-day fight. A reporter asked what McKiernan had done wrong. I said absolutely nothing, that a new strategy required a new commander. When asked why McChrystal was the replacement, I said that he and Rodriguez together brought a unique skill set in both counterterrorism and counterinsurgency.

My usual practice with senior military appointments under both Bush and Obama was to take the officer in for a brief photo op with the president just before my weekly meeting in the Oval Office. My main purpose was to have the president congratulate the appointee and offer his support and confidence. The president knew of McChrystal's extraordinary success in running counterterrorism operations in Iraq and Afghanistan. In official settings, alas, Stan was not relaxed or casual, to say the least. When he met Obama, and the president cracked a little joke, McChrystal remained rigid and unsmiling. After Stan left, Obama smiled and said, "He's very . . . focused."

Even before McChrystal was confirmed by the Senate, I was hearing from Mullen and others about the need for more troops—the president's recent approval of 21,000 more notwithstanding. There was still an outstanding request from McKiernan for another 10,000, among other things. A little over a week after my meeting in Kabul with McKiernan, I attended a deployment orders meeting about staffing Rodriguez's new operational headquarters. (Each week I would meet with the chairman and vice chairman, along with my staff and the Joint Staff, to approve "requests for forces" from commanders all over the world—which units, how many troops, and so on.) I was told that this new headquarters in Kabul would require several thousand more troops, perhaps going well above the presidentially approved number of 68,000. I was surprised by the request and told the group we could not go above the approved number without going back to the president. Once McChrystal was in Afghanistan, he would have to evaluate just how all those people were being used—for example, were there soldiers and Marines doing infrastructure construction or maintenance who could be reassigned to the new headquarters or to the fight?

Meanwhile there weren't enough U.S. civilian advisers and experts, described as so critical to success in the Riedel report. On May 2, Petraeus and Holbrooke cochaired a civilian-military "coordination conference" with representatives from a number of government agencies. The embassy had asked for 421 more people, but Holbrooke asked for an "unconstrained" reanalysis of the civilian requirement down to the provincial and district levels. Holbrooke obviously shared my skepticism about State's ability to expeditiously field a significant number of civilians to Afghanistan. I told the State Department and National Security Staff that I was prepared to provide several hundred civilian experts from Defense and from the military reserve to fill vacancies.

At a Deputies Committee meeting in late May, Tom Donilon reaffirmed the importance of the civilian component and expressed considerable impatience with the size and pace of the civilian surge. Despite the failure of State and others to deliver the needed number of civilian experts, Deputy Secretary of State Jack Lew (in charge of administration) and others did not take advantage of my offer to loan them (and pay for) Defense civilians to fill gaps. The most common response I heard was that our people weren't an exact fit for the open positions. I felt that if a Defense civilian had half the skills or background State was looking for, that would give us 50 percent more civilian capacity than we currently had. On a related issue, I was concerned that a high percentage of the U.S. civilians in Afghanistan were stationed in Kabul, when the greatest need was in the provinces and districts where our military was attempting to clean out the Taliban. They stayed a year—with a number of weeks of vacation time—and nearly all turned over in the summer, often leaving gaps in civilian capability for months and sometimes indefinitely. The numbers and location of civilian experts would remain a source of frustration among our commanders and the rest of us at Defense. (Many of the civilians eventually sent by State did not possess the required skills either; they and too many other civilians spent their entire Afghan tour holed up in the fortified embassy compound.)

I thought there was another potential source of civilian expertise available. I knew of the international outreach programs of most U.S. land-grant colleges and universities, particularly in fields including agriculture, livestock, veterinary medicine, and water resources. Research and practitioner faculty regularly traveled to developing countries and, working in primitive and often dangerous circumstances, made a huge contribution. Repeatedly, I urged Holbrooke and AID officials to reach out to the national president of the land-grant university association to seek his assistance in enlisting help from some of these schools. Unlike many government employees, they would expect and want to be deployed to the countryside to help. The president of that association was Peter McPherson, former president of Michigan State and head of the Agency for International Development from 1981 to 1987 under President Reagan, and I was confident he would make every effort to enlist help from the universities. Like my offer of Defense civilians, though, nothing came of the idea. There wasn't interest at State or AID.

Illustrative of another problem in getting civilian experts into Afghanistan, Secretary of Agriculture Tom Vilsack volunteered to send dozens of specialists to Afghanistan but told me he had no money to cover the cost. Could Defense do so? I had to tell him we could not because of congressional restrictions on transfers of funds among government departments. We could make such transfers only to the State Department.

On June 8, I met with McChrystal, Rodriguez, Mullen, Cartwright, and Flournoy to continue discussions on the new command structure. We needed to take this step-by-step, I cautioned, because of coalition sensitivities, so we would begin with Rodriguez solely as a deputy commander for ISAF through the fall and then see about additionally "double-hatting" him as deputy commander of U.S. forces after New Year's. After I said we needed a better approach to dealing with civilian casualties, I told Stan I wanted him to do a sixty-day review of the situation in Afghanistan, reviewing the personnel we already had and might need. It seemed like a perfectly reasonable, indeed innocuous, request at the time. I said we needed to do the review before I approached the president about any more forces because I couldn't nickel-and-dime him to death. Finally, I warned him that "I feel strongly that too big a footprint [too many U.S. forces] is strategically dangerous." The president and I would rue the day I asked for that review.

The next day was my worst so far with the Obama administration. A meeting with the president began with his approval of our plans to implement the command and control changes in Afghanistan, including Rodriguez's headquarters. I assured him we would come up with detailed plans, get them approved in the interagency process, and then take them to the allies. I then described my request to McChrystal for a sixty-day assessment, including a review of troop levels and newly identified troop needs through the end of the year—things we had not anticipated. I would then come to the president ready to justify any further increase in troop numbers and would not ask again in 2009. The room exploded. The president said testily there would be no political support for any further troop increase—the Democrats on the Hill didn't want one, and the Republicans would just play politics. He recounted how getting approval of the FY2009 supplemental had been harder than they imagined possible. Biden and Emanuel piled on. I was aware of Biden's conviction—and probably that of others in the room—that this request and the McChrystal assessment were part of an orchestrated squeeze play by the military to get the president to approve a lot more troops. I described my own reservations about a big increase in troop numbers but didn't see why two to four thousand more troops should cause so much angst and hostility.

I left the meeting discouraged less about the skepticism regarding more troops than about the total focus on the politics. Biden was especially emphatic about the reaction of the Democratic base. (His remarks reminded me of Cheney's focus on the Republican base when discussing detainee interrogations and Guantánamo.) Not a word was mentioned about doing whatever it took to achieve the goals the president had so recently set or to protect the troops. The president and his advisers all emphasized that before any more troops could be considered, we would have to show success and a change of momentum with the troops we had. I was stunned. The Democrats controlled both houses of Congress, and the White House was running scared. The skepticism I could understand; the politics I couldn't.

McChrystal was confirmed as commander—and authorized for a fourth star—by the Senate on the same day as my ugly meeting in the White House. My earlier strategy of getting him confirmed as director of the Joint Staff and taking care of any potential Senate issues at that time paid off.

Unfortunately, by summer, the Obama foreign policy team was splintering. Biden, his staff, Emanuel, some of the National Security Staff, and probably all of the president's White House political advisers were on a different page with respect to Afghanistan than Clinton, Mullen, Blair, and me. The same people were, to repeat, increasingly suspicious that Mullen, Petraeus, McChrystal, and other senior military officers were trying to box in—"jam"—the president and force him to approve even more troops. Donilon, Denis McDonough, and others were saying openly to people in Defense that "the White House" was not happy with Mullen's performance as chairman "and never have been," and they complained about his frequent interviews on television, even though they were often the ones who would ask him to go on the talk shows. McDonough bellyached to Geoff Morrell about how McChrystal's forthcoming sixty-day assessment would be a "turd," and he went on to say the president shouldn't hear Mullen's views for the first time in the papers and on TV. Rumors about Jones's isolation in the White House and potential exit were rife. Biden, Donilon, and Lute were increasingly at odds with Holbrooke. And as mentioned earlier, the Panetta-Blair relationship had tanked. Jones told me, on his return from a trip to Afghanistan at the end of June, that he had warned Stan that any further request for troops would provoke a "Whiskey Tango Foxtrot" response from the president—military parlance for "What the fuck?" The potshotting and rumormongering by late summer created a volatile atmosphere for considering McChrystal's report.

I had my own growing list of Whiskey Tango Foxtrot issues with the president and others in the administration by this time. After my weekly meeting (accompanied by Vice Chairman Cartwright) with the president on July 15, he asked to see me alone, an increasingly common occurrence. He then dropped a bombshell on me: he intended to meet with General Cartwright privately to ask him if he would stick around and succeed

Mike Mullen as chairman of the Joint Chiefs. I was concerned that any such conversation and arrangement would leak, rendering Mike a lame duck for more than two years—unless, of course, the president's intention was to hasten his departure. I knew nearly everyone at the White House preferred Cartwright's briefing style, which was much crisper than Mullen's. Cartwright could also explain highly technical matters clearly, and his analytical style meshed better with the president's own. But Mullen's high public profile and his independence grated as well. I pleaded with the president not to meet with Cartwright before September or October, until after he and Mullen had both been reconfirmed by the Senate in their positions for another term. When that meeting took place, I suggested the president simply ask Cartwright to remain for the full two years of his second term. (I had proposed his retirement after the first year of his second term only to stagger the chairman's and vice chairman's terms.) I had no problem with the idea of Cartwright succeeding Mullen as chairman at that point.

In early August, I had a long, very direct conversation with Rahm Emanuel in his White House corner office about a list of issues. I had been in that office under many previous chiefs of staff, and the décor remained essentially unchanged, with little that personalized it beyond a few family photos on a credenza behind the desk. In his shirtsleeves, Rahm greeted me cordially as always and offered me a Diet Coke. Ignoring the more formal sofa and chairs in front of his fireplace, we sat down at his conference table. The first issue I raised was a decision by Attorney General Eric Holder that the Justice Department would not defend six Navy petty officers who had been guards at Guantánamo and were being sued by a prisoner there. The sailors had done nothing wrong, but Holder did not want to have to defend the constitutionality of holding prisoners at Guantánamo. The Justice Department had told the sailors the government would pay for their defense by private lawyers, but as I told Rahm, that was not the same as having the full weight of the U.S. government on your side in a courtroom. Everyone in uniform knew that, and it upset them. I told Rahm the president's approach to the military from the day he was elected had been pitch-perfect, but that this decision could strongly and negatively affect military morale and attitudes toward the commander in chief. I also complained that Holder had made this decision without any consultation with me. I told him in language I knew he'd understand that a decision by Justice not to defend innocent American service members was a travesty and a "huge fucking mistake."

I also told Emanuel I was ticked off that Deputy National Security Adviser John Brennan had told the president that additional Reaper drone caps in Afghanistan should be transferred from the military to CIA, without me knowing anything about it. Those were Defense Department assets, I said, and no one in the White House had any business going to the president with such a recommendation without going through the established interagency process. This was part and parcel of an increasingly operational National Security Staff in the White House and micromanagement of military matters—a combination that had proven disastrous in the past. I told Rahm, "I'm a team player, but I'm not a patsy."

Perhaps most important, I told Emanuel that the president needed to "take ownership of the Afghan War," both for the troops and for our allies. My principal concern was not with his public comments on the need for an exit strategy but rather with what he *wasn't* saying. He needed to acknowledge that the war could take years but that he was confident we would ultimately be successful. He needed to say publicly why the troops' sacrifices were necessary. I told Emanuel I would likely come to the president in mid-September for additional "enablers"—more troops for counter-IED, ordnance disposal, route clearance, intelligence, surveillance, reconnaissance, and medics—but that I would try to delay any request for combat units until January. I said that the president did not want to be in the position of turning down assets that had a direct role in protecting the troops' lives. I wasn't trying to "jam" the president; I knew from experience that with the increase to 68,000 troops, more of these support capabilities would be needed.

Emanuel sat patiently and quietly while I vented; then he said he would see what he could do. Although I never raised my voice, I think he could tell how angry I was and chose to exercise uncharacteristic restraint. I would later hear that some of the politicos in the White House worried about my quitting.

In a June 24 videoconference, McChrystal told me for the first time that he had found the situation in Afghanistan much worse than he expected. In the south, he said, insurgents controlled five of thirteen districts in Helmand province, Kandahar was under pressure, and much of the region was "not under our control." The Afghan forces in the south were at only about 70 percent of authorized strength, and there was a big retention problem. In the east, the Haqqani network was expanding its operational reach, "but our guys have a pretty good handle on the situation there." Overall, he said, governance was very bad and creating a lot of problems: "There is no legitimacy." When I asked him if he had enough ISR, his answer provoked the only smiles in the session: "Sir, I am genetically predisposed to never say I have enough."

I first heard that McChrystal was going to ask for a lot more troops from Mike Mullen immediately upon his return from a trip to Afghanistan in mid-July. Mullen said McChrystal might ask for as many as 40,000 additional troops. I nearly fell off my chair. Questions flooded my mind: *Why? What for?* Did he really believe the president would approve that massive an increase so soon after agreeing to an additional 21,000? What about the size of our footprint and the impact on the Afghans? How could I personally reconcile all my public statements expressing concern about our military footprint with supporting McChrystal? Even were I to agree with McChrystal's assessment and recommendation, I had no idea how I could get the president's approval of even a fraction of that number. It didn't take a clairvoyant to see a train wreck coming.

The only time as secretary of defense that I was truly alarmed was when I heard what McChrystal intended. I decided to meet him secretly in Europe on August 2 and hear firsthand what he had to say. Just before the trip, I participated in the president's retreat with the cabinet and senior White House staff. An article in *The Washington Post* on the morning of the thirty-first reported that McChrystal was preparing to ask for a significant increase in troop levels in Afghanistan, a real help as I prepared to spend twenty-four hours interacting with the White House staff.

I climbed aboard my airplane late in the afternoon on the first and flew to Chievres Air Base in Belgium, where I sat down with McChrystal at eight-thirty on Sunday morning for what turned out to be a five-hour meeting. All the other key players were there as well: Mullen, Petraeus (as Central Command commander), Admiral Jim Stavridis (as supreme allied commander, McChrystal's NATO boss), Michèle Flournoy, Rodriguez, and of course, a number of their staff. We met in a very plain, utilitarian conference room at the air base around a large U-shaped table, thus allowing everyone a view of the PowerPoint slides so essential to all military briefings. The enlisted soldiers keeping the coffee pots full and serving food seemed nervous, probably because of the array of four-star admirals and generals in the room. They seemed oblivious to the short, white-haired guy in a blue blazer with no stars.

I began the discussion by underscoring the need to keep the entire troop decision process confidential through its conclusion, which needed to be pushed beyond the Afghan elections on August 20—even though that exceeded my sixty-day deadline for McChrystal's assessment. I said there would be four pressure points associated with any force increase: White House and congressional political opposition, the impact on Iraq, the availability of additional forces and the impact on the already stressed Army and Marine Corps, and the need for additional supplemental funding. I then asked McChrystal eight questions I had prepared on the plane:

- What was the result of your scrub [review] of the 68,000 U.S. troops already in or on the way to Afghanistan? Did you find any that you deemed not necessary or not a high priority?
- Did the alternative strategies you evaluated involve a geographic focus or more sequential or gradual timelines?
- What are the risk trade-offs with a more graduated [slower] timeline?
- How should we look at possible outcomes of the August 20 election, and what impact would they have on the assessment's conclusions?
- What are the political and military risks associated with a larger U.S. footprint?
- A significant further increase in the number of U.S. troops will mean a significant Americanization of the war. What is the expected impact in Afghanistan, NATO, and among other allies?
- Why not wait until the authorized 68,000 troops are in place before asking for more?
- Did your assessment take into account the likely availability of forces?

We spent most of our time on Stan's assessment of the situation, and he repeated to us his belief that the situation was "serious and deteriorating," as he had told me a few weeks earlier. He spoke of Karzai's deficiencies and those of Afghan governance more broadly throughout the country (with some exceptions), the lack of legitimacy, and massive corruption. We talked about civilian casualties and what he intended to do about that, as well as new rules for treating Afghans with respect. He made clear he intended to focus our military effort, as in the past, in the south and east, but he said he would select something like eighty districts and population centers on which to focus our efforts to provide security for the people, "inkblots" on his map where the circles of security would grow until they began to link up. Partnering with the Afghan security forces was critical, and the size and quality of those forces had to increase and improve. It was clear that counterterrorism operations would continue, as well as special operations aimed at taking Taliban commanders "off the battlefield." We also talked about greater military engagement and cooperation with the Pakistanis in a new effort to get them to help go after Taliban safe havens on their side of the border. (I did not share my skepticism that this would work; there was no harm in trying.) These issues would frame the debate inside the administration in the months to come. "Stability in Afghanistan is an imperative," I said. "If the Afghan government falls to the Taliban—or has insufficient capability to counter transnational terrorists—Afghanistan could again become a base for terrorism, with obvious implications for regional stability."

McChrystal said that a new campaign strategy was needed, one that focused on protecting the population rather than on seizing terrain or destroying insurgent forces. He talked a lot about changing the operational culture to interact more closely with the population. He emphasized the urgency of the situation: "I believe the short-term fight will be decisive. Failure to gain the initiative and reverse insurgent momentum in the . . . next 12 months—while Afghan security capacity matures—risks an outcome where defeating the insurgency is no longer possible." I thought to myself that he was right about the need to produce a perceptible shift of momentum in the near term; the status quo would lead to failure. I believed we could produce the shift in momentum, but expanding and improving the Afghan forces would take more time.

We then turned to the issue that everyone there knew had prompted the meeting—the question of more troops. I repeated what I had been saying for a year and a half about the history of foreign armies, the Soviet experience, and my concern about reaching a "tipping point" where the size of our presence and our conduct turned us into "occupiers." McChrystal was ready for the subject. He knew that his chances of getting more troops were nonexistent without my support, and so my concerns had to be alleviated. He said that the size of the force (or footprint) was less important than what you did with it. In and of itself, this wasn't an earthshaking insight. Similar debates took place over troop levels in Iraq. But I had viewed Afghanistan for so long through the lens of the Soviets' experience that his comments had a serious impact on me. If the Afghans could see foreign and Afghan forces working together and providing sustainable protection so they could go about their daily lives and not fear the return of the Taliban, they would not resent their presence. Respect for the Afghans and their customs was critical. He spoke at considerable length on the footprint issue, and when he was finished, while not yet supportive of a big increase in troop numbers, I was at least open to considering it.

I told McChrystal that I wanted him to wait to submit the assessment until after the Afghan election so he could include at least a preliminary evaluation of its impact. He needed to ensure that the military strategy he presented in his assessment focused explicitly on implementing the broader strategy the president had announced in March: "This will be required to achieve the objectives Obama approved." I said he should submit the assessment and troop recommendations separately because I expected the former to leak and we had to hold the latter very closely. I wanted people to focus first on the assessment, how things were going, and on strategy. Having troop options on the table at the same time would totally divert the debate to numbers, and the substance of the assessment would be ignored.

Mullen and I briefed the president on the meeting in the Oval Office on August 4. Biden, Emanuel, and Donilon were also there. We focused on Stan's assessment and the decision-making process to come. I reminded everyone that the troop increase approved in February had preceded the president's decisions on strategy in March. McChrystal's assessment would describe the situation as he saw it and then describe how he would operationally implement the president's March strategy decisions, including the resources required.

I repeated now to the president all that I had said to McChrystal. I told the president that Stan would probably need some additional capabilities for training the Afghan army and some additional enablers—ordnance disposal, counter-IED, medevac, helicopters—but "not a huge number and I'll provide ample justification." I continued, "I understand your priorities this fall—the heavy lift on health care, energy, the budget. I will not add to your burden." At the end of 2009, early 2010, I said, we could evaluate where we were, and I could make further recommendations. I understood the need to justify any increase, I told him; I would not put him in the position of having the appearance or the reality of an open-ended commitment. McChrystal believed that, if properly resourced, he could have the situation in a different place in one year, I said, and the Afghan forces able to secure key population centers within three years.

The president said that he wanted a choice of real options, including not just troop-intensive counterinsurgency. "I would never do that to you," I said. "But whatever we do, we will need more trainers for Afghan forces and more enablers—let's do that in September, and then do a basic review in January—a return to 'first principles.'" I went on to say that combat units wouldn't be ready to deploy before spring anyway, and the real decision was whether to add more combat units or not. In January, we should have a pretty good picture of the effect of the election, whether we could accelerate the recruitment and training of the Afghan army and police, and progress with reintegration of former Taliban fighters.

Obama asked if he had to spend $100 billion a year in Afghanistan. If it was necessary for the security of the United States, he said he would do so. But was that necessary to keep al Qaeda down? Were there alternatives? What about Pakistan? Biden weighed in with his view of the level of congressional opposition to any further increase in troop levels, saying, "The Democrats hate the idea, and the Republicans will just say, 'You're on your own.'" Nothing new there. Emanuel said that the Hill had voted for the war supplemental the preceding May only as a favor to the president, and they wouldn't do it now. The president concluded by asking for "robust options" and saying that he would look at McChrystal's assessment and that we would look deeper at the end of the year or soon afterward into whether we were on the right path. At the end of the session, I said that we would reevaluate progress regularly, something not done in Iraq or Vietnam. The president responded that while North Vietnam had never attacked the United States, there were still points during the war when the basic approach should have been questioned: "I just don't want McChrystal to come in determined to stay on the same path if it's not working." Mullen had the last word: if that was the case, he said, "I would tell you to stop."

That discussion presaged many of the debates we would have in the months to come. I thought the president had been thoughtful and balanced, sensible in his comments and questions. He was aware of the politics but, unlike Biden and Emanuel, not driven by them. The meeting took place on the president's forty-eighth birthday. At Leon Panetta's suggestion, I asked Obama whether he wanted a billion-dollar presidential helicopter or an F-22 for his present. He demurred.

A week and a half later I asked Cartwright whether McChrystal could include an option that would be limited to trainers for the Afghans and enablers, in numbers up to about 7,500 troops. We could then push off a decision on combat forces until January inasmuch as we couldn't deliver them until late spring anyway. In short, as of mid-August, I continued to be focused on a modest increase in troops in the fall and possibly more only after the first of the year, depending on a thorough evaluation of the situation.

Meanwhile Holbrooke was doing his best to bring about the defeat of Karzai in the August 20 elections. Richard had spoken for months about the need for creating a "level playing field" for all presidential candidates in Afghanistan, including ensuring that they all had security, access to independent media, and transportation to campaign around the country. What he really wanted was to have enough credible candidates running to deny Karzai a majority in the election, thus forcing a runoff in which he could be defeated. Unlike the 2004 Afghan presidential election, when the United States offered Karzai unqualified support, in the months leading up to the 2009 election our public position was one of neutrality among the candidates. But Holbrooke and U.S. ambassador to Afghanistan Karl Eikenberry were encouraging the other candidates, meeting and being photographed with them, attending their rallies, and making suggestions. Karzai might not be a great president, I figured, but he sure as hell knew what was going on in his own capital and was well aware of the American efforts to unseat him. Indeed, as Peter Lavoy, the senior intelligence officer briefing the NSC, later told us, Karzai saw the United States—the Obama administration—walking away from him and turned to the warlords and made deals to get reelected.

The election outcome was deeply marred by security problems but also large-scale fraud perpetrated by Karzai. He failed to get the magic 50 percent in the first round but still ended up with a second term. It was all ugly: our partner, the president of Afghanistan, was tainted, and our hands were dirty as well. The senior UN representative for Afghanistan, Ambassador Kai Eide, subsequently gave a report on the election to the NATO defense ministers during which he sat next to me. Before speaking publicly, he whispered to me that while he was only going to say that there was blatant foreign interference in the election, he wanted me to know he had in mind specifically the United States and Holbrooke. Our future dealings with Karzai, always hugely problematic, and his criticisms of us, are at least more understandable in the context of our clumsy and failed putsch.

For two and a half years, I had warned about the risks of a significant increase in the U.S. troop presence in Afghanistan, and during that period we had increased from about 21,000 to 68,000 troops. I was torn between my historical perspective, which screamed for caution, and what my commanders insisted was needed for accomplishing the mission they had been given by the president and by me. Three very different commanders—McNeill, McKiernan, and McChrystal—had all asked for more troops. I believed, with Mike Mullen, that the war in Afghanistan had been neglected and underresourced in the Bush administration. But how many troops were too many before reaching the tipping point in terms of Afghan attitudes and support? Embassy polling showed that in 2005 about 80 percent of Afghans saw us as allies and partners; by summer 2009, after nearly eight years of war, that was down to 60 percent.

As I thought about the tipping point, it seemed to me we had several vulnerabilities with the Afghan population. One was civilian casualties; every incident was a strategic defeat, often caused and always manipulated by the Taliban and then magnified by Karzai. Another was our thoughtless treatment of the Afghans in routine encounters, including U.S. and coalition military vehicles barreling down the roads scattering animals and scaring people. We often disrespected their culture or Islam and failed to cultivate their elders. We collaborated with Afghan officials who were ripping off ordinary citizens. In Kabul and all over the country, we and our coalition partners, as well as nongovernmental organizations, far too routinely decided what development projects to undertake without consulting the Afghans, much less working with or through them on what they wanted and needed. Was it any wonder that Karzai and others complained they had no authority in their own country? Or that even reasonably honest and competent Afghan officials got no respect from their fellow citizens? For all our hand-wringing and hectoring about corruption, we seemed oblivious to how much we were contributing to it, and on a scale that dwarfed the drug trade. Tens of billions of dollars were flooding into Afghanistan from the United States and our partners, and we turned a blind eye or simply were ignorant of how regularly some portion was going to payoffs, bribes, and bank accounts in Dubai. Our own inspectors identified how lousy—or nonexistent—U.S. government controls were. From Karzai on down, Afghans had to shake their heads at our complaints about their corruption when elements of the American government (and almost certainly a number of our closest allies) were paying off them and their relatives as agents and to secure their cooperation. Hillary Clinton and I repeatedly objected to this contradictory behavior by the United States, but to no avail.

An important way station in my "pilgrim's progress" from skepticism to support of more troops was an essay by the historian Fred Kagan, who sent me a prepublication draft. I knew and respected Kagan. He had been a prominent proponent of the surge in Iraq, and we had talked from time to time about both wars, including one long evening conversation on the veranda of one of Saddam's palaces in Baghdad. His essay, "We're Not the Soviets in Afghanistan," subsequently published in *The Weekly Standard*, reminded me of the brutal realities of my first Afghan war. In that conflict, an ill-trained, loutish, and often drunken Soviet army had gradually turned to an out-and-out war of terror on the Afghan people, killing at least a million and creating somewhere between three and five million refugees. (Other accounts put the number as high as seven million.) They tried to upend Afghan culture by redistributing property on a large scale and by trying to destroy "key pillars" in the social structure. As Kagan wrote, "Increasing frustration led to increased brutality, including a deliberate campaign to de-house the rural population (forcing people to concentrate in cities that the Soviets believed they could more easily secure). . . . The Soviets also used chemical weapons, mines, and devices intended to cripple and maim civilians." Kagan wasn't telling me anything I didn't remember about Soviet behavior in Afghanistan in the 1980s; after all, at CIA, I had watched it, reported on it, and beginning in 1986, had a direct part in countering it. What I had not done consciously as secretary of defense, Kagan's essay made me realize, was contrast the behavior of the Soviet troops with our own. As McChrystal had said in Belgium at our meeting, the size of the footprint matters far less than what you do with it. There were reasons to be cautious about more troops, and I still was, but I now saw our experience in a light different from the Soviet one.

My thinking about more troops was further affected by President Obama's speech on August 17 to the Veterans of Foreign Wars. He said, in reference to the war in Afghanistan, "The insurgency in Afghanistan didn't just happen overnight, and we won't defeat it overnight. This will not be quick, nor easy. But we must never forget: This is not a war of choice. This is a war of necessity. Those who attacked America on 9/11 are plotting to do so again. If left unchecked, the Taliban insurgency will mean an even larger safe haven from which al Qaeda would plot to kill more Americans. So this is not only a war worth fighting. This is fundamental to the defense of our people." This was the only time I could recall him being so forthright and committed in terms of prosecuting this war to a successful conclusion. Maybe my comment to Emanuel a few days earlier about the president needing to take "ownership" of the war had penetrated.

Because the Pentagon was more accustomed to Bush's style of decision making than Obama's, the military's proposed timetable for getting a decision on more troops by the end of September was naïve. As planned, McChrystal submitted his assessment to me on August 31. Only Mullen, Petraeus, and Stavridis (at NATO) got copies initially. Petraeus endorsed the assessment the next day and, contrary to later claims, specifically supported Stan's view of the need for both reintegration of lower-level former Taliban fighters into Afghan society and reconciliation with senior Taliban commanders. Flournoy discussed the process with Donilon, and they agreed we would pass the assessment to the NSS right after Labor Day (September 7), and it would then be discussed at limited-attendance meetings of both the deputies and the principals.

Donilon didn't want a firm deadline on resource decisions; he correctly wanted to focus discussion initially on the assessment—as I had hoped would happen—and to make sure we had the strategy right before talking about troop numbers. He said there should be no discussion of the assessment at NATO until the White House was comfortable with it. Stavridis in Brussels agreed to sit on his copy, but he and I would have to deal with a very unhappy NATO secretary general, who expected to be brought into the loop early—a reasonable position, since McChrystal was a NATO commander.

Nobody was going to keep Barack Obama in the dark for a week about what McChrystal's assessment said. Mullen and I met with the president in the Oval Office on September 2 and, as he had insisted, gave him a copy of the report. I told him it did not represent a new strategy but focused on implementing what the president had approved in March. I indicated that the following week I would forward to him the views of Petraeus, Mullen, and the Joint Chiefs, as well as my own, on the way ahead. I promised he would get a full array of options for discussion from McChrystal, noting that there were three elements to the troop issue—combat units, trainers, and enablers (medevac, counter-IED, and the like).

Yet again I told the president I wanted to move quickly on the enablers, sending perhaps up to as many as 5,000. With increased IED attacks and casualties, the message to troops and commanders in delaying the enablers was unacceptable, I said. I requested flexibility to respond to these requests as they came in; I had been sitting on some of them for weeks, to stay under the presidentially imposed troop cap of 68,000. I asked for a decision within a week and offered to report weekly to the NSS on any additional troops sent in this category.

To my astonishment and dismay, the president reacted angrily to my request. Why do you need more enablers? he asked. Were they not anticipated as part of the 21,000? What had changed? Is this mission creep? The public and Congress don't differentiate between combat troops and enablers, he said. Incremental increases lead to a sudden increase in commitment. Any more troops would be a heavy lift in terms of numbers and money. Biden jumped in with the familiar refrain that the Republicans would start calling it "Obama's war." I told them I had gotten a phone call from Senator Joe Lieberman saying that he, John McCain, and Lindsay Graham wanted to be helpful, and I had told Lieberman that they couldn't let the Republicans take a pass on this key national security issue. I told the president I understood his concerns about an open-ended commitment and mission creep but that "war is dynamic, not static. At the end of the year, whatever the troop numbers, we'll reevaluate and change our strategy if it's not working."

Just outside the Oval Office after the meeting, exasperated, I told Biden and Donilon that with respect to the 5,000 enablers, "From a moral and political standpoint, we cannot fail to take action to protect the troops."

I was deeply disturbed by the meeting. If I couldn't do what I thought was necessary to take care of the troops, I didn't see how I could remain as secretary. I was in a quandary. I shared Obama's concerns about an open-ended conflict, and while I wanted to fulfill the troop requests of the commanders, I knew they always would want more—just like all their predecessors throughout history. How did you scale the size of the commitment to the goal? How did you measure risk? But I was deeply uneasy with the Obama White House's lack of appreciation—from the top down—of the uncertainties and inherent unpredictability of war. "They all seem to think it's a science," I wrote in a note to myself. I came closer to resigning that day than at any other time in my tenure, though no one knew it.

During the deliberations over Afghanistan in the weeks to come, events would routinely drag me back to the sacrifices our troops were making and to the obtuseness of many of those at home. One such event occurred two days after I received McChrystal's assessment. That day twenty-one-year-old Lance Corporal Joshua M. Bernard's Marine unit was ambushed, and he was mortally wounded by a rocket-propelled grenade. An Associated Press photographer took a picture of the dying Marine, being tended by two comrades. His wounds were graphically portrayed in the photo. After Bernard was buried ten days later, the AP sent a reporter to talk with his family and tell them they were going to publish the photo. Bernard's father asked that the photograph not be circulated to the news media for publication, saying it would only hurt the family more. The AP's intent to run the photo came to my attention on September 3, and its callousness toward the family both sickened and angered me. From early in my tenure, I had had a good relationship with the press and had spoken publicly and often to military audiences about its importance in upholding our freedom (and identifying problems that needed fixing). But publishing this photo was an outrage as far as I was concerned.

I called Tom Curley, the president and chief executive of the AP, and asked him, in consideration of the father's wishes, not to run the picture. I said at one point in the conversation, "I am the secretary of defense, and I am begging you not to run that picture." I had never begged anybody for anything, but the sacrifice of this young Marine and the anguish of his family had suddenly become very personal to me. Curley said he would review the decision with his editors, but he didn't hold out much hope they would change their minds. I followed up with a letter, in which I said, "The American people understand that death is an awful and inescapable part of war," but publishing the photo would be "an unconscionable departure from the restraint that most journalists and publications have shown covering the military since September 11." I called the decision "appalling" and said that the issue was not one of law or constitutionality but one of "judgment and common decency." The AP was fresh out of common decency that day and put the photo on the wire. Fortunately, most newspapers and other media had better judgment than the AP and refrained from publishing the picture. The AP's insensitivity continues to rankle me.

I formally sent McChrystal's assessment to the president through Jim Jones on September 10, along with a separate paper by McChrystal on why he thought a counterterrorism strategy alone would not work in Afghanistan. At that point, McChrystal was almost certainly the most lethal and successful counterterrorism practitioner in the world. The successes of the U.S. forces under his command in both Iraq and Afghanistan were legion and legendary. The paper I gave to the president was a distillation of years' experience in hunting bad guys. McChrystal wrote that while CT (counterterrorism) operations are highly effective at *disrupting* terrorists, they are not the endgame to *defeat* a terrorist group. "CT operations are necessary to mitigate a sanctuary, but to defeat a terrorist group, host nation capacity must grow to ensure a sustainable level of security. . . . Without close-in access, fix and find methods become nearly impossible. . . . Predator [drone] strikes are effective where they complement, not replace, the capabilities of the state security apparatus, but they are not scalable in the absence of underlying infrastructure, intelligence, and physical presence." Given McChrystal's counterterrorism credentials, I was both astounded and amused in the weeks to come as Joe Biden; his national security adviser, Tony Blinken; Doug Lute; and others presumed to understand how to make CT work better than Stan did.

Along with the assessment, I gave the president the written endorsements and comments from Petraeus, the Joint Chiefs, and Mike Mullen. I said that "they all are essentially of one mind: that McChrystal is the right man, has the right military approach to accomplish the goals set forth in your March 27 decisions, and that he should receive proper resourcing to carry out his plans. As well, they all are, with difference only in degree, convinced that no strategy will work as long as pervasive corruption and preying upon the people continue to characterize governance in Afghanistan." It did not dawn on me at the time that my practice of having the president hear directly from each level in the chain of command, because of the unanimity of the senior military in support of McChrystal's recommendations, in this instance probably only reinforced Obama's and Biden's suspicion of a "military bloc" determined to force the commander in chief's hand.

The same day I gave Jones McChrystal's assessment, I also gave the president a long "eyes only" memo on my own thinking. I began by saying that, with the additional forces he had approved in February and March, I had hoped we would have until early 2010 to see if McChrystal's approach resulted in changed momentum in Afghanistan and, if so, that we would be able to use that to justify continued and perhaps increased support. With the worsening situation the general had identified, and public statements of grave concern by U.S. officials, however, "the debate and decisions—including over resources—I had hoped could be delayed until early next year when we might be able to show some progress are, unfortunately, upon us now. In fact, circumstances have conspired to place us at a historic crossroads during the next few weeks." I added that "as usual," all the options were unpalatable.

The principal alternative to McChrystal's recommendations, I felt, would be Biden's "counterterrorism plus" strategy. I told the president that I thought that strategy had all the disadvantages of a counterterrorism strategy and not enough capability to reap any of the advantages of a counterinsurgency strategy; and "I also don't know how to explain such a strategy to anyone."

I wrote impertinently that any new decision that abandoned his decisions in March or the vow he had made to the VFW in August would be seen as a retreat from Afghanistan, with all the implicit messages that that would send to Afghans, Pakistan, our Arab and NATO allies, Iran, North Korea, and others about American will and staying power: "We need to give it [the March strategy] a chance." Knowing this president, I realized that he, like me, had a number of questions that had to be answered before any decision would be made, and I laid out some of them:

- How do we tie more clearly and persuasively McChrystal's approach to the goal of disrupting, dismantling, and defeating al Qaeda?
- How do we tackle the reality that a corrupt, predatory—and incompetent—Afghan government will significantly affect any good we do in either the military or civilian effort?

- How do we change the subject from "nation-building" with all that implies to a more minimalist objective of capacity-building, particularly in the intelligence, security, and law enforcement areas?
- What can be done about the Pakistanis' unwillingness to take on the Afghan Taliban within their borders?
- How can we cut off funding from the Gulf states to the Taliban?
- How can we get our allies and partners to do more on both the military and civilian side?
- We owe you answers to questions about our current troop deployments: what percentage are actually working daily through or with Afghan counterparts, what percentage are defending terrain without leaving their forward bases, and what percentage is now focused on internal support such as construction and force protection?
- If you agree to more troops, how do we prevent troop levels from inexorably growing, making for the same kind of open-ended increases we saw in Vietnam? How do we reassure the American people we can keep control of this commitment both in troops and time? How does this government impose the discipline on itself to acknowledge when something isn't working and change course? And how do we persuade the Congress and the American people we can and will do this?

The priority, I said, should be to expand the Afghan security forces as quickly as possible. Additional U.S. and allied forces should be considered a temporary "bridge" to train those Afghans while keeping the situation on the ground from deteriorating further, at least until the Afghans could protect their own territory and keep the Taliban and al Qaeda out. I also said we needed a clearer strategy for reintegration of the Taliban. "I am confident of this," I said. "Your strategy—centered on building Afghan security capacity—gives us a chance for success; the more limited alternatives do not." I ended on a very personal note:

Mr. President, you and I—more than any other civilians—bear the burden of responsibility for our men and women at war. I'm sorry to tell you that every day in office makes that burden harder to bear. But, I believe our troops are committed to this mission and want to be successful. Above all, they don't want to retreat, or to lose, or for their sacrifices— and those of their buddies—to be in vain. What we owe them is not only our support, but a clear strategy and achievable goals. I think your

March decisions do that, but we need to explain it better—to them and to the American people. How to do this is one of our principal challenges. I still bear fresh scars from the domestic battle associated with Iraq in my first two years in this job; I am loath to take on another for Afghanistan. But I am more loath to contemplate a Taliban/al Qaeda victory or the implications for us around the world if we are seen to retreat.

During September, several events fractured what little trust remained between the senior military and the president and his staff. On September 4, *The Washington Post* columnist Michael Gerson published an interview with Petraeus in which the general stated flat-out that while there was no guarantee more troops would lead to success in Afghanistan, "it won't work out if we don't" send a lot more. He dismissed the "counterterrorism plus" strategy as insufficient, saying it had been tried before and that the way to target terrorists was with "on-the-ground intelligence," which "takes enormous infrastructure." Petraeus came down squarely in the interview behind McChrystal's approach, "a fully resourced, comprehensive counterinsurgency campaign." Virtually everybody in the Obama White House saw this as blatant lobbying designed to force the president to approve more troops. Their suspicion of Petraeus and his political ambitions was not allayed by the fact that Gerson had been a speechwriter for George W. Bush, something Petraeus denied knowing.

On September 13, the president chaired the first of nine—by my count—very long (two-to-three-hour) meetings on McChrystal's assessment and Afghan strategy. Two days later the Senate Armed Services Committee held a confirmation hearing for Mike Mullen's second term as chairman of the Joint Chiefs of Staff, at which time he forcefully argued for more troops in Afghanistan. He was implicitly critical of the vice president's views, saying we could not defeat al Qaeda and prevent Afghanistan from becoming a safe haven again "from offshore. . . . You have to be there, where the people are when they need you there, and until they can provide for their own security." The president—and everyone else in the White House—was livid, seeing the testimony as another effort by Mullen and the military to force the commander in chief's hand. Rahm told me that the president "used my language" when he heard what Mullen had said. In an effort to calm things down, at a press conference soon thereafter I said the president deserved the right to absorb McChrystal's assessment and have his questions answered, that some of the most important decisions of his presidency were involved and he should not be rushed. I suggested that "everybody should just take a deep breath."

Then the biggest shoe of all dropped. On Monday, September 21, *The Washington Post* published a detailed story by Bob Woodward on McChrystal's assessment, clearly based on a leaked copy. The four-column-wide headline read "McChrystal: More Forces or 'Mission Failure.'" The *Post* had given us advance warning it was going to run the story, and over the weekend Cartwright, Flournoy, and Geoff Morrell negotiated with Woodward and others from the *Post* to remove sensitive numbers, references to intelligence gaps, Special Forces unit designations, and the like. They had some success, but they could not redact the political bombshell the story represented. The story ended with a quote from the assessment: "Failure to provide adequate resources also risks a longer conflict, greater casualties, higher overall costs, and ultimately, a critical loss of political support. Any of these risks, in turn, are likely to result in mission failure." After I left office, I was chagrined to hear from an insider I trust that McChrystal's staff had leaked the assessment out of impatience with both the Pentagon and the White House. If so, I'd be very surprised if Stan knew about it.

Anger and suspicion were further fueled six days later when the CBS-TV program *60 Minutes* aired an interview with McChrystal in which he spelled out in detail how bad he had found the situation in Afghanistan and what needed to be done. The interview had been taped in late summer, long before the debate got under way in the administration, but the timing of its airing was awful.

McChrystal had been invited weeks earlier to give a speech on October 1 in London and asked Mullen whether he should do so, given the furor surrounding the leaked assessment. Mike encouraged him. I did not object. I should have. Stan's speech was innocuous enough, but in response to a question afterward, he dismissed out of hand the option Biden was supporting.

An infuriated president, Mullen, and I repeatedly discussed what he regarded as military pressure on him. On September 16, Obama asked us why all this was being discussed in public. "Is it a lack of respect for me? Are they [he meant Petraeus, McChrystal, and Mullen] trying to box me in? I've tried to create an environment where all points of view can be expressed and have a robust debate. I'm prepared to devote any amount of time to it—however many hours or days. What is wrong? Is it the process? Are they suspicious of my politics? Do they resent that I never served in the military? Do they think because I'm young that I don't see what they're doing?" Mike assured him there was no lack of respect. I said we just needed to shut everyone down until the process was complete.

The president and I then talked alone. I told him Mullen had called both Petraeus and McChrystal after the incidents and thought he had the situation under control. I said Mike's testimony had been a surprise to me, especially since we had reviewed potentially hot topics before his hearing.

Again and again I tried to persuade Obama that there was no plan, no coordinated effort by the three military men to jam him. I said that if there had been a strategy to do that, they sure as hell wouldn't have been so obvious. I reminded him that McChrystal had never had a job before with the kind of public exposure he now had, that he was inexperienced and a bit naïve about dealing with the press and politics. I said Mullen and Petraeus were both on his team and wanted to serve him well; but particularly when testifying, or even when talking to reporters, both felt ethically compelled to say exactly what they thought, however politically awkward. I told the president that Mike's independence had annoyed Bush as well. My assurances fell pretty much on deaf ears, which I found enormously frustrating and discouraging.

The press was reporting a campaign being mounted by the military to force acceptance of McChrystal's recommendations, and Emanuel told me that, according to reporters, there were four different sources saying that McChrystal would quit if he didn't get his way. A wall was going up between the military and the White House. That was bad for the country, even dangerous. I had to fix it. In a conference call with McChrystal and Petraeus on September 23, I told them that the decision the president was facing was conceivably the most significant of his presidency. The experts and politicians in Washington were divided on what to do in Afghanistan. The president was very deliberative and very analytical, and he was going to take whatever time was necessary to work through this decision. If he agreed to provide significant additional troops, he would do everything he could to make it work, though it would be a very

heavy political lift at home. I directed McChrystal to provide his memorandum on force options only to me, the chairman, Petraeus, Stavridis
at NATO, and the NATO secretary general. I said no copies should be
made, and it should not be shared with staff or anyone else, that a leak
would possibly be fatal to Stan's case. I reassured them that the president
was not questioning Stan's assessment or recommendations for further
resources, but rather whether changed circumstances on the ground
required revisiting the strategy he had settled on in March. I ended the
call by emphasizing that we had to actively oppose the perception in the
press and embraced by some in Congress that the president and the military were pitted against each other.

Four days after McChrystal's London gaffe, I gave a speech to the
Association of the U.S. Army in which I mentioned the leaks. I said
it was important to take our time to get the Afghan decision right,
"and in this process it is imperative that all of us taking part in these
deliberations—civilian and military alike—provide our best advice to
the president candidly but privately." Most commentators thought it was
a shot at McChrystal, but my target was far broader. We heard regularly
from members of the press that Biden, Jones, Donilon, McDonough,
Lute, Emanuel, and Axelrod were "spilling their guts" regularly—and
disparagingly—to reporters about senior military leaders, Afghanistan,
and the decision-making process. I was told that *The New York Times*
was besieged by unsolicited White House sources offering their views. I
acknowledged that the Pentagon leaked. But whenever I would complain
about White House leaks, there were bullshit protestations over there of
innocence. Only the president would acknowledge to me he had a problem with leaks in his own shop.

As impatient and frustrated as I would get at different points, not
to mention just being sick of sitting in the Situation Room hour after
hour, day after day, I believe the process on Afghanistan was an important and useful one. In my entire career, I cannot think of any single
issue or problem that absorbed so much of the president's and the principals' time and effort in such a compressed period. There was no angle
or substantive point that was not thoroughly examined. If I were to fault
the process, I would say that vastly more attention was focused on every
aspect of the military effort than—despite Donilon's and Holbrooke's
best efforts—on the broad challenge of getting the political and civilian
part of the equation right. Too little attention was paid to the shortage of

civilian advisers and experts: to determining how many people with the right skills were needed, to finding such people, and to addressing the imbalance between the number of U.S. civilians in Kabul and elsewhere in the country. Nor did we focus on the tension between our ambassadors and commanders in Afghanistan, Eikenberry and McChrystal in particular. During my tenure as secretary, there were three U.S. ambassadors to Kabul; none did well, in my opinion. None could compare to Afghan-born Zalmay Khalilzad, the U.S. ambassador in Kabul from 2003 to 2005, in coaching, counseling, and working with Karzai—or to a couple of CIA station chiefs in Afghanistan. Even Secretary Clinton would speak of Eikenberry's insubordination, that he would not do what she directed. Though both Clinton and I wanted Eikenberry replaced—because his relationship with Karzai was beyond repair and his relationships with both Defense and State were so poor—and repeatedly told Jones so, the ambassador was protected by the White House.

From September through November, over and over again we would rehash the issues and get further into the weeds—details beyond what was needed or appropriate. Broadly, there were three substantive areas on which our many meetings focused. The first was the nature of the threat. What were the relationships between the Taliban, al Qaeda, and other extremist groups in the Afghan-Pakistani border area? Was defeat of the Taliban essential to the defeat of al Qaeda? If the Taliban regained power, would al Qaeda return to Afghanistan? Would a more stable Afghanistan change Pakistan's strategic calculus? The second issue was which strategy for dealing with the threat would be most effective and efficient, COIN or CT-Plus. The key question with COIN was whether there was an Afghan model of governance that would be "good enough" to meet our objectives. Did the government have enough legitimacy in the eyes of its own people to permit our strategy to succeed? In the case of CT-Plus, could it work if the United States lacked the resources on the ground to protect the population and without adequate intelligence to be effective in its counterterrorism strikes? Third, if we stayed with the president's March strategy, how would we know if and when it was time to change course?

Pakistan continued to be a critically important factor in our discussions. If Pakistan was so critical to the success of our strategy, Biden asked, why were we spending thirty dollars in Afghanistan to every one dollar in Pakistan? There was a lot of talk about more military and civilian aid to the Pakistanis. Their military was deeply suspicious of U.S. intentions in Pakistan, believing any effort to increase the number of our uniformed personnel there was part of a nefarious scheme to seize their nuclear weapons. They welcomed our cash and our equipment but not our people. And they were not particularly interested in letting us teach them how to go after targets in their own country. As for civilian assistance, their paranoia and our political ham-handedness reinforced each other. After much political effort, and the leadership of Senators John Kerry and Dick Lugar and Representative Howard Berman, Congress passed a five-year, $7.5 billion aid package for Pakistan. It was a great achievement and just what was needed, especially the multiyear aspect to demonstrate our long-term commitment. Then some idiot in the House of Representatives attached language to the bill that stipulated that the assistance was conditional on the Pakistani military not interfering with the civilian government. Not surprisingly, there was outrage in Pakistan, especially among the military. In a flash, all the actual and potential goodwill generated by the legislation was negated. I knew that nothing would change Pakistan's hedging strategy; to think otherwise was delusional. But we needed some level of cooperation from them.

The president kept returning also to the matter of cost. He observed that the cost of the additional troops McChrystal was requesting would be about $30 billion; yet if he froze all domestic discretionary spending, he would save only $5 billion, and if he cut the same by 5 percent, that would save only $10 billion. He said that if the war continued "another eight to ten years, it would cost $800 billion," and the nation could not afford that given needs at home. His argument was hard to disagree with. The costs of the war were staggering.

By the fifth NSC meeting, on Friday, October 9, some clarity was emerging on the key issues. Panetta set the stage with a simple observation: "We can't leave, and we can't accept the status quo." The president said he thought we had reached "rough" agreement on that but also on what was achievable in terms of taking on the Taliban; that defining counterinsurgency in terms of population security as opposed to Taliban body count was sound; and that the basic "inkblot" strategy was sound—we couldn't resource COIN throughout the country, so we had to deny the Taliban a foothold in key areas.

He then posed the next set of questions. Were the interests of the Afghan government aligned with our own? How could we ramp up training of the Afghan forces to allow us to leave in a reasonable time? How would we transition from clearing out the Taliban in an area to transferring security responsibility there to the Afghans? Did we have a strategy for reintegration of Taliban fighters? What were the timetables, and how did we sustain the effort? If we were not sending enough troops for countrywide counterinsurgency, how did we choose what to protect? How would we deal with Pakistani opposition to our adding troops? I thought these questions in themselves reflected progress in our discussions. Apparently assuming the president was leaning toward approving significantly more troops, Biden jumped in: "What if a year from now this isn't working? What do you do then? Are you increasing the consequences of failing?"

About eight that same Friday night, as I was eating my Kentucky Fried Chicken dinner at home, the president called. "I'm really looking to you for your views on the way forward in Afghanistan. I'm counting on you," he said. Earlier that week Biden had leaned over in the Situation Room and whispered to me, "Be very careful what you recommend to the president because he will do what you say." I spent the weekend deciding what to say.

When I met privately with the president in the Oval Office on October 13, I told him I had thought about his call a lot and had prepared a memo for him offering my thoughts on what he should do. He grinned broadly, stuck out his hand to shake over the bowl of apples on his coffee table, and said, "You have the solution?" I wasn't sure about that, but in the event, one of the most significant decisions of his presidency largely tracked the recommendations in my paper.

I wrote that the Afghan Taliban and al Qaeda had become symbiotic, "each benefiting from the success and mythology of the other, both inside and outside Afghanistan." Al Qaeda clearly believed that a Taliban victory over the United States in Afghanistan would have great strategic benefit for the group.

Because while al Qaeda is under great pressure now and highly dependent on other extremist groups for sustainment, the success of those other groups—above all, the Taliban—would vastly strengthen the message to the Muslim world and beyond that these groups (including al Qaeda) are on the side of God and the winning side of history. What makes Afghanistan and the border area with Pakistan different from Somalia, Yemen, or other possible safe havens is that the former is the epicenter of extremist jihadism—the place where native and foreign Muslims defeated a superpower and, in their view, caused its collapse at home. . . . Taliban success in taking and holding parts of Afghanistan against the combined forces of multiple modern Western armies (above all, the United States)—the current direction of events—would dramatically strengthen the extremist Muslim mythology and popular perceptions of who is winning and who is losing.

I wrote that all three of the mission options we had been discussing were "doomed to fail, or already have." Counterterrorism focused solely on al Qaeda could not work without a significant U.S. ground presence in Afghanistan and the opportunity to collect intelligence that this would afford us. "We tried remote-control counterterrorism in the 1990s, and it brought us 9/11." "Counterterrorism plus," or "counterinsurgency minus," was what we had been doing since 2004, and "everyone seems to acknowledge that too is not working." Fully resourced counterinsurgency "sounds a lot like nation-building at its most ambitious" and would require troop levels, time, and money that few in the United States or in the West were prepared to provide.

I wrote that the core goals and priorities Obama had decided the previous March remained valid and should be reaffirmed. However, *we had to narrow the mission* and better communicate what we were trying to do. We could not realistically expect to eliminate the Taliban; they were now a part of the political fabric of Afghanistan. But we could realistically work to reverse their military momentum, deny them the ability to hold or control major population centers, and pressure them along the Pakistani border. We ought to be able to reduce their level of activity and violence to that which existed in 2004 or thereabouts. I recommended focusing our military forces in the south and east and charging our allies with holding the north and west. Our military efforts should be intended to stabilize the situation in Afghanistan and buy time to expand and train the Afghan security forces, who, despite their many deficiencies, were courageous fighters; many of them were prepared to die—and had died—fighting the Taliban. We should "quietly shelve trying to develop a strong, effective central government in Afghanistan." What we needed, I wrote, was some central government capacity in a few key ministries—defense, interior, finance, education, rural development. We should help broker some kind of "national unity" government or other means to give the Karzai government at least a modicum of legitimacy in the eyes of the Afghan people. We also had to get a handle on corruption. "Our kids must not die so that corrupt Afghan officials can line their pockets."

All this would give us a mission that the public and the politicians could easily understand: "*Deny* the Taliban momentum and control, *facilitate* reintegration, *build* government capacity selectively, *grow* the Afghan security forces, *transfer* security responsibilities, and *defeat* al Qaeda."

I supported McChrystal's request for 40,000 troops, but I offered an alternative of about 30,000 troops. I urged Obama not to place a firm ceiling on the numbers because troop numbers are always estimates, and there are always unplanned needs. Because the fourth brigade combat team McChrystal had requested (bringing his number to 40,000 troops) was needed to replace the Canadians and the Dutch, who were leaving the south in 2010 and 2011, I suggested he leverage our own new commitment to get the allies to provide those replacement troops.

To assure Americans this wasn't an open-ended commitment to a stalemate with constantly rising numbers of troops for years to come, I said I thought it was imperative to pledge that we would review progress at the end of 2010 and, if necessary, "adjust or change our approach." I also wrote that while the deliberative process "has served you well, we cannot wait a month or two for a decision. Uncertainty about the future is beginning to impact Afghans, the Pakistanis, our allies, and our troops."

> In conclusion, Mr. President, this is a seminal moment in your presidency. From Afghanistan to Pakistan, from the Muslim world to North Korea, China, and Russia, other governments are watching very carefully. If you elect not to agree to General McChrystal's recommendations (or my alternative), I urge you to make a tough-minded, dramatic change in mission [in] the other direction. Standing pat, middling options, muddling through, are not the right path forward and put our kids at risk for no good purpose.

Almost two weeks later, on October 26, the president invited Hillary and me to discuss the options. We were the only outsiders in the session, considerably outnumbered by White House insiders including

Biden, Emanuel, Jim Jones, Donilon, and John Brennan. Obama said at the outset to Hillary and me, "It's time to lay our cards on the table. Bob, what do you think?" I repeated a number of the main points I had made in my memo to him. Hillary agreed with my overall proposal but urged the president to consider approving the fourth brigade combat team if the allies wouldn't come up with the troops.

The exchange that followed was remarkable. In strongly supporting a surge in Afghanistan, Hillary told the president that her opposition to the surge in Iraq had been political because she was facing him in the Iowa primary. She went on to say, "The Iraq surge worked." The president conceded vaguely that opposition to the Iraq surge had been political. To hear the two of them making these admissions, and in front of me, was as surprising as it was dismaying.

Rahm charged once again that the military had waged a campaign to limit the president's options to what McChrystal wanted. Seething inside, I ignored him and turned to a question I knew was on the president's mind—why 40,000 more troops were needed if we were narrowing the mission. I said that the early phase of any option other than pure counterterrorism was to reverse the momentum of the Taliban and degrade their capabilities. (A counterterrorism strategy alone could not do that.) The president commented that OMB had told him 40,000 more troops would cost an additional $50 billion or more a year, putting the cost of the overall effort at maybe a trillion dollars over ten years. What were the national security implications of that for the deficit, defense investment, and so on? he asked. He then wrapped up the meeting, saying he wanted to make a decision before his Asia trip (which was to begin on November 12).

Rahm called after the meeting to apologize for the "campaign" comment but said again that the president was feeling boxed in by all the press articles, including one that same day about a Defense war game that purportedly showed the vice president's option wouldn't work. I told Rahm that until that story, the military had been quiet since my public warning to advise only in private, but that had not been true of people at the White House. He admitted, "I know, I know."

Jones came to see me that same day to share his concerns over McChrystal's plans. He had been very quiet during the meetings in the Situation Room. He said, "The idea of 100,000 American troops in RC [regional command] South and RC East blows my mind. There is something missing, the glue that holds it all together. Where is the Afghanistan-wide plan, including the NATO role?" He was also concerned about the inflexibility of the military—either 40,000 troops or none. Jim said that Mullen was seen as responsible for the contentiousness and "has real problems among some at the White House," though not necessarily the president. I went through my familiar commentary again. I said that the notion of some kind of organized campaign was ridiculous, that McChrystal's statement in London was an unscripted answer to a question, and that Mike had admitted that his statement in his confirmation hearing had been a mistake. I said I thought the atmosphere at the White House was getting poisonous, especially on the part of Donilon, who had characterized Mullen and the military as "insubordinate" and "in revolt." It steamed me that someone who had never been in the military and had never even been to Afghanistan was second-guessing commanders in the field on things like why there were helicopters in certain places. Jones acknowledged he had "to get Tom back in the box."

The next day the shit hit a new part of the fan. Roughly three weeks earlier the president had told me that he wanted to talk privately with Vice Chairman of the Joint Chiefs Cartwright to get his personal views on the path forward in Afghanistan. I told him that if it became known, Mullen would feel undercut. I advised Obama to tell no one else, and I suggested he meet Cartwright on a Saturday in the residence. The meeting took place on Tuesday, October 20, while I was in Japan. Several people at the White House were aware of it. Mullen wasn't. A week after the fact, Jones told Mike about the meeting.

Mike came to see me that afternoon, feeling betrayed by Jones, Cartwright, and possibly me. He felt the meeting showed a lack of confidence in him on the part of the president. He asked why the president wouldn't just tell him about wanting to meet with Cartwright (who had been sworn to secrecy). Mike said Cartwright now felt like damaged goods and was wondering how he could stay long-term. I thought Mike might resign. I described the origins of the meeting and my concerns. I admitted I had probably made a mistake in my advice to the president and should have told him to be up-front with Mike. Mullen then asked how he stood with me, and I told him I would not want to remain as secretary without him as my partner, that I had total confidence in him and felt terrible about the whole episode. I added that the president had put all three of us—Mullen, Cartwright, and me—in an awful spot. Mullen and I agreed we each had to talk privately with the president.

Mike wanted clarity on the perceived "campaign" by the military, the president's confidence in him, and the overall White House view of the military. A few weeks earlier the president "had chewed our asses," as Mullen put it, for public military statements. Obama had said, "On Afghanistan, my poll numbers will be stronger if I take issue with the military over Afghanistan policy." That clearly had bothered Mike (as it did me) because it suggested we were on different teams. After our meeting, I called Rahm and asked for fifteen minutes privately with the president the next day. I said it was about a personnel matter but not mine. Rahm asked, "Mike?" I said yes.

I told Obama about my conversation with Mullen and his worry that the president had lost confidence in him. I reported also that Cartwright felt it would be difficult for him to stay on now. I acknowledged to the president that I had given him bad advice. "I should have told you to go ahead and see Cartwright but call Mike first." The president said he could have handled it better, too, and maybe he was not sensitive enough to military protocol because he had never served. But "I feel like I should be able to talk to anyone in uniform as commander in chief," he said. I told him I did exactly that at every post and base without the chain of command present. I told him Mike wanted to stay behind for a private talk with him after our regular meeting that afternoon. Obama said he would give Mike a full vote of confidence but would also repeat his belief that military comments had boxed him in on Afghanistan. Mike later told me they had a good conversation and cleared the air.

This episode serves as a reminder that those at the highest levels of government, tough and experienced people accustomed to the hard knocks of political life at the top in Washington, are still human beings. All of us, in varying degrees, have vulnerabilities, insecurities, and sensitivities. All hate critical press stories that question our motives, integrity, or competence. All, including hardened senior military officers and secretaries of defense, need the occasional pat on the back or gesture of support. And however independent and powerful, we need to know we have the confidence of our boss, especially when he is the president of the United States.

By early November, we were focused on three options: 20,000 additional troops (half for counterterrorism, half for training Afghan forces), the vice president's recommendation; Option 2, McChrystal's proposal for 40,000 more troops; and "Option 2A," my alternative of 30,000 with a push on the allies for 5,000 to 7,000 more. Much would be written later about resentment in the Pentagon over Cartwright helping Biden and his staff craft an alternative plan from McChrystal's. For Mullen, Petraeus, McChrystal, and others, that was probably true. I had no problem with it. My only concern was that, as was his style, Cartwright didn't share much about what he was doing with either the senior civilians (including, at times, me) or the military in the Pentagon, which didn't help things.

Late in our deliberations, we dealt with the important question of how fast additional troops could get into Afghanistan. The original military plan had the deployments spaced out over more than a year. The president correctly pointed out that that could hardly be characterized as a "surge" to recapture momentum. He asked Petraeus how fast the surge had arrived in Iraq. About six months, Petraeus said. Obama decided the arrival of the troops in Afghanistan had to be significantly accelerated. The military leadership ultimately agreed to get most of the troops there by the end of August 2010—a logistical nightmare, but they managed it.

How long would the surge troops stay? The military had been saying that areas cleared of the Taliban would be ready to transition to Afghan government security responsibility within two years. Because the first Marines had arrived in Helmand in the summer of 2009 to take on the Taliban, the president wanted to begin bringing out the surge troops in July 2011. I had opposed any kind of deadlines in Iraq but was supportive of the president's timeline in Afghanistan because I felt some kind of dramatic action was required to get Karzai and the Afghan government to accept ownership of their country's security. I also accepted the military's two-year forecast. I knew well we were not talking about a countrywide transition in July 2011 but, rather, the beginning of a process that would go district by district or province by province. A "conditions-based" date to begin drawing down the surge forces therefore was acceptable to me. To those who said we were inviting the Taliban to just lie low until we left, I said that would only give us more opportunity to accomplish our goals.

In practical terms, a set date to begin drawing down the surge gave Obama something to work with in terms of reassuring both the public and Congress that he was not committing to an open-ended war in Afghanistan. Most Democrats and a growing number of Republicans in

Congress had become increasingly skeptical about the war and its cost, both in lives and in treasure. The politics of the troop increase would be a heavy lift indeed—just as in Iraq in early 2007.

The endgame began on November 6 with a thunderbolt cable to Clinton and the White House from Ambassador Eikenberry in Kabul, which leaked almost immediately. He was dead set against a counterinsurgency strategy and a large infusion of U.S. troops. He said that adding troops was counter to "Afghanization" and "civilianization" of the mission. In his view, Karzai was not an adequate strategic partner, we overestimated the ability of the Afghan forces to take over security, and more troops would only deepen the dependency on us by the Afghan forces. He complained about the lack of a civilian counterpart to the commander of ISAF (McChrystal) and said that he ought to fill that role, not the UN or NATO senior representatives. Eikenberry recommended that we study the situation for several more months while proceeding with development projects.

I thought his recommendations were ridiculous. Analyze for four more months? How do you do development projects without security? The cable ruptured the relationship between McChrystal (and the senior military) and Eikenberry once and for all, both because of the substance but also because Eikenberry had never mentioned either his views or his cable to McChrystal.

On Veterans Day, November 11, we went around and around again on the options. The next day the president called me from Air Force One on his way to Singapore. He said he was focusing on sending two brigade combat teams and not considering a third until the summer of 2010, when we could see what Karzai had done and how we were doing. I urged him to approve all three brigades to demonstrate resolve and to ease military planning. He could then "off-ramp" the third depending on Karzai's actions. He said he'd think about it. He then asked: Were any of the 17,000 in the first tranche of surge troops being deployed because they were needed to support a force of 40,000 more troops? Could some of the third brigade be brought forward to strengthen the second? What were the benchmarks of progress? Could we accelerate both the buildup and the drawdown? How should we treat the civilian and military components together? He said he had posed those questions to the NSS.

As he prepared to end the conversation, he asked me how to adjust his body clock for the Asia trip. I said, "The old-fashioned way—alcohol and Ambien." He laughed and said he'd break out the Johnnie Walker.

On November 13, I invited Emanuel and Denis McDonough to my office to review the president's questions and to make sure Defense and the NSS understood the questions in the same way. They brought Lute with them, and I was joined by Mullen. Rahm told me that my comments on sending three brigade combat teams had gotten the president's attention. I said that sending two brigades would look like the president simply split the difference between zero and four and that, after two months of deliberation, that would be characterized as a "gutless" decision. I was sure that when senior military leaders were asked by Congress to give their personal, professional opinion, they would say two brigades were not enough.

I do not leave big issues to chance. On the fourteenth, I called Hillary in Singapore, told her of my telephone conversation with the president, explained what I'd said about three brigade combat teams, and asked whether she still supported that. She affirmed her strong support and then asked, "Where's Jones?" I said I didn't know, that he had been slippery on this whole matter. She agreed. I told her I'd called because the president might make a decision on his trip and she would be the only strong voice present. She laughed and said she'd do her best.

Our last meeting was on November 23, from eight to ten in the evening. The stage had been set by two opposing papers. The NSS paper recommended that the president approve two brigade combat teams (about 20,000 troops, Biden's proposal) and reserve a decision on the third until July 2010. Mullen, in opposition, wrote a memo to the president, which he sent to Jim Jones, reasserting in the first sentence the need for 40,000 troops; McChrystal was equally adamant. Their unyielding views angered Biden, Jones, and the NSS and portended a break between the president and the military. Mullen was traveling in Europe. When I caught up with him, I said I thought that he, Petraeus, and McChrystal had agreed that my alternative of 30,000 troops plus more allied troops was workable. Mike decided to tear up his memo and redraft it. Fortunately, I had told Jones not to give the original Mullen memo to the president.

The meeting that night was straightforward and lacking in drama. Mullen, Petraeus, and McChrystal were candid in what they said but flexible, affirming their support for whatever the president decided. Hillary strongly supported McChrystal's approach, with UN ambassador Susan Rice, Deputy Secretary of State Steinberg, Mullen, Cartwright, McChrystal, Petraeus, and me supportive of the "maximum leverage" option (my alternative). Biden, Donilon, and Brennan were all opposed. Eikenberry supported more troops but was skeptical that counterinsurgency would work because of the deficiencies of the Afghan government. Emanuel spoke mainly about the political challenge of getting the money to pay for a surge, and the impact on public opinion, health care, the deficit, and other programs. He said getting congressional approval would be difficult.

On November 27, the day after Thanksgiving, the president called me at home in the Northwest for a long talk. He was fine with the 30,000 troops with flexibility "in the range of 10 percent" for additional enablers, but he would not agree to the requests for 4,500 enablers unrelated to the new deployments that had been stacking up on my desk for over two months. He said that pushed the total number to 37,000, which would be hard to sell on the Hill, and it was too close to McChrystal's number for the general to understand he was being given a different number and a different mission. "I'm tired of negotiating with the military," he said. When I expressed my dismay, saying that I'd held off on this need for months pending his decision and now I would have to provide those needed enablers "out of hide," he responded that McChrystal ought to be able to find the necessary troops: "Doug Lute tells me there's a lot of tail to tooth [troops in support roles as opposed to fighters] in Afghanistan." He asked me to return to Washington early for a meeting with him, Mullen, Cartwright, and Petraeus to make sure they were on board: "If they aren't, I will revert to McChrystal's option of 10,000 mostly trainers." We agreed to meet at five on Sunday.

To prepare for that meeting, I held a videoconference with Mullen and Cartwright on Saturday morning and brought them up to speed. "Stan needs to grasp," I said, "that there has been a shift in mission." I repeated the president's threat to go back to McChrystal's smallest troop option. I came away from the videoconference believing everything was okay but worried nonetheless about what McChrystal might say the next day.

I complained to Jones that afternoon that the NSS decision paper for the president was trying to place precise caps on troop numbers, particularly the 10 percent flexibility the president had given me. I told him they should write it just as the president and I had agreed. I then raised the additional 4,500 enablers I had discussed with the president. Jones said he thought the president had just forgotten about them when meeting with "the acolytes" on Friday. He went on to say that "those guys—Emanuel, Axelrod, Donilon, and McDonough—were really deeply involved and stirring the pot." He said he was isolated in the meetings.

I received word that same afternoon that the Sunday meeting with the president had been changed to nine-thirty a.m., thus requiring me to fly all night from the West Coast to make it. I saw the handiwork of the NSS in this and told my staff, "Tell them to go fuck themselves. The president and I agreed on five and that's when I'll be there. If they go at nine-thirty, they'll do it without the secretary of defense." The meeting was changed back to five.

The meeting was unlike any I ever attended in the Oval Office. Obama, Biden, Mullen, Cartwright, Petraeus, Emanuel, Jones, and I were there. Obama said he had gathered the group principally to go through his decisions one more time to determine whether Mullen and Petraeus were on board and fully committed. He said that if not, he would go back to McChrystal's option of 10,000 troops, the option favored by most of his civilian White House advisers. He then went around the room. Mullen and Petraeus said what he wanted to hear. Emanuel—no surprise—stressed the political lift on the Hill and the danger of any daylight between the president and the military. Jones and Cartwright were supportive. I, of course, was pleased to hear my proposal being adopted.

Then there was an exchange that's been seared into my memory. Joe Biden said he had argued for a different approach and was ready to move forward, but the military "should consider the president's decision as an order." "I am giving an order," Obama quickly said. I was shocked. I had never heard a president explicitly frame a decision as a direct order. With the American military, it is completely unnecessary. As secretary of defense, I had never issued an "order" to get something done; nor had I heard any commander do so. Former chairman of the Joint Chiefs of Staff Colin Powell, in his book *It Worked for Me*, writes, "In my thirty-five years of service, I don't ever recall telling anyone, 'That's an order.' And now that I think about it, I don't think I ever heard anyone else say it." Obama's "order," at Biden's urging, demonstrated, in my view, the complete unfamiliarity of both men with the American military culture. That order was unnecessary and insulting, proof positive of the depth of the Obama White House's distrust of the nation's military leadership.

The president announced the troop surge, at West Point on December 1. Clinton, Mullen, Jones, and I accompanied him.

In the end, I felt this major national security debate had been driven more by the White House staff and by domestic politics than any other in my entire experience. The president's political operatives wanted to make sure that everyone knew the Pentagon wouldn't get its way. Jones had told me David Axelrod was backgrounding the press to that effect. I thought Obama did the right things on national security, but everything came across as politically calculated.

After the president's announcement, I wrote a note to myself: "I'm really disgusted with this process, I'm tired of politics overriding the national interest, the White House staff outweighing the national security team, and NSS (Donilon and Lute) micromanagement. May 2010 is looking a lot more likely than January 2011 [in terms of when I would leave]. I'm fed up." When I wrote that, I was frustrated with a valuable process that had gone on way too long.

To be fair, though, national interest *had* trumped politics, as the president made a tough decision that was contrary to the advice of all his political advisers and almost certainly the least popular of the options before him in terms of his political constituents.

On reflection, I believe that *all* of us at the senior-most level did not serve the president well in this process. Our "team of rivals" let personal feelings and distrust cloud our perceptions and recommendations. I believe, for example, that my view of a geographically limited counterinsurgency, combined with aggressive counterterrorism and disruptive Special Forces attacks on Taliban leaders, emphasizing expansion and training of the Afghan security forces, was actually pretty close to what Biden had in mind. The difference between his recommendation for increased troops and mine was the difference in total force between 83,000 to 85,000 troops and 98,000 troops. His number was far above what was required for counterterrorism, and mine was far too small for a fully resourced counterinsurgency strategy. The aggressive, suspicious, and sometimes condescending and insulting questioning of our military leaders—especially by Donilon, Lute, and others at the White House—made them overly defensive, hardening their unwillingness to compromise. White House distrust and dislike of Holbrooke, and Lute's preoccupation with the military side of the equation, contributed to inadequate attention to the civilian component of the Afghan effort.

Contending teams presented alternatives to the president that were considerably more black and white than warranted. A more collegial process, one that tried to identify points of agreement rather than sharpen differences, would have had a more harmonious conclusion and done less damage to the relationship between the military and the commander in chief.

Responsibility for finding the common ground and shaping the deliberations accordingly would normally fall to the national security adviser, Jim Jones. The National Security Staff is supposed to be the "honest broker" in the policy-making process. That was not the case in the Afghan debate. Jones's views, and the even stronger opinions of his deputy, Tom Donilon, and Lute, made the NSS an advocate rather than a neutral party, contributing to a damaging split in the government, with the White House and NSS on one side and the Defense and State Departments on the other.

My anger and frustration with the White House staff and the NSS during the process led me to become more protective of the military and a stronger advocate for its position than I should have been. In retrospect, I could have done more to bridge the differences. Fairly early in the process, after I had talked about a narrower Afghan mission in a principals meeting, Biden wrote me a note at the table saying, "What you outlined is what I've been trying to say." We had breakfast together once that fall at his residence to discuss things, but I could have reached out privately to him more often to find common ground. I don't think we would have agreed on the number of additional troops, but I believe we could have come pretty close on the strategy; that alone would have helped avoid a lot of acrimonious debate.

The rift on Afghan policy would linger for the rest of my tenure as secretary. Biden, Lute, and others in the White House who had opposed the decision would gather every negative bit of information about developments in Afghanistan and use them to try to convince the president that they had been right and the military wrong. That began before the first surge soldier set foot in Afghanistan.

In the middle of our debates over Afghanistan, a tragedy at home was a vivid reminder of the complex dangers we were facing. On November 5, Army Major Nidal Malik Hasan turned on his fellow soldiers, murdering thirteen people and wounding twenty-nine others in a shooting rampage at Fort Hood, Texas. It was the worst such attack ever on a military base in the United States. Hasan had expressed extremist Islamic views and had been in contact with Imam Anwar Al-Awlaki, an advocate of extremist violence residing in Yemen. Hasan's attack on fellow soldiers was a wake-up call for the military to look closely at its own ranks and especially to question why Hasan's expression of extremist views had drawn little scrutiny. The president spoke eloquently at the memorial service at Fort Hood.

Before the service, I met separately with each of the families to express my sympathy and condolences. The father of one victim, Specialist Frederick Greene, invited me to attend his son's funeral in Mountain City, Tennessee. I had wanted to attend the funerals of fallen heroes in their hometowns since becoming secretary, but I had not done so out of concern that my presence would be a distraction and intrude on the privacy of families. I decided to accept Mr. Greene's invitation. Mountain City, a town of about 2,400, is in the far northeastern corner of the state. The nearest airport is near Bristol, Tennessee, about an hour's flight from Washington. I flew there on November 18 with two military assistants (and the always-present security team). I took no staff, no press. We drove across three mountain ridges to get to the remote town. Flags seemed to be hanging from every building. There were many signs acknowledging the life and sacrifice of Specialist Greene. We drove through Mountain City into the countryside to Baker's Gap Baptist Church, a simple but picturesque country church. It was windy, cold, and rainy. The service was at the church cemetery on an adjacent hill. I met with the family privately in the church and then took my seat at graveside under the funeral tent. Fred Greene's wife and two young daughters sat immediately in front of me. As the service proceeded, I could see in my mind's eye other cemeteries in numberless small towns across America, where families and friends had buried local sons who had risked everything and lost everything. When the service ended, I shook hands with the members of the Army honor guard and made the long drive back to the airport.

A little over two weeks later, as I signed the deployment order sending the first 17,000 troops of the surge to Afghanistan, my thoughts returned to that bleak hillside in Mountain City.

CHAPTER 11

Difficult Foes, Difficult Friends

As strange as it may sound, Afghanistan was not an all-consuming issue for the president and his administration in the latter part of 2009; it just seemed so for those of us in the national security arena. Preoccupied at home with a politically troubled health care initiative and the continuing economic crisis, Obama also faced challenges with China, Russia, North Korea, the Arab Middle East and Israel, terrorism—and especially Iran. Unlike Afghanistan, there were generally no serious divisions within the administration on these issues during 2009 and 2010.

By 2009, Iran had become a kind of national security black hole, directly or indirectly pulling into its gravitational force our relationships with Europe, Russia, China, Israel, and the Arab Gulf states. Each key issue related to Iran's nuclear program—preventing the enrichment and weaponization of its nuclear material, imposing sanctions to accomplish that objective, and using missile defense to protect against its potential capabilities—affected multiple countries in different ways. It was like a great web; when we touched one part of the periphery, others would reverberate.

The stakes could not have been higher. Israel's leaders were itching to launch a military attack on Iran's nuclear infrastructure. If they did so, we were almost certain to be drawn in to finish the job or to deal with Iranian retaliatory attacks against Israel, our friends in the region—and probably against the United States as well. The war drums were beating once again. Likely the only way to prevent a third war in the region within a decade—a war possibly more widespread and terrible than those in Iraq and Afghanistan—was to bring enough economic pressure to bear such that Iran's leaders would abandon their aspiration for nuclear weapons.

No relationship is more important to Israel than the one with the U.S. president and leaders of Congress. In that respect, Obama's outreach both to Iran and to the Islamic world more broadly, early in his presidency, scared the hell out of the Israelis. On February 20, Benjamin "Bibi" Netanyahu had again become prime minister, leading a right-wing coalition. I first met Netanyahu during the Bush 41 administration, when I was deputy national security adviser and Bibi, as Israel's deputy foreign minister, called on me in my tiny West Wing office. I was offended by his glibness and his criticisms of U.S. policy—not to mention his arrogance and outlandish ambition—and I told national security adviser Brent Scowcroft that Bibi ought not be allowed back on White House grounds.

Soon after I became CIA director in 1991, I met Ehud Barak, then a lieutenant general and chief of the Israeli general staff. After thirty-five years in the Israeli army, Barak entered politics, became prime minister for a time at the end of the 1990s, and in June 2007 became minister of defense under Prime Minister Ehud Olmert. Barak retained his position when Netanyahu became prime minister in early 2009, so we were both holdover ministers. By the time Bibi took office, my nearly twenty-year-long acquaintance with Barak had become a very good, even close, relationship. We had spoken and met often during my time as Bush's defense secretary and would do so even more frequently during my tenure under President Obama. Barak would travel to Washington to see me about every two months. It was not by accident that even though the political and diplomatic relationship between the Obama administration and Netanyahu remained frosty between 2009 and 2012, the defense relationship remained strong and in every dimension would reach unprecedented levels of cooperation.

Netanyahu's first visit to Washington in his latest incarnation as prime minister, in mid-May 2009, included a meeting and lunch at the White House and a working lunch with me at the Pentagon. He and I focused on military cooperation and a broad discussion of Iran and its nuclear program. Our first no-punches-pulled discussion of Iran came during my visit to Israel in late July, when images of the rigged Iranian election and subsequent repression of the Green Revolution in June were still fresh. Bibi was convinced the Iranian regime was extremely fragile and that a strike on their nuclear facilities very likely would trigger the regime's overthrow by the Iranian people. I strongly disagreed, convinced that a foreign military attack would instead rally the Iranian people behind their government. Netanyahu also believed Iranian retaliation after a strike would be pro forma, perhaps the launch of a few dozen missiles at Israel and some rocket salvos from Lebanese-based Hizballah. He argued that the Iranians were realists and would not want to provoke a larger military attack by the United States by going after American targets—especially our ships in the Gulf—or by attacking other countries' oil facilities. Closing the Gulf to oil exports, he said, would cut the Iranians' own economic throats. Again I disagreed, telling him he was misled by the lack of an Iraqi response to Israel's destruction of their Osirak reactor in 1981 and the absence of any Syrian reaction to destruction of their reactor in 2007. I said the Iranians—the Persians— were very different from Iraqis and Syrians. He was assuming a lot in anticipating a mild Iranian reaction, and if he was wrong, an attack on the Iranian nuclear facilities would spark a war in the region, I said.

These two lines of argumentation would dominate the U.S.-Israeli dialogue over Iran for the rest of my tenure as secretary, though there was not much difference in our intelligence assessments of how far along the Iranians were in their nuclear program, nor in our views of the consequences of Iran acquiring nuclear weapons. Whether (and when) to act militarily and the consequences of an attack would remain contentious.

The last gasp of Obama's engagement strategy with Iran was an ingenious proposal, developed by the United States in consultation with our allies in October 2009, that Iran ship about 80 percent of its known 1.5 metric tons of low-enriched uranium to Russia, where it would be enriched, then sent to France for conversion into fuel rods, and finally sent back to Iran for medical research use in the Tehran Research Reactor. According to the experts, once used in the research reactor, the uranium would be extremely difficult to convert for other purposes—such as nuclear weapons. The proposal was seen as a way to get most of the low-enriched uranium out of the country and rendered useless for weapons, while acknowledging Iran's right to use nuclear reactors for peaceful purposes. France, Britain, China, Germany, Russia, and the United

States supported the proposal, and tentative agreement was reached with Iranian negotiators in Europe on October 22. Iran backed out the next day, having second thoughts about giving up its big bargaining chip—the low-enriched uranium—without, in their view, gaining any strategic benefit. Given French president Sarkozy's open loathing of the Iranian regime, I believe the Iranians also had no intention of putting their uranium in French hands.

The failure to make a deal had significant international consequences. The Obama administration, including me, had seen the deal as a way to get the low-enriched uranium out of Iran and thus buy more time for a longer-term solution. Ironically, but as I had believed it would, the diplomatic effort to reach out to Iran was critical to our success in finding more willing partners in a new, tougher approach.

Central to the new approach would be getting international agreement. The Deputies Committee had met several times in early November and agreed that the United States should first pursue a UN Security Council resolution imposing new economic sanctions on Iran, then widen the net of pressure. The president chaired a National Security Council meeting on November 11—just preceding the important NSC session on Afghanistan—to consider next steps. He said we had to pivot from engagement to pressure as a result of the Iranian rejection of the Tehran Research Reactor initiative, the Iranians' lack of full cooperation with the IAEA inspection of the Qom enrichment facility (a secret facility, the existence of which we revealed to put Iran on its heels and to build support for more sanctions), and their unwillingness to pursue negotiations with the six big powers (France, Germany, Britain, Russia, China, and the United States).

The U.S. ambassador to the United Nations, Susan Rice, felt we were unlikely to get a strong new resolution out of the Security Council. I said that the clock was ticking on both the progress of the Iranian nuclear program and Jerusalem's patience. We needed a new resolution as a foundation for stronger sanctions, and because we didn't expect much anyway, I thought we should accept a diluted resolution if we could get it passed quickly. Then we could develop additional sanctions and other punitive actions beyond the strict terms of the resolution. Militarily, I thought we needed to prepare for a possible Israeli attack and Iranian retaliation and figure out a way to use our actions to send the Iranians a message in parallel to economic pressures.

I had hoped for UN action in January or February; the resolution passed in June 2010. The resolution was better than nothing, but it demonstrated that Russia and China remained ambivalent about how hard to push Tehran. China was leery of losing the significant amount of oil it bought from Iran and, in any event, was in no mood to do anything remotely helpful to the United States after we announced the sale of $6.5 billion in arms to Taiwan at the end of January 2010. Russia, I think, still harbored hopes of future economic and political influence in Iran.

Bush and Obama had said publicly that the military option to stop Iran's nuclear program remained on the table, and it was our job at the Pentagon to do the planning and preparation to ensure that it was not an idle threat. U.S. military leaders were increasingly worried that either the Israelis or the Iranians might take military action with little or no warning and that such an action could require an immediate response from U.S. forces in the Gulf. There would be no time for protracted meetings in Washington or for the president to consult anyone but me, the next person in the chain of command. Other than the U.S. response to a small-scale Iranian "fast-boat" attack on one of our Navy ships, there had been no discussion in either the Bush or the Obama administrations—other than private conversations I had with each president—about momentous decisions that might be required within minutes if serious shooting broke out in the Gulf. It was my view that such a discussion was long overdue.

Accordingly, on January 4, 2010, I sent Jim Jones a memo recommending a highly restricted meeting of the principals to discuss the possibility of a conflict with Iran with little or no advance notice. I wanted to discuss actions we ought to take to strengthen our military posture in the Gulf for Iran-related contingencies, as well as military actions we ought to consider—short of the use of force—to keep the pressure on. I asked in the memo, if Israel attacked Iran, would we help Israel, hinder it, take no action, or conduct follow-up operations (especially if Israel failed to destroy the nuclear sites)? If Iran retaliated against Israel, would we come to Israel's defense? If Iran were to hit U.S. troops, facilities, or interests in retaliation after an Israeli strike, how would we respond? What measures should we take to deter Iranian military actions, to maintain "escalation dominance" (to overmatch any Iranian military action and try to keep the situation from spinning out of control)? Should we emplace forces in advance? How would we respond to closure of the Gulf, terrorism, manipulation of oil prices, and other Iranian responses? Many of these questions and issues had been framed for me by the deputy assistant secretary for defense, Colin Kahl, and his team, whom I greatly admired and relied upon heavily. The questions I posed, and the answers, had not been discussed—in part, I think, because the consequences of a leak could be explosive, both literally and figuratively.

A little over three months later, on April 18, *The New York Times* ran a front-page story asserting that in my January memo I had warned that "the United States does not have an effective long-range policy for dealing with Iran's steady progress toward nuclear capability." A source characterized as a "senior official" described the memo as a "wake-up call." It seemed likely that the authors' (David Sanger and Thom Shanker) source apparently did not provide them with any of the questions I had posed but rather characterized the memo as dealing with policy, strategy, and military options.

Geoff Morrell gave NSC chief of staff Denis McDonough a heads-up about the story before it appeared, and needless to say, he, Donilon, Ben Rhodes (the NSC's strategic communications director), and others at the White House went into a tizzy over a story suggesting that the White House was not properly prepared to deal with Iran. I thought it would be silly to deny the existence of the memo and, in consultation with Morrell, Robert Rangel, and McDonough, agreed to issue a statement clarifying the purpose of the memo. The national press gave the *Times'* story prominent coverage and, regrettably, paid little attention to my statement that the memo was not intended (or received) as a wake-up call but instead had "identified next steps in our defense planning process where further interagency discussion and policy decisions would be needed . . . it presented a number of questions and proposals intended to contribute to an orderly and timely decision making process." (Much later others alleged that the memo called for "containment" of Iran rather than preventing them from getting a weapon. That assertion was also wrong.) The *Times* story was pretty accurate overall, but it did misrepresent my intent and—fortunately—did not deal with the militarily sensitive concerns I had raised.

Three days later I went through many of those concerns in the Oval Office with the president. Biden, Mullen, Jones, Donilon, Brennan, and Tony Blinken, the vice president's national security adviser, were there. I told Obama he needed to consider the ramifications of a no-warning

Israeli attack or Iranian provocation, either of which likely would require a U.S. military response within minutes or hours. I said that the principals had not "chewed" on these issues, and they should. To be better prepared for any eventuality in the Gulf, I told Obama I wanted to take several military steps by November 1, including deploying a second aircraft carrier there, adding better missile defense and radar capabilities, sending a third Aegis destroyer, and forward-positioning other equipment. I asked that the policy issues and added deployments I recommended be addressed urgently, in particular because the military moves required significant lead time. Obama said we should look at options, but he would make no concrete decisions now.

I was put off by the way the president closed the meeting. To his very closest advisers, he said, "For the record, and for those of you writing your memoirs, I am not making any decisions about Israel or Iran. Joe, you be my witness." I was offended by his suspicion that any of us would ever write about such sensitive matters.

Toward the end of May, we discussed the implications of an Israeli attack on Iran, though not as thoroughly as I would have liked. The administration did, however, proceed fairly quickly in important areas mentioned in my memo. It further strengthened our military relationships with key states in the region by providing (or selling) enhanced missile defense capabilities and advanced weapons and made proposals for closer military cooperation. In early February, I traveled to Turkey, where I met with Prime Minister Recep Tayyip Erdogan. We had a long discussion about Iran, during which he said that no country should be denied the right to nuclear technology for peaceful means; he said that he had encouraged the Iranians to be more transparent and cooperate with the IAEA. He was skeptical of the value of further sanctions and thought the Tehran Research Reactor proposal was still a possible course of action. I agreed about the right to peaceful use of nuclear technology "if properly safeguarded" but, in my usual subtle diplomatic way, warned him that if the Iranians proceeded with their nuclear weapons ambitions, proliferation in the region would be inevitable, military action by Israel would be likely, and he would have a war in his neighborhood. I told him it was necessary to proceed with sanctions in order to get Iran back to the negotiating table. Erdogan was interested in missile defenses that would provide coverage of Turkey but wanted to be sure that any initiative was cast in terms of "common security" among allies and not based on a specific threat (such as Iran). I felt I had made little progress with Erdogan; he was just too wary of anything that might provoke the Iranians.

That was plainly not the case at my next stop, to see President Nicolas Sarkozy in France. Sarkozy reminded me of Rahm Emanuel, lithe and short and full of energy—they both sort of explode into a room. Sarkozy went straight to the point: "The Iranians are liars and have been lying from the start." The extended U.S. hand, he said, had been seen in Iran as a sign of weakness. It had led to "a great deal of wasted time." He regretted that new sanctions had not been put in place the preceding fall and asserted, "We are weak. This will all end badly."

In the middle of our meeting, Sarkozy's personal cell phone rang. He answered, holding his hand over his phone and mouth as he talked with his wife, singer and former model Carla Bruni. I had never heard of or experienced a head of government interrupting a meeting to take a personal call. The incident did, I admit, later that evening provoke some amusing commentary between my staff and me.

In early March, I resumed my anti-Iran tour, visiting Saudi Arabia and the United Arab Emirates. Outside Riyadh, I met with the crown prince and deputy prime minister as well as King Abdullah at the king's "farm." I grew up in Kansas, and this wasn't like any farm I had ever seen. We had dinner inside a tent—with crystal chandeliers—that could have held the entire Ringling Brothers circus and then some. The huge, horseshoe-shaped table sat at least a hundred people, and as with Condi Rice's and my dinner with the king a few years earlier in Jeddah, there were at least forty or fifty dishes in the buffet, not counting dozens of desserts. The king and I sat at the head of the table with no one seated near us, but a large television right in front of us was airing an Arab news show. I thought it a bit strange to have the TV on during dinner—until I realized the wily old guy wanted white noise in the background so he and I could speak without being overheard by anyone.

After dinner, we talked privately for a long time about Iran, as I explained to him the president's pivot from engagement to pressure, which the king heartily welcomed, having been opposed to any kind of outreach in the first place. As we talked about sanctions, I encouraged him to consider an overture to the Chinese, proposing that they sharply cut their purchases of Iranian oil, which Saudi Arabia would replace. I made no formal request, and he made no commitment. We discussed upgrading the Saudis' Patriot missile defense systems, and we agreed to discuss further their acquisition of other, more advanced missile defenses. I promised to send the head of the Missile Defense Agency to Saudi Arabia quickly to brief the king and his ministers on these capabilities, which would also make the Saudi missile defense interoperable with our own and that of other countries in the Gulf. We talked about modernization of the Saudi navy.

In that private meeting, the king committed to a $60 billion weapons deal including the purchase of eighty-four F-15s, the upgrade of seventy F-15s already in the Saudi air force, twenty-four Apache helicopters, and seventy-two Blackhawk helicopters. His ministers and generals had pressed him hard to buy either Russian or French fighters, but I think he suspected that was because some of the money would end up in their pockets. He wanted all the Saudi money to go toward military equipment, not into Swiss bank accounts, and thus he wanted to buy from us. The king explicitly told me that he saw the huge purchase as an investment in a long-term strategic relationship with the United States, linking our militaries for decades to come. At the same time, Abdullah was very cautious about any kind of overt military cooperation or planning with the United States that the Iranians might consider an act of war.

I then went to Abu Dhabi, where I met with Crown Prince Mohammed bin Zayed. "MBZ," as we referred to him, is one of the smartest, canniest people I have ever met, very soft-spoken and given to long pauses in conversation. His thoughtful insights on the other Gulf states and on Iran were always useful. We met with a larger group for a few minutes, and then the two of us went outside on his patio to meet privately for an hour or so. We talked about the change in Obama's Iranian strategy from engagement to pressure, making sanctions more effective (a lot of Iranian business was done in the UAE), and about additional missile defense and other military capabilities for the Emirates.

Any sale of relatively sophisticated weapons—especially combat aircraft and missiles—to an Arab state met with opposition in Israel. In the case of the big arms deal I had just concluded with King Abdullah, the Israelis were especially exercised. And it came at a bad time in the relationship. The administration had leaned heavily on Netanyahu in the summer of 2009 to impose a ten-month freeze on building new settlements on the West Bank, as an inducement to get the Palestinians to the negotiating table. Meanwhile construction continued on settlements in

East Jerusalem, which the Israelis consider their sovereign territory. As a result, the Palestinians refused to negotiate. In March 2010—just as I was talking with King Abdullah—the Israelis announced they would continue to build settlements in East Jerusalem, an open slap at the administration, made all the more insulting because Biden was visiting Israel at the time. Secretary Clinton presented an ultimatum to Israel soon thereafter, demanding among other things a freeze on all settlement construction. This led to a notoriously acrimonious meeting between Obama and Netanyahu at the White House on March 26, during which the president bowed out to have dinner with his family, leaving Bibi cooling his heels downstairs.

As these tensions boiled, on April 27, Barak came to see me about the Saudi arms sale. As had become standard practice between us, I greeted his limousine curbside at the Pentagon, escorted him and his delegation up the stairs to my formal dining room, and then I walked him straight through the door to my office, where we met alone, leaving our delegations to chitchat for most of the allotted meeting time. As part of our relationship with Israel, the United States had long pledged that no arms sales to Arab states would undermine Israel's "qualitative military edge" (QME). Barak felt the sale to Saudi Arabia compromised their QME. I told him I thought Israel and Saudi Arabia now had a common enemy—Iran—and that Israel should welcome enhanced Saudi capabilities. I also pointed out that not once in all of Israel's wars had Saudi Arabia fired a shot. I urged that if Israel couldn't see Saudi Arabia as a potential ally against Iran, he should at least tactically concede that its hostility to Iran was in Israel's interest. Pragmatically, I warned that if the Saudis could not buy advanced combat aircraft from us, they would surely buy them from the French or Russians, and the Israelis could be damned sure those countries wouldn't give a second thought to Israel's "qualitative military edge."

We agreed to set up a joint U.S.-Israeli working group to ensure that Israel's QME was not diminished by the F-15 sale to Saudi Arabia and to identify enhanced capabilities we could provide to Israel to satisfy that goal. I reassured Barak that, as I had promised two years earlier to Prime Minister Olmert, we would sell Israel the same model F-35 Joint Strike Fighter we were going to provide our NATO allies. Barak returned to Washington in late June to review progress of the working group and seemed generally satisfied that Israeli interests would be protected by the measures we were considering.

Netanyahu took another view. I met with him at Blair House, the guesthouse on Pennsylvania Avenue that the president uses to host foreign leaders, on July 7. I told him I had my marching orders from the president, and that General Cartwright would lead a senior U.S. team to Israel the following week to talk about military cooperation and needs and to get "specifics about what you need and just how fast you want it." I told Netanyahu we intended to notify Congress soon about the F-15 sale to Saudi Arabia, that we had addressed the QME issues with his defense experts, and that "it would be helpful for Israel to say that there had been an unprecedented effort to take into account Israel's concerns, and that they did not object to the sale." When he complained about the number of F-15s the Saudis would be buying or upgrading, I pointedly asked him, "When did Saudi Arabia ever attack Israel? How long would those planes continue to work without U.S. support? You need to talk to Ehud [Barak] about what we have done to address your concerns!" When Netanyahu asked how to explain to Israelis such a large arms deal with the Saudis, I used the line that the enemy of my enemy is my friend. He replied acidly, "In the Middle East, the enemy of my enemy is my 'frenemy.' "

"What about a counterbalancing investment in our military?" he asked me. "How do we compensate on the Israeli side?" Exasperated, I shot back that no U.S. administration had done more, in concrete ways, for Israel's strategic defense than Obama's, and I listed the various missile and rocket defense programs we were providing or helping to fund, together with stationing an Aegis-class warship with missile defense capabilities in the eastern Mediterranean. Further compensation? "You are already getting air and missile defense cooperation in addition to the F-35. There have been conversations on all of this. This is not new. There has been enormous work done to address your QME. Talk to your defense minister!" I was furious after the meeting and directed Flournoy to call Barak and chew him out for not adequately briefing Bibi on all that we had done to address Israel's concerns. Barak talked to Netanyahu, and by the end of July, Bibi had agreed not to object to the Saudi arms sale—in exchange for more military equipment, including twenty additional F-35s.

Israel lives in a dangerous neighborhood, populated by various groups and countries that are not only its sworn enemies but committed to its total destruction. It has fought four wars against those neighbors, three of them—in 1948, 1967, and 1973—for its very survival. While a few governments, including Egypt's and Jordan's, have found it in their interest to make peace with Israel, the Arab populace—including in those two countries—is more hostile toward Israel than their governments are. I believe Israel's strategic situation is worsening, its own actions contributing to its isolation. The Israelis' assassination of a Hamas leader in Dubai in January 2010, however morally justified, was strategically stupid because the incompetently run operation was quickly discovered and Israel fingered as responsible, thus costing Israel the quiet cooperation of the UAE on security matters. Similarly, the Israeli attack on May 31, 2010, on a Turkish ship carrying confrontational activists to Gaza and the resulting deaths of eight Turks on board, together with Israel's subsequent unyielding response, resulted in a break with Turkey, which had quietly developed a good military-to-military relationship with Israel. These incidents, and others like them, may have been tactically desirable and even necessary but had negative strategic consequences. As Israel's neighbors acquire ever more sophisticated weapons and their publics become ever more hostile, I, as a very strong friend and supporter of Israel, believe Jerusalem needs to think anew about its strategic environment. That would require developing stronger relationships with governments that, while not allies, share Israel's concerns in the region, including those about Iran and the growing political influence of Islamists in the wake of the Arab Spring. (Netanyahu would finally apologize for the Turkish deaths in 2013, opening the way to restoring ties with the Turks.) Given a Palestinian birthrate that far outpaces that of Israeli Jews, and the political trends in the region, time is not on Israel's side.

MISSILE DEFENSE AGAINST IRAN

The United States began working on defenses against ballistic missiles in the 1960s. Stringent limits were imposed on the development and deployment of missile defenses in the 1972 Anti-Ballistic Missile Treaty we signed with the Soviet Union. Even so, the missile defense endeavor received a huge boost in 1983 with President Reagan's announcement of the Strategic Defense Initiative (SDI), intended conceptually to provide a "shield" for the United States against an all-out Soviet attack. Generally speaking, in the years after Reagan's SDI (or "Star Wars") speech, most Republicans supported virtually all missile defense programs and most Democrats opposed them as both unworkable and far too costly. In 2002, as we've seen, President Bush unilaterally withdrew the United States from the 1972 treaty, thereby removing any restrictions on our development and deployment of missile defenses. By the time I became secretary of defense, most members of Congress had come around—with widely varying levels of enthusiasm—to support deploying a very limited capability intended to defend against an accidental launch or a handful of missiles fired by a "rogue" state such as North Korea or Iran. Few in either party supported efforts to field a system large or advanced enough to protect against a mass strike from the nuclear arsenals of either Russia or China, an effort that would have been at once technologically challenging, staggeringly expensive, and strategically destabilizing.

At the end of 2008, our strategic missile defenses consisted of twenty-three ground-based interceptors (GBIs) deployed at Fort Greely, Alaska, and four more at Vandenberg Air Force Base in California. By the end of FY2010, thirty such interceptors were planned to be in place. Those associated with the program had reasonable confidence that the missiles could accomplish the limited mission of knocking down one or a few missiles aimed at the United States. When I became secretary of defense, the president delegated to me, as he had to Secretary Rumsfeld, the authority to launch these interceptors against incoming missiles if there was no time to get his approval.

This was the situation when I recommended to Bush, a few days after I took office, that we approach the Poles and Czechs about cohosting a "third" GBI site on their soil—radar in the Czech Republic and ten ground-based interceptors in Poland. Both countries had shown interest in hosting elements of the missile defense system. Our primary purpose in this initiative was to better defend the United States (and limited areas of Europe) against Iranian ballistic missiles, whose threat was growing.

As I wrote earlier, by the end of 2008 it looked increasingly certain that Czech political opposition to the radar would prevent its construction there. Poland had agreed to host the interceptors immediately following the Russian invasion of Georgia after stalling for more than a year, but their growing demands for U.S. security guarantees beyond our NATO commitment, as well as other disagreements, brought the negotiations to a halt. By the time Obama took office, it was pretty clear that our initiative was going nowhere politically in either Poland or the Czech Republic, and that even if it was somehow to proceed, political wrangling would delay its initial operating capability by many years.

A technically feasible alternative approach to missile defense in Europe surfaced in mid-2009 in the Pentagon (not, as later alleged, in the White House). A new intelligence estimate of the Iranian missile program published in February 2009 caused us in Defense to rethink our priorities. The assessment said the long-range Iranian missile threat had not matured as anticipated, but the threat from Iranian short- and medium-range missiles, which could strike our troops and facilities in Europe and the Middle East, had developed more rapidly than expected and had become the Iranian government's priority. The Iranians were now thought to be capable of nearly simultaneous launches of between fifty and seventy of these shorter-range missiles at a time. These conclusions raised serious questions about our existing strategy, which had been developed primarily to provide improved defenses for the U.S. homeland—not Europe—against long-range Iranian missiles launched one or two at a time. But the Iranians no longer seemed focused on building an ICBM, at least in the near term. And ten interceptors in Poland could at best defend against only a handful of Iranian missiles. The site would easily be overwhelmed by a salvo launch of dozens of shorter-range missiles.

In the spring of 2009 General Cartwright briefed me on technological advances made during the previous two years with the sea-based Standard Missile 3s (SM-3) and the possibility of using them as a missile defense alternative to the ground-based interceptors. New, more capable versions of the SM-3, originally designed to defend our ships against hostile aircraft and shorter-range ballistic missiles, were being deployed on a growing number of U.S. warships and had been used successfully to destroy that falling U.S. satellite during the Bush administration. These new SM-3 variants were still in development, but there had been eight successful tests, and they were considered to be at least as capable against short- and medium-range ballistic missiles as GBIs and could be fully operational years earlier. The SM-3, due to the significantly lower cost than GBIs, could be produced and deployed in large numbers.

There had also been technological advances in airborne, space-based, and ground-based sensors that considerably outperformed the fixed-site radar originally intended for the Czech Republic. These new sensors not only would allow our system to be integrated with partner countries' warning systems, but also could make better use of radars already operating across the globe, including updated Cold War–era installations. Cartwright, former commander of Strategic Command, was a strong and early advocate for a new approach, which was affirmed by the early findings of the Pentagon-led Ballistic Missile Defense Review, begun in March 2009.

Based on all available information, the U.S. national security leadership, military and civilian, concluded that our priorities should be to work with allies and partners to strengthen regional deterrence architectures; to pursue a "phased adaptive," or evolutionary, approach to missile defense within each region, tailored to the threats and circumstances unique to that region; and because global demand for missile defense assets over the following decade might exceed supply, to make them mobile so they could be shifted from region to region as circumstances required.

Independent of these findings and assessments, in preparing the fiscal year 2010 budget, I decided to cancel several huge, expensive, and failing missile defense programs, such as the airborne laser and the kinetic energy interceptor, as described earlier. At the same time, I decided to keep the number of silo-based GBIs in Alaska and California at thirty rather than expanding the deployment to forty-four, and I authorized continued research, development, and testing of our defenses against the long-range-missile threat from Iranian and North Korean missiles. (I also canceled completion of a second field of silos for the GBIs at Fort Greely, but after visiting there a few months later and seeing how close they were to completion, I reversed myself and approved finishing the second field. I was no expert but was always willing to listen to those who were.) Meanwhile, reflecting the new emphasis on regional missile defense, I allocated a great deal of money in the budget to accelerate building the inventory of SM-3 missile interceptors, as well as other regional missile defense systems. I also agreed to fund improved missile defense capability on six more destroyers.

I was determined to increase our capability as quickly as possible to protect our deployed forces and our allies. We briefed Congress on these changes on several occasions between May and July, and the response was generally favorable. The only opposition was focused on my cancellation of several of the big—and failing—development programs.

Those who would later charge that Obama walked away from the third site in Europe to please the Russians seemed oblivious to growing Polish and Czech opposition to the site and, more important, to the reality that the Defense Department was already reordering its missile defense priorities to focus on the immediate short- to medium-range-missile threat. While there certainly were some in the State Department and the White House who believed the third site in Europe was incompatible with the Russian "reset," we in Defense did not. Making the Russians happy wasn't exactly on my to-do list.

In August, the NSS asked the Defense Department to prepare a paper on what had changed to warrant a new direction for missile defense in Europe, and we laid it all out. The principals met on September 1, 2009, and agreed to recommend that the president approve the phased adaptive approach to missile defense in Europe, while agreeing to my proposal to guard against the longer-term threat by keeping open the option for eventually deploying European-based radar and GBIs. The continued investment in GBIs was opposed by some Obama appointees at the State Department and the NSS. We agreed to continue to seek opportunities for cooperation with Russia, including the possible integration of one of their radars that could provide useful tracking data. I formally proposed the Phased-Adaptive Approach in a memorandum to the president on September 11, nearly three years after proposing the third site to President Bush. Times, technology, and threats change. We had to change with them.

Then, as so often happened, a leak made us look like a bunch of bumbling fools, oblivious to the sensitivities of our allies. To date, there had been none of the obligatory consultations with Congress or our allies about what would be the first major reversal of a Bush national security policy and a major shift in the U.S. missile defense strategy in Europe. When we learned on September 16 that the details of the new missile defense approach were in the hands of the press, we had to act quickly to correct that. That evening Hillary dispatched a team of officials from both State and Defense to brief European governments and NATO. The president called the prime ministers of both Poland and the Czech Republic to inform them of his decision and to promise that he was dispatching administration officials immediately to Warsaw and Prague to brief them.

The morning of the seventeenth, the president publicly announced the new approach. In one of those unanticipated and unfortunate coincidences, that month was the seventieth anniversary of the Nazi invasion of Poland. Some news stories asserted that Poland had again been "betrayed," and most suggested that our timing had added insult to injury with the Poles. The president and his domestic advisers clearly wanted me out front to defend this new strategy; I had recommended the earlier approach to Bush and had the credibility to justify a different approach under Obama. It was neither the first nor last time under Obama that I was used to provide political cover, but it was okay in this instance since I sincerely believed the new program was better—more in accord with the political realities in Europe and more effective against the emerging Iranian threat. And I had been successful in preserving the GBI alternative, at least for the time being.

By the time General Cartwright and I sallied forth to the press room to talk about the new program, Republicans in Congress and former Bush officials were all over the airwaves harshly criticizing this "betrayal" of our allies in order to curry favor with the Russians. Senator McCain called the move "seriously misguided." I told the press what had prompted the reassessment and explained the details of the planned system. In response to a question, I said the Russians had to accept that there was going to be a missile defense system in Europe. We hoped they'd join it, but we were going to proceed regardless.

The damage from the leak was manageable in Europe. I thought the Polish and Czech governments were probably relieved that they could avoid a showdown with their parliaments; the plan would have lost for sure in Prague and probably in Warsaw. In my calls with both defense ministers on the eighteenth, I said we still wanted them to be involved with missile defense in Europe.

Under both the Bush and Obama missile defense plans, I thought our goals and those of the Polish and Czech leaders were completely different, although no one ever had the audacity to say so publicly or even privately. *Their* goals were political, having nothing to do with Iran and everything to do with Russia: the U.S. deployments on their soil would be a concrete manifestation of U.S. security guarantees against Russia beyond our commitments under the NATO treaty. *Our* goals under both plans were primarily military: to deal with a rapidly evolving Iranian missile threat, as we repeatedly made clear to them and to the Russians. Indeed, Rice and I had told Putin that if the Iranian missile program went away, so would the need for U.S. missile defenses in Europe. That's why I had offered to Putin in 2008 to delay making the sites operational until the Iranians flight-tested a missile that could reach Europe. Obama would catch hell for saying nearly the same thing to Russian president Medvedev.

The New York Times bottom-lined all this with the headline "Obama Reshapes a Missile Shield to Blunt Tehran," and *The Washington Post* subheadline was "New Plan Designed to Confront Iran's Capabilities More Directly." I never understood the fury of the U.S. critics. The new plan would get defenses operational in Europe and for our 80,000 troops there years earlier than the Bush approach, while still going forward with development of the ground-based interceptors for homeland defense. Obama would still be taking heat for "canceling" missile defense in Europe during the 2012 election.

Obama's new missile defense plan had one unintended, but welcome, consequence. For the first time since before Reagan's "Star Wars" speech, building a limited American missile defense had broad bipartisan support in Congress. That was no small thing.

RUSSIA

The Obama administration's desire to "reset" the relationship with Russia got off to an awkward start. Hillary had her first meeting with Russian foreign minister Lavrov in Geneva on March 6, and someone persuaded her to present him with a big red button, with the word "reset" printed on the top in Russian. Unfortunately, the Russian word on the button actually said "overcharge." This reaffirmed my strong view that gimmicks in foreign policy generally backfire. They are right up there with presidents putting on funny hats—they result in pictures you have to live with forever.

Russian behavior in 2009–10 vis-à-vis Iran was mixed. At one point early on, Medvedev conceded to Obama that the United States had been right about Iran's nuclear and missile ambitions (words that could never have crossed Putin's lips). The Russians would not block efforts to get new sanctions against Iran approved by the UN, even though they would continue to work to water them down. They refrained from sending the Iranians a very sophisticated new air defense system—the S-300—which would have made an attack on Iran's nuclear facilities considerably harder. Putin had promised Bush he would not send the system to Iran and, after Obama became president, actually broke the contract with the Iranians.

When it came to missile defense in Europe, however, the Russians almost immediately concluded that the new approach announced by Obama was potentially a bigger problem for them than the Bush plan had been. They were worried about the possibility of future modifications to the systems that would, in fact, give them capabilities against Russian ICBMs. They came to believe the potential deployment of hundreds of advanced SM-3 missiles that we were planning between 2018 and 2020 posed an even bigger threat to them than the GBIs. From that point—a few weeks after the September announcement—the Russians mounted an even more aggressive campaign against the new approach than they had the old, and they would continue to do so for the rest of my time as secretary and beyond. Discussion of potential partnering on missile defense continued for political purposes on both sides, but in reality, a slim chance had become no chance. Missile defense would continue to be the Russians' principal target in meetings of the NATO-Russia Council and in bilateral meetings with all senior U.S. officials. The Iranian threat simply did not outweigh concerns over their own long-term security. How ironic that U.S. critics of the new approach had portrayed it as a big concession to the Russians. It would have been nice to hear a critic in Washington—just once in my career—say, *Well, I got that wrong.*

With one exception, I played a minor role in the U.S.-Russian relationship during my time in the Obama administration. Where Condi Rice and I had traveled to Russia on several occasions for "two plus two" meetings with our counterparts and to meet with Putin and Medvedev, I visited Russia only once during my two and a half years working for Obama, and that was near the end of my tenure in 2011. There was not a single "two plus two" meeting during that period. I had regular bilateral discussions with Russian minister of defense Serdyukov at NATO sessions when the NATO-Russia Council met, but these rarely lasted more than half an hour and, with translation, provided little opportunity for serious dialogue; he usually had only enough time to poke a stick in my eye over missile defense.

The one exception was negotiation of a new treaty imposing further reductions on the strategic nuclear delivery systems of both countries. I had a personal history with this decades-long endeavor. I had been a junior intelligence adviser to the U.S. delegation negotiating the first such treaty with the Soviets in the early 1970s (SALT I—Strategic Arms Limitation Talks I), and a junior member of the U.S. delegation present in Vienna when President Carter signed the second such treaty in 1979 (SALT II), which was never ratified by the U.S. Senate because of the Soviet invasion of Afghanistan in December 1979. Negotiations for additional limits on both sides' nuclear arsenals continued throughout the 1980s and 1990s (the Strategic Arms Reduction Treaty—START—talks), but not much was actually accomplished. Under Bush 43, the Strategic Offensive Reductions Treaty (SORT, also known as the Moscow Treaty), reducing the nuclear arsenals of both sides to between 1,700 and 2,200 operational deployed warheads, was signed in 2002, to expire at the end of 2012 if not superseded by a new treaty.

In early 2009, SALT, START, and SORT—acronym hell—gave way to "New Start," an Obama administration effort to negotiate the next strategic arms limitations treaty. Medvedev signed on that spring. All the presidents I worked for except Carter found the details of arms control negotiations mind-numbing and excruciatingly boring. Most of the hard work was done by the negotiators and the sub–cabinet level experts in Washington, with only major issues or obstacles put before the principals. The broad outlines of an agreement emerged within a matter of weeks, limiting the number of deployed strategic nuclear warheads to 1,550 and the number of strategic missile launchers and bombers to 800. Included were very important provisions for satellite and remote monitoring—for the first time, monitoring tags would be on each bomber and missile— and for eighteen on-site inspections each year. The Joint Chiefs of Staff and the commander of Strategic Command were supportive of the provisions, as was I. General Cartwright and Jim Miller, principal deputy undersecretary of defense for policy, were expert in the strategic nuclear world and played a prominent role in shaping the views of senior leaders in the Pentagon, including mine.

Agreement was reached on the terms of the treaty on March 26, 2010, and Presidents Obama and Medvedev signed it in Prague on April 8. I informed the president a few days later that at the exact moment of the signing ceremony, the Russian military had been conducting a nuclear attack exercise against the United States. A nice Putin touch, I thought.

Critics of the treaty in the United States wasted no time in describing its purported shortcomings. It was said the treaty would inhibit our ability to deploy missile defenses, to modernize our strategic systems, and to develop capabilities for conventional global strike (using ICBMs with conventional warheads for long-range precision targeting).

Because the treaty limited the number of U.S. and Russian nuclear warheads, the viability of our aging nuclear warheads and production facilities became a growing concern during the ratification process. (A number of our nuclear weapons production facilities had been built for the Manhattan Project during World War II.) Principals had met on several occasions to discuss modernization, not new capabilities. The cost of replacement and upgraded facilities would be significant—$80 billion over ten years. Given Obama's ultimate goal of zero nuclear weapons, the idea of modernization met with stiff resistance at the subcabinet level and in the White House and NSS.

Obama was the fourth president I had worked for who said outright that he wanted to eliminate all nuclear weapons (Carter, Reagan, and Bush 41 were the others). Former secretaries of state Henry Kissinger and George Shultz, former defense secretary Bill Perry, and former senator Sam Nunn had also called for "going to zero." The only problem, in my view, was that I hadn't heard the leaders of any other nuclear country—Britain, France, Russia, China, India, or Pakistan—signal the same intent. If we were going to have nuclear weapons, we'd damn well better ensure they would work and were safe from both terrorists and accidents—and that meant incorporating new designs and technologies.

I spent most of my professional life dealing with the role of nuclear weapons in national defense—beginning with my assignment as an Air Force second lieutenant to the Strategic Air Command. Over the decades, the arguments over the circumstances in which they might be used and how many weapons were needed became highly charged and highly esoteric. The debates sometimes reminded me of medieval theologians arguing over how many angels could dance on the head of a pin. I never believed that nuclear weapons could be used on a limited basis in a war between the United States and the USSR, as a number of others did.

I was a strong advocate of dramatically reducing the massive number of nuclear weapons in our arsenal on the basis of reciprocal agreements with the Soviets and subsequently the Russians. But I do not believe we should unilaterally reduce our nuclear forces. I also believe reducing to very low levels of nuclear weapons—below 1,000 to 1,500—offers the temptation to other powers to exceed those numbers and place us at a disadvantage, at a minimum in terms of perceptions. It is a matter of both global politics and military deterrence.

Led by Senator Jon Kyl of Arizona, a number of senators made clear they wouldn't consider voting for ratification of the New Start Treaty unless the administration put enough money in the budget to pay for upgrading our nuclear facilities and modernizing our weapons. The administration promised the funding, most of which I agreed to provide from the defense budget. (Kyl voted against the treaty anyway.)

During the ratification process and hearings, I (along with Mike Mullen) was placed front and center by the administration to defend the treaty. Clinton, Mullen, and I gave a briefing for all senators on May 6, and then we testified before the Senate Foreign Relations Committee on May 18. Once again the Republican hawk—me—was rolled out to provide political cover for the Democratic president. But as with missile defense, I had no problem with it because I believed the treaty was in our national interest. The key question about the new treaty, I said, was the same one posed during over forty years of strategic arms control: is the country better off with the treaty or without it? During that period, I pointed out, every president felt we were better off with a treaty. Under the treaty, we could maintain a strong ICBM, ballistic missile submarine, and bomber deterrent, and the provisions of the treaty were verifiable. The treaty did not constrain our missile defense programs; it had been buttressed by a credible modernization plan for our nuclear weapons stockpile, for the infrastructure that supports it, and for the necessary funding to carry out these plans; and it did not limit our ability to make essential investments to modernize our strategic forces, including delivery systems, nuclear weapons themselves, and the supporting infrastructure.

Hillary spoke to the political aspects of the treaty and the consequences of not ratifying it, and Mullen talked about its effect on our military, adding the strong endorsement of the Joint Chiefs. The questioning was reasonably civil, the criticism perfunctory—except that Republican

Senator Jim DeMint of South Carolina wanted to bring back Reagan's missile shield. The three of us testified again on the treaty before the Senate Armed Services Committee in mid-June. Before the hearings, I wrote an opinion piece in *The Wall Street Journal* defending the treaty, and then Hillary and I wrote another in mid-November in *The Washington Post*. The two of us, together and separately, had a lot of "quality" time with individual senators through the summer and fall. The treaty was ratified by the Senate in the lame-duck session of Congress just before Christmas 2010. It passed by four votes.

A potentially serious crisis in the U.S.-Russian relationship, unrelated to nuclear arms or Iran, cropped up just when the treaty was under consideration. On June 16, John Brennan grabbed me after a meeting and confided that the FBI had penetrated a Russian "illegals" program in the United States. (Illegals, also known as sleepers, are trained spies sent to another country, where they spend years building a life and well-placed careers so that eventually they can be activated as agents with good access to gather information or influence decisions.) Over a period of years, the FBI had identified four couples of illegals in New York, New Jersey, and Virginia. Seven or eight of the adults were Russian military intelligence (GRU) officers. The immediate problem, according to Brennan, was that the source in Moscow who had identified the illegals to the FBI now needed to get out of Russia immediately. Brennan told me that the current plan was to arrest the illegals, who would be interrogated, tried, and held for a potential swap. The concern was that this would be playing out while the president was meeting with Medvedev—at the White House on the twenty-fourth and at the G-8 meeting in Canada on June 25–26. The potential for a major flap was self-evident. Brennan said there would be a meeting with the president on all of this on Friday afternoon, June 18, and I should be there.

CIA director Leon Panetta filled me in on the details regarding the illegals. Leon was passionate about getting the source out of Russia safely. As a former CIA director, I needed no persuading; we have an obligation to try our best to protect, and save, our sources.

As we took our accustomed places in the Situation Room the next afternoon, there was tension in the air. As happened so often during the Cold War, a spy case threatened to derail a political step forward in the U.S.-Russian relationship. The political and diplomatic players came into the room frustrated and angry about the spy case potentially wrecking their goals with Moscow; the CIA and FBI officials came determined to save the source and prosecute the foreign agents. Panetta and FBI director Bob Mueller informed the president of the planned exfiltration and arrests. The illegals were in the United States under false identities, though none of them had done any spying yet that we knew of. The president seemed as angry at Mueller for wanting to arrest the illegals and at Panetta for wanting to exfiltrate the source from Moscow as he was at the Russians: "Just as we're getting on track with the Russians, this? This is a throwback to the Cold War. This is right out of John le Carré. We put START, Iran, the whole relationship with Russia at risk for this kind of thing?" Biden was adamant that U.S. national security interests would be best served by not acting at all. He strongly believed "our national security interest balance tips heavily to not creating a flap," which "would blow up the relationship with the Russians." Jones agreed and asked if we could hold off on the exfiltration until September. The president, betraying a cynicism (and realism) that had to be deeply offensive to both Mueller and Panetta, said he knew that if we let the illegals go back to Russia, folks in the FBI and at CIA would be mad and probably leak it. "The Republicans would beat me up, but I need to keep a broader perspective on the national interest. Isn't there a more elegant solution?"

Medvedev probably didn't even know about this program, I said, but Putin probably did. If we took down the illegals while Medvedev was here or immediately thereafter, he would be embarrassed and weakened at home: "Maybe there is a way to flip this on Putin." Meanwhile "you must exfiltrate the source on schedule," I said to the president. I suggested Obama meet privately with Medvedev in Canada, give him the list of Russian illegals in the United States with their true Russian names and GRU rank, ask if this kind of thing is part of "reset," and demand that they all be recalled to Russia within forty-eight hours or they would be expelled noisily. This would allow the illegals' children to go back to Russia too. I said this might give Medvedev a trump card with Putin: Why was he doing this? Why did he not tell him? I said we would likely get nothing from interrogations; the illegals had been kept isolated from one another, and we already knew a great deal about the program from the source. Based on past experience, a swap would take a year to negotiate.

The president said he would approve my approach. After he left the meeting, though, the principals talked further and concluded that my recommendation would put Medvedev too much on the spot and agreed—with my concurrence—to suggest that the president proceed with exfiltration of our agent from Russia and then just expel the illegals. This would show decisive action but would not put Medvedev in a potentially embarrassing position. Panetta and Mueller agreed. Panetta added, "The vice president got it all wrong—if the president looked like he didn't take the Russian illegals program seriously, *that* would have jeopardized START and more." The spy story would inevitably leak, he said, and there was no way the Republicans in the Senate would have ratified the New Start Treaty had Obama ignored the Russian illegals. I agreed with Leon.

The illegals were arrested on June 27. Much to my surprise, a swap was swiftly arranged—the illegals for four Russians in prison for spying for the West. The episode, I thought, had ended with no political damage to the president and no damage to the bilateral relationship with Russia—but only because the first instincts of the president and vice president, to sweep the whole thing under the rug, had yielded to a wiser path, and because Obama's other advisers had rejected my initial proposal. I admired the president for moving past his anger and frustration to make a good decision.

While I did not go to Russia for the first twenty-six months of the Obama administration, I did meet regularly with my counterpart, Minister of Defense Anatoly Serdyukov, at NATO. Putin and Medvedev had directed him to reform—and shrink—the Russian military, especially the army; to turn a lumbering, top-heavy Cold War leviathan into a nimble, modern force. He was charged with cutting 200,000 officers and some 200 generals and reducing headquarters personnel by 60 percent. Since retired Russian officers were promised housing, he also had to find or build apartments for all those officers.

Serdyukov had no experience in the security arena. He came to his new post by way of the furniture business and the Russian federal tax service. But his father-in-law, Viktor Zubkov, was a first deputy prime minister and confidant of Putin's, and the longer Serdyukov stayed in his job and the more controversial his reforms, the clearer it became just how strongly he was being protected by both Putin and Medvedev. (Serdyukov later was embroiled in a corruption scandal that resulted in his sacking in November 2012.)

As I went forward with my internal reforms and budget reallocations within the Pentagon, I became increasingly curious about what Serdyukov was doing. And so I invited him to Washington, the first visit by a Russian defense minister in six years. He arrived at the Defense Department on September 15, 2010, and I pulled out all the stops to make him feel welcome, with bands and marching troops. (I probably did that for only a half-dozen visitors over four and a half years.) I set aside the entire day to meet with him, spending the morning on our respective internal defense reforms and the challenges we faced. In my Cold War days, I could never have imagined such a remarkably candid conversation on internal issues and problems taking place between our two countries. Although, as I wrote earlier, Serdyukov did not seem to be a significant player in Russia on foreign policy issues, that September day I came to admire his courage, skill, and ambition in trying to reform his military. One analyst in Moscow was quoted in *The New York Times* as saying, "That which Serdyukov is doing is a challenge to the Russian military culture as a whole, the culture that is based upon the idea of a mass-mobilization army starting with Peter the Great." There was no doubt he had become a hated man among Russia's senior military officers.

Our cordiality changed nothing on the big issue that most divided us—missile defense. And I would continue to annoy Putin. Soon after the Serdyukov visit, I had told my French counterpart, Alain Juppé, that democracy did not exist under Putin, that the government was little more than an oligarchy under the control of the Russian security services, and that although Medvedev was president, Putin still called the shots. That conversation leaked, and of course, Putin took offense. In an interview with CNN's Larry King on December 1, he said I was trying to "defame" either him or Medvedev, and he described me as "deeply confused." I never did get around to polishing my diplomatic skills.

All through 2010, at the bottom of the huge funnel pouring problems from Pandora's global trove into Washington, sat just eight of us who, even though served by vast bureaucracies, had to deal with every one of the problems. The challenge for historians and journalists—and memoirists—is how to convey the crushing effect of dealing daily with multiple problems, pivoting on a dime every few minutes from one issue to another, having to quickly absorb reporting from many sources on each problem, and then making decisions, always with too little time and too much ambiguous information. Ideally, I suppose there should be a way to structure our national security apparatus so that day-to-day matters can be delegated to lower levels of responsibility while the president and his senior advisers focus on the big picture and thoughtfully make grand strategy. But that's not how it works in the real world of politics and policy. And as the world becomes more complex and more turbulent, that is a problem in its own right: exhausted people do not make the best decisions.

ASIA

During each of my first three years in office, I had traveled to the Far East twice, including a visit to China in the fall of 2007. In 2010, I would make the long trip from Washington on five separate occasions.

On any trip to Asia, even if China isn't on the itinerary, it is on the agenda. Improving the military-to-military relationship with Beijing was a high priority. I had first traveled to China at the end of 1980, with then CIA director Stansfield Turner, to implement the 1979 agreement between Jimmy Carter and Deng Xiaoping to begin technical intelligence cooperation against the Soviet Union (to replace the radar sites in northern Iran that CIA lost after the 1979 revolution). That extraordinary relationship had continued uninterrupted over the decades through the ups and downs in the two nations' political relationship. As secretary of defense, I wanted to build a similar relationship—that is, one largely immune to political differences—in the military arena. Above all, I wanted to open a dialogue on sensitive subjects like nuclear strategy as well as contingency planning on North Korea. I was convinced that the prolonged dialogue between Washington and Moscow during our many years of arms control negotiations had led to a greater understanding of each other's intentions and thinking about nuclear matters; I believed that dialogue had helped prevent misunderstandings and miscalculations that might have led to confrontation. In my 2007 visit to China, I tried to lay the groundwork for such a relationship. My Chinese hosts and I decided at that time to build on previous cooperative exchanges with a fairly ambitious list of initiatives, from exchanging officers among our military educational institutions to opening a direct telephone link between ministers and beginning to expand a strategic dialogue. It was clear, though, that Chinese military leaders were leery of a *real* dialogue.

Not much headway was made during the last year of the Bush administration. A pall was cast over the relationship in October 2008, when Bush 43 announced his multibillion-dollar arms sale to Taiwan. Things only got worse in March 2009, when the U.S. Navy ship *Impeccable,* an ocean surveillance ship, was aggressively harassed by Chinese boats in the South China Sea. It was a serious incident and a potentially dangerous one, both because of the Chinese actions and because the Chinese were asserting by those actions that we had no right to be in those waters. We would later conclude that this action had been taken by the People's Liberation Army (PLA) without the knowledge of the civilian leadership in Beijing; we believed the same of their test of an antisatellite weapon some while before. Both were worrisome because of the apparent independent behavior of the PLA. Nonetheless, for the most part, lower-level military and civilian visits and exchanges continued in 2009 as planned. Our primary interlocutor was a PLA air force general, Ma Xiaotian, a deputy chief of the general staff. Or, as we referred to him, the "handler of the barbarians"—us. I would see a lot of him over the years.

During my 2007 visit, I had invited senior Chinese military officials to the United States. On October 26, 2009, General Xu Caihou, vice chairman of the Central Military Commission, finally made the trip. I hosted him and his delegation for dinner at the summer cottage used by President Lincoln several miles from downtown Washington. It was a crowded room, and the seating arrangement gave me my only opportunity to talk privately with Xu. I raised the subject of North Korea. I went into some detail about the risks of instability there and the dangers of its collapse both to China and to the South Koreans, and I said we had a mutual interest in a frank dialogue about what we both would do in such circumstances—including how to ensure that the North's nuclear weapons and materials would be kept secure. It was plain that I was way out of Xu's comfort zone in even raising these subjects. "Thank you for your views on North Korea" was all he said to me in response. We discussed the possibility of my visiting China again in 2010, but as always, the Chinese made clear that all bets were off on our relationship if we continued arms sales to Taiwan. Still, our public statements were largely positive, if only to preserve a good atmosphere for Obama's visit to China the following month.

On January 29, 2010, the Obama administration announced the sale of over $6 billion in arms to Taiwan, including Patriot missiles, helicopters, communications systems for their F-16 combat aircraft, minehunting ships, and other equipment. Everyone knew there would be a strong Chinese reaction. As with the Bush team, we were trying to find the best balance between meeting our obligations to Taiwan and preserving the critically important relationship with Beijing. As long as what we sold to Taiwan could reasonably be described as "defensive," we thought we could minimize the damage with China, and we did. The sale, though, put the military-to-military relationship back on ice.

The most visible casualty was my visit to China. General Xu had invited me to return in 2010, but after the Taiwan arms sales announcement, in a typically Chinese manner they made clear I was unwelcome but wanted me to cancel the visit so they could avoid taking a diplomatic hit. More than a little mischievously, I said from time to time that spring that I was still planning to make the trip. Finally we received official word from China that a visit by me in June would not be convenient. Much was made of this "snub" in the press and its consequences for the broader bilateral relationship.

I went to Singapore in early June for the "Shangri-La" Asia Security Summit, hosted annually by the London-based International Institute for Strategic Studies. The sessions were boring, but the conference attracted senior defense officials from all over Asia and provided a good opportunity to do a lot of bilateral business, and for me to make a major speech. Because my canceled visit to China was the buzz of the conference, I decided to tackle it—and the bilateral relationship more broadly—head-on in my speech. The deputy chief of the PLA general staff, General Ma, representing China, was seated in the front row. I reminded the largely Asian audience that Presidents Obama and Hu had agreed the preceding November "to advance sustained and reliable military-to-military relations" between the two countries. I went on that "the key words here are 'sustained' and 'reliable'—not a relationship interrupted by and subject to the vagaries of political weather." The Chinese breaking off interactions between our militaries because of arms sales to Taiwan, I said, made little sense: "First, U.S. arms sales to Taiwan are nothing new. . . . Second, the United States for years has demonstrated in a very public way that we do not support independence for Taiwan. . . . Finally, because China's accelerating military buildup is largely focused on Taiwan, U.S. arms sales are an important component of maintaining peace and stability in cross-strait relations and throughout the region." I pointed out that Taiwan arms sales had not impeded closer U.S.-Chinese political and economic ties, "nor closer ties in other security areas of mutual interest. . . . Only in the military-to-military arena has progress on critical mutual security issues been held hostage over something that is, frankly, old news."

In the question-and-answer session, a retired PLA general aggressively pursued the Taiwan arms-sales issue. I replied that the Chinese had known full well at the time we normalized diplomatic relations in 1979 that arms-sales to Taiwan would continue. Why, then, I asked, did China still pursue this line? The general's response was as direct as it was revealing. China had lived with the Taiwan arms sales in 1979, he said, "because we were weak. But now we are strong."

Perhaps my most important individual meeting in Singapore was with President Lee Myung-bak of South Korea. I really liked Lee; he was tough-minded, realistic, and very pro-American. (All in contrast to his predecessor, President Roh Moo-hyun, whom I had met with in Seoul in November 2007 and decided was anti-American and probably a little crazy. He had told me that the biggest security threats in Asia were the United States and Japan.) A little over two months earlier, on March 26, the North Koreans, in a brazen provocation, had sunk the South Korean warship *Cheonan*. Lee told me he had warned the Chinese premier that the North must "feel consequences." Failure to act, I said, would encourage Kim Jong-il's successor to show the military he is tough and can "get away with things." Lee agreed and said the UN needed to impose economic and diplomatic sanctions on the North and that we needed show-of-force exercises. I said we were already talking about further exercises, but the United States was willing to follow his lead on timing and their nature. Lee was adamant that there could be no return to the six-party talks on the North's nuclear program "until they admit their wrongdoing and renounce it." I concurred: "Resumption of the six-party talks would be seen as a reward—the sequence must be consequences, then talks."

In its disputes with neighbors, China always prefers to deal with each country individually. They are easier to intimidate that way. Thus the United States looks for opportunities to encourage countries in the region to meet together, including with China, to address these disputes. The Obama administration was particularly active in pursuing this tack, including our own participation wherever possible. Secretary Clinton was very much in the lead. A major step forward in this regard was her planned official visit to Vietnam in July 2010, followed immediately by her participation in the Association of Southeastern Asian Nations (ASEAN) regional forum in Cambodia (where her comments on the South China Sea disputes and the multilateral criticism of China's aggressive behavior would surprise and anger Beijing). While I was in Singapore attending the Shangri-La conference, my Vietnamese counterpart invited me to attend a meeting in Hanoi in October of the ten ASEAN defense ministers, expanded to include the ministers from Australia, China, India, Japan, the Republic of Korea, New Zealand, Russia, and the United States. Because I knew Hillary was going to Vietnam and Cambodia in July, I assumed Washington would have no objection to my going later in the year, and so I accepted the invitation on the spot. This was exactly the kind of forum we wanted to encourage.

After the Singapore conference, I flew to Azerbaijan to try to strengthen its participation in our Afghan supply route through Central Asia—the Northern Distribution Network. I had never been to Baku before, but I knew a fair amount about its history. Its president, Ilham Aliyev, ran the oil-rich country on the Caspian Sea with as strong a hand as his father, Heydar Aliyev, had done. Heydar had run Soviet Socialist Azerbaijan for eighteen years before Mikhail Gorbachev fired him for corruption and expelled him from the Soviet Politburo in 1987. He reinvented himself after the collapse of the Soviet Union and served as president of the country from 1993 to 2003; then his son took over. For all practical purposes, Azerbaijan was a family-run enterprise. I met with Ilham in a huge palace and gave him a letter from President Obama that underscored the importance of the relationship to us and our desire to expand it. Neither the letter nor I mentioned human rights. The main Azeri complaint was that we weren't paying enough attention to them. So just showing up accomplished the main purpose of the visit.

Baku seemed to have one principal thoroughfare, a very wide boulevard with many new and impressive buildings and tony shops. But a few blocks behind that showpiece street was an ancient, dusty, shambolic central Asian city. We ate that night at a traditional restaurant, which served all kinds of grilled meats on a long wooden plank. We were just digging in with gusto when one of my security staff told me the restaurant was on fire. Members of my group began evacuating, but since I saw neither flames nor smoke, I kept eating, along with one or two of my more intrepid comrades. A few minutes later, at about the time I heard the fire engines, my security team made clear they weren't giving me a choice about staying or leaving. I walked out the door just as the first fire truck arrived. I really hated leaving the food behind.

My second noteworthy trip to Asia in 2010 was in mid-July, to South Korea and Indonesia. The main purpose of the visit to Korea was the annual "two plus two" meeting of Secretary Clinton and me and our two Korean counterparts. This meeting took on significant added importance because of the sinking of the *Cheonan*. North Korean leader Kim Jong-il had been ill for some time, and speculation was that the sinking was the bright idea of his twenty-something son, Kim Jong-un, to prove to the North Korean military, as I suggested earlier, that he was tough enough to succeed his father. This line of thinking suggested that other provocations might be coming, so underscoring the strength of our alliance was very important.

Apart from the meetings, an important symbolic part of Hillary's and my program was visiting the demilitarized zone at Panmunjom. We were driven to a hilltop observation post, where we ritually looked through binoculars toward the North's side of the DMZ. (We avoided the embarrassment of an earlier U.S. official who had earnestly looked through the glasses for a photo op, not noticing that the lens caps were still on.) All I could see were trees. At Panmunjom, we entered the small building situated right on the DMZ line, where military representatives from the North and the UN command met. As we were briefed, a very large, menacing North Korean soldier stood outside the window glaring at Hillary and me. We worked hard to keep straight faces, and I resisted the temptation to go to the window and do something quite undiplomatic. Those kinds of offbeat ideas were always going through my head on such occasions; fortunately I mostly resisted them.

The third significant trip was to Hanoi in October for the ASEAN defense ministers-plus meeting. Apart from the unprecedented nature of the gathering itself, there were a couple of notable developments. Eight different ministers spoke up about the need to resolve disputes in the

South China Sea and other international waters peacefully and through negotiations—clear criticism of China, whose defense minister, General Liang Guanglie, was in attendance. All agreed on the need for a "code of conduct" for such disputes. Normally, all this would have elicited a strong reaction from the Chinese, but Liang was clearly under instructions not to create a scene—unlike what China's foreign minister had done in Cambodia the previous July under similar circumstances. Liang, a blustery sort, just sat and took it. It seemed obvious that the Chinese had realized their publicly aggressive approach to issues was isolating them, and therefore they tacked before the wind.

Liang and I met in Hanoi. President Hu was planning to visit Washington the following January and wanted all aspects of the relationship to appear positive. Thus the PLA, and Liang, had obviously been told to be nice to me. He began by referencing Hu's forthcoming visit and said that the overall relationship was positive. He went on to say, "Secretary Gates, I know you place great value on military-to-military relations, and I appreciate that, but the key is to respect each other's core interests and major concerns." He then invited me to visit China early in 2011, making explicit the Chinese desire to have me visit in January before Hu traveled to the United States.

I accepted the invitation, put down my prepared talking points, and spoke straight from the shoulder. "I hope our military-to-military relationship can be shielded from political ups and downs, just as the intelligence relationship has been." I said that a strategic dialogue on nuclear weapons was critical to avoid mistrust and miscalculation, and that there was no substitute for a direct government-to-government dialogue on the subject. "Let's be honest with each other," I continued. "Taiwan arms sales are political decisions and not made by the secretary of defense or Department of Defense, so if our political leaders continue with their relationship despite this disagreement, it seems strange to stop the military-to-military relationship." I reminded him that we had discussed an ambitious list of areas where we could expand our relationship when I visited three years earlier and expressed the hope we could return to it. "There are a lot of opportunities," I said. Always eager for the last word, Liang replied, "Opportunities, yes, but the U.S. should seriously consider our concerns." Similarly interested in getting in the last word, I said, "As in all things, respect for concerns and perspectives is mutual."

While in Hanoi, I gave a speech at the Vietnam national university.

It was unlike anything I had ever experienced. The speech was an unremarkable review of the development of the U.S.-Vietnamese military relationship over the preceding fifteen years. But my reception was quite extraordinary. As I entered the hall, funky dance and disco music was blaring, strobe lights were flashing, and the audience—many young military officers but also a lot of young female students—was applauding, whistling, and carrying on. I knew that the only way I would ever get such a rock star's reception would be at the order of a dictatorship.

DISASTERS

Twice during 2010, the U.S. military was called upon to provide major disaster relief. At 4:53 p.m. local time on Tuesday, January 12, a catastrophic 7.0-magnitude earthquake hit Haiti. Ultimately, three million people were affected and 315,000 killed. As the scale of death and destruction became evident, President Obama placed the highest priority on getting U.S. military assets to Haiti for rescue and relief and to maintain order. While there was never any doubt in my mind that the president's primary motivation was humanitarian, I believed he also wanted to show how fast he could mobilize the U.S. government after a disaster (in contrast to Bush's response to Hurricane Katrina) and to score as many political points as possible both at home and abroad.

The first request from the White House for disaster assistance for Haiti came to Defense early on January 13, and I was told the president wanted a "highly visible, very fast response." He said the deployment didn't have to be perfect, "just get them there as soon as possible." He also wanted to keep tabs on how well we were doing and so asked for daily morning and afternoon reports on our progress. Two U.S. Coast Guard cutters were the first U.S. assistance to get to Haiti on the thirteenth, and that evening two U.S. Air Force C-130 aircraft from the Special Operations Wing landed with emergency supplies, medical units, and communications gear. A team of thirty military engineers, operations planners, and communications specialists also arrived that first day. I had immediately directed several Navy ships to head for Haiti, including the aircraft carrier *Carl Vinson*. Additional Air Force personnel were deployed to reopen the international airport in Port-au-Prince, and I approved "prepare to deploy" orders for a brigade of the 82nd Airborne Division to Haiti, about 3,000 soldiers. There were sixty-six U.S.

military personnel on the island at the time of the earthquake, and they reported that the port was unusable, there was no fresh water, medical care was urgently needed, and many mortuary officers would be needed to deal with fatalities. We began moving heaven and earth to get ships, aircraft, equipment, and people there as fast as possible. I told the commander of Southern Command, General Doug Fraser, "The president considers this our highest priority. Whatever you need, we will get it to you. Don't hesitate to ask."

All this wasn't good enough. When we briefed the president in the Oval Office that night on our actions and plans, he, Donilon, and others were impatient. Mullen and I tried to explain that there was chaos on the island, roads were blocked, air traffic control at the international airport was down, and the port facilities were largely destroyed. Our first priority was to get the airport operating so it could handle a volume of air traffic far beyond its previous capacity. Donilon was especially aggressive in questioning our commitment to speed and complaining about how long we were taking. Then he went too far, questioning in front of the president and a roomful of people whether General Fraser was competent to lead this effort. I've rarely been angrier in the Oval Office than I was at that moment; nor was I ever closer to walking out of that historic room in the middle of a meeting. My initial instinct was to storm out, telling the president on the way that he didn't need two secretaries of defense. It took every bit of my self-discipline to stay seated on the sofa.

By the fourteenth, the Air Force team had cleared the runway at the airport and begun setting up twenty-four-hour-a-day air traffic control. At dawn on January 15, five C-17 cargo aircraft with more communications and air traffic management equipment, as well as 115 Air Force personnel, landed at the international airport and assumed responsibility for restoring air traffic control and expanding the airfield's capacity. From January 16 to 18, 330 aircraft landed at the airport, many times the field's pre-earthquake volume. Half of the flights were civilian relief aircraft, and more than eighty were from other countries. (Our effort at the airport would later be characterized as the largest single-runway operation in history, with 4,000 takeoffs and landings—one every five minutes—in the first twelve days after the earthquake.) The *Vinson* arrived on the fifteenth, with 600,000 emergency food rations and nineteen helicopters. The same day the deputy commander of Southern Command, Lieutenant General Ken Keen, arrived on the island as head of a joint task force to coordinate the U.S. military effort. Over the weekend, several more large U.S. ships arrived with more helicopters and Marines. Within days of the earthquake, we had 17 ships, 48 helicopters, and 10,000 sailors and Marines on the island or off the coast. In Washington, the administrator of the U.S. Agency for International Development, Dr. Rajiv Shah, was appointed overall U.S. coordinator of the relief effort. In this endeavor and in others, I always gave Shah high marks for competence and compassion. He was also easy to work with.

On the other hand, to my chagrin, the president dispatched the NSS chief of staff, Denis McDonough, to Haiti. He arrived on the fifteenth, accompanied by Navy Captain John Kirby, who was press spokesman for the Joint Staff. After the Iran-Contra debacle, I considered NSC involvement—or meddling—in operational matters anathema. I had nothing personal against McDonough, just that such staffers are almost always out of their depth, and the chain of command is blurred when you have someone from the White House in the field who claims to speak for the president. McDonough's purported task was to coordinate communications, but his presence was seen as much more than that. Even Jim Jones, who probably had no say in the decision to send his own subordinate, seemed to recognize this was a bridge too far. He called me a day or two after McDonough's arrival on the island and asked me only partly in jest, "Is our screwdriver too long?" I confided to my staff that I thought this was yet another example of a White House consumed by the crisis of the day and bent on micromanaging—still stuck in campaign mode a year into the presidency.

Our military efforts to assist Haiti were complicated by history and the situation on the island. There was deep suspicion of us in Haiti, for good reason. In 1915, amid political chaos and six Haitian presidents in four years, not to mention Imperial Germany's domination of the island's international commerce, President Woodrow Wilson sent in 330 Marines to safeguard U.S. interests. The United States, for all intents and purposes, ran Haiti until the Marines departed in 1934. In September 1994, President Clinton sent 20,000 troops to Haiti to oust a military junta and restore the elected president, Jean-Bertrand Aristide, to office. Just prior to the arrival of the troops, Jimmy Carter arranged a deal under which the junta gave up power and its leader left the country. Shortly thereafter U.S. troops escorted Aristide into the capital to reclaim his presidency. The U.S. forces left some six months later. And then in 2004, President

George W. Bush sent in 1,000 Marines after the ouster of Aristide (amid allegations that the United States had orchestrated or at least abetted his removal), a force quickly augmented with troops from France, Chile, and Canada.

I had this history in mind as we quickly assembled a huge military force to render assistance. Others remembered the history as well. About the same time the *Vinson* arrived offshore, the French "minister of state for cooperation" publicly accused the United States of again "occupying" Haiti, citing our takeover of air traffic control; both he and the Brazilian foreign minister complained about our giving preferential treatment to U.S. aid flights. There was other international political pushing and shoving over our growing military presence on the island and our control of the airport, and other allusions to our past history in Haiti, but my real concern was the potentially negative impact on Haitians of U.S. Marines and soldiers patrolling the streets and performing security duties. I thought our relief effort gave us the opportunity to improve the long-tarnished image of the U.S. military in Haiti, and I didn't want to blow the chance by taking on missions that might involve the use of force against Haitians.

We also had to work around the collapse of the Haitian government, which had been a fragile and barely functional institution even before the earthquake. How to respect Haitian sovereignty if there was no Haitian leadership or partner? Many officials had been killed, including in the national police, survivors had little or no communications equipment, and President René Préval was initially reclusive and nearly incommunicado. Once he and some of his ministers established offices in the police headquarters at the airport, they formally asked the United States to assume control of the airport, but confusion among the Haitian leaders reigned—including who was in charge of what. That made coordination difficult to say the least.

Our relationship with the UN mission in Haiti was also problematic. The "UN Stabilization Mission in Haiti" (MINUSTAH) had been established in 1994 after the ouster of Aristide. Its roughly 9,000 security personnel from about a dozen countries had been commanded continuously by Brazilian officers. The force commander at the time of the earthquake was Brigadier General Floriano Peixoto Vieira Neto. Keen worked hard to establish a good working relationship with Neto, and after several tense days of jockeying over roles and missions, on

January 22, agreement was reached that MINUSTAH and the Haitian national police would provide domestic security, and the U.S. and Canadian militaries would distribute humanitarian aid and provide security for aid distribution. Our troops were authorized to defend themselves if attacked but otherwise were only to provide a secure environment to get relief supplies to the people.

Criticism that the U.S. military response had been too slow in ramping up came from the press and Congress as well as the White House. We were asked, in particular, why we had not just air-dropped relief supplies to the Haitians. The answer seemed obvious, at least to me. There was the risk that supplies dropped near concentrations of people would actually hit those clamoring to be the first to claim the water and food. Without security and order on the ground, airdrops might provoke riots and widespread violence. We were trying to put in place a relief infrastructure and logistics supply chain that could be sustained for weeks and months. We knew speed was important, but disorganization and more chaos would only hurt the Haitian effort. I told the press on January 15 that I did not see how the United States, and the Pentagon, could have responded any faster.

Some of the forces we deployed to Haiti had been in the pipeline to go to Afghanistan, so I was eager to begin drawing down our relief commitment as early as feasible. Both State and the White House wanted our military there as long as possible. We worked it out amicably, reducing force levels in early May and concluding our efforts in June. I met with the Brazilian defense minister at the Pentagon in early April, and we agreed that, after some "rough patches," we had developed a positive and effective partnership. I give Keen—and General Fraser—a lot of credit for that, and for the overall effectiveness of our relief effort. Looking ahead, though, the task of rebuilding a ravaged, desperately poor, and badly governed Haiti was not a military mission.

The U.S. military also rendered substantial assistance during the historic flooding in Pakistan during the summer of 2010. By late July, one-fifth of the country was underwater, with 20 million people affected and some 2,000 dead. Many of the roads needed to reach victims were destroyed or inundated. Our military help began on August 1–2 with the delivery of food, water filtration plants, and twelve temporary bridges. I then directed the deployment of six CH-47 Chinook helicopters to Pakistan from Afghanistan on August 11. With the arrival of the USS *Peleliu*, we were able to provide a total of nineteen helicopters for rescue and relief, and toward the end of August, the USS *Kearsarge* was deployed to help as well.

Our relief help after a massive earthquake in Pakistan in 2005 had been warmly welcomed and led to an overall, if temporary, downturn in anti-Americanism there. But five more years of war in Afghanistan, drone attacks inside Pakistan, and growing problems between our governments had taken a toll. By summer 2010, 68 percent of Pakistanis had an unfavorable view of the United States. I was therefore extremely nervous about security for our helicopters and their crews. They were operating in northwestern Pakistan in areas such as Swat that were hotbeds of extremist and Taliban fighters. Villagers and even local police and Pakistani military accustomed to attacks by U.S. drones looked upon our military arrival with suspicion, if not outright hostility. I insisted that the Pakistani military have an officer on every flight to explain we were there to help and to organize distribution of supplies as the choppers were unloaded.

The Pakistani press reported that villagers waiting for aid showed no enthusiasm for the crews of our helicopters, and that there were no waves, smiles, or handshakes. Our crews reported some favorable reactions from Pakistanis, but overall there was great suspicion of our motives, and questions as to why we weren't doing more in the way of long-term assistance to improve their roads and bridges. Despite the dour reception, during the first three weeks of August, our aircrews evacuated some 8,000 people and delivered 1.6 million pounds of relief supplies. Nonetheless, anti-Americanism in Pakistan was undiminished.

OTHER DISASTERS

The end of July 2010 brought another kind of flood, from which there would be little relief. On July 25, an online organization named WikiLeaks, created by Julian Assange, posted some 76,000 documents originating from classified Central Command databases in Iraq and Afghanistan. WikiLeaks, as we later learned, operated from computer servers in a number of countries and advertised itself as seeking "classified, censored, or otherwise restricted material of political, diplomatic, or ethical significance." I told reporters on July 29 that the security breach had endangered lives and damaged confidence overseas in the U.S. government's ability to protect its secrets. I said the documents released could have "potentially dramatic and grievously harmful consequences."

From a military standpoint, the release of these documents was much worse than embarrassment. There was a lot of information about our military tactics, techniques, and procedures, as well as the names of Iraqis and Afghans who had cooperated with us. As hundreds of thousands of documents continued to be released through October, we determined that nearly 600 Afghans who had helped us were at risk, and that the Taliban was reviewing the postings to gather the names of those people. Just as worrying was the release of 44,000 documents revealing our tactics for dealing with IEDs, and many others that described our intelligence-collection methods and our understanding of insurgent relationships. There were voluminous documents from Iraq detailing detainee abuses, civilian casualties, and Iranian influence. Nearly all the Joint Task Force Guantánamo documents were released, including all assessments of individual detainees.

The flood assumed a totally different dimension in November when Assange warned that he was going to release hundreds of thousands of State Department documents and cables from more than one hundred embassies. On November 22, he said on Twitter, "The coming months will see a new world, where global history is redefined." He made good on his threat. These cables revealed private conversations between American officials and foreign leaders and other officials, and embarrassingly candid evaluations of those leaders (including above all President Karzai), as well as intelligence-collection priorities, bilateral intelligence relationships, intelligence sources and methods, counterterrorism-related information, and on and on.

Army Private First Class Bradley Manning was quickly identified and charged with downloading the documents from a computer at his base in Iraq and sending them to WikiLeaks. In violation of security rules, he had apparently carried compact discs disguised as music CDs into a secure facility and spent his duty hours downloading the documents from classified networks.

Manning had gotten such broad access to so many databases because, after the Gulf War, and particularly with the wars in Iraq and Afghanistan, there was a concerted effort to make as much information as possible available to every level of command. Huge broadband capacity was developed in both Iraq and Afghanistan, and wide access was provided to all levels. But we would learn, after the fact, that in many forward-deployed areas there was poor physical and operational security in and around facilities holding classified information, a failure to suspend the access to classified information of individuals who displayed behavioral and medical problems, and "weak to no implementation of tools restricting the use and monitoring of network activities." According to the findings of the undersecretary of defense for intelligence in January 2011:

> It is common knowledge that rules are frequently broken in a war zone to accomplish the mission. This may be necessary outside the perimeter and where there is risk of direct hostile action. But these behaviors have extended into garrison culture in forward-deployed areas, where the boredom of routine and limited activity options have exacerbated the problem. . . . The issue is more about compliance than policy—less about what we share and more about how we share it. Compliance is high at the strategic and operational level, but degrades closer to the fight. In forward-deployed areas, many mandatory practices are ignored or standards lowered.

Secretary Clinton had a lot of explaining to do in capitals around the world for a problem caused by the Defense Department. Both she and I noticed that once open and candid interlocutors around the world now turned silent the second they saw an American official take out pen and paper for notes.

I tried to offer some perspective in one press briefing. I pointed out, for example, that these State Department documents demonstrated for everyone to see that there was no significant difference between what American officials said in public and what they said in private. Drawing on my many years of painful experience, I also reminded people that the American government leaks like a sieve—"and always has." I cited President John Adams's lament: "How can a government go on, publishing all their negotiations with foreign nations, I know not. To me it appears as dangerous and pernicious as it is novel." I also recalled that when serious congressional oversight of CIA began in the mid-1970s, many thought foreign services would stop sharing information with us, but it never happened. I said I thought terms being bandied about such as "meltdown," "game-changer," and so on were overstated and overwrought.

Governments deal with the United States because it is in their interest, not because they like us or trust us or because of our ability to keep secrets. Some respect us, some fear us, many need us. We have by far the largest economy and the most powerful military. As has been said, in global affairs, we are the indispensable nation. So, other countries will continue to deal with us. Is this embarrassing? Yes. Awkward? Somewhat. But the longer-term impact? Very modest.

Another disaster, at least as far as I was concerned, was my trip to Bolivia at the end of November 2010 for a meeting of the Conference of Defense Ministers of the Americas. I detested these huge conferences. They are boring beyond words, and little ever results. But because it involves every country in North and South America, the U.S. secretary of defense must go for political and diplomatic reasons. My first such conference, in 2008, was tolerable because it was hosted by the Canadians at the spectacular mountain town of Banff, Alberta. The second, in Santa Cruz, Bolivia, promised to be awful in several respects. In a conference hosted by the government of virulently anti-American leftist Bolivian leader Evo Morales, I foresaw a full day of getting pounded on by my Bolivian hosts and their buddies from Hugo Chavez's Venezuela. When I made known I was considering not attending, both the Canadian and Brazilian defense ministers promised me they would lean on the Bolivians to behave. I took them at their word and showed up on November 21.

The drive from the airport in Santa Cruz to the hotel was the only time as secretary when I was actually uneasy about my personal security. I was discomforted knowing that Morales didn't care if I got killed, and I figured that that attitude might well trickle down to my heavily armed Bolivian military escort. The route was along narrow back roads crowded with cows, chickens, dogs, and people—every corner looking like an opportunity for an ambush right out of Tom Clancy's novel *Clear and Present Danger*. Each time we had to slow or stop, I got a little more nervous. Then we arrived at the un-air-conditioned Hotel Camino Real, which was open to the street. The doctor traveling with us advised us essentially to curl up on the bed in a fetal position and not to touch anything. Don't eat the food, he said. Don't touch the water (even to shower). Don't go outside the hotel. The staff put a fan in my room that was about three feet in diameter and created the sense of sleeping outdoors during a tornado.

My meeting with the Bolivian defense minister wasn't too bad. He clearly had gotten the message from the Canadians and Brazilians. The conference opened, however, with a fifty-five-minute-long welcoming diatribe from Morales. He accused former U.S. ambassadors of backing coup attempts against him and the U.S. consulate of "using machine guns against my administration." He said U.S. embassies all over the world sponsor coups. Then he got personal, looking straight at me and accusing CIA and the Defense Department of being behind all these depredations.

Morales was trying to provoke me into walking out in protest. Tempered by the fires of countless tirades from members of Congress over the years, I sat expressionless throughout Morales's performance. After he finished and departed, a number of Latin American ministers came up to me to apologize because they felt Morales had violated the region's rules for hospitality. I just wanted the damn meeting to end so I could get out of Bolivia. The return trip to the airport was just as exciting and nerve-racking as the trip into town, and I was never so glad to feel that Air Force plane lift off from a runway.

Every administration must deal with difficult allies and difficult foes. I thought President Obama and the administration in 2009 and 2010, for the most part, handled both kinds of relationships well, although I would often cringe at the rhetorical excess of how wonderfully we were doing, especially compared to the Bush administration. Fortunately, the rancor and bitterness of the Afghan debate in late 2009 did not spill over into other areas, and the team worked together better than most I had observed.

There were only two major personnel changes during the period. In May 2010, Denny Blair was forced out as director of national intelligence. He was replaced by my old friend and colleague Jim Clapper. Blair had never been able to develop strong relationships at the White House, and I think the final straw was his single-handed attempt to negotiate an agreement with the French intelligence services limiting activities in each other's country. The idea had zero support anywhere in the administration and, frankly, was considered kind of bizarre.

And then, after publication of Bob Woodward's book *Obama's Wars* in September 2010, Jim Jones left as national security adviser. He had never been a good fit in the Obama White House, as I said, and frankly, I was surprised he lasted as long as he did. I believe the timing of his departure was influenced significantly by Woodward's book. Jones appeared to be a major source; there were many disparaging comments about the rest of the White House staff and even his own staff that could only have come from Jim. Based in no small part on what he had been telling me all along about Donilon, I was quoted as saying that Donilon would be a "complete disaster" as national security adviser. That quote could only have come from Jones. There were a number of other comments I felt had come from Doug Lute, particularly many of the negative references to Mullen and me and to the military's purported efforts to box in the president on Afghanistan. After an auspicious beginning in the Bush administration and although I felt indebted to him for taking on the NSC war coordinator role, Doug had turned out to be a real disappointment in the Obama administration. In both the Bush and Obama administrations, the NSC/NSS seemed to be a rich lode of information for Woodward, a level of cooperation I never understood.

On October 1, the president and I met privately in the Oval Office. He was sitting as usual in a wingback chair in front of the fireplace, and I was seated on the couch to his left. He grabbed an apple from the bowl on the coffee table, took a bite, and then, out of the blue, asked me who should replace Jones. He said he was looking at Donilon, General Cartwright, and Susan Rice. I said, "In the privacy of this room, I suspect Hillary would have a problem with Susan as national security adviser." He laughed and said, "That's well known outside of this room. Hillary's forgiven me, but not the people who came over to me." He then said he had read my comments about Donilon in the Woodward book and asked why I felt so negatively. I told him I had made those comments to Jones after the Afghan review and Tom's disparaging comments about senior military officers—especially during the Haiti operation. Tom had recognized I had a problem with him and called me; we had met privately several months earlier and cleared the air: I said, "I'd be fine with Donilon as national security adviser." I asked the president to tell Tom what I had said. Donilon and I would develop a strong, cordial working relationship, although his suspicion of the Pentagon and the military would not diminish.

I had expected to be another departee in mid-2010. The president and I originally had agreed that I would stay on about a year, and by late

2009, especially after the Afghan travail, I really wanted to leave in the spring of 2010. I intended to tell the president that, right after I returned from a Christmas holiday in the Northwest. He beat me to the punch. Obama called me into the Oval Office on December 16, 2009, the day before I was to fly west. After he shut the door, he said, "I want to talk about you. I'd like you to stay on indefinitely, but that's probably too much to ask of your family. So I'd like you to stay at least until January 2012." He was very generous, saying, "I honestly just don't know where I would even begin to look for a replacement, not just [because of] the effective way you manage the Defense Department but [because of] the other skills and experience you bring to the administration." I told him I was very flattered and that he had preempted me. I told him I had intended to propose in January that I leave at the end of May 2010. I thought we were proceeding reasonably well in Iraq, Afghanistan should be on the right track by then, and we would have completed a second year of budget reforms. "I will have done all I can do," I said, but that I had talked to Becky and that if he said I was needed longer, I would stay until January 2011. He smiled broadly and said, "And we'll evaluate again then." I thought I had ended my sentence with a period, but he ended his with a comma.

That "comma" led to further discussion between us, and I eventually agreed to remain until the end of June 2011. Thinking ahead, I suspected that if I couldn't help him identify a successor, I might get extended until after the 2012 election. And so, in the same meeting on October 1 when I supported Donilon to replace Jones, I told Obama, "I have a seed to plant in terms of my successor—Leon Panetta." I said he had led CIA and OMB and had been White House chief of staff, so he knew how to lead big organizations; he was good with Congress; it was clear from CIA that he cared about the troops; he would continue the Defense reform effort; he would work well with the Joint Chiefs; and he was up to speed on the issues. I said I'd talked to Leon about succeeding me, and he didn't say "Hell, no." "I think he'd be willing to do it for eighteen months." The president responded, "Very interesting. I hadn't thought of that."

Difficult allies and difficult foes were not limited to our relations abroad. I had my hands full with both in Washington, D.C., as well. For me, 2010 was a year of continued conflict and a couple of important White House double-crosses.

CHAPTER 12

Meanwhile, Back in Washington

Don't Ask, Don't Tell

Two thousand ten began inauspiciously for me with the president's State of the Union address, on January 27. I absolutely hated going to this political theater. The president stands before both houses of Congress in the Capitol with packed galleries (the first lady's box is filled with people handpicked to highlight one or another parts of the president's message and always several uniformed military). He tells Congress and the American people that everything in the country is going—or will go—swimmingly with him as president (or at worst, "unprecedented" challenges will be tackled "boldly") and lays out his agenda for the coming year. Major elements of the address are inevitably partisan. His supporters in Congress rise—over and over—to applaud and cheer while the opposition sits on its hands except in the rare moments when the president mentions something they like, or makes the obligatory references to the U.S. military. The Supreme Court justices sit stoically, unsmiling and almost never applauding, never standing except when the president enters and leaves. The Joint Chiefs of Staff follow the lead of the chairman in terms of whether to applaud and whether to stand. Mostly they just sit, rising and applauding only when the troops are mentioned or there is some utterly innocuous declaration about what a great country the United States is. The president's cabinet, on the other hand, must rise with virtually every paragraph and every jab intended to outrage the opposition. I disliked doing these political deep knee bends under both Bush and Obama. Being part of a political cheering squad was embarrassing for me, especially standing to applaud highly controversial domestic initiatives and views. A close observer would have seen how often I was the last to rise and first to sit.

One such moment occurred on January 27, when the president announced toward the end of his address, "This year, I will work with the Congress and our military to finally repeal the law that denies gay Americans the right to serve the country they love because of who they are. It's the right thing to do." I had already agreed that repealing "Don't Ask, Don't Tell" (DADT) was the right thing to do, but in what I considered a serious breach of trust, the president had blindsided Admiral Mullen and me with this announcement, informing us of what he intended to do just the day before the speech. He dropped this bombshell without consulting with the service chiefs of staff, who would have to implement the policy change, and without allowing Mike and me time to consult the chiefs ourselves. All we could do was tell them the announcement was coming. The U.S. military leadership had adamantly opposed gays serving openly since the "Don't Ask, Don't Tell" law had been enacted in 1993, and the service chiefs, if not opposed outright, continued to have strong reservations about the timing and implementation of a change to DADT. The president's preemptive strike, perhaps intended to head off leaks from the Pentagon ahead of the State of the Union, had irked the military—and me—on this sensitive initiative.

My position, as I said earlier, had been clear from the start. I felt that to have legitimacy with the troops, a matter as sensitive as reversing DADT had to be enacted through a change in the law by Congress, the elected representatives of the American people, not through presidential edict or a court order. We also had to give the troops, at every level, the chance to provide their views so we would better understand the challenges facing us and them in implementation. We needed time to train both leaders and troops so there would be minimal, if any, impact on unit cohesion, discipline, morale, or recruitment and retention. The military never gets a "vote" on what it must do, and I was not advocating anything like a plebiscite. But every argument made about what men and women in uniform felt or thought about DADT, pro or con, was either based on assumption or was entirely anecdotal. I would often get questions about DADT from the troops in town halls, and my response was always the same: we would do what the commander in chief and Congress directed, but we had to prepare properly.

In response to a number of lawsuits challenging DADT, the courts seemed to be moving quickly and inexorably toward overturning the law, which would require a change in policy overnight—the worst of all possible outcomes, as I said earlier, because there would be no time to prepare or to train. The challenge I faced was how to juggle all three branches of government: to get the president to hold off from acting pre-emptively through executive action, to get Congress to change the legislation (which in early 2010 seemed unlikely), and to effect change before the courts gave us no choice and no time.

Fortunately Mullen and I, fully aware of the president's determination to eliminate DADT, had asked our staffs to begin preparatory work during the summer of 2009. In June, the Joint Staff gave us a comprehensive briefing on DADT that identified the risks of overturning the policy as: losing control of the change; degraded readiness, unit cohesion, and discipline; implementing a policy for which the force was not prepared; and the unpredictability of implementing a major policy shift in time of war. On the other side of the ledger, the Joint Staff cited several potential mitigating factors: the fact that men and women who join the military expect some reduction in personal freedoms and adjust their behavior accordingly; the determination of gay and lesbian service members "to prove their worth and capability"; force preparation and training with an emphasis on shared values and a focus on commonalities rather than differences; and active leadership at every level. The report offered several alternative approaches to conducting a study of the force and who should lead that study. So while the president surprised us in his State of the Union speech, we were reasonably well prepared to move ahead quickly.

It's a good thing Mullen and I were ready, because six days later, on February 2, both of us were summoned by the Senate Armed Services Committee, chaired by Senator Carl Levin, to testify on DADT. We had met with the president the previous afternoon and outlined what we intended to say and do, and he was supportive. The hearing was a historic moment, and everyone knew it. I opened with the declaration that "I fully support the president's decision." I said the question now was not whether the military would make this change but how best to prepare for it. I announced that, in consultation with Mullen, I had appointed a high-level working group within the Defense Department that would make recommendations in the form of an implementation plan by "the end of this calendar year." A guiding principle of the effort, I continued, would be to minimize disruption and polarization within the ranks, with special attention paid to those on the front lines.

I said the working group would examine a number of lines of study, all proceeding simultaneously:

> First, the working group will reach out to the force to authoritatively understand their views and attitudes about the impact of repeal. . . . Second, the working group will undertake a thorough examination of all the changes to the department's regulations and policies that may have to be made. . . . Third, the working group will examine the potential impacts of a change in the law on military effectiveness.

I told the senators that it would take the better part of a year to accomplish this because the overriding imperative was to "get this right and minimize disruption to a force that is actively fighting two wars and working through the stress of almost a decade of combat." To underscore the importance of the endeavor, I said it would be cochaired by Defense Department general counsel Jeh Johnson and General Carter Ham, the four-star commander of the U.S. Army in Europe, who had previously led soldiers in Iraq. I concluded with a plea to the senators present and to the entire Congress not to politicize the issue.

The high point of the hearing was the statement by Mullen. He began by saying that the Joint Chiefs owed the president their best military advice on the impact and implementation of repeal, and as chairman, he endorsed the process I had laid out. Admiral Mullen's next three sentences, after seventeen years of nearly unanimous senior military opposition to gays serving openly, made history:

> Mr. Chairman, speaking for myself and myself only, it is my personal belief that allowing homosexuals to serve openly would be the right thing to do. No matter how I look at the issue, I cannot escape being troubled by the fact that we have in place a policy which forces young men and women to lie about who they are in order to defend their fellow citizens. For me, it comes down to integrity, theirs as individuals and ours as an institution.

There was an audible gasp in the packed hearing room as Mullen uttered those words. I do not believe anyone expected such a strong, unambiguous personal endorsement of a change in the law from the chairman. But Mullen had put his finger on the fundamental flaw in the 1993 law: it allowed gays to serve in the military, an institution that places the highest possible value on personal integrity, but only by compromising their integrity. Mullen went on to say that while he believed men and women in uniform could and would accommodate such a change, he did not know this "for a fact." The review would provide an opportunity to address that uncertainty.

We appeared before the House Armed Services Committee, chaired by Representative Ike Skelton, the next day. While this hearing was mainly on the budget, there was considerable discussion of repeal of DADT, which Skelton opposed. When a couple of members began arguing with each other about the review, I jumped in. I said I had led three large institutions—CIA, Texas A&M University, and Defense—and I had managed change before. I had done it smart, and I had done it stupid. I had done it stupid, early in my career at CIA, by trying to impose significant change by edict from the top. This review was doing it smart—getting the troops and their families involved and sharing their views.

Reactions to our testimony in both houses were, unfortunately, fairly predictable. Advocates of repeal welcomed the change in views at the top of the Pentagon but expressed concern that we would proceed to drag our heels and delay implementation for years. Opponents, such as John McCain, acidly expressed "deep disappointment" in what we had said, adding that the prospective review would be "clearly biased" because it presumed the law should be changed. Sadly, the issue of repeal, like everything else in Congress, was going to be largely a partisan one, although there were a few outliers in each party. But within a few days after our testimony, I was confident we would have the time to do the review right. Democrats in the Senate clearly did not have the sixty votes necessary to break a Republican filibuster, and even House Speaker Nancy Pelosi said she might hold off a vote until after the midterm elections in November.

Despite my support for the initiative, I shared the concern of the service chiefs about the impact of making the change while we were fighting two wars, with all the stress already on the military. I was especially concerned about the impact on the combat and direct support formations of the Army, Marine Corps, and Special Forces, a relatively small portion of the overall military but the portion that had borne the brunt of the post-9/11 conflicts and where small-unit cohesion and camaraderie were crucial to success and survival. I knew the principal burden of making the new policy work would fall mainly on the same company grade officers and NCOs who were under the most stress. I wanted the troops downrange (in Iraq and Afghanistan) involved in the review as little as possible; I wanted instead to focus on recently returned units. Personally, I hoped we could get past the midterm elections before a vote, though I was quite aware of the hot breath of the courts on my neck. To be honest, I was skeptical Congress would pass repeal. While I wanted the review completed expeditiously, I wanted to avoid roiling the military over a change that I thought might well not happen. Of course, if it did, I would do my very best to lead and implement the change without incident.

Mullen's "personal" testimony complicated life for the service chiefs. They all had been quite public—especially the commandant of the Marine Corps—in opposing repeal anytime soon. They expressed their concerns to me in a meeting in the Tank on February 19, Army chief of staff George Casey and Air Force chief Norty Schwartz being the most outspoken. Casey said he was comfortable with my approach but emphasized the need to consult with the troops and to avoid the appearance that "all of this is a done deal." He added that he wanted to reserve the right to provide "informed military advice," especially if the outcome of the review was to suggest that going forward with a change in DADT was a bad idea. "You can only change culture so much at a time," he said. Schwartz said, "This is not the time for this." Marine commandant Jim Amos expressed his concerns about the risk to unit readiness, then asked me what the chiefs should say if asked their "personal views." I said matter-of-factly, "All you can do is be honest." But I also told them that the review gave them a way to avoid disagreeing either with Mullen or their commander in chief. They could continue to express their concerns but promise to withhold final judgment until after the review was done. All of them were clear with me about one thing: if the law changed, they would implement it effectively.

Thanks to the good work of Jeh Johnson and others, I was able to announce in late March a number of changes, effective immediately, to make application of the existing policy and law fairer. I announced that I would raise the rank of officer authorized to initiate an inquiry or separation because of homosexual conduct to general or admiral. We would revise what constituted "credible information" about a service member's homosexuality to require, for example, that a sworn statement would be necessary and hearsay would not be allowed. We would revise what constituted a "reliable person," upon whose word an inquiry could be initiated, "with special scrutiny on third parties who may be motivated to harm the service member." This was meant to address the problem of jilted lovers and spurned romantic advances, situations in which the accuser used the DADT policy to get revenge by "outing" a service member. Certain categories of confidential information would no longer be used in support of discharges, including information provided to lawyers, clergy, and psychotherapists, medical professionals in furtherance of medical treatment, and public health officials. In effect, these changes limited DADT inquiries and separations to service members who had "outed" themselves intentionally or made little or no attempt to hide their orientation. The military would not consume time and resources trying to ferret out gays and lesbians in the ranks who kept their personal lives to themselves.

As one reporter put it, "There will no longer be an investigatory zeal, a prosecutorial mode, or a policy designed to search for serving gays. A small step, but it will help change the culture." Since 1993, more than 13,500 service members had been discharged for homosexual conduct. Now the number would plummet.

Since Mullen's and my testimony, there had been considerable talk on the Hill about quickly enacting some kind of legislation for repeal. Senator Levin wanted to declare a moratorium on discharges until Congress could act. I wondered how you could declare a moratorium on the enforcement of any law. Fortunately Jeh Johnson backed me up. I made clear to the president and to Emanuel that any effort to legislate DADT before completion of the review was unacceptable to me because it would be perceived as a direct insult by men and women in uniform who had just been told that their views would be sought out before any policy change. It would send the message that neither the president nor the Congress gave a damn what they thought. Obama and Emanuel promised—unequivocally and on several occasions—to oppose any legislation before completion of the review.

By mid-April, we were hearing rumors of quiet side deals being discussed between members of the White House staff and Congress. I met with Rahm on April 21 and told him there were multiple indications from the Senate that White House officials were actively encouraging Senators Lieberman and Levin to move legislatively on DADT in advance of the Defense review. I told Rahm I was getting tired of the White House preoccupation with responding to pressure from gay advocacy groups on DADT without taking into account the impression on the troops that no one "over here" (at the White House) cared about military views and attitudes.

Nine days later Mullen and I repeated our position in a response to a letter from Ike Skelton on the advisability of legislative action to repeal DADT prior to completion of the Defense review: "I strongly oppose any legislation that seeks to change this policy prior to the completion of this vital assessment process." Our concern fell on deaf ears. The politicos at the White House, despite protestations of innocence, continued to negotiate with congressional staffers and outside supporters on the terms of legislation. I knew this because on several occasions during the first part of May, Rahm approached me with one formulation or another to ask if it would work for me. After the assurances from the president and Rahm that they would oppose congressional action before the review was complete, I felt there had been a breach of faith by the White House.

On May 21, Robert Rangel and Jeh Johnson met with White House deputy chief of staff Jim Messina, NSS chief of staff McDonough, and several others from the White House on how to proceed with Congress. Rangel laid out my position (again). Messina said that the president could not publicly declare opposition to congressional action now. He said they had been able to "finesse" and "dodge" the issue over the last several months, but Congress's insistence on taking action was about "to force his hand." Johnson and Rangel explained why Mullen and I felt so strongly about preserving the integrity of the review process and asserted that no matter how "artfully" we rationalized a change of position in a way that could be sold in Washington, "it will not translate well to the world where the troops live—to them it's a simple matter of Congress repealing in advance of the review or not."

On Sunday, May 23, as Rangel, Johnson, and the White House tried to reach agreement on how to proceed with Congress that coming week, Mullen joined me on my porch at home to discuss the state of play. As I puffed on a cigar, I told Mike that Emanuel was pushing me to accept some sort of legislation that would repeal DADT but would delay implementation until after the review was done and recommendations considered. I said it still sent the wrong message to the troops—that Congress didn't care what they thought. Mullen said he had been "diddled" by the White House on an issue where he already was way out in front of the chiefs. He was also deeply bothered by the recently published Jonathan Alter book *The Promise,* which portrayed the White House and the president as distrustful of the military leadership. I responded that I, too, was frustrated and stressed. Afterward I jotted down what I had told him: "The Democrats fear losses in the fall will prevent action on Don't Ask, Don't Tell after the election (and after the review)." They are listening only to the gay and lesbian groups, I had said, and not willing to wait to listen to the troops: "It's all politics, and I've had it."

One last time, on May 24, I tried privately to dissuade the president. I told him that in 1993, the Joint Chiefs, including the chairman, had all come out together against the president on gays serving in the military. I said that seventeen years later Mike and I had gotten the chiefs on board by promising, based on Obama's assurances, that we would have time to complete the review process and there would be no action beforehand. "You're about to blow that up," I said, and "I cannot predict the results." I made no headway, so I threw in the towel. I told the president I could live with the proposed legislative language as a minimally acceptable last resort.

The deal with Senators Levin and Lieberman repealed the 1993 law, but the repeal would not become legally effective until the Defense Department review was complete, its recommendations to prepare for the change fully implemented, and the president, secretary of defense, and chairman of the Joint Chiefs each certified that implementation would not affect military readiness, recruitment, or retention. "I continue to believe that ideally the DoD review should be completed before there is any legislation to repeal the Don't Ask, Don't Tell law," I announced. "With Congress having indicated that is not possible, I can accept the language in the proposed amendment." As CNN's John King reported on May 25, I had "put out a statement that indicates support for it [the amendment], but wow, it is a very, very, very tepid statement." He got that right. While the bill was passed by the Senate Armed Services Committee that week 16–14, it would stall in the Senate. The House Armed Services Committee passed repeal legislation over the objections of its chairman, and the full House voted in favor 229–186. Due to the obstruction of Republicans in the Senate, however, full repeal did not pass until just before Christmas during the lame duck session of Congress—after the review was complete.

Superbly managed by Jeh Johnson and General Ham, the review consisted of a survey sent to 400,000 service members (the original plan was for 200,000, but I told the cochairs to double it), another survey sent to 150,000 military spouses, focus group meetings with Johnson and Ham that involved face-to-face dialogue with nearly 25,000 troops, and a third-party-managed hotline where gay and lesbian service members could offer their views confidentially. The surveys were the largest ever conducted of our military and represented the first empirically based review of military attitudes on gays and lesbians serving openly.

On September 27, I received a first, preliminary report on the results of the surveys. It was encouraging: 15 to 20 percent of respondents said that repeal would have a positive effect, and another 50 to 55 percent said repeal would have little or no effect on their unit's ability to carry out its mission. About a third were opposed. The percentage of those opposed was substantially higher in all-male combat arms units in the Army, among Special Forces of all the services, and in the Marine Corps generally. The survey was helpful in identifying areas of concern that would require special attention in changing our policies and in training prior to repeal. The bottom line, even in the preliminary report, was that opposition to repeal was considerably less than I expected. Implementation of the change would present challenges, but the survey strongly suggested they were manageable. The report, I felt, might just persuade the Senate to pass the legislation.

Just when I thought we had a path forward for repeal of DADT and successful implementation, the courts threw everything into chaos. On September 9, Federal District Judge Virginia Phillips in San Diego ruled that the DADT law was unconstitutional. On October 12, she denied the administration's request to keep the law in place and issued an injunction ordering the military to stop enforcing the law. My worst fear had come to pass. It precipitated the worst confrontation yet between the president and me.

I was in Brussels for a NATO defense ministers meeting when Judge Phillips issued her injunction. The president called me on the thirteenth and said he was prepared to seek a stay of the judge's order, but we needed to figure out a way to "suspend" application of the law long enough to give Congress time to act—"suspended animation," he called it. I said I thought we still had to enforce the law if the judge's decision was stayed by the court of appeals. I suggested that Jeh Johnson, White House counsel Bob Bauer, and Justice Department folks get together to decide what options were available to us "in the context of the law." The president agreed that that group should get together, but there was "a need to find a way to turn the temperature down on the issue."

The battle lines for the next week between the White House and Defense—between the president and me—were drawn that same night, when the attorneys' meeting I had suggested took place. Bauer proposed that Justice seek a stay and appeal Judge Phillips's ruling but also tell the court that we would suspend any further DADT proceedings and/or separations pending a ruling on the appeal by the Ninth Circuit Court (the most liberal in the nation). Johnson and Rangel said such a step was not legally permissible in light of the long Defense Department history in applying the law. They reminded Bauer that the administration had rejected this same rationale in opposing Senator Levin's proposal for a moratorium earlier in the year, and observed the negative impact if the administration suddenly decided not to faithfully enforce the law. The two sides were at an impasse. The White House team said they would reengage with the president.

Even though I was still traveling overseas, arrangements were made for the president and me to talk again on the telephone on October 15. Before the call, Johnson told me it was clear from Bauer that the president "really wants" to suspend separations on a temporary basis while appealing the lower court's decision: he had "thought long and hard about this" over the preceding two days. Johnson told Bauer that I, too, felt strongly and that the president needed to know we were still far apart on the issue.

I talked with Mullen, Johnson, and Rangel from my plane. I told them, "I'm so jet-lagged I'm barely coherent. How do I play the role of constitutional lawyer with a president who is a constitutional lawyer?" Rangel said I just needed to question the wisdom and legal sustainability of suspending separations, not argue the merits of the law itself. "It seems to me that a stay means the law is in effect—all the law," I said. "I think it's black and white: law or no law."

When the president called, he said he still wanted a suspension of separations while the case was heard by the Ninth Circuit. Bauer and Johnson were talking with the Office of Legal Counsel at Justice (the component in the department that tells the government whether its actions are legal) about whether that was possible. The president pretty much ignored my objections.

The president and I reengaged on the issue on October 19 at the White House. I said, "I have a problem enforcing part of the law but not all of it. . . . There is either law or no law—there is no gray area." Mullen agreed. The president leaned forward in his chair and said very firmly, "I strongly disagree. I believe the law is wrong, that the plaintiffs have a stronger case than the government." With barely suppressed anger, he went on: "Two years into my presidency, and there is no action on this. No one can accuse me of being precipitous." He told us to think again and that we would meet again the next day; the matter needed to be decided within the next twenty-four to forty-eight hours. He and I then talked privately for a few minutes, and he told me that he thought the Ninth Circuit, despite its liberal reputation, would reverse the district court's decision. He would need to react somehow, "or the groups [gay activists] will go crazy." He said that suspension of separations during the appeals process would allow him to be seen as doing something to mitigate DADT once the reversal reinstated the policy.

The next day, after an NSC meeting on Afghanistan, the president asked to see Mullen and me in the Oval Office. He asked where we were on DADT, and I said we were in the same place as before. I said I had been told that once it had been determined that a person had engaged in what the law defined as "homosexual conduct," the law was crystal clear in mandating separation. I told the president that, according to Jeh Johnson, "you are proposing to suspend the most directive part of the law." When it was clear there was no give in my position, the president vented: "I won't ask you to sign up to something you're not comfortable with. I'm the leader of the free world, but I can't seem to make anything happen."

During the meeting, the president's voice had been raspy. On the way out of the Oval Office, I unwisely asked him if he was catching cold. He made a dismissive gesture that said, *Don't even try to be friendly with me because I am really angry.* He was as angry with me as I had ever seen him. He felt deeply that the DADT law was wrong, and he was enormously frustrated by his inability to do anything about it. I was a major obstacle, but he was clearly not prepared to order me to do something I thought was wrong.

That same day, October 20, the Ninth Circuit granted the government's appeal for a stay of the lower court's decision, and the DADT law was reinstated. The next day I signed a directive that separations of service members could be approved only by the service secretaries, after coordination with the general counsel and the undersecretary for personnel and readiness. For all practical purposes, it was a suspension of separations, but it upheld the principle that as long as the law was in effect, we would continue to enforce it.

Admiral Mullen and I publicly reported the results of the Pentagon review process on November 30. I summarized it by saying that "for large segments of the military, the repeal of Don't Ask, Don't Tell, though potentially disruptive in the short term, would not be the wrenching, traumatic change that many have feared and predicted. . . . The key to success, as with most things military, is training, education, and above all, strong and principled leadership up and down the chain of command."

I concluded by strongly urging the Senate to pass repeal legislation and to send it to the president for signature before the end of the year. Now that we had consulted the troops, my position on DADT repeal was in line with the White House as far as moving forward with legislation. I ended with a warning meant for Senator McCain and other opponents of repeal: "Those that choose not to act legislatively are rolling the dice that this policy will not be abruptly overturned by the courts." The bottom line of Admiral Mullen's corresponding statement was "This is a policy change we can make."

Mike and I testified before the Senate Armed Services Committee on December 2 on the results of the review. The testiest exchange was when I was asked whether it was a good idea to push for repeal when the survey showed substantial resistance among combat forces. I replied rather brusquely: "I can't think of a single precedent in American history of doing a referendum of the American armed forces on a policy issue. Are you going to ask them if they want fifteen-month tours? Are you going to ask them if they want to be a part of the surge in Iraq? That's not the way our civilian-led military has ever worked in our entire history."

The votes of several undecided senators were influenced by the results of the Pentagon review, and contrary to most expectations even that fall, on December 18 the Senate voted to repeal DADT, and the president signed it into law on December 22. In a not-so-subtle spike of the football, the stage planners at the White House made sure the Marine Corps flag was prominently displayed behind the president as he signed. The massive bureaucratic wheels of the Pentagon began to move with uncommon speed in conforming Defense policies and regulations to the new law and in preparing training materials for the forces. By late February, training was under way for commanders and leaders and then was extended to all two million men and women in uniform. The service chiefs, after all their concern and skepticism, led this massive effort effectively and positively. The new commandant of the Marine Corps, James Amos, who had been, like his predecessor, the most negative toward repeal among the service chiefs, was hell-bent on the Marines being trained best and first.

The training went smoothly, but the certification process was not complete before I left office. The president signed the third and final certification required to bring repeal into effect—Secretary Leon Panetta and Chairman Mike Mullen had already certified—on July 22, 2011, three weeks and two days after I retired. Under the terms of the repeal law, DADT was abolished in the American armed forces on September 22, 2011. The transition went as smoothly as anyone could have hoped. We had turned a page in history, and there was barely a ripple.

Some might argue the transition went so smoothly that our fears and concerns had been greatly overdrawn and that implementation could have taken place much faster. I will always believe implementation proceeded with so few incidents and issues because of the planning and preparation that preceded it.

The War Within (Continued)

Getting the troops in the fight what they needed continued to be a challenge in 2010. In Afghanistan, the all-terrain MRAPs began flowing in early in the year, providing much better—and much needed—protection for the troops when they were in vehicles. We were making considerable progress in getting more aircraft and drones into the theater for intelligence, surveillance, and reconnaissance. But as the strategy changed to emphasize protecting the Afghan people, more troops were moving into hostile terrain on foot. Casualties from IEDs were increasing and the wounds becoming more grievous. When a soldier stepped on an IED, all too often the result was legs and arms blown off, with further blast damage to the groin, pelvis, and abdomen. Dirt and debris was blown into these wounds, further complicating medical treatment. Because of improvements in medevac times and battlefield medicine, most of those so horribly wounded lived and would face years of surgeries and rehabilitation, years of struggle and pain.

I earlier described meeting in the spring of 2009 the wars' first quadruple amputee, Private Brendan Marrocco, wounded in Iraq by an IED. Nearly a year later at Walter Reed, I met the second quadruple amputee, a Marine injured by an IED in Afghanistan. Marrocco, by then with prosthetic arms and legs, was the Marine's hero and role model, giving him hope that he, too, could become functional again. I had signed the orders sending them both into combat, and while it broke my heart to see them like this, their courage and determination to move on with their lives left me in awe.

Months later the cost of war came close to home when my great-nephew e-mailed me that a high school friend of his, Jonathan Blank, from the little town of Augusta, Kansas, had lost both legs in Afghanistan. I visited Jonathan at Bethesda Naval Hospital. He, like Marrocco and so many others I saw, was so young, so vulnerable. And so amazingly tough.

Each visit to a hospital steeled my resolve to drive the Pentagon bureaucracy to do more to protect these kids. The MRAP–all terrain vehicles and intelligence, surveillance, and reconnaissance assets were important but not enough. As we began the Afghan surge, 75 percent of all casualties were due to IEDs, 90 percent of them in the south. And the bombs were getting bigger. In 2008, the average size of an IED was ten kilograms; by early 2010, it was three times that; in 2008, 10 percent had been over seventy-five kilograms, and that number too had nearly tripled by 2010. A growing source of explosives for the IEDs was a common fertilizer, ammonium nitrate, which was trucked in from Pakistan. We had to slow that flow.

There were many technologies and much equipment that could help troops find IEDs before they injured or killed someone, as well as provide more protection for our most exposed outposts. These included hand-held mine and explosive detectors, and large tethered airships (aerostats) providing eyes in the sky over outposts and operations. The wide diversity of the equipment meant that multiple organizations and bureaucratic layers were involved in acquisition and fielding, and that cost time. I wanted these additional capabilities deployed fast enough to match the surge of 30,000 more troops going to Afghanistan in the spring of 2010.

In November 2009, I was made aware of the problems we faced: there was no master integrator of all the capabilities being pushed into the theater; our intelligence analysis was sufficiently focused neither on the enemy's IED tactics and techniques nor on our own approach to disrupting and destroying the IED networks; we had to figure out how better to use the dozens of Liberty surveillance aircraft we had in Afghanistan—especially deciding whether to use them to develop information about the IED networks or to provide coverage for road and troop protection; we needed to get all the Pentagon task forces fused together to focus on the top priorities; we required more analysts and for them to develop targets faster; information about IED detection had to be shared more effectively among the different regional commands in Afghanistan; and we needed to move counter-IED assets faster from Iraq to Afghanistan. The briefing proved, yet again, that the Pentagon was not properly structured to support a constantly changing battlefield or to fight an agile and adaptable enemy.

Once again I went outside the regular bureaucracy to tackle these issues and to do so urgently. On December 4, 2009, I established the Counter-IED Task Force, cochaired by the undersecretary for acquisition, technology, and logistics, Ash Carter, and Marine Lieutenant General Jay Paxton, director of operations for the Joint Staff. Like the MRAP and ISR task forces, this one was to focus on what could be delivered to the theater within weeks and months. Carter and Paxton seized the opportunity with real passion.

Others, however, still needed to have a fire lit under them. I met with the leadership of the Joint Improvised Explosive Device Defeat Organization (JIEDDO)—the organization formed in 2004 to lead department-wide efforts to deal with IEDs—on January 8, 2010, and told them, "Your agency has lost its sense of urgency. Money is no object. Tell me what you need." We still had two wars going on, one of them about to get significantly bigger. Three years into the job, I just couldn't figure out why I still needed to be exhorting people on the urgency of taking care of the troops.

By the end of January, Carter and Paxton had developed plans to disrupt the fertilizer supply chain—now designated HMEs, homemade explosives, including the deployment of nearly 90,000 handheld explosive detectors. They proposed increasing the number of aerostats from thirty to sixty-four by September, growing the number of tower-based sensors at our forward bases from 300 to 420, accelerating the production of MRAP-ATVs, and surging mine detectors and ground penetrating radars; they even had developed plans to fulfill my commitment to our allies that we would provide them with counter-IED training and equipment. Because the kind of detectors needed for a patrol might vary depending on the nature of the mission, instead of every unit getting a standard set of detection equipment, I thought we should have a kind of warehouse at the local level holding every kind of counter-IED kit available so that troops could draw whatever detection or protective devices were most appropriate to that day's mission or a unit's operational environment. Carter and Paxton even figured out a way to do that.

By the end of March 2010, arrangements were in place to buy significantly more minirobots, handheld command-wire detection devices, electronic warfare kits, mine rollers, and explosive trace detectors. No idea for a new technology, technique, or approach was considered out of bounds. But for all the technology, there was common agreement that one sensor worked better at detecting IEDs than anything else: a dog's nose. And so acquiring and training many more dogs became a high priority. New counter-IED capabilities of all kinds just for the surge troops would cost $3.5 billion, and much more for the entire deployed force in Afghanistan. I thought it was worth every cent. The task force continued its efforts into 2011, developing and deploying whatever capabilities might provide better detection and warning of IEDs but also better personal protection for the troops, including developing protective underwear to diminish IED damage to the groin, genitals, and abdomen.

Despite the achievements of this and the other task forces I established, I was still troubled that it was all so ad hoc. I was not fixing the bureaucratic problem, I was bypassing it in the interest of speeding matériel to the battlefield. Ash Carter and I discussed this repeatedly. I asked him to think about how to institutionalize what we were doing. If my successors were unwilling to breach the bureaucratic wall, how could we ensure that future war fighters could get what they needed in a hurry? We needed an acquisition "express lane" at the departmental level to ensure that urgent needs were met. The biggest challenge with the existing system—the Joint Urgent Operational Needs process—was finding the money for those needs. When approved, any such "need" was sent to the most appropriate military service, which was asked to pay for it. All too often the service lacked the money or decided its own priorities were higher and failed to produce the funding. We needed to have a system whereby unfunded battlefield needs would be brought to the attention of the secretary or deputy secretary, who could then direct that funding be found from any source within the entire department. We had not yet formalized this approach when I retired, but I left confident that Carter, who shared my passion for protecting the troops, would make it happen, especially when he was elevated to deputy secretary a few months later.

In dealing with America's vulnerability to cyber attacks on the computers so vital to our critical infrastructure, business, and government, we were in uncharted waters both bureaucratically and legally. There was a deep division within the government—in both the executive branch and Congress—over who should be in charge of our domestic cyber defense: government or business, the Defense Department's National Security Agency, the Department of Homeland Security, or some other entity. There was a split between those whose priority was national security and those whose priority was the protection of privacy and civil liberties. The result was paralysis. Soon after my arrival in office, I asked the department's deputy general counsel for a memo on what kind of cyber attack—by us or on us—would constitute an act of war justifying a response in kind or conventional military retaliation. I was still waiting for a good answer to that question three years later.

The Defense Department was not well organized internally to deal with cyber issues. The director of national intelligence under President Bush, Mike McConnell, had urged me in 2008 to create a separate combatant command to deal with cyber threats. We were just then establishing Africa Command, and I thought the president and Congress would balk at yet another major command. But I made some organizational changes in the fall of 2008 and in June 2009 established Cyber Command as a subordinate component of Strategic Command. I recommended that the president nominate Army Lieutenant General Keith Alexander, the director of the NSA, to run this "subunified" command as well. Its purpose would be to better organize Defense operations in cyberspace, to ensure our freedom of access to cyberspace, and to oversee investments in people, resources, and technology to prevent disruptions of service to the military.

On May 21, 2010, I took the step suggested two years before by McConnell and established an independent Cyber Command with now-General Alexander in command. (Part of my motivation for creating the independent command was to get a fourth star for Alexander, whom I considered one of the smartest, best officers I ever met. Without such a command and promotion, I feared we would lose him to retirement.) I also created a new civilian office to lead policy development and provide oversight to the new command. Overall, thanks to the NSA and other components in Defense devoted to information and cyber security, and with these organizational changes, I felt reasonably comfortable that Defense Department cyber networks were protected, even though they were attacked by hackers many times a day. A major initiative, led by Deputy Secretary Lynn, to get key defense industries to come voluntarily under our cyber umbrella for protection, was also enjoying considerable success. By mid-2010, I thought we had made considerable progress.

Not so in the rest of government. A major issue was the role of the NSA. Specifically, privacy advocates and civil libertarians were loath to use this military intelligence agency to protect cyber networks at home. The real-world implication of their position was creation of some kind of domestic counterpart to the NSA. I thought that was sheer idiocy. Time and again I argued that there wasn't enough money, time, or human talent to create a domestic clone. When we got warning in the summer of 2010 that a major cyber attack was being planned on the United States in the fall, I saw an opportunity to break the stalemate.

I devised a politically risky but potentially successful way to bypass the entire bureaucracy, including the White House staff, and present the president with a solution. To somewhat oversimplify, as secretary of defense I had responsibility for national-security-related cyber matters outside the United States, and under the law, the secretary of homeland security—Janet Napolitano—had responsibility for network protection inside the United States. I invited Janet to lunch. We met on July 7, and I proposed that we assign several of our top people to work together urgently on a plan for her department to be able to use the NSA to defend U.S. domestic cyber networks. My idea was that I would appoint a senior homeland security person—recommended by Napolitano—as an additional deputy director of the NSA, with the authority to use the agency's unique capabilities to protect domestic computer networks. This homeland security appointee would have his or her own general counsel inside the NSA, and together we would build firewalls to protect privacy and civil liberties, to ensure that the wide authority that the NSA had for operating abroad was limited at home.

We met again for lunch a week later to review a preliminary draft proposal. We made some adjustments, and the two of us presented the proposal to the president in the Oval Office on July 27 (unheard-of speed in Washington). We had bypassed everyone else in government—but we told the president the two of us were the ones with operational responsibility, and we could make this work. We told him he could have John Brennan quickly run it through the interagency coordination process (especially the Justice Department) to make sure we hadn't missed something, but that he ought to be able to approve our signing a memorandum of understanding by August 15. Napolitano and I met on August 5 with Brennan in his West Wing basement office, a large but low-ceilinged and cluttered room. With his support in moving the proposal quickly, within three weeks of our meeting with him, the president signed off on the proposal.

Napolitano and I had briefly been able—with the president's support—to part the bureaucratic Red Sea, but the waters soon came crashing back together. Although we fairly quickly made the organizational and personnel decisions and changes at NSA to implement our plan, months later General Alexander told me that Homeland Security wasn't much using the new authority. I don't know why to this day. But because of the failure to make this or something like it work—along with political paralysis in Congress on how to deal with the cyber challenge—the country remains dangerously vulnerable, as my successor starkly pointed out in a speech in 2012.

The process by which the secretary of defense formally conveys presidential authority to use military force to combatant commanders is through the preparation and signature of "execution orders," and they apply to the use of force outside war theaters such as Iraq and Afghanistan. These orders, called EXORDs, usually are quite specific, but there were some on the books from the Bush administration, particularly in the counterterrorism arena, that provided combatant commanders broad authority to launch operations without further authorization—particularly when the opportunity to hit a target might require a very fast decision. In every case, the president had broadly authorized the use of lethal force, but I was uncomfortable with any arrangement where use of that force would catch the president by surprise. Under President Bush, I made clear that whatever the EXORD said, I wanted to be informed of any action beforehand so I could inform the president.

In 2010, I decided we should review all the EXORDs to bring the language in them into conformity with my practice of informing the president in advance. Neither Obama nor his advisers had reviewed the EXORDs approved by President Bush in detail. What I had envisioned as a largely mechanical effort to ensure that the president was properly informed became a broad, time-consuming interagency effort led by an NSS always eager to micromanage the Pentagon. The effort on our side was led by Michèle Flournoy and the assistant secretary for special operations and low-intensity conflict, Mike Vickers. We often had to push back hard to keep the White House and State Department from getting too far into our military knickers, but at the end of a year's work, we had updated the EXORDs, ensured that except in the most extraordinary circumstances the secretary and president would know about operations prior to launch, and had Obama administration buy-in. When we were finished, there didn't seem to be too much unhappiness on the part of the combatant commanders about the curtailment of their unilateral authority to launch military operations.

In a place as big as the Defense Department, something is always going wrong. Most of the time, it's just a bureaucratic screwup. But when our nuclear forces are involved, it can quicken your pulse. The first two such incidents on my watch, as I've described, had led to my firing of the secretary and chief of staff of the Air Force in 2008. In October 2010, at F. E. Warren Air Force Base near Cheyenne, Wyoming, all communications were lost with a squadron of fifty Minuteman III nuclear-tipped intercontinental ballistic missiles. While alternative communications were soon reestablished, no one had informed the secretary of defense or the president when we lost contact with a launch control capsule and fifty ICBMs. And of course, when the communications went down, no one at the base, or at its higher headquarters at Strategic Command, knew at that moment how long they might be down or whether they had been lost due to a technical malfunction, terrorist act, sabotage, or some other scary scenario—or even whether one or more of the missiles might somehow be at risk. In a masterpiece of understatement, Obama allowed as how he would have liked to have known about it. It was a sentiment I shared.

After a massive investigation, a technical problem was found to be the cause and quickly remedied. The missiles had never been outside our control or at risk. I told the president in early November that new regulations were in place providing that in the event of any future problem involving the nuclear force, the national military command center at the Pentagon would be informed within ten minutes, and both the chairman and secretary notified within fifteen minutes of the event. It would be my decision whether to inform the president. It was a sure bet I'd make the call.

Money, Money, Money

Two wars and "Don't Ask, Don't Tell" notwithstanding, I spent more time on the defense budget in 2010 than on any other subject. For all the bleating from Congress about defense acquisition reform, tighter management, reducing waste, and auditable accounting, they made it nearly impossible to manage the Pentagon efficiently. I oversaw the execution or preparation of six defense budgets, and not one was enacted by Congress before the beginning of the fiscal year. Every year we had to operate for anywhere from a few months to an entire calendar year under a "continuing resolution," which, in the absence of an enacted appropriations bill, meant we received exactly the same amount of money as the previous fiscal year, without authority to start any new program. Such madness played havoc with acquisition programs. We were left in a state of near-perpetual financial uncertainty.

On several occasions, political fights over the continuing resolutions led us to the precipice of government shutdowns. Warnings of civilian furloughs had to be issued, and we had to interrupt countless programs and initiatives. Under these ridiculous circumstances, when we had to move money from one account to another to cover a dire shortfall, regardless of the amount, we had to get the approval of four congressional committees; a single hostile staff member could gum up the works for weeks. Congress had no problem expeditiously voting in favor of National Pickle Week, but one task it had to do under the Constitution—appropriate money in a timely way—seemed beyond its grasp. Even eliminating wasteful or obsolete programs was almost always a monumental political lift on the Hill, as I learned in 2009. And each year we would get a defense authorization bill from the Armed

Services Committees that contained about a thousand pages of nearly paralyzing direction, micromanagement, restrictions, and demands for reports. You can imagine why congressional complaints about inefficient management at the Pentagon rang very hollow with me. The legislature played its own significant part in making it so.

For three years, I had endured this congressional incompetence with public equanimity and patience. But I was coming to the end of my tether. Because of the growing effort it took to maintain self-discipline, I increasingly resisted going to the Hill to testify or even to meet with members. Throughout my tenure, before every hearing I held meetings with my staff ostensibly to work through answers to likely questions from members of Congress. Actually, the meetings were more an opportunity for me to cathartically vent, to answer the anticipated questions the way I really wanted to, barking and cursing and getting the anger and frustration out of my system so that my public testimony could be dispassionate and respectful. New members of my staff were sometimes shocked by these sessions, fearful that I would repeat in the hearing what I had just said privately. By 2010, the effectiveness of even these sessions was wearing off. Cuffed and shackled, my heel marks visible in the hallway, I would be dragged to the car and hauled before the people's elected representatives. At least that's how I felt. Robert Rangel warned another member of my team, "You need to give hard counsel to the secretary— that is, telling him to do things when he doesn't want to." He had to be referring to visiting Capitol Hill.

During the first months of 2010, as usual for a secretary, I was dealing with three annual budgets simultaneously—executing the FY2010 budget; defending the proposed FY2011 budget, presented in February; and preparing the FY2012 budget. Beginning with the significant program cuts and caps I announced in April 2009 for the 2010 budget, I was determined to use my remaining time in office to try to shape these budgets to create the versatile military I thought we would need. I also wanted to build on our 2009 success in cutting wasteful and unnecessary programs and activities. However, as I looked at the ever more complex and turbulent world beyond our borders, and remembered history, I had no intention of cutting the defense budget. I readily admit it. As I looked to FY2011 and 2012, what I very much wanted to do was cut bureaucratic overhead and invest the money thus saved in additional and new military capabilities. I continued to hope, as pressures to cut the federal budget deficit built, that if the department operated in this manner, we could avoid the kind of drastic reductions in defense spending that had followed the Vietnam War and the end of the Cold War.

When Congress got around to passing a defense appropriations bill for FY2010 in December 2009 (two and a half months into the fiscal year), they gave us a base budget of $530 billion, $5 billion less than the president's request but still about a 4 percent increase, including inflation. (When asked at one point by a reporter whether I was "gutting defense," I retorted, "In what parallel universe are you living where a four percent increase in the defense budget is a cut?")

For everyone in the executive branch except the president, the Office of Management and Budget is the villain. It recommends to the president how much each agency and department should spend, and it's always lower than the request, sometimes a lot lower in the case of the State Department. Of course, if everyone got what he wanted, we would have a deficit far bigger than the one we have. Defense was no exception. As we worked on the FY2011 budget, OMB director Peter Orszag was telling us to plan for no budget growth beyond the rate of inflation for 2011 and several years beyond that. OMB and I were, shall we say, far apart.

(I shared with Rahm Emanuel a story about the time during the Reagan administration when all the deputy cabinet and agency heads met for dinner at the Justice Department and beforehand saw a live demonstration of the FBI's hostage rescue unit, with the lights going out and the unit walking among us firing blanks at "terrorist" targets. I told everyone afterward I thought it could have been played as a scene right out of Agatha Christie's novel *Murder on the Orient Express,* with the murder victim the deputy director of OMB because everyone in the room would have had a motive for killing him.)

I had several arguments to justify the budget growth we requested. We had already made significant program cuts in 2009, more extensive than ever before, cutting many large programs that were weak, wasteful, or unnecessary. Because no other department had done anything comparable—even proportionately—we deserved some consideration for that. Moreover, our costs rose inexorably. Year in and year out, Defense health care costs would rise $4 billion, military pay raises would cost an additional $3 billion, fuel inflation another $4 billion—in short, the military's basic overhead and operating costs would rise by about $13–$15 billion even if we didn't add a dime for existing or new programs. A broad range of equipment bought during the Reagan years—particularly ships and aircraft—had not been replaced during the defense budget downturn in the 1990s and early 2000s and were coming to the end of their useful lives. After ten years of war, much of our equipment was worn out and would need to be refurbished or replaced. Even the further reductions in overhead I was planning would be inadequate to cover these costs.

My discussions with Orszag and the president on the FY2011 budget began in mid-July 2009. I asked for $558 billion for FY2011, $16 billion more than OMB had proposed. Citing the longer-range factors mentioned above, I also asked for an additional $208 billion for the period from 2011 through 2015. Emanuel, Orszag, and I met privately several times, including once on Rahm's West Wing office patio, where I balanced a sandwich in one hand and PowerPoint slides in the other. After countless meetings through the fall between OMB and the defense budget team, led by our comptroller Bob Hale, it finally fell to me to cut the final deal. I met with Emanuel and Orszag again in Rahm's office on November 23, and we agreed to split the difference for FY2011 at $550 billion (up $8 billion from OMB's original guidance) and a five-year increase of $100 billion over the original OMB number. The president signed on. It was the best budget day I would have as secretary. Everything afterward would go downhill between the White House and me when it came to the defense budget.

The Quadrennial Defense Review (QDR) is a congressionally mandated report—yet another tasking from the Hill that had been introduced since I last left government—that requires a reexamination of defense strategy and priorities roughly every four years. It is a massive undertaking within the department, involving countless military and civilian hours over a period of months. The effort in 2009–10 was led by Michèle Flournoy, with the day-to-day leadership falling to her colleague Kathleen Hicks. The primary complaint about the QDR—other than the blandness that typically characterizes documents based on bureaucratic consensus—in past years had been that its conclusions about strategy and priorities were detached from actual budget decisions. We tried hard but with incomplete success to avoid that pitfall in the 2010 QDR.

On February 1, 2010, I went public with the FY2011 budget, as well as the results of both the QDR and the Ballistic Missile Defense Review. I announced that we would be asking for a base budget of $549 billion and a war supplemental (now euphemistically called "overseas contingency operations") for Iraq and Afghanistan of $159 billion. It added up to a staggering $708 billion.

I said the budget requests and the strategy reviews had several themes. One was continued reform—fundamentally changing the way the department did business: the priorities we set, the programs we funded, the weapons we bought, and how we bought them. I was also introducing a "bracing dose" of realism with regard to risk. I observed that for years, U.S. defense planning and military requirements were based on being prepared to fight two major conventional wars at the same time. I said that that model had been overtaken by events, and we now had to prepare for a much broader range of security challenges, from an adversary's use of new technologies to deny our forces access to "the global commons of sea, air, space, and cyberspace," to the threat posed by non-state groups developing the means to attack and terrorize. I voiced a view I would express repeatedly until I left as secretary:

> We have learned through painful experience that the wars we fight are seldom the wars that we planned. As a result, the United States needs a broad portfolio of military capabilities with maximum versatility across the widest possible spectrum of conflict. This strategic reality . . . directly informed the program decisions contained in the budget.

For the first time, both the budget and the QDR sent the message that prevailing in the wars we were already in had to be our highest priority. This meant more money for special operations, helicopters, ISR, and drones. We would also focus on preventing and deterring future conflicts by increasing investment in regional as well as homeland missile defense, spending more on our ability to train and equip the militaries of other countries, maintaining our nuclear deterrent, and funding the establishment of Cyber Command. We would prepare for possible future conflicts by moving forward with the F-35 Joint Strike Fighter, improving and increasing the shipbuilding program, modernizing our ground forces, and developing new capabilities for long-range strike (including a new bomber). We had to preserve the all-volunteer force, and that required allocating more money for wounded warrior programs, family support programs, and health care benefits.

In the long list of initiatives, including a number of additional program cuts, there were three that were controversial. As with every new aircraft in recent decades, the F-35 Joint Strike Fighter was over budget and behind schedule. The undersecretary for acquisition, technology, and logistics, Ash Carter, presented me with a long list of changes to the program in early 2010 to try to get it back on track. I accepted all his recommendations, including withholding $614 million in performance fees from Lockheed Martin, the lead contractor, and firing the two-star general who had been our program manager and replacing him with a more senior and capable officer. We also reduced the number of planes we would buy in the immediate future. Finally, to compensate for the delays in the program, I agreed with a recommendation to buy more F/A-18 fighters for the Navy so our carriers would not end up short of their full component of aircraft.

The two remaining programs with strong congressional support from my 2009 hit list were the C-17 cargo plane and an alternate engine for the F-35. Despite multiple Air Force studies showing that we had plenty of cargo aircraft, Congress just kept stuffing more C-17s into the budget in order to preserve the jobs on the production line. The Air Force didn't need more, didn't want more, and couldn't afford more. President Obama agreed to back me up with a veto threat on capping the number of C-17s.

As for the F-35 alternative engine, early on Pratt & Whitney had won the competition to build the engines. Needless to say, members who had a General Electric presence in their districts and states weren't happy about that and put money in the budget to fund development of an alternative—produced, of course, by GE, partnering with Rolls-Royce. In no time, Defense was spending hundreds of millions of dollars each year to support a program that, again, we didn't want, didn't need, and couldn't afford. Facts and logic play no part in debates on the Hill when jobs at home are at stake, and so members and I would go around and around on the extra engine. Here, too, the president agreed to support my decision with a veto if necessary. When a reporter asked me if I was sure the White House would back me up with a veto, I responded, "I don't go out on a limb without looking back to see if there's a guy back there with a saw."

The initial face-off on both issues came when Mike Mullen and I presented the budget to the Senate and House Armed Services Committees on February 2 and 3. Among the members with strong views one way or the other, when it came to issues involving defense programs, the two committees (and the Appropriations Committees as well) were largely split not by party or ideology but, with a few exceptions, by the location of the pork. I suppose the two issues also ended up becoming a test of wills between Congress and the president over who had a final say on defense acquisition. Congress had held the upper hand for a long time, and now it was being challenged. At one point, Representative Neil Abercrombie, a longtime Democratic congressman from Hawaii, said that I and the executive branch needed to learn that Congress made the final decisions on acquisition issues. I replied, maybe a little confrontationally, "Only if you have sixty-seven votes"—the number needed in the Senate to override a presidential veto.

Undeterred, the House Armed Services Committee put $485 million for the extra engine into its bill, along with more C-17s—and repeal of "Don't Ask, Don't Tell," exactly the scenario I had worried about in terms of getting a presidential veto. The House committee, in which Democrats were a majority, was prepared to fight for the extra engine until the last dog died, but after months of debate and confrontation, the newly Republican-controlled House—led by Tea Party members—in February 2011 killed the program. A full vote in the Senate led to the same result. Proponents of buying more C-17s gave up the ghost more easily. So I had put two more notches on my budget gun. I had now secured congressional approval of all thirty-three program cuts or caps I had announced in April 2009, a record.

The history of Defense Department acquisition and development of new programs is rich in over-cost, overdue, and flawed programs. There have been enough studies on how to fix the problem to fill a room, and repeated attempts at legislative remedies have been made, including as recently as 2009. Ash Carter and I spent a lot of time talking about the problem, and I concluded that the principal fixes were pretty straightforward: make sure there is competition for contracts, but real competition, not the kind Congress likes where everybody wins (such as proposals on the Hill to split the Air Force tanker buy between Boeing and Airbus/ EADs or for the F-35 alternative engine); have experienced and tough government contract negotiators, people with really sharp pencils; in big, long-term programs—excluding current wartime needs—wherever possible, build prototypes of new equipment, and don't start production until testing is complete and problems have been resolved; freeze requirements early in the process (anybody who has ever added a room onto his house knows that if you change the plans after construction begins, it will cost you an arm and a leg; same thing with warplanes and ships); demand accountability—be willing to fire government project managers or contractor managers if programs go off the rails; finally, the secretary of defense has to get his (or her) hands dirty overseeing all this, getting knowledgeable enough about the big programs, and keeping up to speed on progress to be able to know when to blow the whistle if things go awry.

Responsibility for overseeing acquisition cannot be delegated to the deputy secretary, as has so often been the case in the past. This is not about micromanagement, it's about accountability in leadership. Too many top executives in business and government think the details are beneath them, often with calamitous results. Frankly, I did not involve myself in acquisition issues in the Bush administration apart from urgent wartime needs, but I changed course early in the Obama presidency.

As we began to prepare the FY2012 budget in the spring of 2010, my sense of foreboding about Defense's budgetary future turned to alarm as I listened to the debates in Congress, followed the media, and listened to Obama. I believed our budget would remain flat at best and probably decline. To afford the weapons programs and equipment that I strongly believed we had to buy, we would need to find the money internally. Defense's base budget—not counting funding for the wars—had nearly doubled during the previous decade, and I believed the Pentagon had forgotten how to make tough decisions and to prioritize. We needed to begin to change a culture of spending into a culture of savings. This, then, required a new, even more aggressive examination of every part of the Defense Department. Thus began the "efficiencies" initiative of 2010.

I hoped to set the tone for what we would do in a speech on May 8 at the Dwight D. Eisenhower Library. Eisenhower, one of my great heroes, had told the Pentagon he wanted it cut down to "a Spartan basis," noting that "I say the patriot today is the fellow who can do the job with less money." I said in my speech that I found it compelling that under Eisenhower real choices were made, priorities set, and limits enforced—even in the face of a superpower adversary like the Soviet Union. The post-9/11 "gusher of defense spending," I warned, "has been turned off and will stay off for a good period of time." Accordingly, the department had to take a hard look at every aspect of how it was organized, staffed, and operated—indeed, every aspect of how it did business. I concluded: "The goal is to cut our overhead costs and to transfer those savings to force structure [military capabilities] and modernization. . . . What is required is not more study. Nor do we need more legislation. It is not a great mystery what needs to change. What it takes is the political will and willingness, as Eisenhower possessed, to make hard choices."

Three and a half years into the job, I had again declared war on the Pentagon—on the 40 percent of its spending that went to overhead, on layers of bureaucracy that put as many as thirty layers of staff between me and an action officer, on unnecessary programs, on too many generals and admirals for the size of our forces, on too many senior civilians in the department, and on too many contractors.

Most of my predecessors railed about the same problems. But most were trying to cut budgets, and some, including Robert McNamara, had come up with dramatic reform and restructuring initiatives that were imposed by fiat on the military services. These efforts, not surprisingly, met with significant resistance from the military. My strategy was different. I told the services that the money they saved through changing their way of doing business and cutting overhead I would return to them to invest in military capabilities. As with the program cuts and caps in 2009, the services would be deeply involved in the process. Critically important was getting agreement in advance from the president and the new director of OMB, Jack Lew, that we could keep all the savings from these efforts to reinvest in military capabilities. They were both supportive.

Between mid-May and mid-December, I chaired nearly sixty meetings ranging from half an hour to nearly eight hours on the efficiencies initiative. We delved into every aspect of the Pentagon. I was intending to bring about a cultural shift—"How do we make this place more efficient, make staffs more lean, flatten decision making, and pay more attention to cutting unnecessary costs." I did not want to wait eighteen months until FY2012 to begin implementing these changes; I wanted to identify things we could begin to do right away.

I went public with the first changes on August 9, 2010. Among other decisions, I announced we would:

- reduce funding for service support contractors by 10 percent a year for three years;

- freeze the number of positions in the office of the secretary of defense, Defense agencies, and the combatant commands for three years (except for hiring additional acquisition professionals);
- freeze the number of senior civilian executive and general and flag officer positions while a task force came up with recommendations to reduce general officer and flag positions by at least 50 and civilian executive positions by 100;
- impose dramatic cuts in funding for myriad reports and studies, as well as for outside advisory boards and commissions;
- reduce funding for Defense intelligence contracts, freeze the number of senior executive positions in Defense intelligence organizations, and carry out a "zero-based" review of all Defense intelligence missions, organizations, relationships, and contracts;
- eliminate organizations that performed duplicative functions or had outlived their usefulness.

To underscore the importance I attached to making these changes, I said that I intended that all the initiatives lead to operational plans or measurable results within 90 to 120 days, and I appointed Robert Rangel and Hoss Cartwright to cochair the effort.

While collectively the measures amounted to an earthquake inside the department, only my recommendation to close the Joint Forces Command in Norfolk, Virginia, was controversial on the outside. Its role was to infuse, or occasionally compel, "jointness"—the military services working together—in everything the military did: train joint forces, create joint doctrine, and experiment with that doctrine. I said those goals remained important, but much progress had been made since the command was created, and it no longer required a four-star combatant command, 2,800 military and civilian positions, 2,000 contractors, and a billion-dollar budget to accomplish the mission. The Virginia congressional delegation went wild. A couple of the congressmen became my worst enemies on the Hill and would remain so throughout the rest of my tenure as secretary.

Even as we were devising and implementing these efficiencies that summer and fall, we were negotiating with OMB over the size of the FY2012 budget. My proposal was exactly the same set of numbers that former OMB director Orszag and I had agreed to—and the president had blessed—in November 2009. Under a new director, Jack Lew, OMB walked away from that agreement and proposed instead a $20 billion reduction from our request and wanted to cut the five-year defense program by $148 billion in projected spending. It quickly got ugly.

On November 24, I gave the president a long memo summarizing our progress on the efficiencies initiative since my August announcement, reporting that the military services had indeed come up with $100 billion in overhead savings over five years, to be applied to increasing our capabilities. I also said we had identified a further $20 billion in department-wide savings over the same time period, which we intended also to plow back into "tooth." I briefed him in more detail on November 30, with Mullen, Lew, and Donilon present. With regard to the dispute with OMB over the current and future budget numbers, Obama told me to "work out" the number with OMB. I met with Lew for an hour on December 3, and while the meeting was friendly, we didn't make much progress.

On December 14, Obama met with me, Cartwright, Lew, and Donilon for the budget endgame. I offered to cut our FY2012 request to $555 billion and make further cuts of $63 billion over the following five years— a considerable concession, I thought, given our agreement of the previous year. The president said we had to do better. He talked about the budget crisis and the deficit and cuts he was making to domestic programs. He said he couldn't slash domestic spending and leave Defense with real growth. I reminded him that he had agreed we could keep all the savings we identified for reinvestment. I said I recognized the challenges facing the country, but that Defense should get credit for the cuts we had already made.

At that point, I intemperately told Obama that I could break the Defense Department, put hundreds of thousands of people out of work, and wreck programs, but that wasn't in the country's interest. He then asked Lew and me to continue talking.

The next morning I called Lew and told him we could cut another $1 billion (to $554 billion) for FY2012 and a total of $78 billion over the five years—"and that's it." The president called me after lunch and was somewhat apologetic, saying with respect to our meeting the day before, "At least you didn't yell at me."

That same afternoon, the fifteenth, I was waiting alone in Donilon's office for my regular weekly meeting with him and Hillary (they were both in with Obama) when the door opened and the president walked in carrying a gift-wrapped package. He gave it to me, and I unwrapped an expensive bottle of vodka. Enclosed was a handwritten note: "Dear Bob, Sorry I drive you to drink. Barack Obama." It was a very thoughtful peace offering.

In truth, I was extremely angry with President Obama on the afternoon of the fourteenth. I felt he had breached faith with me both on the budget numbers for FY2012–16 that Orszag, Emanuel, and I had agreed on—with Obama's approval—in the fall of 2009, and on the promise that Defense could keep all the efficiencies savings for reinvestment in military capabilities. I felt like all the work we had done in the efficiencies effort had been unrewarded and, further, that I had been forced to break my word to the military services. As in the spring with "Don't Ask, Don't Tell," I felt that agreements with the Obama White House were good for only as long as they were politically convenient.

In the end, we got about the same amount of money—roughly $530 billion—in FY2011 as in FY2010. Budgetary pressure on Defense would only increase for the rest of the time I was secretary and well beyond.

Nonetheless, we continued our efficiencies endeavor. On January 6, 2011, I gave a status report to the Pentagon press corps detailing the savings each of the services had made to reach the $100 billion mark. I outlined an additional $78 billion in savings that came from department-wide reductions, mainly in information technology, contracting, workforce size, general officer and flag officer positions, civilian executive positions, and intelligence organizations. I announced the cancellation of a number of additional procurement programs, the most controversial of which was the Marine Corps decision to cancel the expeditionary fighting vehicle, an amphibious assault vehicle that had proven far more costly than anticipated and that would have excessively high operating costs.

I then elaborated the areas in which the services would invest their overhead savings: a new long-range bomber for the Air Force; modernizing the Army's battle fleet of armored vehicles; and additional ships, F/A-18s, and unmanned strike and surveillance aircraft for the Navy. I said we would make more investments in long-range and regional missile defense. As it turned out, I was able to return virtually all of the $100 billion in savings to the services for "must pay" bills such as fuel price increases, and for reinvestment. The $78 billion in departmental savings was applied to the reduced budget levels in the future. The effort to reallocate funds through the efficiencies initiative had been successful, but actually realizing those savings would require very tight discipline and top-down managerial toughness for the entire projected five-year period. That would be a high hurdle indeed.

I have long believed that the way to change bureaucratic culture and performance is not through reorganization but by affecting day-to-day operations and ways of doing things. You need to get at the essence of what people are doing and encourage, incentivize, or force them to alter behavior. The crux of what I was trying to accomplish through the efficiencies effort was to pry open all the components of the defense budget that cost hundreds of billions of dollars but didn't get close scrutiny either within the Pentagon or by Congress. We needed to get at that daily "river of money" running through the building, as my Bush-era deputy Gordon England had so eloquently put it. We made a beginning, but only that.

As the Defense Department continues to face deep budget cuts, the effort to cut overhead costs must be intensified; as we learned from the "efficiencies" exercise, such efforts can succeed only if enforced from the top with regular reporting and strict accountability.

Respite

My last full year as secretary, 2010, was my toughest because of the multiple fronts on which I was fighting. The only thing that kept me going was getting out of the Pentagon and being around the troops. There is not much about being secretary of defense in wartime that is fun, but there *are* moments.

In May, I helicoptered into an open area at Eglin Air Force Base in Florida as a couple of hundred exhausted, hungry men training to be Army Rangers emerged from the deep woods to assemble for a few words from me. One of my key staff people, Ryan McCarthy, had been a Ranger captain, and he alerted me that these guys had not eaten or slept in days and were filthy and barely conscious. He told me that ordinarily they would not remember me or my visit. But, he said, if you bring them frozen Snickers candy bars, they will never forget you. He added that I should make the soldiers eat while I was talking because if they didn't, their instructors would take the candy away from them after I left. I'll never forget the look on those soldiers' faces as we hauled coolers full of

Snickers bars out of the helicopter to pass out to them. Months later I was still hearing from parents and friends of those soldiers who had heard about my visit.

In August, I visited the Marine Corps Recruit Depot San Diego, watched new recruits in training, and spoke to several hundred brand-new enlisted Marines at their graduation ceremony. I was amazed how many of their parents were present. I then visited the Naval Special Warfare Center in San Diego, where sailors undergo the toughest training imaginable in the hope of becoming Navy SEALs. Only 67 out of the previous entering class of 180 graduated. The fifth week of training—"Hell Week"—is the toughest. I arrived at the end of that week and had the pleasure of telling the sailors that it was over and they had survived to continue their training. These aspiring SEALs were a mess: having gone days without food or sleep, they were hollow-eyed, freezing, and barely able to stand. Formed up on the beach, they were covered head to toe in sand, unshaven, a little drool here and there, snot running out of their noses. I was proud to shake every filthy hand. These young men, like the Ranger trainees and so many others in uniform, are the best our country can produce. Being able to thank them personally was, for me, one of the greatest honors of being secretary of defense.

In the spring of 2010 I began a speaking campaign to impart to young people in uniform my views on how they should think about their military careers and what kind of officers they should become. I wanted to talk with them about the military challenges I thought they would face, the same challenges I was trying to get their four-star leaders and Congress to address. I began in April with visits to the Air Force Academy in Colorado Springs, the Naval Academy in Annapolis, and West Point. At each academy, I spent nearly an hour in each of two classrooms, taking questions from the cadets and midshipmen and talking about the future.

My main messages were delivered in lectures to the entire student body of cadets and middies. At each academy, I talked about the great officers of the past in their branch of service who had the "vision and insight to see that the world and technology had changed," understood the implications of that change, and then pressed ahead at the risk of their careers in the face of "incredible fierce institutional resistance." I spoke about how each of these officers had put his career on the line "to speak truth to power," and I said they must be willing to do so as well. I also warned them: "In most of these cases, integrity and courage were ultimately rewarded professionally. In a perfect world, that should always happen. But sadly, in the real world it does not, and I will not pretend there is no risk. You will, at some point or another, work for a jackass. We all have. That is why speaking up often requires courage. But that does not make taking a stand any less necessary for the sake of our country."

I told the aspiring young officers at the academies that the complexity of the twenty-first-century battlefield would require leaders of great flexibility, agility, resourcefulness, and imagination, leaders willing to think and act creatively and decisively in different kinds of conflict than we had prepared for during the previous six decades—precisely the qualities I had found in Petraeus, Odierno, McChrystal, Dempsey, Austin, Rodriguez, Chiarelli, and others. I urged them to reject service parochialism, convention, and careerism and instead "to be principled, creative, and reform-minded" on and off the battlefield.

I believe the ever-changing complexity of the world in the years ahead and the agility and adaptability of our adversaries make the willingness of our officer corps to challenge orthodoxy and conventional thinking essential to our success, and that is the message I wanted to convey to the cadets and midshipmen. I would tell both cadets and generals that we must not stifle the young officers and NCOs coming back from the wars. They had been forced to be innovative, adaptable, independent, and entrepreneurial and to take responsibility. Our future depended on keeping them in the services and sustaining those same characteristics at home that we had so valued on the battlefield. All these were messages I would continue to preach until I left office, and I would damn sure make certain the officers I recommended to the president to lead the military in the years to come understood and shared those same views.

At the end of my remarks, I always thanked the young officers-to-be for their service. And then, my voice breaking each time, I said, "I consider myself personally responsible for each and every one of you as though you were my own sons and daughters. And when I send you in harm's way, as I will, I will do everything in my power to see that you have what you need to accomplish your mission—and come home safely."

Perhaps my voice broke because I knew that on my return to Washington, as always, I would have to turn again to the wars in Iraq and Afghanistan. And send more of those kids in harm's way.

CHAPTER 13

War, War . . . and Revolution

December 2009 marked the end of the third year of my deployment to the Washington combat zone. It began with the president's announcement at West Point that the United States would surge 30,000 troops to Afghanistan, followed by my spending two full days of hearings on his announcement before the House and Senate with Hillary and Mike. The president had made a tough call on Afghanistan knowing there would be heavy political fallout. Hardly anyone in Congress was happy with his decisions. Republicans, led by McCain, disliked the deadlines—that troop drawdowns would begin in July 2011 and that our combat operations would end by 2014. A few of the president's fellow Democrats were guardedly supportive, but most were critical and some were downright hostile. At our hearings, the antiwar protesters were out in full force, sitting both at the dais and in the audience. As difficult as I found the House Armed Services Committee, its members were model statesmen compared to those of the House Foreign Affairs Committee, a number of whose members from both parties I again found extraordinarily rude and nasty; as a committee, I thought, it had more than its fair share of crackpots on both the left and the right. I didn't envy Hillary having to deal with them routinely. The day after the hearings, opponents of the war fingered me as responsible for the president's decisions and decided, according to the magazine *The Nation,* "It's time to fire Robert Gates."

It was with great relief that a few days later I flew to Afghanistan and Iraq. We had a full contingent of press on the plane, and as usual, I met with them during the flight. There, for the first and only time I was secretary, I said with respect to Afghanistan, "We're in it to win it." I had always been careful to avoid using terms like *winning* or *victory* because in the case of both wars, I knew such terms had become politically loaded, and that even the best possible outcome would not look to most Americans like winning or a victory. I preferred to use less politically fraught terms like *success* or *accomplishing the mission*. There would be nothing like the German or Japanese unconditional surrenders at the end of World War II, or even the Iraqi capitulation in 1991. But on that plane trip to Afghanistan after the president's speech at West Point, I just felt the troops needed to hear someone say that they weren't putting their lives on the line for some kind of "reconciliation."

Foreign travel, especially to war zones, by a secretary of defense is routinely tightly scripted, meticulously planned, and executed with military precision. Not this trip. In Afghanistan, I hoped to visit a Stryker brigade in the south that had lost thirty soldiers, but I was grounded in Kabul because of bad weather. I did have lunch with ten of our younger NCOs. I was struck both by the airmen's positive attitude about the Afghans they were training and also by their observation that desertion was a problem because some Afghan trainees were disgusted by their officers stealing part of their salaries. I always learned real "ground truth" like this from our troops. And then, just hours before my private meeting with President Karzai, there had been another incident that allegedly involved our coalition operations and civilian casualties. Karzai never waited for the facts before drawing conclusions, so the atmosphere for my meeting wasn't the best. Still, he and I got along well, and we had a good conversation. An important element of the strategy, I told him, was the need for Afghans to accelerate the recruitment of more young men into their security services. I played to his ego, saying he was the first president of a democratic Afghanistan—the father of his country—and he needed to be constantly encouraging young men to do their patriotic duty to defend their country. He vigorously nodded his agreement, although little came of the conversation.

As usual, he was more supportive in private than in public. He threw me a curve ball in our joint press appearance immediately afterward, saying that Afghanistan would not be able to support its own security forces financially for "fifteen to twenty years"—not a message any American wanted to hear. I tap-danced with the press to avoid the appearance of a major disconnect between us, saying that we could not abandon Afghanistan after our combat operations ended in 2014 and that I anticipated continued assistance. But it was apparent to all that Karzai had blindsided me. *New York Times* columnist Maureen Dowd was traveling with us on that trip, and she wrote a few days later, in her typical sharp-edged style, "Puppets just aren't what they used to be." Karzai was no puppet, but the United States probably hadn't had a more troublesome ally in war since Charles de Gaulle in World War II, perhaps because both were nearly totally dependent on the United States and both deeply resented it.

That evening I took my staff to the CIA's equivalent of an officers' club, which had much better food than the military provided—and adult beverages. One of the CIA officers who ate with us that night, a very bright young woman, was among the seven agency people killed in a Taliban ambush three weeks later, a tragic reminder that a lot of Americans not in uniform were also putting their lives on the line in this fight.

The next day, December 10, we were in Iraq, where our role in the war was beginning to wind down. There had been successful provincial elections in January 2009, with international election monitors present in every single constituency. In accordance with the Status of Forces Agreement signed by Bush and Maliki in December 2008, all U.S. combat forces had withdrawn from Iraqi towns and cities by the end of June. General Ray Odierno was well along with planning for the transition of our combat forces to "assistance and advisory" brigades and the withdrawal of some 70,000 U.S. troops and their equipment by the end of August 2010—all the while continuing to hunt down terrorists, train the Iraq security forces, and promote reconciliation among Iraqi politicians. It was a massive and complex undertaking, and the performance by Ray and his team was outstanding.

I was scheduled to meet with Maliki right after my arrival, but he was instead spending six hours of quality time getting scorched by the Council of Representatives—the Iraqi parliament—for his government's failure to prevent several recent terrorist bombings. When our meeting was canceled, the reporters with us characterized it as Maliki "blowing me off." I knew from personal experience that Maliki would much rather be meeting with me than getting shellacked by legislators.

The major topic of my meetings with Iraqi leaders was the national election to be held the following March. After a protracted stalemate, the

Council of Representatives had passed an elections law in early November. The elections would determine 325 members of the council, which would then choose a president and prime minister. Politicking was well under way. In my meeting with the Presidency Council—President Jalal Talabani (Kurd), Vice President Adel Abdul Mahdi (Shia), and Vice President Tariq Al-Hashimi (Sunni)—I asked Talabani if Iraq's neighbors were interfering in the elections. "Yes, everyone is interfering," he said. "Iran, the Gulf States, Syria, Turkey. Only Kuwait is not." Hashimi was his usual dour self, complaining that the violence was "no joke," the government was unable to do anything about the attacks, the security team needed to be reshuffled, and the people were disappointed and angry. Hashimi was a habitual complainer, but inasmuch as he was the only senior Sunni official, he had legitimate gripes. When he said the Presidency Council was being marginalized by Maliki, I suspected there was a lot of truth to that.

Maliki rescheduled the meeting with me for early the next morning. We discussed the violence, and he assured me the security forces were working well together. He asserted that al Qaeda did not pose a "great danger to us" but did want to disrupt the elections—"their last opportunity." We talked about the standoff between the central government in Baghdad and the Kurdish Regional Government (KRG) over control of the city of Kirkuk. I told Maliki I was going to Irbil, the Kurdish capital, that afternoon and would urge President Masoud Barzani to play a constructive role.

I was struck in Irbil by the signs of prosperity, including a lot of foreign-financed construction. I thanked Barzani for his help in devising the compromises that allowed the election law to pass, and I assured him of continuing U.S. friendship. I pointedly told him we were committed to preserving Kurdish security and prosperity "within a unified Iraq." Barzani replied that messages of support from Obama, Biden, and me had been the first such clearly conveyed to him (a statement I knew to be untrue from my Bush days) and had allayed longtime concerns about how the United States viewed the Kurds in Iraq. He said the KRG would always be "a part of the solution" and that "we are committed to national unity if the government in Baghdad is committed to the constitution." I stressed to him, as I had to the Presidency Council, the need to form a unity government as soon as possible after the election. Delay would only aid the worst extremists in Iraq. I assured him that we would be happy to do anything we could do to help resolve internal differences among the political factions. I then returned to Washington, D.C., and *its* political factions.

The Iraqi elections took place on schedule on March 7, 2010. There was little violence and a good turnout, but no party even came close to a majority. Maliki's coalition came in second with 89 seats in the Council of Representatives, while former interim prime minister Ayad Allawi's party came in first with 91 seats. The new parliament convened on June 14, with its primary task to select a new prime minister to form a government, but no candidate could muster a majority of the votes. Maliki was determined to remain as prime minister and refused to support Allawi (also Shia) even though he had won more seats. The result was a stalemate, with Maliki remaining as prime minister until someone could muster a majority in the parliament. That stalemate would continue for six months, despite the best efforts of Biden, Odierno, and U.S. ambassador Chris Hill to broker a compromise. Finally, Maliki's government was unanimously approved on December 21. The absence of a return to the kind of sectarian violence that followed the 2005 election was a mark of significant progress.

As President Obama had decided a month after his inauguration, the U.S. combat role in Iraq ended on August 31, 2010, nearly seven and a half years after we invaded. For Americans, the war in Iraq was finally over. Since the March 20, 2003, invasion, 4,427 American troops had been killed and 34,275 injured. Of the 3,502 killed in action, 1,240 died on my watch; of the 31,894 wounded in action, 9,568 had been hurt while I was secretary. During the preceding two years, we had withdrawn nearly 100,000 troops, closed or transferred to the Iraqis hundreds of bases, and moved millions of pieces of equipment out of the country.

The president marked the end of the war, the combat mission named Operation Iraqi Freedom, with a visit to Fort Bliss, Texas, on the thirty-first and with an address to the American people from the Oval Office that evening. He lauded the troops and their sacrifice and noted that because of them "Iraq has the opportunity to embrace a new destiny, even though many challenges remain." He spoke of the huge cost in lives and treasure America had paid to put the Iraqis' future in their own hands, of his own opposition to the war, and of its contentiousness in the United States. He discussed Afghanistan and his strategy there and concluded with his views on the need to tackle the many challenges at home. He hit all the political bases in his remarks, and he certainly could not be accused of waving a "mission accomplished" banner marking the end of the Iraq War.

I, too, gave a speech on August 31, to the American Legion in Milwaukee. I, too, waved no banners: "This is not a time for premature victory parades or self-congratulation, even as we reflect with pride on what our troops and their Iraqi partners have accomplished. We still have a job to do and responsibilities there." I observed that the opportunities in front of the Iraqis had been purchased "at a terrible cost" in the losses and trauma endured by the Iraqi people, "and in the blood, sweat, and tears of American men and women in uniform." I left the hall and immediately boarded an airplane to Iraq.

I landed at the gigantic Al Asad Air Base in western Iraq, once home to 22,000 Marines. It was now a ghost town, its long runways used mainly for ferrying soldiers home. I visited U.S. troops in nearby Ramadi, the scene of some of the most vicious fighting of the war. The reporters accompanying me asked if the war had been "worth it," and I responded—in "markedly anti-triumphal remarks," as they would write—that while our troops had "accomplished something really quite extraordinary here, how it all weighs in the balance I think remains to be seen. . . . It really requires a historian's perspective in terms of what happens here in the long run." I added that the war would always be clouded by how it began—the incorrect premise that Saddam Hussein had chemical and biological weapons and an active nuclear weapons program. In stark contrast to the cosmic questions posed by the press, the troops were mainly interested in retirement and health benefits and hardly mentioned the war.

Later the same day, September 1, Biden and I presided over the inauguration of the new U.S. training and advisory mission in Iraq, Operation New Dawn, and the change of command ceremony in which Ray Odierno handed responsibility to his successor, General Lloyd Austin. The ceremony was held in Al Faw palace, crowded with American and Iraqi commanders and as many troops as could be stuffed into the ornate hall built for Saddam. We all made speeches. Biden's was the longest as he paid tribute to Odierno, his family, and the troops. (It was a little awkward listening to the vice president, knowing that he had vigorously opposed the military surge that had made this relatively peaceful transition possible.) My remarks focused primarily on Odierno's accomplishments, noting that without his leadership as Multi-National Corps commander under Petraeus in 2007 and his ability to turn plans into results on the ground, "we would be facing a far grimmer situation outside these walls today, and more broadly a strategic disaster for the United States." I recalled asking him to return to Iraq as overall commander in the fall of 2008; he subsequently kept a boot on the neck of al Qaeda in Iraq and expanded the capabilities of the Iraqi army and police, all while overseeing the drawdown, restructuring, and repositioning of U.S. forces. I also welcomed Lloyd Austin. In addition to praising the troops, both Biden and Odierno called upon the Iraqi government to end its squabbling and get on with forming a government and addressing the country's challenges. During the speeches, I noticed that my jet-lagged senior staff sitting in the front row, to a man, had fallen sound asleep.

Fifty thousand U.S. troops would remain in Iraq, deployed in six "advise and assist" training brigades, with all American forces scheduled to depart Iraq by the end of December 2011 unless there was a new agreement of some sort with the Iraqis. During my remaining time in office, 26 more Americans would be killed in action in Iraq, and another 206 wounded in action. But the war that President Bush in November 2006 asked me to help salvage and that President Obama two years later asked me to help end was over. The future of Iraq was up to the Iraqis. I was indescribably proud of what our troops and their commanders at every level had accomplished, against all odds at home and in Iraq itself.

AFGHANISTAN

As I've said, the president had made a tough decision on the surge in Afghanistan in November 2009, and he had, for all practical purposes, made me, Mullen, Petraeus, and McChrystal swear a blood oath that we would support his decision. Unfortunately, Biden and his staff, the White House staff, and the NSS apparently had not taken the same oath of support. From the moment the president left West Point, they worked to show he had been wrong, that the Pentagon was not following his direction, and that the war on the ground was going from bad to worse. The president's decision clearly had not ended the rancor and division over war strategy inside the administration, or the White House–NSS suspicion of the senior military—and me—on this issue. Indeed, the suspicion seemed to have increased.

Everything each side said and did was perceived through this distorted prism. A big issue in the fall 2009 debate had been the need to get the additional 30,000 U.S. troops into Afghanistan quickly, as had been done in Iraq in 2007. The logistics challenges in Afghanistan were beyond daunting, but Mullen, Petraeus, and the military's logistics professionals pretty much pulled it off. When the Defense Department informed the White House in January that the last few thousand troops might not arrive until early September, we were accused of having misled the president. Almost none of the critics in the White House or the NSS— whose ranks were filled primarily by former Hill staffers, academics, and political operatives—had ever managed anything, and so there was no understanding of or sympathy for the challenges involved in what we were trying to do, only an opportunity to accuse us of walking away from our commitments to the president.

Biden, Donilon, Lute, and others bridled when McChrystal referred to his strategy as "counterinsurgency," accusing him of expanding the mission the president had given him. But words that had been so carefully parsed in the White House debate were not adequate to explain the mission to 100,000 soldiers and Marines, and the core of that mission was, in fact, counterinsurgency, albeit with fairly tight geographical and time limits. Troops risking their lives need to be told that their goal is to "defeat" those trying to kill them. But such terms were viewed in the White House as borderline insubordinate political statements by generals trying to broaden the president's strategy. Biden publicly asserted that the drawdowns beginning in July 2011 would be "steep." I said I thought they would, and should, be gradual. When I said in testimony on the Hill that the president always had "the freedom to adjust his decisions" with respect to the timing and pace of drawdowns, it was interpreted by administration skeptics as my saying that the drawdowns might not begin in July.

The same skeptics in the West Wing and the NSS second-guessed McChrystal's decision to secure several key villages in Helmand early in the campaign. They argued that the significant population center in the south was Kandahar. This was coming from the same critics who had wanted to avoid counterinsurgency—which is focused on population centers—and had demanded a "proof of concept" for his overall strategy.

The gap between the White House and senior Defense leaders became a chasm. Early in 2010, it had widened as the White House criticized the

U.S. military relief effort in Haiti, the repeal of "Don't Ask, Don't Tell" was playing out, I resisted major cuts in the FY2011 defense budget, and I wrote my memo on shortcomings in our preparations for a possible conflict with Iran. While the military's every move in Afghanistan was examined through a microscope, and we were under great pressure to speed the surge, no comparable attention was paid to the civilian side. Commanders in the field were the most insistent in pleading for more civilian expertise, citing one example after another where even a small number of U.S. diplomats or development experts would make a dramatic difference in provincial capitals, villages, and rural areas. One of the few things the NSC principals had agreed upon the previous fall was that a significant increase in the number of American civilian experts was essential to success, but the numbers trickled in far too slowly. Donilon would occasionally raise the problem with Hillary or her deputies in principals' meetings, but little came of it.

We at Defense certainly at times contributed to White House suspicions. For example, overly optimistic statements by McChrystal and others about the early success of military operations in and around the village of Marjah in Helmand—in particular, the claim of an Afghan "government in a box" ready to insert—gave ammunition not only to skeptics inside the government but also to the press. The more our commanders touted any success in the field, the more the NSS looked for evidence they were wrong. We should have done a better job of explaining what we were doing on the ground to implement the president's decisions, although God knows we tried. Neither side was really listening.

In mid-January 2010, I made my second and last trip to Pakistan. Mike Mullen and Richard Holbrooke had devoted significant time and energy to cultivating the Pakistanis, reassuring them we wouldn't abandon them and trying to get them to work more closely with us on the Afghan-Pakistani border. No administration in my entire career devoted more time and energy to working the Pakistanis than did President Obama and all his senior team. On January 21–22, I met with President Asif Ali Zardari, Prime Minister Yousaf Raza Gilani, and most important, the chief of the army general staff, General Ashfaq Parvez Kayani. My message was consistent: we were committed to a long-term strategic partnership; we needed to work together against the "syndicate of terror" placing Afghanistan, Pakistan, and India at risk; we needed to remove safe havens on both side of the border; Pakistan needed to better control anti-Americanism and harassment of Americans; and the Pakistani army's "extra-judicial killings" (executions) were putting our relationship at risk. In a speech at Pakistan's National Defense University, I took direct aim at the many conspiracy theories circulating about us: "Let me say, definitively, the United States does not covet a single inch of Pakistani soil. We seek no military bases and we have no desire to control Pakistan's nuclear weapons."

The visit was for naught. I returned convinced that Pakistan would work with the United States in some ways—such as providing supply lines through Pakistan, which were also highly profitable—while at the same time providing sanctuary for the Taliban and other extremists, so that no matter who came out on top in Afghanistan, Pakistan would have influence. If there was to be any reconciliation, the Pakistanis intended to control it. Although I would defend them in front of Congress and to the press to keep the relationship from getting worse—and endangering our supply line from Karachi—I knew they were really no ally at all.

If you'll remember, in recommending a surge of 30,000 troops to the president the previous fall, I was counting on our coalition partners in Afghanistan to contribute an additional 6,000 to 7,000 troops, which would get us close to the 40,000 McChrystal had requested. At a NATO defense ministers meeting in Istanbul on February 4–5, 2010, I leaned hard on my colleagues to find at least 4,000 more trainers to send to Afghanistan. I told them that effectively training a sizable Afghan security force was the exit strategy for all of us. I promised our allies more training to deal with IEDs and offered to make available to them counter-IED technologies we had developed. I then visited Ankara, Rome, and Paris to urge leaders in those governments to do more. The European governments eventually contributed an additional 8,000 to 9,000 troops. Even with this new infusion, though, we remained short of trainers needed to build up the Afghan army.

Two organizational changes in Afghanistan in early 2010 helped the allied effort considerably. The U.S. leadership had long thought that having a senior NATO civilian in Kabul to partner with the military commander would be important. Earlier efforts along these lines had not been successful, but in January the British ambassador to Afghanistan, Mark Sedwill, was appointed to the senior civilian role. He would prove a valuable partner for the ISAF commander and a useful influence both in Brussels and in Afghanistan.

The second change was solving the U. S. command and control problem once and for all—for the first time, to bring all American forces (including both special operations and the Marines) under the U.S. theater commander, at last establishing "unity of command." I told McChrystal at the February defense ministers meeting that I wanted him to be like Eisenhower in World War II and have complete command of all forces in the theater. Toward the end of February, I told Mullen and Petraeus the same thing. To accomplish this, Petraeus said, getting the Marines under McChrystal's command was "the Holy Grail." After deferring for too long to multiple senior military voices supportive of or resigned to the status quo, I simply directed the command change. By late spring, every American in uniform in Afghanistan was under McChrystal's command. It had taken far too long to get there, and that was my fault. I had fired several senior officers and officials because once they had been informed about a serious problem, they had not acted aggressively to solve it. I had been guilty of doing the same damn thing with respect to Afghan command and control.

As we surged troops into Afghanistan and McChrystal honed our military strategy, his staff began to tackle a problem that had concerned me all along—the inadequacy of our intelligence on the ground. McChrystal's intelligence chief, Major General Michael Flynn, prepared a report detailing our ignorance of tribal, social, and political relationships in local areas, and our lack of understanding of power relationships and familial and clan connections. His diagnosis was on target as far as I was concerned, and I thought his proposals to remedy the situation made sense, including having our troops on the ground report what they learned as they went into villages, met with tribal elders, and brokered local deals. My only concern with Flynn's remarkable analysis was that in January 2010, he published it in a think-tank journal so that everyone, including our adversaries in Afghanistan, could read about our deficiencies. Still, he was on the money in a critically important part of our effort.

I traveled once again to Afghanistan in early March and, as usual, met with Karzai. The prospects for reconciliation with the Taliban and reintegration of their fighters into Afghan society were much on everyone's mind, especially Karzai's, since he had convoked a national peace conference in late April. I told him we supported reconciliation but that it had to be on his terms, not those of Taliban chief Mullah Omar. He should negotiate from a position of strength, and I suggested he could probably do that by the coming autumn. I informed him that the request for an additional $30 billion needed to fund the surge would be before Congress about the time of his visit to the United States in May. "You could help Secretary Clinton and me," I told him.

As always, though—sorry to be predictable on the subject—the high point of the trip was getting out of Kabul to see the troops. I was flown to Forward Operating Base Frontenac near Kandahar to visit the 1st Battalion of the 17th Infantry Regiment, a Stryker unit that had suffered twenty-one killed and sixty-two wounded in its successful campaign. Roughly one out of seven soldiers in that unit had become a casualty. As a memorial to the fallen, they had set up a tepee with shelves along the sides holding photographs of those who had been killed, along with small mementos and coins left by comrades and visitors like me to honor them. It was, I thought, a sacred place, and I stayed in there alone for several minutes.

My spirits were revived by lunch with 10 junior enlisted soldiers and then a meeting with 150 of their buddies. As always, they were refreshingly candid. They were concerned about the tighter rules for engaging the enemy to prevent civilian casualties. Although they understood the consequences of hitting innocent people, they wanted to be able to fire more warning shots. They wanted more female soldiers to help search houses. They said the Afghan army troops were "good but lazy" and the Afghan national police were "corrupt and often stoned." Someone always caught me off guard in these exchanges, in this case a soldier who said there was a design flaw in the soldiers' combat uniform (fatigues)—the crotches tore out too easily crossing fences. He added with a smile, "It's not a problem in the summer, but it can get a little breezy in the winter." I allowed as how I probably wouldn't have heard about that problem back in the Pentagon. (It turned out the Army was aware of this problem and had already ordered replacements.)

I was then flown to Combat Outpost Caferetta in northeastern Helmand province to see the 3rd Battalion, 4th Marine Regiment. Captain Andy Terrell led me on a walk through the town of Now Zad, once home to 30,000 people and a former Taliban stronghold so laced with IEDs as to render it uninhabitable. The Marines had taken Now Zad the previous December and cleared most of the mines, at a great cost in double amputations. I was told that about a thousand residents had returned, and economic life was reviving. As I walked down the dusty main street, a few shops were open with a handful of men and boys standing around. I wondered, as I saw the significant number of Marines throughout the town and noted the paucity of open shops and the absence of livestock, whether this was a show for my benefit, or whether my visit and the presence of so many Marines to guard me had simply led people to hide. There was no question about the courage and grit the Marines had shown in taking this town or of the sacrifices they had endured. The question in the back of my mind was simply whether it had been worth what it cost them.

Before leaving Afghanistan the next day, I visited Camp Blackhorse, outside Kabul, one of the largest training camps for the Afghan army. Afghan defense minister Abdul Rahim Wardak met me there wearing a three-piece suit. He escorted me to various training demonstrations. I took a few minutes to thank the U.S. soldiers who were trainers there and then spoke to several hundred Afghan trainees through an interpreter. Wardak insisted that I end my remarks with a few encouraging words in Pashto. He wrote them out phonetically for me on a card. I gave it my best shot, which I suspected was none too good, and to this day I don't know what I actually said to them. Presumably it was nothing too insulting because they didn't appear offended.

My comments to the press on this trip weren't exactly brimming with optimism. I told those traveling with me to Now Zad that my visit there had reinforced my belief that we were on the right path, "but it will take a long time." "People need to understand there is some very hard fighting, very hard days ahead. . . . The early signs are encouraging, but I worry that people will get too impatient and think things are better than they actually are." No one could accuse me of looking at Afghanistan through rose-colored glasses. I'd seen our soldiers and Marines and what they'd accomplished, but I also understood what lay ahead for them.

Obama made his first trip as president to Afghanistan on March 28, 2010. He was on the ground for six hours, meeting with Karzai and with American troops at Bagram Air Base. His appearance gave a boost to Karzai, even as the U.S. president delivered some tough messages on corruption, drug trafficking, and governance. They also discussed reconciliation with the Taliban. The troops gave him a tumultuous welcome. Jones later told me angrily that a senior embassy official had told the Afghans prematurely about the visit and that not long after the president's plane departed Kabul, a rocket hit the tarmac less than a quarter mile from where it had been parked.

The divide over Afghanistan between State and Defense on one side and the White House and the NSS on the other, smoldering since December, flamed again at the beginning of April. Mullen and Michèle Flournoy returned to Washington from separate trips to Afghanistan, both deeply disturbed by what they had seen. Flournoy came to see me on April 2 to express her concerns about Ambassador Eikenberry's skepticism regarding the president's strategy, his treatment of Karzai, and State-NSS wrangling over who was in charge of the civilian side of the war effort. Mullen shared those concerns. A few days later I told Hillary I wanted to use my regularly scheduled time with the president that week to discuss these issues and asked if she would join me. She said yes. Jim Jones asked if the three of us could meet first without the president to come up with some ways forward. I said okay.

The next day I was discussing a sensitive personnel matter in private with the president when he asked me about Afghanistan. I told him I had agreed with Jones not to discuss my concerns with him—Obama—until Jones, Clinton, and I met. Obama said, "Consider that overruled." So I said that Eikenberry seemed convinced the strategy Obama had approved would fail. I said the ambassador, and others, had to deal more positively with Karzai, especially in public statements. It was a matter of Afghan sovereignty and pride. The Department of State and the White House/NSS were wrestling for the steering wheel on the civilian side, I continued, and this was going to take the entire effort into a ditch. Obama was quite reserved in his response, commenting only that the principals needed to work out the turf issue.

A few minutes later Clinton, Mullen, Donilon, and I met with Jones in his office. I repeated my concerns with added vigor and details. I said Eikenberry's pervasive negativity radiated throughout the embassy and was like a general telling troops going into a fight that the campaign would fail. I was very critical of his, and the White House's, treatment of Karzai, reminding all that Karzai knew we had interfered in the election the previous fall and noting that press secretary Robert Gibbs's public statement that very morning—that the United States might withdraw the invitation for Karzai to visit Washington in May—had been a horrible mistake. (Gibbs was reacting to Karzai's public statement that if foreign-

ers didn't stop meddling in Afghanistan, he might join the Taliban—
yet another of his many impulsive public statements that caused all of
us heartburn.) I then described the White House–State problem as we
saw it from Defense. Mullen endorsed what I had said, adding that we
would be looking at rule of law, corruption, and governance issues in a
few months, and yet there were no plans. "The civilian side is not happening," he said.

Hillary had come to the meeting loaded for bear. She gave a number
of specific examples of Eikenberry's insubordination to herself and her
deputy, Jack Lew, including refusals to provide information and plans.
She said, "He's a huge problem." She agreed with me on the administration's treatment of Karzai. Then she went after the NSS and the White
House staff, expressing anger at their direct dealings with Eikenberry
and offering a number of examples of what she termed their arrogance,
their efforts to control the civilian side of the war effort, their refusal
to accommodate requests for meetings, and their refusal to work with
Holbrooke and his team. As she talked, she became more forceful. "I've
had it," she said. "You want it [control of the civilian side of the war], I'll
turn it all over to you and wash my hands of it. I'll not be held accountable for something I cannot manage because of White House and NSS
interference."

At that point, I asked Jones how many people Doug Lute had working for him on the NSS. About twenty-five, Jones said. I angrily said that
the entire professional NSC staff under Bush 41 had been about fifty
people. "When you have that big an operation at the NSS," I told him,
"you're doing the wrong things and looking for ways to stay busy." The
National Security Staff had, in effect, become an operational body with
its own policy agenda, as opposed to a coordination mechanism. And
this, in turn, led to micromanagement far beyond what was appropriate. Indeed, on one visit to Afghanistan, I spotted a direct phone line
to Lute in the special operations command center at Bagram Air Base.
I ordered it removed. On another occasion, I told General Jim Mattis at
Central Command that if Lute ever called him again to question anything, Mattis was to tell him to go to hell. I was fed up with the NSS's
micromanagement.

Both Donilon and Jones were generally quiet in the face of Hillary's
and my criticism, though Donilon said that Holbrooke's team refused to
work within the interagency process. Jones said, "You want a meeting,

you get one." Further, he said, if the secretaries of state and defense and the chairman of the Joint Chiefs thought Eikenberry should go, "then he should go."

It was a real air clearing. I called Jones the next day to ask if we would discuss all this with the president. He said yes. But it had become clear that Eikenberry and Lute, whatever their shortcomings, were under an umbrella of protection at the White House. With Hillary and me so adamant that the two should leave, that protection could come only from the president. Because I could not imagine any previous president tolerating someone in a senior position openly working against policies he had approved, the most likely explanation was that the president himself did not really believe the strategy he had approved would work.

I could understand the president's skepticism even if I didn't agree with it. I did not believe that Karzai would change his stripes, Pakistan would stop hedging, corruption would appreciably diminish, or the U.S. civilian surge would actually materialize. Just the same, if I had ever come to believe the military part of the strategy would not lead to success as I defined it, I could not have continued signing the deployment orders.

The consistent irony of our NSC meetings, I thought, was that we spent most of our time dissecting the one part of the strategy that actually was working pretty well—the military operations and training of Afghan security forces—while neglecting the same kind of searching examination of those elements that weren't working. Obama's skepticism toward McChrystal's implementation of the strategy was apparent in virtually every meeting that spring. In a videoconference with Mullen and me in early May, Stan expressed his frustration with an NSC meeting the preceding day. He told us he was struck by the negativity and confusion over counterinsurgency expressed there. He said he intended to go through his operational plans for the Kandahar offensive again "so that they better understand it. . . . I am concerned the president doesn't understand the campaign plan" for Kandahar. I replied that those advising him at the White House were looking at our operations "through a soda straw" and seemed to have a hard time grasping the larger picture. That said, I knew that if the president didn't understand the campaign plan, that was our fault at Defense. I told McChrystal I would try to get him some time with the president to talk about the plan.

Meanwhile Hillary's and my complaints about how Eikenberry as well as White House officials were treating Karzai (especially in public) began to have some effect. Karzai had no use for Eikenberry, Holbrooke, or Biden, and his relationship with Obama was a distant one. McChrystal got along best with him, with Clinton and me coming next. In any event, the White House began to soft-pedal the public criticism of our "ally" in April.

On May 10, 2010, Karzai and a number of his ministers arrived in Washington for a "strategic dialogue." It began with a dinner that night hosted by Hillary, where everyone was on their best behavior. The next morning a number of cabinet ministers from both sides met for two hours at the State Department to discuss every aspect of our bilateral relationship. I spent another ninety minutes with the Afghan ministers of defense and interior at the Pentagon. I had developed a strong partnership with Defense Minister Wardak, a Pashtun who had been a national leader in the anti-Soviet mujahideen resistance in the 1980s. He was often eloquent, in an old-fashioned way, in expressing gratitude for our efforts in Afghanistan, and he was easy to work with—once I convinced him his forces did not need F-22s, just one of which would have consumed his entire budget. The president met with Karzai on the twelfth, and after they made statements to the press, the two delegations had lunch at the White House.

Those at the White House involved in orchestrating the visit, including NSS chief of staff Denis McDonough and Deputy National Security Adviser Ben Rhodes, were on pins and needles worrying about an outburst from Karzai. He had expressed a desire to visit our wounded soldiers at Walter Reed Army Medical Center, to go to Arlington National Cemetery, and then to visit Fort Campbell, Kentucky, to thank deploying soldiers and their families. White House officials opposed the visit to Fort Campbell, saying they wanted attention to revert to domestic affairs after three days of nonstop Karzai and Afghanistan. I think they were mainly nervous about what Karzai might say at Fort Campbell. I objected, and they relented. Karzai was at his very best at Walter Reed and at Arlington. I met him in Section 60 at Arlington, where many of those killed in Iraq and Afghanistan are buried, and he was deeply moved as we walked amid the headstones.

The next day I met him at Fort Campbell. Escorted by Major General J. F. Campbell, commander of the 101st Airborne Division, we went to a hangar where some 1,300 soldiers and their families were waiting. From a raised dais surrounded by three-foot-high metal crowd control fences, Karzai expressed his gratitude for all the United States had done to help Afghanistan since 2001. He told the audience that there were "many miles to go, but we are already better thanks to you," and promised that someday Afghan families would come to Fort Campbell "to thank you." The crowd of soldiers and family members exploded into a remarkable cheering standing ovation. Karzai was stunned and, energized, stepped off the dais, shook hands along the fence, and then leaped over the fence—nearly falling—to mingle in the crowd and get photos with families. It was an amazing sight. We eventually dragged him away to another building, where he spoke quietly to about 200 soldiers deploying to Afghanistan that day. He thanked them "for what you are doing for me and my country" and then shook every hand. As Karzai's plane lifted off from Fort Campbell and his visit to America ended, I could only hope the positive feelings on both sides would last awhile. I thought his visit had been a triumph, and I told him so.

In Afghanistan, McChrystal continued executing his plan to devastate the Taliban on their home turf in southern Afghanistan, first in Helmand and then in Kandahar province. After focusing his efforts in the south, he would swing the main effort to the eastern part of the country along the Pakistani border. The surge forces were just beginning to arrive in Afghanistan in May and June, but the pessimists were in full cry. They had plenty of ammunition. The operation to clear Marjah and surrounding areas of Taliban had taken longer than planned (and touted) by the military, and the campaign to clear Kandahar was also unfolding more slowly than expected. (McChrystal was moving more slowly in the Kandahar campaign than originally planned to ensure that more Afghan troops would be working with us and that local authorities were better prepared to offer services when security improved—lessons learned from Marjah.) There had been no real improvement in the standing of the Afghan government outside Kabul, with little or no central government presence in the provinces and villages and continuing corruption at every level—perhaps most harmfully by local officials and police, who routinely shook down ordinary Afghans. Adjudication of local and family disputes, an essential role for Afghan officials, was the occasion for yet more bribes. There were still too few Afghan soldiers and police for real partnering. Obama's announcement that the United States would begin withdrawing our forces in July 2011 was widely interpreted as an end date, so many Afghans just hunkered down to wait for our departure.

In making his decisions in November 2009, the president had said his national security team would review progress of the new strategy in December 2010. As I said earlier, if we couldn't see real progress, then we had to be willing to change our approach. By early June, Biden and others in the White House were already pushing us to rethink the strategy.

Because of mounting political pressure both in Washington and in Europe to show security progress in Afghanistan by the November NATO summit in Lisbon, I was worried that NATO ambassadors in Brussels and the NSS in Washington would conclude *they* should decide which parts of the country were ready to transition to Afghan control. So I was blunt at the June NATO meeting in Brussels in arguing that any announcement of which provinces to transition should depend solely on recommendations from McChrystal, senior NATO representative Ambassador Mark Sedwill, and the Afghan government, based on criteria and metrics they developed. I said the timing of transition must remain dependent on local security conditions and Afghan capacity to govern. I asked the ministers to remember that "transition is the beginning of a process without a predictable timeline; it is not a rush for the door."

Five days later Mullen and I testified before the Senate Appropriations Committee, ostensibly about the FY2011 budget. Much of the hearing focused on Afghanistan. Mike and I took issue with the negative tone of reporting from Afghanistan and reminded the senators that the surge forces were still arriving. When asked whether the surge could work, I wearily replied, "I must tell you I have a certain sense of déjà vu because I was sitting here getting the same questions in June 2007 when we had just barely gotten the surge forces into Iraq." We warned that this was going to be a long, hard fight, but that McChrystal "is convinced, confident that he will be able to show that we have the right strategy, and we are making progress, by the end of the year." Mullen said all the indicators were moving in the right direction, "as tough as it is." We highlighted Karzai's formal approval of the Kandahar operation just days earlier. The same day Petraeus and Flournoy testified before the Senate Armed Services Committee along the same lines, then appeared for a second day, Petraeus having fainted at the hearing the day before. In both hearings, the July 2011 drawdown date was hotly debated, with all of us saying that drawdowns would begin on that date, the pace to be determined by "conditions on the ground." Unrelievedly, the president's strategy in Afghanistan—and the performance of the U.S. military commander there—was under heavy pressure both from his staff and Biden in the White House and from the news media. We were barely holding our own. Then disaster struck.

Late in the afternoon of Monday, June 21, Mullen called to tell me the magazine *Rolling Stone* was publishing an article, "The Runaway General," about McChrystal that was potentially very damaging. He sent the article to my office, and as I read it, I wondered what in the world Stan had been thinking to give this reporter such access. The article cited one aide as describing McChrystal's first meeting with Obama as a "10-minute photo op. . . . Obama clearly didn't know anything about him, who he was. Here's the guy who's going to run his fucking war, but he didn't seem very engaged. The Boss was pretty disappointed." Another staff aide is quoted as calling Jim Jones a "clown" who remains "stuck in 1985." Most egregiously, the article portrayed the general mocking the vice president. "'Are you asking about Vice President Biden?' McChrystal says with a laugh. 'Who's that?' 'Biden?' suggests a top adviser. 'Did you say: Bite Me?'" The article by Michael Hastings was harshly critical of the entire Afghan strategy, and I knew the quotes about Biden, the president, and Jones would be dynamite at the White House.

About five p.m., Stan called me to apologize for the article. Deeply fearful of its impact on the war, for once I couldn't contain my anger: "What the fuck were you thinking?" McChrystal offered no explanation, didn't say he or his staff had been misquoted or that the article was distorted in any way. The four-star general replied essentially as he had been taught as a cadet at West Point—"No excuses, sir."

My heart sank. I knew that McChrystal's critics in the White House could put his command in jeopardy. Jim Jones called twice that evening to let me know the White House was getting very "spun up" about the article, a classic understatement.

The next afternoon I was scheduled to meet privately with the president about potential successors for me, Mullen, and Cartwright. Before the meeting, Biden called and, I thought rather defensively, said, "I didn't rile him [Obama] up last night, I just asked him if he'd seen the article." Biden told me that McChrystal had called him to apologize for the comments in the article.

I went in to see the president a little after three p.m. on the twenty-second. The first words out of his mouth were "I'm leaning toward relieving McChrystal." He went on to say, "Joe [Biden] is over the top about this." (So much for Biden's credibility.) I said I was going to see Stan the next morning and would tell him that if he were in any position but commander ISAF, I would fire him myself. But, I went on, "I believe if we lose McChrystal, we lose the war." I said I feared that any successor would take three to four months to get confirmed, get to Afghanistan, and get up to speed. This loss of momentum, in light of the timelines the president had set, the fragility of the Kandahar campaign, and Stan's special relationship with Karzai, I said, would be "irrecoverable."

The president told me my concerns were valid, but he had to think about the institution of the presidency. He said, "Let's talk substance." He then reinforced my worst fears. He said, "I don't have the sense it's going well in Afghanistan. He [McChrystal] doesn't seem to be making progress. Maybe his strategy is not really working." Hearing the president express doubt about the strategy he had approved six months earlier, just as many of the surge troops were arriving in Afghanistan, and his lack of confidence in his commander and the strategy floored me. These feelings did not spring from a magazine article but had been there all along. I replied that the effort was proving harder and taking longer than anticipated, but McChrystal had just briefed forty-four NATO defense ministers in Brussels and all expressed confidence that we were on the right track. "They trust him. And I believe we are making progress and will be able to demonstrate that we are on the right path in December."

Obama then asked, "What if Petraeus took command?" I told Obama that if Dave would do it, it would address my worst fears—Petraeus knew the campaign plan, knew Karzai, knew the U.S. military leaders in Afghanistan, knew the Europeans, and knew the Pakistanis. I said that under the circumstances, that would be the best possible outcome. Petraeus could hit the ground running, and his reputation would itself bring new energy to the campaign.

I still urged the president to hear out McChrystal. I said McChrystal would offer a letter of resignation and affirm his support for the president's policy. I urged the president "to flay him" but then be generous and turn down the resignation, and tell Stan he had one last chance. As I left the Oval Office, I was pretty sure the president would not do as I had suggested.

The personal warmth, confidence, and trust that Obama consistently showed me—often at difficult moments between us—never ceased to surprise. Our meeting originally had been scheduled to talk about succession planning at Defense, and when we finally turned to it, I told him I planned to leave early in 2011. I probably had been his most contentious, difficult, and stubborn cabinet member; and yet the president then told me, in the same meeting where he said he was about to fire a field commander I had recommended to him, that he wanted me to stay for at least the remainder of his first term. "I know that's not possible," he said. "How about January 2012?" I reminded him that when we had talked the previous December, I'd said that this timing wouldn't work because it would be hard to get a quality person to serve for potentially only one year. I also said he didn't want a defense secretary nomination before the Senate early in the presidential primary season, thus providing Republicans an opportunity to use the hearings to attack his national security policies. Obama agreed, then suggested I remain until the end of June 2011, a logical time to leave as we began the transition in Afghanistan. I said okay. As I reflected on the meeting, I was moved by the president's generous treatment of me. I probably owed *him* a bottle of vodka.

After that meeting, I went downstairs to the Situation Room for a principals' meeting. When it was over, I told Hillary I thought the president was going to relieve McChrystal and was thinking about Petraeus as a replacement. She thought Petraeus was a great idea.

When I returned to the Pentagon, I took a call from Karzai, who earlier had had a videoconference with the president. He urged leniency for McChrystal: "I like him. He serves your objectives clearly and purposefully in Afghanistan. I have never had such a clear understanding and productive relationship with any other officer as I have with him." Karzai said he knew about our system of civilian control but expressed the hope that "this very fine gentleman" could stay in Afghanistan. I told him I would pass along his comments to the president, and that I shared his high regard for McChrystal, but that he had "committed a very serious breach of discipline." I said I hoped the matter would be resolved quickly to avoid prolonged uncertainty.

At eight-thirty the next morning, Mullen and I met with McChrystal. I again told him, "If you were in any other job than commander in Afghanistan, I'd fire you myself. How could you put the entire war effort at risk with such a stupid decision?" I told him the president was leaning toward relieving him and that the proper thing to do was to offer to resign. Stan said only, "I'll do what's best for the mission." He then left to see Obama.

Just after ten a.m., the president called to tell me he had relieved McChrystal and told me to "come over right away to discuss the way forward." Mullen and I raced to the White House and joined Obama, Biden, Emanuel, Jones, and Donilon in the Oval Office. We reviewed a list of other possibilities for commander—Marine General Jim Mattis, then commander of Joint Forces Command; Army Lieutenant General Dave Rodriguez, McChrystal's second-in-command; Marine Lieutenant General John Allen, deputy commander at Central Command; and General Odierno. All present agreed that only Petraeus would work. I said Petraeus was in the White House for a meeting, and the president said, "Get him up here."

While those two met, the rest of us went to the Situation Room to wait for a scheduled meeting with the president on Afghanistan. Thirty minutes passed. Mullen, Donilon, and I began to look nervously at one another, wondering if something had gone wrong in the Obama-Petraeus meeting. At 10:50, the president came in and told the assembled senior team that Petraeus was the new commander, and he would have full freedom to make military recommendations. Obama expected frankness. He said Dave supported the strategy but could make recommendations for changes, which the president would consider. He then delivered a very stern lecture about divisions within the team, sniping, and leaks. He demanded that everyone get on board. The president wanted to announce the change immediately in the Rose Garden. It all happened so fast that Petraeus had to leave a phone message for his wife that he was headed back overseas.

Because we had another principals' meeting in the early afternoon, Mullen, Clinton, Petraeus, and I remained in the Situation Room after the Afghanistan meeting to discuss the civilian side of the equation. It was a somber gathering given the drama that had just taken place. We were still trying to fathom the consequences for the war in Afghanistan. Hillary suggested Ryan Crocker as our new ambassador, replacing Eikenberry. (Crocker had been ambassador in Iraq and a close partner of Petraeus's during the surge.) We all agreed he'd be terrific if he was willing to do it. Hillary said she would raise the idea with the president that afternoon. She later told me that Obama did not want to move on the ambassador's job until the dust had settled with the military changes, but he had authorized her to reach out very quietly to Crocker. At Clinton's suggestion, Petraeus called Crocker that evening and reported back to us that Ryan had not said no, but there were some conditions, including that Holbrooke had to go. But the protective umbrella over Eikenberry at the White House was still up, and Crocker would not become ambassador for more than a year.

McChrystal, whose civilian media adviser had thought the general should reach outside the mainstream media to discuss his mission in Afghanistan, had handed Biden and his other adversaries at the White House and the NSS the opportunity to drive him from command. Giving access to the reporter writing for *Rolling Stone*—a reporter who subsequently would also write very critical articles on both Petraeus and Lieutenant General William Caldwell, in charge of training Afghan security forces—was a terrible blunder. An Army inspector general investigation later concluded that the Army officers on McChrystal's staff had not made the derogatory comments; nor had the general heard directly the statements in question. (I would hear subsequently that some of the comments in the article were attributable to non-Army members of his staff.) The Department of Defense inspector general reviewed the Army report and, while finding shortcomings in that investigation, concluded that "not all of the events at issue occurred as reported in the article." The magazine stuck by its reporter.

Whatever actually happened or was said, McChrystal's refusal to defend himself—to give me any ammunition to use on his behalf—made it impossible for me to save his job. But to this day, I believe he was given the bum's rush by Biden, White House staff, and NSS who harbored deep resentment toward his unyielding advocacy the previous fall of counterinsurgency and a huge troop surge in Afghanistan; who interpreted his public comments back then as "boxing in" the president; and who continued to oppose the strategy approved by the president and the way McChrystal was implementing it. I am convinced the *Rolling Stone* article gave the president, egged on by those around him in the White House, and himself distrustful of the senior military, an opportunity he welcomed to demonstrate vividly—to the public and to the Pentagon—that he was commander in chief and fully in control of the military. Absent any effort by McChrystal to explain or to offer mitigating circumstances, I believe the president had no choice but to relieve him. The article simply was the last of several public missteps by the general in the political minefield, a risky battlespace where he had little combat experience. At his retirement ceremony in late July, I told the audience, "As he now completes a journey that began on a West Point parade field nearly four decades ago, Stan McChrystal . . . does so with the gratitude of the nation he did so much to protect, with the reverence of the troops he led at every level, with his place secure as one of America's greatest warriors."

McChrystal's departure and Obama's stern lecture did nothing to diminish the split at the highest levels of the administration over Afghanistan. Petraeus made a couple of early moves that had positive effect on the battlefield. To reduce civilian casualties, McChrystal had issued restrictive guidelines about when troops could fire and when air strikes could be called in for support. Unfortunately, to be sure they were compliant with his intent, every subordinate level of command added a margin of error on the restrictive side. The result was that the troops on the front line felt exposed and vulnerable, unable to defend themselves adequately. Petraeus issued a new set of guidelines that were less restrictive and explicitly forbade anyone to add further limitations. This helped morale. Also, while McChrystal had always supported targeting specific Taliban commanders and officials, Petraeus significantly stepped up the intensity of these attacks. By the end of August, we were beginning to see signs of progress in the counterinsurgency effort around Kandahar—above all, a significant decline in Taliban activity—as well as the impact of stepped-up attacks against the Taliban leaders. We had long done both, but the added troop numbers enabled us to show some better results.

Whatever was happening on the battlefield, the debate at home was already beginning to rev up over how fast U.S. forces should withdraw beginning in July 2011. Democrats in Congress were urging steep reductions right away, a view held by Biden and the usual suspects at the White House and the NSS. Mullen, Petraeus, and I reminded everyone that the last of the surge troops were just arriving, and we needed time to show what they could accomplish; the drawdowns would begin as the president said, but they should be gradual. As he had at dicey moments in Iraq, Petraeus now went public, granting interviews to major newspapers in August in which he talked about gains that had been made in routing the Taliban from traditional strongholds in the south and in training Afghan troops. He asked for patience and time, two commodities in short supply in Washington, D.C.

I again visited Afghanistan in early September, flying in from the change of command ceremony in Baghdad. There were several very touchy issues to discuss privately with Karzai. I explained to him what had happened with McChrystal. We then discussed his edict that essentially required all private security contractors to leave Afghanistan, including those guarding development projects intended to help the Afghan people. He had been privately expressing his concerns to U.S. officials about the behavior of these men for many months, and as happened all too often, we didn't pay enough attention until he blew up and we faced a crisis. Another perennial issue was corruption, this time not the penny-ante stuff that was alienating average Afghans but rather reports that the Kabul Bank's Afghan chairman and others had looted the bank of anywhere from $800 million to $1 billion. The bank's troubles were additionally a problem because electronic payments to Afghan soldiers, police, and most civil servants were paid through the bank, and if it collapsed, we would have a huge problem. Karzai furiously asserted that he had taken corrective actions, that he had briefed Petraeus and Eikenberry, but that leaks from our embassy had led to a panic and the withdrawal of huge sums. Karzai said that the U.S. embassy "doesn't understand the Afghan public" and that he resented Afghan officials "being summoned" to meetings at the embassy. I assured him we would work with and through him on issues and be respectful of Afghan sovereignty. I also told him his government needed to implement corrective measures regarding the Kabul Bank in a way that was credible to the international community and our Congress.

The next day, September 3, I flew to Kandahar to see things for myself. At Camp Nathan Smith, Brigadier General Nick Carter briefed me on what his forces were doing in and around Kandahar City, as well as the surrounding areas—Arghandab, Panjawi, and Zheray, all longtime Taliban strongholds—and the next steps he planned to take in securing the populated areas. We spent a lot of time discussing the local strongman, Ahmed Wali Karzai (AWK), the president's half-brother. He was powerful and regarded as notoriously corrupt, but every time Hillary or I asked for evidence of his criminality, the intelligence community had nothing to offer. Carter captured the near-term challenge well, I thought. He said that for the foreseeable future, the choice facing us was a theocracy run by the Taliban or a "thugocracy" run by the likes of AWK. He said that working with AWK offered the best way to show results quickly against the Taliban. I told Carter that "if working with AWK helped keep our troops alive and succeed in their mission, then that's no contest."

At Combat Outpost Senjaray, twelve miles west of Kandahar, I spent an hour having lunch with ten junior enlisted soldiers. A private first class named Brian told me his wife had stepped on a nail back home, but the Navy hospital nearby, at China Lake, had refused to treat her even with a military ID because she didn't have the right Tricare (military insurance program) policy. She was told she could go across the hall and sign up for the right policy, but it would take a month to process the paperwork. When she gave up and went to a private doctor to be treated, she was told she was lucky not to have gotten blood poisoning. This was exactly the kind of bureaucratic bullshit that set my hair on fire. I told Brian to send an e-mail to Marine Lieutenant Colonel Kris Stillings, a member of my staff who was notetaker at the lunch. When Stillings e-mailed him back that I would get answers for him, the PFC responded, "Even though I am just a private in this vast military world, it's nice to see that you and the Sec-Def will always take care of the little guy." I was so moved by his humility, I sent him the only e-mail I ever sent a soldier:

> Brian, Lt. Col. Stillings has shared with me your exchange of e-mails with him. The facts of your wife's medical treatment as you report them are completely unacceptable to me and we will follow up vigorously.
>
> Brian, you may be "just a private in this vast military world," but you and those like you are the backbone of America's military. Just sitting and talking with you and your fellow soldiers at COP Senjaray— and experiences like it with other troops of similar rank—is the most inspiring thing I do. And being able to do everything I can to look out for you all is the most satisfying thing I do each day. You may be "just a private," but you and those like you are the only reason this Secretary of Defense continues to do this job. Whatever else you accomplished today, you and your buddies provided renewed inspiration for an old Secretary of Defense.

Brian's wife would get a personal apology from the commander of the Navy hospital at China Lake, and I was told changes would be made to prevent such a recurrence at any other military hospital. Several new washing machines were helicoptered into COP Senjaray a few days later, and their Wi-Fi was fixed; both had been requested by the soldiers at lunch. If only the bigger problems were so easy to tackle.

On this trip, I heard two stories that brought a smile. A joint U.S.-Afghan patrol had come upon a stolen pickup truck parked near a tree, and everyone concluded it was probably a truck bomb planted by the Taliban. An Afghan soldier decided to fire a rocket-propelled grenade at the truck to blow it up. He missed the truck and hit the tree, where it turned out a Taliban fighter had been hiding. The Taliban was blown out of the tree and onto the truck, which promptly detonated. A nice, if unintended, carom shot. Separately, I was told of a report that Taliban commanders in the Sangin area of Helmand had instructed their fighters not to engage U.S. Marines in large-scale attacks: "Taliban fighters say U.S. Marines are unkillable and invincible. . . . The Marines are insane. They run toward the sound of our guns rather than run away."

I came away from my visits to Camp Nathan Smith and COP Senjaray impressed with the commanders and their sense that they had the right strategy and enough forces to implement it. Cautious as always, though, I told the press, "Everybody knows this is far from a done deal. There is a lot of hard fighting to go. But the confidence of these young men and women that they can be successful gives me confidence." I observed that the question to be addressed in the December review would be whether the strategy was working—was there enough evidence of progress to indicate we were on the right track? "Based on what I've seen here today, I'm hopeful we will be in that position." I also said I thought it would take two or three more years of combat before we could transition to a purely advisory role.

A couple of weeks later, because of the continuing negative public narrative about the course of the war, I sent the House and Senate Armed Services Committees a report on my trip, something I had never done before. I affirmed that we had well-understood, clear objectives. I told them that 85 percent of the Afghan army was now partnered with coalition troops, and that the Afghans had led a successful operation against a Taliban stronghold outside Kandahar, an area never taken by the Soviets. I reported on briefings I had received at Camp Nathan Smith about increasing numbers of Afghans reporting IEDs, working with us to build schools and bazaars, and sending their children to school. I said that our approach "is beginning to have cumulative effects and security is slowly expanding," although tough fighting still lay ahead and challenges remained in the areas of governance and corruption. I said that a big problem was the fear of many Afghans that we were leaving, causing them to hedge their bets. "We must convince the Afghans that both the United States and NATO plan to establish a strategic partnership with

Afghanistan that will endure beyond the gradual transition of security responsibilities." I concluded, "In contrast to some past conflicts, what I find is that the closer you get to this fight, the greater the belief we are moving in the right direction."

Despite my own cautious optimism, I had come to realize, as I suggested earlier, that both Presidents Obama and Karzai, whose commitment to the strategy was essential to success, were both skeptical if not outright convinced it would fail. (Bush had seemed to believe wholeheartedly that the Iraq surge would work.) I wondered if we had gotten the strategy and the resources right in Afghanistan too late, after patience there and in the United States had run out. Had the diversion of attention and resources to the invasion of Iraq sown the seeds for future failure in Afghanistan? I believed we had to succeed there because the stakes were higher than perhaps any other senior official in the government understood. For Islamic extremists to defeat a second superpower in Afghanistan would have devastating and long-lasting consequences across the entire Muslim world. For the United States to be perceived as defeated in Afghanistan at the same time we were suffering an economic crisis at home would have grave implications for our standing in the world. Nixon and Kissinger had been able to offset the consequences of U.S. defeat in Vietnam with the dramatic openings to Russia and China, demonstrating that we were still the colossus on the global stage. The United States had no such opportunities in 2010.

In early October, the president announced that Jim Jones would be leaving and that Tom Donilon would become the new national security adviser. Despite our disagreements, Donilon and I had developed a solid working relationship since the air-clearing between us months earlier, and I welcomed his appointment (although he continued to harbor deep suspicion of the senior military and the Pentagon). He had access to and great influence with both Obama and Biden, was comfortable disagreeing with them, and was considered an insider by the rest of the senior White House staff. As with his counterpart in the Bush administration, Steve Hadley, I bridled at the number of meetings Tom summoned us to attend in the Situation Room—but then, the world was a mess and required a lot of tending to.

My last autumn as secretary was a busy one, with the wrap-up of the "Don't Ask, Don't Tell" review and all the court actions surrounding DADT; a trip to Vietnam and Belgium (a NATO meeting); another to Australia, Malaysia, and Iraq; and my unforgettable visit to Santa Cruz, Bolivia. We had to deal with a very dangerous crisis beginning on November 23 when the North Koreans unleashed an artillery barrage at the South Korean island of Yeonpyeong. South Korea had suffered such provocations for thirty years with restraint, but North Korea's sinking of its warship *Cheonan* the previous March had produced a change in attitude in the South, and there were demands for retaliation against the shelling, especially since several innocent South Korean civilians had been killed. South Korea's original plans for retaliation were, we thought, disproportionately aggressive, involving both aircraft and artillery. We were worried the exchanges could escalate dangerously. The president, Clinton, Mullen, and I were all on the phone often with our South Korean counterparts over a period of days, and ultimately South Korea simply returned artillery fire on the location of the North Koreans' batteries that had started the whole affair. There was evidence the Chinese were also weighing in with the North's leaders to wind down the situation. The South Koreans and we agreed to carry out a naval exercise together—led by the aircraft carrier *George Washington*—in the Yellow Sea to assert our freedom of navigation. Never a dull moment.

The president had insisted all along that he wanted the December review of progress in Afghanistan to be low-key, avoiding the spectacle of the preceding year. Petraeus kicked off the review at the White House on October 30 with a briefing for Donilon and Lute. He had the usual packet of PowerPoint slides. One showed where the surge troops had been deployed; another highlighted that the Afghan security forces had doubled in size to more than 260,000 since 2007. Then he focused on the Kandahar campaign. He said among other things that the current operations were Afghan-led and that nearly 60 percent of the forces involved were Afghan. He was particularly enthusiastic about the "Afghan Local Police" initiative, in which young men were recruited in villages, trained and equipped, and returned to those same villages. The key was keeping them connected to the regular police and Afghan authorities so they didn't turn into independent militias. The early results had been quite encouraging.

The U.S. senior military leadership had pledged to the president that they should be able to clear, hold, and transition to Afghan security forces places where our troops had been deployed within two years. By the fall of 2010, about a third of the country and an even higher percentage of the population had in fact already been transitioned to Afghan security responsibility. Our two years would expire in Helmand the following July. Although these deadlines grated on the military, that was the deal we had made with the president. I could understand Obama's insistence on keeping to the commitment. If we couldn't get the job done in two years, how many years would it take? Down that path lay an open-ended conflict with potentially many more years of fighting. We had agreed on a strategy, and we were going to stick to it. The president would fulfill his part of the bargain despite his reservations, but he would make sure we did too.

The NATO summit in Lisbon on November 20–21 was a milestone in the alliance's involvement in Afghanistan. Karzai, who attended the Afghan part of the meeting, had proposed at his inaugural a year earlier that foreign forces end their combat role by the end of 2014, transitioning security responsibility for the entire country to the Afghans—not coincidentally, at the end of Karzai's last year in office. Obama had embraced that date two weeks later in his December 2009 announcement, and the member nations of the alliance did so as well in Lisbon in November 2010. At the same time, they promised to continue helping Afghanistan with military training and equipment, as well as civilian assistance, after 2014.

The president made a surprise visit to Afghanistan just over a week later on December 3. Weather prevented him from helicoptering from Bagram Air Base into Kabul to have a working dinner with Karzai, but the two talked on the telephone. The president spent several hours chatting with U.S. troops, visiting wounded at the medical facility on the base, and meeting with Petraeus and Eikenberry. There was grumbling among the Afghans about the president not making the dinner with Karzai, and some as well among our military about him not getting off the air base and visiting a forward operating base, where the fighting troops were. I thought both criticisms unwarranted, particularly in the latter case. Had I been asked, I would have recommended against him going to a FOB because of the risk; secretaries of defense are expendable, but presidents are not.

I arrived in Afghanistan four days later, partly to get a last personal update before the review concluded, and partly to visit the troops before the holidays. Major General J. F. Campbell, commander of the 101st Airborne and Karzai's and my host the previous May at Fort Campbell, provided a realistic picture of the tough fight in the east. There were some areas, like the Pesh River Valley, he said, where a long-term U.S. troop presence was actually destabilizing. The locals hated both us and the Taliban, and we were better off leaving them alone. He told me he needed more intelligence, surveillance, and reconnaissance and more firepower to go after fighters coming across the border from Pakistan. He said he saw progress every day, "but it's gonna take time."

I spent two full days with the troops on this trip, the first in Regional Command–East and the second in the south. At Forward Operating Base Joyce, near the Pakistani border, I presented six silver stars, testimony not only to the bravery of the recipients but to the intensity of the fight in eastern Afghanistan.

We helicoptered next to Forward Operating Base Connolly, southwest of Jalalabad, still in the east. This was probably the most emotional troop visit I made as secretary. The week before, six soldiers in one platoon at this FOB had been killed by a rogue Afghan policeman, and I met alone with eighteen soldiers of that platoon. We sat on folding chairs in a tent, and I quietly told them we would do everything humanly possible for the families of those who had been killed, that I had some idea how hard this was for them, and that they had to keep focused on the mission. We talked for about fifteen minutes. I thanked them for their service and signed memory books they had for each of the six. After some briefings, I then spoke to 275 soldiers. I was barely holding it together. I told them I was the guy who signed the orders that sent them here, "and so I feel a personal responsibility for each and every one of you." I said that to all the troops I talked to, but after my meeting with the platoon, I felt the need to go further. "I feel the sacrifice and hardship and losses more than you'll ever imagine. You doing what you do is what keeps me doing what I do." Choking up, I then said something I had never said before and, embarrassed, never said again: "I just want to thank you and tell you how much I love you."

I returned to Washington to yet another fight over Afghan policy. As I've said, the president had made it clear both publicly and privately that the December review was intended simply to examine progress and to identify where adjustments were needed. His intent was then for a small group, early in 2011, to examine the way forward more fundamentally. Unfortunately, the Lute-directed NSS paper prepared for the December review basically questioned whether any progress had been made at all, as he attempted to relitigate the president's decisions of a year earlier. Clinton and I were furious. Lute had told our representatives that the NSS "had the pen" for the report and resisted attempts by State and Defense to include dissenting views. I told Donilon the NSS might have the pen, but it couldn't have its own foreign policy. The analytical papers prepared by the interagency group were pretty balanced and included a number of positive developments in Afghanistan. But it was the NSS overview paper, which everyone outside the NSS thought was too negative, that would dominate the process. Some of the "adjustments" it proposed appeared to question the strategy itself rather than identify how to make it work better.

I regretted that the Defense leadership and Lute had come to have such an adversarial relationship. As I wrote earlier, Pete Pace and I had twisted Lute's arm to get him to take on the newly created job of NSC war czar at the White House in 2007, charged with coordinating the military and civilian components of the wars in Iraq and Afghanistan. Obama had asked him to remain in the same role. The relationship between him and the senior military leadership began to deteriorate, though, early in the new administration, as he was increasingly viewed as an advocate for views contrary to those of the Joint Chiefs, the field commanders, and me. His disparaging comments to Bob Woodward, for *Obama's Wars*, about senior military leaders and me didn't exactly win him friends in the Pentagon either. The longer he stayed at the White House, and the more senior officers and Defense civilians saw him as an adversary, the more difficult it became for him to return to a promising future in uniform. I got along personally with Doug, always believed he served both Bush and Obama loyally, and felt badly that his bridge back to the Pentagon burned.

The day after I returned from Afghanistan, Saturday, December 11, the principals met for two hours on the draft review. I accused the NSS of trying to "hijack" the policy with its overview paper, which, I said, was not balanced. In fact, it wasn't even consistent with the topic-specific papers prepared by the NSS itself, based on contributions from other departments and agencies. I argued that the NSS could not just override the views of Defense, State, and CIA. Rather, where there was disagreement on progress, I contended, it should be made explicit—"we shouldn't have to fight for a week to get our views included." I took issue with the NSS assertion that "the pace of the strategy is generally insufficient" and said that the paper fundamentally mischaracterized certain elements of Petraeus's strategy. Panetta disagreed with the NSS assessment of the al Qaeda effort, as did Hillary on the civilian component of the strategy.

The review did have one positive outcome. State had been requested to prepare a paper on corruption in Afghanistan, and I was told that Hillary had personally redrafted major elements. The analysis was the best I had ever seen on the topic. The paper said there were three levels of corruption that needed to be addressed: (1) corruption that was predatory on the people—for example, shakedowns by the national police and bribes for settlement of land disputes; (2) high-level, senior leadership corruption; and (3) "functional" corruption—common bribes and deal making. I said the paper set forth exactly the right way to look at the problem and that, given an overall and deeply ingrained culture of corruption that was highly unlikely to end anytime soon, we needed to focus on those aspects that mattered most to our success—low-level corruption that alienated the Afghan people and high-level corruption that undermined confidence in the entire government. Hillary and I both again raised the contradiction between (not to mention the hypocrisy of) U.S. payments to Afghan officials and our public stance on corruption. We ran into a stone wall named Panetta. The CIA had its own reasons not to change our approach.

On December 16, the president appeared in the White House press briefing room flanked by Biden, Clinton, Cartwright, and me. He began by paying tribute to Richard Holbrooke, who had tragically died three days before from a torn aorta. The president then went on to summarize the review, saying that the United States was "on track to achieve our goals" in Afghanistan and adding that "the momentum achieved by the Taliban in recent years has been arrested in much of the country, and reversed in some key areas, although these gains remain fragile and reversible." He reaffirmed that U.S. forces would begin withdrawing on schedule the next July. He added that al Qaeda was "hunkered down" and having a hard time recruiting, training, and plotting attacks, but that "it will take time to ultimately defeat al Qaeda, and it remains a ruthless and resilient enemy bent on attacking our country." The president and vice president decamped as soon as Obama finished reading his statement, leaving the other three of us to take questions. In response to a question as to whether the review "sugarcoated" the picture in Afghanistan, Clinton replied, "I don't think you will find any rosy scenario people in the leadership of this administration, starting with the president. This has been a very, very hard-nosed review." I was asked about the pace of the July drawdowns, and I said we didn't know at that point: "The hope is that as we progress, those drawdowns will be able to accelerate."

Yet again the contending forces within the administration, like medieval jousters, had armored up and clashed on Afghanistan. Yet again the president had mostly come down on Hillary's and my side. And yet again the process had been ugly and contentious, reaffirming that the split in Obama's team over Afghanistan, after two years in office, was still very real and very deep. The one saving grace, as strange as it might seem, was that this fundamental disagreement on Afghanistan never became personal at the most senior level; nor did it ever spill over into other issues, where the national security leadership continued to work together quite harmoniously. But a new source of contention was about to emerge early in 2011, and this time the internal battle lines would be drawn very differently. I would even find myself in agreement with the vice president, a rare occurrence in both the Bush and Obama administrations.

THE ARAB REVOLUTION

The history of revolutions is not a happy one. Most often repressive authoritarian governments are swept out, and power ends up in the hands not of moderate reformers but of better-organized and far more ruthless extremists—as in France in 1793 (the Reign of Terror), Russia in 1917 (the Bolsheviks), China in 1949 (Mao), Cuba in 1959 (Castro), and Iran in 1979 (Ayatollah Khomeini). In fact, it is hard to think of a major exception to this fate apart from the American Revolution, for which we can largely thank George Washington, who rejected a proffered crown, refused to march the army against Congress (however tempting on occasion that must have been for him), and voluntarily gave up command of the army and then the presidency. Revolutions and their outcomes are usually a surprise (especially to those overthrown) and damnably hard to predict. Experts can write about economic hardship, demographic problems such as a "youth bulge," pent-up rage, and "prerevolutionary" conditions, but repressive governments often manage such conditions for decades. Thus was the Obama administration—and everyone else in the world (including every Arab government)—surprised by the "Arab

Spring," a revolution that shifted the political tectonic plate of the Middle East.

Sometimes revolutions are triggered by singular and seemingly isolated events. This was the case in the Middle East, where, on December 17, 2010, in the small Tunisian town of Sidi Bouzid (overrun by German panzers in 1943 on their way to defeating American forces at the Kasserine Pass), a poor twenty-six-year-old street vendor named Mohammed Bouazizi set himself on fire after being harassed and humiliated by a police officer. He died three weeks later. His mother, according to a *Washington Post* reporter, said, "It was not poverty that made her son sacrifice himself. . . . It was his quest for dignity." In an earlier time, before cell phones, Facebook, and Twitter, what happened in the village usually stayed in the village. But not now. A cell phone video of a subsequent protest demonstration in Sidi Bouzid was posted online and went viral across Tunisia, sparking more and larger demonstrations against the regime of President Zine al-Abidine Ben Ali, a dictator in power for more than twenty years. The video was spread throughout the Middle East not only by the Internet but also by the Qatari-owned television network Al-Jazeera, which was equally detested by authoritarian governments in the region and by the administration of Bush 43. Less than a month later, on January 14, Ben Ali was ousted and fled to Saudi Arabia. According to news reports, more than sixty political parties were created within two months, but the best organized and largest by far was the Islamist Ennahda Party (which would win 41 percent of the vote in elections held ten months later to select a Constituent Assembly charged with drafting a constitution).

President Obama's first official statement on developments in Tunisia was on the day of Ben Ali's ouster, January 14, when he condemned the use of violence against peaceful demonstrators, urged all parties to avoid violence, and called upon the government to respect human rights and hold free and fair elections in the near future. He devoted one sentence to Tunisia in his State of the Union address on January 25, saying that the United States "stands with the people of Tunisia and supports the democratic aspirations of all people."

Young, Internet-savvy Egyptians read Facebook pages and blogs about developments in Tunisia and in the latter half of January began to organize their own demonstrations at Tahrir Square, a huge traffic circle in downtown Cairo, to protest the authoritarian regime of Hosni Mubarak, Egypt's president for nearly thirty years. The first large demonstration was on the same day as the State of the Union address, and the peaceful protests would grow daily as more and more Egyptians of all ages and backgrounds joined. The administration was divided on how to respond, with the NSS staff—perhaps sensitive to the criticism of some conservatives and human rights activists that Obama had been too slow and cautious in reacting to developments in Tunisia—urging strong support for the demonstrators in Tahrir Square.

On January 28, Mike Mullen called me at home to tell me the president had joined a principals' meeting that afternoon on the Middle East peace process and turned immediately to events in Egypt. Mike walked next door to my house and briefed me on the meeting. He said that the deputies, led by NSS members Denis McDonough, John Brennan, and Ben Rhodes, had proposed "very forward leaning" support of the protesters in Egypt and a change of leadership there. According to Mullen, Biden, Clinton, and Donilon had urged caution in light of the potential impact on the region and the consequences of abandoning Mubarak, an ally of thirty years. The president, Mike went on, was clearly leaning toward an aggressive posture and public statements.

Alarmed, I called Donilon and asked to see him first thing the next day, a Saturday. He said the president might call me that night. The president didn't call, and I met with Donilon at eight-thirty a.m. on the twenty-ninth. I reminded him that I had been sitting in the office he now occupied with Zbigniew Brzezinski when the shah of Iran was overthrown in 1979, and I spoke about the role the United States had played in that revolution. I expressed my great concern that we were entering uncharted waters and that the president couldn't erase the Egyptians' memory of our decades-long alliance with Mubarak with a few public statements. Our course, I said, should be to call for an orderly transition. We had to prevent any void in power because it likely would be filled by radical groups. I said we should be realistically modest "about what we know and about what we can do." Donilon reassured me that Biden, Hillary, he, and I were on the same page. All of us were very concerned that the president and the White House and NSS staffs were leaning hard on the need for regime change in Egypt. White House staffers worried about Obama being "on the wrong side of history." But how can anyone know which is the "right" or "wrong" side of history when nearly all revolutions, begun with hope and idealism, culminate in repression and bloodshed? After Mubarak, what?

The internal debate continued through the weekend. I missed a principals' meeting on Saturday afternoon because of a commitment in Texas, but former ambassador to Egypt and retired career diplomat Frank Wisner was dispatched to Egypt by the president on Sunday to meet with his old friend Mubarak and deliver a message from the president: start the transition of power "now."

That same morning I made the first of multiple calls to my counterpart in Egypt, the minister of defense, Field Marshal Mohamed Hussein Tantawi. I urged him to ensure that the army would exercise restraint in dealing with the protesters and to support political reforms that would protect the dignity of the Egyptian people. He was quite gracious and reassuring, saying that the Egyptian military's primary mission was to defend Egypt and secure critical facilities, "not to harm its people or shed blood in the streets." I told him we were concerned about the government's lack of decisive action to develop a political solution to the crisis and that, without moving toward a political transition—including "meaningful discussion" with key members of the opposition—Tantawi would likely be hard-pressed to maintain stability in Egypt. "Nothing bad will happen to Egypt, I assure you," he said.

The afternoon of February 1, the principals met again with the president, and there was a heated debate about whether he should call Mubarak and, if so, what he should say publicly about the call. We interrupted the meeting to watch Mubarak's televised speech to the Egyptian people. He said he would change the constitution, not run for president again (his term would expire in the fall), begin a dialogue with the opposition, and appoint a vice president—in short, he promised to do exactly what the administration had asked him to do through Wisner. Timing is everything, though, and I would often wonder whether, if Mubarak had made that speech two weeks earlier, the outcome for him might have been very different. What he promised was now too little, too late.

NSS staffers McDonough, Brennan, and Rhodes, and the vice president's national security adviser, Tony Blinken, all argued the president should call Mubarak and tell him he should leave office in the next few days. We needed, they said yet again, "to be on the right side of history."

Biden, Clinton, Mullen, Donilon, and I were in strong agreement, urging caution. We had to consider the impact of such a statement throughout the region. What would come next?

I asked what would happen if Mubarak didn't leave. The president would have scored a few public relations points that would, at the same time, have registered with every Arab friend and ally we had in the entire region, all of whom were authoritarian to one degree or another. Thirty years of American cooperation with the authoritarian government of Egypt, I said, could not be wiped out by a few days of rhetoric. Besides, people in the region didn't pay any attention to our—I wanted to say "your"—rhetoric anymore. If we humiliated Mubarak, I warned, it would send a message to every other ruler to shoot first and talk later. What if he did go? I asked. Who then? A military dictatorship? Would we have promoted a coup d'état? If you wanted to be on the right side of history, I argued, let Mubarak depart from office with some dignity, turning over power to elected civilians in "an orderly transition." That would send the message to others in the region that we wouldn't just "throw them to the wolves." I repeated, "We have to be modest about what we know and what we can do."

All the meeting participants finally agreed that the president should call Mubarak and congratulate him on the steps he had announced and urge his early departure. I argued that Obama should not use the word "now" in asking for a change but rather the more vague phrase "sooner rather than later." The suggestion was rejected. All of the senior members of the team recommended against the president going public with the call and what he said to Mubarak. The president overrode the unanimous advice of his senior-most national security advisers, siding with the junior staffers in terms of what he would tell Mubarak and in what he would say publicly. He telephoned Mubarak and, in a difficult conversation, told Mubarak that reform and change had to begin "now," with Press Secretary Robert Gibbs saying the next morning that " 'now' started yesterday."

The telephone lines between Washington and the Middle East were, by this time, burning up. The previous week there had been demonstrations in Oman, Yemen, Jordan, and Saudi Arabia. Biden, Clinton, and I were either calling or being called by our counterparts across the Middle East with regard to events in Egypt and in the region. On the second, I talked with Crown Prince Salman bin Hamad al-Khalifa of Bahrain and Crown Prince Mohammed bin Zayed of the UAE. The latter, whose insights and judgment I had always regarded highly, gave me an earful, saying that he was getting mixed messages from the United States, that the message from the vice president and me was not the same as what he was hearing from the White House or the media. He went on that "if the regime crashes, there is only one outcome, which is Egypt to become a Sunni version of Iran." He said that the U.S. stance reminded him of the days of Jimmy Carter during the fall of the shah, "and Obama's message needs to be tuned differently." He did not disagree that Mubarak had moved too late, but "we are here." We agreed to talk every few days.

With violence increasing in Cairo, I talked to Tantawi again that day, stressing the need for the transition "to be meaningful, peaceful, and to begin now," and for a wide spectrum of the opposition to be included. I expressed concern that if the transition process did not proceed quickly, the demonstrations would continue, food shortages and economic conditions would worsen, and the emotions of the Egyptian people would heighten—all of which could well lead to the situation spinning out of control. Tantawi said that pro-Mubarak demonstrators had gone to Tahrir Square to show support for Egypt's longtime leader and that there had been clashes between the pro- and anti-Mubarak forces. "We will make efforts to terminate them soon," he assured me, referring to the clashes (or so I hoped). I commended him for the military's handling of the protests "so far" and urged continued restraint.

I had lunch that day with White House chief of staff Bill Daley, who had been in the job less than a month. He was smart, tough-minded, open, honest, and funny. Over sandwiches, he told me that he had been doing a press roundtable and "pontificating" about Egypt when he thought to himself, *What the fuck do I know about Egypt?* Daley said he had had the same thought looking at Ben Rhodes at the NSC meeting the day before. I responded that I thought Ben believed in the power of Obama's rhetoric and the effectiveness of public communication but was oblivious to the dangers of a power vacuum and the risks inherent in premature elections where the only established and well-organized party was the Muslim Brotherhood. Moderate, secular reformers needed time and help to organize. I told Bill that all our allies in the Middle East were wondering if demonstrations or unrest in their capitals would prompt the United States to throw them under the bus as well.

Contrary to Tantawi's assurances, violence escalated that day, with pro-Mubarak thugs riding horses and camels into the crowds of demonstrators at Tahrir Square, lashing out with sticks and swords, creating a panic. The next day gunmen fired on the protesters, reportedly killing 10 and injuring more than 800. Our information, admittedly sketchy, suggested that these attacks were enabled, encouraged, and/or carried out by pro-Mubarak officers from the Ministry of the Interior. I called Tantawi again on the fourth. Courageously, I thought, he had gone on foot into Tahrir Square that morning to reassure the demonstrators that the army would protect them. He had been well received and so was very upbeat when I called him. He emphasized there had been no more violence. I asked about reports that Interior forces had lost discipline and attacked their fellow Egyptians. Tantawi rather carefully answered that "if the allegations were true, it is no longer an issue."

The demonstrations at Tahrir Square continued, intensified, and spread to other parts of Egypt over the next several days despite the efforts of the new vice president, Omar Suleiman, to negotiate with representatives of the opposition. Biden talked with Suleiman on February 8, urging him to move forward with the negotiations, to eliminate laws that had been used to maintain the authoritarian government, and to show that Mubarak had been sidelined. Biden later told me Suleiman had complained that it was hard to negotiate with the young people in Tahrir Square because they had no leaders. Mubarak again addressed the nation on February 10. Most Egyptians—and we—thought he was going to announce his resignation, but to the contrary, he said that while he would delegate some of his powers to Suleiman, he would remain as head of state. Afterward I thought to myself, *Stick a fork in him. He's done.* We were all alarmed as Egyptian anger and frustration boiled over. Donilon asked me to call Tantawi to see if we could find out what was going on. The hour was very late in Egypt, but Tantawi took my call. I said it was unclear to us whether Suleiman was acting as president. Tantawi said Suleiman would "execute all powers as acting president." I asked about Mubarak's status and whether he was still in Cairo. Tantawi told me that preparations were being made "for his departure from the palace, and there is the possibility he will leave for Sharm el-Sheikh." He reassured me yet again that the army would protect the people, and I again stressed that it was critical the government implement its commitments to reform.

At six o'clock the next night, February 11, Suleiman announced that

Mubarak had resigned and that the Supreme Council of the Egyptian Armed Forces would assume control. The next day the Supreme Council promised to hand over power to an elected civilian government and reaffirmed all international treaties—a subtle way to reassure Israel that the new government would adhere to Egypt's bilateral peace treaty. On the thirteenth, the council dissolved the parliament, suspended the constitution, and declared it would hold power for six months or until elections could be held, whichever came first.

Six weeks later, I arrived in Cairo to meet with Prime Minister Essam Sharaf, in office three weeks, and Tantawi. Both were, I thought, unrealistically upbeat. I asked Sharaf how they intended to give the many different groups vying for power the opportunity to organize and get experience so they could run credible campaigns. I added that a leading role for the Muslim Brotherhood would send shivers around the region and be a deterrent to foreign investment. Tantawi, who was in the meeting, answered, "We don't think the Muslim Brotherhood is that powerful, but they are one of two organized groups [Mubarak's National Democratic Party was the other], so people will need some time to be able to organize themselves as a party and share their positions."

The next day Tantawi told me that neither the Muslim Brotherhood nor others would have the upper hand: "The Egyptian people will have the upper hand in everything and we will encourage them." Again I asked whether the leaders of the revolution would have the time and space to organize themselves into competitive political parties for the elections. He replied, "We will give them *reasonable* time for political organization" but added that the longer the government waited to hold elections, the worse it would be for the economy. He told me that tourism, Egypt's main source of hard currency, had fallen since January by 75 percent. I told him the U.S. government thought they would be better off electing a president before electing a parliament as a way of providing secular leadership of the country, which, in turn, could help buy time for alternatives to the Muslim Brotherhood to emerge. Tantawi replied that they had been consulting constitutional experts, who told them to hold the parliamentary elections first. When I asked him about rogue elements of the Interior Ministry and extremists showing up to create problems, he was blandly reassuring: "There are no real problems." His confidence would not be borne out by subsequent events.

Crown Prince Mohammed bin-Zayed's concern about an Islamist

takeover in Egypt initially seemed to have been warranted. In elections that fall, the Muslim Brotherhood and the ultraconservative Islamist Salafist Party, respectively, won 47 percent and 25 percent of the seats in the new parliament—together, nearly three-quarters of the seats. After promising not to nominate a candidate for president, the Muslim Brotherhood reneged and ran Mohammed Morsi, who was elected in June 2012. Not long afterward he "retired" Tantawi, ostensibly taking control of the military. During the fall of 2012, Morsi declared that his decisions could not be reviewed by the courts, a move back toward authoritarianism, but the public outcry forced him to back off, at least partly and for the time being. The new constitution, drafted by an Islamist-dominated constituent assembly, established the role of Islamic (Sharia) law in principle, but the extent of its application was unclear.

As of summer 2013, Morsi has been ousted by the Egyptian army, the Muslim Brotherhood is under attack, and the military—which has led Egypt since 1952—is openly running the country again. Whether they will give genuine democratic reform another chance remains to be seen. While it is hard to believe the clock can be turned back to 2009, Egypt is likely to face difficult days ahead. As I warned, the best organized and most ruthless have the advantage in revolutions.

On February 15, 2011, four days after Mubarak resigned, a group of lawyers in the capital of Libya—Tripoli—demonstrated publicly against the jailing of a colleague. A growing number of other Libyans, perhaps emboldened by what they had seen happen in Tunisia and Egypt via Facebook and other social media, joined the protesters during the ensuing days. Muammar Qaddafi's security forces killed more than a dozen on February 17, and armed resistance to the government began the next day in Benghazi, in eastern Libya. Unlike the mostly nonviolent revolutions in Tunisia and Egypt, what began as a peaceful protest in Libya quickly turned into a widespread shooting war between the government and the rebels, and the casualties mounted. The rebels within days gained control of important areas in the east and launched attacks elsewhere across the country.

The ruthlessness with which Qaddafi responded to the rebels prompted a statement on February 22 by the UN Security Council condemning the use of force against civilians, and calling for an immediate end to the violence, and steps "to address the legitimate demands of the population." The council also urged Qaddafi to allow the safe passage of international humanitarian assistance to the people of Libya. That same day the League of Arab States suspended Libya's membership. On February 23, Obama repeated comments he had made the previous week, condemning the use of violence, and announced that he had asked his national security team for a full range of options to respond. He sent Secretary Clinton to Europe and the Middle East to consult with allies about the situation in Libya.

International pressure to stop Qaddafi's killing of Libyans and for him to step down mounted quickly. The Security Council acted again on February 26, demanding an end to the violence and imposing an arms embargo on the country and a travel ban and assets freeze on Qaddafi, his family, and other government officials. Politicians in Europe and Washington were talking about establishing a "no-fly zone" to keep Qaddafi from using his aircraft against the rebels, and they were becoming increasingly enthusiastic about getting rid of him. Another regime change.

The lineup inside the administration on how to respond to events in Libya was another shift of the political kaleidoscope, this time with Biden, Donilon, Daley, Mullen, McDonough, Brennan, and me urging caution about military involvement, and UN ambassador Susan Rice and NSS staffers Ben Rhodes and Samantha Power urging aggressive U.S. action to prevent an anticipated massacre of the rebels as Qaddafi fought to remain in power. Power was a Pulitzer Prize–winning author, an expert on genocide and repression, and a strong advocate of the "responsibility to protect," that is, the responsibility of civilized governments to intervene—militarily, if necessary—to prevent the large-scale killing of innocent civilians by their own repressive governments. In the final phase of the internal debate, Hillary threw her considerable clout behind Rice, Rhodes, and Power.

I believed that what was happening in Libya was not a vital national interest of the United States. I opposed the United States attacking a third Muslim country within a decade to bring about regime change, no matter how odious the regime. I worried about how overstretched and tired our military was, and the possibility of a protracted conflict in Libya. I reminded my colleagues that when you start a war, you never know how it will go. The advocates of military action expected a short, easy fight. How many times in history had that naïve assumption proven wrong? In meetings, I would ask, "Can I just finish the two wars we're already in before you go looking for new ones?"

I had four months left to serve, and I was running out of patience on multiple fronts, but most of all with people blithely talking about the use of military force as though it were some kind of video game. We were being asked by the White House to move naval assets into the Mediterranean to be prepared for any contingency in Libya. I was particularly concerned about moving an aircraft carrier out of the Persian Gulf area to accommodate this request. I ranted with unusual fervor during a meeting at Defense on February 28 with Mike Mullen and others. As usual, I was furious with the White House advisers and the NSS talking about military options with the president without Defense being involved: "The White House has no idea how many resources will be required. This administration has jumped to military options before it even knows what it wants to do. What in the hell is a 'humanitarian corridor'? A no-fly zone is of limited value and never prevented Saddam from slaughtering his people." I made the point that, to date, the focus of the opposition in Tunisia, Egypt, and Libya had been their own authoritarian, corrupt regimes. I expressed the worry that U.S. military intervention risked making us (and Israel) a target for those demonstrators.

"Don't give the White House staff and NSS too much information on the military options," I said. "They don't understand it, and 'experts' like Samantha Power will decide when we should move militarily." At the same time, I authorized moving significant Air Force assets in Germany to bases in Italy and several additional Navy ships into the Mediterranean. I was adamantly opposed to intervening in Libya, but if the president so ordered, it was my responsibility to make sure we were ready. I was blunt and stubborn, but I wasn't insubordinate.

On March 1, John McCain lambasted the Obama administration for its handling of events in the Middle East. On Libya, he said, "Of course we have to have a no-fly zone. We are spending over $500 billion, not counting Iraq and Afghanistan, on our nation's defense. Don't tell me we can't do a no-fly zone over Tripoli." Mike Mullen and I held a press conference the same day, and our comments underscored the distance between McCain's views and our own. My answers reflected my caution. When asked about U.S. military options in Libya, I replied that there was no unanimity in NATO for the use of armed force, that such an action would need to be considered very carefully, and "our job is to give the president options." To that end, I said I had ordered two ships into the Mediterranean, including the USS *Ponce* and the amphibious assault ship USS *Kearsarge,* to which I was sending 400 Marines. Asked about the potential follow-on effects of a no-fly zone, I said that all options beyond humanitarian assistance and evacuations were complex, and I repeated my other concerns. Mullen echoed testimony that same morning by Central Command commander General Jim Mattis that enforcing a no-fly zone would first require bombing radar and missile defenses in Libya. Mike and I both pointed out that we had seen no evidence that Qaddafi was using aircraft to fire on the rebels. When asked about the strategic implications of the events in Tunisia, Egypt, and Libya, I said these changes represented a huge setback for al Qaeda by giving the lie to its claim that the only way to get rid of authoritarian governments in the region was through extremist violence.

More than any other previous event, a hearing before the House Appropriations Defense Subcommittee (HAC-D) on March 2 confirmed for me that my decision to leave my post in June was the right one. I had simply run out of patience and discipline and a willingness to "play the game," as illustrated by two exchanges during that hearing. The first was in response to several members pressing me about why we wouldn't just declare a no-fly zone in Libya. I responded with uncharacteristic force and a borderline disrespectful tone: "There is a lot of, frankly, loose talk about some of these military options" in Libya. It's more than just signing a piece of paper, I said. "Let's call a spade a spade. A no-fly zone begins with an attack on Libya to destroy its air defenses. A no-fly zone begins with an act of war." I went on, "It's a big operation in a big country" and it's impossible to say how long it would take or how long it would have to be sustained. I said the U.S. military could do it if ordered by the president, but I warned it would require more planes than were found on a single aircraft carrier.

Several weeks earlier I had asked our four committees of jurisdiction in Congress for approval to transfer about $1.2 billion from several accounts in order to pay for significant additional ISR capabilities requested by Petraeus for Afghanistan. Three of the four committees had approved, but HAC-D, chaired by Bill Young, a Republican from Florida, had not. I learned that Young had blocked approval because the bulk of the transferred funding was to come from the Army's Humvee budget. (The Army neither wanted nor needed more of those vehicles.) Young had told me the problem would be worked out before the hearing, but it had not been. I couldn't understand his actions, so I entered the hearing room prepared to do something I had never done: publicly and directly criticize the chairman of one of my most important oversight committees.

At the end of my prepared statement on the budget, I noted that the reprogramming request for ISR had been submitted a month earlier. "Mr. Chairman, our troops need this force protection equipment and they need it now. . . . Every day that goes by without this equipment, the lives of our troops are at greater risk. I urgently want to get these items under contract so that I can get these important capabilities to Afghanistan." I said that cuts Congress was proposing to our FY2011 budget and uncertainty over another continuing resolution left us no source of money for the reprogramming other than the Humvee program. I concluded, "We should not put American lives at risk to protect specific programs or contractors." Young and the committee staff were infuriated by the public criticism. One staffer subsequently said, "Gates was pretty unprofessional at our hearing. . . . It is outrageous. I think it was unacceptable. He was out of line." Another called my comments "a cheap shot." Young said in an interview later that day that he had "no back-home interest in Humvee production." But *Washington Post* writer Dana Milbank wrote the next day that AM General—the manufacturer of the Humvee—"happens to be Young's third-largest campaign contributor. Its executives have funneled him more than $80,000."

I disliked going after Young like that. He was an old-school gentleman, was always gracious toward me, and had long been a strong supporter of the military and especially the troops; he and his wife often visited our wounded in the hospitals. But after more than four years as secretary, I was fed up with the usual forelock-tugging deference to special interests and pet projects among members of Congress, especially when they got in the way of providing urgently needed help to our commanders and troops. Within a couple of days, Young and I talked on the telephone, and then our staffs worked out a deal—the usual course of action in getting something done with Congress. In the end, $614 million of the $864 million I had requested was transferred from the Humvee program.

As the conflict inside Libya heated up, so did the internal debate inside the administration. The most immediate challenge was the exodus from Libya of tens of thousands of foreign workers of many nationalities—mostly Egyptian—to Tunisia because of the fighting. For a new and weak Tunisian government, 90,000 refugees posed a growing problem. The State Department wanted the U.S. military to establish an "air bridge" to fly these people to Egypt. The size of the undertaking was daunting and, to be effective, would require a number of U.S. aircraft that were already supporting two wars, as well as a lot of Americans on the ground in both Tunisia and Egypt to support the effort. Pointing out these challenges once again made Mullen and me the skunks at the garden party. At a principals' meeting on Libya the evening of March 2, Donilon told me the president wanted me to provide an air bridge from Tunisia to Egypt to move the Egyptian refugees. Biden then jumped in and said, "No, the president orders you to do the bridge." I'd had enough of Biden's "orders." "The last time I checked, neither of you are in the chain of command," I said. If the president wanted to deploy U.S. military assets, I made clear, I needed to hear it from him directly, not through the two of them. At the Pentagon, I went further, telling Mullen and Robert Rangel that no military options were to be provided to White House or NSS staff without my approval, "especially any options to take out Qaddafi." Ultimately, many nations were involved in sending aircraft to evacuate the refugees, including several from us.

Although Obama stated in a press conference on March 3 that Qaddafi "must go" and, as the days passed, the pressure to act militarily grew, it was clear that the president was not going to act alone or without international sanction. He wanted any military operations to be under NATO auspices. At a NATO defense ministers meeting on March 10 in Brussels, where the first subject we discussed was Libya, I told Secretary General Anders Rasmussen privately that we supported planning for a no-fly zone but would need a UN Security Council resolution and explicit regional participation: "This can't be seen as a bunch of Americans and Europeans intervening in a sovereign Arab state without sanction." I told him we needed to be able to answer such questions as: Why were we intervening in Libya and not in other civil wars? Was it because of oil? Rasmussen asked me if a no-fly zone would be effective. Keeping his planes down shouldn't be a problem, I said, but it was tough to keep helicopters down with a no-fly zone. Rasmussen shared with me his concern that Germany would not agree to any NATO action on Libya, mainly because it wanted the European Union to be in the lead. Admiral Jim Stavridis, supreme allied commander Europe, told me that a no-fly zone had to be limited to the coastal area of Libya, but that would cover 80 percent of the population. He said it would require a couple of days of bombing to destroy the air defense system and then, to sustain a no-fly zone, at least forty fighters, twenty tanker aircraft, and other support aircraft. (In the event, we needed a lot more.)

Most ministers were supportive of creating a no-fly zone. Still, they spoke about the importance of keeping Afghanistan as the first priority, the need for Arab League support and participation vis-à-vis Libya, and the need to be ready to act by moving planes and ships into position. As Rasmussen had predicted, Germany was not helpful and even opposed relocating some ships, though Stavridis could do that on his own authority. For all the talk, though, the allies were not yet prepared to act.

I flew from Brussels to Bahrain, the headquarters of the U.S. Fifth Fleet. Violence there had begun with a "Day of Rage" demonstration in the capital, Manama, on February 14, during which two were killed. Before the protest, the king (a Sunni) had offered economic concessions, but the Shia—70 percent of the population of Bahrain—wanted political reform. On the seventeenth, the government launched a crackdown at the Pearl Roundabout in Manama, a big traffic circle somewhat akin to Cairo's Tahrir Square. Six protesters were killed. I called the crown prince, Salman, who told me that Arab rulers in the Gulf saw Bahrain as a proxy in the struggle with Iran and that the lesson they took from events in Tunisia and Egypt was that those governments had erred by showing weakness. Salman nonetheless believed the royal family had to be the voice of moderation. He had met with the Shia al-Wifaq opposition leaders the night before the violence, and they demanded constitutional changes, removal of the prime minister, and political reform. Salman said he was ready to become prime minister if asked and that the road map forward must include Shia representatives in the government. Salman was, I thought, the voice of reason. Unfortunately, he was powerless.

I arrived in Manama late on March 11, aware that there had been widespread demonstrations and clashes between antigovernment Shia protesters and pro-government loyalists that day that reportedly had left hundreds injured. My visit had been intended as a show of support for the kingdom's royal family, but the message I delivered was hardly welcome. Separately, I told the crown prince and the king that as their strategic partner for more than sixty years, we were deeply concerned about Bahrain's stability. I told them that they needed to take credible steps toward genuine political reform and to empower moderate voices for change, if they were going to avoid being overtaken by events. I told them that "baby steps won't do." Mubarak had finally embraced change, I said, but he was two weeks too late: "Time is not on your side."

I told the king that developments in the Middle East had come because the regimes had failed to address the legitimate grievances of their people. Iran did not start the unrest but could exploit it. He needed to let the crown prince go forward with the national dialogue and be an example to the entire region, since there were hard-liners on both sides. I suggested to both the crown prince and king that they find a new and different role for the prime minister, who was disliked by nearly everyone but especially the Shia; lift constraints on the media as well as on civil society and human rights groups; announce the results of the investigation into the deaths of demonstrators in a timely and transparent way; move forward in integrating the Shia into the security services and Bahrain defense force; and promote basic civil rights in the social, media, and political arenas. Bahrain had a chance to show the region how to deal with public and political pressures and how to preserve stability, I said. "There can be no return to the status quo ante. You are a close ally, we are prepared to defend you against Iran, and we want to help you here as well. As you make difficult decisions to address the concerns and aspirations of your people, we will stand with you."

The crown prince and king both were positive in their responses to my suggestions, but the royal family was split, and the hard-liners had the edge. The Sunnis in Bahrain, and elsewhere in the Gulf, were watching apprehensively. The ineffectiveness of my diplomacy became apparent two days after I left Manama, when more than a thousand Saudi troops moved into Bahrain to ensure that the royal family and the Sunnis remained in control.

The same day I was in Bahrain, the Arab League voted to call upon the UN Security Council immediately to impose a no-fly zone in Libya and to protect the Libyan people and foreign nationals in Libya. It also asked for UN cooperation with the Libyan opposition's Transitional National Council, headquartered in Benghazi. On the plane home from

Bahrain, I told reporters that if we were directed to impose a no-fly zone, we had the resources to do it. But, I continued, "the question is whether it is a wise thing to do. And that's the discussion that's going on at a political level."

The situation in Libya forced everyone's hand. Qaddafi's forces began to have some military success and pushed east. By March 14, there was real danger they could soon move on Benghazi, and few doubted that the city's capture would lead to a bloodbath. The president convened the NSC on the afternoon of March 15. He was not happy with the options his advisers offered. He was particularly frustrated when Mullen described for him why a no-fly zone likely would have little effect on the movement of ground forces or in protecting innocent civilians. He told the NSS to come up with better options, and then he, Mullen, and I left for a meeting and dinner with the combatant commanders. Afterward he reconvened the NSC for another two hours. It was plain that to slow or stop Qaddafi's eastward military progress, a Security Council resolution would need to authorize not just a no-fly zone but also "all necessary means" to protect civilians. Qaddafi's bloodthirsty rhetoric about killing "the rats" in Benghazi, the action of the Arab League, and strong British and French pressure for NATO to act, I think, together persuaded the president that the United States would need to take the lead at the UN and in organizing the military campaign to stop Qaddafi.

On March 17, the principals met for an hour and a half, and then we met with the president. We rehashed all the arguments, and then the president went around the room one last time. Biden, Mullen, Donilon, Daley, Brennan, McDonough, and I opposed getting involved. Clinton, Rice, Power, and Rhodes argued we had to. The president said it was a close call, but we couldn't stand idly by in the face of a potential humanitarian disaster—he came down on the side of intervention. There would be no use of American ground forces, except for search and rescue if one of our pilots went down over Libya, or if Qaddafi made a move to use his chemical weapons. We would take the lead in destroying Qaddafi's air defenses but then scale back our involvement, primarily helping others to sustain the no-fly zone. The active participation of Arab air forces was essential, even if their numbers would be small. Rice was directed to pursue a tougher UN resolution that would provide for the protection of civilians, thus allowing us to bomb a broad range of Libyan military and command-and-control targets (the latter including Qaddafi's residences). In a private side conversation with me after the meeting, the president said the Libyan military operation had been a 51–49 call for him.

Rice worked a near-miracle at the UN in securing the tougher Security Council resolution. Russia, China, Germany, India, and Brazil abstained. The air campaign against Qaddafi began March 19. It was supposed to be a highly coordinated operation, but French president Sarkozy wanted a little extra publicity, so he sent his planes in several hours before the agreed start time.

The president would have been justified in thinking there was broad support in Congress for what he intended to do. On March 1, the Senate had unanimously passed a resolution calling on the UN Security Council to impose a no-fly zone and to protect civilians in Libya. There was vocal and bipartisan support on the House side as well. He gathered some of the congressional leaders in the Situation Room midday on March 18, and several others were piped into the room via speakerphone. Obama told them about the military role we would play and the limits he had set. There was no real disagreement. The president asserted that he had the authority to act in Libya under the War Powers Act without congressional approval but that he was complying with the provisions of the act in terms of notifying Congress.

When considering military intervention, presidents virtually never consider the cost—Obama included, when it came to Libya. I received estimates that the Libyan operation as we planned it would cost between $800 million and a billion dollars through September. Even the Defense Department didn't have that kind of cash lying around, especially since Congress was funding us under a yearlong continuing resolution at about $20 billion less than the president's proposed budget. The debate between us and OMB was whether to add the Libya cost to the FY2011 war supplemental, send Congress a separate supplemental request, or force us to find the money internally.

As is usual when the president makes a momentous decision, the White House wanted key cabinet members blanketing the Sunday talk shows. I avoided that onerous duty the first weekend because I left for Russia and the Middle East on the nineteenth. As I was flying back to Washington on March 25, the White House communications gurus proposed I go on all three network shows the next Sunday to defend the president's decisions on Libya. Exhausted from the trip, I agreed to do two of the three. Then I took a call from Bill Daley, who pushed me hard to do the third show. I told Daley I'd make him a deal—I would do the third show if he'd agree to get funding for the Libya operation included in the Overseas Contingency Operations (OCO) appropriation (the war supplemental). I said, "I'll do Jake Tapper if you'll do OMB." Daley whined, "I thought it would cost me a bottle of vodka." I shot back, "Bullshit. It's going to cost you $1 billion." Daley had the last laugh. The president and OMB director Jack Lew refused to approve moving the Libya funding into the OCO. The Defense Department had to eat the entire cost of the Libya operation.

President Obama's position on his authority to launch military action was rather different from candidate Obama's in 2008, when he had stated unequivocally that "the president does not have the power under the Constitution to unilaterally authorize a military attack in a situation that does not involve stopping an actual or imminent threat to the nation." In fact, there had been a vigorous debate within the administration over whether he had the authority—without congressional action—to sustain the intervention in Libya for more than sixty days, with the Justice Department and the general counsel of the Defense Department arguing that he did not. He chose to go with the opinion of the White House counsel and State Department legal adviser, that the engagement fell short of "hostilities" as defined in the War Powers Act and therefore the mission could be continued indefinitely without permission from Congress. A small minority of Republicans and Democrats on the Hill strongly objected to this assertion of presidential power, but there was never a serious challenge to the legality of the president's actions.

There was a challenge, however, to the limitations Obama had placed on the military mission. In a televised speech at the National Defense University on March 28, he explained why he had decided to intervene in Libya, offered justification for acting there and not in such conflicts elsewhere, and described the limited nature of the U.S. military mission. He made clear that we would transfer leadership of the military operation to NATO two days later and reduce the level of our involvement, and he explicitly stated that using the military to bring about Qaddafi's removal would be a mistake.

Mullen and I caught the full blast of congressional blowback on those limitations when we testified before the House and Senate Armed Services Committees on March 31. The ranking Republicans in both houses—McCain in the Senate and Buck McKeon in the House—asked why the military mission fell short of regime change. I replied that we had to differentiate between political goals and the military mission. The military mission authorized by the UN was to establish a no-fly zone and protect civilians, whereas the U.S. political goal was to get rid of Qaddafi. McCain was bitterly critical of the president's decision to turn over the military mission to NATO and reduce our support after the initial destruction of Qaddafi's air defenses, saying that would only make it harder to achieve our policy goals. We should, he said, do whatever was necessary to succeed in Libya, short of sending in ground troops. Senator John Cornyn of Texas said he wished the president had gone to Congress before he went to the UN; he added that the mission in Libya was unclear, that NATO wouldn't be able to finish the job on its own, and that there was no plan post-Qaddafi. When he asked me about the "ill-defined endgame," I responded that the last thing America needed was another enterprise in nation-building, other countries ought to take responsibility for Libya, and "I don't think we ought to take on another war."

At another point in the hearing, I acknowledged that I was preoccupied with "mission creep" in Libya and that, given our wars in Iraq and Afghanistan, I needed help from Congress to limit our role. The House committee was far more critical than the Senate of the president's failure to get congressional approval for the Libya action. Members also pressed me on the cost. I said we had nineteen ships and 18,000 troops committed to the operation, and the cost for the first eleven days was about $550 million, and probably $40 million a month going forward. I agreed with several members that "we should not overestimate our ability to influence" what would happen after Qaddafi fell. I acknowledged we knew little about the rebels, but "we know a lot about Qaddafi and that is reason enough to help them."

The hearings were awkward for me because many of the members were raising precisely the concerns I had raised during the internal administration debates. Asked if the situation in Libya involved our "vital national interests," I honestly said I did not think so—but our closest allies felt that it affected their vital interests and therefore we had an obligation to help them. When asked whether there would be U.S. forces on the ground in Libya, I impetuously and arrogantly answered, "Not as long as I'm in this job." The response was a further reflection of my diminishing discipline in testifying. I simply should have said that the president had been quite firm in prohibiting the use of American ground forces.

I later confided to my staff that I had considered resigning over the Libya issue. I told them I had decided not to leave because I was so close to the end of my tenure anyway; it would just look petulant. Frustrated, I said I had tried to raise all the issues for which the administration was being criticized—an open-ended conflict, an ill-defined mission, Qaddafi's fate, and what came after him—but the president "had not been interested in getting into any of that." I was, moreover, at the end of my tether with White House–NSS micromanagement. The same day the military campaign began, I started to get questions at a principals' meeting from Donilon and Daley about our targeting of Libyan ground forces. I angrily shot back, "You are the biggest micromanagers I have ever worked with. You can't use a screwdriver reaching from D.C. to Libya on our military operations. The president has given us his strategic direction. For God's sake, now let us [Defense] run it." My well of patience had gone dry.

All twenty-eight NATO allies voted to support the military mission in Libya, but just half provided some kind of contribution, and only eight actually provided aircraft for the strike mission. The United States ultimately had to provide the lion's share of reconnaissance capability and most of the midair refueling of planes; just three months into the campaign, we had to resupply even our strongest allies with precision-guided bombs and missiles—they had exhausted their meager supply. Toward the final stages, we had to reenter the fray with our own fighters and drones. All this was the result of years of underinvestment in defense by even our closest allies.

Libya's population of 6.4 million is made up of a mix of ethnic groups and indigenous Berber tribesmen. It has been occupied, dominated, or governed over the past 2,500 years by the Phoenicians, Greeks, Romans, Muslims, Ottomans, Italians, British, and French. Its three historical regions—Cyrenaica, the eastern coastal area; Tripolitania, the central and western coastal area centered on Tripoli; and Fezzan, the southwestern part of the country—were politically unified only in 1934, and the autonomy of the regions was reduced largely through Qaddafi's repression (although even at his strongest, he had to pay close attention to tribal politics). In short, Libya as a unified entity is a relatively recent phenomenon, created by foreigners. Problems abound there. Can a weak central government hold the country together in the face of long-standing centrifugal pressures? We shall see.

I believe we are in the early stages of what is likely to be a very long period of instability and change in the Arab world. Above all, we must stop pretending to ourselves that we can predict (or shape) the outcome. At a White House meeting at the end of March 2011, U.S. ambassador to Syria Robert Ford asserted that "Assad is no Qaddafi. There is little likelihood of mass atrocities. The Syrian regime will answer challenges aggressively but will try to minimize the use of lethal force." He would be proven horribly wrong.

Fundamental questions remain unanswered. Will free elections in the Arab countries inevitably lead to Islamist-dominated governments? Will those governments, in time, revert to authoritarianism? Will the military reverse the outcome of elections that bring Islamists to power (as in Algeria and Egypt)? The absence of democratic institutions, the rule of law, and civil society in virtually all Arab states—and the challenges facing secular reformers—do not provide much reason for optimism. Will freely elected governments be able to make the hard decisions necessary to bring economic growth and alleviate the grim existence of most Arabs? If not, will they turn to extreme nationalism, blame Israel and the United States, or ignite sectarian violence as a diversion from their domestic failures? Can states whose boundaries were artificially drawn by foreigners and that are composed of historically adversarial tribal, ethnic, and religious groups—above all, Iraq, Syria, and Libya—remain unified absent repression? Will the monarchies and emirates strive to preserve the internal status quo, undertake gradual but real reform, or face their own violent challenges to stability and survival? I believe the only way the United States will find itself "on the right side of history," as these revolutions and their aftermath unfold, is to continue to articulate our belief in political freedom and human rights, and to affirm that government exists to serve the people and not the other way around, as well as our belief in the superiority of a regulated market economy. Beyond that, we will have to deal with each country individually, taking into account its specific circumstances and our own strategic interests.

As I had told President Bush and Condi Rice early in 2007, the challenge of the early twenty-first century is that crises don't come and go—they all seem to come and stay.

CHAPTER 14

At War to the Last Day

I knew I wouldn't be able to coast through my last six months as secretary, but as I flew back to Washington, D.C., from Christmas vacation, I had no idea how hard it would be right up to the last days. The Arab revolutions beginning in January and our subsequent military operations against Libya were daunting enough. But there were still big internal fights coming over the next steps in both Iraq and Afghanistan; another budget battle looming; major issues with China, Russia, and the Middle East; getting the president's agreement on a new chairman of the Joint Chiefs; and, conducting a daring—and dangerous—raid into Pakistan. I had no choice but to sprint to the finish line.

CHINA, RUSSIA, AND THE MIDDLE EAST

When Chinese defense minister Liang invited me in October 2010 to return to China, as I said earlier, he explicitly asked me to make the trip before President Hu Jintao's state visit to the United States in late January. Liang's restrained behavior at that fall meeting of Asian defense ministers in Hanoi and in our bilateral discussions there indicated that the People's Liberation Army had been told to help set a positive atmosphere for Hu's trip. When I arrived in Beijing on January 9 (thirty years after my first visit), it was obvious the Chinese were pulling out all the stops to make my visit a success. From closed-off roads and highways to banquet sites, I was given head-of-state treatment. They had been stand-offish for three years because of our arms sales to Taiwan, but now they welcomed me warmly.

In every meeting, I emphasized the importance of strengthening the military-to-military relationship, including a strategic dialogue covering nuclear weapons, missile defense, space, and cyber affairs. An on-again, off-again relationship served no one's interests. Sustained and reliable ties insulated from political ups and downs were, I said, essential to reduce miscommunication, misunderstanding, and miscalculation. I also warned that North Korea's nuclear and missile programs had reached a point where the president had concluded they represented "a direct threat to the United States," and we would react accordingly if they did not stop. I said that after thirty years of patiently enduring North Korea's lethal provocations, public opinion in South Korea had changed with the sinking of their warship and shelling of their islands. They intended to react forcefully to such provocations in the future, and that raised the risk of escalating hostilities on the Korean peninsula. The Chinese should weigh in with North Korea to stand down. I also made clear our view that China's continued aggressive response to operations of U.S. aircraft and ships operating in international airspace and waters in the South China Sea could lead to an incident that neither country wanted. We were within our rights, and they should back off. Of course, I couched all I said in diplomatic terms full of sweetness and light (I could do that when the occasion demanded), but they understood what I was saying.

All my interlocutors supported strengthening the military-to-military relationship in principle but were hesitant about a sustained, formal, high-level diplomatic-military strategic dialogue, arguing that there were already multiple mechanisms for such discussions. Given the sensitive agenda I had proposed, I think the PLA leaders were reluctant to sign on to a dialogue that would include Chinese civilian officials from the party and the Foreign Ministry. (It reminded me of the Soviet general in the strategic arms talks in the early 1970s who complained to the U.S. delegation head that he should stop talking about the detailed capabilities of Soviet missiles and nuclear weapons because the civilians on the Soviet side weren't cleared for that information.) They didn't want to dampen the atmosphere of my visit, so they didn't reject the strategic dialogue idea; they just said they'd study it.

While each senior Chinese official was careful to frame his comments on other topics positively, they had some tough messages of their own. Liang said the military relationship had been "on again, off again" for thirty years. There had been "six ons and six offs." The offs were due to U.S. arms sales to Taiwan and to "harmful discriminating actions against China," such as our surveillance operations. On these two issues, he said, "there is no space for compromise or discretion when it comes to our core interests." We should make mutual respect, trust, reciprocity, and benefit the guiding principles of our military relationship, he said, and "mutual respect means accommodating our core interests." I got the point about core interests.

I went through all the familiar points about Taiwan. On surveillance, I told him we did it near many countries worldwide, including Russia, and that the Russians did it to us, and neither country considered these activities as hostile acts. I said the United States did not consider China an enemy or Cold War–style rival, but I warned that since August 2010, PLA aircraft had on several occasions come very close to our planes—I showed him a photograph of a PLA fighter closing to within thirty feet of one of our aircraft—which raised the risk of a serious incident. We then faced the press together, and Liang was exceptionally positive. He said we had reached consensus on a number of issues; the talks had been positive, constructive, and productive; and a healthy military relationship was in both our interests. He announced that the chief of the PLA general staff—Admiral Mullen's counterpart—would visit the United States that spring. I essentially said ditto.

The chosen "bad cop" for my visit was the foreign minister, who treated me to a long, condescending, and occasionally threatening diatribe that covered all the bases: Taiwan, surveillance, North Korea, U.S. naval deployments around Korea, and China's need to build up its military defenses. I responded in kind.

Vice President Xi Jinping (then President Hu's likely successor) responded to my concerns about North Korea with some candor by acknowledging that the situation had become a concern for both China and the United States and, further, that the recent escalation of tension and continued enrichment of uranium "had put the six-party talks in a grim and grave situation." Xi said China had made every effort to mediate and to keep the United States informed of those efforts. He added that a denuclearized and stable Korean peninsula was in everyone's interest.

He raised U.S. arms sales to Taiwan almost in a perfunctory way. He, like others, downplayed China's strength and economic success, saying that while China's economy was the second largest in the world, GDP per person was one-tenth that of the United States, and that the gap between rural and urban China was even bigger. Liang had commented that China's military was two to three decades behind "advanced" militaries—meaning the United States and our strongest NATO allies—and was "not a military threat to the world."

Despite President Hu's desire to have my visit be picture-perfect to pave the way for his state visit to Washington just a little over a week later, in a remarkable display of chutzpah, the PLA nearly wrecked both trips. Just hours before my meeting with Hu, the PLA rolled out for the first time publicly its new J-20 stealth fighter. Photos of the plane hit the Chinese press about two hours before my session with Hu. As one of my China policy experts insightfully expressed it, "This is about as big a 'fuck you' as you can get." There was some talk among my team about canceling the rest of the visit or part of it, or ignoring the insult. U.S. ambassador to China Jon Huntsman, seconded by my senior China policy expert, Michael Schiffer, came up with the best approach: as I had been embarrassed, I should turn the tables and embarrass the PLA.

I met with President Hu midafternoon on January 11 in the Great Hall of the People, in a reception room roughly the size of Grand Central Station. The two of us sat at the head of a horseshoe-shaped arrangement of overstuffed easy chairs in which we and our colleagues wallowed, a setting that required us both to use microphones. After Hu's opening pleasantries and recital of standard Chinese talking points, I noted to Hu that everyone had been focused on ensuring as positive an atmosphere as possible for his visit to Washington, but I had noticed in the Chinese media a few hours earlier reports of the rollout of the PLA's new stealth fighter. I told Hu the U.S. press was trying to figure out the significance of this test in the middle of my visit and just before his trip. I said I was worried that the U.S. press would present the test as a negative development in the relationship and asked the president of China to advise me on how to explain the test to them. Hu laughed nervously as he turned to his military aides and asked, Is this true? A furious discussion broke out on the Chinese side involving Liang, his deputy General Ma, and others. The Chinese civilians in the room had known nothing about the test. A Chinese admiral seated farthest from Hu passed word back up the line that it had been a "scientific research project." After several minutes of chatter on the Chinese side, Hu adamantly assured me that the rollout had been a "previously scheduled scientific test" having nothing at all to do with my visit—or his. I suspected the PLA would have given me a different explanation. That the PLA would pull such a politically portentous stunt without telling Hu in advance was worrying, to say the least.

Central Military Commission vice chairman General Xu (earlier my guest at Lincoln's cottage in Washington) hosted a dinner for me in the same guesthouse where Hu had hosted President Obama, with several of China's most famous singers as the entertainment. Baijiu, Chinese "white lightning," flowed as toasts were made. Both Xu's and Liang's wives were present, as was Becky, and decorum was largely maintained. Our entire crew visited the Great Wall the next day, the highway shut down by troops the entire distance for my motorcade. One of the traveling press bought a small backpack at a gift shop near the wall with Obama's picture on it dressed in a Mao jacket and wearing a PLA hat. I persuaded the journalist to sell it to me, and I presented it to the president upon my return. I told him it would validate what a lot of Republicans already thought about him. He laughed.

Hu's visit to the United States began a week later and went off without a hitch. But high-level cordiality and professions of cooperation cannot mask the reality that the U.S.-Chinese relationship faces serious challenges. China continues to invest a growing portion of its budget in new military capabilities and technologies—including highly accurate antiship cruise and ballistic missiles, diesel and nuclear submarines, antisatellite capabilities, and stealth fighters—designed to keep U.S. air and naval assets well east of the South China Sea and Taiwan. They are building a navy that, while far inferior to that of the United States globally, could be a serious problem for us in Northeast and Southeast Asia. Beijing learned from the Soviet experience, I believe, and has no intention of matching us ship for ship, tank for tank, missile for missile, and thereby draining China financially in a no-holds-barred arms race with the United States. They are investing selectively in capabilities that target our vulnerabilities, not our strengths. The Chinese are becoming increasingly aggressive in asserting territorial claims over much of the South China Sea and islands close to Japan. And they continue to challenge U.S. air and naval surveillance missions, even though we operate in international airspace and waters. Their cyber-attack capabilities are advanced and getting better, and they are targeting both our military and our civilian networks every day. All in all, this is a relationship that will require careful and skilled long-term management by leaders on both sides if we are to sustain our partnership in some areas (for example, economic) and keep competition in other areas from becoming adversarial. A robust American air and naval presence in the Pacific, especially in East Asia, will continue to be necessary to reassure our friends and allies but also to ensure peaceful resolution of disputes.

When I arrived in Russia for the last time as secretary a day after the bombing in Libya started, I began in St. Petersburg, capital city of the Russian Empire from its founding on the Baltic Sea by Emperor Peter the Great in 1703 until the Bolshevik revolution in 1917. First stop was the Russian Naval Museum, to give a lecture to about 200 middle-grade Russian naval officers. The atmosphere was barely more welcoming than for my speech at the Russian General Staff Academy in October 2007; no applause when I was introduced and tepid applause when I finished. This time, though, the questions were not confrontational but curious. What did we see as the greatest threat? Was I streamlining the U.S. Defense Department? What role would the Navy play in U.S. security? What about joint operations and joint combat training with Russia? How about Russian naval officers attending U.S. military institutions? What was the most significant event for me as secretary? I left the session somewhat heartened by the prospect for future U.S.-Russian military exchanges and cooperation.

I then motorcaded to the Peter and Paul Fortress, the original citadel of the city, where I had been invited to fire the "noon cannon," set off daily since the days of Peter the Great. Following the ceremony, I visited the Peter and Paul Cathedral on the grounds, burial place of most Russian tsars. As someone who had studied Russian history all my adult life, seeing these sights was a pleasure that had been denied me for decades because of the Cold War and my CIA career.

The next day, March 22, I flew to Moscow to meet with Defense Minister Serdyukov and President Medvedev. Putin was traveling. Libya was on everyone's mind, especially in light of an unusual public difference of opinion between Putin and Medvedev. The day before, Putin had told some factory workers in central Russia that the UN resolution on Libya "reminds me of a medieval call for a crusade." Medvedev had taken issue with that statement: "Under no circumstances is it acceptable to use expressions that essentially lead to a clash of civilizations—such as 'crusade' and so on." He also defended his decision not to veto the Security Council resolution.

The Russians later firmly believed they had been deceived on Libya. They had been persuaded to abstain at the UN on the grounds that the resolution provided for a humanitarian mission to prevent the slaughter of civilians. Yet as the list of bombing targets steadily grew, it became clear that very few targets were off-limits and that NATO was intent on getting rid of Qaddafi. Convinced they had been tricked, the Russians would subsequently block any such future resolutions, including against President Bashar al-Assad in Syria.

Both Serdyukov and Medvedev expressed concern about growing civilian casualties in Libya as a result of our air strikes. I urged them not to believe Qaddafi's claims about large-scale civilian deaths. We were taking every possible precaution to avoid such casualties and believed that very few Libyan civilians had been hurt or killed by our aircraft and missiles. I wanted the Russians to know that we believed Qaddafi was forcing civilians into buildings that were obvious targets and also that he was placing the bodies of people he had executed at the bombing sites. Medvedev said he was not happy to see NATO jets and missiles operating in Libya, but these actions were "the result of Qaddafi's irresponsible behavior" and his "blunders." He expressed concern that the conflict would go on indefinitely but was "not convinced things will calm down while Qaddafi is in power." Medvedev then repeated what he had told Vice President Biden in Moscow just two weeks earlier: "Land operations in Libya may have to be considered." He said Biden had told him that was impossible. Medvedev then worried aloud that "if Libya breaks up and al Qaeda takes root there, no one will benefit, including us, because the extremists will end up in the north Caucasus" part of Russia.

Missile defense was the other main subject of discussion during my visit. Medvedev had made new proposals for NATO-Russian cooperation in this area at the NATO summit in Lisbon the preceding November, and he had followed up with a letter to Obama. Serdyukov began our discussion by noting that Medvedev's letter had said it was "high time" for a breakthrough in this area. Among other things, Medvedev had proposed a "sectoral approach"—that is, Russian missile defense systems would protect Russia and "neighboring states," thus "minimizing the negative impact of the U.S. system on Russia's nuclear forces." There should be a legally binding agreement assuring that U.S.-NATO missile defenses would not weaken or undermine Russia's nuclear deterrent. I told Serdyukov we were interested in the proposals Medvedev made at Lisbon. Building on Serdyukov's suggestion for operational data exchanges, I proposed that we establish two missile defense data centers, one in Russia and one in western Europe, where both Russian and NATO officers would be assigned. The centers could do collaborative planning, establish rules of engagement for missile defense, develop preplanned responses to various missile threat scenarios, and carry out joint exercises focused on countering common missile threats.

I met with Medvedev that evening at his modernistic dacha outside Moscow. He insisted that Russia needed legal guarantees that missile defenses were not aimed at Russia. "Either we reach agreement or we increase our combat potential," he said. I repeated what I had told Serdyukov about the impossibility of getting a legal agreement ratified by the Senate and that the Baltic states would never accept Russian responsibility for their security. I knew that the Russians' concern over Obama's new missile defense approach was focused on the danger posed by future improvements to our SM-3 missile systems. I told Medvedev I understood their concerns. He and I both knew the early phases were of no concern to Russia, but as the United States continued to develop more advanced capabilities, "over time we can persuade you that nothing we have in mind will jeopardize Russia's nuclear or ballistic missile capabilities."

Medvedev said he was grateful that Obama was president, that "I can work with him, make deals, and respect each other when we disagree." He acknowledged that the Iranian threat was real. As we parted, he wished me "success in this part of your life and the next one. May they both be interesting."

My program in Russia concluded with a dinner cruise that evening on the Moscow River, hosted by Serdyukov. It was an elegant affair, reciprocating a similar cruise I had hosted for him on the Potomac the previous year. On my last night in Russia as secretary of defense, as we glided by the Kremlin, I thought about the remarkable path I had followed during the forty-three years since I began work as a junior Soviet analyst at CIA two days before the USSR invaded Czechoslovakia.

Had Putin allowed Medvedev to run for reelection as president in 2012, the prospects for the Russian people and for the U.S.-Russian relationship would be far brighter. I felt that Medvedev understood Russia's deep internal problems—economic, demographic, and political, as well as the absence of the rule of law, among others—and had realistic ideas about how to deal with them, including the need to more closely align Russia with the West and to attract foreign investment. However, Putin's lust for power led him to shoulder Medvedev aside and reclaim the presidency. I believe Putin is a man of Russia's past, haunted by lost empire, lost glory, and lost power. Putin potentially can serve as president until 2024. As long as he remains in that office, I believe Russia's internal problems will not be addressed. Russia's neighbors will continue to be subject to bullying from Moscow, and while the tensions and threats of the Cold War period will not return, opportunities for Russian cooperation with the United States and Europe will be limited. It's a pity. Russia is a great country too long burdened and held back by autocrats.

I flew from Moscow to Egypt, a visit described earlier, and then on March 24 to Israel. The day before, there had been a terrorist attack on a bus in Jerusalem, leaving one dead and thirty-nine injured. Rocket attacks on Israeli towns from Gaza were continuing, and a little over a week before my visit the Israelis had seized a ship carrying fifty tons of rockets and missiles to Gaza, including missiles from Iran. Political unrest across the Middle East had not interrupted the security threats to Israel.

I had not been to Israel since July 2009, although Defense Minister Ehud Barak visited me in Washington every two or three months. As I said earlier, we had developed a close relationship and were very candid with each other. After a formal welcoming ceremony at the ministry in Tel Aviv (seeing the Stars and Stripes and the Star of David flying together always moved me), we went to Barak's office to meet privately. I was there primarily to reassure the Israelis of American steadfastness in the midst of the political earthquake under way in the Middle East.

I opened the conversation by expressing condolences over the terrorist attack, to which Barak simply replied, "We will respond shortly to what happened."

For once, we had more than Iran to discuss. He was interested in my meetings in Egypt, and the bombing of Libya, which had begun just a few days before. He was, naturally, very concerned about developments in the region. He told me Egypt was losing its grip on the Sinai peninsula and hoped it was only temporary because of the potential for large-scale smuggling of weapons into Gaza. I told him that both Tantawi and the prime minister in Cairo had reaffirmed to me their commitment to the Egyptian peace treaty with Israel and said that they would continue to work with the Israeli government. Speaking as a friend, I said now was the time for Israel not to hunker down but to act boldly in the region—to move on the peace process with the Palestinians, to reconcile with Turkey, and to help Jordan. I added that the good news about the turmoil in the region was that it was not about Israel or the United States—"No one is burning U.S. or Israeli flags, yet"—but about internal problems in the Arab countries, and we needed to make sure that that remained the focus. Barak said the best approach on Libya would be to keep hitting the military until they turned on Qaddafi. He hoped the regional turmoil would spread to Iran, where he said the mullahs were celebrating Mubarak's fall and the increase in oil prices because of the broad unrest. We need to accelerate the sanctions, he continued, in order "to help this earthquake to reach Tehran."

Barak asked about Obama's view of events in the region, and I told him that while some in the United States thought the president wasn't tough enough in international affairs, I totally disagreed. Obama had sent 60,000 troops to Afghanistan and had now attacked Libya. He was aggressively pursuing al Qaeda. While he was willing to talk with adversaries such as Iran, I said, "when push comes to shove, he is willing to push back and protect the interests of the United States and our allies."

At a subsequent joint press conference, Barak said that the security relationship between Israel and the United States had never been stronger, and that cooperation between his ministry and the U.S. Department of Defense was unprecedented. On the unrest across the Middle East, he said that nothing like what was going on had been seen since the collapse of the Ottoman Empire, and it was a moving and inspiring phenomenon. He added, though, that "a pessimist in the Middle East is an optimist with experience."

The next morning we drove up the Israeli coast to Caesarea for a breakfast meeting with Prime Minister Netanyahu. Caesarea was built by King Herod the Great a few years before the birth of Christ, and I would have liked to explore some of the ruins, but business left no time for pleasure. There were about twenty people at the breakfast, so both Netanyahu and I stuck pretty close to our script, although the prime minister understandably took a very tough line on the need to respond forcefully to the recent terrorist attacks. We talked about the continuing problem of Iran and, of course, about Libya and the political unrest across the region. The Israelis clearly were nervous about events, seeing considerable potential for trouble and little opportunity for outcomes that were in Israel's interest. As I had with Barak, I urged Netanyahu not to go into a defensive crouch but to seize the moment with bold moves in the peace process. Bibi wasn't buying.

I ended my visit with an eighty-minute motorcade to Ramallah in the Palestinian West Bank to meet with Prime Minister Salam Fayyad. It was the first time a U.S. secretary of defense had made such a trip. As I left Israeli-controlled territory, the motorcade rolled into a large fenced area and then, inside that, a sizable enclosure with high concrete walls. Everybody but me had to transfer to Palestinian armored vehicles for the drive to Ramallah. I suppose I was allowed to continue on in my own vehicle as a courtesy. Even so, my security team was pretty edgy at this point. When I met with Fayyad, he complained that although Palestinian security had never been better—we had trained them—there had been an increase in Israeli military incursions. Further, he said, violence by Israeli settlers—including "outright terrorism"—had been on the rise, but the Israeli authorities had "done nothing to rein it in." I shared with Fayyad what I had told Netanyahu about using the regional turmoil to take bold steps for peace, adding that progress would require bold steps by the Palestinians as well. I thought my comments had about the same effect on Fayyad as they had on Netanyahu.

Less than two weeks later, I made my last visits to Saudi Arabia, Iraq, and the UAE. After a particularly productive conversation in 2010, King Abdullah of Saudi Arabia had asked me to stop by and see him whenever I was in the region, "even if only for an hour." I had done just that in early March, and now I was back again less than a month later. We met for nearly two hours at his palace in Riyadh, a huge white marble building. His office was about ten times the size of my Pentagon office and ornately decorated with dark wood and eight crystal chandeliers. In a meeting attended by many, we agreed that the bilateral military relationship was strong and affirmed that the $60 billion arms sale he and I had concluded was on track. The king said modernization of their eastern navy (in the Persian Gulf) was the next project.

Pleasantries done, the king excused virtually everyone else, and the two of us, and the Saudi ambassador to the United States, Adel Al-Jubeir, who interpreted, privately turned to Egypt and Iran. The king, in his late eighties, was not in good health physically—he still enjoyed smoking cigarettes—but was very sharp mentally. I walked into the meeting knowing that he was very upset with the United States for what he saw as our abandonment of Mubarak and our failure to fully support other longtime friends and allies, such as Bahrain, facing similar unrest. In fact, there had been loose talk by some senior Saudis about fundamentally altering the relationship with the United States and developing closer relations with other big powers such as China and Russia.

Reading from notes, Abdullah had a stark message for me and for the president:

- Our two countries have had a strategic relationship for seventy years. I value it and support all facets.
- The relationship is essential to the security of the world.
- America's reputation is at stake. Events in Egypt and in the early stages in Bahrain have affected America's reputation in the world.
- Some are comparing the treatment of Mubarak to the abandonment of the Shah.
- I believe this is wrong, but you have to manage the perception.
- You should look at how your friends view you.
- Individuals in both the U.S. and Saudi governments are saying things that cast doubt on the relationship. We must not allow them to succeed. The relationship has been tested and not broken by temporary events.
- Iran is the source of all problems and a danger that must be confronted.

He concluded by saying that his message was intended to be supportive.

While we favored democratic reform, I said, the United States had not been the cause of the uprisings in Tunisia, Egypt, Libya, or Bahrain. These were the protests of people who had been forced to live too long under autocratic governments. I said our only advice to the Egyptian government, and to the protesters, had been to avoid violence and to embrace peaceful reform. I had told the king of Bahrain that stability there required reform led by the royal family. And while Iran had not caused the protests, I said, it was exploiting them for its own purposes.

After a long discussion of the unrest, the king again said the Gulf region's leaders were bothered by the way the United States had turned its back on Mubarak and that, in light of talk of putting him on trial, the United States should protect him. I was noncommittal.

As we parted, Abdullah said he had "heard rumors I hope are not true—that you are leaving." I said that I was leaving in a few months, to which the king replied, "Make it a few years." I joked that President Obama insisted that I still looked healthy, but I had told him that was just on the outside. And then we parted company for the last time.

MILITARY SUCCESSION

One of the most significant responsibilities of the secretary of defense is recommending to the president officers to fill the highest positions in the military. It is a complicated business, involving not just picking the right person for each job but ensuring that the appointments are equitably distributed among the four services and dealing with the "daisy chain" of vacancies that cascade from each appointment. These senior personnel decisions usually are made months in advance because of the need to identify replacements and the uncertainty of every confirmation process.

As I said earlier, in July 2009, the president told me that he wanted to talk to Hoss Cartwright about succeeding Mike Mullen in 2011 as chairman of the Joint Chiefs of Staff. Obama, like Bush, had quickly come to admire Cartwright. The White House staff and the NSS also liked working with him. I let the chairman's succession issue simmer for nearly a year. However, by early summer 2010 time was growing short for me to act, inasmuch as I thought I would be leaving by the end of the year. I thought there was zero chance Obama would nominate Petraeus as chairman. The White House didn't trust him and was suspicious that he had political ambitions. An alternative candidate for chairman I had in mind was Army General Marty Dempsey, then leading the Army's Training and Doctrine Command. Previously he had commanded a division in Baghdad during the bloody first year of the Iraq occupation, led the training of Iraqi security forces, and had served superbly as the deputy commander and then acting commander at Centcom. I wanted very much to ensure that the next chairman or vice chairman had commanded in Iraq or Afghanistan. For my own job, my short list included Hillary, Colin Powell, Panetta, and New York mayor Michael Bloomberg.

Obama and I seriously discussed the succession issue in an hour-long private meeting on October 1, 2010. He began by asking yet again whether there was any chance of my staying on longer. I simply said, "Please don't." I asked him, once more, if Petraeus was not a possiblity as chairman. Obama replied that pulling Petraeus out of Afghanistan would be a problem, especially with drawdowns set to begin in July 2011. I told Obama that Cartwright was willing to stay on either as national security adviser or as chairman. A big fan of Cartwright's, I nevertheless felt obligated to share again with the president my concerns about Cartwright's relationships with the other chiefs and his propensity to hold information close. Cartwright had told me he would prefer the national security adviser's job as a new and different challenge. Obama said he needed "to talk to him," and he would do so on several occasions. At the end of the meeting, I again urged the president to think about Panetta as my successor.

The president was sold on Cartwright as the next chairman, and as so often, I was being difficult. I kept thinking about having assigned Dave McKiernan to a job that did not play to his strengths and worried about doing the same to Cartwright.

On April 4, 2011, the president told me I could still change my mind about leaving. During our meeting he said that Hillary had told him the previous day, "You're not leaning hard enough on Bob." I told him, "I'm spent. I'm just out of gas." I then recommended that he nominate Marty Dempsey as chairman. The previous fall, not knowing how the chairman's succession would play out, I had recommended that the president nominate Dempsey to be the new chief of staff of the Army, and he had done so. I proposed he nominate Panetta as my successor and Petraeus to take his place at CIA. (Petraeus had surprised me shortly before by expressing his interest in the CIA job.) I told Obama I thought he could wait until mid-May to announce the military choices, but that I wanted to go public with my firm departure date by the end of April.

Dempsey was sworn in as Army chief of staff on April 11. I called him to my office the next day to tell him I was recommending him to the president to be the next chairman of the Joint Chiefs. He was flabbergasted. I shared with him the challenges I believed he would face, particularly with the budget, and said that he would need to lead the chiefs as a team, maintain their cohesion, and help the new secretary manage the relationship between the senior military and the president.

On April 28, in the East Room of the White House (where Abigail Adams once hung the presidential laundry), the president announced that I would leave on June 30 and be replaced by Panetta. Panetta would be replaced at CIA by Petraeus, and Petraeus as commander in Afghanistan by Marine General John Allen. Eikenberry would be replaced as ambassador to Afghanistan by Ryan Crocker. We were all on the dais with the president, along with the vice president, Hillary, and Mullen. The president invited each of us involved in the changes to say a few words, and we were all quite disciplined. For my part, I thanked President Obama for "asking me to stay on—and on and on."

On Memorial Day, I stood with the president in the Rose Garden at the White House as he announced his intention to nominate Dempsey and Admiral Sandy Winnefeld as chairman and vice chairman of the Joint Chiefs, and Ray Odierno as chief of staff of the Army. Two weeks later I announced that I would recommend Admiral Jon Greenert as the next chief of naval operations. He would be my last personnel recommendation to the president.

When it was all done, I felt I had left the president with the strongest possible team of military leaders to face the daunting challenges ahead. It was a legacy that made me proud.

The Bin Laden Raid

During my first three and a half years as secretary of defense, the hunt for Osama bin Laden had been dormant as far as senior policy makers were concerned. While there was lip service to the priority of finding him, there were seemingly no new leads, and our focus in Afghanistan was on fighting the Taliban, not on finding Bin Laden. When Obama early in his presidency directed a more concentrated effort to get the world's most notorious terrorist, I thought it was an empty gesture without new intelligence information on his whereabouts. In the summer and early fall of 2010, I did not know that a small cell of analysts at CIA had acquired a lead on a courier thought to be in contact with Bin Laden. In the end, he would be found not through the $25 million reward or a new agent with firm evidence of his location, and certainly not through any help from the Pakistanis. Bin Laden was found through old-fashioned detective work and long, painstaking analysis by CIA experts. There would be a lot of heroes in the Bin Laden raid and even more people in Washington who would take credit for it, but without those extraordinary analysts at CIA, there would have been no raid.

The story of the raid by now has been told countless times. Here is my perspective. Sometime in December 2010, Panetta came to see me and privately informed me of his analysts' belief they had found Bin Laden's location. Leon would update me from time to time, and then in February 2011 he invited the commander of the Joint Special Operations Command, Vice Admiral Bill McRaven, to CIA headquarters to begin a collaborative effort to strike the suspect compound in Abbottabad, Pakistan. McRaven's special operators had been carrying out similar raids virtually every night for years inside Afghanistan to capture or kill Taliban commanders, and had the requisite skills and experience to carry out the strike successfully.

The president and his seniormost national security team met multiple times in March and April to debate whether to strike the compound. Joe Biden and I were the two primary skeptics, although everyone was asking tough questions. Biden's primary concern was the political consequences of failure. My highest priority was the war in Afghanistan, and so my greatest worry was that no matter what happened during the raid, as a result the Pakistanis might well shut down our vital supply line from Karachi to Afghanistan (carrying 50 percent of our fuel and 55 percent of our cargo), withdraw permission for us to overfly Pakistan, and take other steps that would have a dramatically negative impact on the war effort. A successful raid would be a humiliation of the worst kind for the Pakistani military. The Abbottabad compound was thirty-five miles from the Pakistani capital of Islamabad, six miles from a nuclear missile facility, and within a couple of miles of the Pakistan Military Academy (their West Point), the boot camps and training centers for two storied Pakistani regiments, a Pakistani intelligence office, and a police station.

I was also concerned that the case for Bin Laden being at the compound was entirely circumstantial. We did not have a single piece of hard evidence he was there. As we probed the analysts about how confident they were Bin Laden was in the Abbottabad house, the estimates ranged from 40 to 80 percent. As a former CIA analyst, I knew those numbers were based on nothing but gut instinct. As the president said at one point, "Look, it's a fifty-fifty proposition no matter how you look at it." From my vantage point, we were risking the war in Afghanistan on a crapshoot.

Our discussion of the raid was influenced by the arrest in late January of a CIA security officer named Raymond Davis in Lahore, Pakistan. His car was full of weapons, spy gear, and pictures of Pakistani military installations when he was stopped by two motorcyclists who pointed guns at him. Davis shot and killed both. He was arrested at the scene. By mid-March, a deal had been struck, payments were made to the families of the two men Davis had shot, and Davis was released. But white-hot public anger in Pakistan at the United States had not abated. Another such infringement on Pakistani sovereignty would almost certainly get very ugly. And we were thinking about a beaut.

There were three possibilities for a strike at Abbottabad—a special operations raid, bombs, and a limited, small-scale strike from a drone. The advantage of the last two options was that they posed the lowest risk of a Pakistani reaction. One big disadvantage was that we would not know if we had actually killed Bin Laden. The military planners initially proposed a massive air strike using thirty-two 2,000-pound bombs. Even though we persuaded them to scale that down, there was still a high likelihood of civilian casualties in the surrounding residential neighborhood. The drone attack was attractive because any damage could be confined to the compound, but it still would require a high degree of accuracy and, importantly, the drone had not been fully tested. The special operations raid, the riskiest option, also offered the greatest chance of knowing for sure we had gotten Bin Laden and offered an opportunity for gathering up all the intelligence about al Qaeda operations he might have with him. I had total confidence in the ability of the SEAL team to carry out the mission. My reservations lay elsewhere.

I laid out my concerns in detail at a meeting with the president on April 19. Succeed or fail, the raid would jeopardize an already fragile relationship with Pakistan and thus the fate of the war in Afghanistan. I said that while I had complete confidence in the raid plan, I was concerned that the case for Bin Laden's presence in the compound was purely circumstantial. "It is a compelling case," I said, "for what we want to do.

I worry that it is compelling *because* we want to do it." I worried that Pakistani Inter-Services Intelligence (ISI) was aware of where Bin Laden was and that there might be rings of security around the compound that we knew nothing about or, at minimum, that ISI might have more eyes on the compound than we could know.

The worst-case scenario was that the Pakistanis could get a number of troops to the compound quickly, prevent extraction of our team, and take them prisoner. When I asked Vice Admiral McRaven what he planned to do if the Pakistani military showed up during the operation, he said the team would just hunker down and wait for a "diplomatic extraction." They would wait inside the compound and not shoot any Pakistanis. I then asked what they would do if the Pakistanis breached the walls: "Do you shoot or surrender?" I said that after the Davis episode, and given the high level of anti-Americanism in Pakistan, negotiating the release of the team could take months or much longer, and meanwhile we'd have the spectacle of U.S. special operators in Pakistani custody and perhaps even show trials. Our team couldn't surrender, I said. If the Pakistani military showed up, our team needed to be prepared to do whatever was necessary to escape. After considerable discussion, there was broad agreement to this, and as a result, additional MH-47 helicopters and forces were assigned to the mission. McRaven later expressed his appreciation to me for raising the issue.

I expressed caution about the operation based on personal experience and the historical record. I recalled the Son Tay raid in 1970 to rescue some 500 American prisoners of war in North Vietnam; despite a well-executed mission, the intelligence was flawed, and no U.S. prisoners were at the camp. I had been executive assistant to CIA director Stansfield Turner in the spring of 1980 when the attempt was made to rescue the hostages at the American embassy in Tehran. Operation Eagle Claw, a failure in the desert that left eight American servicemen dead, was aborted because of helicopter problems and then became a disaster when a helicopter crashed into a C-130 refueling aircraft on the ground. I had gone to the White House with Turner the night of the mission, and it was a searing memory. I remembered a cross-border mission into Pakistan by U.S. forces in the fall of 2008 that was supposed to be a quick and clean in-and-out, but the team ended up in an hours-long firefight and barely made it back across the border into Afghanistan. The Pakistani reaction had been so hostile that we had not undertaken another such operation since. In each case, a great plan, even when well executed, had led to national embarrassment and, in the case of Eagle Claw, a crushing humiliation that took years for our military to overcome.

I believe Obama thought from early in his presidency that my long experience in the national security arena was an asset for him. Now I told him in front of the rest of the team that perhaps in this case my experience was doing him a disservice because it made me too cautious. He forcefully disagreed, saying my concerns were exactly what he needed to take into account as he weighed the decision.

No one thought we should ask the Pakistanis for help or permission. In every instance when we had provided a heads-up to the Pakistani military or intelligence services, the target was forewarned and fled, or the Pakistanis went after the target unilaterally, prematurely, and unsuccessfully. We all knew we needed to act pretty quickly, whatever we did; everyone was scared to death of a leak. There was considerable discussion about whether to wait and see if CIA could get more proof that Bin Laden was at the compound, but the experts told us that was highly unlikely.

Who should have overall authority for executing the raid was never in question. If it was carried out under Defense Department authority, the U.S. government could not deny our involvement; CIA, on the other hand, could. To preserve at least a fig leaf—granted, a very small leaf—of deniability, we all agreed that when the time came, the president would authorize Panetta to order the operation. Defense periodically would loan—"chop"—forces to CIA for operations, so this was a familiar practice.

The final meeting was on April 28. The plan, if approved, was to launch the raid two days later. Most of us, including the president, were scheduled to attend the White House Correspondents' Dinner that night, one of Washington's springtime rituals in which press, politicians, and officials all dress up and pretend to like one another for at least a few hours. Someone raised the question of how it would look if all of us rose from our tables and left at the same time because of something that had happened relating to the raid. The point was also made that yukking it up when our servicemen were risking their lives in a daring operation was not desirable. Hillary was forceful in saying there should be no change in the plan and those of us going to the dinner should do so. The president strongly agreed. (As it turned out, weather forced delay of the raid by a day, and we would all later get credit for our poker faces at the dinner.)

Finally, the president went around the table and asked each person for his or her recommendation. Biden was against the operation. Cartwright and I supported the drone option. Panetta was in favor of the raid. Everyone else acknowledged it was a close call but also supported the raid. The president said he would make a decision within twenty-four hours.

The next morning Undersecretaries Michèle Flournoy and Mike Vickers came to my office to try to persuade me to support the raid option. There were no two people whose judgment I trusted more, so I listened closely. After they left, I discussed the raid with Robert Rangel. I then shut the door to my office to think about everything the three of them had said. After a few minutes, I called Donilon and asked him to inform the president that I now supported the raid. The president had made the decision to go ahead an hour or so earlier.

Midday on Sunday we gathered in the Situation Room. We were all tense, bantering nervously. The stakes involved were enormous, and yet at this point, we all knew we were just spectators. For such a sensitive operation, it seemed to me there were a lot of people in the room. Panetta remained at CIA to monitor the action. Across the hall, in a small conference room, Air Force Brigadier General Marshall Webb was monitoring a video feed of the Abbottabad compound, and an Army sergeant was keeping a detailed log of audio reports he was hearing over headphones. Someone had told the president about the video feed, and he crossed the hall to the small room, grabbed a chair, and sat in a corner, just to Webb's right. As soon as the rest of us realized where he had gone, we joined him. Biden, Clinton, Denis McDonough, and I sat at the table, with Mullen, Donilon, Daley, John Brennan, Jim Clapper, and others standing around the edges.

When early in the raid a helicopter went down, I cringed as I remembered the attempted Iranian rescue mission thirty years before. At first, we feared disaster, but the pilot skillfully managed the crash-landing, and all the SEALs aboard were okay; the mission continued. We could track every move until the team entered the house, and then in the most critical moments of the raid, we could see and hear nothing. After an unimaginably long fifteen or so minutes, we heard the message "Geronimo—EKIA," enemy killed in action. McRaven had told us earlier that the only way Bin Laden would be taken alive was if he greeted the SEALs naked and with his hands up. Other than a shared sigh of relief, there was little reaction in the room. The SEAL team still had to get out of the compound and get back across the border to Afghanistan, which involved a helicopter-refueling stop in a dry streambed.

After nearly forty minutes, the SEALs were headed out of the compound, some escorting women and children beyond the walls for safety as others took time to plant explosives and blow up the downed helicopter. It was a huge blast, and we could be confident not many Pakistanis anywhere close were now still asleep. And then the team was on its way, one helicopter carrying the remains of Bin Laden, another carrying the forensic evidence that proved who he was—and what turned out to be a mound of intelligence. Even after the helicopters had returned safely, there was no celebration, no high-fives. There was just a deep feeling of satisfaction—and closure—that all the Americans who had been killed by al Qaeda on September 11, 2001, and in the years before, had finally been avenged. I was very proud to work for a president who had made one of the most courageous decisions I had ever witnessed in the White House.

As on nearly all such dramatic occasions, there was a light moment. When the SEALs got Bin Laden to the base in Jalalabad, McRaven wanted to measure his height as part of making sure we had the right man. When no one had a tape measure, he had a six-foot-tall SEAL lie down beside the body. The president would later quip that McRaven had no problem blowing up a $60 million helicopter but couldn't afford a tape measure. He would later present the admiral with one attached to a plaque.

Before we broke up and the president headed upstairs to tell the American people what had just happened, I reminded everyone that the techniques, tactics, and procedures the SEALs had used in the Bin Laden operation were used every night in Afghanistan and elsewhere in hunting down terrorists and other enemies. It was therefore essential that we agree not to release any operational details of the raid. That we killed him, I said, is all we needed to say. Everybody in that room agreed to keep mum on details. That commitment lasted about five hours. The initial leaks came from the White House and CIA. They just couldn't wait to brag and to claim credit. The facts were often wrong, including details in the first press briefing. Nonetheless the information just kept pouring out. I was outraged and, at one point, told Donilon, "Why doesn't everybody just shut the fuck up?" To no avail.

Soon after the raid was over, the White House released the now-famous photo of all of us watching the video in that small conference room. Within hours, I received from a friend a Photoshopped version with each of the principals shown dressed in superhero costumes: Obama was Superman; Biden, Spiderman; Hillary, Wonder Woman; and I, for some reason, was the Green Lantern. The spoof had an important substantive effect on me. We soon faced a great hue and cry demanding that we release photos of the dead Bin Laden, photos we had all seen. I quickly realized that while the Photoshop of us was amusing, others could Photoshop the pictures of Bin Laden in disrespectful ways certain to outrage Muslims everywhere and place Americans throughout the Middle East and our troops in Afghanistan at greater risk. Everyone agreed, and the president decided the photos would not be released. All the photos that had been circulating among the principals were gathered up and placed in CIA's custody. As of this writing, none has ever leaked.

The Pakistani reaction was bad, although not as bad as I had feared. There were public anger and demonstrations, but probably the biggest impact was the humiliation of the Pakistani military. The one respected institution in the country was considered by many Pakistanis to have been either complicit in the raid or incompetent. The fact that our team had penetrated 150 miles into Pakistan, carried out the raid in the middle of a military garrison town, and then escaped without the Pakistani military being the wiser was an awful black eye. Pakistani investigations of the raid focused far more on who in Pakistan had helped us than on how the world's most notorious terrorist had lived with impunity on their soil for five years. The supply lines to Afghanistan remained open.

Four days after the raid, I visited the SEAL team that had carried it out, and they gave me a detailed briefing. (It was my second meeting with many of them.) I congratulated them and said I had wanted to thank them in person for their extraordinary achievement. I told them that earlier in the day I had encountered the mother of one of the seventeen sailors who had been killed in the al Qaeda attack on the USS *Cole*. She had told me that if I met with the SEAL team, she wanted me to thank them for avenging her son. I did so. The SEALs shared with me their concerns about the leaks, particularly the fact that reporters were nosing around their communities trying to find them. They were worried about their families. I said we would do whatever was necessary to protect them—although I thought to myself that a reporter who approached one of these guys' families likely would find himself in the middle of his worst nightmare.

I shared with them my respect for the president's courage in making the decision to go forward with the mission. I reminded them that President Carter had perhaps gambled his presidency on such a mission in 1980, and it had failed. Obama had taken a significant risk, and thanks to those in that room, he had succeeded. I said I knew they had just returned from a deployment to Afghanistan a few months before the raid and would be heading out again in the summer. I thanked them and asked them to thank their families for me for "supporting you and your service." I concluded by saying that the SEALs in that room truly gave meaning to George Orwell's observation that "people sleep peaceably in their beds at night only because rough men stand ready to do violence on their behalf."

A final observation on the raid: its success was the result of decisions and investments made over the preceding thirty years. Lessons learned from the disaster in Iran in 1980 led to the creation of the Joint Special Operations Command and development of the training and equipment that undergirded the success at Abbottabad. In 1986, as deputy director in charge of analysis at CIA, I agreed to provide more than a dozen analysts to the new Counterterrorism Center in the clandestine service, an unprecedented and controversial assignment of analysts to help inform and plan counterterrorist operations. I had no idea then that we had laid the foundation for such a historic success by those analysts' successors twenty-five years later.

Cutting the Defense Budget: Math, Not Strategy

Halfway through FY2011, Congress as usual had not passed an appropriations bill—we were still operating on a continuing resolution (CR), which meant a budget of about $530 billion instead of the $548 billion the president had requested. As I wrote earlier, that year we would have six different continuing resolutions and finally a yearlong CR representing an $18 billion cut that we would have to absorb in the last few months of the fiscal year. The world's largest and most complex organization was being funded hand to mouth, living paycheck to paycheck. It was also apparent that Congress would not jump our budget from $530 billion in FY2011 to $553 billion in FY2012, as we were requesting.

On March 15, 2011, I gathered the senior military and civilian leadership of the department to begin planning for the dire prospects ahead. I described a stark future:

> I am of the view that the budget pressures we are facing are not because of a conscious political or policy decision to reduce our defense posture or withdraw from global obligations. I think it reflects a rather superficial view that the federal government is consuming too much of the taxpayer's money and that as part of the government, we share an obligation to reduce that burden. The debate that is taking place is largely free of consequences and certainly from any informed discussion of policy choices. As I have said before, this is more about math, not strategic policy decisions. . . . If the nation decides to cut defense spending, then that is a decision we will honor and carry out to the best of our ability. But we have an obligation to do everything we can to inform that decision with consequences, choices, and clarity on how any such cuts should be done to protect the nation's interests.

I added that I thought we would not be doing our job right if we obscured the consequences of big reductions by quietly making thousands of small cuts—"salami-slicing"—across the whole department. Significant choices and decisions needed to be made. We had to force the politicians, I said, to face up to the strategic military consequences of their budget math. For once, we had to abandon the military's traditional "can do" culture and make clear what we "can't do."

On April 12, I was summoned to Bill Daley's office for a meeting with him and OMB director Jack Lew. My budget people had learned from OMB that we were going to be hit with another major cut. Lew told me the president was going to make a speech on the budget and deficit reduction the next day and wanted to announce he would cut Defense by $400 billion over ten years. I was furious. I pointed my finger at Daley and said, "This White House's word means nothing!" I reminded them that my December 2009 agreement with Emanuel and Orszag had been thrown out, and now the new agreement I had reached with Lew and the president just four months earlier was being thrown out as well. I reminded Daley of his unfulfilled promise regarding funding for the Libyan operation. "You didn't get us a fucking dime," I told him.

Again, a decision with monumental consequences was being driven by a presidential speech of which I was given one day's advance notice. I told Daley and Lew this was math, not strategy. It would have a big impact on the morale of the forces and send a big strategic message abroad: "The United States is going home, cut a deal with Iran and China while you still can." The only way to cut that much, I continued, was to get rid of both people and equipment, at a time when we needed to refurbish worn-out equipment from two wars, replace aging Reagan-era ships and planes, and buy a new Air Force tanker. I proposed that the president should be vague in his speech. He should say something to the effect that Defense had cut nearly $400 billion in programs over the past two years and would be asked to do the same again over the next ten to twelve years. Have him ask us, I urged, to assess our strategy, mission, and force structure and make recommendations for his decisions based on that review.

That afternoon I met with the president. He described the desperate economic circumstances facing the country and said that, as he cut domestic spending, Medicare, and Medicaid (little or none of which he has done as of this writing), he couldn't leave out defense. He said that the Republicans would be okay with that, but not the Democrats. The best politics, he said, would be for him to lie back and stay out of the budget fight. There was no gain in it politically for him. (How many times over the years had I heard presidents, beginning with Richard Nixon, say they were doing the politically hard thing for the good of the country, when in reality it was obvious they were doing the politically easy thing?) I made the same argument to Obama that I had made to Daley and Lew: What did he want us to stop doing? I advised him to keep in mind that the enemy always gets a vote. Suppose, I said, once you make these cuts, "Iran forces you into a real war"? I spoke from the heart: "The way we will compensate for force cuts today in the next war is with blood—more American kids will die because of our decisions."

Obama told me that he was not asking Defense to match domestic cuts dollar for dollar, maybe one for ten. (Such a one-sided ratio was never in the cards.) Arguing further was pointless, so I shifted focus to how the defense budget would be cut. In the hours between my meetings with Lew and Daley and the president, my staff and I had drafted a paragraph for the president to use in the speech that I thought made his points but mine as well. There was some jockeying over the language, but given where he was headed on our budget, what he said the next day came out as well as I might have hoped:

> Just as we must find more savings in domestic programs, we must do the same in defense. Over the last two years, Secretary Gates has courageously taken on wasteful spending, saving $400 billion in current and future spending. I believe we can do that again. We need to not only eliminate waste and improve efficiency and effectiveness, but conduct a fundamental review of America's missions, capabilities, and our role in a changing world. I intend to work with Secretary Gates and the Joint Chiefs on this review, and I will make specific decisions about spending after it's complete.

As I walked out of the Oval Office, I thought to myself that I wouldn't be around to complete this review, but I had to make the fight on the cuts. With defense spending at 15 percent of all federal expenditures (it had been over 50 percent when Eisenhower made his speech about the military-industrial complex), the lowest percentage since before World War II, I was convinced the defense budget was a very modest part of the nation's fiscal problems. Political reality demanded that the military be cut, but at what cost to the troops and to our national security? Did those playing with the math ever consider that? Were they looking at what was going on in the rest of the world?

During my remaining weeks in office, I played both sides of the street. Internally, I organized the comprehensive review with a hoped-for completion by the end of summer. We structured the review to address four broad areas of possible reductions: more "efficiencies," a combination of further reductions in overhead costs but also cutting programs that were not critical to the future; reducing or cutting capabilities for highly specialized but lower-priority purposes where generic capabilities could be made to work, and also cutting specialized missions such as counternarcotics and building security capacity in developing countries; changes in the size and composition of our forces, which would be the most difficult internally—could we accept reductions in forces that would make fighting two simultaneous conflicts tougher? Should we reduce our ground forces?; and last, a bundle of possible changes in military compensation and benefits. While I told the department's senior leadership that I was not comfortable with a defense budget that would grow at only the rate of inflation for ten years, I went on to ask, "With every other agency of government on the chopping block, can we credibly argue that a $400 billion cut (or 7 percent) from the over $6 trillion presently planned for defense over the next decade is catastrophic and not doable?" I began including Panetta in meetings on these issues in early June, since he would lead the effort as of July 1. Happily, Leon and I saw eye to eye on the comprehensive review.

While fulfilling my responsibilities to the president inside the Pentagon, I used my last public speeches to warn Americans about the consequences of significant reductions in defense capabilities. In a commencement speech at Notre Dame on May 22, I said that we must not diminish our ability or our determination to deal with the threats and challenges on the horizon because ultimately they must be confronted. "If history—and religion—teach us anything," I warned, "it is that there will always be evil in the world, people bent on aggression, oppression, satisfying their greed for wealth and power and territory, or determined to impose an ideology based on the subjugation of others and the denial of liberty to men and women." I noted my strong support of "soft" power, of diplomacy and development, but reminded the audience that "the ultimate guarantee against the success of aggressors, dictators, and terrorists in the twenty-first century, as in the twentieth, is hard power—the size, strength, and global reach of the United States military."

Two days later I spoke at the American Enterprise Institute (AEI), a conservative think tank in Washington, where various scholars had been critical of the earlier program cuts I had made. Ironically, I was at AEI to warn against further cuts to defense. I told the audience I had spent the last two years trying to prepare our defense institutions for the inevitable decrease of the defense budget. When looking at our modernization programs, I said, "the proverbial 'low-hanging fruit'—those weapons and other programs considered most questionable—have not only been plucked, they have been stomped on and crushed." What remained was needed capabilities. Those programs, I warned, should be protected "unless our country's political leadership envisions a dramatically diminished global security role for the United States." I urged that across-the-board cuts—"the simplest and most politically expedient approach both inside the Pentagon and outside of it"—be avoided and that future spending decisions be based on hard choices focused on priorities, strategy, and risks. The worst outcome would be to cut the budget deeply while leaving the existing force structure in place, an approach I said would lead to the kind of "hollowed-out" military of the late 1970s: ill trained, ill equipped, and ill prepared. The Pentagon had to be honest with the president, Congress, and the American people that a smaller military would be able to go fewer places and do fewer things. "To shirk this discussion of risks and consequences—and the hard decisions that must follow," I asserted, "I would regard as managerial cowardice."

The comprehensive review would be completed under Panetta and Dempsey's leadership and provide a road map for further cuts. It would prove critically important because the Budget Control Act passed by Congress and signed by the president in August 2011 would reduce defense spending by $485 billion over the ensuing ten years and, through a "sequestration process," expose the military to an additional potential cut of nearly $600 billion. Math, not strategy, had prevailed after all.

As I suggested earlier, the global security environment is becoming more complex, more turbulent, and in some instances, more dangerous—and the military challenges more diverse. The military capabilities of our longtime allies are shrinking fast, and those of potential adversaries are growing. Yet our security needs and responsibilities remain global. Earlier significant cuts in defense spending following major conflicts, including after the Cold War, were made because the world scene had changed significantly for the better, at least in the short term. But in 2011, neither the state of the world nor the state of our military justified significantly less spending on defense.

The problem with the defense budget, as I saw it, is not its size but how it gets spent. It's not that we have too many planes, warships, submarines, tanks, and troops; rather, we load up every possible piece of equipment with every possible technology, and then they are so expensive, we can buy only a small number. Defense is not disciplined about eliminating programs that are in trouble, overdue, and over budget. The Pentagon spends far too much money on goods and services that make only a tangential (if any) contribution to military capabilities—overhead, or "tail." Congress requires the military services to keep excess bases and facilities and to buy equipment that is no longer needed or is obsolete. And the personnel costs of the all-volunteer force are skyrocketing: health care costs alone have risen in a decade from about $12 billion to nearly $60 billion.

My effort between 2009 and 2011 to cut or cap weak, failing, or unnecessary programs and to find "efficiencies" was all about spending the defense budget more wisely, to force more dollars into actual military capabilities. If the budget is slashed and the problems I just described are not addressed, disaster and tragedy lie ahead. And when the next war comes, as it surely will, our men and women in uniform will pay the price for managerial cowardice, political parochialism, and shortsightedness.

My Last Fights: Ending Two Wars

I had lost the argument on Libya. I had lost on the budget. I had had a tough but—I thought—successful run for four years. The last six months were turning out very differently.

As 2011 began, we were wrestling with continuing internal Iraqi disagreement on formation of a government, an increase in attacks on our embassy and other targets by powerful Iranian-provided improvised rocket-assisted munitions (IRAMs), and planning for the post-2011 U.S. presence in Iraq.

The IRAMs were not going to threaten the security gains that had been made, but they had the potential to cause a lot of American casualties, and they reflected increased targeting by Iranian-supported extremists of our troops and diplomats. The Iraqis were making little effort to stop the attacks. In January, I asked General Austin, our commander in Iraq since the preceding September, in a videoconference if he had the authority to go out and kill those firing the IRAMs. He said he was trying to get the Iraqis to do it but would use our troops if he had to. I responded, "If you get the opportunity to kill them, do it." I asked for a menu of possible actions we could take against the Iranians and their minions in Iraq. I was cautious about going to war with Iran over its nuclear program, but I wouldn't stand for Iranians killing our troops in Iraq.

The principal question surrounding Iraq that spring, however, was the size of the U.S. military and diplomatic presence after December 31, when—according to the agreement Bush 43 had concluded with

Maliki—all our troops had to be out of the country. Any continuing U.S. military presence would require a new agreement with the Iraqis. I met with Mike Mullen, Austin, our ambassador to Iraq, Jim Jeffrey, and others on January 31. Jeffrey and Austin said that Maliki wanted a U.S. troop presence after December but was doubtful he could get the Council of Representatives to approve a status of forces agreement (legal protections for our troops when stationed in foreign countries). In fact, all the key Iraqi leaders wanted a continuing U.S. military presence, Austin said, but as in 2008, no one wanted to take the political risk of saying so publicly or leading the political fight. Jeffrey said he was looking at a post-December State Department presence of about 20,000, many of them for security.

On February 2, in the middle of the Egypt crisis, the principals were to meet in the Situation Room to discuss all this. I believed that 40,000 Americans—20,000 civilians, 20,000 troops—would be a very hard sell, both in Washington and in Baghdad. Mullen said that Austin was trying to get the numbers down, but we were still looking at a three-to-five-year transition in Iraq. We agreed that if we stayed, we needed to keep our capabilities for intelligence, air defense, logistics, and counterterrorism.

At the principals' meeting later that day, I said "Whoa" when we quickly dived into the details. Basic questions had to be answered first, including whether we all agreed we wanted a U.S. military presence in Iraq after December 31? (I did.) To what extent did State's plans after December 31 depend upon a U.S. military presence? What if Congress wouldn't approve the money for State? As so often, I said, the NSS was already in the weeds micromanaging before basic questions had been addressed.

To a certain extent, as in the Afghan debate in the fall of 2009, I found myself in a different place from both the White House advisers and the military commanders. Recognizing the huge political roadblocks, I believed a substantial U.S. military presence was needed post-2011 to help keep Iraq stabilized, to continue training and supporting their security forces, and to signal our friends in the region—and Iran—that we weren't abandoning the field. Accordingly, I asked Austin to prepare force options below 20,000. He came back in mid-March with options for 15,000 troops (which would forgo any U.S. presence in southern Iraq) and 10,000 (which would severely limit the support we could provide for the embassy). The lower option would result in virtually no U.S. troops on the political fault line around Kirkuk between the central government and the Kurds, an area of continuing potential confrontations. Sustaining helicopter support both for our forces and especially for the embassy was vital since it was still too dangerous for civilians to move around Iraq in vehicles.

I made my fourteenth and last visit to Iraq in early April. I couldn't help but reflect on how far we had come in four and a half years—and on the cost of that progress. I flew into Baghdad from Saudi Arabia and helicoptered to the distinguished visitors' quarters. As we flew over the city, I marveled at how much had changed since December 2006. The security forces and police were all Iraqi now. There were traffic jams. The parks were filled with families. The markets were bustling. Life had returned to the city.

With each successive visit, my basketball-court-size bedroom had one or another new amenity, like hangers in the closet. The primitive plumbing, however, was the same. After showering the next morning, I looked in the mirror, and to my horror, my white hair had turned yellow. There had been something strange in the shower water, and now, with a full day of meetings and an interview with Katie Couric of *60 Minutes* ahead of me, I looked like someone had peed on my head. Iraq continued to surprise me in new and different ways until the very end.

Apart from wanting to thank the troops, the primary purpose of my trip was to tell the Iraqi leaders they had to make some decisions quickly about whether they wanted us to stay after the end of the year. I reviewed with Prime Minister Maliki the areas in which his forces were deficient: counterterrorism, intelligence, air defense, logistics, training, and capabilities for external defense. Noting that most Iraqi leaders had privately expressed their support for a post-2011 American presence, I asked if he would describe for me his strategy for building support in the Council of Representatives. At the end of our meeting, I warned him that if U.S. soldiers kept getting killed by extremist groups and he did not approve operations to capture or kill those responsible, I had directed General Austin to exercise our right to self-defense under the security agreement and to go after them unilaterally. I had the same messages for Sunni deputy prime minister Saleh al-Mutlaq and for President Talabani. "The clock is ticking," I said. "Time is short. You need to figure out whether you want some U.S. troops to remain after December. You can't wait until October or even this summer to figure it out." I also told Talabani that Iraq's leaders needed to reach private agreement to support one another on this issue in public.

In my meetings with junior enlisted troops, they asked me about numerous news reports on the latest budget crisis in Washington and rumors that the troops might not get paid. I told them, "Let me just say you will get paid. All smart governments throughout history always pay the guys with guns first."

By mid-April, the president asked Austin to explore the feasibility and risks of having 8,000 to 10,000 troops remain in Iraq. There was some grumbling in Defense over the low number; I thought we could make that work. But the thumb twiddling continued in both Baghdad and Washington, and in June, as I prepared to leave, the number of troops that might stay on as well as the size of our embassy post-December were totally up in the air.

I don't know how hard the Obama administration—or the president personally—pushed the Iraqis for an agreement that would have allowed a residual U.S. troop presence. In the end, the Iraqi leadership did not try to get an agreement through their parliament that would have made possible a continued U.S. military presence after December 31. Maliki was just too fearful of the political consequences. Most Iraqis wanted us gone. It was a regrettable turn of events for our future influence in Iraq and our strategic position in the region. And a win for Iran.

As you will recall, the president had put all of us on notice in the late fall of 2010 that, while he wanted a low-key and swift review of the Afghan strategy in December, he intended to return to the subject in the spring. He didn't wait that long. He gathered Biden, Clinton, Mullen, Donilon, Lute, and me (and other White House and NSS staff) in the Oval Office on January 20 to begin the strategy review. The key subjects were the troop drawdowns in July and determining what our presence should be in Afghanistan after 2014. Did we want bases? Would we continue to conduct counterterrorism operations? What is "Afghan good enough"? How big should the Afghan national security forces be? How much would they cost, and who would pay for them? Petraeus and the Defense Department were proposing an Afghan force level between 352,000 and 378,000. The president expressed his displeasure that those numbers had leaked, again making it look like the military was trying to "jam" him.

He wondered how our strategy for pursuing "reconciliation" with the Taliban might play out and fit with Karzai's and Pakistani general Kayani's view. Obama said we needed a political strategy to accommodate or work around Karzai and Kayani.

It was as if we had never stopped arguing since 2009. The vice president jumped in aggressively, saying the strategy in Afghanistan could never succeed, there was no government, corruption was rampant, and Pakistan was still providing sanctuaries. He proclaimed that neither Karzai nor Kayani wanted a big Afghan army. I countered.

The internal fight heated up again on March 1, when Biden convened a meeting at his residence to push for a dramatic troop drawdown. The residence is a big Victorian-era house on the grounds of the Naval Observatory, first occupied by Vice President Nelson Rockefeller in the mid-1970s. As always, Biden was warm in welcoming us, a cordial host. When we got down to business, he asked whether the strategy had succeeded enough so we could "think bigger about transition sooner." Could we meet our strategic goals with less "input" over the next two years? He argued again that no one wanted an Afghan army of 300,000 or more and that our commitment in Afghanistan was limiting our ability to deal with both Iran and North Korea. He contended that both public opinion and Congress were becoming more negative about the war. (In my view, virtually no effort had been made by the White House to change that attitude during the fifteen months since the president's decisions on the Afghan surge.)

The temperature of the Afghan debate rose further a few days later, provoked in no small part by a cable from the U.S. ambassador to NATO, Ivo Daalder, reporting that Petraeus had told a NATO meeting that the transition to Afghan security leadership would "commence" everywhere by the end of 2014, a statement that seemed to contradict the president's intention that the security transition be completed by then. When the president saw that cable, it looked to him like another case of military insubordination. As a result, the president opened an NSC meeting on March 3 with a blast: "I am troubled by people popping off in the press that 2011 doesn't mean anything. . . . My intention is to begin the security transition in July 2011 and complete it by the end of 2014. We will think through the glidepath [of troop drawdowns], but I will push back very hard if anyone proposes moving the drawdowns to the right [delaying them]. I prefer to move to the left [accelerating them]. I don't want any recommendations trying to finesse the orders I laid out." He concluded, "If I believe I am being gamed . . ." and left the sentence hanging there with the clear implication the consequences would be dire.

I was pretty upset myself. I thought implicitly accusing Petraeus (and perhaps Mullen and me) of gaming him in front of thirty people in the Situation Room was inappropriate, not to mention highly disrespectful of Petraeus. As I sat there, I thought: *The president doesn't trust his commander, can't stand Karzai, doesn't believe in his own strategy, and doesn't consider the war to be his. For him, it's all about getting out.* Biden continued to egg him on, and his staff missed no oppertunity to pass him inflammatory news clips and other information raising questions about Petraeus and the senior military leaders.

I called Donilon two days later to express my concern that the vice president was poisoning the well with the president with regard to Petraeus and Afghanistan. I said I thought Biden was subjecting Obama to Chinese water torture, every day saying, "the military can't be trusted," "the strategy can't work," "it's all failing," "the military is trying to game you, to screw you." I said we couldn't operate that way. I asked how the Daalder cable could be sent in to the president without someone checking its accuracy. I said, if he or the president had been concerned about the cable, why didn't they call me instead of posturing in front of thirty people "who will inevitably leak how the president imposed his will on the military" and about mistrust of the military in the White House?

My fuse was really getting short. It seemed like I was blowing up—in my own, quiet way—nearly every day, and no longer just in the privacy of my office with my staff. As we've seen, I had blown up at Donilon and the vice president at a meeting on Libya on March 2 and at House Defense Appropriations chair Bill Young on the third, had come close to openly arguing with the president in the NSC meeting that same day, and had gone off on Donilon again on the fifth. Partly, I think, I was just exhausted from the daily fights.

As the debate in Washington over the pace of troop drawdowns cranked up, I wanted to get a firsthand report on how the campaign was going. I also needed to talk with Karzai about the overall relationship and our post-2014 relationship. In addition, I wanted to reassure Afghans that the drawdowns beginning in July would be gradual, that there would still be many American troops fighting in the fall.

Tensions between the United States and Karzai were running particularly high when I arrived on March 7, following the deaths the preceding week of nine young Afghan boys in an American air strike. I had a long private meeting with him late that first afternoon. I apologized profusely for the deaths of the boys and, as I had so often before, described for him the extraordinary measures we were taking to avoid civilian casualties. With regard to the security transition, I told him I shared his concerns about foreign governments and organizations operating independently of the Afghan government, creating parallel structures. I also recognized the intrusiveness of ISAF troops and operations on the daily lives of Afghans. The solution, I said, was for the Afghans gradually to assume leadership for security. While NATO would provide recommendations on which places were ready to transition, I said, Karzai should have the final approval authority.

I said the Afghan security forces were critical for transition. The United States had budgeted $12.8 billion to train, equip, and sustain those forces for the coming year, but how, I asked him, could that be sustained long term? Maybe over time Afghanistan could maintain a small regular army plus a large national-guard-type organization. I told Karzai I believed a long-term U.S. presence in Afghanistan would be important for his country but also in the interest of regional stability. We did not want permanent bases, I made clear, but perhaps we could share some facilities with the Afghan security forces. He had spoken of a binding agreement between us, but I told him it had taken Congress five years just to ratify defense-technology-sharing agreements with the British and Australians. What we needed was a mutual commitment to an enduring U.S. presence.

Partnerships must be of mutual value to last, I said, raising the level of my intensity. He and I had been working together for more than four years, I said, and I had been his advocate and defender throughout. "I have listened to you" on civilian casualties, on more respect for Afghans, on respect for Afghan sovereignty, on private security contractors, and most recently, on the provincial reconstruction teams. "But my efforts are not helped when you blame us for all of Afghanistan's problems. We are your ally and partner. We protect your government, and we saved your life. Your criticisms are making a long-term relationship more difficult to sustain in the United States and elsewhere." Looking ahead, I said, we needed to work together on transition and the Kabul Bank. In February, Dexter Filkins had published a devastating exposé of the looting of the bank in *The New Yorker*. I told Karzai he could not ignore it or blame earlier audits or the United States or the international community. I told him that if he did not address the bank problem or continued to blame us, it would undermine efforts to agree on any strategic partnership. I said the bank issue provided "an opportunity for you to stand up for your people." Not for the first time, I warned him that he had people around him who exploited his worries and concerns, who tried to get him angry and upset at us, and who propounded all kinds of ridiculous conspiracy theories.

Karzai's responses in the meeting and then at dinner led me to wonder if he listened to anyone *but* the conspiracy-minded. He said he had heard that the United States wanted to weaken Afghanistan, to create many small states in its place. U.S. efforts to build the Afghan Local Police (ALP) and to work with local leaders could "be very destabilizing," he added. In the war on terror, he claimed, it was never clear whether the United States wanted Pakistan strong or weak. The Chinese view, he said, was that the United States wanted to strengthen Afghanistan against Pakistan and to use India against China. What is the "real" American agenda? he asked. He carried on at some length about the "radicalization" of the Pashtuns, wondering who was behind it. The Indians, he said, thought it might be the United States or the United Kingdom. To all this and more, knowing the futility—and risks—of challenging him in front of a roomful of people, I responded only that he "needed to get his relationship with the United States straight in the very near future."

Before and after the Karzai meeting, I met at length with Petraeus, Rodriguez, the operational commander, and others to pose questions I felt would be at the heart of the White House discussions in the coming weeks. I asked about their expectations for the spring and summer campaigns, whether the Pakistanis were actually making a difference, and how we might discourage our allies from pulling out of Afghanistan prematurely.

The day after the Karzai encounter was an emotional one. I flew to Camp Leatherneck in southern Afghanistan and visited the medevac unit there. Pilots, medics, and doctors described what they had been able to do with the additional assets we had provided them, the lives they had been able to save. Every day those crews put their lives on the line to save our troops; to say they are heroic doesn't do them justice. Talking with them fueled my gratitude for what had been accomplished but reignited my fury at those in the Pentagon who had fought the medevac initiative with such vigor.

I flew to Sangin in northern Helmand province, scene of some of the toughest fighting of the Afghan War. At Forward Operating Base Sabit Qadam, I met with Marines of the 3rd Battalion, 5th Marine Regiment. Twenty-nine Marines had been killed and 175 wounded in five months clearing Sangin, the heaviest losses of any battalion in the entire war. Accompanying me was my new senior military assistant, Marine Lieutenant General John Kelly. Kelly's son Robert had been one of those twenty-nine killed. Kelly met privately with the Marines of his son's platoon, who gave him a picture of Robert taken a few hours before he was killed and signed by all the Marines in the platoon.

The commanders in Sangin expected a resurgence of violence during the summer. I told the press, "The Taliban will try to take back much of what they have lost, and that in many respects will be the acid test." Rodriguez told reporters accompanying me, "We think they'll be returning this spring to a significantly different environment than when they left last year." I told the Marines at Sabit Qadam that they had written "in sweat and blood" a new chapter in the Marine Corps' roll of honor. I added, "Every day I monitor how you are doing. And every day you return to your base without a loss, I say a little prayer. I say a prayer on the other days as well."

During the worst of the battalion's fight in Sangin, when they were taking such significant casualties, some in the Pentagon had suggested the unit be pulled out of the line. Commanders in the field strongly recommended against it, and I had deferred to their judgment. I thought to myself at Sabat Qadam that pulling them out would possibly have been one of my worst mistakes as secretary of defense. These Marines had been hit hard, very hard. But despite their terrible losses, they were very proud they had succeeded where so many others had failed. And justifiably so.

My last troop visit on the trip was to Combat Outpost Kowall, just north of Kandahar. The area had long been a Taliban stronghold. I walked a few hundred yards to a nearby village to meet with the elders and take a look at the Afghan Local Police unit there. The ALP, mentioned previously, was an initiative pushed by Petraeus that recruited men from local villages and trained them as a local security force to keep the Taliban away. There were farm animals around and, more significantly, lots of children and women out and about, unique in my visits to rural Afghanistan. There were a number of troops lining the road about twenty-five yards apart, and again, for the first time in my experience, about half were Afghans. The village council greeted me, and I met with about twenty of the ALP. I was encouraged when told by the village council that the ALP had worked so well, other nearby villages were starting to participate.

After leaving Kowall, I told the press with me that I was very encouraged and felt that "the pieces were coming together." "The closer you get to the fight, the better it looks." I thought but didn't say that I only wished some of the skeptics working in the White House and the NSS would get a little closer to the fight and be a little less reliant on Washington-based intelligence assessments and press reports.

After the killing of Bin Laden, there was a frenzy of commentary about whether that success would allow us to get out of Afghanistan faster, and if not, why not. There were several Principals Committee meetings on issues relating to Afghanistan and Pakistan in April, but the decisive discussion about how many troops to withdraw and at what pace was not to occur until June.

I made my twelfth and final visit to Afghanistan in early June. Support for the war was steadily dropping at home. On May 26, House Democratic leader Nancy Pelosi had given a speech in which she said Americans had done our job to help the Afghans, and "it is time to come home." That posture wasn't new for her, but twenty-six Republicans joining most House Democrats in voting for an amendment calling for an exit strategy and accelerated withdrawal was. The measure failed by 215–204. One of my goals during this last trip was to make the case, through the press accompanying me, for a gradual drawdown of troops, so as to not jeopardize the troops' hard-won gains. I warned Karzai how fragile support for the war was in Washington and mentioned his "constant criticism."

The main purpose of the visit, though, was to say thanks and goodbye to the troops. I visited five different forward bases over two days, including spending the anniversary of D-Day, June 6, with units of the 4th Brigade of the 101st Airborne Division. I shook hands and had photos taken with some 2,500 soldiers and Marines. Choking back tears, at the end of each visit I said the same thing:

More than anybody except the president, I'm responsible for you being here. I'm the person who signed the deployment papers that got you here, and that weighs on me every day. I feel your hardship and your sacrifice and your burden, and that of your families, more than you can possibly know. You are, I believe, the best our country has to offer. My admiration and affection for you is limitless, and each of you will be in my thoughts and prayers every day for the rest of my life.

I participated in the first White House session on drawdowns by videoconference. It was very discouraging. Briefers talked about the weakness of the Afghan central government, the poor performance of the Karzai government, the dependence of the Afghan forces on ISAF, and the lack of progress on reconciliation. To my chagrin, both Panetta and Clapper said that another year or two of effort still would not lead to a satisfactory outcome. Petraeus was recommending that the final elements of the surge be withdrawn in December 2012. Biden said the president should withdraw 15,000 troops by the end of 2011 and the remaining 15,000 of the surge by April 2012 or July at the latest, before the next "fighting season."

I responded on the video screen by asking whether the strategy was to get out of Afghanistan at all costs or to achieve some level of success for the president and the country. I said the critics were too focused on Karzai and the central government, that the situation was far better than it had been a year earlier. The war was not open-ended, I said. The surge would end in 2012, and we faced a deadline of 2014.

Donilon was so concerned that Biden had convinced the president to withdraw the entire surge by April or July 2012 that he helped me get a private session with Obama a few days after my return from Afghanistan. I started with my bottom line: I recommended he announce a drawdown of 5,000 between July and December 2011 and the return of all surge troops by the end of summer 2012—late September. This would, I said, be consistent with his decision to surge for between eighteen and twenty-four months. I said the full surge had been in place only since late summer 2010—just nine months. I said the strategy was working and that you couldn't generalize across the entire country. A quarter of the Afghan population was under Afghan security, and our troops had a much more positive view of the Afghan army than did intelligence assessments. Kabul was now safer than Baghdad, and the Afghans had primary security responsibility there. Karzai was a challenge, I said, but we had a new start with Ryan Crocker as ambassador, and in any event, we had successfully managed around Karzai when necessary. The coalition was strong, our costs were declining sharply—from $40 billion in FY2012 to $25–$30 billion in FY2013. This most certainly was not an endless war. We needed to retain our confidence, act in a measured way. Afghanistan would be messy, just as Iraq still was, but the commanders in the field, many journalists, and NATO leaders believed we were achieving success. "The more time you spend in Afghanistan," I told the president, "the closer to the front you get, the more optimistic people are."

I then tackled Biden's proposal to withdraw all surge forces by April 2012. I reminded Obama that the vice president had never accepted the 2009 decision, had never thought about the consequences if his approach failed. I said if Obama were to announce the withdrawal of all 30,000 surge troops by April, he would signal to the Afghans, the Taliban, the Pakistanis, the allies, and the world that the United States had concluded it could not be successful and was pulling the plug nine months into the surge. I continued that if he opted for April or even July, the entire force would be focused on withdrawing, on choosing which areas to leave exposed, on defense, and on meeting the deadline. The surge effort would largely be over before the first soldier came out. I reminded him that the logistics were complicated and that we would be looking at pulling 40,000 to 50,000 troops out of Iraq by December, another 15,000 from Afghanistan by then as well, and another 15,000 by April. I said I thought the troops would feel betrayed by such a decision: "After all their losses, they are convinced they are winning and thus would consider their sacrifices in vain." Confidence and morale were high, I said, but a precipitous withdrawal of the surge troops would lead them to believe that their successes were neither understood nor appreciated. "I know you want to end this war," I told him, "but how you end it is of critical importance. To pull the entire surge out before the end of summer would be a tragic mistake."

Biden was relentless during those few days in pushing his view and in attacking the integrity of the senior military leadership. A White House insider told me he was telling the president, They'll screw you every time. Biden was said to be pushing Donilon really hard, accusing him of being "too fucking even-handed." I considered that a high compliment for a national security adviser. Tom continued to be deeply suspicious of the military, but he wanted to do what was in the best interests of the president and the country. His willingness and courage to challenge both Obama and Biden when he thought they were mistaken was a great service, including to them.

The president met with the team on June 17. I repeated most of what I had told him privately. Clinton argued forcefully that withdrawing the surge by April or July 2012 would signal we were abandoning Afghanistan. It would, she said, shock the Afghans, encourage the Taliban, and encourage ordinary Afghans to hedge their bets. We would have to cede control of some areas, and it would take all the pressure off the Taliban to seek a political solution. She recommended withdrawing 8,000 troops by December 2011, with the rest of the surge coming out by December 2012, the "pace and structure . . . linked to political negotiations." We had to leverage the drawdown, she said, to pressure both the Taliban and the Afghan government. At the end, the president said he wasn't sure we needed the surge for another fighting season, especially since we would still have nearly 70,000 troops there. He would ponder on it.

The decisive meeting was on June 21, nine days before I stepped down. The president walked into the Situation Room, sat down, and declared that he intended to withdraw 10,000 troops by the end of December and the remaining 20,000 of the surge by July 2012. "You're welcome to try to change my mind," he said. Petraeus and Mullen described the risks associated with that timetable. I said that a July completion of the surge withdrawal meant the surge troops would have no 2012 summer fighting season at all since the planning for their withdrawal would pull them out of the line in April and May. The vice president argued strongly for July—"though I prefer earlier"—because the fighting season would still be under way in September and therefore finishing the surge then would be illogical. (I didn't ask what that would make a July withdrawal.)

Hillary said with conviction that the entire State Department team preferred December but she could live with September because I had suggested it. (I knew Obama wouldn't agree to Petraeus's proposed December timeline; at least late September would get us through much of the fighting season.) Panetta said that CIA's analysts unanimously agreed the surge troops should stay until then. Leon then put on his experienced "Washington hand" hat and told Obama that "speaking politically," all of Defense, State, and CIA were recommending September or later. "Do you really want to go forward with July against all that?" The president then went around the room. Clinton, Mullen, Petraeus, Panetta, Donilon, McDonough, and I all supported the end of September. Biden, Blinken, Lute, Rhodes, and Brennan supported July or earlier. Not one person outside the White House favored a withdrawal by July or earlier.

The president decided to withdraw 10,000 troops by the end of December 2011 and the remainder of the surge by the end of summer 2012. He turned to me, Hillary, Mullen, and Petraeus and asked, "If I decide this, will you support it publicly?" All but Petraeus said yes. He said that he had a confirmation hearing for CIA director in two days and that he was certain he would be asked his professional military judgment about the decision. He intended to say that the scheduled withdrawal was "more aggressive" than he liked. The president said that was okay and in fact would be helpful. But he then asked Dave, Will you say it can succeed? How can you have confidence the plan will succeed if I decided December but not September? Dave got argumentative with Obama at that point, and I came within a whisker of telling him to shut up. He had gotten most of what he wanted, and I believed we had avoided a much worse outcome.

The next day the president announced his decisions. He spoke encouragingly of the progress of the war:

> Thanks to our extraordinary men and women in uniform, our civilian personnel, and our many coalition partners, we are meeting our goals. . . . We're starting this drawdown from a position of strength. . . . The goal that we seek is achievable and can be expressed simply: No safe haven from which Al Qaeda or its affiliates can launch attacks against our homeland or our allies. . . . Tonight we take comfort in knowing that the tide of war is receding. . . . And even as there will be dark days ahead in Afghanistan, the light of a secure peace can be seen in the distance. These long wars will come to a responsible end. . . . America, it is time to focus on nation-building here at home.

Eight days later I resigned as secretary of defense. My first fight as secretary had been over Iraq. My last was over Afghanistan. My entire tenure was framed by war. I had served longer than all but four of my predecessors and had been at war every single day. It was time to go home. My wars were finally over.

CHAPTER 15

Reflections

T hroughout my four and a half years as secretary of defense, I was treated by Presidents Bush and Obama with consistent generosity, trust, and confidence. They both gave me the opportunity and honor of a lifetime in serving as secretary. With only a few exceptions, members of Congress—both Republicans and Democrats—were respectful and gracious toward me, both privately and publicly. Overall, the press coverage of me and my actions was substantive, thoughtful, and by Washington standards, positive and even gentle. In both administrations, I liked—and enjoyed—nearly everyone I worked with at the White House, the National Security Council, other departments and agencies, and above all, the Department of Defense. Treated better for longer than almost anyone in a senior position I could remember during the eight presidencies in which I served, why did I feel I was constantly at war with everybody, as I have detailed in these pages? Why was I so often so angry? Why did I so dislike being back in government and in Washington?

It was because, despite everyone being "nice," getting anything of consequence done was so damnably difficult even in the midst of two wars. From the bureaucratic inertia and complexity of the Pentagon to internal conflicts within the executive branch, the partisan abyss in Congress on every issue from budgets to the wars, the single-minded parochial self-interest of so many individual members of Congress, and the magnetic pull exercised by the White House and the NSS, especially in the Obama administration, to bring everything under their control and micromanagement, all made every issue a source of conflict and stress—far more so than when I had been in government before, including as director of central intelligence. I was more than happy to fight these fights, especially on behalf of the troops and the success of their mission; at times, I relished the prospect. But over time, the broad dysfunction in Washington wore me down, especially as I tried to maintain a public posture of nonpartisan calm, reason, and conciliation.

I have described many of these conflicts in these pages. I have tried to be honest about where I think I fell short, and I have tried to be fair in describing the actions and motivations of others. I am confident some, if not many, will feel that I have further fallen short in both respects, especially to the degree I have been critical. So in concluding this very personal memoir, I want to rise above specific issues and reflect on the broader drama under two presidents in which I was a leading member of the cast.

THE WARS

I was brought in to help salvage the war in Iraq and, as it turned out, to do the same in Afghanistan—in short, I was asked to wage two wars, both of them going badly when I reported for duty. When I arrived in Washington, we had already been at war in Afghanistan longer than the United States had been in World War II, and at war in Iraq longer than our participation in the Korean War. Afghanistan would become the nation's longest foreign war, Iraq the second longest. By the end of 2006, America was sick of war. And so was Congress.

In an earlier time, people would speak of winning or losing wars. The nearly seventy years since World War II have demonstrated vividly that while wars can still be lost (Vietnam, nearly so in Iraq), "winning" has proved difficult (from Korea to the present). In December 2006, my goals in our wars were straightforward and I think relatively modest, but they still seemed nearly unattainable. As I believe I have already made clear, in Iraq, I hoped we could stabilize the country in such a way that when U.S. forces departed, the war there would not be viewed as a strategic defeat for the United States, or as a failure with global consequences; in Afghanistan, I sought only an Afghan government and army that were strong enough to prevent the Taliban from returning to power and al Qaeda from returning to use the country again as a launching pad for terror. These goals were more modest than President Bush's, especially since I thought establishing democratic rule and effective governance in both countries would take far more time than we had. I believe my minimalist goals were achieved in Iraq and remain within reach in Afghanistan as of this writing.

Had I been secretary of defense during the winter of 2002–3, I don't know whether I would have recommended that President Bush invade Iraq. Because I am widely characterized as being a "realist" in foreign policy—like my mentors Brent Scowcroft and Zbigniew Brzezinski, both of whom opposed the invasion—many people assume I opposed the war or somehow would have prevented the debacle that followed had I been in a position of influence. But it would be disingenuous to say with ten years' hindsight that I would have been opposed, especially since I publicly supported the decision at the time. With my CIA analyst's background, I might have questioned the intelligence reporting on weapons of mass destruction more aggressively. Perhaps I would have made the same arguments against attempting regime change and occupying Iraq that I made before the Gulf War in 1990–91. I certainly hope that, following the initially successful invasion, I would have been able to prevent or mitigate some of the disastrous decisions that followed. But this is all speculation on my part.

What *is* clear ten years later, though, are the huge costs of the Iraq War. It lasted eight years, more than 4,000 American lives were lost, 35,000 troops were wounded (the number of Iraqis in both categories many times that), and it easily cost over $1 trillion. The overthrow of Saddam and the chaos that followed in Iraq eliminated Iran's worst enemy and resulted in a significant strengthening of Tehran's position in the region—and within Iraq itself. I cannot honestly claim I would have foreseen any or all of that.

As I often said while in office, only time will tell whether the invasion of Iraq was worth its monumental cost. The historical verdict, I suspect, will depend on how Iraq evolves and whether the overthrow of Saddam comes to be accepted as the first crack in decades-long Arab authoritarianism that will eventually bring significantly greater freedom and stability to the entire Middle East. However the question is ultimately answered, the war will always be tainted by the harsh reality that the public premise for invasion—Iraqi possession of chemical and biological weapons as well as an active nuclear program—was wrong.

As much as President Bush detested the notion, our later challenges in Afghanistan, especially the return of the Taliban in force by the time I became defense secretary, were, I believe, significantly compounded by the invasion of Iraq. Resources and senior-level attention *were* diverted from Afghanistan. U.S. goals in Afghanistan—a properly sized, competent Afghan national army and police, a working democracy with at least a minimally effective central government—were embarrassingly ambitious (and historically naïve) when compared to the meager human and financial resources committed to the task, especially before 2009. We were not effective early on in building the Afghan security forces. The number of Afghan troops we envisioned initially was far too low. We allowed rotating commanders to change training plans and approaches midstream, and too often we tried to build the Afghan forces in our own image, not based on a more sustainable indigenous design. The training effort did not really take off and begin to yield success until 2008. We remained woefully ignorant about the relationships and history among key tribes, clans, villages and provinces, individuals, families, and power brokers.

President Obama simply wanted the "bad" war in Iraq to be ended and, once in office, the U.S. role in Afghanistan—the so-called good war—to be limited in scope and duration. His fundamental problem in Afghanistan was that his political and philosophical preferences (not surprisingly shared by his White House advisers) conflicted with his own pro-war public rhetoric (especially during the presidential campaign and even in papers prepared during his presidential transition), the nearly unanimous recommendations of his senior civilian and military advisers at State and Defense, and the realities on the ground in Afghanistan.

One positive result of the continuing fight over Afghan strategy in the Obama administration was that the debate and resulting presidential decisions led to a steady narrowing of our objectives—our ambitions—there. I had believed this necessary as early as my job interview with Bush in November 2006.

Obama's decision to dramatically increase the number of U.S. troops in Afghanistan in late 2009 was, as we have seen, based on a number of assumptions agreed upon by his top advisers: that the Pakistanis could be induced to change their hedging strategy, Karzai could be coached to become a more effective president, Afghan corruption could be reduced, and the Afghan central government's reputation among the people and its capabilities could be improved. The challenges to achieving those goals were fully debated leading up to the president's major troop escalation in the fall of 2009. Still, I think there was a good deal of wishful thinking in the Obama administration that we might see some improvements with enough dialogue (with Pakistan) and civilian assistance to the Afghan government and people. When real improvements in those nonmilitary areas failed to materialize, too many—especially in the White House and the NSS—concluded the president's entire strategy, including the military component, was a failure and were eager to reverse course.

On the other hand, I pushed hard for the troops requested by McChrystal because I became convinced that my own minimalist objectives could be achieved without significant improvements in those other, nonmilitary arenas. If our troops, combined with larger and more capable Afghan forces, could provide security for much of the population, then the other improvements could follow over time. If there was one useful lesson from Iraq, I thought, it was that security for much of the population could, indeed must, precede other progress. This was why I could not sign on to Biden's counterterrorism strategy: "whack-a-mole" hits on Taliban leaders were not a long-term strategy. By the same token, the blended counterterrorism-counterinsurgency strategy to provide security for population centers like Kandahar probably should have been implemented with a tighter focus geographically, paying less attention to sparsely populated areas, such as parts of Helmand.

Many argue today that the strategy shift and associated troop increase that Obama approved in late 2009 was a big mistake. I continue to believe it was the right decision. By 2008, the Taliban had regained the momentum in Afghanistan as the United States applied what was essentially a "counterterrorism-plus" strategy that allowed large swaths of the country (particularly in the south and east), including some key population and economic centers, to fall under Taliban domination if not outright control. Despite a near-doubling of the international troop presence in Afghanistan during the Bush administration after I became defense secretary, we were not winning. Our approach was a formula for stalemate, or worse.

The deployment of 21,000 more U.S. troops in February–March 2009 was in response to a request toward the end of the Bush administration from commanders and was intended to blunt the Taliban 2009 offensive and, secondarily, as I've said, to help provide some protection for the elections later that year. It was a request Bush was prepared to approve, but he held off at the request of the incoming Obama team. That force was not sized by the military to accomplish the strategy—the mission— Obama decided upon in February. In February and March, the president, I, and virtually all the senior leaders in Washington, including in the Pentagon, thought we were finished adding forces in Afghanistan. But McChrystal's summer assessment for the first time put a true military price tag on achieving the broad objectives Obama had decided upon.

What was clear by fall was that the alternative paths forward in Afghanistan were either a significant increase in forces or a dramatic scaling back of our presence and our mission, the alternatives I proposed to Obama in my October 2009 memo. Despite all the arguments I heard then and all the commentary I have read since, I have not seen critics of Obama's decision spell out precisely what would have been the consequences of standing pat in a losing posture, or the consequences of turning to a quite different strategy with a significantly smaller U.S. military presence. In the latter case, no one has spelled out how that approach would have been able to prevent a Taliban return to power throughout much, if not all, of Afghanistan and the reestablishment of al Qaeda there. The December 2009 decisions and related troop surge provided sufficient military forces to break the stalemate by rooting the Taliban out of their strongholds and keeping them out while training a much larger and more capable Afghan army.

Obama was much criticized by conservatives and hawkish commentators for announcing that the troop surge in Afghanistan would begin to be drawn down in July 2011, and that all U.S. combat troops would be withdrawn and all responsibility for security transferred to the Afghans by the end of 2014. Inside the military, there was also much grumbling about the numerical limits he placed on troops. I believe Obama was right in each of these decisions.

After eight years of war in Afghanistan, Congress, the American people, and the troops could not abide the idea of a conflict there stretching into the indefinite future. The "war of necessity" to punish and root out those responsible for 9/11 had become an albatross around the nation's neck, just as the war in Iraq had, and by 2009 public and congressional patience was nearly gone. By adopting Karzai's deadline of full transfer of security responsibility from foreign forces to Afghans by the end of 2014, the president made clear to Americans—and to our troops—that this was not an endless war. Just as I had bought more time for the surge in Iraq by foreshadowing troop withdrawals, with the deadlines Obama politically bought our military—and civilians—five more years to achieve our mission in Afghanistan.

The timelines also finally forced a narrowing of our objectives to those attainable in that time frame. I was convinced that we could dramatically weaken the Taliban and strengthen the Afghan army during that period—and if not, then we probably never could. The deadline put the Afghan government and security forces on notice that they had to step up their game, for their own survival if nothing else. To the argument that the 2014 deadline signaled to the Taliban how long they had to wait before taking over, I said at the time that they had at least five years of hard fighting ahead of them, including against advanced Western armies, and that every day the Taliban chose to "wait us out," they would grow weaker as the Afghan forces grew stronger.

In deciding to begin drawing down the surge in July 2011, the president transformed our commanders' estimate that they could transfer places they had seized from the Taliban to Afghan security within two years into a mandate. I had hoped that the drawdowns in the last six months of 2011 would have been smaller than the president decided. Still, overall U.S. troop strength in Afghanistan did not fall below pre-surge levels until September 2012, more than three years after the first Marine surge arrived in Helmand. The surge was sustained in Afghanistan twice as long as in Iraq.

Inside the Pentagon, the U.S. troop cap in Afghanistan of 101,000 was highly unpopular, viewed as a seemingly arbitrary political restriction on forces available to the field commander. It grated badly especially on the Army and Marine Corps. I think that Obama and his ever-suspicious staff welcomed the numbers approach—and a cap—because it gave them a mechanism to prevent the military from sneaking in more troops under the guise of "enablers."

For me, managing the troop cap was just one more challenge in trying to achieve military success in Afghanistan. Every week after the Afghan surge began, I met with the chairman and Joint Staff to ensure that we would not exceed the number of troops the president had approved. This accounting process became a huge chore, consuming countless man-hours, and commanders felt their hands were tied by a political decision on troop levels. I was convinced, however, that without these controls, the number of deployed troops would steadily inch upward, not as part of some military ruse to get more troops but because of the inexorable pressures from commanders as other assets were required. (I remembered vividly how Bush's surge went from 21,500 to 30,000.) Virtually every military commander in history has wanted more troops to enhance the prospect for victory—and to reduce his forces' casualties through overwhelming power (as happened in the Gulf War). Given this reality, and the level of mistrust of the military at the White House, including by Obama, I believe the cap was the only way to avoid having the president wake up one morning and discover there were 130,000 troops in Afghanistan rather than the 101,000 he had approved. Of course, this added to hard feelings in the Pentagon about Obama and the White House.

The outcome in Afghanistan remains to be determined. By most accounts, the training of the Afghan military is going well, and security responsibility is steadily being transferred to them. But how the endgame plays out after more than a decade of war will determine whether there is a good prospect of success in achieving our now-limited objectives, or whether the entire effort and all the sacrifice will have been for nothing. Contrary to popular belief, the Afghan government and army held together pretty well for nearly two years after the Soviets withdrew, but civil war began when Russian aid ended with the collapse of the Soviet Union. For us, the chance of success will be significantly enhanced with a modest continuing NATO military presence after 2014 for training, logistics, intelligence, air support, and counterterrorism—along with financial support for the Afghan security forces. If we signal early that we will support such a role, it will inform friends, foes, and those on the fence that we will not repeat our strategic mistake in the early 1990s of abandoning Afghanistan. We know all too well the consequences of that mistake.

THE CIVILIAN-MILITARY RELATIONSHIP

The relationship between senior military leaders and the civilian commander in chief—the president—is often a tense one. This was true of my experience under both Bush and Obama (as it has been true pretty much throughout American history). A major task of the secretary of defense is to help manage that relationship and to ensure that the president listens to professional military advice that he may not want to hear, and that the senior officers offer their best and most candid advice and obey loyally, especially when they are overruled.

In wartime, disagreement is inevitable because the president is ultimately accountable for success or failure and must sustain at least some level of public and congressional support. At the end of 2006, Bush overruled the field commander, the chairman and all the Joint Chiefs, and the Middle East and Central Asia regional (Centcom) commander in ordering the surge. He replaced the secretary of defense, the Centcom commander, and the field commander essentially at the same time. The war in Iraq was going badly, and he acted courageously and boldly to change course. Obama similarly acted courageously and boldly at the end of 2009 when he ordered the Afghan surge, the impetus for which came from the military. In so doing, Obama overruled the policy and domestic political concerns of his vice president and virtually all the senior White House staff. Then, contrary to the advice of his generals, he imposed timelines to avoid the impression (and potential reality) of endless war and to sustain political support in Congress and among the public. Both presidents were willing (at least on my watch) to replace commanders they thought were not succeeding.

During my tenure as secretary, Bush was willing to disagree with his senior military advisers on the wars, including the important divergence between the chiefs' concern to reduce stress on the force and the president's higher priority of success in Iraq. However, Bush never (at least to my knowledge) questioned their motives or mistrusted them personally. Obama was respectful of senior officers and always heard them out, but he often disagreed with them and was deeply suspicious of their actions and recommendations. Bush seemed to enjoy the company of the senior military; I think Obama considered time spent with generals and admirals an obligation.

While I was secretary, senior officers greatly added to the inherent tension with both Bush and Obama by all too frequent public statements that were seen by the two presidents as unnecessary and inappropriate, creating unwanted (and sometimes unnecessary) political problems at home, limiting options abroad, and narrowing the commander in chief's freedom of decision. Bush was repeatedly angered by public statements from Mullen (on Iraq and Afghanistan), Fallon (Iran), and others, as Obama was repeatedly critical of Mullen, Petraeus, McChrystal, and others. Congress demands that senior officers provide their "personal and professional military opinion" on issues when requested during testimony. Although sometimes what they said aggravated Bush and Obama, it was only rarely that I heard either criticize an officer testifying under those circumstances. It was when those opinions were offered to the press or in public speeches that the presidential blowtorch came out.

Generals and admirals speaking out and angering a president is nothing new. (George Patton and Douglas MacArthur come to mind.) I believe the country and public support for the military and its missions are well served by hearing firsthand from our senior military leaders. But I think the frequency and number of officers speaking out has been steadily increasing, and unwise decisions about content, timing, and specific forums have unnecessarily aggravated their always-delicate relationship with the president.

For some reason, more and more senior officers seem compelled to seek a high public profile and to speak out, often on politically sensitive issues or even on matters beyond their area of responsibility (not to mention expertise). Some in the military establishment appear to have embraced the notion that modern military leaders should also be "strategic communicators." This trend accelerated when Petraeus achieved superstar status during the Iraq War. The increasingly accepted theory is that "getting the message out"—in television profiles, op-eds, speaking tours, think-tank speeches—is part of the duties of high command. Interestingly, when Petraeus arrived to take command in Baghdad, he corrected a member of his staff who complained of a "strategic communications problem." No, we have a "results problem," Petraeus said, and when the violence in Iraq declined dramatically under his leadership, the strategic communications problem took care of itself.

Enabled by the ample availability of war funding, a strategic communications/public relations cottage industry cropped up around the Pentagon and the combatant commands, a bonanza for consultants who produced questionable results for those in the military paying for their services. The *Esquire* (Fallon) and *Rolling Stone* (McChrystal) episodes represented the most damaging end of the spectrum. On the other end of the spectrum, I never understood why top admirals and generals felt compelled to go on Facebook, to tweet and blog, usually about their daily schedule and activities, typically a mundane chronology of meetings, travel, and generic pronouncements. To me, that diminishes their aura of rank and authority. It is par for the course now for politicians, university administrators, and corporate executives. But I think the military is different, or at least should be.

When it comes to civil-military tensions, politicians and policy makers are equally culpable. Because the military is held in such high regard, political leaders and civilian appointees all too often succumb to the temptation to "put a uniform out there" to sell their decisions to the public, knowing that a military officer is far less likely to be criticized and questioned skeptically. Politicians, even in the White House, can't have it both ways.

I was quite comfortable in my relationships with senior officers. They were, individually and collectively, the finest, brightest, most selfless and dedicated people of great integrity with whom I have ever been privileged to work. I hope to count many among them as friends for the rest of my life (even after this book). As is obvious, I shared the view that too many talked too much publicly, and I cautioned some and personally reprimanded a few. Still, I felt that service chiefs and other senior generals and admirals were candid with me, willing to disagree and argue their case forcefully, and yet quite disciplined in falling into line once I made a decision. Based on everything I know, senior military leaders rarely tried to "end-run" me with the press or Congress.

The challenge for any secretary, especially in wartime, is to strike the right balance between building team spirit and maintaining an open, close working relationship with the senior military while not getting too "buddy-buddy." He must instill a culture of accountability. An effective secretary is not a congenial chairman of the board but rather a demanding, tough chief executive whose daily life is often filled with life-and-death decisions.

I always treated senior officers respectfully. I had ways of making my displeasure known—usually a deepening silence and grim expression— but I never shouted. I never belittled. I never intentionally embarrassed anyone. I always listened and often adjusted my opinions and decisions in response to the advice and counsel of senior officers. I valued the opinions and experience of the chiefs and the combatant commanders. Both Pete Pace and Mike Mullen were true partners in that I don't think I ever made a consequential decision without consulting them first. But

I fired enough senior officers that everyone in the Defense Department knew there was a line not to be crossed.

I saw firsthand the age-old reality that the qualities important for military leadership and success in war are not the same as those required in peacetime. In war, boldness, adaptability, creativity, sometimes ignoring the rules, risk taking, and ruthlessness are essential for success. These are not characteristics that will get an officer very far in peacetime. Over the ten years of the Iraq and Afghan wars, too many officers were assigned to command positions because the stateside personnel system identified them as "next in line" rather than because they were selected as best qualified for the combat mission. And too many talented officers who achieved real battlefield success were rotated out of command in Iraq and Afghanistan too soon simply to keep the personnel system running smoothly. When we are in a fight, field commanders and the combatant commanders should be given the authority to relieve underperformers or keep good officers in command. In wartime, I believe the routine peacetime officer-assignment process should be set aside and senior field commanders should be empowered to choose their subordinate commanders. The failure to do this was, in my view, consistent with the peacetime mentality that pervaded the entire Defense Department, business-as-usual the order of the day among senior civilians and even among most generals and admirals, even as the troops were fighting and dying. I should not have allowed it.

Running the Defense Department

The Department of Defense is the largest, most complex organization on the planet: three million people, civilian and military, with a budget, the last year I was there, of over $700 billion. Nearly everyone there is a career professional, with considerable job security. Every major part of the organization—budget, acquisition programs, and policy—has a constituency both inside and outside the Pentagon. Local and state officials, members of Congress, lobbyists, industry, retired senior officers—everyone has an oar in the water, many of them pulling in different directions. So how does a secretary gain control, then establish and implement an agenda for change?

Above all, if a secretary actually intends to run the Pentagon—and make real changes—as opposed to presiding over it, he must be selective in identifying his agenda, and both realistic and single-minded in developing strategies for achieving each specific goal. Exhortations to be more efficient or to achieve some broad goal are akin to shouting down a well. Very specific objectives, with tight deadlines and regular in-person reports to the secretary himself, provide the only way to get people focused and to ensure they are performing. The organization must understand that the secretary is personally invested in these issues and determined to drive the process to specific outcomes. This was what I did during the first two years with regard to MRAPs, ISR, medevac, wounded warrior care, and other changes to help those fighting the wars in Iraq and Afghanistan. As noted repeatedly, I also held regular videoconferences with our commanders in Baghdad and Kabul to closely monitor progress in the two wars, to ensure that their needs were being met by the Pentagon, and to keep them informed about the Washington battlespace. It was the same approach I took to the big cuts and caps I implemented in programs in the spring of 2009, and then in the efficiencies effort in 2010.

In implementing an agenda for change, the secretary cannot delegate the hard work to the deputy secretary, who simply doesn't have the clout in the building, at the White House, or in Congress to push through changes on big issues. The secretary has to master the details and fully understand the issues and problems. The challenge is to maintain a high-level, broad perspective, understand enough details to make sensible and executable decisions, and then delegate responsibility for implementation. "Microknowledge" must not become micromanagement, but it sure helps keep people on their toes when they know that the secretary knows what the hell he's talking about. If the secretary of defense doesn't do all of this, he becomes a "kept" man at the Pentagon, enjoying all the accouterments of position and authority—the big plane, massive entourages, lots of ceremonies and speeches—but held hostage by the military services, the Pentagon bureaucracy, and his own staff, without the knowledge or influence to effectively lead the department in new directions, much less put the place on a war footing.

In every aspect of running the department, the senior civilians and political appointees are critically important. I have not given due credit in these pages to those civilians who played a key role in everything I did—and accomplished—as secretary. Career professionals and political appointees, men and women, worked countless hours to prepare me for meetings and helped shape decisions, then saw to their implementation.

I depended on these civilians to help me frame the agenda for change, to help me come up with specific strategies for accomplishing each initiative. Their insights, dedication, and skills are critical assets that any secretary of defense and the American public must always value. Because while the military trains and equips our forces, provides professional military advice to the civilian leadership, and, when necessary, fights our wars, it is the Defense civilians who make the entire giant enterprise work—or not. First on the list for pay and hiring freezes, furloughs, and firings when the budget is being cut, they are the enduring backbone of the department. I have often criticized the Pentagon bureaucracy in these pages, but given the right leadership and clear direction, these public servants can move mountains. Anyone who wants to reform the Pentagon had better remember that these civilians are essential to success. They were for mine.

CONGRESS

I was always schizophrenic about Congress. In the abstract, I saw it as a critical check on the executive branch and guarantor of our freedom. For that reason, I had long been a strong advocate of effective congressional oversight. As secretary, I consistently tried to be respectful of the role of Congress and responsive to its requests and views. I urged my civilian and military subordinates to behave similarly. Early in my tenure as secretary, I told cadets and midshipmen at the military academies that as officers, they would need to remind their subordinates that Congress was one of two pillars of our freedom (the other being the press), a coequal branch of government that under the Constitution "raises armies and provides for navies." Many senators and congressmen were longtime supporters of men and women in uniform, and we had an obligation to be "honest and true" in reporting to them. In my first senior staff meeting as secretary, I said I wanted a strong, respectful, and positive relationship with Congress. I also knew that the Founding Fathers had created a system of government designed primarily for the preservation of liberty, not for efficient or agile government.

On a day-to-day basis, I believe, in that last regard, that the Founders succeeded beyond their wildest aspirations. Congress is best viewed from a distance—the farther the better—because up close it is truly ugly. And nearly every day I was secretary, I was dealing with Congress up close.

As I wrote earlier, I have less reason to complain about Congress than just about anyone who has served in the executive branch. Over four and a half years, the Armed Services and Appropriations Committees—as well as the congressional leadership and others—almost always treated me with respect and civility. The exceptions I can count on the fingers of one hand. But it seemed like every day, in nearly every way, we were in conflict that went well beyond the expected, healthy friction between two coequal branches of government.

In the Bush administration, the fights with Congress were mostly over Iraq troop levels, timetables and deadlines, and war budgets. As I turned my focus to budget and program matters under President Obama, I was more or less continuously outraged by the parochial self-interest of all but a very few members of Congress. Any defense facility or contract in their district or state, no matter how superfluous or wasteful, was sacrosanct.

I suppose I should have known better going in, but I was constantly amazed and infuriated at the hypocrisy of those who most stridently attacked the Defense Department for being inefficient and wasteful but would fight tooth and nail to prevent any reduction in defense activities in their home state or district no matter how inefficient or wasteful. However, behavior that was simply frustrating to me in 2009–10 will seriously impair our national security in the years ahead as the defense budget shrinks: failure to cut or close unneeded programs and facilities will drain precious dollars from the troops and our war-fighting capabilities.

A second source of frustration, as you might suspect, was the failure of Congress to do its most basic job: appropriate money. I prepared five budgets for Congress from 2007 to 2011, and *not once* was a defense appropriations bill enacted before the start of the new fiscal year. The impact of this, and the associated "continuing resolutions"—which kept the funding level at the previous year's appropriations and did not allow for starting any new program—was dramatically disruptive of sensible and efficient management of the department. This was an outrageous dereliction of duty.

I was exceptionally offended by the constant adversarial, inquisition-like treatment of executive branch officials by too many members of Congress across the political spectrum—a kangaroo-court environment in hearings, especially when the press and television cameras were present. Sharp questioning of witnesses should be expected and is entirely appropriate. But rude, insulting, belittling, bullying, and all too often highly personal attacks by members of Congress violated nearly every norm of civil behavior as they postured and acted as judge, jury, and executioner. It was as though most members were in a permanent state of outrage or suffered from some sort of mental duress that warranted confinement or at least treatment for anger management. I had to put up with less of this Queeg-like behavior than almost anyone, but I was infuriated by the harsh treatment of my subordinates, both civilian and military. The temptation to stand up, slam the briefing book shut, and quit on the spot recurred often. All too frequently, sitting at that witness table, the exit lines were on the tip of my tongue: *I may be the secretary of defense, but I am also an American citizen, and there is no son of a bitch in the world who can talk to me like that. I quit. Find somebody else.* It was, I am confident, a widely shared fantasy throughout the executive branch. And it was always enjoyable to listen to three former senators—Obama, Biden, and Clinton—trash-talking Congress.

Uncivil, incompetent in fulfilling basic constitutional responsibilities (such as timely appropriations), micromanagerial, parochial, hypocritical, egotistical, thin-skinned, often putting self (and reelection) before country—this was my view of the majority of the United States Congress.

It required an extraordinary effort on the part of Robert Rangel to keep me from erupting in a hearing but also to do the necessary courtesy calls, outreach, and day-to-day schmoozing with members. Robert had been a staff member of the House Armed Services Committee for years, including serving as its staff director, and so he had a longer and different perspective than I did—fortunately. He was better able to set aside (or ignore) members' behavior—he was used to it—and kept focused on our fundamental dependence on members' goodwill and legislative actions. With his wise and restraining hand, the clenched teeth behind my smile when on the Hill remained well hidden. It was just another battlefield in my wars.

What Rangel knew, and persuaded me to heed, was that a secretary of defense faces a steep uphill battle to be successful if he or she does not have a strong, nonpartisan relationship with Congress and respect among the members. From slow-rolling (or opposing) confirmation of Defense nominees, to conducting intrusive and time-consuming investigations, imposing legislative restrictions, opposing budget proposals, holding protracted hearings, and much more, Congress can truly make a secretary's life miserable. And so for four and a half years, I dutifully marched to the Hill to meet with the leadership, the party caucuses, committee leaders, and individual members. I behaved myself in hearings, letting my respectful demeanor implicitly draw the contrast with the boorishness of the members. Future secretaries would do well to remember Rangel's guidance, despite the outrageousness of their situation.

While American politics has always been a shrill, partisan, and ugly business going back to the Founding Fathers, we have rarely been so polarized and so unable to execute even the basic functions of government, much less tackle the most difficult and divisive problems facing the country. I believe that is due to the incessant scorched-earth battling between Congress and the president (I saw it under both Bush and Obama) but even more so to the weakening of the moderate center of both parties in Congress. Progress in America historically has come from thinkers and ideologues on both the left and the right, but the best of those ideas have been enacted into law through compromise. Now moderation is equated with lacking principles, and compromise with "selling out." This problem goes deeper than personalities, and I have seen it intensify greatly since first arriving in Washington in 1966. As secretary, I greatly missed the "bridge builders," most of whom left Congress because of their own frustrations in the House and Senate.

The paralytic polarization we face today is the result of changes—some structural, some historical, some outside the control of government— that have taken root over several decades, and it will not be undone simply by changing the cast of characters. It is due, first, to a highly partisan congressional redistricting process, through which more and more seats—all but perhaps 50 or 60 out of 435—are safe for either the Republican or Democratic party. As a result, the really consequential campaigns are the party primaries, where candidates must cater to the most hardcore ideological elements of their base.

Addressing the country's most intractable and complex problems requires consistent strategies and their implementation across multiple presidencies and congresses, and that requires bipartisanship. The best historical example of this was the Cold War, when, despite great differences in tactics and approaches, the basic contours of the strategy to contain the Soviet Union remained in place through nine successive presidential administrations of both political parties. Now the party that wins typically seeks to impose its agenda on the other side by brute political force. Compromise is the victim, as are the bipartisan strategies and policies that can—and must—be sustained over a number of years to deal successfully with the country's most serious challenges.

Contrary to conventional wisdom, the decline of congressional power brokers is to be mourned, particularly the committee chairs, who might have been tough partisans but were also people who could make deals and enforce those agreements on their committees and their party caucuses. The so-called reform of going from appointing committee chairmen based solely on seniority to electing them in the caucuses has proved worse than the disease, weakening the role of Congress in governing.

Another congressional change for the worse has been the shift to a three-day workweek—Tuesday through Thursday. Gone are the days when members shared group houses, played poker or golf together, and often ate dinner together. The families of members got to know one another and made friendships across the political spectrum. Now, with barely three days in town each week, they barely know members of their own party, let alone others from across the aisle. It's hard to build trust and the relationships necessary to get things done under these circumstances.

There have been vast changes in the composition and role of the news media over the decades, and that is a cause for concern as well. When I first entered government nearly forty-eight years ago, three television networks and a handful of newspapers dominated coverage and, to a considerable degree, filtered the most extreme or vitriolic points of view. Today, with hundreds of cable channels, blogs, and other electronic media, too often the professional integrity and long-established standards and practices of journalists are diluted or ignored. Every point of view—including the most extreme—has a ready vehicle for rapid dissemination. And it seems the more vitriolic the opinion, the more attention it gets. This system is clearly more democratic and open, but I believe it has also fueled the coarsening and dumbing down of our national political dialogue.

These discouraging elements of our democracy and civil society are well entrenched. But presidents and members of Congress are not helpless in confronting either the polarization or paralysis. They could start by restoring civility and mutual respect; by listening to and learning from one another; by curbing the purposeful distortion of facts; and by not pretending to have all the answers and demonizing those who differ. And by putting country before self and before party.

THE PRESIDENTS

It is difficult to imagine two more different men than George W. Bush and Barack Obama. We have a long tradition in America of electing a president, celebrating him for a few days, and then spending four or eight years demonizing him, reviling him, or blindly defending him. From George Washington on, there has scarcely been a president of any consequence—including those we consider our greatest—who has not faced the most scurrilous attacks on his policies, patriotism, morals, character, and conduct in office. So it has been with both Bush and Obama.

Clearly, I had fewer issues with Bush. Partly, that is because I worked for him in the last two years of his presidency, when, with the exception of the Iraq surge, at least in national security affairs nearly all the big decisions had been made. He had already made his historical bed and would have to lie in it. (He always seemed comfortable with that.) He would never again run for political office, and neither would his vice president. I don't recall Bush ever discussing domestic politics—apart from congressional opposition—as a consideration in decisions he made during my time with him, though it should be said that his sharp-elbowed political gurus were nearly all gone by the time I arrived. I encountered an experienced, wiser president beginning the last lap of his political race. By early 2007, Vice President Cheney was the outlier on the team, with Bush, Rice, Hadley, and me in broad agreement on virtually all important issues.

With Obama, however, I joined a new, inexperienced president facing multiple crises and determined to change America's approach to the world—and the wars we were in—and equally determined from day one to win reelection. Domestic political considerations therefore would be a factor, though I believe never a decisive one, in virtually every major national security problem we tackled. The White House staff—including the chief of staff, Rahm Emanuel and Bill Daley; Valerie Jarrett; David Axelrod; Robert Gibbs; and others—would have a presence and a role in national security decision making that I had not previously experienced (but which, I'm sure, had precedents). Under these circumstances, the surprise was how little disagreement on national security policy there was among the most senior members of the team, except over Afghanistan—at least until early 2011. On issue after issue—Iraq, Russia, China, Iran, Pakistan, the Middle East—the president, vice president, Clinton, Jones, Donilon, and I were usually on the same page. And where there were differences, including dealing with the Arab Spring, there was none of the emotion or rancor associated with Afghanistan.

President Obama and I did cross swords. Our disagreements on the defense budget in 2010 and 2011 were explicit, and often discussed face-to-face. I could understand the pressures on him as a result of the nation's deep economic problems, but I was frustrated that what I regarded as the agreement with him on future budget levels made in late 2009 was so quickly abandoned a year later, and then a subsequent agreement was abandoned just a few months after that. Our "negotiations"—if one can so describe discussions between a president and a cabinet officer—over budget levels, in fact, marked a fundamental difference between us: I wanted to restructure defense spending to make it more efficient and disciplined, reducing bureaucratic overhead and waste and canceling weak programs in order to preserve and enhance military capability. I did not want to cut the overall budget itself. As I have made clear, I believed that an increasingly complex, turbulent, and unstable world required sustaining the U.S. military at a high level of capability and readiness; we just needed to be a lot smarter in how we spent our money to achieve that purpose. The president felt that defense could and should be cut on its merits, but also to give him political space with his own party and constituents to cut domestic spending and entitlements. (At least that's what he told me.) I believed Defense was not a major factor in the size of either the national debt or the annual deficits, and that developments in the rest of the world provided ample reason to sustain and enhance our military capabilities; if we had to reduce our budget, we should be allowed to do so slowly and with a wary eye on the global security environment.

I never confronted Obama directly over what I (as well as Clinton, Panetta, and others) saw as the president's determination that the White House tightly control every aspect of national security policy and even operations. His White House was by far the most centralized and controlling in national security of any I had seen since Richard Nixon and Henry Kissinger ruled the roost. I had no problem with the White House and the NSS driving policy. As I had witnessed time and again, the big bureaucracies rarely come up with significant new ideas, and almost any meaningful departures from the status quo must be driven by the president and his national security adviser—whether it was Nixon and Kissinger and the openings to the Soviet Union and China, Carter and the Camp David accords, Reagan and his outreach to Gorbachev, or Bush 41 and the liberation of eastern Europe, reunification of Germany, and collapse of the Soviet Union.

Just as Bush 43 had driven the Iraq surge decision in late 2006, I had no issue with the White House and the NSS driving the policy reevaluation early in 2009 on Afghanistan. But I believe the major reason the protracted, frustrating Afghan review that fall created so much ill will was due to the fact it was forced on an otherwise controlling White House by the theater commander's unexpected request for a large escalation of American involvement. It was a request that surprised the White House (and me) and provoked a debate that the White House neither sought nor wanted, especially when it became public. I think Obama and his advisers were incensed that the Department of Defense—specifically the military—had taken control of the policy process from them and threatened to run away with it. That partly accounts for the increased suspicion of the military at the White House and the NSS. The Pentagon and the military did not consciously intend to snatch the initiative and control of war policy from the president, but in retrospect, I can now see how easily it could have been perceived that way. The White House saw it as a calculated move. The leak of McChrystal's assessment and subsequent public commentary by Mullen, Petraeus, and McChrystal only reinforced that view. I was never able to persuade the president and others that it was not a plot.

I had served in the White House on the National Security Staff under four presidents and had strong views as to its proper role. I had come to learn that White House/NSS involvement in operations or operational details is usually counterproductive (LBJ picking bombing targets in Vietnam) and sometimes dangerous (Iran-Contra). The root of my unhappiness in the Obama administration was therefore not NSS policy initiatives but rather its micromanagement—on Haitian relief, on the Libyan no-fly zone, above all on Afghanistan—and I routinely resisted it. For an NSC staff member to call a four-star combatant commander or field commander would have been unthinkable when I worked at the White House and probably cause for dismissal. It became routine under Obama. I directed the commanders to refer such calls to my office. The controlling nature of the Obama White House, and its determination to take credit for every good thing that happened while giving none to the people in the cabinet departments—in the trenches—who had actually done the work, offended Hillary Clinton as much as it did me.

These issues did not begin under Obama. There has been a steady trend toward more centralized White House control over the national security apparatus ever since Harry Truman considered his principal national security advisers to be the secretaries of state and defense. (That they were Dean Acheson and George Marshall certainly helped.) But even Truman initially had opposed legislation creating the National Security Council, convinced that Congress was trying to impose "cabinet government" on him. Since then the presidential staff assigned to national security has increased many times over. As recently as the Scowcroft-led NSC staff in the early 1990s, professional staff numbered about fifty. Today the NSS numbers more than 350.

The controlling nature of the Obama White House and the NSS staff took micromanagement and operational meddling to a new level. Partly, I think, it was due to the backgrounds and résumés of the people involved. For most of my professional life, top NSC positions went to people who may have aligned with one party or the other, but they had reputations in the foreign policy and national security arenas that predated their association with the president—either from academia (such as Henry Kissinger, Zbigniew Brzezinski, Condi Rice) or longtime service in the military, intelligence, or foreign policy arenas (such as Frank Carlucci, Jim Jones, Colin Powell, Steve Hadley, Brent Scowcroft, and me). Inevitably there were some politically or personally connected handlers as well, but they were the exceptions. Obama's top tier of NSS people, though, was heavily populated with very smart, politically savvy, and hardworking "super staffers"—typically from Capitol Hill—who focused on national-security-related issues only as their careers progressed. This changed profile may explain, in part, their apparent lack of understanding of or concern for observing the traditional institutional roles among the White House, the Pentagon, and the operational military.

Stylistically, the two presidents had much more in common than I expected. Both were most comfortable around a coterie of close aides and friends (like most presidents) and largely shunned the Washington social scene. Both, I believe, detested Congress and resented having to deal with it, including members of their own party. And so, unfortunately, neither devoted much effort to wooing or even reaching out to individual members or trying to establish a network of allies, supporters— or friends. They both had the worst of both worlds on the Hill: they were neither particularly liked nor feared. Accordingly, neither had many allies in Congress who were willing to go beyond party loyalty, self-interest, or policy agreement in supporting them. In this, they had more in common with Jimmy Carter and Richard Nixon than with LBJ, Ford, Reagan, and Bush 41. Nor did either work much at establishing close personal relationships with other world leaders. Bush did somewhat more of this than Obama, but neither had anything like the number of friendships cultivated by Ford, Reagan, and Bush 41. (I don't know about Clinton; I wasn't there.) Both presidents, in short, seemed to me to be very aloof with respect to two constituencies important to their success in foreign affairs.

Both were generous, kind, and caring when it came to men and women in uniform and their families. Both presidents—and their wives—devoted significant time and energy to helping the wounded and all military families. Helping those families was particularly important to Michelle Obama and Jill Biden. Both presidents regularly, privately, visited our wounded at hospitals and met with families of the fallen. No one could have asked either to do more or to care more. As was fitting.

Their relationship with me was friendly and relaxed but businesslike. President Obama had much more occasion than Bush to be angry with me, but by the standards of Johnson and Nixon—whose wrath could be semiterrifying even to the most senior officials—Obama was civil in his impatience, never nasty, cutting, or personal. And the squall always passed quickly. At times, I'm sure he treated me better than I deserved.

I witnessed both of those presidents make decisions they believed to be in the best interest of the country regardless of the domestic political consequences, both thereby earning my highest possible respect and praise. Although, as I've said, political considerations were far more a part of national security debates under Obama, time and again I saw him make a decision that was opposed by his political advisers or that would be unpopular with his fellow Democrats and supportive interest groups. I liked and respected both men.

On War

Until becoming secretary of defense, my exposure to war and those who were fighting wars had been at a distance, from antiseptic offices at the White House and at CIA. But I had read much history about war and its glories, follies, and horrors. Serving as secretary of defense made the abstract real, the antiseptic bloody and horrible. I saw up close the cost in lives ruined and lives lost.

Several lessons, none new to me, were hammered home during my four and a half years as defense secretary. Above all, the unpredictability of war—that once the first shots are fired or first bombs fall, as Churchill said, the political leader loses control. Events are in the saddle. It seems that every war is begun with the assumption it will be short. In nearly every instance, going back far into history, that assumption has been wrong. And so it happened again in Iraq and Afghanistan, as swift and successful regime changes gave way to long and bloody conflicts. In light of history, how could anyone have been surprised that our wars in Iraq and Afghanistan took unanticipated turns?

I was reminded, too, that nearly always, we begin military engagements—wars—profoundly ignorant about our adversaries and about the situation on the ground. We had no idea how broken Iraq was when we invaded and took control of the country. We did not grasp that after eight years of war with Iran, the Gulf War with us, and twelve years of harsh sanctions, the Iraqi economy, society, and infrastructure were shattered. The facade of Saddam's regime misled us with regard to what we were letting ourselves in for, just as his facade with respect to possessing weapons of mass destruction misled us. We had no idea of the complexity of Afghanistan—tribes, ethnic groups, power brokers, village and provincial rivalries. So our prospects in both countries were grimmer than perceived, and our initial objectives were unrealistic. And we didn't know that either. Our knowledge and our intelligence were woefully inadequate. We entered both countries oblivious to how little we knew.

I was also reminded that no country is fully prepared for the next war. Secretary Rumsfeld said you go to war with the army you have. But the Defense Department was unconscionably slow in identifying and providing the equipment to make the Army and Marine Corps into the force we needed in Afghanistan and Iraq. That slowness, that business-as-usual peacetime mentality, cost lives.

Usually we don't get to choose and almost never accurately predict the kind of war we will fight next. I am always amused when I hear a senior military officer or a politician declare that we will never fight certain kinds of wars again. After Vietnam, our defense "experts" avowed we would never again try to fight an insurgency, yet we have done so in both Iraq and Afghanistan. We are hearing the same claim now. Those who assert we will fight only certain kinds of wars in the future forget history and the reality that our enemies, as I've said, always have a vote, as do future presidents. In the forty years since Vietnam, our record in predicting where we will be militarily engaged next, even six months out, is perfect: we have never once gotten it right, not in Grenada, Haiti, Panama, Libya (twice), Iraq (twice), Afghanistan, the Balkans, or Somalia. When it comes to predicting future conflicts, what kind of fights they will be, and what will be needed, we need a lot more humility.

Wars are a lot easier to get into than out of, a point I hope I have made clear. Those who ask about exit strategies or what happens if assumptions prove wrong are rarely welcome at the conference table when the fire-breathers argue we must act militarily—as they did when advocating an invasion of Iraq, intervening in Libya and Syria, or bombing Iranian nuclear sites. The argument against military action is almost never about capabilities but whether it is wise. As Petraeus said early on in Iraq, "Tell me how this ends." Too often the question is not even asked, much less answered.

My time as secretary of defense reinforced my belief that in recent decades, American presidents, confronted with a tough problem abroad, have too often been too quick to reach for a gun—to use military force, despite all the realities I have been describing. They could have done worse than to follow the example of President Dwight D. Eisenhower. During his presidency, the Soviet Union became a thermonuclear power, China became a nuclear power, and there were calls for preventive nuclear war against both; the Joint Chiefs unanimously recommended that he use nuclear weapons to help the French in Vietnam; there were several crises with China related to Taiwan; a war in the Middle East; a revolution in Cuba; and uprisings in East Germany, Poland, and Hungary. And yet after Eisenhower agreed to the armistice in Korea in the summer of 1953, not one American soldier was killed in action during his presidency.

Too many ideologues call for the use of the American military as the first option rather than a last resort to address problems. On the left, we hear about the "responsibility to protect" as a justification for military intervention in Libya, Syria, the Sudan, and elsewhere. On the right, the failure to use military force in Libya, Syria, or Iran is deemed an abdication of American leadership and a symptom of a "soft" foreign policy. Obama's "pivot" to Asia was framed almost entirely in military terms as opposed to economic and political priorities. And so the rest of the world sees America, above all else, as a militaristic country too quick to launch planes, cruise missiles, and armed drones deep into sovereign countries or ungoverned spaces.

I strongly believe America must continue to fulfill its global responsibilities. We *are* the "indispensable nation," and few international problems can be addressed successfully without our leadership. But we also need to better appreciate that there are limits to what the United States— still by far the strongest and greatest nation on earth—can do in an often cruel and challenging world. The power of our military's global reach has been an indispensable contributor to peace and stability in many regions and must remain so. But not every outrage, every act of aggression, every oppression, or every crisis can or should elicit an American military response.

I wrote in my first book in 1996 that, contrary to conventional wisdom, the biggest doves in Washington wear uniforms. This is because our military leaders have seen the cost of war and its unpredictability, and they have too often sent their troops in harm's way to execute ill-defined or unrealistic presidential objectives, with thin political support that evaporated when the going got tough or the fight became prolonged. Just as it did in "the necessary war" in Afghanistan.

There is one final lesson about war that we too often forget. We are enamored of technology and what it can do because of advances in precision, sensors, information, and satellite technology. A button is pushed in Nevada, and seconds later a pickup truck explodes in Mosul. A bomb destroys the targeted house on the right, leaving intact the one on the left. War has become for too many—among them defense "experts," members of Congress, executive branch officials, and the American public as well—a kind of arcade video game or action movie, bloodless, painless, and odorless. But as I told a military audience at the National Defense University in September 2008, war is "inevitably tragic, inefficient, and uncertain." I warned them to be skeptical of systems analysis, computer models, game theories, or doctrines that suggest otherwise. "Look askance," I said, "at idealized, triumphalist, or ethnocentric notions of future conflict that aspire to upend the immutable principles of war, where the enemy is killed, but our troops and innocent civilians are spared; where adversaries can be cowed, shocked, or awed into submission, instead of being tracked down, hilltop by hilltop, house by house, block by bloody block." I quoted General William T. Sherman that "every attempt to make war easy and safe will result in humiliation and disaster." And I concluded with General "Vinegar Joe" Stilwell's warning that "no matter how a war starts, it ends in mud. It has to be slugged out—there are no trick solutions or cheap shortcuts."

We must always be prepared and willing to use our military forces when our security, our vital interests, or those of our allies are threatened or attacked. But I believe the use of military force should always be a last resort and our objectives clearly and realistically defined (as in the Gulf War). And presidents need to be more willing and skillful in using tools in the national security kit other than hammers. Our foreign and national security policy has become too militarized, the use of force too easy for presidents.

The Troops

Most of the public attention with regard to men and women in uniform seems to fall to one end of the spectrum or the other—the heroes are extolled for their valor and sacrifice, and those who have disgraced the uniform in some way are condemned. The latter, fortunately, are small in number. The former, the heroes, to me are countless. I know that if everyone is a hero, then no one truly is. I concede the term is thrown around far too casually. Most troops signed up in a time of war and did their job ably and honorably, without fanfare or much recognition. There is no doubt that those who fought bravely, those who saved the lives of their comrades often at the risk of their own, those who were wounded, and those who fell are all heroes. But how, then, to describe the hundreds of thousands who went to Iraq and Afghanistan, did their duty, then returned to their families and must live with the nightmare of war for the rest of their lives? What about the medics, doctors, and nurses who have had to deal with so many shattered bodies and minds? Or the aircrews who have been at war since 1991? Or the logistics experts for whom performing miracles became a routine day's work? Or the Special Forces among whom seven or eight or ten tours of duty were common? Or all those troops who had to endure fifteen-month tours? Wherever I went in the world, these men and women were standing watch for all of us. For some, it is a career; for all, it is a calling.

There will always be a special place in my heart for all those who served on the front lines in Iraq and Afghanistan, most in their twenties, some in their teens. I never imagined that I would be responsible for overseeing two wars and for seeing to the well-being of those fighting them. On each visit to the war zones, as I would go to joint security stations in Baghdad or even forward operating bases and combat outposts in Afghanistan, I knew I wasn't being exposed to the true grim reality of our troops' lives, and so I could not fully appreciate what those in the fight endured daily. But I saw enough. My imagination—and all those lunches with young troops—filled in the blanks. And I could only contrast their selfless service and sacrifice with so many self-serving elected and nonelected officials back home.

When I was asked in October 2006 if I would be willing to serve as secretary, I said that because all of those kids out there were doing their duty, I had no choice but to do mine. The troops were the reason I took the job, and they became the reason I stayed. Being called "the soldiers' secretary" because I cared so much about them was the highest compliment imaginable. I never, for one moment, forgot that tearful mother's plea in the hotel restaurant before my confirmation hearings: "For God's sake, bring them back alive." That plea drove me, just as the troops inspired me. When I was at my lowest, they lifted me up.

I came to believe that no one who had actually been in combat could walk away without scars, some measure of post-traumatic stress. And while those I visited in the hospitals put on a brave front for me, in my mind's eye I could see them lying awake, alone, in the hours before dawn, confronting their pain and their broken dreams and shattered lives. I would wake in the night, think back to a wounded soldier or Marine I had seen at Landstuhl, Bethesda, or Walter Reed, and in my imagination, I would put myself in his hospital room and I would hold him to my chest, to comfort him. Silently, in the night at home, I would weep for him. And so my answer to the young soldier's question in Afghanistan about what kept me awake at night: he did.

I always assumed that my predecessors during wartime felt every bit as deeply as I did about the men and women on the front lines, the wounded, the fallen, and their families. But ironically, the scale of earlier wars—World War II, Korea, and Vietnam in the last eight decades—and the number of wounded and killed in those conflicts precluded my wartime predecessors from establishing the kind of personal connection to the troops or to their families that became so important to me. When 1,000 young Americans were being killed every month in Vietnam, reading hometown news coverage of each casualty and handwriting condolence letters were impossible. And so, perhaps because our losses were comparatively so much smaller than in previous wars, I could and did become emotionally bound to the troops.

During World War II, General George Marshall once told his wife, "I cannot afford the luxury of sentiment, mine must be cold logic. Sentiment is for others." Icy detachment was never an option for me. Because of the nature of the two wars I oversaw, I could afford the luxury of sentiment, and at times, it overwhelmed me. Signing the deployment orders, visiting hospitals, writing the condolence letters, and attending the funerals at Arlington all were taking a growing emotional toll on me. Even thinking about the troops, I would lose my composure with increasing frequency. I realized I was beginning to regard protecting them—avoiding their sacrifice—as my highest priority. And I knew that this loss of objectivity meant it was time to leave.

The day before I stepped down as secretary, I sent a message to every man and woman wearing the American military uniform because I knew I could not speak to or about them at my farewell ceremony without breaking down. I repeated my now-familiar words: "Your countrymen owe you their freedom and their security. They sleep safely at night and pursue their dreams during the day because you stand the watch and protect them. . . . You are the best America has to offer. My admiration and affection for you is without limit, and I will think about you and your families and pray for you every day for the rest of my life. God bless you."

I am eligible to be buried at Arlington National Cemetery. I have asked to be buried in Section 60, where so many of the fallen from Iraq and Afghanistan have been laid to rest. The greatest honor possible would be to rest among my heroes for all eternity.

Acknowledgments

Above all, I wish to thank President Bush and President Obama for their trust and confidence in asking me to serve as secretary of defense. It was the honor of a lifetime to serve my country and the two of them in that role. I dedicated this book to the men and women of the United States armed forces, and I thank them for inspiring me every day I was secretary. As I have written in these pages, they are the best America has to offer. I also want to thank General Pete Pace and Admiral Mike Mullen for their friendship and partnership throughout this adventure. It was a great blessing to have these two men by my side every day. I also could not have asked for more capable, professional, and personable colleagues than the service chiefs, combatant commanders, and field commanders with whom I was privileged to work. I want to express special appreciation to my senior military assistants Lieutenant General Gene Renuart, Lieutenant General Pete Chiarelli, Lieutenant General Dave "Rod" Rodriguez, Vice Admiral Joe Kernan, and Lieutenant General John Kelly. Each was a mentor and a friend.

I also want to thank the senior civilians in the Department of Defense: Deputy Secretaries Gordon England and Bill Lynn, the secretaries of the Army, Navy, and Air Force with whom I worked, and the undersecretaries and their career and appointed colleagues whose support, expertise, and counsel I relied upon every day. Words cannot adequately express my appreciation—and dependence upon—those in my immediate office, Robert Rangel and Delonnie Henry (who served four secretaries), Geoff Morrell, Ryan McCarthy, and Christian Marrone, and the NCOs who subtly but effectively managed us all.

In writing this book, I have relied on my personal papers and notes, as well as notes taken by my staff. Where I quote individuals in conversations or meetings, the source is either notes from one of my staff who was present or my own notes made during or immediately after the event.

I want to thank Robert Storer, chief of the Records and Declassification Division at the Pentagon, for his help in reviewing my classified documents, and to the commander and staff at Whidbey Island Naval Air Station for providing the facilities for that review. Appreciation is also due to Mike Rhodes, director of administration and management, and Mark Langerman, chief of the Office of Security Review, at the Defense Department for their professional and expeditious review of the manuscript and photographs.

I want to thank Staff Sergeant Tim Brown and First Lieutenant Dan Moran for permission to use their photographs.

I asked several people to review parts or all of the manuscript, and want to thank them for taking the time and effort to help me: Robert Rangel, Pete Chiarelli, Geoff Morrell, Thayer Scott, Ryan McCarthy, Steve Hadley, Eric Edelman, Michèle Flournoy, and Harry Rhoads. Obviously, responsibility for any errors or mistakes is mine alone.

Special thanks as well to Wayne Kabak of WSK Management, who began representing me twenty years ago and has become a close friend, adviser, and counselor. I also want to express heartfelt appreciation to Jonathan Segal of Alfred A. Knopf, a superb editor and guide. It has been a special pleasure working with him. I also want to thank Sonny Mehta, Paul Bogaards, Meghan Houser, Chip Kidd, Lisa Montebello, Cassandra Pappas, and Michelle Somers at Knopf for their important contributions to this book.

Thanks are due to my able assistant, Keith Hensley, for all his help in the final stages of preparing this book. Without his technical expertise, I would have been lost. I want also to express my gratitude to Bill and Vicky Yarcho and Chris and Wendy Belanger, close friends in the Northwest who helped us so much during my years as secretary.

Finally, neither this book nor the experience it recounts would have been possible without my wife, Becky, whose patience and understanding as I was writing were surpassed only by her patience and understanding through my tenure as secretary of defense and forty-seven years of marriage.

Index

Illustration Credits